# BYRON : *A Biography*

VOLUME I

# BYRON

## A BIOGRAPHY

By

Leslie A. Marchand

*VOLUME I*

*ALFRED A. KNOPF : NEW YORK : 1957*

*L. C. catalog card number: 57–7547*

THIS IS A BORZOI BOOK,
PUBLISHED BY ALFRED A. KNOPF, INC.


*Published simultaneously in Canada by McClelland & Stewart Limited. Manufactured in the United States of America.*

FIRST EDITION

*To my wife, Marion Hendrix Marchand*

# PREFACE

WHAT need is there for another biography of Byron? If we may trust the record of Lady Blessington, Byron himself had an answer: "People take for gospel all I say, and go away continually with false impressions. *Mais n'importe!* it will render the statements of my future biographers more amusing; as I flatter myself I shall have more than one. Indeed, the more the merrier, say I. One will represent me as a sort of sublime misanthrope, with moments of kind feeling. This, *par exemple,* is my favorite *rôle.* Another will portray me as a modern Don Juan; and a third . . . will, it is to be hoped, if only for opposition sake, represent me as an *amiable,* ill-used gentleman, 'more sinned against than sinning.' Now, if I know myself, I should say, that I have no character at all. . . . But, joking apart, what I think of myself is, that I am so changeable, being everything by turns and nothing long, —I am such a strange *mélange* of good and evil, that it would be difficult to describe me."

It is true that every generation has had its own concept and interpretation of Byron since the constellation of *Childe Harold* broke upon the world in 1812. To his contemporaries he was at once titillating and shocking, and they lamented and moralized upon the sad spectacle of his "wasted powers," while they read avidly each succeeding installment of *Don Juan.* Thomas Moore, who published in 1830 the first extensive edition of Byron's letters and journals, "with notices of his life," set the tone of the nineteenth-century picture of the "*amiable,* ill-used gentleman." It is surprising with what persistence traditional views (and errors), once established, are repeated from the same old sources decade after decade. This view was scarcely disturbed by Harriet Beecher Stowe's scandalous revelations about the Byron marriage and separation, or by the new material and insights presented in the biographies of Karl Elze and J. Cordy Jeaffreson.

The reinterpretations in the first quarter of the twentieth century were precipitated largely by the publication of Rowland E. Prothero's fine edition of the *Letters and Journals* (containing several hundred new letters and other material); Lord Lovelace's *Astarte,* with its letters of Byron to Augusta, which raised anew the question of the relations of Byron with his half-sister; and *Lord Byron's Correspondence,* edited by John Murray, which contained the important letters of Byron to Lady Melbourne, Hobhouse, and Douglas Kinnaird. Ethel C. Mayne's was the first full-length biography (1924) to make use of this material. Miss Mayne, in writing her life of Lady Byron (1929), and André Maurois, in preparing his life of Byron (1930), both had access to the Lovelace papers, which have since become unavailable to biographers.

But what is there now to justify another life of Byron? The simple answer is that since Maurois's *Byron* was published nearly twenty-seven years ago, much new material, extensive and important, has come to light. Some of this—such as Byron's letters to the Countess Guiccioli included in the Marchesa Iris Origo's *The Last Attachment* and the fifty or more new Byron letters in the two-volume Murray edition, *Byron: A Self-Portrait,* edited by Peter Quennell—has been published since I began my labors more than ten years ago. But much of first importance yet remains unpublished, and the newly published material has not been incorporated in any complete biographical account.

It has been my aim to evaluate my source materials, old and new, as if they were all new, and not to give undue weight to some letter or document merely because it has not been used before in a biography of Byron. The value of the new material has often been that it fills in missing parts of the jigsaw puzzle or gives more meaning to what had to be guessed at before. Where it was possible I have tried to go to original sources, to consult manuscript documents and letters, even when they have been published, for there have been numerous errors, omissions, and suppressions in the published record of Byron's life.

I have sometimes been asked what my thesis is. That always astounds me, and annoys me a little, because the assumption behind it seems to be that the biographer should explain everything in terms of some one dominant humor. My reply generally is that I have no thesis and have consciously avoided formulating one. Too many biographies, including lives of Byron, have been written to prove a thesis. I think it important for the biographer not to have a preconceived single notion of the character he is attempting to delineate. Because I have tried to be objective, I have been taxed by some readers of my manuscript with not presenting a very favorable picture of Byron. That too astounds me, for my feeling is that in my total view I have revealed his essential virtues more strikingly than have most other biographers. My only thesis is that Byron was a human being, shaped by the strange combination of his inherited traits and his unnatural upbringing, but essentially likable, disarmingly frank in his confessions of his own peccadilloes, with a delightfully fresh observation of human character and human frailties and a unique facility for lucid and concrete expression. I have come to feel that Byron is not, as he has been accused of being, more inconsistent than most men and women—only more honest in acknowledging his inconsistencies. That is what startles and delights the sympathetic reader aware of the human penchant for reticence and rationalization.

Is Byron alone not allowed to yawn with impunity, without his loyalty or his love being called into question? Unless we recognize the fact that wayward fancies and true loyalty may coexist, that these fancies or ineffable longings, stronger in Byron than in other less romantic and poetic personalities but present to some degree in all of us, may be reconciled with the strongest attachments, we will continue to misread Byron's character and his life. Byron's greatest offense was his honesty in giving expression to what many feel but most suppress or refuse to acknowledge. It is always a characteristic of the kind of hypocrisy that Byron attacked to think that putting irregular conduct into words is more reprehensible than the acts themselves.

One of the commonest clichés of biography and criticism is that Byron was a poseur. I think that view arose in part because his contemporaries, and later the Victorians, wanted desperately to justify their liking for him and his poetry and hence fell in very readily with the contention of Thomas Moore, his first biographer, that he was not as bad as he pictured himself, that he was striking an attitude, a Satanic pose, for effect and deliberately to shock the British public. It is undeniable that Byron did at times delight in shocking the British public, but not so much by striking an attitude or assuming emotions he had not, at least in some unguarded moments, felt, as by telling embarrassing truths about himself and, by implication, about human nature in general. Unlike many other nineteenth-century biographical subjects, Byron did not try to suppress the facts of his life—it was his friends who did so—but his spirit cast such a spell that few who knew him destroyed his letters or other evidence. There are notable exceptions, of course, such as the burning of the famous "Memoirs" in the fireplace at John Murray's when the news of Byron's death reached England. It is perhaps understandable that his friends were then a little confused and slightly hysterical. Byron wrote to Moore in 1820 concerning these Memoirs, which he had written to please himself and had given to Moore to help him out of a financial difficulty: "Over these latter sheets I would leave you a discretionary power; because they contain, perhaps, a thing or two which is too sincere for the public. . . . if *you* (as most likely) survive me, add what you please from your own knowledge; and, *above all, contradict* any thing, if I have *mis*-stated; for my first object is the truth, even at my own expense." John Cam Hobhouse, who perhaps knew Byron better than did any other of the poet's friends, commented in the margin of his copy of Moore's life of Byron: "Very true."

I think the facts of Byron's life which have recently come to light will tend to confirm the view that he was in his poetry even more autobiographical than he has been supposed—that the moods, though not all the literal account of adventures, of Childe Harold and of Manfred, as of Beppo and Don Juan, were all his at one time or another. The great mistake has been not to recognize that Byron was speaking in sober earnest when he wrote:

"All convulsions end with me in rhyme. . . ." And again: "I can never get people to understand that poetry is the expression of *excited passion*, and that there is no such thing as a life of passion any more than a continuous earthquake, or an eternal fever." The failure to heed the poet's own words has made Byron seem inconsistent to many in his own day as well as later. People who expected to find in him the moody Childe Harold, the proud and brooding Manfred, or perhaps the Corsair, as Trelawny apparently did, were surprised with the exuberance of his spirits and his anything but misanthropic behavior when they met him. And those who looked for the jeering cynic were frequently struck by his courtly behavior to women and his ability to discuss serious subjects seriously and without a leer.

The fact may be that perfect consistency is, in the last analysis, the greatest pose of all in human beings. We all, whether aware of it or not, suppress to a certain extent (perforce—and often with the best of social reasons) those wayward tendencies in our nature which we think our families, our friends, or our neighbors would not approve of. And it is precisely when Byron with his frankness surprises in us some of these instincts and moods common to mankind (and womankind) that he furnishes a wholesome katharsis.

But what fresh light does all the new material throw on Byron's life and character? One thing that seems to emerge more clearly than ever before, principally from hitherto unpublished letters to Byron, is that he had an extraordinary capacity for friendship, and that all his friends, men and women alike, were devoted to him. And finally, further study of biographical details strengthens the conviction of the essential honesty and self-honesty of Byron. He had a kind of "desperate integrity" (to borrow a phrase from a twentieth-century critic) in little things as well as big—in literature as well as in life—and all other things seem less important. As we become better acquainted with him, we are inclined to accept his idiosyncrasies and his deviations from approved conduct as we would those of a friend—in fact, as his own friends did.

To what extent I too have become bewitched by Byron, the reader may decide for himself. Certainly I owe him a great debt.

He took me on a fascinating pilgrimage "through Europe to the Ætolian shore" and beyond in search of biographical material.[1] He has introduced me to charming and interesting people—has given me new friends with common interests in half a dozen countries. But (as a biographer) I owe him more: he wrote a legible hand, though scrawling; he dated his letters (no "Wednesday at four"); and he kept practically all letters sent to him.

What strikes a traveler following Byron's trail is the extent and persistence of his European reputation. Not only in the houses where he lived—I was surprised to find so many still standing, and all remembered—but also in the living tradition there are evidences of the impact he made in Italy and Greece. It is a commonplace that Byron came to know Italy and the Italians better than did any other English poet. Shelley and his friends lived to themselves. Even the Brownings lived in a rather self-sufficient circle in Florence. But I think it is less generally realized how much better Byron knew Greece and the Greeks than did most English travelers to that country. In Greece it is easy to recapture the spell that the sunshine, the tavernas, the hospitality of the islands, the friendly peasants and their donkeys with orange-laden panniers, the shepherds on the hills with their picturesque capotes, the caïques that ply the blue waters of the Corinthian gulf must have cast on the young Byron. It is easy to feel this spell even now, for many of the fundamental aspects of life in Greece have not changed since Byron heard the wild Albanian war songs or stood on Colonna's cliff gazing at the isles of Greece. And the traveler soon finds that the name of Byron still has a magic power in that land, even among people who have never read a line of his poetry.

It is the personality of Byron that finally captures the imagination, whether one sees it through his egocentric poetry, through his letters, or through the eyes of his contemporaries. One American critic has said that Byron "was too idealistic to refrain from blowing bubbles, and too realistic to refrain from pricking them."[2] This seems to furnish the key to the paradox of Byron's

[1] For details of that pilgrimage, see Richard D. Altick: *The Scholar Adventurers* (New York, 1950), Chapter XII, "On the Trail of Byron."
[2] Hoxie Neale Fairchild: *The Romantic Quest* (New York, 1931), p. 370.

personality, and to explain many of the seeming contradictions of his nature. For Byron struck the human balance between idealistic aspiration and realistic disillusionment. And he refused to ignore any note of feeling in the gamut that runs from one to the other, his self-honesty compelling him to record every nuance of the "mobility" of his nature. This accounts for Byron's continued human appeal through all the changes in literary taste and swings of the intellectual pendulum. When more intransigent idealists and equally austere realists have palled or passed out of favor, Byron has remained a refreshing spirit attuned to every time and every clime.

New source materials for a life of Byron, in public and private collections, are so abundant that the problem of selection has been a difficult one.[3] In America large and important collections of Byron letters and Byroniana have been made available to me in the Henry W. and Albert A. Berg Collection of the New York Public Library, the Pierpont Morgan Library, the Yale University Library, the Houghton Library of Harvard University, the University of Texas Library, the Henry E. Huntington Library, and the William Andrews Clark Memorial Library of the University of California at Los Angeles. To the respective curators and librarians of these collections I am indebted for permission to quote from unpublished manuscripts. I wish particularly to thank Mr. John D. Gordan of the Berg Collection, Mr. Frederick B. Adams of the Morgan Library, Mr. William A. Jackson of the Houghton Library, Mr. Robert F. Metzdorf of the Yale Library, Mr. Lawrence Clark Powell of the Clark Library, Mr. H. C. Schulz of the Huntington Library, and Miss Fannie Ratchford of the University of Texas Library. To numerous librarians in the two hemispheres I owe a debt difficult to acknowledge adequately. Not the least of my obligations is to the staff of the Rutgers University Library. I wish also to thank Mr. John S. Mayfield of Washington, D.C., and Dr. Gregg M. Sinclair of Honolulu for allowing me to quote from Byron letters in their possession. I am grateful to Mr. Mayfield also for calling my attention to much useful material. Mr. James M. Osborn of New Haven, Connecti-

[3] For details, see "Unpublished Sources" at the end of Volume III.

cut, has kindly allowed me to borrow his copy of Moore's life of Byron and to quote from E. H. Coleridge's marginalia in the volumes. And to Professor Chauncey B. Tinker I am indebted for making available to me several Byron letters in his private collection.

From European collections I gathered between five and six thousand microfilm frames of manuscript materials, in addition to many notes. To Lord Abinger I am grateful for permission to make copies of a number of letters of the Shelley circle which have important references to Byron. The Keeper of Manuscripts of the British Museum has given me permission to quote from a number of manuscripts in the Egerton, Ashley, and Additional MSS. I am indebted to the librarians of the Nottingham Free Public Library and the Roe-Byron Collection at Newstead Abbey, and of Trinity College Library, Cambridge, for permission to quote from manuscripts in their collections.

I should like to thank Sir Charles Hobhouse for permission to quote from the manuscript diaries of John Cam Hobhouse, and to express my gratitude in particular to Mr. and Mrs. John Hobhouse, who made these diaries available to me in their home.

Sir Harold Nicolson, who has long been an enthusiastic Byronian, allowed me to transcribe Hobhouse's marginal notes in his copy of Moore's life of Byron (now in Sir Harold's possession), kindly read my last chapters in manuscript, and extended to me many courtesies during my researches on Byron.

To the Murrays, who have the finest Byron collection in existence, I am, like all Byron scholars, indebted for many favors. Sir John Murray gave me access to innumerable boxes of Byroniana, provided me an office in which to examine them, and allowed me to have more than sixteen hundred microfilms made from the manuscripts in his possession. And I have a happy recollection of helping Mr. John Grey Murray carry a stack of Byron letters over two feet high to his home, where we examined them during a pleasant week end. To Sir John I am grateful for permission to quote from letters and documents in his collection and for the devotion of much of his time and effort to the reading of my manuscript. I am also indebted to him for allowing me to use copyright material.

Mr. Duncan Gray and Miss Violet W. Walker of the Free Public Library of Nottingham have helped my work in a number of ways. Miss Walker directed me through Newstead Abbey and the Roe-Byron Collection. The late Lord Byron (10th Baron) and Lady Byron entertained me at Thrumpton Hall, showed me their Thorwaldsen bust of Byron, and introduced me to Colonel Chaworth-Musters and his family. The Chaworth-Musters family in turn invited me to spend a week end at Annesley Hall, where Byron used to visit their ancestor Mary Chaworth.

Mr. Cuthbert Becher Pigot, great-nephew of Elizabeth Pigot, Byron's friend at Southwell, showed me his Byron relics and allowed me to make copies of some Byroniana in his possession. And the late Mr. H. K. Grant shared with me his researches into the Scottish ancestry of Byron and sent me some useful books.

In Geneva, Mr. Arnold A. L. Armstrong, former British Consul, gave me the benefit of his wide knowledge of the Genevese background of Byron, as did also Professor H. W. Häusermann, Professor of English at the University of Geneva.

In Italy, I had the privilege of examining Byron's Italian letters to the Countess Teresa Guiccioli, Teresa's manuscript *"Vie de Lord Byron en Italie,"* and many other items in the Gamba collection, through the courtesy of the Marchesa Iris Origo, who was then preparing her *The Last Attachment,* the story of Byron and the Countess Guiccioli. The Marchesa has also rendered me valuable service by furnishing me with copies of Italian documents, answering innumerable questions, and finally reading the typescript of my Italian chapters. The Marchesa Origo's friend Signorina Elsa Dallolio has given me valuable help, particularly in arranging for the microfilming of Teresa Guiccioli's *"Vie."* To Professor Manara Valgimigli, Librarian of the Biblioteca Classense, Ravenna, I am indebted for permission to quote from the *"Vie."*

I am grateful to Signora Vera Cacciatore, librarian and curator of the Keats-Shelley Memorial in Rome, for helping me to get microfilms of manuscripts in the library and for many courtesies beyond the line of duty. My thanks are due also to Mr. William Wilson, sometime director of the British Information Office in Venice, for arranging for me to see the Palazzo Mocenigo and to examine documents in the Museo Correr; and to Professor Mario Praz, the Marchesa Enrica Viviani Della Robbia, and Signora F. Farini-Cini for various courtesies in furtherance of my research.

My recollection of the hospitality I met with in Greece is livelier than my memory of the names of many who aided my research in one way or another. I felt almost as if I were the recipient of the gratitude the Greeks owed to the memory of Byron. Of those who helped me most I must mention Miss Joan Clarke of the British Information Office in Athens, who assisted me to make contacts which were extremely useful in my work; Mr. Nassos Tzartzanos, who helped to arrange for the microfilming of various documents; Mr. Emm. Protopsaltis, Curator of the Archives of the State, who translated many documents in the archives for me and gave me permission to quote from them; Mr. Dam. Kyriasis, who allowed me to microfilm letters from his fine collection of manuscripts; Mr. K. Th. Dimaras, who called my attention to much useful material in Greece; Mr. Linos Politis, professor and scholar, who gave me much aid and encouragement; Mr. Michael D. Volonakis, who shared with me his knowledge of Byron in Greece; and the librarians of the British School of Archæology and the Gennadion Library. While speaking of the Greeks, I should mention the very great service rendered me by Mr. George Savidis, then a student at Cambridge, who translated and summarized for me a number of Greek documents and letters in the Murrays' Byron collection in London.

I owe a special debt to the memory of the late Newman Ivey White, the Shelley scholar, who generously gave up his intention to write a life of Byron after learning of my researches in England, and who as generously offered me material that had been prepared for him.

To American Byron scholars I also owe much. Professor C. L. Cline at the University of Texas supplied me with much new material which he was using in his *Byron, Shelley and their Pisan Circle.* I am grateful for various kinds of assistance to Professors Willis W. Pratt, Guy Steffan, and Ernest J. Lovell, Jr., Byronians all, and all of the University of Texas.

To Miss Marion Kingston (now Mrs. M. J. Stocking) I am

grateful for making available to me a list of Byroniana in the Abinger papers, which she catalogued, and to Professor Edward McAleer my thanks are due for transcribing references to Byron in some letters of Mrs. Mason (Lady Mountcashell). Professor James A. Notopoulos of Trinity College, Hartford, Connecticut, has given me valuable aid by translating certain Greek documents and by making available to me his researches on Greek folk songs relating to Byron and a contemporary account of Byron by a soldier in the Greek Revolution.

For a medical analysis of Byron's lameness and last illness I am indebted to Dr. P. D. Genovese of Indianapolis and Dr. Nolan D. C. Lewis, Director of Research in Neurology and Psychiatry at the New Jersey Neuro-Psychiatric Institute.

For information and encouragement I am grateful to Mrs. Doris Langley Moore, long a Byron enthusiast; Mr. André Maurois, who has had a constant interest in Byron since he wrote his biography, the last full-length life of the poet; Michael Joyce, biographer of John Cam Hobhouse; Edmund Blunden, now Professor of English at the University of Hong Kong; Lady Rosalie Mander, biographer of Trelawny; Professor E. R. Vincent of Corpus Christi College, Cambridge; Peter Quennell, biographer and editor of Byron's letters; Professor T. G. Ehrsam of New York University, who warned me away from Byron forgeries; Dr. David V. Erdman, now Editor of Publications of the New York Public Library; Professor Cecil Lang of Yale University; Professor Gilbert Highet of Columbia University; Miss Mabel A. E. Steele, curator of the Keats collection at the Houghton Library, Harvard University; Mr. W. Douglas Seymour, collector of Byroniana in the Nottingham area; the late Dr. William A. Borst, who gave me much information about Byron's "First Pilgrimage"; and Mr. H. B. Forster, formerly of the British Council of Patras, Greece, who made some researches for me on Byron in the Ionian Islands.

I must express my gratitude to innumerable scholars in Byronian and related fields who have given me the benefit of their researches, have called my attention to useful material, and have sent me offprints of articles. Where I have used the material I have given credit to them in the notes.

I wish to make grateful acknowledgment to the members of the Rutgers University Research Council, whose several grants made the writing of this book possible. My first extensive grant from the Research Council launched my *annus mirabilis* (1947–8) by providing me leisure and money to follow Byron's trail through Europe in search of biographical material; the second (1950–1) gave me a year's leave in which to write. My special thanks are due to the Director of the Council, Professor William H. Cole, and to Professor Donald F. Cameron, University Librarian, who first fostered my project.

For corrections in the manuscript and for helpful suggestions I am indebted to Mr. Herbert Weinstock, Executive Editor at Alfred A. Knopf, Inc. And for lending his keen eye to the reading of proofs I wish to thank my colleague, Paul Fussell, Jr.

I can never adequately thank my wife, Marion Marchand, for molding her life to the exigencies of authorship in her home for six years, for assisting in the herculean task of cutting in half a manuscript which in the first draft ran to over one million words, in checking quotations, and in suffering through proofs and index. Whatever the "rewards of authorship" may be, she deserves them equally with the author.

LESLIE A. MARCHAND

# ACKNOWLEDGMENTS

FOR PERMISSION to quote from copyrighted books and periodicals, my thanks are due to the following individuals and publishers:

The Countess of Airlie's executors and A. P. Watt & Son—for quotations from *In Whig Society*, by Mabell, Countess of Airlie (published by Hodder and Stoughton, Ltd., 1921).

George Allen & Unwin, Ltd.—for quotations from *The Diary of Dr. John William Polidori*, edited by W. M. Rossetti (published by Elkin Mathews, 1911).

Appleton-Century-Crofts, Inc.—for quotations from *The Friend of Shelley*, by H. J. Massingham (published by D. Appleton & Co., 1930).

Ernest Benn, Ltd.—for quotations from *The Complete Works of Percy Bysshe Shelley*, edited by Roger Ingpen and Walter E. Peck, 1928–9.

Jonathan Cape, Ltd.—for quotations from *The Last Attachment*, by Iris Origo, 1949; and *Byron*, by André Maurois, 1930.

The Cresset Press—for quotations from *The Autobiography of Leigh Hunt*, edited by J. E. Morpurgo, 1949.

J. M. Dent & Sons, Ltd.—for quotations from *Henry Crabb Robinson on Books and Their Writers*, edited by Edith J. Morley, 3 vols., 1938.

Harvard University Press—for quotations from *Byron, Shelley and Their Pisan Circle*, by C. L. Cline, 1952.

The Macmillan Company, New York—for quotations from *His Very Self and Voice*, edited by Ernest J. Lovell, Jr., 1954.

Major Edward C. Mayne and A. P. Watt & Son—for quotations from *The Life and Letters of Anne Isabella Lady Noel Byron*, by Ethel Colburn Mayne (published by Constable & Co., Ltd., 1929).

The modern Language Association of America—for quotations from articles in *PMLA*.

Sir John Murray—for quotations from books in which he holds copyright.

Sir Harold Nicolson—for quotations from *Byron, the Last Journey* (published by Constable & Co., Ltd., 1924).

Oliver & Boyd, Ltd.—for quotations from *The Journal of Sir Walter Scott,* edited by J. G. Tait, 1950.

Professor Willis W. Pratt and Miss Fannie Ratchford, curator of the Rare Books Collections of the University of Texas—for quotations from *Byron at Southwell,* by Willis W. Pratt, 1948.

The Richards Press, Ltd.—for quotations from *The Byron Mystery,* by Sir John C. Fox (published by Grant Richards, Ltd., 1924).

Routledge & Kegan Paul, Ltd.—for quotations from *Byron, the Poet,* edited by Walter A. Briscoe (published by Routledge & Sons, Ltd., 1924).

Martin Secker & Warburg, Ltd.—for quotations from *Byron in Perspective,* by J. D. Symon (published by Frederick A. Stokes Co., New York, 1925).

The University of Iowa—for quotations from *My Leigh Hunt Library: the Holograph Letters,* by Luther A. Brewer, 1938.

University of Oklahoma Press—for quotations from *Mary Shelley's Journal,* 1947; *The Letters of Mary W. Shelley,* 2 vols., 1944; *Maria Gisborne & Edward E. Williams,* 1951—all edited by Frederick L. Jones; and *John Bull's Letter to Lord Byron,* edited by Alan Lang Strout, 1947.

Yale University Press—for quotations from *Lord Byron's First Pilgrimage,* by William A. Borst, 1948.

# CONTENTS

## VOLUME ONE



## VOLUME TWO

VOLUME THREE

# ILLUSTRATIONS

## VOLUME ONE

## VOLUME TWO

## VOLUME THREE

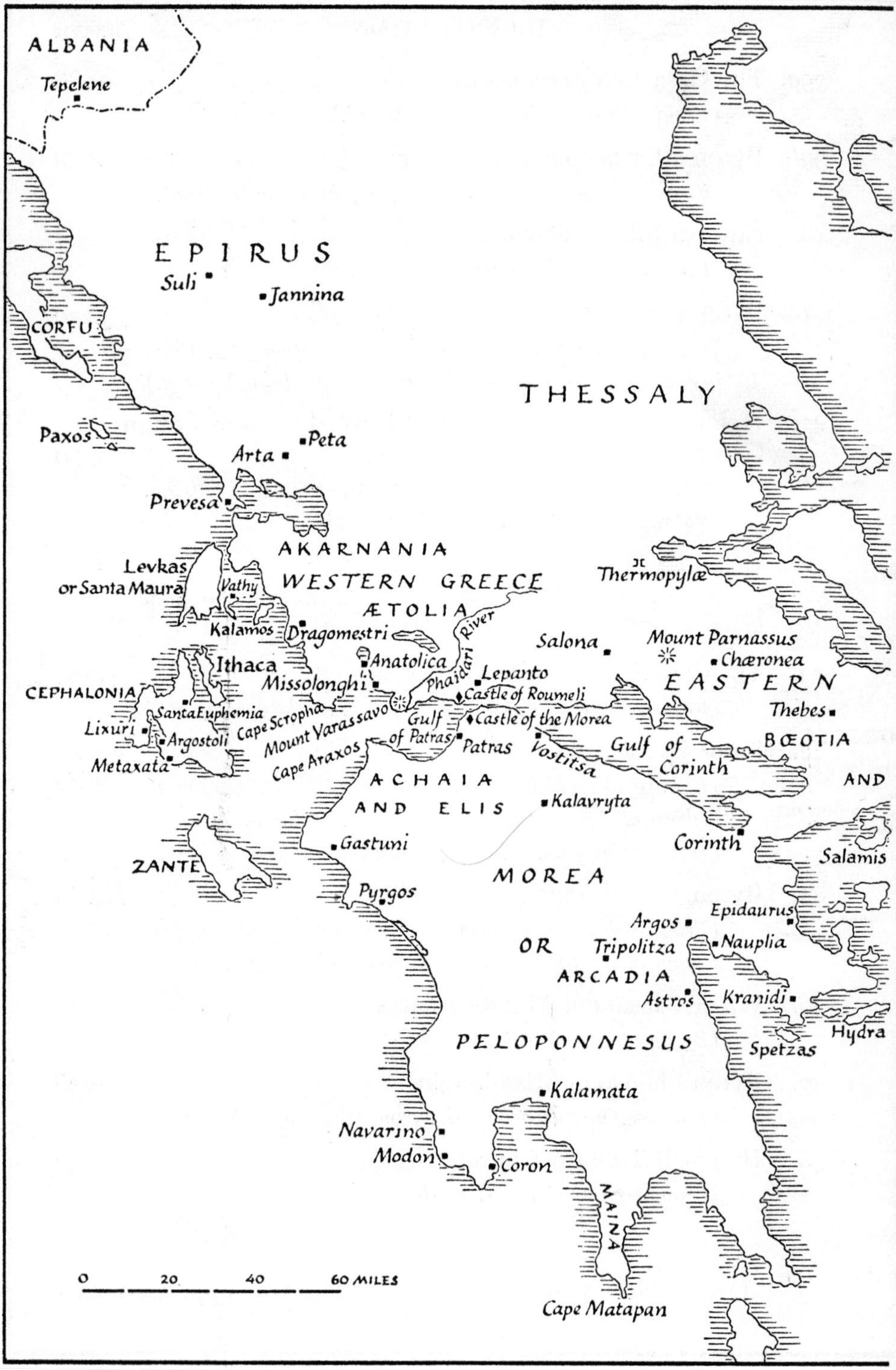
ALBANIA
Tepelene
EPIRUS
Suli
Jannina
CORFU
THESSALY
Paxos
Arta
Peta
Prevesa
AKARNANIA
Levkas
or Santa Maura
Vathy
WESTERN GREECE
ÆTOLIA
Thermopylæ
Kalamos
Dragomestri
Phaidari River
Salona
Mount Parnassus
Chæronea
Ithaca
Anatolica
Lepanto
CEPHALONIA
Missolonghi
Castle of Roumeli
EASTERN
Santa Euphemia
Cape Scropha
Castle of the Morea
Thebes
Lixuri
Argostoli
Mount Varassavo
Gulf of Patras
Patras
Vostitsa
Gulf of Corinth
BŒOTIA
Metaxata
Cape Araxos
AND
ACHAIA
AND ELIS
Kalavryta
Corinth
ZANTE
Gastuni
Salamis
MOREA
Pyrgos
Epidaurus
Argos
OR
Tripolitza
Nauplia
ARCADIA
Astros
Kranidi
Hydra
PELOPONNESUS
Spetzas
Kalamata
Navarino
Modon
Coron
MAINA
0 20 40 60 MILES
Cape Matapan

Samothrace
Sestos
Abydos
Mount Athos
Hellespont
(Dardanelles)
Plains of
Troy
MITYLENE
OR LESBOS
ÆGEAN
SEA
EUBŒA
CHIOS
Smyrna
GREECE
Marathon
ATTICA
Athens
Piræus
Cape Colonni
(Sunium)
Kea
Paros
Antiparos
NAXOS

# BYRON : *A Biography*

VOLUME I

# NOTES

*Superscript numbers from 1 to 9 in the text refer to notes at the foot of the page which are explanatory or of general interest; the superior characters* $^{n}$ *in the text refer to notes of bibliographical or scholarly interest (chiefly source identifications), which are indicated by page and line at the back of each volume.*

# CHAPTER I

## *To 1788*

## The Byrons and the Gordons

GEORGE GORDON, the sixth Lord Byron, was descended from two of the most colorful strains in the history of the British aristocracy. The Byrons, who with some uncertainties trace their ancestry back to the Buruns, contemporaries of William the Conqueror, seem to have grown more irresponsible with each generation, until the summit of social irregularity is reached in the character and conduct of the great-uncle and the father of the poet, if not indeed in the poet himself. The Gordons of Gight, Byron's maternal ancestors, display a startling record of violence rare even in the annals of Scottish lairds. Beginning with Sir William Gordon, first of the House of Gight, who fell at Flodden Field in 1513, they presented through the seventeenth century a spectacle of unrestrained barbarity which rivaled the Newgate Calendar. Signs that they were subsiding into a civilized state appeared only a little before the line ran out with Byron's mother, Catherine Gordon, the unlucky thirteenth to hold the castle and lands in Aberdeenshire.

Thomas Moore has perpetuated among biographers of Byron the saying that "In the character of the noble poet the pride of ancestry was undoubtedly one of the most decided features."[1] But Byron had a realistic and not always sanguine appreciation

[1] Moore, I, 1. John Cam Hobhouse, however, who knew Byron longer and associated with him more intimately than did Moore, wrote in the margin of his copy of Moore, opposite this passage: "This may be true but I never perceived it."

of what his ancestors had contributed to his character. He was sometimes inclined to boast of his Scottish descent from James I, but in the main it was the longer line of his paternal ancestry which held his interest and stimulated his imagination.

The first members of the Byron family in England are supposed to have been Ernegis and Radulfus (Ralph) de Burun, large landholders in the north of England in the time of the Conqueror. Whether he came in that overladen ship with William I or not, Ralph, whom some genealogists believe to be an ancestor of the poet, is mentioned (for his landed estates) in Domesday Book.[2] By the time of Henry II (1165–1189) the spelling "Byron" had been fixed.

Little is known of the Byrons before the sixteenth century except the extent of their lands.[n] Although they were well established in Nottinghamshire by the time of Henry VIII, the picturesque seat that has been associated with the name ever since came through the favor of that monarch to Sir John Byron. He must have been one of Henry's loyal supporters, for he was created Steward of Manchester and Rochdale and Lieutenant of the Forest of Sherwood. And on the dissolution of the monasteries Henry sold to "our beloved servant John Byron of Colewyke," for the nominal sum of £810, "all the house and site, ground and soil, of the late Monastery or Priory of Newstede within the Forest of Sherewode in our said County of Notingham," together with large holdings of the monks in the adjoining Papplewick and Hucknall Torkard and in the surrounding country and forest.[n] The new owner was not cheated, for the annual income of the property was then valued at £219. 18*s.* 8*d.*[n]

The Priory of Newstead was founded by Henry II, probably between 1163 and 1173, for Canons Regular of the Order of St. Augustine, known as Austin Canons or Black Canons, for the color of their robes. The exact date of the foundation charter is not known, and there is no direct evidence for the popular legend

[2] Byron the poet referred, somewhat inaccurately, to a few of his early ancestors in his poem "On Leaving Newstead Abbey." And again in *Don Juan* (X, 36) he wrote of the first of the clan:

*Erneis, Radulphus—eight-and-forty manors . . .*
*Were* their *reward for following Billy's banners. . . .*

that Henry founded the Abbey in remorse for the murder of Thomas à Becket in 1170.[n] In the nearly four hundred years before the property came to the Byrons, the Canons had built a handsome gray stone Gothic church and, adjoining it, the extensive halls of the Priory surrounding a square cloister that enclosed an open court with a fountain in the middle. Sir John had no great difficulty in converting it into an extensive country estate. He and his descendants may have used the stone of two walls of the church as a quarry ready to hand for alterations and repairs,[n] for when the poet first saw Newstead in 1798 there remained nothing but the front or west wall and the south side of the nave, which was also the wall of the main structure of the Priory.

A bar sinister was cast on the escutcheon (but not included in the coat of arms, perhaps because the dishonor was later rectified by marriage with the lady) by this same Byron who was the first owner of Newstead. His *filius naturalis* (by Elizabeth, daughter of William Costerden and wife of George Halghe, and subsequently Sir John Byron's second wife) inherited the estates by deed of gift in 1576, his illegitimacy preventing the ordinary legal inheritance.[3] He too acquired the title of Sir John when Queen Elizabeth knighted him in 1579, and he became something of a legendary character in his day for his lavish entertainment and for that remarkable hirsute adornment which won him the sobriquet of "Little Sir John with the Great Beard." [n]

The second Sir John to hold Newstead was not oppressed by his illegitimate birth, for he married Alice, daughter of Sir Nicholas Strelley, a neighboring gentleman, and apparently lived in great state at the Abbey, where he increased his expenses by maintaining a troop of players. A later Sir John Byron, a faithful though not very successful general of Charles I, was created Baron Byron of Rochdale in the county of Lancaster on October 24, 1643. The Byrons lost most of their property in the Civil War.

[3] If Byron the poet knew of this "blot on the 'scutcheon" he never referred to it, and he was not reticent about the *faux pas* either of himself or of his ancestors. John Galt was the first to point to the bar sinister in the Byron lineage (p. 16). The translator of Elze's *Lord Byron* gives in an appendix (pp. 435–8) the whole evidence for the charge of illegitimacy from the Herald's Visitation of the County of Lancaster (1567).

Lord Byron followed Charles II into exile, serving as superintendent-general of the house and family of the Duke of York, later James II, and died childless in Paris in 1652. According to Pepys, Lord Byron served the exiled monarch in another way of which he was perhaps not conscious, for his second wife, Eleanor, is mentioned in the famous *Diary* as having been the seventeenth mistress of Charles II when abroad. She may have been trying to recover the fortunes of the Byron family, drained by the wars, for Pepys records that she did not leave Charles till she had extorted from him an "order for £4000 worth of plate to be made for her; but by delays, thanks be to God! she died before she had it." [n]

After the death of his older brother, Sir Richard Byron succeeded to the Barony. His epitaph in Hucknall Torkard church records that with his brothers he faithfully served Charles I in the Civil War and that they "suffered much for their loyalty, and lost all their present fortune; yet it pleased God so to bless the honest endeavours of the said Richard Lord Byron that he repurchased part of their ancient inheritance." [n] Newstead Abbey, sequestered by the Parliament but restored on the accession of Charles II, continued to be the seat of the Byrons. Richard's only surviving son, William, became the third Baron. He had in 1661 married Elizabeth, daughter of John Viscount Chaworth of Ireland, thereby establishing the link of blood relationship between the poet and Mary Chaworth, and also the cousinship of William Chaworth with the fifth Baron Byron, who killed him in a duel in 1765.

The fourth Lord took three wives in succession. The third, who was the poet's great-grandmother, Frances, daughter of William Lord Berkeley, may have contributed more to the waywardness and eccentricity of her descendants than all the Byrons. We know little enough about her, but all her descendants displayed irregularities of behavior not before observed in the Byron line.

Six children were born to the fourth Baron Byron and Frances Berkeley: William, the fifth Lord; John, who had a stormy career as a commodore and later as an admiral in the Navy and who became the grandfather of the poet; three younger sons who died early; and Isabella, the eldest child, whose first husband was

Henry, fourth Earl of Carlisle, progenitor of the Lord Carlisle who was the poet's guardian during his minority.

Born in 1722, the fifth Lord Byron came to the title at the age of fourteen on the death of his father. He entered the Navy and became lieutenant of the *Victory* under Admiral Balchen, but had the good fortune to leave the ship just before she was lost on the rocks of Alderney.[n] He had married Elizabeth, heiress of Charles Shaw of Besthorpe Hall, Norfolk, in 1747, but he frequently left Newstead for London, where he was known as a rake (probably from his once having tried to carry off Miss Bellamy, the actress).[n]

Already before his fortieth year his extravagances had begun to make him a legendary figure among his tenants and neighbors. Both in town and country he lived luxuriously and indulged every whim. Old Joe Murray, his most trusted and devoted servant for many years, reported that his "dear late Lord, whenever there were any very rare and costly articles of vertu or art on sale in London, would order horses to his carriage and set out at a moment's notice to purchase them." [n] In 1749, only two years after his marriage, he built among the trees on a rise overlooking the lake a miniature castle, said to be the scene of many concerts and gay parties. During his later years of seclusion, when fantastic popular legends grew out of the common gossip about the "Wicked Lord," it was called "Folly Castle" and was darkly hinted to be the rendezvous for unspeakable orgies.[n]

It may have been during this same period that, nostalgic for his Navy days, he built two turreted forts on the banks of the upper lake and waged, with the aid of his servants, mimic naval warfare upon them from small armed vessels.[n] His follies had already drained the resources of Newstead when Horace Walpole visited him in 1760. This lover of the Gothic found the Abbey delightful, but was shocked that the park had been stripped of its trees. ". . . the present Lord has lost large sums," he wrote, "and paid part in old oaks, five thousand pounds worth of which have been cut near the house." [n]

Handsome as a Byron and ruddy as a country squire, Lord Byron loved the congeniality of the London clubs. Once a month a group of Nottinghamshire gentlemen dined at the Star and Garter tavern in Pall-Mall. On January 26, 1765, Lord Byron, then in his middle forties, was present at the monthly gathering. Near him sat his kinsman and neighbor William Chaworth of Annesley Hall. Heated with claret after dinner, they got into an argument as to the best way of preserving game. The dispute was broken up by the others, but not before Mr. Chaworth had uttered some words that sounded like a veiled challenge. When Lord Byron went out the door he found Mr. Chaworth waiting for him at the top of the stairs and tempers flared up again. They asked for an empty room. A waiter opened a door, left a candle, and then departed. Taking no chances in the darkened room, Chaworth drew his blade and made the first thrust, entangling his sword in the left side of Lord Byron's waistcoat. Thinking he had wounded or killed his adversary, Chaworth came close, and Lord Byron shortened his sword and ran him through the belly near the navel.

Chaworth died the next day, making no more damaging statement than that he had been a fool to fight in a darkened room and that he was glad he had not to answer for another man's life. Though pressed by his friends, he never said that the fighting was unfair. Chaworth was a better swordsman than Lord Byron, whose weapon was the pistol.

The coroner's jury gave a verdict of "Wilful Murder," and Lord Byron was sent to the Tower. When he was tried by his peers on April 16 and 17 in Westminster Hall, the interest ran so high that tickets of admission were said to have sold for as much as six guineas.[n] Lord Byron defended himself with a prepared statement that was clear and objective. He admitted the irregularity of the fighting in the dimly lighted room, but pointed to the provocation of Mr. Chaworth and the fairness of the combat considering the circumstances. One hundred and nineteen lords voted "Not guilty of murder, but guilty of manslaughter," and four simply "Not guilty." [n]

Following the notoriety of the trial, Lord Byron found it unpleasant to visit London. When compelled to go on business, according to one story, "he travelled with the utmost privacy, taking the feigned name of Waters." [n] If he felt much remorse for killing his kinsman, it must have worn off before long, nor did he withdraw from the world until some time later when poverty and quarrels had soured his relations with most of his neighbors.

In October 1770, more than five years after the duel, Joe Murray witnessed a grand and expensive celebration at Newstead in honor of the coming of age of the only son and heir of his master, when "a vessel rigged and equipped was brought over land from one of our ports all the way to Newstead . . . she had 21 guns and discharged them on the occasion in question, the report being heard all over Nottingham and some of the adjoining counties." [n]

It was not long, however, before an event occurred which disturbed his lordship much more than did the duel. He had no doubt counted on the marriage of his son to Miss Danvers,[n] a lady of large fortune, to extricate him from financial difficulties, but shortly before the wedding the undutiful boy eloped with his first cousin, Juliana Elizabeth Byron, daughter of the impecunious Admiral. From that time forward the already crotchety old Baron became more unsocial, and by his own strange behavior encouraged those popular legends of the "Wicked Lord" which persisted long after his death. Like his famous great-nephew later, he always carried pistols, and it was reported that on one occasion when his neighbor Sir John Warren came to dine, he found pistols placed on the table as if they were a customary part of the dinner service.[n] And Byron the poet recorded that his uncle always kept in his bedchamber the sword with which he had killed Chaworth.[n]

While there is undoubtedly no truth in the tales that were told of his throwing Lady Byron into the pond, or of his shooting a coachman for a minor offense, pitching the corpse into the coach with his wife, and then mounting the box and driving off,[n] he did make himself obnoxious enough so that she left him. Perhaps he had already taken into his favor the servant Elizabeth Hardstaff, commonly referred to as "Lady Betty," who served him faithfully and ministered to his whims for the rest of his life, and who had the dubious benefit of being the chief legatee in his will signed in 1785 (his wife died in 1788).

Joe Murray related that "His Lordship always dined quite alone and for some years one and the same Bottle of Claret was kept by me by his Lordship's order the cork drawn and when the cloth was removed his Lordship cried aloud, 'Joe, put the claret on the table.' . . . The Claret was daily removed . . . and reappeared on each successive day but never touched." [n] More timber was sold until the forests were denuded, the "Pilgrim" or "Druid" oak near the gatehouse being saved only by the intervention of some benevolent purchasers. In addition, the old lord is said to have killed twenty-seven hundred head of deer in the park and sold them for very little to the markets in the neighboring town of Mansfield.[n] In 1784 he illegally leased the coal mines on the Rochdale estate in Lancashire, which had been in the Byron family since the time of Edward I, for the annual rental of only £60.[n] Byron the poet was troubled most of his life with litigation over the estate.

The old lord had cut all ties with his relatives after the marriage of his son, though his niece Mrs. Charles Leigh (daughter of the Admiral) long continued to visit him.[n] When his grandson was killed at the siege of Calvi in 1794, his grand-nephew George Gordon Byron (or George Byron Gordon, as he was called in Scotland), then six and one-half years old, became heir presumptive to the ancient Byron estates. The old lord, shut up in solitude and engrossed in feeding the crickets he had tamed and taught to crawl over him,[n] had no interest in "the little boy in Aberdeen."

The fourth Baron's second son, John, grandfather of the poet, was scarcely less spectacular in his career, though considerably more genial in his personality than his brother the "Wicked Lord." Born at Newstead Abbey on November 8, 1723, he left school early and entered the Navy, perhaps to escape the consequences of some such escapade as that hinted at in a gossip column of a later time where it is said that at school "his bedmaker evinced his abilities in the field of Venus." [n] At any rate, early in 1740, while he was not yet seventeen, he embarked as midshipman on board the *Wager*, one of the ships sent out under Commodore Anson to harass the Spanish in the South Seas. The shipwreck, starvation, and hardships he encountered on that voyage he described in his *Narrative*, published in 1768.[n] The *Wager*, totally unseaworthy, was wrecked on May 14, 1741, on the rocky coast of Patagonia, north of the Strait of Magellan. The unspeakable privations of the seamen before they reached the mainland of Chile, where they were held three years by the Spanish government, are related with typical eighteenth-century reserve. Without wincing, Byron tells of making a meal on the paw and skin of a favorite dog, an incident that his equally hardy descendant took almost verbatim from his "grand-dad's 'Narrative'" and used with ironic relish in the scene of the shipwreck in *Don Juan*.[n]

Allowed to return to England in 1746, John Byron achieved rapid successes both at sea and on land. Soon, however, after several amorous adventures, he settled on shore, and in August 1748 married his first cousin Sophia Trevanion at her home town of Carhais in Cornwall. Her mother was a sister of Frances Berkeley, who had married the fourth Lord Byron.[4] Sophia Byron was apparently a lady of considerable charm and intelligence. She was long an intimate friend of Mrs. Thrale (later Piozzi), the friend of Dr. Johnson, with whom Mrs. Byron was a favorite.[5] She bore nine children to her nautical husband, the first son being the scapegrace father of the poet.

"Hardy Byron," as his sailors called him, was not yet through with his adventures. Again in 1764, then a commodore, he put to sea as commander of the *Dolphin*, which with the *Tamar* began a voyage of discovery that took him through the Strait of Magellan and around the globe. This voyage was something of a fiasco. In the neighborhood of the strait he saw, according to his journal, some giant natives whom later voyagers could never find. Sailing westward from Magellan, Byron miraculously avoided all but a few of the northernmost islands with which those seas are crowded. His biographer wrote "It now seems almost wonderful how these ships could have sailed through this part of the

[4] There were several first-cousin marriages in addition to this in the Byron family: the Admiral's daughter Juliana Elizabeth married William, son of the fifth Baron, her father's brother; Augusta Byron, the poet's half-sister, married her first cousin Colonel George Leigh, son of her father's sister Frances. There were also several marriages of cousins among the Gordons. Byron's first boyish "passion" was for his distant cousin Mary Duff; his second for his first cousin Margaret Parker; his third for another distant cousin, Mary Chaworth.

[5] There are frequent references to Sophia Byron in the letters of Mrs. Piozzi.

ocean without making grander discoveries; but they appear to have held a straight course westward, intent only on getting the voyage over." [n]

By the time he was promoted to the rank of Rear-Admiral in 1775 (his highest rank was Vice-Admiral, 1778) he had encountered so many storms that he came to be known as "Foulweather Jack." At his home in the west of England he had a reputation for hospitality and liberality. And tales of his gallantry were circulated with relish. One of these thinly veiled stories, concerning "Miss Betsy G——n" and her "Nautical Lover," was published in 1773. Betsy, a chambermaid with superior education and beauty, was caught in her master's bed and dismissed, whereupon the Admiral, unwilling to relinquish her charms, found lodgings for her in London and continued to visit her. When his wife followed him to her retreat, he found her more secluded quarters. It is touchingly reported that she "rejected considerable sums of money for temporary gratifications, and even settlements" and remained faithful to her "Nautical Lover." [n] Perhaps Mrs. Thrale had this or some similar escapade in mind when she referred later to her intimate friend Sophia Trevanion as "wife to the Admiral, *pour ses péchés*." [n]

Before the Admiral died in 1786, his eldest son, John ("Mad Jack"), had so far exceeded him in gallantry, in scandal, and in extravagance as to cause the old seaman to disinherit him.

Born at Plymouth on February 7, 1756, John Byron, the father of the poet, was first sent to Westminster School and later to a French military academy, where he probably learned the language and acquired a taste for the "pastimes and prodigalities" that made him notorious while still a young man. His father bought him a commission in the Guards and he served for a time with the British forces in America. But by 1778 he was back in London, where he devoted himself to the pursuits of the man of fashion. He was handsome and brave but apparently without feeling or principle in his amours, for it is said that to pay his gambling debts he did not hesitate to levy contributions upon the ladies who favored him.[n]

The profligate son was only twenty-two when in the summer of 1778 he met one of the most captivating belles of the London drawing-rooms, the accomplished and beautiful Lady Carmarthen, wife of Francis, then a marquis and afterwards fifth Duke of Leeds. She was the only child and heiress of the last Earl of Holderness, a man of cultivation and learning who had assisted in the education of the eldest sons of the King. Born Lady Amelia d'Arcy, and holding the title of Baroness Conyers in her own right, she had superior education and talents. It is likely, however, that the self-assured and handsome Guardsman was, at least at first, as much interested in her fortune as in her natural attractions, for he had already outrun the purse and patience of his family. And he could not have been unaware that her father at his death on May 16 of that year had left her for life an estate that yielded £4,000 a year.

According to an account in a contemporary "scandal sheet," [n] the Marchioness was lacking neither in experience nor in aggressiveness when she met Captain Byron. She was, the report goes, only nineteen when, having set her heart on the apparently indifferent Marquis, she had contrived through a female relation to entice his interest and accomplish her purpose of marrying him. For a while they were blissfully happy, and she bore him three children before her fateful meeting with the Captain in 1778. Soon, however, domestic bliss began to pall on the young Marquis and he turned more and more to gaming and masquerades. In jealousy and resentment "she yielded to the impulse of her complicated passions, and with one of her own domestics, planted the antlers on his lordship's brow."

According to the scandalous narrative, while the Marquis was absent in the country his lady one day was persuaded to make a trip to Coxheath when Captain Byron was of the party.[6] At first she showed him a genuine or feigned indifference and even made him the butt of her wit, but soon succumbed to his charm and became entirely infatuated with him, casting aside all pru-

[6] The author of the gossip column refers to Byron as "Captain B." Some time after his return from the American campaign, and probably before he eloped with the Marchioness, Captain Byron sent a request to Major General Picton for permission to dispose of his captain-lieutenancy in the 12th Regiment of Foot, and to retire on the half-pay of a lieutenant. (The document was sold at the Union Art Galleries auction, April 25, 1934.)

dence and discretion. The Marquis, returning before he was due, learned that the Captain and the Marchioness were gone for the day to dine at Barrowhedges, and he set out in pursuit, but they were warned and made their escape.

The frustrated Marquis returned home in a rage and ordered the doors locked against the Marchioness. The next day the Captain prepared apartments for her and she sent for her clothes and jewels, which were delivered to her messenger. ". . . at the same time she requested of his lordship, in a card, to favour her with the last new *vis-à-vis* he had given her: to this request he also consented, having previously ordered his coach-maker to obliterate the arms." [n]

Captain Byron married the lady on June 9 of the following year (the Marquis had secured a divorce by act of Parliament), whether at the insistence of her family and friends or whether induced by her charms and devotion (and income) it is difficult to say. After retiring for a time to her house near Doncaster, [n] the pair went to France to escape the éclat of the scandal. It was convenient also to evade the English creditors who were always in pursuit of the gay Captain.

That the madcap Byron was devoted to his heiress in his fashion seems probable, for they lived together in France until her death on January 26, 1784. She bore him three children, [n] the last and only one to survive beyond infancy being Augusta, the poet's half-sister, born in 1783. The poet later replied to an accusation that his father's "brutal conduct" had caused the greatest misery and remorse to the Marchioness and that she died literally of a broken heart: "So far from being 'brutal,' he was, according to the testimony of all those who knew him, of an extremely amiable and (*enjoué*) joyous character, but careless (*insouciant*) and dissipated. . . . It is not by 'brutality' that a young Officer in the Guards seduces and carries off a Marchioness, and marries two heiresses. It is true that he was a very handsome man, which goes a great way." [n]

Captain Byron was soon sufficiently recovered in spirit and immersed in debt (his wife's £4,000 a year was lost to him after her death) to leave the carefree life of Paris for the chilly shores of England, once more in search of an heiress. Knowing that the happy hunting-ground for fortunes in the marriage market was to be found in the ballrooms of Bath, the handsome Captain appeared in that city in the spring of 1785 and no doubt cut a considerable figure, his natural grace heightened by French manners and speech. What choice he had is not known, but he met and soon turned the head of Catherine Gordon of Gight. Though her fortune of more than £23,000, "doubled by rumour,"[7] may not have been the largest in the Bath market, certainly it must have seemed the most accessible to the blasé, suave Captain. Catherine Gordon was an inexperienced Scottish girl of twenty seeking excitement and flirtation in the city of fashion and wealth. She had come to Bath early in 1785 to buy some jewelry, attend Lindsay's dancing parties, and in short to see life on a larger scale and in a freer atmosphere than was possible in Banff, where she had lived with her grandmother since the death of her parents. Mrs. Duff, wife of the Admiral, was then living in Bath and could introduce her into society. There seems to have been a family scheme to save the heiress from Scottish fortune-hunters, but ironically she succumbed to the blandishments of a more subtle adventurer.[n] Though in the bloom of youth, she was rather plain and coarse, "awkward in her movements, provincial in her accent and manner,"[n] and, as her son later said, "haughty as Lucifer." But, hard-pressed as he was, Captain Byron saw opportunity knocking at his door and seized it. With his elegant dancing he swept the poor country girl off her feet, and on May 13, 1785, they stood before the rector, John Chapman, in the church of St. Michael's, Bath, and for the second time Byron was united with an heiress.[n] If visions of his beautiful Marchioness troubled him on that occasion, he brushed them away, for he had married the mistress of Gight and the silly girl had not even insisted on a marriage settlement.

If in her naïveté and pride Catherine Gordon boasted to her Johnny Byron of the long, distinguished line of her ancestry,

[7] Leslie Stephen, article on Byron in *D.N.B.* Under forced sale to pay the debts of Captain Byron, her property was finally converted into a total sum in money of £23,430, and that is the figure usually given of her value as an heiress when Captain Byron met her, but the property was probably worth much more, possibly in excess of £30,000.

she may have amused the bored Romeo, though he was more interested in the cash value of her estate than in her pedigree. She could have pointed to Gordons (or Gordouns) in France at the time, or even before, the Buruns established themselves on English soil under the Conqueror. But that branch of the numerous Gordon family from which she was most proud to be directly descended dated from 1490, when Sir William Gordon traded the lands of Aboyne to his elder brother for the estate of Gight, which lay in the valley of the River Ythan about thirty miles north of Aberdeen.[n] Sir William was the third son of George, second Earl of Huntly, by his second wife, Princess Annabella Stuart, daughter of James I of Scotland.

But if Catherine had known the whole history of her lawless and barbaric clansmen, she could hardly have taken pride in their deeds. From their beginnings through the sixteenth century the Gight Gordons had a record of violence and banditry, of feuding and murder, which pales into insignificance the peccadilloes of the Byrons. Altogether they were an ill-starred family.

With due allowance for the lawlessness of the time and place, the Gight Gordons were among the most notorious of the Scottish lairds for their defiance of law and order. Sir George Gordon, the second laird, on October 12, 1564, with his son and eighteen others, was arraigned before the Privy Council for the "crewale invassion of William Con of Auchry and hurting and wounding of him in divers parts of his body to the great effusion of his blude; and striking and draging with a brydill three of Con's cottars and otheris."[n]

There are even more evidences of the brutalities of the lairds of Gight and their followers in the archives of the seventeenth century. Their feuds with the Mowats and the Hays are a token of the fierce audacities of the clans. In 1601, the Mowats having complained of the depredations and destructive raids of the Gordons, a messenger of the Privy Council was sent with letters against William Gordon (then the fifth laird) charging him to answer for certain crimes. The messenger would have been shot had not the laird been restrained. Hurling him into the hall, William seized the letters, cast them into a dish of broth, and with a dagger at his heart forced the officer to "sup and swallow thame." [n]

The wars of the Covenant gave the Gordons a happy chance to enter into some large-scale raids. Like the Byrons in England, they were Royalists, and they combined politics with plunder. But by the end of the seventeenth century or the beginning of the eighteenth, the establishment of more stable government and the cooling of the hot blood of the clans, under a regime that substituted peaceful trade and commerce for banditry and encouraged a cultivation of civilizing arts, gradually developed more sober traits in the Gordons of Gight. Probably as important in modifying their character during the next century was the intermarriage with other families which provided a leavening of literary traditions, Scots caution, and commercial astuteness, and a *soupçon* of wit and the lighter graces. In stressing the Gordon ancestry of Byron it should not be forgotten that he was related by blood and by direct descent to several other leading northern Scottish families.[n]

The ninth laird married his kinswoman Elizabeth Urquhart, who came of a family that produced several distinguished men, the most famous of whom was Sir Thomas, the sixteenth-century translator of Rabelais. Their only offspring was a daughter, Marie, who became the tenth "laird." When she married Alexander Davidson in 1701, her husband took the surname of Gordon and the insignia of the family of Gight, legal steps having been taken to keep the family name alive.[n] (The same provision later caused Byron's father to take the name of Byron Gordon.) It is not surprising that the riotous Gordons had run so far into debt that after Alexander Davidson had paid £40,000 the Gight family creditors still pursued him.[n] The son of this union, Alexander Gordon, the eleventh laird, married into a family as different from that of the Gordons as could be imagined. His wife was Margaret Duff (1720–1801), cousin of the first Earl of Fife and grandmother of Byron's mother. Her brother was the great-grandfather of Byron's Mary Duff, the poet's first childhood love. It was a family of canny Scots who achieved a remarkable commercial success. The Duffs, with ready money always at hand, were the bankers of the north.

The eleventh laird fathered fourteen children before he was drowned in the River Ythan on January 24, 1760, under circumstances that suggested suicide. The biographer of the Gordons remarks skeptically of the report in the *Aberdeen Journal* which said he had drowned while bathing: "Scotsmen in 1760 had not become slaves to the tub so much as to induce them to bathe in ice-covered rivers in the depths of winter." [n]

The eldest son, George Gordon, succeeding as the twelfth laird of Gight, brought more Innes blood into the family by marrying his second cousin Catherine, daughter of Alexander Innes, Sheriff-Clerk and Provost of Banff. Catherine Innes's mother was an Abercromby, so the strain of another northern family of note was mingled with that of the Gordons.

The twelfth laird had three daughters, but only Catherine Gordon was living when her father died in 1779, leaving her heir to a moderate fortune, a decaying castle, and a curious combination of ancestral traits.

The bride of Captain Byron had few intellectual endowments to compensate for her plainness and the rolling gait that made her conspicuous. She had been brought up by her grandmother Margaret Duff Gordon, a pious and ignorant old woman called by courtesy "Lady Gight," and had spent some time with the family of General Abercromby of Glassaugh, a kinsman and trustee for her mother. Catherine's education was inferior to that of most young girls of her social station in Scotland. Her Calvinistic training made her superstitious, a believer in ghosts, fortune-telling, and second sight. Though her letters were often forceful and direct when the subject moved her, her spelling and grammar displayed an astounding illiteracy. She was fond of gossip and was given to fits of melancholy followed by capricious outbursts of passion during which she would favor her hearers with some choice unrestrained language in the dialect of her native Buchan.[8] Her vanity gave her a fondness for finery

[8] Rev. W. Rogerson: "Lord Byron's Connection with Aberdeen," *Bon Accord*, May 8, 1902, p. 5. Sir Walter Scott recollected seeing Catherine Gordon at the theater in Edinburgh before her marriage when she was overcome by one of her emotional excesses. "It was during Mrs. Siddons's first or second visit to Edinburgh. . . . When the curtain fell, a large proportion of the ladies were generally in hysterics. I remember Miss Gordon of Gight,

and show which invited ridicule. But her affectionate nature and goodness made her steadfast in her sentimental attachments.

Where the Byrons spent their "treaclemoon," as their son later called the days following his own "fatal marriage," is not known. No doubt it was financed by the heiress and was spent somewhere far from the Captain's creditors. Mrs. Byron must have known that her relatives, especially her parsimonious and careful grandmother, would not be happy about her marriage. But by July of 1785 the Byrons were back in Scotland and already established at Gight. Perhaps the bridegroom was eager to take stock of his wife's property. By the middle of the summer Catherine, it seems, was already frightened by his free spending and was trying to check it.

But since she could never resist him, the Captain proceeded to lay waste the Gordon inheritance. For almost a year they continued to live in the ancient and already dilapidated castle. They were visited at Gight in September by Alexander Russell, Mrs. Byron's cousin, son of the commissioner of her estates. The young cousin, then only seventeen, was at once attracted by the suave and experienced Captain of the Guards and a little scandalized by the French freedom and prodigality that he had introduced into the sober Presbyterian life of the community.

When the boy arrived on Friday, September 23, Mr. Byron was out shooting. The visitor was shocked to see an English translation of Rousseau's *Nouvelle Héloise* on the table and guiltily picked it up to while away the hours before dinner. Mrs. Byron took *Peregrine Pickle* to read and her young cousin carried off "Eloisa" and read a great deal in it with uneasy relish. The next day it rained heavily. In the evening, "Piper come. Mr. and Mrs. Byron, Sally [a servant girl] and I danced, a long time without stopping. . . . Mr. B. very droll. . . . out to other room got three girls dancing Mr. B. took them in and made them

---

in particular, harrowing the house by the desperate and wild way in which she shrieked out Mrs. Siddons's exclamation, in the character of Isabella, 'Oh my Byron! Oh my Byron!' . . . The remarkable circumstance was, that the lady had not then seen Captain Byron. . . ." (Quoted, Moore, I, 614n.) The drama was Southern's *The Fatal Marriage,* in which the leading character is named Biron.

dance." At 10:40 young Russell drank some punch with Mr. Byron and went to his room. "11:30 piper still going and dancing. Mrs. B. was in bed. I afraid he will break Sabbath, too near it already."[n] But to his relief they stopped just before 12:00.

The recklessness of the spendthrift Captain was a shock to the cautious gentry. The reputation Johnny Byron had earned among his neighbors is indicated in a popular ballad of the time:

*O whare are ye gaeing, bonny Miss Gordon?*
*O, whare are ye gaeing, sae bonnie and braw?*
*Ye've married, wi' Johnny Byron*
*To squander the lands o' Gight awa'.*
*This youth is a rake, frae England is come;*
*The Scots dinna ken his extraction ava;*
*He keeps up his misses, his landlords he duns,*
*That's fast drawn the lands o' Gight awa'.*[n]

By the summer of 1786 Captain Byron had indeed squandered the lands of Gight away. The £3,000 in cash which Catherine Gordon had when she was married had been spent, and her other disposable property sold at a sacrifice on forced sale. And within a year after the marriage £8,000 had been borrowed on a mortgage on the estate. Spendthrift though he was, the Captain could hardly have found ways to waste so much money in Scotland, even with high festivity every night in the great hall. The probable solution to the mystery is that, there having been no marriage settlement, his previous creditors pressed him for what they could get. A change of residence seemed in order. The last trace of the Byrons in Scotland dates from March 1786. According to an advertisement in the *Aberdeen Journal* of March 13, Mr. Byron Gordon was trying to raise money by leasing "The Mains of Gight,"[n] and during that month the couple went through a second marriage ceremony in the Scotch form, no doubt for legal reasons connected with the sale of the estate, and not to appease local sentiment.[9]

They had left for England some time during the spring, pos-

[9] Moore, I, 7n. It may have been then that the Captain took the name of Byron Gordon, a step made legal and necessary for the inheritance of the Gordon property when the ninth laird's only child, a daughter, married.

sibly in April, when Captain Byron heard of the death of his father, the Admiral.[n] If he had any hope of profiting considerably from the will, however, he was soon disillusioned. Perhaps it was then that the Byrons took the house in South Warnborough, Hampshire, where they appear in August. In the meantime the gallant Guardsman turned up in London, but with the shadow of a debtor's prison looming over him he was not so gay as usual.[n]

Having narrowly escaped the jailer, he no doubt found country life more wholesome. From his mother's birthplace, Carhais in Cornwall, where he had gone on "business" (perhaps to extract money from his mother's relations there), he wrote on August 22 to the commissioners, urging them to dispose of Gight as soon as possible and to remit some money.[n]

Mrs. Byron's friends in Scotland were already feeling sorry for her. And the poor lady was indeed in a pitiable situation. Completely under the spell of her scamp of a husband but knowing from bitter experience that he would soon leave her destitute, she appealed to her kinswoman Miss Urquhart of Craigston, lacking the temerity to approach the commissioners directly:

"It is by Admiral Duff and Mr. Russell of Montcoffer's advice that we sell the estate. You know they are commissioners, and if they act as my friends they should see that there is a proper settlement made upon me, the best that I could wish or expect would be 10,000£., and I would have that settled in such a manner that it would be out of Mr. Byron's power to spend, and out of my own power to give up to him, though I should wish to have the power of spending it myself, or to leave it to anybody I pleased. . . .

"I should not wish to appear in it myself, or Mr. Byron should know that I wrote or spoke to anybody upon the subject, because if he did he would never forgive me. . . ."[n] Her anxiety on this count was so great that she asked that the reply be sent under cover to her maid.

The following year Gight was bought by the third Earl of Aberdeen for his son, Lord Haddo.[n] The purchase price was £17,850, and all that could be salvaged after the mortgage and

Mr. Byron's most pressing creditors had been paid was wisely kept in Scotland by Mrs. Byron's careful kinsmen and business agents. They took the precaution of putting what brakes they could on the reckless dissipation of the balance, which must have been £7,000 or £8,000. While the arbiters in Edinburgh were trying to negotiate a scheme to keep some part of it in trust, the agent for the commissioners cannily doled out small remittances, but still it dwindled frighteningly.

It is possible to catch only fleeting glimpses of the Byrons in 1787. No doubt they were only a few jumps ahead of the bailiff most of the time. On July 10 the Hon. Jean Duff wrote from Cowes, Isle of Wight: "Mr. and Mrs. Byron have taken a house in this place. He has hired a vessel and gone to the coast of France." [n] The reason for that sudden move was later explained by Mrs. Byron's attorney, who in February of the following year was examining the intricacies of the Captain's borrowings: "Last summer Mr. Byron proposed paying off his debts but when he got hold of £700, being the balance left of the last £1000 you sent Mrs. Byron, which would have been sufficient then for that purpose, he set off with it for Paris and in two months had not a guinea left. . . ." [n]

On September 9, Captain William Abercromby added an item to the family gossip: "Mrs. Byron is big with Bairn for certain. He is off to France for debt, where she, unhappy woman, must follow soon." [n] By that time Captain Byron was without a sou and was glad to have his wife join him in Paris with what was left of her savings from the remittance from Scotland. The short sojourn of Mrs. Byron in France could not have been very happy. While her husband spoke French and was at home in French society, she knew not a word of the language. Several hundred pounds of new debts were piled up during the two or three months that they were in Paris. The Captain's daughter by the Marchioness, Augusta, then four years old, was taken from his sister and put under the care of Mrs. Byron, who nursed her through a serious illness. Yet the poor pregnant woman was still loyal to the Johnny Byron who had already caused her so much heartache and anxiety.

If pre-natal influences count for anything, how potent and

disturbing must have been those which worked on the unborn poet. Financial worries increased daily, while the Captain's spending continued unabated. Captain George Anson Byron, then living at Chantilly, was persuaded to pay some of his brother's debts, and the Paris banker Mr. Perregaux was prevailed on to advance £200.[n]

When her time approached, Mrs. Byron returned to England accompanied by Augusta, whom she soon placed with her grandmother Lady Holderness, the mother of the Marchioness. At Boulogne on her way she visited R. C. Dallas (whose sister had married George Anson Byron), who later wrote in his *Recollections:* ". . . she was pregnant, and stopped at Dover on crossing the Channel."[n] But she could not have stayed there long, for on December 14 Mr. Watson, Edinburgh Agent for the Arbiters of the Gight Estate, had "remitted to London on account of Mrs. Byron, who is lying-in there, £50, 5s."[n] She had already taken lodgings in London for her accouchement.

# CHAPTER II

## *1788–1798*

## England and Scotland

CONSTANTLY harassed by financial worries, Mrs. Byron rented a furnished back drawing-room on the first floor at 16 Holles Street, and prepared for her confinement. In this respectable but inexpensive lodging in the short lane connecting Oxford Street and Cavendish Square [1] she was visited on January 1, 1788, by a Mr. John Leslie, who described himself as "a very near relation." He had been appointed by the Edinburgh agent of the commissioners to dole out money as needed by the Byrons.[n] The balance from the sale of Gight had now dwindled to £5,768, and negotiations were not yet completed to stop the drain on the capital by establishing a trust.[n] Mr. Leslie reported to the agent, Mr. James Watson: "She tells me that she expects to be brought to bed in two or three weeks & wished for some Money, I gave her a draft on my Banker for Twenty Guineas on your acct. . . . She tells me she expects Mr. Byron in London every day.—and that he goes to Scotland on business with you."[n] Mrs. Byron herself wrote to the agent the next day: "I don't want much and if there was to be large sums it would only be thrown away as it was before."[n]

The Captain did indeed arrive in England early in January,

[1] The number of the house was later changed to 24. Toward the end of the nineteenth century the house, which bore a metal medallion indicating that it had been the poet's birthplace, was torn down. The large drapery establishment of John Lewis & Co. later occupied the site. During the blitz of the Second World War almost the whole street was bombed out.

pausing at Dover to draw some money and probably to survey the scene before proceeding cautiously to London without encountering any creditors. It is only through his debts and the reports of the financial agents that his movements can be traced. He spent part of the next three months hiding in the country, venturing into London on Sunday, when by English law the debtor had immunity, to wheedle money from his poor wife or to have a conference with one of the agents. Whether he dared the duns to witness the birth of his son on Tuesday, January 22, will perhaps never be known. That he was hovering near is indicated by the fact that there is no record of his being in Scotland before February 2, though he was eager to go there on business.*n*

A nurse, Mrs. Mills, a man-midwife, Mr. Combe, and a Dr. Denman were employed to look after the expectant mother.*n* The father cannot have been very helpful, for it has been recorded that "the midwife and the nurse were engaged on the recommendation of a total stranger."[2] Whether or not he was "born in bitterness and nurtured in convulsion" (as Byron wrote later of his own daughter),*n* Mrs. Byron's first and only offspring came into the world with a physical handicap that caused him much bodily suffering and mental agony, and that probably did more to shape his character than it will ever be possible to calculate. He was born with a caul and, what was worse, with a deformed right foot.[3] John Hunter the surgeon was called in for advice and recommended a special shoe that he thought would

[2] R. E. Prothero: "The Childhood and School Days of Byron," *Nineteenth Century,* Jan. 1898, p. 68. Prothero cites this as evidence of the friendlessness of Mrs. Byron in London. He says elsewhere that "the midwife and the nurse were recommended by Mrs. Hanson." (*LJ,* I, 8n.) This was the wife of John Hanson, solicitor, of 6 Chancery Lane, who was later to become the poet's attorney and man of business.

[3] Prothero records that the caul, supposed by sailors to be a lucky charm against drowning, was sold by the nurse, Mrs. Mills, to Captain James Hanson, brother of John Hanson. But it did not save him when H.M.S. *Brazen* foundered in a storm off Newhaven on Jan. 26, 1800. (*LJ,* I, 9n.) Despite all the witnesses who said, after Byron's death, that it was the left foot, it is safe to take his mother's word that it was the right. All the evidence points to its being a conventionally clubbed foot, the heel being drawn up and the sole of the foot being turned inward. (See Chapter III, pp. 54–5.)

enable the boy, when old enough, to walk without difficulty, though he offered no hope of an actual cure.[4]

It is not certain whether Captain Byron returned from Scotland in time to see his son christened in the near-by Marylebone parish church on February 29, or whether he would have ventured to leave his hiding-place for such a public event.[5] The godfathers named on the occasion were of Mrs. Byron's choosing, the Duke of Gordon and her kinsman Colonel Duff of Fetteresso (both probably in absentia), and she gave the child the name of her father, George Gordon.[n]

Captain Byron's affairs were daily growing worse, nor did that stop him in the least from piling up new bills. On the same day that his son was christened, Mr. Beckett, a London attorney, gave a report to the Edinburgh agent, at the request of Mrs. Byron, on her husband's old and new debts. He found that "nothing less than £1300 will make Mr. Byron a free man," and warned that "discharging the present debts would only be paving the way to the accumulation of fresh ones."

And he revealed to the agent that the poor woman was again asking others to protect her from her own weaknesses in the face of her husband's demands: "Mrs. Byron is afraid that she has not the resolution to refuse any request Mr. Byron may make to her personally, but she begs that the Trustees or Arbiters if they have the power will not take notice of any application from her through Mr. Byron or otherwise but as far as in them lays protect her present property. . . ."[n]

It was at Mrs. Byron's own urging that a settlement was finally made early in March securing £4,222 of the remaining

[4] *LJ,* I, 11n. Writing later to her sister-in-law, Mrs. Leigh, Mrs. Byron said that "Mr. Hunter saw George when he was born." (Symon, p. 38.) John Hunter was a noted anatomist and surgeon who had specialized in the study of the rupture of the Achilles tendon. Jeaffreson (p. 22) has inferred from Mrs. Byron's letter that Hunter attended her at her accouchement, but the greater likelihood is that he was called in as a specialist after it was found that the child had a deformed foot.

[5] The parish register, which reads: "Baptisms in the year 1788: March 1st, George Gordon, son, of John Byron Esq. & Catherine, b. 22 inst.," has two clerical errors. Elze (Appendix B, p. 440) notes that the clerk forgot that it was leap year, when February had 29 days, and that he wrote "22 inst." instead of "22 ult."

capital against further inroads of creditors. Of this, £3,000 was invested at five per cent under the care of trustees for Mrs. Byron, the principal being inalienable during her lifetime, and £1,222 was left as a burden on the estate, the annual interest (£55. 11*s.* 1*d.*) going as a life annuity to her grandmother Duff.[6] There still was a surplus for the payment of Mr. Byron's debts and for their present support, but (perhaps because of the warnings they had received from Mrs. Byron herself) the arbiters were slow to send it.[n]

A pitiful picture of the household in Holles Street is drawn in a letter of Mr. Beckett to Edinburgh on March 11: the penniless mother with a clubfooted baby in her arms; her husband, whose insatiable demands she could never deny, sneaking in on Sunday from his secret lodging in the country, looking for a remittance that had not arrived. Until it came he would "be obliged to be at hide and seek."[n] On March 20, Mrs. Byron herself wrote to Watson, asking to what purpose the arbiters were keeping Mr. Byron in suspense. Five days later she renewed the appeal, asking Watson to urge the arbiters to consider "that they are keeping Mr. Byron and me here at an expense we can by no means afford and that the time I have taken this house for is up in a fortnight and that I must leave London then & pray how am I to leave it without a farthing in short you may tell them if they delay sending me any money a week after you receive this I shall be reduced to the greatest misery."[n]

The movements of the Byrons for the next year are completely shadowed in mystery, though it is likely that the character of their existence changed little. It is logical to suppose that they went into the country a few steps ahead of the bailiff, that they moved frequently for strategic reasons, and that finally, probably sometime in 1789, Mrs. Byron left the spendthrift Captain and went to Aberdeen, where she and her baby could live comfortably enough on the £150 per annum secured her under the settlement.

[6] Moore, I, 7n. Moore says the capital of the life interest set up for the grandmother was £1,122, but Symon (p. 34) points out that it was originally £1,222 and was later reduced by Mrs. Byron's appealing to the trustees for £100 in Jan. 1791 after she had been further drained of money by her husband.

Of the captivating Mr. Byron we catch a characteristic glimpse in the summer of 1789. He had taken a house on the coast of Kent near Folkstone, where he was visited by William John Byron, the grandson of the "Wicked Lord." [n] This eighteen-year-old heir apparent to the title and estates of the ancient Byron line, who like his father had been *persona non grata* to the old lord at Newstead, found his uncle altogether delightful and had no criticism to make, though he was perfectly aware of the precarious life he lived. He wrote to his other uncle, George Anson Byron, on August 4: "Your brother took a small house at Sandgate Castle [n] this summer where I stayed some time with him & we had a very fine Lugger all the time so that we were at Sea a great deal and in France but since that he has been very near taken up and put into prison at Boulogne [n] but now he is gone down to Scotland and I am sure I wish he may make a long stay as it is by much the safest place for him." [n]

By August 1789, then, it seems that Mrs. Byron had her problem husband back on her hands. What their life was like in the small lodging she had taken in Queen Street it is not difficult to imagine.[7] In these close quarters, with a maid, Agnes Gray, a pious Bible-reading Presbyterian, to look after the little lame boy, the Byrons lived an uneasy and cramped existence for a while, the Captain reduced to asking his wife for spending-money and she upbraiding him for wasting her inheritance. Stern necessity alone kept him in this narrow and unpleasant environment. He was no longer master of Gight, where the evening punch and the pipes playing until midnight made the raw Scottish winter seem less unbearable. Shut up with this uncouth woman who scolded him constantly in her broad Scots, he, the most amiable of men in good company, became irritable too. The bickering

[7] Bulloch (p. 132 [296]) says she lived in Virginia Street for a time "apparently with a Mrs. Cruickshank, 'on the shore,' to whom she wished a letter addressed to her in January, 1791." If this is right she moved there after Captain Byron left her for the last time in 1790. On the other hand, Symon (p. 31) says: "It is common knowledge that Mrs. Byron lodged for a time in Virginia Street, next with a Mr. Anderson in Queen Street. . . ." But he gives no evidence, and we know from Moore and others that she was in Queen Street while her husband was with her. Her landlord was James Anderson, a perfumer. (Symon, p. 34.)

continued, no doubt intensified by the squalling of the young George Gordon, then nearing his second birthday. The ill-matched couple soon separated and dwelt at opposite ends of Queen Street. Relieved from the aggravations of constant contact, they lived more amicably and visited and drank tea with each other.[n] Though she could fly into a tantrum when he asked her for money, Mrs. Byron often indulged in ridiculous displays of affection for her Johnny Byron. And the same extremes of uncontrollable anger and demonstrative affection marked her behavior both then and later toward her son. When the Captain could stand no more of his wife's company he ceased to call, but he was reduced to writing her for a guinea.[n] Mrs. Byron was flattered that he asked the nurse, when he saw her on the street, about the "bairn," and she plied Agnes with eager questions, expressing the "tenderest anxiety" for her spouse.[n] But when he asked her to send the child to his own lodgings for a visit, she feared to put the boy in his hands. The nurse, however, who knew the characters of both the boy and his father, urged her to it, saying that if he kept George one night he would not want him for another. She was quite right; once was enough. At this early age the boy displayed a temper equal to his mother's. When she scolded him angrily one day for soiling a dress he had just put on, he stood for a while in a silent rage and then tore the garment from top to bottom.[n]

After some weeks of this life the Captain was eager to escape. As soon as he could get a draft from his sister, Mrs. Leigh, who sent him most of her pin money, he sought a more congenial society.[n] When he was gone, Mrs. Byron was desolate. She remembered the maddening things he could do and say, however, as well as his attractions, and she assuaged her passionate grief by a mingled hatred and love of the son who reminded her of him. "My mother," the poet recalled, "when she was in a rage with me, (and I gave her cause enough,) used to say, Ah, you little dog, you are a Byron all over; you are as bad as your father!" [n] But the next moment she was covering him with kisses.

Captain Byron, it seems, returned once more to Aberdeen in the late summer of 1790 with one purpose in view: to get enough money to go to France again. It is a sufficient indication of the hold he had over his wife when he appealed to her "personally" that during his stay in Aberdeen she had gone into debt to the extent of £300. In spite of all her experience with him, and despite the needs of herself and her son, she was putty in his hands. On September 8, 1790, John Byron Gordon, "late of Gight," "intending to go abroad for some time," signed a power of attorney authorizing his wife to withdraw from the Earl of Aberdeen, to whom Gight had been sold, £100 of the £1,222. 10*s.* left with him to pay the annuity to Mrs. Byron's grandmother.[n] No doubt "Mad Jack" already had his money, and this instrument was for the purpose of enabling Mrs. Byron to repay earlier borrowings. By the time she received the money, the shameless John Byron was established in the house which his sister, Mrs. Leigh, owned at Valenciennes, and was dallying with chambermaids and actresses. His wife and son never saw him again.

Unperturbed by the French Revolution, this incorrigible playboy wrote to Mrs. Leigh on December 1, 1790: "As for me, here I am, and in love with whom? A new actress who is come from Paris, she is beautiful and played last night in *L'Epreuve Villageoise*. . . . As for Madame Schoner—she fairly told me, when drunk, that she liked me, and I really do not know what to do. . . . No duns appear, as Fanny bites them all, and I am never at home. . . . For my Amours, these are all finished and everybody says 'je suis très amoureux but très inconstant.[']. . . and, I believe, I have had one third of Valenciennes, particularly a Girl at L'Aigle Rouge, an Inn here[.] I happened to [be] there one day when it rained so hard. . . . She is very handsome and very tall, and I am not yet tired." [n]

At this point he was quite deaf to the piteous pleas of the wife he had beggared. In desperation Mrs. Byron wrote on January 21, 1791, to his sister, presumably then in London: "Though I have not the pleasure of being personally known to you, I hope you will forgive this trouble. Some time ago I wrote to Mr. Byron, telling him I had not a farthing in the world nor could I get any at present, and begging him to ask you to lend him thirty pounds or forty pounds to send to me, to which he returned for answer that he could not think of asking you as you had been so good to him but that he had wrote to a person that he hoped would send it me. This was only to put me off, as I don't know a person in the world that would advance that sum for him but yourself and though it is all owing to the debts I became bound to pay for him for the extravagant way he would live when he was here which my income could not afford that I am in this situation. . . ." She and her son had nothing to live on, she repeated in her agitation, "as the people I am due money to have got arrestments on my income and I cannot receive it till I pay them." Then, swallowing her pride, she asked for a loan of thirty or forty pounds, assuring her sister-in-law twice over: "I will pay you honestly in May." [n]

Mrs. Leigh, no doubt ashamed of her brother's conduct, must have been touched by this pathetic appeal, sealed in red wax with the motto of the proud Gordons: "*Je ne change qu'en mourant.*" Though her answer is not extant, she seems to have replied kindly and probably contributed money to aid the impoverished household in Aberdeen, and a friendly correspondence ensued. But Jack Byron was quite unrepentant and was interested only in money for his own now desperate needs. Writing again to his sister from Valenciennes on February 16, he spoke cavalierly of his wife and made the only reference to his son to be found in his correspondence: "With regard to Mrs. Byron, I am glad she writes to you. She is very amiable at a distance; but I defy you and all the Apostles to live with her two months, for, if any body could live with her, it was me. . . . For my son, I am happy to hear he is well; but for his walking, 'tis impossible, as he is club-footed." [n]

On March 27 Mrs. Byron wrote Mrs. Leigh that her son was "very well, and really a charming boy," [n] and in May her correspondent sent an invitation to accompany her to France, but of course the poor woman could not go. Perhaps it was just as well, for her husband was sinking lower and lower in degradation and debt. By summer his appeals must have passed the patience even of his sister, tragic as he made his plight seem. "I am really without a shirt. . . . I have not a sou." [n]

On August 2, 1791, his self-made tragedy came to an end. On

June 21 he had made a will, leaving Mrs. Leigh £400 to be paid out of the hypothetical effects of his deceased father and mother, and, perhaps ironically, appointing his son, "Mr. George Gordon, heir of my real and personal estate, and charge him to pay my debts, legacies, and funeral expenses."[n]

Mrs. Byron was grief-stricken. When she heard the news, her anguished cries could be heard in the street.[n] She wrote to Mrs. Leigh on August 23: "I do not think I shall ever get the better of it;—necessity, not inclination, parted us, at least on my part, and I flatter myself it was the same with him; and notwithstanding all his foibles, for they deserve no worse name, I ever sincerely loved him. . . . You say he was sensible to the last. . . . Was he long ill, and where was he buried? Be so good as to write all those particulars, and also send me some of his hair. . . . I was not well before, and I do not think I shall ever recover the severe shock I have received. It was so unexpected. If I had only seen him before he died! Did he ever mention me? I am unable to say more."[n]

George was three and one-half years old when his father died, and less than three when he saw for the last time, but he later told Thomas Medwin: "I was not so young when my father died, but that I perfectly remember him; and had very early a horror of matrimony, from the sight of domestic broils . . . . He seemed born for his own ruin, and that of the other sex."[n]

Mrs. Byron drew her shattered life together with a great deal of courage and lived within her narrowed income. Broken as she was by the events of the past six years, which had reduced her from a proud Gordon heiress to an impoverished widow living in cramped lodgings with her lame son, she devoted herself unselfishly to his care. First of all she must see what could be done with his foot. On May 8 she had written to Mrs. Leigh, who was then in London, for her aid in getting "a proper shoe for George's foot as I cannot get a right one made here." She enclosed a letter for Mr. Hunter the surgeon: "Nothing but want of money prevents me sending him up to London for Mr. Hunter to see his foot, as I am perfectly sure he would walk very well if he had a proper shoe and indeed Mr. Hunter said to me that his foot would be very well in time if he could have a proper shoe. . . ." [n]

Again on May 31 she gave Mrs. Leigh more details of her son's deformity: "George's foot turns inward, and it is the right foot; he walks quite on the side of his foot." [n]

The boy early developed a sensitiveness to his lameness, perhaps because his mother upbraided him for it in her exasperated moods. Moore tells a story of a nurse who, encountering Agnes Gray and her charge on one of her walks, remarked: "What a pretty boy Byron is! what a pity he has such a leg!" Flaring up immediately, his eyes flashing with anger, the child struck at her with his little whip, shouting: "Dinna speak of it!" [n]

Putting still further liens on her income, Mrs. Byron borrowed enough to furnish a flat of her own, taking the whole first floor at 64 Broad Street, a respectable thoroughfare in the heart of the new town. This flat, which she rented from a Mr. Leslie (perhaps the kinsman who had visited her in London before the birth of her son), provided a separate bedroom for herself, another for her son, and one for Agnes Gray, as well as a living-room and a large kitchen.[n]

How much influence his nurse had on the formation of Byron's infant mind it is difficult to say. The stories told in later years by her sister Mary (or May) Gray, who succeeded Agnes when the latter married, should be taken with some caution, for May was finally dismissed for misconduct. That Agnes treated him with kindness and tried to instill in him the dogmas of her own harsh Calvinistic creed seems probable. But she also introduced him to the poetry of the Psalms, the first and twenty-third being the earliest that he memorized.[n]

Mrs. Byron was not always in a tantrum, and there is ample evidence that she loved her son and that she sacrificed her own comfort to give him every advantage her poverty permitted. The chronological vagueness of early accounts of Byron's childhood has left the impression that his mother habitually threw the fire tongs at her son's head or broke dishes over it. But most of these spectacular performances belong to the period of his obstreperous youth in England. In his early years George, though mischievous, high-strung, and sensitive, had a loyal and affectionate nature. He was responsive to kindness and was easily manageable by those who understood him and who appealed to his sympathy or his sense of justice. In those qualities and in his early experiences as a schoolboy were founded his extraordinary facility for friendship and his ardent support of the cause of the underdog (to which a sense of his own deformity may well have contributed).

Byron's curious combination of aristocratic pride on the one hand and liberal sympathy on the other may have originated in Mrs. Byron's influence and teaching. He wrote John Murray in later years: "My Mother (who was as haughty as Lucifer with her descent from the Stuarts, and her right line, from the *old Gordons, not* the *Seyton Gordons,* as she disdainfully termed the Ducal branch,)" always reminded him "how superior *her* Gordons were to the Southron Byrons." [n]

And on the other side, there is the record of her sympathy with the popular cause in the French Revolution. Writing to Mrs. Leigh on November 29, 1792, while Louis was still in prison, she said she would not want to go abroad in the present state of affairs. "I am very much interested about the French, but I fancy you and I are on different sides, for I am quite a Democrat and I do not think the King, after his treachery and perjury, deserves to be restored." [n]

Byron could not have failed at this period to imbibe something of the staunchly held opinions and prejudices of his mother. And the whole environment of his Aberdeen years conditioned him to the views of the lower-middle-class Scottish world with which he was daily associated in the streets and later at school. Though she was related to some of the best families in the northern counties, Mrs. Byron recognized that now she was only a poor relation, and she did not hold her head too high above her neighbors.

Certainly there was nothing aristocratic about the first school to which she sent her son. In a narrow lane known as Long Acre very near the house in Broad Street, a Mr. John Bowers kept a mixed and noisy school in a grimy warehouse-like room,

EARLIEST PORTRAIT OF BYRON, AT THE AGE OF SEVEN

MRS. BYRON (BYRON'S MOTHER)

poorly lighted, with a low ceiling and dusty floor whose holes were an invitation to the rats.[8]

Mrs. Byron may have been attracted by its nearness and economy or the prospect it offered of keeping her son off the streets. The "little boy with the red jacket and the nankeen trowsers" had often been turned out of the courtyard of near-by Marischal College, where he had wandered to play.[n] In his own reminiscences of Aberdeen, Byron wrote: "I was sent at five years old, or earlier, to a School kept by a Mr. *Bowers,* who was called '*Bodsy* Bowers' by reason of his dapperness. It was a School for both sexes. I learned little there, except to repeat by rote the first lesson of Monosyllables—'God made man, let us love him'—by hearing it often repeated, without acquiring a letter. Whenever proof was made of my progress at home, I repeated these words with the most rapid fluency; but on turning over a new leaf, I continued to repeat them, so that the narrow boundaries of my first year's accomplishments were detected, my ears boxed (which they did not deserve, seeing that it was by *ear* only that I had acquired my letters), and my intellects consigned to a new preceptor."[n]

During the next year, under more competent instructors, he learned to read. First there was "a very decent, clever, little Clergyman, named Ross, afterwards Minister of one of the Kirks . . . . Under *him* I made an astonishing progress, and I recollect to this day his mild manners and good-natured pains-taking.

"The moment I could read, my grand passion was *history;* and why, I know not, but I was particularly taken with the battle near Lake Regillus in the Roman History, put into my hands the first."[n]

Next he had for a tutor "a very serious, saturnine, but kind young man, named Paterson."[n] Byron said he was "the son of my Shoemaker, but a good Scholar, as is common with the Scotch. He was a rigid Presbyterian also. With him I began Latin in Ruddiman's Grammar, and continued till I went to the 'Grammar School.' "[n]

[8] Moore, I, 11; Rogerson: *Bon Accord,* May 29, 1902, IV, 8. The books of this school show that Mrs. Byron paid only a guinea for the period from Nov. 19, 1792, to Nov. 19, 1793.

Before he was entered there, however, news came indirectly to Mrs. Byron which was to change the whole course of life for herself and her son. The young man who had gone sailing with her husband when he was staying at Sandgate Castle in 1789 had been killed by a cannon ball at the battle of Calvi in Corsica on July 31, 1794, and her own son, at the age of six and one-half, was heir presumptive to the title and estates of the "Wicked Lord."[9] Mrs. Byron began to hold her head a little higher, to visit with more confidence some of her relations, and to renew her contact with Mrs. Leigh, the one member of the Byron family with whom she had corresponded. On November 23, 1794, she wrote: "I should have supposed you would have wrote before now to have inquired after your newphew [*sic*]. He is a fine boy and very well and walks and runs as well as any other child. I hear that Mrs. Parker[1] is dead and that your newphew [*sic*] Lord Byron's grandson is dead, but I have not been informed of it from any of the family."[n] It is significant that she never signed herself "Byron Gordon" in writing to Mrs. Leigh, but always "C. Byron."

Writing again on December 8, Mrs. Byron opened her mind more fully on the subject that was increasingly absorbing her attention: "You know Lord Byron. Do you think he will do anything for George, or be at any expense to give him a proper education; or, if he wish to do it, is his present fortune such a one that he could spare anything out of it?"[n]

But the old lord was then too far sunk in debt and misanthropy to be impressed with such an appeal even if Mrs. Leigh, who was on more friendly terms with him than was any other member of the family, ever laid it before him.

[9] Newton Hanson, in an unpublished manuscript narrative of Byron's early life, Murray MSS., gives the date of the death of the "Wicked Lord's" grandson. At the time of Byron's birth two lives, that of this grandson and of Byron's own father, stood between him and the heirship to the peerage. Hobhouse's statement in the margin of his copy of Moore that "at his birth there were six lives between him and the title" seems quite unaccountable, unless Byron himself had had that impression and told Hobhouse so.

[1] Mrs. Parker was not dead, for Byron's first extant letter was addressed to her on Nov. 8, 1798. Charlotte Augusta Byron, youngest sister of Byron's father, married Christopher Parker, later a Vice-Admiral in the Navy. Her daughter, Margaret, was one of Byron's early loves.

Mrs. Byron took the precaution to enlist legal advice in her son's interest. Through an Aberdeen attorney, Alexander Crombie, she employed James Farquhar, who had represented Buchan, Montrose, and other Aberdeenshire constituencies in Parliament, and who was then living in London, to keep an eye on the Byron property and the activities of the old lord at Newstead.[n] Clutching at straws, she even alienated the friendship of Mrs. Leigh by inquiring too closely into the settlement of the estate of her brother (Mrs. Byron's late husband). Having conceived the notion, fantastic enough, that a sum had come to the estate on the death of his mother, she persisted with a kind of peasant suspicion in demanding an exact accounting.[n]

During the term of 1794–5, young George, then approaching his seventh birthday, was entered at the Aberdeen Grammar School in the Schoolhill, a short walk from Broad Street. Aberdonians were proud of their school, which was so old that no record remained of its foundation. The schoolhouse was then what was considered a modern building. Constructed in 1757, it was a low one-storied gray stone structure in the form of an "H," the public school being in the center and the four classrooms occupying the wings. The small playground in the front within the fence could not have accommodated the 150 boys who attended in Byron's day, but they may have wandered outside to play with their marbles, buttons, hand-balls, or peg tops.[n]

As Byron recalled the school, "It was divided into five classes, taught by four masters, the Chief teaching the fifth and fourth himself . . . and Monitors are heard by the Head Masters." [n] In his time the only branch of study was Latin, taught in the traditional manner that made lessons a deadly chore. Geo. Bayron Gordon, as his name was entered on the rolls in 1796 [n] (indicative perhaps of the pronunciation of the Aberdonians), did not exert himself and remained in the respectable middle of the class or just below, though in the fourth class he had risen to fifth from the top in a group of twenty-seven boys.[n]

Writing, though an expected part of every schoolboy's education, was then an "extra." After the morning's work at the Grammar School, the boys whose parents could afford it rushed across a churchyard to Mr. Duncan's writing school, and from twelve to one practiced the neat round hand with sharp ascending capital "M" and "N" that one sees in Byron's first letter to be preserved.[n] Either while in Aberdeen or after he went to England, he studied French long enough to get an adequate reading knowledge of it, though he would never venture to speak it.[n]

Byron had already begun to read widely before he left the Grammar School. There were two booksellers, Angus and Brown, whose shops in Aberdeen he could have frequented, and his mother, who had read *Peregrine Pickle* on stormy nights at Gight, may have been a subscriber to the New Circulating Library. But travels and histories rather than novels (though he later said he had read some four thousand volumes of fiction) appealed to him most. And the ponderous tomes that he read then made such an impression on him that he remembered them years later. He once jotted down in the margin of his copy of Isaac D'Israeli's *The Literary Character:* "Knolles, Cantemir, De Tott, Lady M. W. Montague, Hawkins's Translation from Mignot's History of the Turks, the Arabian Nights, all travels, or histories, or books upon the East I could meet with, I had read, as well as Ricaut, before I was *ten years old.*"[n] Knolles's *Turkish History* was recalled by him again only a few weeks before his death as "one of the first books that gave me pleasure when a child; and I believe it had much influence on my subsequent wishes to visit the Levant, and gave, perhaps, the oriental colouring which is observed in my poetry."[n]

As he recalled it, he had read the *Arabian Nights* first, and then the histories and travels. "After these, I preferred the history of naval actions, Don Quixote and Smollett's novels, particularly Roderick Random, and I was passionate for the Roman History. When a boy, I could never bear to read any Poetry whatever without disgust and reluctance."[n]

Under the tutelage of Agnes Gray, and later of her sister May, he had read with some thoroughness most of the books of the Bible. ". . . I am a great reader and admirer of those books," he later wrote John Murray, "and had read them through and through before I was eight years old,—that is to say, the *Old* Testament, for the New struck me as a task, but the other as a pleasure."[n]

He was less impressed with the solemnities of preaching and religious ceremonies. His mother took him regularly to St. Paul's Chapel in Aberdeen. A lady who sat behind them one Sunday "observed the poet (then about seven or eight years old) amusing himself by disturbing his mother's devotions; he every now and then gently pricked with a pin the large round arms of Mrs. Byron, which were covered with white kid gloves."[n]

But the drama of the Old Testament continued to intrigue him.[2] The story of Cain and Abel early captured his imagination. He later wrote in the preface to his own drama of *Cain:* "Gesner's 'Death of Abel' I have never read since I was eight years of age, at Aberdeen. The general impression of my recollection is delight. . . ."[n]

The problem of evil as something inborn was readily fostered by the Calvinistic teaching of his nurse and his Presbyterian tutors, and was fortified as he learned more of his own ancestors. The fascinating idea that he was predestined to evil was strengthened at this time or not long after by his reading a semi-gothic novel by John Moore called *Zeluco* after its misanthropic hero-villain, fated to perform dark deeds by forces beyond his control. The book made a deep impression on him, for in the preface to the first two cantos of *Childe Harold* he confessed that "the outline which I once meant to fill up for him [Harold] was, with some exceptions, the sketch of a modern Timon, perhaps a poetical Zeluco."[n] Zeluco, like Byron, lost his father at an early age, and "very soon after his death, he indulged, without control, every humour and caprice; and his mistaken mother applauding the blusterings of petulance and pride as indications of spirit, his temper became more and more ungovernable, and at length seemed as inflammable as gunpowder, bursting into flashes of rage at the slightest touch of provocation."[n]

But it was in retrospect that the parallels with his own life in *Zeluco* struck him. Whatever inward impressions he may have been storing up, he gave the outward appearance to his class-

[2] Goethe told Crabb Robinson he believed Byron "was indebted for the profound views he took of the Bible to the ennui he suffered from it at school." (*Robinson*, I, 372.)

mates, Thomas Moore says, of a normal boy, "lively, warm-hearted, and high-spirited . . . passionate and resentful, but affectionate and . . . fearless, and (as one of them significantly expressed it) 'always more ready to give a blow than to take one.'" He was quick to defend those persecuted by others, and to pay off debts of insult or offense to himself. He one day returned home breathless, and answered the servant who asked him what he had been about, "with a mixture of rage and humour, that he had been paying a debt, by beating a boy according to promise; for that he was a Byron, and would never belie his motto, *'Trust Byron.'*" [n]

No doubt he thrashed more than one boy who dared to make references to his lameness, though he had so far overcome his sensitivity to it as to take part in games which required running, such as "bases," and on one occasion, in a sense of bravado and kinship with another boy who had a similar handicap, he said in a good-humored mood: "Come and see the twa laddies with the twa club feet going up the Broad-street." [n]

While he mingled freely with his classmates on a plane of equality and entered into their games, his mother had already begun to make him conscious of his superior destiny, not only as a descendant of the Gordons, but also now more particularly as heir to the Byron peerage. She chanced one day to be reading part of a speech in the House of Commons in his presence when a friend who was there turned to the boy and said: "We shall have the pleasure, some time or other, of reading your speeches in the House of Commons." "I hope not," he replied; "if you read any speeches of mine, it will be in the House of Lords." [n]

Mrs. Byron had probably continued to be on good terms with the Fetteresso Duffs, and her uncle Alexander Russell of Montcoffer had aided her as administrator when she was trying to stem the tide of her husband's debts. Little "Geordie" may have been taken to Fetteresso even before his schooldays, for Mrs. Byron was no doubt eager to show him to his godfather, who lived in the fabulous old castle a few miles south of Aberdeen.[n]

If Mrs. Byron's grandmother, Margaret Duff Gordon, the dowager "Lady Gight," had cut her acquaintance during her unhappy marriage, the old lady now forgave her, for there is record of at least one visit made by mother and son to their relations at Banff. The summer holiday of the Grammar School was only three weeks. It was probably during one of these short vacations, possibly in 1795, that Mrs. Byron took her bairn to see his great-grandmother. His mother had caused his portrait to be drawn that year by John Kaye.[3] The demure, almost angelic profile of the seven-year-old boy with curly hair down to his shoulders gives no indication of a mischievous nature. But if any of the legends of his sojourn at Banff are to be believed, he earned his appellation of "that little deevil Geordie Byron." It is recorded that, while at Banff, George dressed a pillow in his clothes and threw it out the window to frighten his mother and her aunt Abercromby, and that when at the aunt's insistence he was punished, he butted her like a goat "for meddling." [4]

Byron himself has left the best account of his first love affair. Sometime in his eighth year he met his distant cousin Mary Duff.[5] He had the impression that she was a year older, a not uncommon error for a boy to make, but actually she was born in the same year as he was and was slightly younger.[6] He apparently saw her during the visit to the Duffs and again in Aberdeen. Years later, he wrote in his diary: "I have been thinking lately a good deal of Mary Duff. How very odd that I should have been so utterly, devotedly fond of that girl, at an age when I could neither feel passion, nor know the meaning of the word." He recalled that he had been nearly convulsed by his mother's

[3] This is apparently the earliest portrait of Byron. It is reproduced in *Bon Accord,* June 19, 1902, p. 4. Moore mentions another "by Kay of Edinburgh" painted in the same year, showing him equipped as an archer. (Moore, I, 37.)

[4] Rogerson: *Bon Accord,* June 19, 1902, p. 5. According to local tradition, Byron threatened to pull the red nose of the doctor who came to bleed him.

[5] Her great-grandfather was a brother of his great-grandmother, Mrs. Duff Gordon. Byron told Pryse Gordon (*Personal Memoirs,* II, 321): "we met at the dancing-school," but whether this was in Aberdeen or at Banff is not clear.

[6] Byron is quoted by Pryse Gordon as saying: "She is a year older than I am." (*Personal Memoirs,* II, 321.) And Finlay, to whom he spoke of her at Missolonghi, reported that Byron told him he was six and she nine. (Stanhope, 2nd ed., p. 522.) But in *The Book of the Duffs* (p. 246) it is stated that Alexander Duff, her father, married in 1787, and that his eldest daughter, Mary, was born in 1788.

announcement, when he was sixteen, that Mary Duff was married. "Now what could this be?" he asked himself. "I had never seen her since . . . her removal to her grandmother's at Banff; we were both the merest children. I had and have been attached fifty times since that period; yet I recollect all we said to each other, all our caresses, her features, my restlessness, sleeplessness, my tormenting my mother's maid to write for me to her. . . .

"How the deuce did all this occur so early? where could it originate? I certainly had no sexual ideas for years afterwards; and yet my misery, my love for that girl were so violent, that I sometimes doubt if I have ever been really attached since. . . . How very pretty is the perfect image of her in my memory—her brown, dark hair, and hazel eyes; her very dress!" *n*

To convalesce from an attack of scarlet fever George was taken by his mother in 1795 or 1796 for a holiday in the valley of the Dee about forty miles above Aberdeen. They lodged with a farmer named James Robertson near Ballaterich.[7] The boy wandered in the country and came to love the mountain scenery of the Scottish highlands. The beautiful Deeside invited his rambles, and Loch-na-garr (Lachin y Gair) and Morven were visible in the distance. Perhaps he rode, for his deformity would have prevented him from climbing much. He wore the Gordon tartan, dark blue crossed with lighter shades of green and blocked off with thin yellow lines. "But my 'heart warms to the tartan,' " he once wrote to Walter Scott, "or to anything of Scotland, which reminds me of Aberdeen and other parts. . . ." *n* Thenceforth his most nostalgic recollections of Scotland centered about Deeside and the surrounding mountains.

The summer holidays were short, but on Wednesday and Saturday half-holidays the boy could roam about the vicinity. It is a mistake to suppose that Byron was not happy in Aberdeen. Except for an occasional flare-up, his mother treated him indulgently, and allowed him much freedom. It was only a short walk to the harbor and the open shores of the windy North Sea,

[7] *Poetry*, I, 192n.; Rogerson: *Bon Accord*, June 26, 1902, p. 14. Byron wrote Scott of his love for the highlands, "about Invercauld and Braemar, where I was sent to drink goat's fey in 1795–6, in consequence of a threatened decline after the scarlet fever." (*LJ*, VI, 6. Letter of Jan. 12–27, 1822.)

but the estuaries of the Dee and the Don were protected enough to give ample practice in the swimming that early became Byron's favorite sport.[8] It was an easy ride of a mile or two to the ancient stone arch over the Don, known as the Brig o' Balgounie. On the way through the Old Town the boys on their ponies would pass King's College and the ancient granite-and-sandstone cathedral. The bridge, though built in the fourteenth century, was solid enough. Its sixty-two-foot pointed arch spanned a deep pool in the river, protected by woods.

"The brig of Don," Byron recalled, "near the 'auld toun' of Aberdeen, with its one arch, and its black deep salmon stream below, is in my memory as yesterday. I still remember, though perhaps I may misquote, the awful proverb which made me pause to cross it, and yet lean over it with a childish delight, being an only son, at least by my mother's side. The saying as recollected by me was this, but I have never heard or seen it since I was nine years of age:—

> '*Brig of Balgounie,* black's *your* wa',
> *Wi' a wife's* ae son, *and a mear's* ae foal,
> *Doun ye shall fa'!*' " [n]

George had passed his tenth birthday when exciting news reached Mrs. Byron from England: the old Lord Byron was seriously ill. She lost no time in writing to her Aberdeen attorney, Alexander Crombie: ". . . do what you think proper or what those you may consult think proper to secure his property from embezzlement as there are only servants at Newstead." [n] Crombie conveyed Mrs. Byron's wishes to James Farquhar in London, who in turn wrote to Samuel Bolton, an attorney in Nottingham, saying that he was authorized by the mother of Lord Byron's heir "to do what may be needful in behalf of the Boy." [n]

On April 2, Bolton reported that the old lord was "declining very fast." The lawyer had arranged to be "instantly acquainted with his death by a person who lives very near Newstead Abbey & goes Errands for the family." [n] In the early days of April

[8] In *Childe Harold* Byron, addressing the sea, wrote:

> *From a boy*
> *I wanton'd with thy breakers. . . .* —Childe Harold, *IV*, 184.

the correspondence flew back and forth between London and Nottingham. Like vultures the attorneys hovered over the dying man.

The end came at one o'clock on the morning of May 21, and Bolton was already on his way to Newstead when his clerk relayed the news to Mrs. Byron through Crombie.[n] The day after the ten-year-old boy in Aberdeen was told that he was now the sixth Baron Byron of Rochdale, he asked his mother, perhaps to stem the overenthusiastic pride with which she retailed the news to the neighbors and the schoolmasters, "whether she perceived any difference in him since he had been made a lord, as he perceived none himself." [n]

But the greatest embarrassment came when his new title, "Dominus de Byron," was pronounced without warning or previous explanation in the Grammar School. "Unable to give utterance to the usual answer 'adsum,'" Moore records, "he stood silent amid the general stare of his schoolfellows, and, at last, burst into tears." [n] Hobhouse noted: "Byron himself told me that he was sent for by the master of the school who gave him some cake & wine & told him that his paternal great uncle was dead and he was now a lord—Byron added that the little treat and the respectful manner of the master gave him at once high notions of his new dignity." [n]

Farquhar had hoped that Mrs. Byron could come to Newstead immediately, but she could not uproot herself so easily. He would take all steps necessary to protect the interests of her son, he reported on June 1, and as the appointment of guardians and a receiver was under the jurisdiction of the Court of Chancery, "I have all along (since you first consulted me on the Business) advised with my Friend John Hanson Esqr. of Chancery Lane (an Eminent Chancery Solicitor). . . . By his advice it was that I applied to Mr. Bolton." [n] Thus John Hanson stepped into the affairs of Byron and soon became indispensable as practical guardian and general business agent.

Unacquainted with legal formalities, Mrs. Byron was incensed at the necessity of proving her marriage. It gave her "considerable uneasiness," Crombie wrote, "that she should be connected with people who could make such an unhandsome insinuation." [n] On

June 8 he gave Farquhar a detailed report on Mrs. Byron's affairs. "Mrs. Byron is desirous . . . to have a Nobleman joined with her as Guardian to her Son. . . . I wish you would consult Mr. Hanson whether Mrs. Byron would be entitled on application to the Chancellor to a certain allowance out of her Son's Estate beside for her maintenance. I am told that when the Estates are let this will exceed £2000 per Ann.—Mrs. Byron's present income is no more than the Interest of £3000 . . . per Ann. And she owes me about £300 & to Lord Aberdeen £100 being money advanced partly before her husband's death and partly since for buying furniture &c. by this means she has only at present about £100 yearly after paying the Interest of her debt and setting apart a sinking fund for discharging the Principal—she will also have the interest of £1200 more on the Death of her grandmother but all this will not be sufficient for enabling her to live in that respectable state she is entitled to from the rank of her Son . . . but I do not think that she will reside at Newstead." [n]

Everyone had underestimated the debts and encumbrances piled upon the estate by the late lord. On June 4, Hanson had a conference with Mr. Robert Aisley, the executor, who feared he would not be reimbursed for his expenses in proving the will. "I am apprehensive we shall have to bury the poor Lord ourselves after all," Hanson wrote to Farquhar.[n] In the meantime Lord Byron's remains languished at Newstead while Aisley and the attorneys held daily conferences in London with Mr. Stubbs, the old lord's business agent. When it was decided that there was money enough to bury him, Hanson went down to Newstead, leaving on the 14th and staying twelve days. On Saturday, June 16, the bones of the "Wicked Lord" were finally laid to rest with those of his ancestors in the Church at Hucknall Torkard.[n]

In the meantime Mrs. Byron and her son were having a busy time in Aberdeen, arranging their affairs, selling the furniture in the flat at 64 Broad Street, and making final visits to friends and relations. The furniture brought her £74. *17s. 7d.*[n] Little is known of their movements during the summer, but it has been suggested that they gave up the Aberdeen house after hearing of the old lord's death and took a suburban cottage called Honeybrae. Agnes Gray had married several years before (she had two children by 1798, the first named for her young charge, George Gordon) and had been replaced by her sister May. The gossip of the Grays and their descendants accounts for the local tradition that Byron spent some time with his first nurse at Woodside, and that there he presented a gold watch to his namesake.[n]

Despite his later romantic dreams of his Scottish childhood, "Scotch plaids, Scotch snoods, the blue hills, and clear streams,"[n] it is difficult to know what the young lord's feelings were on leaving his homeland. His bickerings with his mother, which had never been more than flashes of anger on both sides, did not prevent him from harboring affectionate feelings for her. After speaking of his precocious childish love for Mary Duff, he recorded in his journal in 1813: "In all other respects, I differed not at all from other children, being neither tall nor short, dull nor witty, of my age, but rather lively—except in my sullen moods, and then I was always a Devil. They once (in one of my silent rages) wrenched a knife from me, which I had snatched from table at Mrs. B.'s dinner (I always dined earlier), and applied to my breast . . . just before the late Lord B.'s decease."[n] Those who saw him only in his rages no doubt got a warped impression, and it is easy to account for his reputation as "Mrs. Byron's crockit deevil."[n] But there was a softness and shyness in him not taken into account by these observers, and an amiable desire to please and to be liked. When his sensitivities were not aroused he could be an agreeable companion, despite the fact that he was already a spoiled child. He had a lively intelligence, a fondness for reading in fields that captured his interest, a natural curiosity, and a sense of humor. It seems probable that, on the whole, he had a happy childhood in Scotland. In his later journals and in his poetry he never intimated that he had not. At the phrase "Auld Lang Syne," he wrote, all Scotland flew up before him:

*But I am half a Scot by birth, and bred*
*A whole one. . . .*[n]

Toward the end of August, Mrs. Byron made final arrangements for meeting John Hanson at Newstead. The young lord and his mother, accompanied by May Gray, left Aberdeen by coach, crossed the Dee, and headed southward. Byron's hopes were buoyed by the excitement of his new status and the prospects of life across the border.

# CHAPTER III

## *1798–1801*

## Newstead, Nottingham, London

FOUR miles south of Mansfield, and still about 130 miles from London on the Great North Road, the coach from Aberdeen carrying three eager passengers stopped at the Newstead tollgate. Mrs. Byron, enjoying the drama of the occasion, asked what nobleman lived on the adjoining estate. "It was Lord Byron's, but he is dead," the woman at the gate replied. "And who is the heir now?" the proud mother asked. "They say it's a little boy that lives at Aberdeen." At this point May Gray could contain herself no longer. "This is him, God bless him!" she exclaimed, turning to kiss the embarrassed young lord.[n] Driving past the gatehouse and continuing along a road that passed the forlorn stumps of once great oaks, and farms sadly run down, they had gone nearly two miles when, rounding a little hill, they saw the gray walls of the old Abbey facing a lake. Even in its dilapidated state it was impressive, the ruins of the Gothic church giving a romantic charm to the massive structure. Both the ten-year-old boy and his mother were captivated by it at first sight and wanted to live there, though the old lord had left it in complete decay.

Swinging around the fountain which had been removed by the earlier Byrons from the court of the cloister and placed before the entrance, they were greeted by Mr. and Mrs. John Hanson, who had left London on August 27 to meet them there.[n] As they looked over the park and the spacious but gloomy halls, their determination to dwell in this seat of the Byrons was strengthened. But Hanson tried to dissuade them, for on the rear side of the court the building was roofless, and the monks' reception hall and the grand refectory were stuffed with hay for the cattle that had been stabled in the entrance hall and the Priory parlor.

The creditors of the old lord had seized everything the law allowed, including much of the furniture. The 3,200 acres of the estate, including the park, the forest, mills, public houses, quarries, lime kilns, and sixteen farms, were so encumbered that the total income from rents, then not exceeding £850 a year, had been drained by debts and attorneys' fees.[n] And now to make necessary repairs to the Priory and the long-neglected farm buildings, to survey the property and set new rents, and to disentangle the legal knots tied in it under the fifth Baron's regime would take most of the income for at least the first year. Hanson's bill alone before the end of 1798 was £148. 19*s.* 7*d.*, and he had paid the executor £29. 11*s.* 9*d.*[n]

But it was the end of August and the park was lovely. The two lakes glistened and "Folly Castle" and the forts offered irresistible attractions to a ten-year-old boy. In contrast with the narrow flat in Aberdeen even the scullery of the old Abbey seemed palatial and the inconveniences small sacrifice for the freedom and spaciousness these surroundings offered. Perhaps the Gothic tales the young lord and his mother had read increased their desire to inhabit the monastic ruins. Reluctantly they drove on to Nottingham, where Byron relatives were waiting to receive them.

Hanson wrote to Farquhar: ". . . it would be better for her to take a House or Lodgings in or near London till the Affairs are arranged and it is known what she is to have allowed her, The Young Lord is a fine sharp Boy not a little spoilt by Indulgence but that is scarcely to be wondered at." [n]

But the spoiled boy's wishes were granted. It was decided that Mrs. Byron could live at Newstead, at least until affairs were settled, repairs made, and a suitable renter found for the manor. Hanson installed the young lord and his mother in the Abbey and saw a great deal of his little charge in the days that followed. The attorney took the young lord, proudly riding his pony, to see the neighbors, and introduced him to the Clarkes at Annesley Hall. Mrs. Clarke had a little girl by her first husband, Mr. Chaworth, a descendant of the William Chaworth who had been killed by the "Wicked Lord Byron" in the famous duel. If Byron saw his distant cousin Mary Chaworth on this occasion, he probably thought little about her, for she was two years his senior, and his romantic thoughts were still in Scotland. Mrs. Byron told Mrs. Hanson that Byron had no regrets at leaving his former home "excepting the scenery and one associate, a little girl named Mary Duff." [n] When Mary Chaworth came over one day to dine at Newstead, Byron still professed a decided indifference. Hanson said jokingly: "Here is a pretty young lady—you had better marry her." "What, Mr. Hanson," Byron replied, "*the Capulets and Montagues intermarry?*" [n]

The attorney soon perceived Byron's unusual qualities. Hanson's son recorded: "Lord Byron seemed to have taken a great hold upon his fancy for one so young and he spoke of him with admiration. . . . There either was at Newstead when little Ld. Byron arrived there or he br[ough]t with him from Scotland a large Wolf Dog called Woolly. It was a great Pet of Byron's. One Day the Dog from some cause or other outrageously offended him, perhaps it bit him or attempted to do so, however his countenance became suddenly pale, he rushed into the Abbey, seized a loaded gun or pistol of the Keeper's with which he hurried back to the Dog in the Garden, seized hold of him and threw him on his back exclaiming, Woolly you have done so & so, you shall *die* Woolly. My father used to say the decision of character displayed, his action & expression, & the emphasis with which he uttered the determination, the reflexion in the midst of his passion were so finely depicted that he should never forget it as long as he lived. He did not slay the Dog, arresting as it were his fixed resolve on the very verge of its destructive execution." [n]

On his return to London Hanson made arrangements with Robert Aisley, the old lord's executor, for Mrs. Byron to pay a small rental for the furniture remaining at the Abbey with an option to purchase it later.[n] In a short while the young lord was happily settled as a nobleman on his country estate. He already felt himself a landed gentleman. Shortly after arriving from

Aberdeen, he had planted a young oak [1] in the park on the green sloping down to the lower lake, visible from the great windows of the old refectory, which in their best days the earlier Byrons had used as a grand drawing-room. He was proud of the Byron arms with the mermaid and the chestnut horses surmounting the ancient motto: "Crede Byron." [2] With a generous hand he dealt out largess to his relatives in town. On November 8 he addressed his aunt, Mrs. Parker, daughter of the Admiral, to let her know that "the potatoes are now ready and you are welcome to them whenever you please." He is sending home to Mrs. Parkyns, he says, the pony which "is now quite well but too small to carry me." He has also sent some game, "a young Rabbit which I beg Miss Frances will accept off." The letter is in the copybook hand he had learned at Mr. Duncan's in Aberdeen. In a postscript he says: "I hope you will excuse all blunders as it is the first letter I ever wrote." [3]

Early in the following year, however, Byron was in Nottingham, staying with the Parkyns family, whence he wrote his mother a letter which shows that at the age of eleven he was already beginning to take seriously his responsibilities as a young nobleman. He had had no instruction since he had left Aberdeen, and Mrs. Byron in her present financial state apparently hesitated to employ a tutor, but her son wrote: "Mr. Rogers could attend me every night at a separate hour from the Miss Parkynses, and I am astonished you do not acquiesce in this Scheme which would keep me in Mind of what I have almost entirely forgot. I recommend this to you because, if some plan of this kind is not adopted, I shall be called, or rather branded with

[1] Moore, I, 101. Moore says he "had an idea that as *it* flourished so should *he*." Returning some years later and finding it choked with weeds, he wrote his sentimental poem "To an Oak at Newstead."

[2] The Heralds' description runs: "*Arms*—Arg., three bendlets enhanced gu. *Crest*—A mermaid with her comb and mirror all ppr. *Supporters*—Two horses of a chestnut colour ppr. hoofs or. *Motto*—Crede Byron." (Burke's *Peerage* [1949 ed.], p. 321.)

[3] *LJ*, I, 6–7. Mrs. Parker's daughter Margaret was one of Byron's early loves, who inspired his "first dash into poetry." Mrs. Parkyns appears to have been an aunt, or second cousin, perhaps a daughter of the Admiral's brother George Byron.

the name of a dunce, which you know I could never bear." [n]

May Gray had been left in Nottingham to care for the boy, particularly while he was receiving treatments for his lame foot from Lavender, a practitioner who called himself a surgeon, and who apparently tried to straighten the deformed limb by rubbing it with handfuls of oil and then screwing it up in a wooden machine that gave the patient excruciating pain. Dummer Rogers, "Teacher of French, English, Latin, and Mathematicks," did take over the instruction of the young lord for several months in 1799.[n] With him Byron read parts of Virgil and Cicero, sometimes with his foot in such a tortured position that the tutor could not help feeling sympathy. One day Rogers said: "My lord, I don't feel comfortable at having you sitting opposite me there, in such pain as you must be." Byron replied: "Never mind, Mr. Rogers, you shall not see any signs of it in me." [n]

Rogers in later years told Moore how Byron got revenge on Lavender, a pompous pretender to knowledge, for the torment suffered at his hands. One day in a mischievous mood the boy set down the letters of the alphabet at random but spaced to look like words and asked Lavender what language it was. Not wishing to profess ignorance, the quack replied with assurance: "Italian," whereupon Byron roared with laughter at the gullible impostor.[n]

Byron still found time to enjoy the freedom of his estate at Newstead. No tenant had appeared to take the ramshackle and roofless Abbey, and Mrs. Byron continued her residence there. On holidays and at other times the young lord returned to play the grand seigneur. There was much to interest a boy on the premises. The fifth Baron's fatal sword "of Iron and Steel, of the Value of Five Shillings," [n] which had been used in the duel with Mr. Chaworth, was still there.[n] The old lord's pistols were also fascinating playthings, and young Byron imitated his predecessor by practicing pistol shooting (a habit which he continued through life) and by always carrying small loaded pistols in his waistcoat pockets.[n]

He was less happy in Nottingham, where, part of the time living with relatives and for a while with a Mr. Gill in St. James's Lane, he had to suffer not only the torture, the pretensions, and the insolences of Lavender,[4] but also the neglect and liberties of the maid May Gray.

Hanson, constantly occupied with the tangled affairs of the Byron estate, left London on June 30 (1799) to meet the surveyor at Newstead and to transact other business. A short while before, he had called on Byron's kinsman, the Earl of Carlisle, to try to persuade him to become the guardian of the young lord during his minority. The Earl, at first reluctant because of the amount of business it might entail, and because the Byrons were total strangers to him, at length succumbed to the zeal of the attorney for his protégé. But he consented only to act in an advisory capacity.[5]

Hanson had already seen the necessity of getting the spoiled boy who had so much promise away from his mother and into an environment in which he would have both kindness and discipline and could get a more systematic education. Moreover, it was evident that Lavender was merely torturing him without doing him any good, and it was important to get him to London, where his foot could be examined by competent medical men. When the attorney left Newstead in the second week of July, he took Byron with him in his carriage, May Gray being sent along by Mrs. Byron to look after the wardrobe and the bandages for the lame foot.

Byron saw London for the first time since he was an infant on July 12, 1799, when the carriage rolled through Old Brompton to the house at Earl's Court, Kensington, that Hanson had purchased from the executors of the famous John Hunter.[6] There was a dramatic moment when the young lord entered the room

[4] Lavender, though he was listed in the Nottingham Directory in 1814 as a "surgeon," was actually "trussmaker to the general hospital." (*LJ*, I 7n.)

[5] Hanson narrative, Murray MSS. The 5th Earl of Carlisle was a son of Admiral Byron's elder sister, Isabella, who had married the fourth Earl. He was thus the first cousin of Byron's father.

[6] John Hunter (1728–1793), anatomist and surgeon, built the house in 1764. There he maintained an anatomical museum and a considerable menagerie of wild animals, whose carcasses he anatomized when they died. He was appointed surgeon extraordinary to George III in 1776. The Hansons lived in the house until 1804. It was natural that John Hunter, the most famous surgeon of his day, should have been brought into consultation when Mrs. Byron's newborn son was found to have a clubfoot.

where the Hanson children were eagerly waiting to see him. All eyes were upon him, but he seemed little abashed while his friend, the father of the family, was in the room. Then Hanson's seven-year-old daughter exclaimed with gravity and emphasis: "Well he is a pretty Boy however!" He must indeed have made an impression on the Hanson children. Though he was lame and had already a tendency to portliness, he had inherited the handsome lineaments of his father. Newton Hanson noted that he was "remarkably chested and from the tip of finger to finger was a lengthy span, hence [he was] a good swimmer." He no doubt still spoke with a pronounced Scottish accent which the English schools had not yet erased.

The next day Hanson had a long conference with Lord Carlisle and with Dr. Baillie on Byron's education and the best treatment of his foot. And on the 15th the boy was taken to meet his guardian. On this visit he was obviously ill at ease. Though he was generally tractable in Hanson's hands, he was reluctant to go, possibly because he knew Dr. Baillie had been asked there to meet him, and he did not want his foot discussed before Lord Carlisle. The Earl spoke to him kindly, but after they had been there a very short time, Byron turned to Hanson and said: "Let us go." [n]

On the 17th of July Hanson took his charge to Dr. Baillie's house, where a full examination was made of his foot. It was the opinion of Baillie, Newton Hanson recorded, "that if the proper means had been taken at the first in Infancy the malformation might have been brought round. The right foot was inverted and contracted as it were in a heap and of course did not go fully and flatly to the ground. But as it grew if it had at first been forced into a frame by constant and gradual pressure on the inside to the right side and also pressed down on the instep much if not the whole of the Evil might have been cured. But little could be done after the lapse of ten or eleven years. . . . Mr. Sheldrake however of the Strand . . . attended Lord B. and made him some instruments for his foot which were continued in use for a short Time but were afterwards given up for a Boot which he constructed for him." [7]

[7] Hanson narrative, Murray MSS. However the therapeutics of Dr. Baillie

Though all the Hansons became attached to the young lord, they soon discovered they had a firebrand on their hands when his pride or sensitivities were touched. One day at Earl's Court, when Lord Portsmouth was on a visit, they were witnesses to one of Byron's fits of sudden anger. The party was lounging around in the conservatory after breakfast when "Lord P. took the liberty of pulling Ld. Byron's ears in his usual rough way though in fun. There happened to be some large shells laying near to Byron and he instantly seized one of them and threw it with all his might at the Earl. Fortunately it missed him . . . but it not only frightened Lord Portsmouth very much but everyone else. I think my father and two or three others were present. Mrs. Hanson interfered and tried to pacify Lord P. by saying Lord B. did not do it intentionally my Lord, whilst Lord Byron kept reiterating he did do it intentionally and he would teach a fool of an Earl to pull another Noble's ears. However the affray was afterwards made up and the parties shook hands and were very good friends." [n]

Byron's lameness, according to Newton Hanson, considerably

---

may appear to modern surgeons, the description given here of the nature of Byron's deformity points clearly to some form of clubfoot. The evidence coincides exactly with that of the most reliable witnesses: Byron's father, who said he had a clubfoot (*LJ*, I, ix); his mother, who said: "George's foot turns inward, and it is the right foot; he walks quite on the side of his foot" (*LJ*, I, 11n); and Dr. Millingen, the only one of the doctors at Missolonghi who has left a record of the nature of Byron's deformity: "The foot was deformed, and turned inwards; and the leg was smaller and shorter than the sound one. Although Lord Byron preferred attributing his lameness to the unskilful treatment of a sprained ankle, there can be little or no doubt, that he was born club-footed." (Millingen, p. 143.) It is true that Millingen, like several others who wrote years after the subject of their observation was dead, said it was the left foot, but it would be easier to confuse right and left than to forget the nature of the deformity and the appearance of the foot. Dr. James Kemble, who made a careful examination of Byron's boots, now at John Murray's, and all the other evidence, concluded that "Byron's lameness was due to congenital club-foot of the Talipes Equino-varus type, affecting the right foot only." (James Kemble: "Byron: His Lameness and His Last Illness," *Quarterly Review,* Vol. CCLII [Oct. 1931], p. 235.) Dr. Matthew Baillie (1761–1823) was an eminent morbid anatomist, nephew of the great anatomists William and John Hunter and brother of the poetess Joanna Baillie. He later took a house in Grosvenor Street and became physician extraordinary to George III.

restricted his movements and turned him to reading. "In the morning till about one o'clock he would lie upon the sofa quite lost in his book. Then he would start up, put, or sometimes throw the book down and be in high spirits and ready for a romp, as completely divested of all thought of his book or of what he had been reading as if he had never been so engaged."[n]

Mrs. Byron had represented to Hanson while he was at Newstead the difficulty of her situation. Half of the money she had received from the sale of her furniture in Aberdeen had been spent on the journey to Newstead.[n] And her income had been reduced to £122 a year. If she was to pay the doctor's bills and give Byron a proper education, she would have to receive some aid. On his return to town Hanson at once drew up a petition to the King for Mrs. Byron, which she signed and sent to the Duke of Portland, and on the attorney's suggestion the Earl of Carlisle wrote in support of the petition. On August 24 the Duke replied that Mr. Pitt had been given orders that a provision of £300 a year should be made to her out of the Civil List.[n]

After consulting with Lord Carlisle, Hanson chose a school for Byron in the quiet residential suburb of Dulwich about seven miles from the heart of London. It was run by a Scotsman, Dr. Glennie, recommended by Hanson's friend Mr. Farquhar, an Aberdonian who had first managed Mrs. Byron's business affairs in London. Dr. Glennie kept a small number of boys at his house in Lordship Lane. On August 22, Hanson accompanied Byron to Dulwich, and on the 1st of September he reported to Mrs. Byron that her son was settled at the school, where he had a private room and was comfortable.[n]

Byron, it is clear, had cast his spell over Hanson, who wrote: "I entertain a very great affection for Lord Byron, and I trust I shall not be considered solely in my professional character, but as his Friend. . . . He has Ability and a quickness of Conception and a correct Discrimination that is seldom seen in a youth, and he is a fit associate of men, and choice indeed must be the Company that is selected for him."[n]

In this same letter Hanson told Mrs. Byron a story of the misbehavior of May Gray, who had been sent back to Newstead, which must have disturbed her profoundly. "I assure you,

Madam," he wrote solemnly, ". . . her conduct towards your son while at Nottingham was shocking, and I was persuaded you needed but a hint of it to dismiss her. Mrs. Parkyns, when I saw her, said something to me about her; but when I found from dispassionate persons at Nottingham, it was the general Topic of conversation, it would have ill become me to have remained silent.

"My honourable little companion, tho' disposed to retain his feelings, could not refrain, from the harsh usage he had received at her hands, from complaining to me, and such is his dread of the Woman that I really believe he would forego the satisfaction of seeing you if he thought he was to meet her again. He told me that she was perpetually beating him, and that his bones sometimes ached from it; that she brought all sorts of Company of the lowest Description into his apartments; that she was out late at nights, and he was frequently left to put himself to bed; that she would take the Chaise-boys into the Chaise with her, and stopped at every little Ale-house to drink with them. But, Madam, this is not all; she has even—traduced yourself." [n]

Hanson had not told the whole story, however. He kept the secret which he had extracted from the boy and only revealed it after Byron's death. Reflecting on his youth, Byron wrote in his "Detached Thoughts": "My passions were developed very early—so early, that few would believe me, if I were to state the period, and the facts which accompanied it." [n] Commenting on this precocity in love, the poet's friend Hobhouse later wrote: "With the respect to the early development of these propensities in Byron I am acquainted with a singular fact scarcely fit for narration but much less romantic and more satisfactory than the amour with Mary Duff." [n]

And the nature of this "less romantic" fact is revealed in a note written by Hobhouse after talking with Hanson in 1824: "When [Byron was] nine years old at his mother's house a free Scotch girl used to come to bed to him & play tricks with his person—Hanson found it out & asked Lord B—who owned the fact—the girl was sent off—" [8]

[8] Hobhouse notes titled "Lord Byron" with his manuscript diary of the sum-

It seems then that the blows Byron suffered at the hands of May Gray were psychological rather than physical. It is possible also, however, that she did lay hands on him in anger if he protested against her low company when she had been drinking, for she might have felt that the intimacies he had shared with her would prevent him from complaining of her conduct to his mother.

Byron's first months at Dulwich must not have been unhappy ones, for the discipline was not too strict, he found some agreeable companions, and he slept in Dr. Glennie's own study, where he had access to the books. Sheldrake attended him to apply an instrument designed by Dr. Baillie to straighten his foot. Though it probably did not give him as much pain as he had suffered at the hands of Lavender, he was quite as unwilling to submit to the inconvenience and constraint. Hobhouse said: "This instrument he wore with much impatience and one day threw it into a pond." [n] Late in November Byron wrote to Hanson: "I am at present very well and my foot goes but indifferently; I cannot perceive any alteration." [9]

Dr. Glennie's account of Byron's stay at Dulwich savors a little of reminiscence sweetened too much with deference to the boy's rank and his later fame. "I found him enter upon his tasks," Glennie says, "with alacrity and success. . . . His reading in history and poetry was far beyond the usual standard of his age, and in my study he found many books open to him. . . .

---

mer of 1824. If Byron was nine years old when this sex-play began, it must have gone on some time before Byron revealed it to Hanson. This experience with an apparently pious girl who had taught him to read the Bible may have been an additional shock and in part the foundation of his lifelong hatred of cant and hypocrisy in religious people.

[9] *LJ*, I, 11. Moore, after talking with the Glennies, when gathering material for his life of Byron, recorded in his *Diary:* "Mr. and Mrs. Glennie, under whose care he was for near two years (I think), affirm positively that it was a club-foot, and that he was born with it. Sheldrake used to come to put on the iron; the leg, they say, was not wasted, and the iron went up only a short way. When I mentioned to them his saying to me that he was never altogether free from pain in it, they said he suffered no such pain at that time, and that it must be, perhaps, from his efforts to disguise the deformity that the inconvenience was felt, when I knew him." (Moore: *Memoirs,* July 10, 1827, II, 625.)

He showed at this age an intimate acquaintance with the historical parts of the Holy Scriptures, upon which he seemed delighted to converse with me, especially after our religious exercises of a Sunday evening; when he would reason upon the facts contained in the Sacred Volume, with every appearance of belief in the divine truths which they unfold." [n]

Byron was much behind the other boys in the systematic study of Latin grammar, and was probably not very patient in toiling through the work which was necessary before he could make any progress in the English schools. He was stimulated to some effort, however, by the example of a very clever boy by the name of Lowes with whom he became friendly. But some of the other boys ridiculed the young lord's boasting of the superiority of his lineage to the more recent peerages and gave him the nickname of "the Old English Baron." [1]

It was arranged that Byron should spend the Christmas holidays with the Hansons at Earl's Court. He had grown fond of the household where he was admired and catered to by young and old, and he had no desire to return to Newstead while May Gray was still there. Writing to Hanson toward the end of November, he said: ". . . since you are going to Newstead, I beg if you meet Gray send her a packing as fast as possible." [2]

Hanson visited his young friend at Dulwich before he and his wife left on November 27 for the north, and, though they did not return until the first week in January 1800, Byron had a very merry time with the Hanson children, who were left under the not too strict chaperonage of John Hanson's older sister. Newton Hanson wrote an account of Byron's first school holiday in Lon-

[1] Moore: *Memoirs,* July 10, 1827, II, 625. Also Moore, I, 46–7. *The Old English Baron* was a popular gothic tale by Clara Reeve, first published in 1777.

[2] *LJ,* I, 10. Mrs. Byron apparently had not yet acted on Byron's appeal through Hanson to have May Gray discharged. This suggests that she may have listened to May's side of the story, for she knew that Byron was obstreperous and difficult to control. Mrs. Byron had written to Hanson on November 28: "As to Byron's coming with you, if it is now the Holydays I shall be happy to see him, if it is not, I do not wish it, as his education has been too much interrupted since he has been in England." (Unpublished letter, Huntington Library.) But the boy was glad of the excuse to remain in London.

don: "Lord Byron was then rather sedate, fond of reading, and contemplative, yet we [Newton and his brother Hargreaves were then home from school] had occasionally some brisk Gambols together when our Books were laid aside and we had dashed out of doors. Among others was the climbing up of one of the high Pyramids which was one of the curiosities of the spot erected by Hunter. . . .

"Tho' contrary to our parole of Honour to my Aunt I fear, we occasionally advanced too far in the lower regions [of the house], for on one occasion I remember Byron had so far excelled in the art of teasing as to bring out from her Habitation a fiery and violent old woman (a very good cook I have no doubt) in full Chase after us and with a weapon in her hand that I verily believe w[oul]d have been cruelly used in her rage if she had come up with Byron. By great good luck and his agility he did manage to get clean of her, but whilst retracing her Steps and venting her disappointment the latter exclaimed 'You a Lord—indeed you a Lord, I wonder who the d——l ever made you a Lord.'" [n]

Mrs. Byron, having finally sent May Gray back to Scotland, accompanied the Hansons on their return to London, partly to be on hand for business conferences with Hanson and Lord Carlisle and partly to be near her son. They arrived about the middle of January and she remained for a few days at Earl's Court until Byron went back to Dr. Glennie's. Newton Hanson observed that "Mrs. Byron showed a great fondness for her Son, but it was occasionally interspersed by a contrary Disposition. She was certainly fickle in her Humour and Treatment of him but on the whole they were very fond of each other.

"Byron had a sad Trick of biting his Nails which sometimes used to call forth from his Mother sudden and violent Ejaculations of Disgust accompanied by a Box on the ear or Hands." [n]

Mrs. Byron, her income now increased by £300, took lodgings in Sloane Terrace, about two miles from the Hansons. On January 16 she met her son's guardian, Lord Carlisle, for the first time when Hanson brought them into conference on matters relating to the estate. There is no record of the immediate impression she made on him, but she was soon to render herself obnoxious to both the Earl and the attorney. Her gaucheries, her volatile temper, her desire to interfere with Byron's education made her stay in London an embarrassment for her son and a nuisance to Lord Carlisle, Dr. Glennie, and Hanson.

Once in London, she could not leave her son alone, but was constantly taking him home to Sloane Terrace and keeping him from Saturday to Monday, contrary to the wishes of Dr. Glennie, though she was aware that he was behind the other boys and should devote his whole time to study. She would sometimes even keep him out of school for a week at a time. Perhaps she was merely acquiescing in the wishes of the young scamp, who was averse to discipline and who knew how to melt her resistance as his father before him had done. Dr. Glennie was ready enough to blame Mrs. Byron, who was uncouth and frequently made a scene when she came to the school. He accused her not only of interfering with the school discipline, but also of gathering around her son a circle of young acquaintances not likely to improve his manners.[n]

Byron apparently accompanied his mother to Nottingham and Newstead during the summer vacation of 1800, for that was the date he assigned to his "first dash into poetry," inspired by "the ebullition of a passion for my first Cousin Margaret Parker . . . one of the most beautiful of evanescent beings. I have long forgotten the verses, but it would be difficult for me to forget her. Her dark eyes! her long eye-lashes! . . . I was then about twelve—She rather older, perhaps a year. . . . I do not recollect scarcely any thing equal to the *transparent* beauty of my cousin, or to the sweetness of her temper, during the short period of our intimacy. She looked as if she had been made out of a rainbow—all beauty and peace.

"My passion had its usual effects upon me: I could not sleep, could not eat; I could not rest; and although I had reason to know that she loved me, it was the torture of my life to think of the time which must elapse before we could meet again—being usually about *twelve hours* of separation!"[n]

In this experience and in the very different one with May Gray there is a clear indication of two parallel developments in Byron's relations with women, both awakening his sensibilities at an abnormally precocious age, and both with tremendous implications to his later life. It is strange how little account has been taken of Byron's plain statement that his passions were developed very early and that this "caused the anticipated melancholy of my thoughts—having anticipated life." [n] Now one of these developments, associated in his mind with both the Mary Duff and the Margaret Parker affairs, stimulated him to a "dash into poetry" and became the constant symbol to him of the ideally beautiful unpossessed love, the sort of image that usually develops in adolescence but that in Byron was a dominating vision between the years of eight and twelve. It had numerous counterparts or embodiments male and female during the rest of his life. The other, the premature sexual awakening, caused disillusionment, the melancholy which springs from physical disgust and the failure of a real experience to measure up to the ideal. The first carried him into love with young girls and boys; the second into the cynical search for "fine animals" like the baker's wife in Venice.

Back at Dulwich, his mind filled with visions of the dark eyes of Margaret Parker, Byron found the routine of Latin grammar less and less supportable; and Mrs. Byron, torn between her knowledge that he should study without interruption and her impulse to cater to his whims, continued to keep him at home for extended periods. Glennie appealed to Hanson, who summoned the aid of Lord Carlisle: "I have taken upon me to desire Mr. Glennie not to permit Mrs. Byron to take him out of his House without a written order from your Lordship." [n] When Mrs. Byron was denied the privilege, too often abused, of the usual Saturday visit, she broke out into "such audible fits of temper as it was impossible to keep from reaching the ears of the scholars and the servants." After one of these displays Dr. Glennie heard one of Byron's classmates say to him: "Byron, your mother is a fool." The resigned reply of the embarrassed son was "I know it." [3]

[3] Moore, I, 32. Hobhouse recorded that "His mother bred him so foolishly, now kicking and now kissing him, that Hanson took him away by force to Dulwich school—She fell in love with a French dancing master at Brompton & laid a plan for carrying B to France—The Frenchman called at Dulwich

Her violence soon caused Lord Carlisle to throw up his hands and say to Mr. Glennie: "I can have nothing more to do with Mrs. Byron,—you must now manage her as you can." [n] Hanson, who had all along done his utmost to cultivate the Earl's interest in his ward, felt completely thwarted by Mrs. Byron's outrageous conduct and by Byron's shyness.

Byron again spent the Christmas holidays at Earl's Court with the Hansons, with whom by this time he had thoroughly ingratiated himself. The attorney was more and more delighted with the boy as his mind developed, and he was willing to make excuses for his slowness in routine studies. Thinking that he should have the advantage of a public school, soon after the holidays he took the matter before Lord Carlisle, suggesting Harrow, to which the Earl saw no objection. On January 25, 1801, Hanson went down to Harrow and had an interview with Dr. Joseph Drury, the headmaster, giving him an enthusiastic account of his young friend, admitting "that his education had been neglected; that he was ill prepared for a public school"; but adding "that he thought there was a *cleverness* about him." [n]

After a second interview with Lord Carlisle, the matter was settled, and Hanson informed the none too happy Dr. Glennie that he should prepare his pupil, as far as was possible in the time, for entrance to Harrow after the Easter holiday. It is unlikely that the boy applied himself very seriously to Dr. Glennie's intellectual offerings, however, for he was thoroughly sick of Dulwich by this time. Writing to his cousin George Byron on February 24, he announced: "I am going to leave this damned place at Easter and am going to Harrow." [n]

Hanson was also worried about Byron's foot, which had not shown the improvement he expected. During the Christmas holidays he had arranged meetings with Dr. Baillie and with a Dr. Maurice Laurie of Bartholomew's Close, who had been brought into consultation, and to whom Dr. Baillie thenceforth turned over the practical care of the case, though he continued to give advice. They came together to Earl's Court, and under

---

to take him away but the master would not let him go." (Manuscript narrative entitled "Lord Byron" in the Hobhouse diary of the summer of 1824.)

Dr. Baillie's supervision Dr. Laurie constructed what was apparently a kind of brace intended to straighten the foot by gradual pressure. But Byron was as impatient of using it as he had been of wearing the instruments of Sheldrake. Whenever his "flow of spirits" impelled him to active movements, he threw the brace aside or neglected to wear it.[n]

Toward the end of April, Hanson took his protégé to Harrow and introduced him to Dr. Drury. The attorney's partiality in describing the boy had scarcely prepared the headmaster for his first meeting with this singular young lord. Handsome, with a finely chiseled countenance and sensitive blue-gray eyes, curly auburn hair, and small ears, he was inclined to be haughty and reserved, with the touchy independence of spirit of one who had never responded willingly to the reins of discipline. And yet in his clear eyes Dr. Drury, who had a wide and tolerant knowledge of boys, could perceive behind the shyness a responsiveness to kindness and proper handling. After Hanson's departure Drury took Byron into his study and tried to draw him out "by inquiries as to his former amusements, employments, and associates, but with little or no effect;—and I soon found that a wild mountain colt had been submitted to my management. But there was mind in his eye. . . . His manner and temper soon convinced me, that he might be led by a silken string to a point, rather than by a cable;—on that principle I acted." [n]

A few months past his thirteenth birthday Byron was thus launched upon the rough-and-tumble life of a public school. He knew that his training was deficient and that he was behind most of the boys of his own age. And he soon discovered that only physical defense would gain him immunity from the animal cruelties inflicted upon any deformity in that environment. In addition, he was just entering upon the emotional and physical developments of adolescence. It is little wonder that Byron hated Harrow during his first years there. Self-willed and passionate when aroused, he was at bottom soft, almost feminine in his emotional attachments, remarkably generous, and full of boyish ambition and idealism. The crucible of Harrow in the next four years fixed as much as it modified these traits.

# CHAPTER IV

## *1801–1805*

## The Harrow Years

AT THE beginning of the nineteenth century Harrow-on-the-Hill was a pleasant country village eleven miles northwest of the heart of London. At the top of the hill stood the famous school founded in 1571 by John Lyon. It shared with Eton the distinction of a long history and rivaled it in popularity with the aristocracy. A surprising number of young lords and scions of earls and dukes were Byron's contemporaries at Harrow. Dr. Drury, who was fifty-one when Byron entered, had been with the school for over thirty years, and had been headmaster since 1785. He had built up a reputation for fairness, and he and his masters crammed with impartiality into the heads of lords and commoners (the middle class was well represented in the school) a respectable knowledge of Latin and Greek.

When Byron rode up the hill with John Hanson on that April day in 1801, he saw a high, rather ungainly building with small windows and sharp gables on top. A wall separated it from the churchyard of the tall-spired fourteenth-century church of St. Mary's. The shy boy with the brace on his foot could not have been reassured if he saw on the playground the strange boys with tall broad-brimmed black hats, open collars, frock coats with tails, and tight-fitting trousers.

But Drury, foreseeing the embarrassment Byron would suffer if he were placed with boys younger than himself, assigned him his own son Henry as tutor until he should have made sufficient progress to be placed among boys of his own age. Living in the house of Henry Drury (then one of the younger masters), Byron did not at first associate much with the other boys, for "a degree of shyness hung about him for some time." *n* Unused to any kind of discipline, this "wild mountain colt" was rebellious and unruly and quickly resented the master's attempt to put any restraint on him, though he usually responded well enough to the headmaster's "silken string."

It was the first time he had been thrown with boys of his own rank, and he was proud to associate with them but a little awed by the older ones. His earliest friends were younger boys and those of humbler station. Edward Noel Long, who was to be one of Byron's most intimate friends at Harrow and later at Cambridge, arrived at the same time, and they had the common bond of being newcomers together. Long wrote to his father on May 1: "There is another, Ld. Byram [*sic*] a lame fellow just come he seems a good sort of fellow." *n* Robert Peel and his brother William were also contemporaries. Twenty years later Byron wrote in his "Detached Thoughts": "Peel, the Orator and Statesman . . . was my form fellow, and we were both at the top of our remove. . . . We were on good terms, but his brother was my intimate friend. . . . As a Scholar, he [Peel] was greatly my superior: as a declaimer, and Actor, I was reckoned at least his equal. As a school boy *out* of school, I was always *in* scrapes, and *he never;* and *in School* he *always* knew his lesson, and I rarely; but when I knew it, I knew it nearly as well. In general information, history, etc., etc., I think I was *his* Superior, as also of most boys of my standing." *n*

It was inevitable that the lame boy with a great deal of pride and a delicately balanced chip on his shoulder should come to blows with some of his fellows, for fists were honorable weapons among Harrovians. Taunts at his deformity may have initiated the combats, though he never said so,[1] but, whatever the cause, he fought like a little demon as he had done in Aberdeen. He himself later confessed that in his early days at Harrow he was "a most unpopular boy," but that he had fought his way very

[1] Leigh Hunt wrote (*Lord Byron*, I, 151) of Byron's lameness that "the usual thoughtlessness of schoolboys made him feel it bitterly at Harrow. He would wake, and find his leg in a tub of water."

NEWSTEAD PRIORY, NOTTINGHAMSHIRE

NEWSTEAD PARK

*HARROW SCHOOL, 1816*

honorably.[n] It is only fair, however, to record the statement of Sir Thomas Bernard, a contemporary who once shared a bedroom with him and who said he was "a terrible bully." [n] But against this must be set the stories of his championing smaller boys—George Sinclair,[n] Peel,[n] Lord Delawarr, and William Harness,[2] who was lame from an accident. One of his schoolfellows remembered him as "a clever, plain-spoken, and undaunted boy." [n] Byron boasted that he had lost only one battle out of seven, and that one because his antagonist had practiced some unfairness; with the others he was always friendly afterward.[n]

Most of Byron's Harrow friendships were to ripen later. His first months of fighting his way left him unhappy, and he hated the school, though there was some exhilaration in forcing respect by his own pluck. He had the intelligence necessary for the prescribed work, but no enthusiasm for the daily grind of lessons. He described himself as idle but "capable of great sudden exertions (such as thirty or forty Greek Hexameters, of course with such prosody as it pleased God), but of few continuous drudgeries." [n] By the end of June, Dr. Drury had placed him in the fourth form, at the top of the remove, together with Long, Peel, and Clayton, whom Byron described as "another School Monster of learning, and talent, and hope . . . he was certainly a Genius." [n]

The summer holidays were a welcome relief. Mrs. Byron had given up her lodgings in Sloane Terrace and had taken a room with a Mrs. Massingberd at 16 Piccadilly. Her son stayed with her occasionally, though it was her wish that he should spend the holidays again at Earl's Court. Actually he divided his time during the summer between his mother and the Hansons.[n] On August 4, Hanson arranged for Drs. Baillie and Laurie to visit him at 16 Piccadilly.[n] For his use at Harrow the doctors had devised a shoe with a brace round the ankle, and they continued to bandage the foot.

[2] L'Estrange: *The Literary Life of the Rev. William Harness,* p. 4. Byron one day saw him being bullied by a boy much older and stronger and said to him: "Harness, if any fellow bullies you, tell me; and I'll thrash him if I can." Another story of Byron's interference is that of his thrashing Lord Herbert for bullying Thomas Dundas, Byron's comment being: "I like licking a Lord's son." (Minchin: *Old Harrow Days,* p. 193.)

Later in the summer Byron accompanied his mother to Cheltenham and visited the Malvern Hills, the only thing in England that reminded him, "even in miniature, of a mountain," and he longed again for the Scottish Highlands. "After I returned to Cheltenham," he wrote in a note to *The Island,* "I used to watch them every afternoon, at sunset, with a sensation which I cannot describe. This was boyish enough: but I was then only thirteen years of age, and it was in the holidays." [n]

By September they were back in London, and Mrs. Byron proceeded to Brighton, where she spent the autumn and early winter. Dr. Laurie had convinced her that the treatment of her son's foot had been beneficial, but the doctor's bill shocked the poor woman, who faced the prospect of giving up a large share of her own income indefinitely for a problematical advantage to her son. Hanson had secured from the Court of Chancery a grant of £500 a year for Byron's education, payable in quarterly installments to his mother, whose pension was reduced to £200 and was paid very irregularly.[n] As Byron's expenses and his lavish habits grew, his mother's financial difficulties became acute, and she was frequently obliged to write Hanson for advances on her quarterly payments.

Writing from Brighton to Dr. Laurie on September 21, Mrs. Byron complained that the doctor's bill "comes extremely high at the rate of a hundred and fifty pounds a year and two guineas a visit to Harrow I think a great deal of Money. I am however sensible that Lord Byron certainly walks better than he did, therefore you may continue your visits to him at Harrow. . . ." [n] But the boy was careless and reluctant to submit to treatment. On December 7, Dr. Laurie, after his visit to Harrow, reported: ". . . I found his foot in a much worse state than when I last saw it,—the shoe entirely wet through and the brace round his ancle quite loose; I much fear his extreme Inattention will counteract every exertion on my part to make him better. I have only to add that with proper care and bandaging, his foot may still be greatly recovered; but any delay further than the present vacation—would render it folly to undertake it." [n]

The difficulty was that Byron would never allow his foot to prevent him from doing what other boys did, and, while he was never much of a sportsman (except in swimming, in which he excelled), he would try his hand at everything and became a fair cricketer. Though he was frequently in mischief, he was not always fighting. He began to make friends, which was not difficult for him when he set his mind to it, for he was amiable, generous to an extreme with those he liked, and eager for others to like him. His penchant for steadfastness in his friendships caused him to remember his Harrow intimates with fondness years after. In retrospect he recalled that "P. Hunter, Curzon, Long, and Tatersall, were my principal friends. Clare, Dorset, Cs. Gordon, De Bath[e], Claridge, and Jno. Wingfield, were my juniors and favourites, whom I spoilt by indulgence." [n] All of his older friends were commoners. But most of these friendships were those of his last year or two at Harrow. He became most intimate with Long during his Cambridge days. Byron early developed a taste for being the patron and benefactor, and that was the basis of many of his Harrow friendships. To be a fag or to depend on others was intolerable, though he got through it somehow.

He spent the Christmas holidays with his mother in Half Moon Street, but often went to the Hansons at Earl's Court. It may be that he met his half-sister Augusta during that holiday, though their first correspondence is of a later date. Mrs. Byron had written to Augusta on October 18, extending rather frosty condolences on the death of her grandmother Lady Holderness, but assuring Augusta of "the unalterable regard & friendship of myself and son." Byron, she said, "often mentions you to me in the most affectionate manner, indeed the goodness of his heart and amiable disposition is such that your being his Sister had he never seen you would be a sufficient claim upon him. . . . Your Brother is at Harrow school and if you wish to see him I have now no desire to keep you asunder." [n] During the following year Augusta took an increasing interest in her brother and in his progress at Harrow.

Early in February 1802, Byron and Hargreaves Hanson returned to Harrow and Mrs. Byron went to Bath, where she had friends and where she could bask in the melancholy memory of the days not long since when she had been courted there by the irresistible Captain Byron. The young idler at Harrow scribbled in his notebooks and wrote translations of simple Greek words in his volumes of Xenophon and the Greek plays while waiting for the holidays.[3]

Mrs. Byron seems to have returned to London for the Easter or the summer holidays, for Byron reminded Pryse Gordon, when he met him in Brussels in 1816, that they had taken a ride in Hyde Park together fourteen years before, "when I came to town to spend the holidays with my poor mother."

"At fourteen," Gordon wrote, "he was a fine, lively, restless lad, full of fire and energy, and passionately fond of riding. . . . though he was a spoiled child, and had too much of his own way, he never did any thing intentionally to disoblige or vex . . . [his mother],—at least so she has often told me." [n]

Byron again spent the end of the summer holidays with his mother at Cheltenham. Mrs. Byron wrote to Hanson on September 5 to ask if he could accommodate her son with a bed for one night on his way to Harrow on the 21st.[n]

Harrow in the new term was less strange, for he was beginning to make more friends, again with younger boys and those who leaned on him for protection. It was during this year that he first met William Harness. Harness was only twelve at the time, no doubt overwhelmed by the kindness of the young lord, and flattered by the friendship which he remembered as being "uniformly affectionate" and without "a single instance of caprice or unkindness." [n] Byron was touched by the boy's devotion, and was moved to indite some verses to Harness, but the lines were destroyed before his friend saw them.

The adolescent proclivity for versifying was burgeoning in the young Byron, now in his fifteenth year, for, despite his turbulent disposition, he had a serious side hardly suspected by his classmates. Hanson had noted and admired his facility in clever epigram and satiric rhyme; that was something that he could turn out readily on occasion for his classmates. But the senti-

[3] Moore, I, 59. That Byron was already doing a good deal of writing is indicated by his later statement that he had begun a drama "at thirteen years old, called 'Ulric and Ilvina,' which I had sense enough to burn." (*Poetry*, V, 338.)

mental emotions that stirred him called for a more self-revealing verse that was not meant for casual eyes. These moods of melancholy found their proper milieu in the Harrow churchyard, where he used to sit under an elm for hours on a flat blue limestone tomb which covered the remains of one John Peachey, Esq., of the island of St. Christopher's.[n] There on the brow of the hill that commanded a view of the valleys and wooded hills he could daydream or, in the graveyard setting, with the melancholy reminders of mortality all about, abandon himself to mournful thoughts of the death of his beautiful cousin Margaret Parker, news of which had just reached him. Why had "The King of Terrors seiz'd her as his prey"? Not even the autumn splendor of the Middlesex hills could win him from disturbing reflections on "That clay, where once such animation beam'd." "Hush'd are the winds, and still the evening gloom," he began, but he knew it was a dull and conventional thing he was writing, not at all matching the depth of the feeling stirred by "the memory of that beauteous face."[n]

But more than contemplation of early death stirred in his mind. Some vague perception of the satisfactions of poetic composition as an outlet for emotion and a deliverance from the imperfections of life had begun to form in his consciousness.

The daily life of Greek translations became more and more irksome. He sought relief in pranks that got him into trouble with Henry Drury, who found his pupil increasingly difficult to handle. Only by "many serious conversations" with Byron and frequent admonitions to his son to have patience could the headmaster prevent an open breach before the Christmas holidays. Henry Drury had complained of Byron's "Inattention to Business, and his propensity to make others laugh and disregard their Employments as much as himself."[n]

The holidays came as a relief to both master and pupil. Byron went to visit his mother, who had gone back to Bath. Although she was finding it difficult to pay Byron's Harrow bills, provide for the care of his foot, and maintain herself in modest lodgings, Mrs. Byron was determined to give her son a good holiday. Apparently she tried to recapture for his sake some of the gaieties of Bath that she had known in her girlhood. She took him to a masquerade given by Lady Riddel. Perhaps inspired by some of the Oriental travel books he had read in Aberdeen, he dressed as a Turkish boy.

In fact he was enjoying the life in Bath so much that he thought very little about Harrow until the time approached for his return, and then he could not face the prospect of going back to Henry Drury's. His mother wrote Hanson on January 19: "Byron *positively* refuses to return to Harrow to be Henry Drury's *Pupil* as he says he has used him *ill* for some time past. . . . You may perhaps be surprized that I don't force him to return but he is rather too old and has too much sense for that." [n]

Byron finally agreed to return in the middle of February as the pupil of Mr. Evans, and the turbulent waters were quieted for a time. He was then fifteen, but there is no evidence that he studied more or that he mended his behavior, though with a new master the friction was lessened. His friendship with the Earl of Clare, who was then only eleven, began in this year and lasted in a kind of idealized nimbus for the rest of his life. Byron wrote in his "Detached Thoughts": "My School friendships were with *me passions* (for I was always violent), but I do not know that there is one which has endured (to be sure, some have been cut short by death) till now. That with Lord Clare began one of the earliest and lasted longest, being only interrupted by distance, that I know of. I never hear the word '*Clare*' without a beating of the heart even *now*, and I write it with the feelings of 1803–4–5 ad infinitum." [n]

Another of his favorites was the Duke of Dorset. John Wingfield (a son of Lord Powerscourt) was one of Byron's fags to whom he was even more attached.[n] No doubt the pride of being a patron to younger boys who looked up to him enhanced the pleasure of these friendships for Byron, and his boyish vanity was flattered by the fact that some of them were scions of rank that exceeded his own. But no rank or family distinction contributed to the satisfactions of his friendship with other "juniors and favourites" whom he "spoilt by indulgence" such as Charles Gordon, a fellow Scot from Abergeldie, and John Cecil Tattersall, who saved him from the butt end of a musket in a skirmish with some town rustics.[n] It was inevitable that among so many favorites jealousies and feelings of neglect should have complicated these passionate schoolboy attachments. The Earl Delawarr, one of the most touchy of his young protégés, had already been wounded through envy and pride when Byron returned to Harrow in February 1803, and needed the soothing flattery of verse to assuage his hurt feelings.[n]

After the Easter holiday the old feud with Henry Drury flared up again. Byron wrote indignantly to his mother, who had left Bath and gone back to Nottingham, that his former master had "behaved himself to me in a manner I neither *can* nor *will bear*. . . . I have been *idle* and I certainly ought not to talk in church, but I have never done a mean action at this School to him or *any one*." [n]

Mrs. Byron sent the letter on to Hanson with an appeal to him to settle the business. Dr. Drury, in apologizing for his son, added a note of praise for Byron: "He possesses, as his letter proves, a mind that feels, and that can discriminate reasonably on points in which it conceives itself injured." [n] The conversation he had with Byron gave the boy a renewed esteem for the headmaster, for in his next letter to his mother (June 23) he said: "I have been placed in a higher form in this School to day, and Dr. Drury and I go on very well." [n] Though he deplored the boy's laziness in routine studies, Dr. Drury had already begun to recognize some of the qualities of Byron's mind. When Lord Carlisle summoned him to tell him of Byron's reduced expectations of property, and to ask about his progress, Drury said: "He has talents, my lord, which will *add lustre to his rank.*" "Indeed!!!" uttered with considerable surprise, was Lord Carlisle's only reply.[n]

Byron's property, in truth, was not what he and his mother had expected when they first heard of the death of the "Wicked Lord." Hanson had been busy trying to make a survey and to raise the rents. A certain amount of planting and repairs had been done, and search had been made for a suitable tenant for Newstead Abbey during Byron's minority. A Mr. Clay had occupied the Abbey for a while in 1802. When he left, two maiden ladies made application through Hanson's friend Lord Grantley to live there temporarily until they could find a house, and on October 28 Hanson wrote to Owen Mealey, the gardener and caretaker,[4] announcing that he had given permission to "the two Miss Launders of Bosford to take up their Abode at Newstead until we can meet with a proper Tenant." [n] Early in December 1802 they had moved in with all their furniture.

Though they had not taken a lease, the Launders had some notion of living at Newstead until Byron came of age, but on January 11, 1803, Lord Grey de Ruthyn, a young man of twenty-three, applied to lease the property, and Hanson, after giving the ladies first refusal, soon closed with him.[n] He was to have the mansion house and park for the five years of Lord Byron's minority for £50 a year.[5]

Mrs. Byron had gone to Nottingham late in April for the purpose of finding a house near to Newstead where she could live economically and make a home for her son during his holidays. While Owen Mealey, the Newstead caretaker, was out scouring the county for a suitable place, she took a small lodging at Park Row in Nottingham. But on May 30 she wrote to Hanson: "I have taken a House at Southwell called Burgage Manor, with a garden and ground just as I could wish but I shall not go to it till July." [n] In the meantime, to the scandal of the community, she became involved in Nottingham politics on the wrong side, supporting the liberal Whig candidate in the Parliamentary election against the respectable Tory, who of course won. Mrs. Byron had not forgotten her sympathy for the popular party at the time of the French Revolution.[n] On July 21 she moved into Burgage Manor and prepared to receive her son for the summer holiday.[n]

Despite occasional battles, life at Harrow was running more

[4] Hanson had engaged Owen Mealey and sent him to Newstead in November 1798. (Hanson and Birch accounts, Murray MSS.) Many amusing details about the estate during Byron's minority are contained in his letters (quite ungrammatical and freely phonetic in spelling). These and other manuscript letters to Hanson from Newstead are in the British Museum (Eg. 2612 and 2613).

[5] Eg. 2612, ff. 52, 53. Mrs. Byron's tenant was the nineteenth Baron Grey de Ruthyn, who had inherited his title through his mother, a daughter of the third Earl of Sussex. Lord Grey was to pay the taxes and buy the furniture that had been left by the old lord.

smoothly than it had for some time for the young lord. He was on excellent terms with Dr. Drury and was beginning to enjoy a certain popularity. The Hansons came down for Speech Day in July, and on the 26th Byron left London for Southwell by Newark on the mail coach. Burgage Manor was a pleasant three-story wooden house with a garden and some trees. It faced a small green at the end of the main street of the sleepy little town of three thousand inhabitants. In contrast with Harrow and London, Byron found it very dull. At the end of a few days he could stand it no longer and rode off to Newstead, which was only twelve miles distant. Lord Grey had sent word through Hanson, soon after he signed the lease in April, that Byron would be welcome at Newstead if he wished to spend any time there.[n] Grey had taken possession by July 2, but he left almost immediately on a trip to York, Harrogate, and Scarboro, from which he did not expect to return until October.[n]

On August 2, Byron established himself with Owen Mealey, who reported to Hanson that he "Boards and Sleeps at my House he talks of Stoping a Month here." [n] Riding over the estate that would one day be his country place gave him a romantic rapport with his ancestors. Remembering the days when the Byrons had lived lavishly in the great halls, he gave a dinner for the tenants (possibly at Mealey's or at a near-by inn). Mrs. Byron allowed him five pounds for the occasion, but he spent far more; the bill was forwarded to Hanson.[n]

The young lord soon found a much greater interest at Annesley Hall, three or four miles to the west. When he rode there on his pony with Hanson in 1798, Mrs. Clarke's daughter Mary Chaworth was a gangling child of twelve; now she was in her eighteenth year, gay and full of fun, with all the charm of a young girl in the freshness of early maturity, and a beauty that cast a halo about her for the youth not yet sixteen. Byron's drollery and satiric wit may have amused her, and his obvious admiration must have flattered the girl, who could have no real romantic interest in him, for she was already engaged to John Musters, a dashing young fox-hunting country squire with elegant manners.

Soon Byron was riding over every day from Newstead, and

in a short time was utterly and miserably in love. Without committing herself, Mary could be very amiable and a little flirtatious. To the girl newly awakened to her womanhood there was a little pleasurable sexual excitement, perhaps subconscious, perhaps sublimated into friendly feeling, in playing with this lame boy with the handsome face. After all, he was a distant cousin and she could treat him as a brother. To pass the day with him riding over the hills, taking along a girl cousin for the sake of respectability, was innocent enough and did not prevent her from dreaming of the more mature love of Mr. Musters while the boy looked adoration from his earnest eyes. Occasional "accidental" physical contacts, the pressure of a hand or a knee, could be idealized into an unforgettable memory by the adolescent boy, whose awakening erotic impulses had already been stimulated by the sentimentalized sensuousness of Thomas Moore.[6] "When I was fifteen years of age," Byron later recalled, "it happened that in a Cavern in Derbyshire I had to cross in a boat (in which two people only could lie down) a stream which flows under a rock, with the rock so close upon the water, as to admit the boat only to be pushed on by a ferry-man (a sort of Charon), who wades at the stern stooping all the time. The Companion of my transit was M.A.C., with whom I had been long in love, and never told it, though *she* had discovered it without. I recollect my sensations, but cannot describe them—and it is as well." [n]

By the middle of September he was so enamored that he could not leave, though he knew it was time to go back to Harrow. His mother had appealed to him to return to Southwell to make his preparations, and, not unaware of what was going on, she cast some aspersions on the company he kept. He replied: "I know it is time to go to Harrow. It will make me *unhappy;* but I will *obey*. . . . I am sorry you disapprove my Companions,

[6] Byron wrote to Moore, June 9, 1820: "I have just been turning over *Little,* which I knew by heart in 1803, being then in my fifteenth summer. Heigho! I believe all the mischief I have ever done, or sung, has been owing to that confounded book of yours." (*LJ,* V, 42.) Moore had published pseudonymously in 1801 *The Poetical Works of the Late Thomas Little.* Nine editions appeared by 1808. Moore's verses were full of pretty voluptuous phrases: "her ripe lips," "rapture's rite," "my Julia's burning kiss," etc.

who, however, are the first this County affords, and my equals in most respects; but I will be permitted to chuse for myself. . . . Those that I most love live in this County; therefore in the name of Mercy I entreat this one day to take leave. . . ." [n]

He remained at Mealey's until October 9. On the 10th the caretaker of Newstead wrote to Hanson: "Lord Byron left here on yesterday he has been here since the second of August and he talks of Coming again next week. . . . My Lord has been a very great Hindrance to me since he has been here." [n] Poor Mealey was sent on errands and made to groom his lordship's horse for the daily rides with Mary Chaworth. Lord Grey had not returned, and Byron went to Southwell to appease his mother, but he was soon back at the Abbey, for he could not stay away long from Annesley. He grew tired of riding over to Newstead at night and concocted a story of a "bogle" he had seen as an excuse for spending the night. Thereafter for some time he slept at Annesley.[n]

Drury had inquired of Hanson the reason for Byron's failure to return to Harrow. Hanson finally got a despairing reply from Mrs. Byron: "I cannot get him to return to school, though I have done all in my power for six weeks past. He has no indisposition that I know of, but love, desperate love, the *worst* of all *maladies* in my opinion. In short, the Boy is distractedly in love with Miss Chaworth, and he has not been with me three weeks all the time he has been in this county, but spent all his time at Annesley." [n] She urged Hanson to try to move him if she failed, but Mrs. Byron had capitulated to her son's wishes before another week passed. On November 7 she wrote Hanson: "Byron is really so unhappy that I have agreed, much against my inclination, to let him remain in this County till after the next Holydays." [n]

The young lover at Annesley was growing restive and moody, for he was forced to realize that "Her sighs were not for him." [7] To be a younger brother to Mary Chaworth was not enough.

[7] "The Dream." Stanzas 2 and 3 of this poem, written while Byron was in Switzerland in 1816, give an idealized but probably basically true picture of this early love episode that made such an impression on his mind. "She was his life," he wrote, ". . . upon a tone,/ A touch of hers, his blood would ebb and flow,/ And his cheek change tempestuously—his heart/ Unknowing of its cause of agony./ But she in these fond feelings had no share. . . ."

The fresh gaiety of their companionship had worn off, and Mary found the sulky boy a little tiresome as a serious suitor. He sat in idle reverie, toying with his handkerchief; he spent hours firing his pistols at the wooden door under the stairway to the garden terrace. In spite of his handsome features, his tendency to corpulence made him appear an awkward schoolboy.[8] His haughty bearing and turn for satire did not please her, and Mary found him intolerable in his pettish moods.

Still, she was flattered by his admiration. He delighted to hear her play his favorite piece, the Welsh air "Mary Anne." He tried to arouse her interest by boasting of a locket given him by some lady admirer, but he did not have the finesse to touch the chords of jealousy skillfully. She may have been annoyed that her friendship with this boy was a common subject of gossip. Late one night Byron, according to Moore, "either was told of, or overheard, Miss Chaworth saying to her maid, 'Do you think I could care any thing for that lame boy?' " In a spasm of rage and chagrin he rushed out of the house and never stopped until he was back at Newstead.[9] But he could not put Mary Chaworth out of his mind so easily. He told Medwin later: ". . . those were days of romance! She was the *beau idéal* of all that my youthful fancy could paint of beautiful; and I have taken all my fables about the celestial nature of women from the perfection my imagination created in her—I say created, for I found her, like the rest of the sex, any thing but angelic." [n]

Mrs. Byron went to Newstead frequently and cast a critical eye over the estate. As she and her son walked about the park or rode over the farms, she felt that Hanson's management was

[8] Moore, I, 55–6. Moore's notes from his conversations with Mary Chaworth (Mrs. Musters) indicate that she found Byron's vanity a little offensive. "Was proud of his beauty; used to say, 'I think I'm a good-looking fellow.' " (*Prose and Verse,* p. 432.)

[9] Moore, I, 56. Hobhouse was skeptical of this incident, at least as Moore told it. He wrote in the margin at this point: "I do not believe this story." But Moore says it came from Byron's "Memoranda," meaning the famous Memoirs that were burned. And in his notes he recorded the substance of his conversation with Mrs. Musters: "Thinks it possible she might have said what he mentioned in his Memoirs: 'What! me care for that lame boy!' " (*Prose and Verse,* p. 431.)

not all that it should be, and she began to question his handling of the business of the inheritance. What had he done in five years to make the property pay its own way and become a source of income against Byron's coming of age? Without mincing words she posted a letter to the attorney on November 17 which must have made him a little uneasy: "The House at Newstead it is my opinion will soon be in ruins, and the Park is in a Deplorable State. . . . I think every tenant ought to be restricted properly and then it is not in their power to do mischief. . . . I hope Lord Grey will be a good Tenant, but still it ought to be *put out of his power to be a bad one.*"[1]

Byron's thoughts were elsewhere. The decay of the Abbey and the grounds matched his melancholy mood. The heroic deeds of his ancestors offered solace and recompense for the failure of his adventure at Annesley.

*Through thy battlements, Newstead, the hollow winds whistle:*
*Thou, the hall of my Fathers, art gone to decay;*
*In thy once smiling garden, the hemlock and thistle*
*Have choak'd up the rose, which late bloom'd in the way.*[n]

Byron was ready to leave the scene of his chagrin and the home of his ancestors as well, but Lord Grey had returned to Newstead by November and made him welcome at the Abbey. Grey was a pleasure-loving spoiled boy eight years older than Byron, truculent and high-tempered and given to quarreling with underlings. His great interest was in shooting.

Byron had been at loose ends since he left Annesley. He could not go back to Harrow until after the holiday, and he preferred remaining at Newstead as the guest of Grey to being bored at Southwell. On November 29, Mealey reported to Hanson: "Lord Byron is at Newstead with Lord Gray they goe

[1] Hanson narrative, Murray MSS. Hanson had attended many conferences in London, but nothing had yet been done about the recovery of the Lancashire coal mines at Rochdale, illegally leased by the "Wicked Lord." After long negotiations, the estates of the wife of the fifth Baron at Weymondham in Suffolk, which had been in a legal tangle since the death of the old lord's grandson in 1794, were surrendered to the Byron estate in January 1802. The Duke of Portland had given a mortgage on his estate for £1,000, on which over five years' interest was due to the Byron estate. (Hanson and Birch accounts, Murray MSS.)

out those moonlight nights and shuitt Pheasants as they sit at roost. . . . Lord Byron says that his mother says that you ought to have taken the rents before now as he is loosing the Interest of his money by laying in the farmers hands so long and a great deal more that I can better explain to you when you Come down." Mealey ended the letter with a cry of distress which showed how annoyed he was by the whims of the young lord: "I hope to God you will Come down very soon to put things to Rights here. The most of all me time has been taken up waiting of Lord Byron since the first of august when I tell him that you will blame me not to attend to the work he says he [does not] Care that he must be waited on." *n*

Byron stayed on through the holidays. On December 28, Mealey wrote resignedly: "Lord Byron is still at Newstead talks of stoping till towards his birthday." *n* But before that day something had happened at Newstead that gave Byron an emotional shock. He left with a determination never to have anything to do with Lord Grey again, and though Byron would never reveal the nature of the offense, he hinted at it clearly enough to make it obvious that the sensuous young lord had made some kind of sexual advance which disgusted his younger companion.[2]

At the end of January 1804, shortly after his sixteenth birthday, Byron was back at Harrow. Mary Chaworth was still very much in his thoughts. He was further behind than ever in his studies, and, aside from the old and new friendships of Harrow, he had little relish for the school. Several experiences of the past year had matured him beyond his years, but he remained a spoiled boy in his attitude toward the disciplines of school life.

Just before the Easter holiday Byron's half-sister Augusta wrote to Hanson to inquire about her brother.[3] She had to leave London

[2] Byron's own references to Lord Grey (quoted later) furnish sufficient indirect evidence. Hobhouse wrote in the margin of his copy of Moore opposite the statement that "An intimacy . . . soon sprung up between him and his noble tenant": "and a circumstance occurred during [this] intimacy which certainly had much effect on his future morals."

[3] There is no clear indication of when Byron first met Augusta. Prothero says: "Augusta Byron seems scarcely to have seen her brother between his

before he passed through on his way to Southwell, but an affectionate letter drew from him a warm response immediately on his arrival at Burgage Manor on March 22: ". . . I hope you will not attribute my neglect to a want of affection, but rather to a shyness naturally inherent in my Disposition." He asked her to consider him "not only as *a Brother* but as your warmest and most affectionate *Friend.* . . . you are *the nearest relation* I have in *the world both by the ties of Blood* and *affection.*" She had confided in him that she was engaged to their cousin George Leigh. ". . . Trust to your Brother," Byron wrote, "and be assured that he will never betray your confidence. . . . tell him that I already consider him as my Friend, for whoever is beloved by you, my amiable Sister, will always be equally Dear to me." And he ended by inquiring about old Joe Murray, who after the death of the fifth Baron had been taken into service by the Duke of Leeds, Augusta's half-brother, for "*while I live,*" he wrote grandiosely, "*he shall never be abandoned In his old Age.*"[4] Assured of affection, Byron had found someone in whom he could confide. As he grew more critical of his mother, this tie was the more warmly welcomed. In the glow of this confidence his deepest feelings flowed out in a revealing correspondence during the next year.

Life was dull in Southwell, he told her; "not being on terms of intimacy with Lord Grey I avoid Newstead, and my resources of amusement are Books, and writing to my Augusta." The reason for his avoidance of Lord Grey he could not bring himself to confide, though it haunted him like a theme that is repulsively attractive and he referred to it frequently. "I am not reconciled to Lord Grey, *and I never will.* He was once my

---

infancy and 1802." (*LJ*, I, 18 n.) Their correspondence in 1804 presumes some previous meeting in person, possibly during Byron's holidays spent in London.

[4] *LJ*, I, 19–22. Augusta Byron, after the death of her grandmother Lady Holderness, divided her time among several close relatives: Lady Mary Osborne, daughter of the Duke of Leeds (by a second wife after the Marchioness of Carmarthen eloped with Captain Byron, Augusta's father); her half-brother George, who succeeded his father as sixth Duke of Leeds; her cousin, the Earl of Carlisle, Byron's guardian; and General and Mrs. Harcourt.

*Greatest Friend*, my reasons for ceasing that Friendship are such as I cannot explain, not even to you, my Dear Sister, (although were they to be made known to any body, you would be the first,) but they will ever remain hidden in my own breast. They are Good ones, however, for although I am *violent* I am not *capricious* in my *attachments*." [n] What increased his chagrin and widened the already increasing gap of sympathies between Byron and his mother was the fact that Mrs. Byron had taken up with Lord Grey in his absence and had become foolishly infatuated with him.

Mrs. Byron's interest in Lord Grey had not escaped the watchful Mealey. After reporting to Hanson that Grey was attempting to drain the ponds to get the fish out, he wrote: "He is very thick with Mrs. Byron and Lord Byron is displeased at it." [n]

On the eve of his departure for Harrow Byron wrote his sister again. The gloom of the place still enveloped him, but the anticipation of his escape buoyed him up. He was nervous about his first public oration on the coming Speech Day. ". . . I do not dislike Harrow," he confessed. "I find *ways* and *means* to amuse *myself very pleasantly* there. . . ." Then in a facetious humor he added: "My mother Gives a *party* to night at which the principal *Southwell Belles* will be present, with one of which, although I don't as yet know whom I shall so far *honour, having never seen them*, I intend to *fall violently* in love . . . then you know in the course of a few weeks I shall be quite *au désespoir*, shoot myself and Go out of the world with *éclat*. . . ." [n]

Despite the bravado and assumed gallantry of his letter to his sister, he subsided into the bashful boy at the party that night. One of the guests was Elizabeth Pigot, a girl several years older than Byron whose family lived in the house across the green. "The first time I was introduced to him," she told Moore, "was at a party at his mother's, when he was so shy that she was forced to send for him three times before she could persuade him to come into the drawing-room, to play with the young people at a round game. He was then a fat bashful boy, with his hair combed straight over his forehead, and extremely like a miniature picture that his mother had painted by M. de Chambruland. The next morning Mrs. Byron brought him to call at our house, when he still continued shy and formal in his manner. The conversation turned upon Cheltenham, where we had been staying . . . and I mentioned that I had seen the character of Gabriel Lackbrain very well performed.[n] His mother getting up to go, he accompanied her, making a formal bow, and I, in allusion to the play, said 'Good by, Gaby.' His countenance lighted up, his handsome mouth displayed a broad grin, all his shyness vanished, never to return, and, upon his mother's saying 'Come, Byron, are you ready?'—no, she might go by herself, he would stay and talk a little longer. . . ." [n] From that time he felt perfectly at home in the Pigot house. But the next day he left for London.

Back at Harrow he relapsed into the mischievous schoolboy. Writing to his mother early in May, he complained of the malice of Martin Drury (Henry had not interfered with him since the difficulties of the year before), who was "continually reproaching me with the narrowness of my fortune, to what end I know not. . . . I have as much money, as many clothes, and in every respect of appearance am equal if not superior to most of my school-fellows, and if my fortune is narrow, it is my misfortune, not my fault."

And then with a bravura revealing unexpected depths of ambition and with a sudden spate of rhetoric, he continued: ". . . the way *to riches, to greatness* lies before me. I can, I will cut myself a path through the world or perish in the attempt." [n]

Byron put such energy into the coming Speech Day preparations as to win the warm praise of the headmaster. ". . . Dr. D[rury], my grand patron," Byron wrote in his "Detached Thoughts," "had a great notion that I should turn out an Orator, from my fluency, my turbulence, my voice, my copiousness of declamation, and my action. I remember that my first declamation astonished him into some unwonted (for he was economical of such), and sudden compliments, before the declaimers at our first rehearsal." [n] What surprised Drury was that "he suddenly diverged from the written composition, with a boldness and rapidity sufficient to alarm me, lest he should fail in memory as to the conclusion. There was no failure. . . ." [n]

When the important day came for the speeches (July 5, 1804) he acquitted himself very well. Byron took the role of Latinus in a three-part dialogue from the eleventh book of Virgil's *Æneid*. He had first taken the part of Drances, but he suddenly changed his mind and gave it up to another boy, possibly for fear of ridicule from the taunt of Turnus (spoken by Peel): "*Ventosâ in linguâ, pedibusque fugacibus istis,*" which might turn attention to his lameness.[5]

In the upper forms Byron came to like Harrow, having gained the confidence and friendship of the older boys and the respect and often the devotion of the younger ones who were his favorites. He wrote in 1821: "I always *hated* Harrow till the last year and half, but then I liked it." [n] The outbreaks of turbulence were only occasional storms upon the otherwise smooth seas of his life at Harrow. He read extensively and his mind was full of daydreams that seemed much more important than the "drilled dull lesson, forced down word by word/ In my repugnant youth." [6]

"At School I was . . . remarked for the extent and readiness of my *general* information," Byron wrote. This information was "so great on modern topics, as to induce a suspicion that I could only collect so much information from *reviews*, because I was never *seen* reading, but always idle and in mischief, or at play. The truth is that I read eating, read in bed, read when no one else reads; and had read all sorts of reading since I was five years old. . . ." [n]

It seems probable that Byron, like Dr. Johnson, "tore the heart out of a book." Moore was tremendously impressed with the "range and variety of study" represented in the list of "writers whose works I have perused in different languages," taken from a memorandum book of Byron dated "November 30, 1807." In addition to a formidable array of historical works, he listed biographies of Charles V, Cæsar, Sallust, Marlborough and Eugene, Tekeli, Bonnard, Bonaparte, "all the British Poets,

[5] Moore, I, 41. Turnus said to Drances: "Will thy bravery ever be in that windy tongue and those timorous feet of thine?"

[6] *Childe Harold*, IV, 75. Byron's satire on Don Juan's education (*Don Juan*, I, 39–44), though by no means an accurate picture of his own, suggests at least what some of his reading may have been at Harrow.

both by Johnson and Anderson," Rousseau's *Confessions*, lives of Cromwell, of Charles XII, Catherine II, Newton, and a dozen more; Blackstone and Montesquieu on Law; in philosophy, Paley, Locke, Bacon, Hume, Berkeley, Drummond, Beattie, and Bolingbroke ("Hobbes I detest"); in poetry, "All the British Classics . . . with most of the living poets, Scott, Southey, &c.—Some French, in the original, of which the Cid is my favourite.—Little Italian.—Greek and Latin without number"; in divinity, "Blair, Porteus, Tillotson, Hooker,—all very tiresome"; and miscellanies such as the *Spectator* and *Rambler*. As early as 1803, Byron had discovered the poetry of Alexander Pope.[n]

"All the books here enumerated I have taken down from memory," Byron added. "I recollect reading them, and can quote passages from any mentioned . . . the greater part of the above I perused before the age of fifteen. . . . I have also read . . . about four thousand novels, including the works of Cervantes, Fielding, Smollett, Richardson, Mackenzie, Sterne, Rabelais, and Rousseau," and he mentions Burton's *Anatomy of Melancholy* as "most useful to a man who wishes to acquire the reputation of being well read" because of its "amusing and instructive medley of quotations." [n]

Hobhouse, who knew Byron more intimately than did Moore, commented skeptically: "Certainly he did *not* read these books," but later he wrote more cautiously: "As Lord Byron says he read these volumes I am inclined to believe the fact, but it is certain he never gave any sign of this knowledge afterward." [n]

On July 2, Mrs. Byron wrote proudly to her kinswoman Miss Abercromby: "Byron will not return from Harrow till the end of this month, he is to speak about this time . . . I long to see him, he is much improved in every respect. He is truly amiable and passes his time I am informed very differently from most young people, he writes a great deal [of] Poetry. . . ." [n]

Though he was restive at his mother's vagaries, Byron had not yet cut the apron strings. He was destined for Southwell for the summer holidays, but he hoped to prolong his Harrow associations long enough to ride north with some classmates. To his embarrassment, however, Mrs. Byron came to London, canceled the reservations he had made through Hanson for July 25 on the Edinburgh Mail, kept him with her several days at Mrs. Massingberd's, 16 Piccadilly, and took him home to Burgage Manor on the 28th.[n]

Southwell seemed a little more tolerable since he had met the Pigot family. Through the Pigots he met other Southwell people, including some young ladies who were eager to cultivate the acquaintance of the young lord. Among these was Julia Leacroft, who was fond of staging private theatricals in her father's drawing-room. Byron had no interest in going to Newstead as long as Lord Grey was there. He discovered a considerable library in the home of his mother's landlord, Mr. Falkner, which he ran through eagerly. Among the books was the *Autobiography* of Lord Herbert of Cherbury, a diplomat and philosopher of the seventeenth century, whose views had influenced Locke and the eighteenth-century Deists. The frank egoism of this handsome and vain would-be Casanova, prouder of his duels and his gallantries than of his learning, "engaged and interested him" immediately.[n] Southwell was more agreeable than he had supposed, and he became so obliging that Mrs. Byron was surprised and pleased. Together they "bespoke" a play on August 8.[n]

But Byron's efforts to calm the gale of his mother's temper were fruitless. Byron sent to Augusta his complaints "against my tormentor, whose *diabolical* disposition (pardon me for staining my paper with so harsh a word) seems to increase with age, and to acquire new force with Time. The more I see of her the more my dislike augments; nor can I so entirely conquer the appearance of it, as to prevent her from perceiving my opinion; this, so far from calming the Gale, blows it into a *hurricane*. . . ."[n]

The intensity of the feud between mother and son was no doubt increased by Mrs. Byron's continuing to see Lord Grey and insisting that Byron be reconciled to him. While Byron was away, she had made frequent trips to Newstead, and her courting of Lord Grey was the gossip of the County. Mealey kept Hanson well informed of what was going on: "Mrs. Byron and him is greater than ever he has dined with her several times since you left here, and whatever he says is right with her when he writes to her it is my dear Mrs. Byron."[n]

After he had had time to reflect Byron wrote to Augusta: "In former days she spoilt me; now she is altered to the contrary; for the most trifling thing, she upbraids me in a most outrageous manner, and all our disputes have been lately heightened by my one with that object of my cordial, deliberate detestation, Lord Grey de Ruthyn. . . . once she let drop such an odd expression that I was half inclined to believe the dowager was in love with him. . . ." [n]

When he could, he escaped to the Pigots'. It was a pleasant, restful household that required no pretense and imposed no emotional strain. Elizabeth Pigot had at first a disinterested fondness for the boy. With her he did not have to play the suitor and he could be frank and genuine, and yet the womanly warmth of her attention was pleasing to his self-esteem.

They exchanged books and wrote verses, lightly flattering, slightly romantic, to each other. It was a new experience for Byron. There was a frank tenderness mixed with playfulness in their relationship. They talked of love, but in speculative generalizations which seemed just far enough from the personal to be safe. Byron borrowed her copy of *Letters of an Italian Nun and an English Gentleman,* in which she had written a quatrain beginning "Away, Away—your flattering arts." He returned it with some verses in reply that violated their code, for they were both personal and flattering: "For he who sees that witching grace,/ That perfect form, that lovely face;/ With eyes admiring, oh! believe me,/ He never wishes to deceive thee. . . ." But she was ashamed and a little fearful lest they should be seen by others, and she tore out the leaf.[n]

But before the end of August she had left Southwell for an extended absence, and he felt desolate in the dull town. Writing to thank her for some drawings of his coat of arms, he reminded her of the "watch-riband and purse" she had promised to knit before he left for Harrow.[n] The theater at Southwell offered some diversion, and one evening he had attended Miss Leacroft to the play, but the town bored him and the atmosphere at home was depressing when it was not explosive. His thoughts turned again to Annesley Hall. He needed something more than a light flirtation to break his heart upon. Mary Chaworth was promised to another, but the agony of rejected love was perferable to ennui.

Perhaps it was at this time that he paid his farewell visit to Annesley, which Moore says took place during this year [7] "(as he himself used to relate) on that hill near Annesley which, in his poem of 'the Dream,' he describes so happily as 'crowned with a peculiar diadem.'" [n] Seeing where her thoughts were, he said with attempted calmness: "The next time I see you I suppose you will be Mrs. Chaworth." [8] Her chilling reply was "I hope so." [n]

Such an emotional crisis left him spent, almost on the verge of hysteria, for his passions were violent. At Burgage Manor there was no one in whom he could confide. It is possible that it was while these frustrations were tormenting him that Mrs. Byron, piqued by his treatment of Lord Grey, told him one day: "Oh, Byron, I have had a letter from Edinburgh, from Miss Abercromby, and your old sweetheart Mary Duff is married to a Mr. Co[e] [Cockburn]." Recalling this years later, Byron wrote: "I really cannot explain or account for my feelings at that moment; but they nearly threw me into convulsions, and alarmed my mother so much, that after I grew better, she generally avoided the subject—to *me*—and contented herself with telling it to all her acquaintance." [n]

Byron was glad to escape from Southwell early in September. Before returning to Harrow, he went on a week's shooting trip with Hanson.[n] After such a turbulent summer both mother and son must have felt some relief at the parting. Byron confessed later to Augusta: "I am sorry to say the old lady and myself don't agree like lambs in a meadow, but I believe it is all my own fault,

[7] Both Medwin and Moore are so vague in their chronology that it is difficult to know which meetings were in 1803 and which in 1804. Medwin (I, 66) quotes Byron as saying: "I returned to Harrow . . . more deeply enamoured than ever, and passed the next holidays at Newstead [Southwell?]. I now began to fancy myself a man, and to make love in earnest. Our meetings were stolen ones, and my letters passed through the medium of a confidante. A gate leading from Mr. C . . . . .'s grounds to those of my mother, was the place of our interviews. But the ardour was all on my side. I was serious; she was volatile. She liked me as a younger brother, and treated and laughed at me as a boy. She, however, gave me her picture, and that was something to make verses upon."

[8] Musters, like Byron's father, took his wife's name on his marriage, but the name was later changed to Chaworth-Musters.

I am rather too fidgety, which my precise mama objects to, we differ, then argue, and to my shame be it spoken fall out a *little*, however after a storm comes a calm. . . ."[9]

The disenchantments of the past year had wrought changes in the growing boy, bringing to the surface an adolescent cynicism as a transparent cloak for wounded vanity. Writing to Augusta, he offered sympathy for her distress (her uncle General Leigh was putting obstacles in the way of her marriage to his son). Then he added: "But really, after all (pardon me my dear Sister), I feel a little inclined to laugh at you, for love, in my humble opinion, is utter nonsense, a mere jargon of compliments, romance, and deceit. . . ."[n]

The atmosphere at Harrow now seemed more congenial than any he had hitherto known. "My friends are not numerous, but select," he told Augusta; "among them I rank as the principal Lord Delawarr . . . do you know the family at all? Lady Delawarr is frequently in town, perhaps you may have seen her; if she resembles her son she is the most amiable woman in Europe."[1]

[9] *LJ*, I, 40. Letter of Oct. 25, 1804. Moore recalled from Byron's Memoirs an account of one of these quarrels, supposedly of an earlier period, though it might have happened at this time. Byron was sometimes amused at his mother's violence, Moore says, "and when Mrs. Byron, who was a short and corpulent person, and rolled considerably in her gait, would, in a rage, endeavour to catch him, for the purpose of inflicting punishment, the young urchin, proud of being able to outstrip her, notwithstanding his lameness, would run round the room, laughing like a little Puck, and mocking at all her menaces." (Moore, I, 25.) It is not unlikely that such tormenting of his mother goaded the enraged woman into taunting him with his deformity. Moore says that in his Memoirs Byron "described the feeling of horror and humiliation that came over him, when his mother, in one of her fits of passion, called him 'a lame brat.'" (Moore, I, 25–6.) He remembered the episode with bitterness, and Moore is probably right in assuming that it had much to do with the conception of his drama *The Deformed Transformed* with its often quoted opening:

*Bert*[*ha*]. *Out, hunchback!*
*Arn*[*old*]. *I was born so, mother!*

[1] *LJ*, I, 41. Letter of Oct. 25, 1804. Colonel Wildman, one of Byron's classmates, who later bought Newstead Abbey from him, told Moore that he thought Byron's passion for Delawarr, Clare, Dorset, and Wingfield was influenced much by their being brother nobles. Moore records: "W[ildman], being a monitor, one day had put Delaware [*sic*] on his list for punishment. B. coming up to him, said, 'W[ildman], I find you have got Delaware [*sic*] on your list; pray don't lick him.' 'Why not?' 'Why, I don't know, except that

Rejected by the girl he loved most desperately, the first serious love of his maturity, Byron turned to the reassuring affection of his Harrow friends. To them he did not appear awkward and lacking in the gallantries and graces demanded by fickle young women. He understood them, and they talked the same language, uncomplicated by the vagaries of feminine pretenses that drove him to forced witticisms, or to morose and sullen resentment. And so Byron developed a penchant for the society of younger boys, especially those like Clare and Delawarr whose handsome faces gave him something of the same æsthetic satisfaction he felt in the presence of beautiful women. If sexual attraction entered into his feelings, he was unaware of it or, thinking of his experience with Lord Grey, he put it out of his mind as repugnant and easily sublimated it in terms of affectionate camaraderie.[2] But these Harrow friendships were seldom mild and easygoing; they

---

he is a brother peer; but pray don't,' &c." Moore adds: "W[ildman] *did.*" (Moore: *Prose and Verse*, p. 416.) Hobhouse wrote in the margin opposite this in his copy of Moore: "I do not believe Byron would be such a fool as to say this."

[2] How early Byron was aware of the sexual implications of these passionate friendships it is difficult to know: possibly before he left Harrow, probably while he was at Cambridge, and certainly while he was in Greece on his first pilgrimage. There seems little doubt, if one considers dispassionately the total evidence now available, that a strong attraction to boys persisted in Byron from his Harrow days throughout his life. But there is no evidence that he felt guilt or shame about any of the friendships formed at Harrow. Hobhouse, however, who knew him from his Cambridge days, and who apparently was well aware of this tendency in Byron, wrote in the margin where Moore was glossing over the Harrow friendships with younger favorites: "M. knows nothing or will tell nothing of the principal cause & motive of all these boyish friend[ships]." Byron's attraction to women, however, did, on the whole, fulfill his emotional needs much more extensively and through longer periods of his life, though it was not necessarily stronger in individual instances. The reader may judge for himself from the evidence in later chapters how strong this tendency was in Byron. These facts have long been known. Looked at without moral hysteria, they help to explain a great deal in Byron's character and his relations with both men and women. Various friends noted the feminine qualities in Byron. Moore recorded in his diary on July 7, 1827: "In the evening some talk with D. Kinnaird about Byron; a great deal of the woman about Byron, in his tenderness, his temper, his caprice, his vanity. Chantrey's remark upon this; the soft voluptuous character of the lower part of his face, and the firmness of the upper part." (Moore: *Memoirs*, II, 624.)

were fraught with jealousies, heartaches, and sometimes ruptures.

And his volatile emotions were stirred in other ways. In his wide reading he had already dipped into Rousseau and some of the Deistic philosophers, and in a rebellious frame of mind he had expressed some views not quite orthodox which easily shocked some of the conventional-minded boys, who taunted him with the fighting name of "Atheist." While at Harrow (he told Medwin), "I fought lord Calthorpe for writing 'D . . . . d Atheist!' under my name. . . ." [n]

After his recent difficulties with his mother, Byron was drawn closer and closer to Augusta, for he felt he could unburden himself to her without divulging secrets outside of the family. The growing recognition of the gulf that had widened between mother and son is apparent in Byron's constant recurrence to the theme in his letters to Augusta through the autumn. On November 2 he wrote: ". . . she is so hasty, so impatient, that I dread the approach of the holidays, more than most boys do their return from them. . . . You, Augusta, are the only relation I have who treats me as a friend; if you too desert me, I have nobody I can love but Delawarr. If it was not for his sake, Harrow would be a desert, and I should dislike staying at it." [n]

On November 11 he followed up the topic that was weighing on his mind almost to the point of obsession: ". . . she [Mrs. Byron] has an excellent opinion of her personal attractions, sinks her age a good six years, avers that when I was born she was only eighteen. . . . But I am now coming to what must shock you . . . when she has occasion to lecture me . . . she does not do it in a manner that commands respect. . . . But she flies into a fit of phrenzy, upbraids me as if I was the most undutiful wretch in existence, rakes up the ashes of my *father*, abuses him, says I shall be a true Byrrone, which is the worst epithet she can invent. Am I to call this woman mother? " [n]

Augusta lost no time in writing to Hanson, expressing the wish that Byron might spend the holidays with him, so that Lord Carlisle might "see more of him and shew him more attention than he has hitherto, being withheld from doing so from the dread of having any concern whatever with Mrs. Byron." She added with sisterly pride: "I think the Letters he writes me *quite perfect* and he does not express one sentiment or idea I should wish different. . . ." [n]

Byron conspired with Augusta and Hanson to spend the holiday in town without arousing the suspicion of Mrs. Byron that it was her son who particularly desired it. Augusta apparently had shown some of Byron's letters to Lord Carlisle, who, seeing that the boy's views of Mrs. Byron coincided very well with his own, warmed toward him considerably.

Early in December Mrs. Byron received a letter from Dr. Drury, who, she wrote to Hanson, "speaks highly of my son, but he does not think it proper he should remain longer at Harrow." [n] Hanson communicated the news to Augusta, who wrote anxiously recommending a conference with Lord Carlisle on Byron's future.

Before leaving for the holiday Byron had said his farewells at Harrow. To the distress of his mother, he had left all his books there and had bequeathed several to the Library.[n] After consulting Lord Carlisle, Hanson wrote to Dr. Drury, who then replied frankly: "During his last residence at Harrow his conduct gave me much trouble and uneasiness; and as two of his Associates were to leave me at Christmas, I certainly suggested to him *my wish* that he might be placed under the care of some private Tutor previously to his admission to either of the Universities. This I did no less with a view to the forming of his mind and manners, than to my own comfort." [n] Drury was himself retiring at Easter, and could not give his time to Byron in the last few weeks of his stay as he had in the past. But if Byron's friends desired to hazard the experiment, Drury would not refuse to receive him.

There the matter rested during the holidays, which Byron spent at the Hansons'. It was the first complete holiday he had spent in London for at least two years, and he enjoyed his freedom. He went several times to see the "Young Roscius," the thirteen-year-old boy actor, who was making such a sensation at Covent Garden that the guards had to be called out to keep order in the crowds pressing in to get a view of him. Byron was rather pleased with the excitement, though critical of the actor.[n] What Byron's other occupations and diversions were during the holiday is not known. According to Moore, "During one of the Harrow vacations he passed some time in the house of the Abbé de Rouffigny, in Took's-court, for the purpose of studying the French language. . . ."[3]

Mrs. Byron had fondly expected that he would spend part of the holiday with her. But Byron's seventeenth birthday (January 22, 1805) came and passed and he was still in London and his future was as yet undecided. On the 23rd his mother wrote pathetically to Hanson: "As soon as there is a tolerable day I beg you will send Byron down—I shall be quite unhappy till I see him."[n]

Hanson wrote his excuses for Byron on January 29. "He seems now to think that his not returning to Harrow would after what has been said amount in the opinion of his Friends to an Expulsion and as that idea hurts him very much and he has a great wish to speak in the Summer he seems bent upon his returning. . . ."[n] At the same time Hanson, having at last seen Lord Carlisle, appealed to Drury to take Byron back at Harrow until June.

Before the end of January Augusta's greatest wish had been fulfilled. Her brother had actually dined with Lord Carlisle on the 26th, "and on further acquaintance I like them all very much," he reported.[n] Augusta was delighted. She wrote with enthusiasm to Hanson: "You will easily believe that he is a *very great favourite of mine* . . . the more I see and hear of him the more I *must* love and esteem him."[n]

At Harrow, where he returned early in February, Byron resumed his old ways, but the greatest trouble he caused in the school arose from his loyalty to Dr. Drury, who was retiring in

[3] Moore, I, 61 n. Moore may have drawn his information from the none too accurate anonymous "Byroniana" which appeared in the *Literary Gazette* on May 24, 1828: "For the purpose of studying the French language, Byron passed three vacations, of six weeks each, at the Abbé de Rouffigny's in Took's Court (then the *foyer* of all the French emigrants, of whom about 200 or 300 lived in the neighbourhood), where he occupied two small apartments. . . . There are no anecdotes worth relating of him at this period, save that he was little given to study, and spent much of his time in fencing, and greatly annoyed the Abbé by making so much noise in his house. The worthy Abbé did not discover in him any indications of that talent which was to astonish the world—but put him down as a boisterous Pickle."

March. There were three candidates for the vacancy: Mark Drury, younger brother of the headmaster, Benjamin Evans, who had been Byron's tutor, and George Butler. Byron took no part in the movements for any of the three candidates, though he was at first inclined to favor Evans. Wildman led the faction for Mark Drury, then under master, as a gesture of loyalty to the retiring headmaster. An astute boy who knew Byron's character told Wildman: "Byron will not join because he will not act second to any one, but you can secure him by giving up the leadership to him."[n] Wildman stepped down and Byron became the leader of the Drury party. When Butler was appointed there was a rebellion which, however, did not break out in full force until after the Easter holiday. The boys expressed their esteem for Dr. Drury by presenting him with plate worth 330 guineas.[n]

The holiday began on April 3, but Byron was in no hurry to return to Southwell, though he felt in duty bound to visit his mother, whom he had not seen since September. He was already beginning to think of the university. He wrote Augusta: "Mr. H. Recommends Cambridge; Ld. Carlisle allows me to chuse for myself, and I must own I prefer Oxford. But, I am not violently bent upon it. . . ."[n] He lingered in town as long as he dared before going north.

Southwell was as dull as ever, and he was once more subjected to the caprices of Mrs. Byron, who had accumulated many reproaches to heap upon his head. At first he could speak lightly of "the Eloquence of a *near relation* of mine" in writing to Hargreaves Hanson,[n] but before he had been there two weeks a tempest broke, and though he tried to write of it jestingly to Augusta, it is apparent that he had reached the end of the rope and would no longer be treated as a boy. ". . . I contrived to pass my time in peace, till to day, when unhappily . . . I said that Southwell was not *peculiarly* to my taste. . . . I assure you upon my *honour*, jesting apart, I have never been so *scurrilously*, and *violently* abused by any person, as by that woman, whom I think I am to call mother, by that being who gave me birth, to whom I ought to look up with veneration and respect, but whom I am sorry I cannot love or admire."[n]

Byron finally escaped from Southwell on May 1 and spent a

week in London before returning to Harrow (Dr. Butler had postponed the opening of the summer term until the 8th). He was in no hurry to subject himself to the authority of the new headmaster. It was his intention, he told Augusta, to remain in town until the 10th "on purpose to hear our *Sapient* and *noble Legislators* of Both Houses debate on the Catholic Question, as I have no doubt there will be many *nonsensical,* and some *Clever* things said on the occasion." [n] Despite his flippant style, Byron was seriously interested in hearing the speeches, perhaps to get some ideas for the coming Speech Days. Since his first triumph, oratory had been the accomplishment in which he desired to achieve distinction, and he realized that it would not be long before he too might take his seat in the House of Lords.

Back at Harrow, Byron soon organized the resistance against Dr. Butler. No particular act of the new head was offensive, but warmth of feeling for Dr. Drury prompted a rebellion in which Byron was the ringleader. The rebels wrote up in conspicuous places throughout the school: "To your tents, O Israel!" ; they dragged the desk of the headmaster to the middle of the school and burned it; and some of the bolder ones even laid a train of gunpowder under a passage in the school with the intention of blowing up the whole building, but were dissuaded from setting it off by an appeal to spare the hall where their fathers and grandfathers had carved their names on the walls. [n]

Byron's opportunity for conflict with Dr. Butler was increased by the fact that though he was not his pupil he lived in the headmaster's house, and did everything he could to annoy him. On one occasion he tore down the blinds of the window in Butler's hall. When confronted with the deed and asked why he had done it, he said defiantly that they darkened the hall. But, according to Moore, "Afterwards . . . when Butler threatened him, [he] cried and blubbered like a child." [n] The feud continued through the term. Byron turned to writing satires which he circulated among the senior boys, ridiculing Butler as Pomposus.[n] When Byron received the customary invitation to dinner, issued by the headmaster to the senior boys at the end of the term, which had always been considered as a kind of royal command, he sent a refusal.[n]

The comradeship of opposition had brought Byron closer to his upper-form classmates, and his younger favorites, Clare, Wildman, Dorset, Delawarr, Gordon, De Bathe, and Claridge (the last had just entered), looked up to him as patron and friend. He was now a leader in the school, and the prospect of leaving it saddened him. The hold of Harrow on his affections had imperceptibly strengthened as his home ties weakened. ". . . I so much disliked leaving Harrow," he wrote in his "Detached Thoughts," "that, though it was time (I being seventeen), it broke my very rest for the last quarter with counting the days that remained."[4]

He had a new sense of time as fleeting. To seize a moment of it and savor its associations (or perhaps only to salvage something from the dull hours of study), he wrote on the first leaf of his *Scriptores Græci:* "George Gordon Byron, Wednesday, June 26th, A.D. 1805, 3 quarters of an hour past 3 o'clock in the afternoon, 3d school,—Calvert, monitor, Tom Wildman on my left hand, and Long on my right. Harrow on the Hill."[n]

But he spent less time in brooding on the Peachey stone now. He was oftener on the cricket field or in "Duck Puddle," and in the evening he joined in the conviviality at the local inn, "Mother Barnard's," where he lost his self-consciousness in roaring out: "This bottle's the sun of our table."[n] And the coming Speech Days absorbed his interest. Back in February, while Drury was still there, he had chosen for the first Speech Day on June 6 one of the most coveted parts, the dramatic and passionate speech of Zanga over the body of Alonzo, from Young's tragedy of *The Revenge.*[5] He was eager for Augusta to hear him, but he waited too long to apprise her of the date. He considered her now his only relative. Writing to comfort her for a sharp epistle she had received from Mrs. Byron charging her with ingratitude, Byron

[4] *LJ*, V, 445. Byron's mischief-making had not prevented him from being in a position of prestige. According to the Bill Book of 1805, he is listed as a monitor and third boy in the School. (Minchin: *Old Harrow Days*, p. 310.)

[5] *LJ*, I, 28–9 n. In 1805 Kemble was playing the part of Zanga to applauding audiences. Washington Irving was "*completely* overpowered" by Kemble's acting of the part. (Letter of Oct. 26–9, 1805, *The Journal of the Rutgers University Library*, Vol. X, [Dec. 1946], p. 25.) It is possible that Byron had seen the performance and wished to emulate the great actor.

said of his mother: "She is as I have before declared certainly mad (to say she was in her senses, would be condemning her as a Criminal), her conduct is a *happy* compound of derangement and Folly." [n]

On his return from Cambridge, where he went on July 1 to enter his name in Trinity College, he gave timely notice to his sister of the next Speech Day, July 4. "*I beg, Madam,*" he wrote, "you may make your appearance in one of his Lordships most *dashing* carriages, as our Harrow *etiquette,* admits of nothing but the most *superb* vehicles, on our Grand *Festivals.*" [n] This time Byron had chosen to declaim an impassioned passage from *King Lear.* Augusta, however, apparently did not appear. He put so much nervous energy into the delivery of his speech that at the end he was overcome by the exertion and was obliged to quit the room.

The days were running out, and he wanted to make the most of them. As the term neared its close, there were farewells to be said and gifts to be exchanged with his favorites. These passionate friendships were fraught with hurt sensibilities, for Byron's capacity to sink himself in the feeling of the moment made each one "dearest" in turn, and a sense of slight at times was inevitable. Lord Clare was wounded because Byron paid more attention to some of his newer intimates. Byron, on his side, could be just as jealous. He had taken offense on one occasion because Clare addressed him as "my dear Byron" instead of "my dearest." But the quarrel was soon made up.[6]

The final day came. Henry Long, younger brother of Byron's friend Edward Noel Long, arrived for the festivities in time to meet Byron descending the steps of the school after participating in the rite of carving his name on the wall in the old fourth-form room. Young Long recorded that "during some further conversation, he introduced an oath, and I took an opportunity after-

[6] Moore, I, 50 n. Byron wrote later on the back of one of Clare's letters: "This and another letter were written, at Harrow, by my *then* and, I hope, *ever* beloved friend, Lord ** [Clare], when we were both schoolboys, and sent to my study in consequence of some childish misunderstanding,—the only one which ever arose between us. It was of short duration . . . our first and last quarrel." (Moore, I, 50.) Byron's lifelong idealized friendship for Clare, Moore thought, was sustained in part by their separation, which eliminated causes of friction. (Moore: *Prose and Verse,* p. 411.)

wards to put the question to my brother, do boys at Harrow swear? 'Well,' he said, 'sometimes, you've just heard an instance of it.' We went together to the fighting ground and on looking over the wall 'There Sir,' said Byron, 'that is the spot where I hope your blood will often be shed.' "[n]

As he left Harrow, Byron was not fully aware of the changes which had taken place in him, especially in the past year and a half. When Augusta saw him, she perceived the difference. "In the year 1804," Byron wrote in his "Detached Thoughts," "I recollect meeting my Sister at General Harcourt's in Portland Place. I was then *one* thing, and *as* she had always till then found me. When we met again in 1805 (she told me since), that my temper and disposition were so completely altered, that I was hardly to be recognized. I was not then sensible of the change, but I can believe it, and account for it." [n]

Byron tried to prolong his school experiences and associations as long as possible. By assiduous attendance on the cricket field, and perhaps by some partiality of his friends, he had realized his ambition of playing in the final game of the year against Eton. The match took place in London on August 2, 1805, on the old cricket ground in Dorset Square. Henry Long wrote: "The most curious thing was, that Lord Byron, though lame, was one of the eleven: he was always ambitious of doing as other boys but in this instance, was obliged to have somebody to run for him." [7] Byron's own account of the day, which he sent off to his friend Charles Gordon the moment he reached Southwell two days later, indicates what pride he took in his prowess in the game,

[7] MS. recollections of Byron, Berg Collection, New York Public Library. Long adds: "It was principally on account of his [not? or desire of?] being on a par with everybody else, that he devoted himself so much to swimming in which art he was certainly a proficient." Byron's foot had so far improved that he could now wear a common boot (over a corrective inner shoe). (Moore, I, 37.) Apparently after his first year at Harrow he ceased to take treatments and have his foot bandaged by Dr. Laurie, though as late as July 1, 1803, he was asking to have Sheldrake send shoes and an "instrument" for his foot. (Hanson narrative, letter of Mrs. Byron to Hanson.) The inner shoe took the place of the iron brace around the ankle. Dr. James Kemble, who examined two of Byron's inner shoes now at John Murray's, says that one is for a boy of eleven and the other for one of eighteen. (James Kemble: "Byron: His Lameness and His Last Illness," *Quarterly Review*, Vol. CCLII [Oct. 1931], p. 235.)

and with what undergraduate assumptions of manliness he relished the rowdy party which followed: "We have played the Eton and were most confoundedly beat; however it was some comfort to me that I got 11 notches the 1st Innings and 7 the 2d, which was more than any of our side except Brockman & Ipswich could contrive to hit. After the match we dined together, and were extremely friendly, not a single discordant word was uttered by either party. To be sure, we were most of us rather drunk and went together to the Haymarket Theatre, where we kicked up a row. . . ." [8] The next evening he set off for Southwell. His schooldays were over, but his thoughts still turned back to Harrow and to his young admirers there. His "dearest friend" at the moment was Charles Gordon of Abergeldie, to whom he played the young lord, issuing him a pretentious invitation which showed how seriously he took his position in the world and to what fatuous boasting his ego could sometimes lead him: ". . . when I have finished my *Classical Labour,* and my minority is expired, I shall expect you to be a frequent visitor to Newstead Abbey, my seat in this county which is about 12 miles from my mother's house where I now am. There I can show you plenty of hunting, shooting and fishing. . . ." [n]

Byron's dreams still turned to Mary Chaworth, though he kept his thoughts about her to himself. Toward the end of August, Miss Chaworth had married John Musters. Mrs. Byron knew where to touch her son in revenge for his taunting. An eyewitness, possibly Elizabeth Pigot, described the scene for Moore: "His mother said, 'Byron, I have some news for you.'—'Well, what is it?'—'Take out your handkerchief first, for you will want it.'—'Nonsense!'—'Take out your handkerchief, I say.' He did so, to humour her. 'Miss Chaworth is married.' An expression, very peculiar, impossible to describe, passed over his pale face, and he hurried his handkerchief into his pocket, saying, with an affected air of coldness and nonchalance, 'Is that all?'—'Why, I

[8] *LJ,* I, 70–1. Letter of Aug. 4, 1805. Prothero says in a note: "At this match Lord Stratford de Redcliffe remembers seeing a 'moody-looking boy' dismissed for a small score. The boy was Byron." According to Minchin (*Old Harrow Days,* p. 316), who has taken his figures from Wisden's *Almanack,* Byron's score was 7 in the first and 2 in the second innings.

expected you would have been plunged in grief! '—He made no reply, and soon began to talk about something else." [n]

But his feelings found relief in verse. Reading Burns's *Farewell to Ayreshire* with Miss Pigot one day, he was attracted by the meter and said: "Let me try it." Taking a pencil, he wrote two stanzas which were a clear enough indication of where his thoughts were wandering:

*Hills of Annesley, Bleak and Barren,*
*Where my thoughtless Childhood stray'd,*
*How the northern Tempests, warring,*
*Howl above thy tufted Shade!*

*Now no more, the Hours beguiling,*
*Former favourite Haunts I see;*
*Now no more my Mary smiling,*
*Makes ye seem a Heaven to me.*[n]

On September 23, Byron escaped from Southwell. He arrived in London the next day.[n] Although he was not due at Cambridge until October 24, he sought a less disturbing environment for his final preparations.

# CHAPTER V

## *1805–1807*

## Cambridge, Southwell, and London

WHEN I went up to Trinity, in 1805, at the age of seventeen and a half," Byron wrote to John Murray many years later, "I was miserable and untoward to a degree. I was wretched at leaving Harrow, to which I had become attached during the two last years of my stay there; wretched at going to Cambridge instead of Oxford (there were no rooms vacant at Christchurch); wretched from some private domestic circumstances of different kinds, and consequently about as unsocial as a wolf taken from the troop." *n*

Though the ambitions and romantic idealisms of his earlier years had subsided, or were at least temporarily buried, a sense of being prematurely cast adrift obsessed him. ". . . it was one of the deadliest and heaviest feelings of my life to feel that I was no longer a boy," he wrote in his "Detached Thoughts." "From that moment I began to grow old in my own esteem; and in my esteem age is not estimable." *n*

He arrived at Trinity at the last moment before lectures began. On October 26 he asked the elder Hanson to order him "4 Dozen of Wine—Port, Sherry, Claret, and Madeira, one dozen of each. I have got part of my furniture in, and begin to admire a College life. Yesterday my appearance in the Hall in my State Robes was *Superb,* but uncomfortable to my *Diffidence.*[1] You may order the

[1] The nobleman had special privileges at Cambridge in Byron's time, and he wore a distinguishing garb, a hat instead of the academic cap, and a gown with elaborate gold embroidery. But when Byron had Gilchrist of Cambridge paint his portrait in his full regalia he carried in his hand the regular academic "mortar-board" with a rich gold tassel.

Saddle, etc., etc., for the 'Oateater' as soon as you please. . . ." *n*

He had secured rooms in the southeast corner of the Great Court of Trinity, rooms that opened on a wide staircase of the tower round which one might drive a coach and six.[2] Byron always liked spacious quarters. That was one reason the great halls of Newstead appealed to him. There was spaciousness in the Court of Trinity too. It was the largest of all the courts in the colleges of England, for Trinity had had royal favor since its foundation by Henry VIII in 1546. In these surroundings Byron began to feel in better spirits immediately. "I am now most pleasantly situated in *Super*excellent Rooms," he wrote his sister on November 6, "flanked on one side by my Tutor, upon the other by an old Fellow, both of whom are rather checks on my *vivacity*. I am allowed 500 a year, a Servant and Horse, so Feel as independent as a German Prince who coins his own Cash, or a Cherokee Chief who coins no Cash at all, but enjoys what is more precious, Liberty." *n*

Augusta was still his confidante, for she could be counted on to appreciate his cleverness and listen sympathetically to the expansion of his ego. He had just had a fiery letter from "the *Court* at *Southwell*" because he would not turn off his servant Frank (Francis Boyce), who had obtained money on false pretenses from a Nottingham tradesman.*n* ". . . in future I shall avoid her *hospitable* mansion," he wrote Augusta, "though she has the folly to suppose She is to be mistress of my house when I come of [age]." He apologized for the dullness of his letter, since the effects "of last nights Claret have no [t gone] out of my head, as I supped with a large party." *n* He was still on the high tide of enjoyment of his new situation when he wrote Hargreaves Hanson on November 12: "College improves in every thing but Learning. Nobody here seems to look into an Author, ancient or modern, if they can avoid it." *n*

The Reverend Thomas Jones, Byron's tutor, though nearing retirement, had been considered something of a firebrand in his

[2] Byron's rooms were in Merton-hall Corner, commonly called Mutton-hall Corner. A circular stairway went around the tower and ended in a turret where Byron later kept his bear. (See *Alma Mater; or, Seven Years at the University of Cambridge. By a Trinity-Man* [J. M. F. Wright], I, 165–7.)

younger days. In 1786 he had been one of "the Ten" younger Fellows who had made a successful stand against the Master and the Seniors in the matter of laxity in Fellowship elections. The rebellion brought about the public rather than private examination of Fellowship candidates.

While the conscientiousness of Jones and a few others had raised the morale and the scholarly standards of Trinity, there was still a remnant of eighteenth-century contempt for learning which Byron had immediately sensed on his arrival, particularly among the nobility and gentlemen-commoners, of whom Trinity drew more than any other college with the possible exception of St. John's. Long custom and some lingering rules had given the scions of nobility easy exemption from attendance at lectures, exercises, and examinations. They were expected to be idle and to hold themselves apart from other students. For the most part, they availed themselves of the immunities of their position and were the ringleaders in breaches of discipline and in all the dissipations then expected of the young aristocracy, particularly excessive drinking of wine, gaming, and wenching.[n]

There was not, however, the class distinction or snobbery that might have been expected in such an environment. Wordsworth had found Cambridge in 1787–91 more democratic in spirit than the rest of England.

> *And wealth and titles were in less esteem*
> *Than talents, worth, and prosperous industry.*[n]

Although Byron had associated with his fellow peers at Harrow and felt some snobbish pride in their friendship, not one of his closest friends at Cambridge was titled. It might have been different had he gone to Oxford with Lord Clare and other Harrow nobles. But at Cambridge, though he mingled at first with the blasé young idlers among whom were no doubt many spoiled sons of the nobility, he did not feel at home with them.

Swept along by the current of riotous life in which he had suddenly been immersed, Byron soon felt discontented, but had not the strength or guiding purpose to tear himself from it. Writing to Hanson on November 23, he analyzed his situation with remarkable clarity. ". . . Study is the last pursuit of the Society;

the Master[3] eats, drinks, and sleeps, the Fellows *Drink, dispute* and *pun;* the Employment of the Under graduates you will probably conjecture without my description. I sit down to write with a Head confused with Dissipation which, tho' I hate, I cannot avoid. I have only supped at Home 3 times since my Arrival, and my table is constantly covered with invitations, after all I am the most *steady* Man in College, nor have I got into many Scrapes, and none of consequence." [n]

Byron's attachment to Edward Noel Long, his Harrow friend who came up to Trinity at the same time, was based on wider interests than were common among his drinking companions. "We were rival swimmers," Byron wrote, "fond of riding—reading—and of conviviality. We had been at Harrow together; but —*there,* at least—his was a less boisterous spirit than mine. . . . At Cambridge—both of Trinity—my spirit rather softened, or his roughened, for we became very great friends. . . . Though Cam's is not a very translucent wave, it was fourteen feet deep, where we used to dive for, and pick up—having thrown them in on purpose—plates, eggs, and even shillings. I remember, in particular, there was the stump of a tree (at least ten or twelve feet deep) in the bed of the river, in a spot where we bathed most commonly, round which I used to cling, and 'wonder how the devil I came there.' Our evenings we passed in music (he was musical, and played on more than one instrument, flute and violoncello), in which I was audience; and I think that our chief beverage was soda-water. In the day we rode, bathed, and lounged, reading occasionally." [n]

Even in the company of his gayer companions Byron stole time for reading. Among his friends the first year at Trinity was William Bankes, to whom he later referred as "my collegiate pastor, and master, and patron." Bankes, he said, "ruled the roast—or rather the *roasting*—and was father of all mischiefs." [n] But, writing to Bankes in 1820, he recalled that Scott's poetry "I redde for the first time in my life in your rooms in Trinity College." [n]

Byron had found a pleasanter routine of idleness than he had

[3] William Lort Mansel was Master of Trinity from 1798 to 1820. He was a well-known pluralist, being Bishop of Bristol at the same time that he was holding the Trinity post.

ever enjoyed at Harrow. Riding out to the weir above Grantchester (still called Byron's pool) with his friend Long, he could escape the depression of spirits that followed the nightly carousing with his too hospitable companions. While the novelty of this convivial life lasted, however, he wrote of it so vividly to Hanson that the solicitor became alarmed and apparently hinted that if he did not behave, Mrs. Byron might come to Cambridge. That, together with an intimation in Hanson's letter that the allowance he had been led to expect would be made by the Court of Chancery for furniture and repair of his rooms would not be forthcoming, elicited an angry reply from Byron, so cutting as to discourage any more fatherly advice from his poor business agent and friend. "Mrs. Byron and myself are now totally separated, injured by her, I sought refuge with Strangers, too late I see my error, for how was kindness to be expected from *others,* when denied by a *parent?*" Alarmed by the prospect of a visit by his mother (he remembered the scenes she had made at Dr. Glennie's school), he added: ". . . the instant I hear of her arrival I quit Cambridge, though *Rustication* or *Expulsion* be the consequence."

His indignation reached its height, however, in the matter of the allowance, for he thought Hanson had deceived him. "Still, Sir, not even the Shadow of dishonour shall reflect on *my* Name, for I will see that the Bills are discharged; whether by you or not is to me indifferent, so that the men I employ are not the victims of my Imprudence or your Duplicity. I have ordered nothing extravagant; every man in College is allowed to fit up his rooms. . . ." Then he felt a little repentant, for he remembered Hanson's many favors. "In the course of my letter I perhaps have expressed more asperity than I intended, it is my nature to feel warmly, nor shall any consideration of interest or Fear ever deter me from giving vent to my Sentiments, when injured, whether by a Sovereign or a Subject." [n]

Hanson was deeply wounded, but he had the good sense to write a reasoned reply which appealed to Byron's sense of fair play. Byron, quick to make amends, was forthright in his apology. And then in an access of confidence in his old friend and adviser he confessed fully what he had intimated before concerning his relationship with his mother. "I declare upon my honor that the Horror of entering Mrs. Byron's House has of late years been so implanted in my Soul, that I dreaded the approach of the Vacations as the *Harbingers* of *Misery.*" *n*

Byron participated in the Cambridge vices with something more resembling a feeling of duty to his position than joy and eagerness for pleasure. "I took my gradations in the vices with great promptitude," he later wrote, "but they were not to my taste; for my early passions, though violent in the extreme, were concentrated, and hated division or spreading abroad. I could have left or lost the world with or for that which I loved; but, though my temperament was naturally burning, I could not share in the common place libertinism of the place and time without disgust." *n*

While he had not wasted his substance on light loves, as was customary among the gayer Cambridge men, Byron seems to have spent lavishly in other ways, for when he went to London for the Christmas vacation he was badly in need of money. The "best allowance in College" he had found not enough, for on December 27 he appealed to Augusta, confessing his extravagance and urging the greatest secrecy on her. He did not ask to borrow from her. "All I expect or wish is, that you will be joint Security with me for a few Hundreds a person (one of the money lending tribe) has offered to advance . . . the reason of this requisition is my being a Minor, and might refuse to discharge a debt contracted in my nonage." *n*

This is the first intimation of Byron's involvement with the moneylenders, from whom in the next three or four years he borrowed until his debts ran into the thousands. Augusta was naturally frightened, and at first proposed to present him with a sum sufficient to pay his debts, but that he would not accept. Writing to her on January 7, 1806, he hinted at some mysterious and painful cause of melancholy unrelated to his need for money, which he declined to disclose since "it arises from what you could not alleviate. . . . Suffice it to know, that it cannot spring from Indisposition, as my Health was never more firmly established than now, nor from the subject on which I lately wrote, as that is in a promising Train, and even were it otherwise, the Failure would not lead to Despair. You know me too well to think it is *Love;* & I have had no quarrel or dissention with Friend or enemy, you may therefore be easy, since no unpleasant consequence will be produced from the present Sombre cast of my Temper." *n*

The specific causes of that melancholy are clouded in mystery. It is possible, however, to make a reasonable surmise from Byron's own statements in his "Detached Thoughts" and in his later letters dealing with this period. After speaking of his disgust at the libertinism of Cambridge which threw his heart back upon itself, casting him "into excesses perhaps more fatal than those from which I shrunk, as fixing upon [one] (at a time) the passions which, spread amongst many, would have hurt only myself," he says: "If I could explain at length the *real* causes which have contributed to increase this perhaps *natural* temperament of mine, this Melancholy which hath made me a bye-word, nobody would wonder; but this is impossible without doing much mischief." *n*

He had told Augusta it was not *Love* that caused his distress. In one sense that was true, for he had not become emotionally involved with anyone of the opposite sex since the disappointment of his love for Mary Chaworth. And both his desire to prevent his sister from supposing that he was in any scrape with a woman and his reluctance to use the term in describing his present perturbation made him shy away from the word though he could not avoid the fact. He later acknowledged both word and fact more frankly, however. Referring to E. N. Long in his diary of 1821, he wrote: "*His* friendship, and a violent, though *pure*, love and passion—which held me at the same period—were the then romance of the most romantic period of my life." *n*

And he confided to Elizabeth Pigot that while he was at Cambridge he had met and had become romantically attached to John Edleston, a choirboy at Trinity Chapel.[4] "His *voice* first at-

[4] The Rev. William Harness recorded in a manuscript note (see *LJ*, I, 131; and *Poetry*, I, 66) that Byron saved Edleston from drowning and that this began their acquaintance. If this had happened, Byron would hardly have been shy of mentioning it. Of course, that event might have taken place later. Since Byron met him in October 1805, soon after his arrival at Cambridge, he must first have noticed him in the choir of Trinity Chapel.

tracted my attention, his *countenance* fixed it, and his *manners* attached me to him for ever. . . . I certainly love him more than any human being, and neither time nor distance have had the least effect on my (in general) changeable disposition. . . . He certainly is perhaps more attached to *me* than even I am in return. During the whole of my residence at Cambridge we met every day, summer and winter, without passing *one* tiresome moment, and separated each time with increasing reluctance. . . . He is the only being I esteem, though I *like* many."[5]

Thus he wrote in July 1807, a year and a half after that melancholy January when the separation from Edleston oppressed him. Writing to Hobhouse in October 1811, just after he had heard of the death of Edleston, he said: "At present I am rather low, and don't know how to tell you the reason—you remember *E.* at Cambridge—he is *dead*—last May—his Sister sent me the account lately—now though I never should have seen him again (and it is very proper that I should not) I have been more affected than I should care to own elsewhere."[n] And he recurred to the theme again the following week: "I am very low spirited on many accounts. . . . The event I mentioned in my last has had an effect on me, I am ashamed to think of. But there is no arguing on these points. I could 'have better spared a better being.' Wherever I turn, particularly in this place [he wrote from Cambridge], the idea goes with me. I say all this at the risk of incurring your contempt; but you cannot despise me more than I do myself. I am indeed very wretched, and like all complaining persons I can't help telling you so."[n]

It seems quite possible then that the disconsolate and reckless mood of January 1806 may have been engendered by thoughts of the Cambridge chorister, two years his junior, who had become devotedly attached to him.[6] At this point, raising money

[5] *LJ*, I, 133–5. Letter of July 5, 1807, to Elizabeth Pigot. Under the passage concerning the "violent, though *pure* love and passion" E. H. Coleridge, editor of the seven-volume edition of Byron's poetry, wrote in his copy of Moore's life of Byron (now in the possession of James M. Osborn of New Haven, Conn.): "A reference, doubtless, to Edleston."

[6] Either at this time or later, Edleston presented Byron with a cornelian. "He offer'd it with downcast look,/ As *fearful* that I might refuse it. . . ." ("The Cornelian," first published in *Fugitive Pieces*, Dec. 1806.) Byron's generosity

by signing his bond for exorbitant interest to the "sordid Blood-suckers" was in itself a matter of indifference. The papers would be ready for signing when Augusta came to town, "or if you feel an inclination to retreat, do not let affection for me counterbalance prudence." [n] As matters turned out, however, Augusta did not sign as collateral guarantor, either because she did not come to town in time, or because, contrary to Byron's stipulations, she consulted Lord Carlisle and Hanson and they advised against it. At any rate, Byron did not communicate with his sister for some months. In the end Mrs. Massingberd, his landlady at 16 Piccadilly, and her daughter became joint security for the loan.[n]

As early as January 11, Mrs. Byron took alarm, for her son's bills began coming in "to double the amount I expected; he went and ordered just what he pleased here, at Nottingham, and in London. However, it is of no use to say anything about it, and I beg you will take no notice. I am determined to have everything clear within the year, if possible." [n] The new term at Cambridge began on February 5, but Byron stayed on in London. It may be that the loan was not yet concluded; or there may have been other reasons connected with his personal impasse that caused him to avoid an immediate return to the University. Needing

---

in return may have contributed to his desperate need for money at the end of 1805.

Whatever Byron's feelings may have been later, however, after the sophistication of his Eastern travels, there seems little reason to doubt the truth of his statement, already quoted, that his feeling at the time for Edleston was a "violent, though *pure,* love and passion"—in other words, a romantic attachment. And the best evidence is that the most idealized of Byron's attachments were those that still bore the aura of innocence, such as his love for Mary Duff, Margaret Parker, and Mary Chaworth.

It seems probable that the lines "To E——," first published in *Fugitive Pieces,* are addressed to Edleston. This second poem in the volume, following "On Leaving N[ew]st[ea]d," is given the date "November, 1802," but the probable date of composition is November 1805, shortly after he had met Edleston. The poet reassures his friend that his higher birth can make no difference: "Our *souls* at least congenial meet,/ Nor can *thy* lot *my* rank disgrace." Moore (I, 44) has conjectured that the poem was addressed to "the son of one of his tenants at Newstead," probably thinking of his later attachment to Robert Rushton, but Byron had not been at Newstead, except briefly while he was courting Mary Chaworth, since he visited his mother there in 1800.

some kind of physical activity, he began to frequent the rooms of Henry Angelo, the famous fencing-master,[7] and through him he met Gentleman Jackson, the pugilist and ex-champion, who shared rooms with Angelo at 13 Bond Street. Byron was soon taking lessons in their respective arts, and he formed friendships with them and with their strange assortment of high-class demi-monde associates in theatrical and sporting circles.

Augusta was thoroughly disturbed. She had sent an urgent appeal to Hanson to call on her on February 12, and on the 18th she wrote: "I own *I* perfectly despair of my Brother ever altering his Tone to me—for when one has put oneself very much in the wrong, it is very difficult to get right again." *n*

By February 26, Byron had concluded his business with the moneylenders. He received his few hundred pounds at ruinous interest and seemed confident that he could get more when he needed it. He had paid his Harrow debts and also £231 of College bills (£75 of which he expected Hanson to repay, as it had been spent for furniture). "I happen to have a few hundreds in ready Cash by me," he reported with a kind of malicious glee to his mother; ". . . but I find it inconvenient to remain at College, not for the expence, as I could live on my allowance (only I am naturally extravagant); however the mode of going on does not suit my constitution. Improvement at an English University to a Man of Rank is, you know, impossible, and the very Idea *ridiculous*." Then he broke the news that he wished to spend a couple of years abroad. " 'Tis true I cannot enter France; but Germany and the Courts of Berlin, Vienna & Petersburg are still open, I shall lay the Plan before Hanson & Lord C." He would like to go with her consent and have a tutor of her furnishing, but he would go in any case. "I intend remaining in Town a Month longer, when perhaps I shall bring my Horses and myself down to your residence in that *execrable* Kennel. I hope you have engaged a Man Servant, else it will be impossible for me to visit you. . . ." *n*

Mrs. Byron was of course frantic. In the meantime, Byron was

[7] Angelo had first made Byron's acquaintance at Harrow, where he taught him fencing (*LJ*, I, 99 n), and Byron, according to a contemporary account, had already during his Harrow vacations spent some time in his rooms in London.

living the gay life in town which money in the pocket had put within his reach. On February 28, Augusta had been vexed to see him at the play when he ought to be "employing his time more profitably at Cambridge." [n]

And in a letter of 1821 he referred to "a little circumstance which occurred when I was about eighteen years of age. There was then (and there may be still) a famous French 'entremetteuse,' who assisted young gentlemen in their youthful pastimes. We had been acquainted for some time, when something occurred in her line of business more than ordinary, and the refusal was offered to me (and doubtless to many others), probably because I was in cash at the moment. . . . The adventure on the tapis, it seems, required some caution and circumspection. Whether my venerable friend doubted my politeness I cannot tell; but she sent me a letter couched in such English as a short residence of sixteen years in England had enabled her to acquire. After several precepts and instructions, the letter closed. But there was a postscript. It contained these words:—'Remember, Milor, that *delicaci ensure everi succés.*' " [n]

Perhaps the Madame had some reason for doubting Byron's "delicaci," for he had entered into his dissipations with the reckless cynicism of one who was trying to prove his power over women despite the fact that he was "the little lame boy," or, it may be, to prove to himself that he could find in feminine embraces an escape from his too compelling involvement with Edleston.

His poor mother was hysterical with apprehension. She saw him following in his father's footsteps and ruining himself before he was of age. "That Boy will be the death of me, & drive me mad," she wrote in desperation to Hanson. "I never will consent to his going abroad. Where can he get Hundreds; has he got into the hands of Money lenders, he has *no feeling, no Heart.* This I have long known; he has behaved as ill as possible to me for years back, this bitter Truth I can no longer conceal, it is wrung from me by *heart rending agony.* . . . God knows what is to be done with him—I much fear he is already ruined; at *eighteen! ! !*—Great God, I am distracted I can say no more." [n]

The plan for going abroad did not materialize. Perhaps it was only a passing fancy after all, for Byron did not mention it again in letters to Hanson or to his mother. And by March 10 he had gone through his "hundreds" and was asking Hanson to raise £500 to help him pay his borrowings. He appealed to Hanson's business sense, asking that he borrow for him at a reasonable interest to keep him from paying one hundred per cent to the moneylenders.[n]

By this time he was probably also somewhat bored by his life in town. There was, after all, amusement at Cambridge: swimming contests with Long, convivial suppers, and his comfortable quarters. On April 10 he wrote a curt note to Hanson: "In a few Days I set off for Cambridge and will trouble you for £200 due to me since Lady Day last as that alone delays my departure."[n]

But he was no sooner back at Trinity than his prodigalities began anew. Mrs. Byron duly reported them with distress to Hanson: "Lord Byron has given £31 10s. to Pitt's statue.[8] He has also bought a Carriage, which he says was intended for me, which I *refused* to accept of, being in hopes it would stop his having one."[n] But of course it did not stop him. One extravagance led to another. He had to have equipment to go with the carriage, not only horses and harness but also servants appropriately clothed, and then a new silver hunting watch, gold chain, gold seal, key, and engraving, which he purchased for a total of £13 on May 5, probably as a gift.[n]

Byron tried to combine the pleasures of Cambridge and London while he had money in his pockets. Apparently he had invited the gentlemanly fencing-master Henry Angelo to come to Cambridge to give instruction as he had done at Harrow, but the Mayor of the town, Mr. Mortlock, had refused Angelo permission to set up rooms in Cambridge. Byron wrote to Angelo to express his regret and his indignation at the stupid Mayor. He would communicate with Lord Altamont and they would see what could be done "to bend the obstinacy of the *upstart* magistrate."[9]

[8] Pitt, who died early in 1806, had been a kind of patron of Trinity and a frequent visitor at Trinity Lodge. Thirty guineas was a large sum to donate, even if Byron had not been heavily in debt, but he always had to do things with a flourish.

[9] *LJ*, I, 99–100. Letter of May 16, 1806. Lord Altamont, who later became

If Byron ever attended a lecture at Cambridge, he found it too dull to mention in his correspondence. Nor did he do any systematic reading, though among his bills for the first term is an item for £20. 17*s.* 6*d.* for books. But he was busily writing verses, some of which he refurbished for his first volume of poems.

Byron had become gracious in his correspondence with Hanson again, and on June 16, having some debts to pay before his departure, he asked politely for his quarterly allowance of £125, which was due about that time.[n] Hanson sent the money on the 28th, but Byron was still in Cambridge on July 8. On that day he wrote to Mrs. Massingberd, who apparently was trying to negotiate another loan for him: "I am detained in Cambridge by the painting of my carriage, nor take my departure till Saturday [July 13]."[n]

With no ready cash in his pocket and no prospect of getting any, Byron did not remain long in London, but was forced, against his strongest inclinations, to return to Southwell.[1] Quarrels with his mother were inevitable. He was in no mood to be scolded for his extravagances or to be questioned about his dealings with moneylenders.[n] He escaped as often as he could across the green to the Pigots', where he had made a fast friend of Elizabeth's brother John, on vacation from his study of medicine at Edinburgh. Byron was preparing a little volume of his poems, some that he had written while he was at Harrow and others of a more recent composition. He had already taken them to the

---

the second Marquis of Sligo and who saw Byron in Athens in 1810, was then a student at Jesus College. He had probably joined with Byron in inviting Angelo to Cambridge.

[1] We have one glimpse of Byron in London, recorded by Henry Angelo: "In the year 1806, one night in the month of July, I was seated with Lord Byron in the last row of the front boxes, at Coleman's Theatre [the Haymarket]; the heat was so intense as to oblige us to keep the box door open during the intervals of the acts, when a young man, with a blustering air and *noli me tangere* look, intruded himself on the same seat. As soon as the curtain drew up, his Lordship told him, in a firm yet polite manner, that the box was already full; he nevertheless tenaciously persisted in keeping his place: some words ensued, but seeing that he was still determined to maintain his position, Lord Byron, being next the door, pushed him *sans cérémonie* into the lobby." (*Angelo's Pic Nic,* pp. 16–17.)

printer John Ridge in the neighboring town of Newark, when a domestic explosion occurred that sent him flying back to London on the 7th of August, "departing in my Carriage & four, without *'Beat of Drum'* in the *'Dead of the Night,'*" as he wrote his friend Long on the 9th from 16 Piccadilly.[n]

The Pigots had assisted him in his flight from "Mrs. Byron furiosa," as he described her facetiously to John. "Oh! for the pen of Ariosto," he continued, "to rehearse, in epic, the scolding of that momentous eve. . . . What a group!—Mrs. B. the principal figure; you cramming your ears with cotton, as the only antidote to total deafness; Mrs. —— in vain endeavouring to mitigate the wrath of the lioness robbed of her whelp. . . ." He urged Pigot to keep his lodging secret.[n] But, as he was staying at his usual rooms in Piccadilly, it seems apparent that he did not really expect his mother to follow him.[n]

The next day, however, to his surprise, Mrs. Byron turned up at Mrs. Massingberd's, having made the arduous journey to London to find out just what her wayward offspring was up to, and particularly how deeply he had involved himself with the money-lenders. "This gunpowder intimation of her arrival (confound her activity!)," Byron wrote to Elizabeth Pigot, "breathes less of terror and dismay than you will probably imagine, from the volcanic temperament of her ladyship. . . ."[2] He sent Elizabeth, who was dealing with the printer for him, a correction in the first poem in the volume, "On Leaving Newstead Abbey." And to her brother he sent some stanzas "improper for the perusal of ladies" to be printed separate from his other compositions.[3]

[2] *LJ,* I, 103. Letter of Aug. 10, 1806. Hobhouse wrote in the margin of his copy of Moore: "B. started in a chaise and four and she followed in a chaise and pair poor soul said B."

[3] *LJ,* I, 104. Letter of Aug. 10, 1806. These stanzas may have been those addressed "To Mary," included in *Fugitive Pieces* and the cause of the suppression and burning of the edition. This "Mary" has never been identified. The Pigots knew her, but never revealed her name. Byron had apparently already been sowing some wild oats in the neighborhood. Years later local gossips said that "when Byron lived at Southwell he kept a mistress in the house in the Bullpit, now occupied by Mr. Richardson . . . and that the young poet used to ride over on horseback to visit her." (Unpublished letter of Thomas M. Blagg, author of *Newark as a Publishing Town.*) If the poem is based on fact, which seems likely, this Mary had already caused him

A week later he announced a victory; Mrs. Byron was returning to Southwell and he was proceeding to Worthing on the Sussex coast. He expected to be back in Southwell by the middle of September, and in the meantime ordered the printing of his poems suspended, for he intended to give them an entirely new form.[n]

On August 18 he was still in London, but was just setting out for Worthing to visit his friend Long. His poems, probably then in proof, were to be sent on to London.[n] Byron actually found Long at Little Hampton, about eight miles from Worthing, where he was spending the holidays with his family. His arrival made a deep impression on Edward Long's younger brother Henry, who left a convincingly realistic picture of the young lord appearing on the scene with great éclat. "Lord Byron had with him his horses, and his dog Boatswain[4]—he established himself at the Dolphin Inn, why he did not take up his quarters at the Beach House Hotel, I know not. The Dolphin was but a poor place in a dirty village, and the only one there in those days. . . . Lord B. was fond of practising with pistols, and on the first day of his arrival, he was engaged in firing at oyster shells by the Pier. From this pier on one occasion, the dog Boatswain leapt into the river, a feat which my brother could not prevail upon his dog Fish to perform. . . . Occasionally a game of cricket was the order of the day, if mere batting and bowling between the two, deserves the name. I remember the wickets were pitched not far from Mother Zebedee's baths, and there I was compelled to fag out for the balls, constantly called by Lord Byron, 'young shaver.' Bathing of course was carried on daily, with great vigour —here Lord Byron was in his element, and I had good reason, to know his excellence in the art of swimming for he was very fond of carrying me about on his back. There I sat like Orion on the

to be "Rack'd by the flames of jealous rage." She had "quickly sought a second lover." She was not the first one who had blessed him, but she was the dearest, and he recalled the ecstasies of their relationship, hoping she would regret him, "And smile to think how oft were done,/ What prudes declare a sin to act is. . . ." (*Fugitive Pieces*, pp. 17–19.)

[4] This seems to be the first mention of Byron's favorite Newfoundland dog, which he probably acquired at Southwell. On his tomb at Newstead Byron recorded that he was born in May 1803.

Dolphin with this difference that in my case the poet was undermost."

Young Long recalled that his brother and Byron, having stripped off "every thing excepting their drawers and shirts . . . jumped from the end of the pier at the bottom into the river, which as it was now nearly low water was running out with fearful rapidity; they shot out to sea, and were carried to such a distance as I could barely discern their heads, popping up and down like little ducks upon the sea—by making an immense semicircle, which as the tide runs out very far on that coast, it was absolutely necessary, they at last arrived in safety at the spot where the machine was prepared to receive them. . . . I recollect one day at dinner when talking about the respective ages of the two friends, Lord Byron remarked 'I believe I am one month the senior.' The words, and the expression of the lips and the tone of voice, which always appeared to me somewhat haughty and conceited, has impressed this circumstance indelibly on my memory." *n*

Byron was back in Southwell in September. There with his carriage and horses, his groom and his valet, he no doubt cut a considerable figure in the little town while his mother fumed helplessly at his extravagance. He was still absorbed in revising his volume of poems, and he soon became involved in some private theatricals with the Pigots and some of their friends, including Julia Leacroft, the indefatigable organizer of theatrical performances in Southwell. Byron was to take a part and was asked to write a prologue, but before rehearsals began he and John Pigot set off for the resort town of Harrogate in Byron's own carriage with post horses. He had sent his groom ahead with his two saddle horses, Brighton and Sultan, and the bull mastiff Nelson. Boatswain rode beside the valet Frank on the box of the carriage.

Pigot later described for Moore this Byronic interlude: "The bull-dog Nelson, always wore a muzzle, and was occasionally sent for into our private room, when the muzzle was taken off, much to my annoyance, and he and his master amused themselves with throwing the room into disorder. There was always a jealous feud between this Nelson and Boatswain; and whenever the latter came into the room while the former was there, they instantly seized each other; and then, Byron, myself, Frank, and all the waiters that could be found, were vigorously engaged in parting them,—which was in general only effected by thrusting poker and tongs into the mouths of each." [n] But one day Nelson escaped into the stableyard and fastened his fangs in the throat of a horse, and Frank had to shoot him with one of Byron's pistols.

Life at Harrogate was anything but wild. All the while Byron was poetizing, and he and Pigot were memorizing their parts for the play. "Lord Byron can say *all* his part," Pigot wrote his sister, "and I *most* of mine. He certainly acts it inimitably." [n] Byron had seen a beautiful Quaker who inspired some verses to be included in his volume.

On the return from Harrogate Byron wrote between stages a prologue for the play. He entered wholeheartedly into the production of the amateur group, which had chosen Cumberland's *Wheel of Fortune,* a heroic drama that gave ample scope to Byron's love for histrionic rhetoric. He had the leading role of Penruddock, the gloomy disappointed lover of Arabella Woodville (Miss Ann Bristoe). He mouthed the heroic passages with gusto, frequently bringing down the house with his acting. Byron also played the lead (Tristram Fickle) in Allingham's *Weathercock* in the second play of the evening's offering. Miss Bristoe played the heroine again.

Through October Byron was working on his poems, sending them off to Ridge, the printer, in Newark, as he copied and revised old ones or wrote new. At the same time he was paying court and writing verses to several of the Southwell belles, especially to Julia Leacroft, in the dining-room of whose home the plays were represented, and to Ann Houson. To none of these Southwell flirtations did Byron give more than cynical attention. Since his frustrated passion for Mary Chaworth he felt that the capacity for romantic attachments had been burned out of him. Most of his verses addressed to the Southwell girls were essays in gallantry and accusations of infidelity and fickleness.

Of the thirty-eight poems in Byron's privately printed volume which appeared in its final form some time in November [n] without the author's name and with the title *Fugitive Pieces,* about half were composed during his Harrow years or his first residence at Cambridge. The opening piece was "On Leaving N—st—d," written in 1803. Included were such diverse pieces as his elegy to his cousin Margaret Parker, several school exercises and translations, four rather warm love poems addressed to a mysterious "Caroline" in 1805, his satire on Dr. Butler as "Pomposus" ("On a Change of Masters at a Great Public School"), two satires on personalities and practices at Cambridge ("Thoughts Suggested by a College Examination" and "Granta, a Medley"), and the frankly erotic poem "To Mary," which apparently he had not at first intended to include in the volume.[n] This Mary, to whom he addressed two other poems in the same volume, was, as Moore tells us (probably on the authority of Elizabeth Pigot), "of an humble, if not equivocal, station in life." She had "long, light golden hair, of which he used to show a lock, as well as her picture, among his friends."[n] It is possible that Byron met her in London rather than in Southwell. Writing a little later to John Pigot of the reaction to his "*unlucky* poem" which had caused him to be "pronounced a most *profligate sinner,* in short a '*young Moore,*'" he says: "The adventures of my life from sixteen to nineteen, and the dissipation into which I have been thrown in London, have given a voluptuous tint to my ideas; but the occasions which called forth my muse could hardly admit any other colouring."[5]

The second poem to the voluptuous maiden ("To Mary, on Receiving Her Picture") is somewhat more romantic in tone, but the third ("To a Lady, Who Presented the Author a Lock

[5] *LJ*, I, 112–13. Letter of Jan. 13, 1807. While Hobhouse was sitting for his portrait in 1832, he told Benjamin Robert Haydon, the painter, that "Moore, in his 'Life of Byron,' had certainly pretended that Byron's early life with those amiable girls in Nottingham had been virtuously passed, and that had he continued such female connections his vices might have been less; and that had he followed the advice of Hodgson, the parson, it would have been better for him, &c. 'Now,' said Hobhouse, 'this Hodgson was, on the whole, the most dissipated of the set'; that Byron came to college perfectly initiated after these innocent experiences in Nottingham; and that neither he (Hobhouse) nor Matthews could teach Lord Byron anything, for of the three he was certainly the most advanced." (*Benjamin Robert Haydon: Correspondence and Table-Talk*, ed. F. W. Haydon, II, 367–8.) But Byron's initiation in the vices came probably earlier even than Hobhouse supposed, certainly as early as his sojourn in London in the early months of 1806.

of Hair, Braided with his Own, and Appointed a Night in December to Meet Him in the Garden") suggests amazingly the realistic vein of his mature satires. Some lines seem almost like trial verses for such a sophisticated poem as *Beppo.*

The rest of the poems, mostly addressed to his Southwell friends, were written as the occasion or mood dictated and dated in October or November. The moods of gallantry or light cynicism predominate, but some, like "The Tear" and "The Cornelian," appeal to the softer sentiments. What has not been sufficiently stressed, however, is that this first volume of Byron had as much realism and satire as sentiment and romance. It was only after certain "ladies in years" and his clerical friends had taken offense at his franker effusions that he filled his first volume meant for the public with the romantic and melancholy poems which fixed his bent and determined his reputation until his Italian exile freed him finally from English restraints. His verses to John Pigot in *Fugitive Pieces* give the advice of a Don Juan:

> *At first she may* frown *in a pet;*
> *But leave her awhile,*
> *She shortly will smile,*
> *And then you may* kiss *your* coquette.

In his second poem to Pigot, "To the Sighing Strephon," he is even more the roving gallant:

> *Whilst my blood is thus warm,*
> *I ne'er shall reform,*
> *To mix in the Platonist's school;*
> *Of this I am sure,*
> *Was my passion so pure,*
> My mistress *must think me* a fool.
>
> *Though the kisses are sweet,*
> *Which voluptuously meet,*
> *Of kissing I ne'er was so fond,*
> *As to make me forget,*
> *Though our lips oft have met,*
> *That still there was* something beyond.

Byron had not returned to Cambridge for the autumn term, partly because his finances were not in a state to allow him to live there as he wished, and partly no doubt also because he was pleasantly occupied in Southwell. His success in the amateur theatricals was a salve to his vanity, and being the cynosure of several pairs of not unattractive female eyes was agreeable enough. But chiefly his volume of poems absorbed his attention, and nothing in the academic life at Cambridge compelled him to hurry back. He had contrived a truce with Mrs. Byron sufficient to make life bearable, especially since he spent much of his time out of her presence.

During his visits to Southwell the Pigot house across the green had become Byron's adopted home. The fact that he escaped there usually as soon as he rose in the morning helped him to avoid many quarrels with his mother. In the Pigots' parlor he could improvise imitations of his favorite poets, Camoëns and Thomas Moore, and Elizabeth would copy them out for him. He was still shy when he saw new faces, and if he saw strangers approaching the house, Elizabeth recalled, "he would instantly jump out of the window to avoid them." *n*

He had already established the habit of late retiring and late rising that remained with him the rest of his life. His favorite recreations were swimming and diving and firing at a mark with pistols, and these practices too he continued until his death. His delight in firearms and swords was always very great. He kept a small sword by the side of his bed and when he awoke in the morning amused himself by thrusting it through the bed-hangings.*n*

By November Byron was thinking of returning to Cambridge. But at the end of the month he was still at Southwell and had apparently given up his plan. Owen Mealey wrote to Hanson on November 24, after giving account of the thievery and other misdeeds of Byron's valet, Francis Boyce: "Lord Byron is at Southwell, and I bleve means to stay there all the winter." [6]

[6] Unpublished letter, Roe-Byron Collection, Newstead Abbey. (Quoted in part, in Catalogue, 1937, C. 4, p. 55.) Byron was reluctant to believe that his servant was dishonest, and from Cambridge he wrote indignantly to his mother when she presented him with the evidence. Mealey gave Hanson the

By this time *Fugitive Pieces* was in its final form, and Byron presented a copy to the Reverend John Thomas Becher, Vicar of Rumpton and Midsomer Norton, Notts., who had given him fatherly advice and encouragement in his versifying. No sooner had Becher seen the poem "To Mary" than he wrote a protest to Byron. Perhaps he thought it would be taken better by the author if he couched it in verse. Byron's first reaction was one of annoyance and pique, though it seems incredible that he could not have foreseen the repercussions in the respectable clerical society of Southwell of such lines as

*Now, by my soul, 'tis most delight*
*To view each other panting, dying,*
*In love's* extatic posture *lying,*
*Grateful to* feeling, *as to* sight.

He dashed off, partly in apology and more in self-justification, an "Answer to some elegant verses sent by a friend to the author, complaining that one of his descriptions was rather too warmly drawn." His plea was juvenile but not unreasonable: "Can youth then hush the dictates of the heart?/ Precepts of prudence curb, but can't controul,/ The fierce emotions of the flowing soul." His argument was essentially the same one he used later to defend *Don Juan*. His muse, he said, was "the simple Truth." [n]

Although he resented the criticism, Byron had been awakened to the light in which his verses would be viewed by the old ladies of Southwell, some of whom had already seen a copy of the *Fugitive Pieces* or heard of the scandalous nature of the volume and had begun to gossip. The same day that he wrote the reply to Becher (November 26) he called in all the copies that he had given to friends in Southwell and burned the lot.[n] Only four copies escaped the flames. In spite of the strictures he had made on it, the Reverend John Becher kept his copy.

details of "how Lord Byrons vallet has served him which is now in the House of Correction he has taken 15 of his new Shirts besides Neck handkerchiefs. Several pairs of Silk Stockings and several other things besides Money that Lord Byron gave him to pay small bills at Cambridge which he has left unpaid." Francis Boyce (Frank) was ordered transported for a term of seven years.

John Pigot, who had gone back to his medical studies in Edinburgh, kept his, but at Byron's request tore out the poem "To Mary." One copy Byron apparently retrieved later from Elizabeth Pigot and used in preparing his next privately printed volume, which he started almost immediately.[n]

Byron's hurt pride had not been soothed, however, and while he was at work on the new volume he wrote two more defenses of his position against the local censors. In the first, "To a Knot of Ungenerous Critics," his chief attack is upon "a portly Female," "impelled by private pique," who was the leader of the busybodies raising the specter of scandal in the town.[n] This was followed shortly after by his "Soliloquy of a Bard in the Country," a more clever and somewhat more detached satire, though it has a few personal attacks on Becher and on a certain "coxcomb" physician who had been active in gossip. He had the good sense not to publish either poem, though he probably circulated them among his friends. But it is characteristic of Byron that he could write thus in pique of his friends and yet remain on amicable terms with them. In fact, he had a great deal of respect for the judgment of Becher and conferred with him frequently while assembling the poems in the new volume.

In an effort to make his muse more chaste, Byron omitted some of the amorous poems and passages, including "To Mary," one of the poems "To Caroline,"[n] and the stanza already quoted from "To the Sighing Strephon." In deference to Becher he also omitted from one of the poems "To Caroline" a stanza beginning "No jargon of priests o'er our union was muttered." Discretion further prompted the substitution of fictitious names for some of the poems addressed to the young ladies of Southwell. "To Julia" (Leacroft) was changed before the printing of the new volume to "To Lesbia," and a number of other substitutions were made to avoid obvious identifications.

The general effect of these excisions and prunings was to make the second volume more sedate and at the same time less distinguishable from any other juvenile collection of sentimental and imitative verse. Of the twelve poems added, "The First Kiss of Love" probably had the most freshness and lyrical lilt, while "Childish Recollections," nostalgic reminiscences of his

Harrow associations and friends, lapsed into the stilted language of conventional couplets. Sincere as may have been his tributes to Dr. Drury, to Clare, Wingfield, Tatersall, Delawarr, and Edward Long, the artificiality of the style did not give Byron an opportunity to display his talents for realism, incisiveness, or humor. Southwell had effectively diverted his true bent, and the new volume was, as he rather bitterly confessed to John Pigot, "*vastly* correct and miraculously chaste." [n]

While he was revising his poems, and writing more, a task which occupied most of December, he was roused to indignation by the action of Hanson's partner Birch, who, in an effort to force Byron to return to Cambridge, had withheld the income allotted by the Court of Chancery. Byron expressed his feelings in a caustic letter to Hanson.[n] If he had had any intention of returning to College, this attempt to force his hand would have set him against it. But his poetry now interested him much more than the University.

*Poems on Various Occasions*, as he called the revised volume, was printed by S. and J. Ridge in an edition of about one hundred and was ready for distribution early in January 1807.[n] By the 6th, Byron was at Dorant's Hotel, London, where he had gone in all probability to try to raise some money. His first move was to write to Hanson for an advance on his allowance, which was not due until March 25.[n] At the same time he was busy distributing copies of his poems and writing new ones addressed to some of the Southwell belles.

In the meantime Byron had been in touch with the money-lenders again through Mrs. Massingberd, who on the 16th sent him their proposal: he was to receive three thousand pounds and to pay five thousand when he came of age, and to pay interest if he could not repay the loan within six months after that time. Out of the three thousand she proposed that he should pay off the loan which she had contracted to pay when she went security for him for his first loan the year before.[n] According to Byron's statement to Hanson later, the lenders refused to advance money on Mrs. Massingberd's security (there was already a lien on her property) without the addition of another name. Mr. Dorant, the proprietor of his hotel, then consented to sign, and Byron received the money after protesting the exorbitancy of the charges, and left a sum with Dorant to pay the interest.[7]

Hopelessly in debt, Byron returned to Southwell toward the end of January. In a reckless mood, he was soon in trouble of another sort. He had for some time been paying court of a cavalier kind to Julia Leacroft, apparently with the knowledge of her family, who would not have been averse to entrapping the young lord into marriage with their daughter.

Having heard the story from Byron, Hobhouse wrote in the margin of his copy of Moore: "It was at this place [Southwell] that he learnt not only his first lessons in sensuality but had an opportunity of seeing to what base expedients self-interest will resort—one of the families he mentioned winked at an intercourse between him and [one] of the daughters in hopes of entangling him in an unequal marriage."[8] It was no doubt the same episode that Byron referred to in a letter to Elizabeth Pigot the following summer: "As for the village 'Lass'es' of *every*

[7] Mrs. Byron got wind of what was going on and wrote Hanson on Jan. 31, 1807: "Mrs. M. is now trying to get my son into another *Scrape* that is to borrow more money. She is certainly a Dupe herself, or *wishes to make* him one. I know her income has been seized for the payment of the Annuity." She asked Hanson to try to stop the transaction. (Hanson narrative, Murray MSS.)

[8] Hobhouse perhaps referred to Byron's early "lessons in sensuality" from May Gray (see Chapter III). Byron maintained, however, that the "Mary" of the fleshly poems of *Fugitive Pieces* was a London and not a Southwell girl. When he reprinted "To a Lady Who Presented the Author a Lock of Hair," Byron added a note to refute the rumor which had disturbed Julia Leacroft's father, that the line "Since Juliet first declared her passion" referred to his daughter: "In the above little piece the author has been accused by some *candid readers* of introducing the name of a lady from whom he was some hundred miles distant at the time this was written; and poor Juliet, who has slept so long in 'the tomb of all the Capulets,' has been converted, with a trifling alteration of her name, into an English damsel, walking in a garden of their own creation, during the month of *December*, in a village where the author never passed a winter." But Byron was apparently in Southwell in December. Mr. Leacroft would have been still further incensed had he known as well as Byron did Otway's *Venice Preserved*, for the reference in Byron's poem to "a sea-coal fire" was from a couplet which Byron frequently quoted in his letters:

*Give but an Englishman his whore and ease,*
*Beef and a sea-coal fire, he's yours for ever.*
(Act II, Scene iii.)

description, my *Gratitude* is also unbounded, to be equalled only by my *contempt*. I saw the *designs* of all *parties* while they imagined me *every thing* to be *wished*." [n]

Alternate moods of depression, ambition, and reckless indulgence seized Byron as he dragged out the winter and spring rudderless in Southwell. And yet a native compulsion to kindness and a sense of justice warred with his weaknesses. At the same time that he had been indulging in reckless gallantries (or so he liked to make them appear in writing to his friends—one must never take Byron quite at his word in such things, for he always became more emotionally involved than he pretended), he was trying to get King's Clemency for his servant Frank, whom he had paid a lawyer £20 to prosecute.[n]

Byron wrote the Earl of Clare on February 6: "I have been *transporting* a servant, who cheated me,—rather a disagreeable event;—performing in private theatricals;—publishing a volume of poems . . . making love,—and taking physic. The two last amusements have not had the best effect in the world; for my attentions have been divided amongst so many fair damsels, and the drugs I swallow are of such variety in their compositon, that between Venus and Æsculapius I am harassed to death." [9]

Byron had already begun the strict reducing regimen which for the next few months he carried on with almost fanatical zeal. In that time he pared down the stoutness that had persisted since his entrance to Harrow to a slenderness that he maintained with little variation until he relaxed and grew fat again in Venice in 1818. He had been at his heaviest during the autumn of 1806, having reached 202 pounds, a tremendous weight for a man of only moderate height (five feet eight and one-half inches). It may be that his desire to succeed as a Lothario encouraged him to undertake his spartan regime, which besides dieting consisted of "violent exercise, *much* physic, and *hot* bathing." [1]

[9] *LJ*, I, 116–19. Hobhouse's comment at this point in his copy of Moore is: "all true and decisive as to the silly romances of T. M. respecting the purity of Lord Byron."

[1] *LJ*, I, 127. Letter of April 1807 to John Pigot. Byron must have been aware that his stoutness made him hardly a graceful Romeo. Describing himself in his satiric poem "Prim Mary Ann," he says: "His form was stout, & his

In January, after negotiating the loan in London, Byron had paid £150 to the Reverend Thomas Jones, his tutor, to apply on his College debts of the previous year. Jones apparently admonished him for not returning to Trinity College, for Byron wrote the tutor on February 14 with a freedom that verged on petulance: "I have not pursued my College studies, I have pursued none. . . . I have other reasons for not residing at Cambridge. I dislike it, I was originally intended for Oxford. My guardians determined otherwise. I quitted the society of my earliest associates who are all 'Alumni' of the latter to drag on a weary turn at a place where I had many acquaintances but few friends. I therefore can never consider Granta as my Alma Mater, but rather as a Nurse of no very promising appearance on whom I have been forced against *her* inclinations and contrary to *mine*."[n] There was no doubt a good deal of rationalization in this argument. Byron's real reasons for not returning to Cambridge were probably more complicated; certainly stronger motives than those here mentioned were his lack of money and the inertia that generally made it difficult for him to leave a place where he was once established. His financial situation was ever more perilous. His mother, in an attempt to keep him from borrowing more from the moneylenders, was negotiating a loan of £1,000 among her relatives in Nottingham, to be secured by her Scottish property.[n]

Despite his complaints, Byron was agreeably employed in Southwell. Between flirting and versifying he kept despondent thoughts at bay except at intervals. The fact that melancholy generally dominated his verses has given a wrong impression of Byron as a gloomy youth. He was full of animal spirits and still boyish a great deal of the time, as Elizabeth Pigot knew. In some exuberant verses labeled "Egotism" addressed to J. T. Becher,

---

shoulders were Broad." A ledger in the possession of Messrs. Berry, St. James's Street, where a record of weights was kept for the convenience of customers, gives the following weights for Byron: Jan. 4, 1806 (boots, no hat), 13 stone 12 lbs. (194 lbs.); July 8, 1807 (shoes), 10 stone 13 lbs. (153 lbs.); July 23, 1807 (shoes), 11 stone (154 lbs.); Aug. 13, 1807 (shoes), 10 stone 11½ lbs. (151½ lbs.); May 27, 1808 (shoes), 11 stone 1 lb. (155 lbs.); June 10, 1809 (shoes), 11 stone 5¾ lbs. (159¾ lbs.); July 15, 1811 (shoes), 9 stone 11½ lbs. (137½ lbs.). (*LJ*, I, 27n.)

"written between one and two, after *midnight*," on February 25, he summed up his defiant hedonism:

> *Some sage* Mammas *with gesture haughty*
> *Pronounce me quite a youthful Sinner—*
> *But* Daughters *say, "although he's naughty,*
> *You must not check a* Young Beginner!" [n]

Though *Poems on Various Occasions*, like the earlier volume, was intended only for private circulation, Byron was proud enough of his versifying to want to get a wider audience and more expert opinions than Southwell afforded. He sent to John Pigot in Edinburgh a copy to be presented to Henry Mackenzie, author of *The Man of Feeling*. Mrs. Byron, with a mother's pride in her son's authorship (though he had tried to keep from her the poems in the first volume), sent two copies to Augusta, who had not the courage to show them to Lord Carlisle.[n]

Byron was most pleased with the encomiums of his Harrow and Cambridge friend Edward Noel Long, whom he had pictured fondly as "Cleon" in "Childish Recollections." He was annoyed, however, because Long had shown his "poor effusions" to Bankes, who delighted too much in repartee. And he was still more concerned about another matter: ". . . pray keep the subject of my '*Cornelian*' a *Secret*." [n]

The mischievous William Bankes apparently sent Byron an unsolicited critique of measured praise and considerable frankness. Bankes was "very good-natured," Byron later told Lady Blessington, but he was "not much of a flatterer." [n] In his reply Byron gave a rather strained welcome to such frank criticism, for he was "*cloyed* with insipid Compliments." But he added: "I have a better opinion of your Judgement & Ability, than your *Feelings*." Nevertheless, he assured him: "Your further Remarks, however *Caustic*, or bitter to a palate vitiated with the *Sweets* of *Adulation*, will be of Service. . . ." At the same time he let Bankes know that on the same day he received his critique, he "was honoured with the Encomiums of *Mackenzie* the celebrated author of the 'Man of Feeling'. . . ." In extenuation of the despondency of some pieces and the eroticism of others he had a ready explanation: "Many of them were written under great

Depression of Spirits, & during severe Indisposition, hence the gloomy Tone of the Ideas.—We coincide in opinion that the '*Poesies Erotiques*['], are the most exceptionable, they were however, grateful to the *Deities,* on whose altars they were offered, more I seek not." [n]

Hanson had complimented him on his verses, but had suggested that his true forte was in oratory, for he had his mind set on Byron making a name for himself as a public figure. Byron's reply was that he could do nothing in the oratorical line until he came of age. And then he explained why he lingered in Southwell, a place which he abhorred. "The Fact is I remain here because I can appear no where else, being *completely done* up. *Wine* and *Women* have *dished* your *humble Servant,* not a *Sou* to be *had;* all *over;* condemned to exist (I cannot say live) at this *Crater* of Dullness till my *Lease* of *Infancy* expires. To appear at Cambridge is impossible; no money even to pay my College expences."

Byron was still carrying on the rigorous system of thinning which he described to Hanson in the same letter: "I have lost 18 LB in my weight, that is one Stone & 4 pounds since January. . . . However don't be alarmed; I have taken every means to accomplish the end, by violent exercise and Fasting, as I found myself too plump. . . . I wear *seven* Waistcoats and a great Coat, run, and play at cricket in this Dress, till quite exhausted by excessive perspiration, use the Hip Bath daily; eat only a quarter of a pound of Butcher's Meat in 24 hours, no Suppers or Breakfast, only one Meal a Day; drink no malt liquor, but a little Wine, and take Physic occasionally. By these means my *Ribs* display Skin of no great Thickness, & my Clothes have been taken in nearly *half a yard.*" [n]

While he was working on his new volume of poems, a disconsolate letter from Edward Long, his old Cambridge crony, who had entered the Guards and felt that his happiest days were over, opened the floodgates of Byron's reflection on his own situation. "To be plain with Regard to myself," he wrote, "Nature stampt me in the Die of Indifference. I consider myself as destined never to be happy, although in some instances fortunate. I am an isolated Being on the Earth, without a Tie to attach me to life, except a few School-fellows, and a *score of females*." His reading and reflection had made him skeptical of the beliefs that offered comfort to others. "Of Religion I know nothing, at least in its *favour*. We have *fools* in all sects and Impostors in most; why should I believe mysteries no one understands, because written by men who chose to mistake madness for Inspiration, and style themselves *Evangelicals*?" He concluded: "I am surrounded here by parsons and methodists, but, as you will see, not infected with the mania. I have lived a Deist, what I shall die I know not; however, come what may, *ridens moriar*." [n]

He was detained in Southwell only by the publication of his poems, he told Long, and they would not be complete until June. The volume for the public was becoming more serious and less personal. About twenty of the earlier occasional verses were being deleted and he was substituting, in addition to imitations and translations from Anacreon and Virgil, such melancholy and nostalgic poems as "Lachin Y Gair," recalling the lost romance of his Scottish summers, "Elegy on Newstead Abbey," a too serious recital of the heroic deeds of his ancestors, and "The Death of Calmar and Orla," an imitation of Ossian. Nothing was left of the humor and realism that compensated in some measure for the juvenility of his first volume. When Byron approached the public it was with a trepidation that snuffed out most of the sparks of original talent. What remained in the volume was imitative, sentimental, and mawkish enough to invite the ridicule of the reviewers. The title, *Hours of Idleness*, was supplied by the printer Ridge.[n]

As his volume approached completion, Byron was growing restive and was seeking an opportunity to escape from Southwell. But he could not return to Cambridge without money to pay his bills. When it seemed unlikely that Mrs. Byron could raise a £1,000 loan from her relatives, Byron in a fit of renunciation proposed selling his horses, and made "plans of Œconomy that I much fear will be laid aside if the Money is procured," Mrs. Byron said shrewdly.[n]

The loan was finally agreed upon, but as the money had not been received by June 11, Byron asked Hanson for an advance of three quarters of his allowance so that he could go to Cambridge and clear his debts.[n]

When he descended upon Cambridge on June 27 with his usual vivacity, he had two surprises for his friends and acquaintances: his new volume of poems and a loss of weight that made him scarcely recognizable. "I have been here two days," he wrote Long on the 29th, "& find very few of my old acquaintances, except Erskine, Campbell, Hobhouse &c &c. none of them knew me at first my figure & visage are of such preternatural Longitude. . . . Edleston called on me last night. . . . I think he is much grown & rather improved." [n]

He expected to be in London on Saturday, but as usual lingered longer than he had anticipated. "I quit Cambridge with little regret," he wrote Elizabeth Pigot, "because our *set* are *vanish*ed, and my *musical protégé* before mentioned has left the choir, and is stationed in a mercantile house of considerable eminence in the metropolis. You may have heard me observe he is exactly to an hour two years younger than myself. I found him grown considerably, and as you will suppose, very glad to see his former *Patron.* He is nearly my height, very *thin,* very fair complexion, dark eyes, and light locks. My opinion of his mind you already know;—I hope I shall never have occasion to change it. . . . The University at present is very gay from the fêtes of divers kinds. I supped out last night, but eat (or ate) nothing, sipped a bottle of claret, went to bed at two, and rose at eight. I have commenced early rising, and find it agrees with me. The Masters and the Fellows all very *polite,* but look a little *askance*—don't much admire *lampoons*—truth always disagreeable." [2]

When Byron wrote again on July 5 his plans had changed. A week at Cambridge with new and old friends had made it seem agreeable enough so that he determined to go back for another year, "as my rooms, etc., etc., are finished in great style, several old friends come up again, and many new acquaintances made; consequently my inclination leads me

[2] *LJ* I, 132. Byron imagined, perhaps without cause, that the university authorities would be offended by his "lampoons" on Cambridge in "Thoughts Suggested by a College Examination" and "Granta, a Medley."

MARY CHAWORTH

JOHN CAM HOBHOUSE

forward. . . ." [n] Byron's changes of plans frequently seemed casual, but there was always a strong emotional force directing his inclinations.

On this occasion his meeting with John Cam Hobhouse and Charles Skinner Matthews no doubt fixed his resolve to continue residence at Cambridge. Both were as full of mischief as Byron himself, but both had uncommon intellectual interests and abilities—something that Byron had not found among many of his drinking companions at Cambridge. Hobhouse, son of Benjamin Hobhouse, M.P. from Bristol who was created a baronet in 1812, had come up to Trinity College in 1806 from Westminster School. He had read widely in historical and political fields, had formed liberal Whig opinions, and had political ambitions and literary aspirations. Byron had met both Hobhouse and Matthews the year before, probably through Bankes, but they were not friends. "It was not till 1807," Byron wrote, ". . . that I became one of Matthews's familiars, by means of Hobhouse, who, after hating me for two years, because I wore a *white hat*, and a *grey* coat, and rode a *grey* horse (as he says himself), took me into his good graces because I had written some poetry. I had always lived a great deal, and got drunk occasionally, in their company—but now we became really friends in a morning."

Byron had known Matthews in his first year at Cambridge, but not intimately. During his absence from College, Matthews had occupied his spacious rooms in the corner of the Great Court of Trinity, with Byron's furniture, "and Jones, the tutor, in his odd way, had said, on putting him in, 'Mr. Matthews, I recommend to your attention not to damage any of the moveables, for Lord Byron, Sir, is a young man of *tumultuous passions*.' Matthews was delighted with this; and whenever anybody came to visit him, begged them to handle the very door with caution; and used to repeat Jones's admonition in his tone and manner. . . . Jones's phrase of '*tumultuous passions*,' and the whole scene, had put him into such good humour, that I verily believe that I owed to it a portion of his good graces." [n]

Although Matthews was Hobhouse's particular friend and in most respects much more intimate with him than with Byron, there were certain areas in which Matthews entered into rapport with Byron more readily than did the more sober and less bold John Cam. "As he [Matthews] was very free in his speculations upon all kinds of subjects," Byron wrote, "although by no means either dissolute or intemperate in his conduct, and as I was no less independent, our conversation and correspondence used to alarm our friend Hobhouse to a considerable degree." [3]

What appealed to Byron was that the mischief of Matthews was generally interfused with wit. Stories of his escapades at Cambridge and elsewhere are legion. Byron has recorded a few. Matthews was one of the "band of profane scoffers," led by Bankes,[n] who used to rouse the Master of Trinity, Lort Mansel, with the taunt "We beseech thee to hear us, good *Lort!*"—"Good *Lort* deliver us!" [n]

In this company Byron was full of high spirits and facetiousness, and this mood was reflected in his letter to Elizabeth Pigot on the eve of his going up to London. "My life here has been one continued routine of dissipation—out at different places every day, engaged to more dinners, etc., etc., than my *stay* would permit me to fulfil. At this moment I write with a bottle of claret in my *head* and *tears* in my *eyes;* for I have just parted with my *'Cornelian,'* who spent the evening with me. As it was our last interview, I postponed my engagement to devote the hours of the *Sabbath* to friendship:—Edleston and I have separated for the present, and my mind is a chaos of hope and sorrow. Tomorrow I set out for London. . . ."

But it was not to be a permanent parting. He revealed his plans to the sympathetic Miss Pigot: "I rejoice to hear you are interested in my *protégé;* he has been my *almost constant* associate since October, 1805, when I entered Trinity College. . . . He departs for a *mercantile house* in *town* in October, and we shall probably not meet till the expiration of my minority, when I shall leave to his decision either entering as a *partner* through my interest, or residing with me altogether. Of course he would

[3] Byron wrote later (to R. C. Dallas) that Matthews, though a man of "most astonishing powers," was "a most decided atheist, indeed noxiously so, for he proclaimed his principles in all societies." (*LJ,* I, 338. Letter of Aug. 21, 1811.)

in his present frame of mind prefer the *latter,* but he may alter his opinion previous to that period;—however, he shall have his choice." Then he added the sentence already quoted: "I certainly love him more than any human being, and neither time nor distance have had the least effect on my (in general) changeable disposition. In short, we shall, put *Lady E. Butler* and *Miss Ponsonby* to the blush, *Pylades* and *Orestes* out of countenance, and want nothing but a catastrophe like *Nisus* and *Euryalus,* to give *Jonathan* and *David* the 'go by.'" He concluded: "My *protégé* breakfasts with me; parting spoils my appetite—excepting from Southwell."[4]

In this same letter he gave Elizabeth a light account of his social life at Cambridge: ". . . upset a butter-boat in the lap of a lady—look'd very *blue—spectators* grinned—'curse 'em!' Apropos, sorry to say, been *drunk* every day, and not quite *sober* yet . . . sad dogs all the *Cantabs.* Mem.—*we mean* to reform next January. This place is a *monotony of endless variety*—like it—hate Southwell. Has Ridge sold well? or do the ancients demur? What ladies have bought?"[n]

Byron had forwarded a copy of *Hours of Idleness* to Lord Carlisle, who sent a polite and encouraging note, though he had not read the volume. He expressed "a sincere satisfaction in finding you employ your leisure in such compositions."[n] Byron no doubt had an uneasy eye on the reviewers when he put his name to the volume, "By George Gordon, Lord Byron, A Minor." The deprecating tone and mock modesty of the Preface could hardly have been better calculated to spur critical attacks. The poems were "the fruits of the lighter hours of a young man, who has lately completed his nineteenth year. As they bear the internal evidence of a boyish mind, this is, perhaps, unnecessary

[4] Lady Eleanor Butler, sister of the seventeenth Earl of Ormonde, and Sarah Ponsonby, cousin of the Earl of Bessborough, lived together in the Vale of Llangollen for fifty years (1779–1829). Charles Mathews (*Memoirs,* III, 150–1) described their appearance at the theater in 1820: "They came twelve miles from Llangollen, and returned, as they never sleep from home. . . . As they are seated, there is not one point to distinguish them from men . . . the upper part of their habits, which they always wear, even at a dinner-party, made precisely like men's coats; and regular black beaver men's hats."

information." Some were written during illness and depression of spirits. While this would not excite praise, it might "arrest the arm of censure." " 'To do greatly', we must 'dare greatly.' " " 'I have pass'd the Rubicon,' " he wrote grandly, "and must stand or fall by the 'cast of the die.' " Though he knew his poems were imitative, there was no intentional plagiarism. "Poetry, however, is not my primary vocation; to divert the dull moments of indisposition, or the monotony of a vacant hour, urged me 'to this sin.' " He would be content if he achieved "a posthumous page in 'The Catalogue of Royal and Noble Authors.' . . . With slight hopes, and some fears, I publish this first, and last attempt. . . . It is highly improbable, from my situation, and pursuits hereafter [he would be declaiming in the House of Lords, or directing affairs of state, for that was still at the bottom of his mind], that I should ever obtrude myself a second time on the Public. . . ." He would "rather incur the bitterest censure of anonymous criticism, than triumph in honours granted solely to a title." [n]

One of Byron's reasons for going up to London was to see that his poems got distributed and found their way into the hands of reviewers. He settled down for some weeks at Gordon's Hotel in Albemarle Street to enjoy being an author and to enter again into the delights of the town, made more pleasant by his long residence at Southwell. On the 13th he sent a boasting budget of his pastimes and plans to Elizabeth Pigot. He no doubt tried to impress the country girl, and possibly stretched the account of the gaiety in which he participated.

He was pleased at the sale of *Hours of Idleness*. "I hear many of the London booksellers have them, and Crosby has sent copies to the principal watering places." [n] Crosby was the London agent of Ridge, the Newark bookseller who printed Byron's poems. He was, as Byron soon discovered, also the publisher of a magazine called *Monthly Literary Recreations*, in the July number of which it "chanced" that there appeared a very favorable notice of *Hours of Idleness*. In the same number was Byron's review of Wordsworth's *Poems* (2 vols., 1807).[5]

[5] *LJ*, I, 137n. Byron evidently took the earliest opportunity to make the acquaintance of Crosby and to suggest ways of increasing the circulation of

By August he could report to Elizabeth that his poems were getting the favorable attentions that warmed his ego. Though the town was beginning to empty, "things wear a most promising aspect, & a Man whose works are praised by *Reviewers*, admired by *Duchesses*, and sold by every Bookseller of the Metropolis, does not dedicate much consideration to *rustic readers*." He spoke with elation of the review in *Monthly Literary Recreations*, "where my *Bardship* is applauded far beyond my deserts. I know nothing of the critic, but think *him* a very *discerning gentleman*, & *myself* a *devilish clever fellow*." Moreover, his cousin Lord Alexander Gordon had told him that the Duchess of Gordon, his mother, had bought the poems and admired them with the rest of the fashionable world, and wished to meet him. ". . . in every Bookseller's I see my *own name*, and *say nothing*, but enjoy my *fame* in *secret*.—My last Reviewer, kindly requests me to alter my determination of writing no more." In his intervals of leisure, after two in the morning, he had written 380 lines of blank verse on Bosworth Field.[n]

While Byron was in London, his sister Augusta tried again to effect a reconciliation. She had written her brother on his arrival in town, she told Hanson, requesting ten minutes' conversation with him, but received no reply. Now she made her pathetic appeal to the attorney: ". . . will you tell me if you think there is the slightest hope of his forgiving me. . . . I am *perfectly wretched* at his continuing angry & you know there is not anything I would not do to regain his good opinion and affection, which I trust I don't *quite deserve* to have lost. . . ."[n]

But Hanson's relations with Byron were not such as to make him an effective mediator. Byron suspected him of holding back his allowance or of making it difficult for him to collect an advance on it, and Hanson's proposal to make Mrs. Byron his treasurer, probably for the £1,000 borrowed for Byron's use, did not improve his feelings toward the lawyer.

---

his poems. It may have been Byron's idea that there was a potential market for the poems of a young lord at the principal watering-places. The review of Wordsworth was tempered and did not at all assume the contemptuous tone which Byron later took in *English Bards and Scotch Reviewers* or the caustic and ridiculing one of *Don Juan*. (The review is reproduced in *LJ*, I, 341–3.)

There is no indication that a reconciliation with Augusta came about at this time, or that Byron met her during the summer. On August 11 he announced to Elizabeth Pigot a grand scheme for a tour of the Scottish Highlands with a friend who would accompany him to Edinburgh in his carriage. They would hire a vessel on the coast and visit "the most remarkable of the Hebrides; and, if we have time and favourable weather, mean to sail as far as Iceland. . . ." [n] To be in trim in case of a squall at sea he had been swimming in the Thames from Lambeth to Blackfriars and had made a total distance of three miles.[6] The whole scheme of course was somewhat fantastic, the sort of thing that may have been concocted by two young college men at midnight in their cups. They were to leave the following Sunday (August 16), but on the 20th Byron was in Cambridge. The scheme had been proposed as early as the summer of 1805 and had become a joke among his friends. Elizabeth Pigot wrote to her brother on one occasion: "How can you ask if Lord B. is going to visit the Highlands in the summer? Why, don't *you* know that he never knows his own mind for ten minutes together? I tell him he is as fickle as the winds, and as uncertain as the waves." [n]

In the meantime, Byron would enjoy life as he could at Cambridge. Probably disgruntled by the fact that the rules prevented him from keeping his newly acquired bulldog Smut in his College chambers, he bought a tame bear (the College had no specific statute against keeping bears) and lodged him in the turret or small hexagonal tower above his rooms in "Mutton-hole Corner." He enjoyed the sensation he made when he took bruin for walks on a chain like a dog. He announced with pride to Elizabeth Pigot: "I have got a new friend, the finest in the world, a *tame bear*. When I brought him here, they asked me

[6] This may or may not have been the occasion that Leigh Hunt described in his *Lord Byron and Some of His Contemporaries* (2nd ed., I, 1–2): "The first time I saw Lord Byron, he was rehearsing the part of Leander, under the auspices of Mr. Jackson the prize-fighter. It was in the river Thames, before he went to Greece." Hunt noticed "a respectable-looking manly person, who was eyeing something at a distance. This was Mr. Jackson waiting for his pupil. The latter was swimming with somebody for a wager. I forget what his tutor said of him; but he spoke in terms of praise."

what I meant to do with him, and my reply was, 'he should *sit for a fellowship.*' . . . This answer delighted them not." [n] The fame of this bear spread far. When Hewson Clarke ridiculed Byron's poems the following year in *The Satirist,* he wrote some mocking verses called "Lord B——n to his Bear." And he appended a note: "This bear, which is kept in one of his rooms at Trinity, is a great favourite of his Lordship's; and, if report say true, he has been seen to hug it with all the warmth of fraternal affection!" [n] The bear's fame lasted at Trinity long after Byron left. The incident which brought about the rustication of the bear before he got his Fellowship is related by a later student who lived in Byron's rooms: "Poor Bruin peeping out one day from this retreat, bestowed so ardent an embrace upon a 'small College-man,' that his lordship was constrained, at the suggestion of the Tutor, to 'cut' him. So attached, however, were this singular pair, that the whole power of the Tutor was scarcely able to divide them." [n] Byron eventually sent the bear to Newstead to join a growing menagerie.

Thomas Jones having died before Byron returned to Trinity in October 1807, the Reverend George Frederick Tavell became the mentor of the eccentric young lord. In *Hints from Horace* Byron devoted a couplet to a recognition of the trials of the poor man:

*Unlucky Tavell! doomed to daily cares*
*By pugilistic pupils, and by bears. . . .* [n]

Although Byron liked to give the impression that he was engaged in constant drinking, gambling, and dissipation, he must have devoted only the fringes of his interest and time to those pursuits which were the core of Cambridge life. Casually at the end of his letter to Elizabeth he gave an indication of how his time had been occupied. "I have written 214 pages of a novel—one poem of 380 lines, to be published (without my name) in a few weeks, with notes,—560 lines of Bosworth Field, and 250 lines of another poem in rhyme, besides half a dozen smaller pieces. The poem to be published is a Satire."

And he had been watching the reviews of *Hours of Idleness.* He had been "praised to the skies in the *Critical Review,*" but his poems had been mercilessly ridiculed in the October number of *The Satirist,* edited by Hewson Clarke, a sizar of Emmanuel College, Cambridge. Byron pretended to bear the harsh criticism like a philosopher, since it helped the sale of the book: "it keeps up controversy, and prevents it being forgotten." [n] But it cut more deeply than he would admit, and he took several opportunities to strike back at Clarke. [n]

Ridge was already urging a new edition, and on November 11 Byron wrote to give him instructions for it. He had the wisdom to order the egoistic and mock-modest Preface suppressed entirely. He would omit some poems and add others, as he had done before. The dedication was finally addressed to the Earl of Carlisle, from "his obliged ward and affectionate kinsman," for the Earl had written a second and flattering letter on December 7, praising *Hours of Idleness,* and had sent him a copy of his own "few trifles." [n]

Byron no doubt did a good deal of miscellaneous reading while at Trinity, though more of his spare time now went into writing. Conscious of his comparative neglect of reading since his schooldays, he sat down on November 30 and recorded in a memorandum book the remarkable list of the solid works of literature and history which he had read since his fifth year. He noted that "the greater part of the above I perused before the age of fifteen. Since I left Harrow I have become idle and conceited, from scribbling rhyme and making love to women." [n] There is evidence, however, that when he did read it was with care and critical attention. In his copy of Owen Ruffhead's *The Life of Alexander Pope,* which he owned while at Cambridge, he wrote marginal commentaries.[n] On a flyleaf at the beginning he scrawled: "Of Pope's pithy conciseness of style Swift—no diffuse writer himself—has so emphatically said—

*For Pope can in one couplet fix*
*More sense than I can do in six."*

Where Ruffhead wrote that Pope's "natural benevolence suggested to him that he could not better serve the interest of society, than . . . by writing a book to bring mankind to look upon this life with comfort and pleasure," Byron underscored the word "mankind," and wrote in the margin: "A malignant race with Christianity in their mouths and Molochism in their hearts." [7]

Of Byron's associates during the new term, several with whom he became most intimate were distinguished by their serious interest and their ambition in politics and literature. William Bankes, the "father of all mischiefs," was gone; Matthews, amusing and brilliant but too indolent and skeptical to harness himself to any serious purpose, was no longer resident at Cambridge, and Byron saw him chiefly in London and elsewhere. While Hobhouse valued Matthews for his superior intelligence, Byron appreciated him most as a companion in facetious wit and hilarious pranks. Matthews introduced Byron to another Cambridge wit, Scrope Berdmore Davies, then Fellow of King's College.[n] Davies was already well known at the gaming-tables as well as in fashionable drawing-rooms in London, and it was probably through him that Byron was first introduced to gambling. A crony of Beau Brummell and other dandies, he had the entree of the best society but preferred the company of men of brilliant intellect like Matthews. It was after Byron left Cambridge that he came to be most closely associated with Davies.

With little solid knowledge of political principles, but with liberal leanings and an "opposition" mind, Byron was drawn into the Cambridge Whig Club.[8] It was there perhaps that his

[7] Byron was of course very familiar with Pope's poetry, and he was already molding his satire on Pope's model. Byron probably studied the Classics less at Cambridge than he had at Harrow. The famous Greek scholar Richard Porson was still there as Regius Professor of Greek, but Byron's only recollection of him was not of conversation on the Classics. He wrote Murray from Venice in 1818: "I remember to have seen Porson at Cambridge, in the Hall of our College, and in private parties, but not frequently: and I never can recollect him except as drunk or brutal, and generally both: I mean in an evening, for in the hall he dined at the Dean's table. . . . but I have seen him in a private party of undergraduates, many of them freshmen and strangers—take up a poker to one of them, and heard him use language as blackguard as his action." (*LJ*, IV, 200. Letter of Feb. 20, 1818.) In the margin of his copy of Moore, Hobhouse wrote opposite the reference to Porson's taking a poker to a student: "He did so to Byron himself [when] J.C.H. was present."

[8] In an unpublished letter to E. N. Long, n.d. (postmark Nov. 23, 1807), Houghton Library, Harvard University, Byron wrote: "there is a Whig Club here, of which Tavistock wants me to become a member." Hobhouse later

friendship and admiration for Hobhouse ripened. But their literary interests drew them together most closely at this time. Each had written a satire. Byron's was the poem which had already reached 380 lines on October 26. This was no doubt the "Dunciad" on all the living authors in the manner of Pope and Gifford to which Byron had given the title "British Bards." Hobhouse had thrown all his ideas concerning the corruptions of political and social life (measured against the stoical virtues of the ancients) into an imitation of the Eleventh Satire of Juvenal.[n] Byron wrote on December 22 to Crosby, the London bookseller who had sold a goodly number of copies of *Hours of Idleness:* "A Friend of mine of this University, & son of a member of Parliament, has a Satire in imitation of Juvenal ready for the press, but as it is hardly considerable enough to fill a volume, I have consented to publish a poem of mine in conjunction with his, and we wish to know if you will undertake the publication. . . . Mine is of the same nature, but original, and contains above four hundred Lines, with several notes; the subject, the poetry of the present Day.—It must be published (if at all) anonymously. . . ."[n] But the satires were not then published, possibly because Ben Crosby, Ridge's London agent, smelled in Byron's work, "if not gunpowder, at least half a dozen libels."[n]

Another literary friendship developed at this time between Byron and Francis Hodgson, who in October had been appointed resident tutor at King's College. Though he was then a master at Eton and did not come into residence at Cambridge until after Christmas, he had many friends at the University and often visited there. Hodgson, seven years older than Byron, shared with him an enthusiasm for Dryden and Pope and had great facility in versifying, though he tended to be too diffuse. He had been a schoolfellow of Henry Drury at Eton, and of Matthews and Scrope Berdmore Davies, all of whom were to be increasingly prominent in Byron's orbit in the next few years. Hodgson's father

told John Murray that there "were but ten" in the Club and named among them: "Mr. W. Ponsonby, Mr. George O'Callaghan, the Duke of Devonshire, Mr. Dominick Browne, Mr. Henry Pearce, Mr. Kinnaird [Douglas Kinnaird, later Byron's banker and close friend], Lord Tavistock, Lord Ellenborough, Lord Byron, and myself." (*LJ*, IV, 500. Letter of Nov. 1820.)

had been vicar at Croyden, where he was frequently visited by his friend William Gifford, onetime editor of the *Anti-Jacobin* and later editor and a leading critic of the *Quarterly Review*. Such literary connections must have been particularly interesting to Byron, who had already paid Gifford the compliment of imitating his satires the *Mæviad* and the *Baviad* in his own castigation of modern writers.

Hodgson, who was an excellent classical scholar, published in 1807 a translation of Juvenal which was given some attention in the *Edinburgh Review*. Byron called upon him to correct his own classical allusions and quotations. Yet in many ways this friendship was one of Byron's strangest. Hodgson's moral earnestness and sometimes humorless conventionality were at complete odds with Byron's skeptical proclivities, and still more with those of the "profane scoffers" Matthews and Davies, to whom Hodgson was equally attached. But Byron always enjoyed having someone to shock (he had already practiced on the Reverend J. T. Becher in Southwell). And Hodgson, knowing that Byron had a good heart, clung to the hope of converting him to orthodoxy. Like so many of Byron's friends who were closely associated with him in his early manhood, Hodgson came to be utterly devoted to him. On his side Byron did not speak or act with condescension and always had respect for Hodgson's learning, though he sometimes wrote to him with complete freedom and lack of restraint with regard to his own beliefs and conduct.

But Byron's new-found intellectual life at the University soon came to an end. With the usual request for an advance on his allowance and an immediate loan of twenty pounds, he wrote Hanson on December 2 to say that he hoped to "take my New Years Day dinner with you *en famille*."[n] At the Christmas holidays, 1807, he left Cambridge not to return, except for an occasional visit to his cronies, until he went down for his M.A. the following summer. During this final term at Trinity and in the first months of the following year Byron cemented his friendship with Hobhouse, Matthews, the droll Scrope Davies, and Hodgson. Nothing that he carried away from Cambridge was more tangible or more lasting.

# CHAPTER VI

## *1808–1809*

## London and Newstead

STILL busy with the revision of his poems and the preparation of the new volume, Byron settled at Dorant's Hotel in London at the beginning of 1808 and was soon enjoying the life of an author and man about town.

With assumed nonchalance, he was anxiously watching the reviews of *Hours of Idleness.* On January 20 he received an effusively flattering letter from Robert Charles Dallas, who claimed kinship with the young lord.[1] The fawning tone and moral advice might have offended Byron had he been less avid of praise for his poems. Dallas was the sort of person whom Byron in other circumstances might readily have pilloried as a dullard, but politeness and flattery generally neutralized his critical acids. With less ability than Hodgson, Dallas prided himself on his literary achievements. He had written poems, a tragedy, *Moral Essays,* and a number of novels, including *Percival, or Nature Vindicated,* the object of which was "to improve the heart, as well as to please the fancy, and to be the auxiliary of the Divine and the Moralist." Having read Byron's poems, he felt "irresistibly impelled" to pay tribute to "the effusions of a noble mind in strains so truly poetic." He wrote: "Your poems, my Lord, are not only beautiful as compositions, they bespeak a heart glowing with honour, and attuned to virtue, which is infinitely the higher praise."[n]

Byron's reply was designed to express ample gratitude for

[1] Dallas's sister Charlotte had married Byron's uncle, George Anson Byron.

praise from "a man of acknowledged genius," but to quash any hopes that Dallas might have of reforming him. "The events of my short life have been of so singular a nature, that, though the pride commonly called honour has, and I trust ever will, prevent me from disgracing my name by a mean or cowardly action, I have been already held up as the votary of licentiousness, and the disciple of infidelity." [n] The next day, January 21, Dallas wrote praising Byron's candor and expressing confidence that he would someday reform.[n] And this elicited a flippant rejoinder designed to shock the sanctimonious correspondent.

"In morality, I prefer Confucius to the Ten Commandments, and Socrates to St. Paul (though the two latter agree in their opinion of marriage). In religion, I favour the Catholic emancipation, but do not acknowledge the Pope. . . . I believe truth the prime attribute of the Deity, and death an eternal sleep, at least of the body. You have here a brief compendium of the sentiments of the *wicked* George, Lord Byron. . . ." [n]

But this did not stop Dallas, who called on Byron within a few days, dined with him several times, and was perfectly delighted with his new acquaintance, being convinced that he was basically good but had been corrupted by the "pridelings of intellect" at the University. Byron on one occasion turned the conversation into a different channel when one of his companions (perhaps Matthews or Scrope Davies) started to make a butt of the moralizing Dallas.[n] This was another of those strange friendships which Byron was capable of forming with men of most disparate intellects and points of view. Dallas, more than thirty years his senior, became devoted to Byron, aided him, sometimes officiously, in putting his poems through the press, and was a frequent caller for several months.

At the same time Byron had other and more congenial friends in several spheres. He began to cultivate his old Harrow associates again. Henry Drury, to whom Byron had been obstreperous as a schoolboy, now called, perhaps at the instance of Hodgson, his close friend, who felt he knew Byron's worth. In his insecurity, with no clear goal before him, Byron clung to the image of Harrow as a symbol of the happiest times of his boyhood. There in his last two years he had belonged to a community much more closely knit than anything he had encountered at Cambridge, where he still felt a stranger in spite of the bacchic comradeship. He renewed his friendships with Wingfield, with William Harness, and with Delawarr, to whom he had apologized after a misunderstanding. Henry Drury invited a number of the old Harrovians to visit him at the school. One visit led to another, and during the spring and summer Byron made several pilgrimages to Harrow, recapturing fond remembrances of his past and enjoying the sense of being looked up to by the younger boys.

Another escape was already being planned in his mind: a grand tour beyond the confines of Europe. "In January *1809*," he wrote De Bathe, "I shall be twenty one & in the Spring of the same year proceed abroad, not on the usual Tour, but a route of a more extensive Description. What say you? are you disposed for a view of the Peloponnesus and a voyage through the Archipelago? I am . . . very serious with regard to my own Intention which is fixed on the *Pilgrimage*. . . ." [n]

In the meantime, he was increasingly nettled by the reviews of his poems. Despite his feigned indifference, Byron was extremely tender of adverse criticism. The only really caustic critique so far had been the article in *The Satirist* the previous October.[n] He had not forgotten that, and was biding his time for a reply in his own satire. But in January there was published in the *Monthly Mirror* a bit of ridicule that touched him in a sensitive spot: "If this was one of his lordship's *school exercises* at Harrow, and he escaped whipping, they have there either an undue respect for lords' bottoms, or they do not deserve the reputation they have acquired." [n] This, appearing just before his first Harrow visit, must have put him in a particular rage.

In great agitation Byron wrote to Long on January 28: "I have sent to Mr. Twiddie [?] demanding whether he is the author of the article in question or not, and if he refuses a satisfactory answer, my second, Davies, has a challenge to Deliver. ——We shall probably meet near Harrow, as if I fall, I should like 'to die where I was [roused?]' and if Mr. Twiddie takes his departure, I shall breakfast with Harry Drury, instead of Pluto.—" This was written at four o'clock in the afternoon. At half past five he added a postscript: "Davies is returned, Mr.

Twiddie was not at home, but D. is to call tomorrow early in the morning & bring me an answer." [2] Perhaps the delay saved him from Pluto. Either Byron cooled off by morning or Mr. Twiddie satisfied him off the field of honor, for nothing more is heard of the matter.

Pinched for money as usual, Byron had determined not to return to Cambridge. "I am now in my one and twentieth year, and cannot command as many pounds," he complained to Hanson just after his birthday. ". . . my Debts amount to three thousand, three hundred to Jews, eight hundred to Mrs. B. of Nottingham, to coachmaker and other tradesmen a thousand more, and these must be much increased, before they are lessened." [n]

Lack of cash at this period must have been peculiarly galling to Byron, who liked to be able to distribute largess with a free hand. Generosity was always his greatest extravagance. He had already given £200 to the sycophantic Dallas.[n] Now that he was living as a man about town, entertaining people as careless with money as Scrope Davies and some of his theatrical cronies, he must make a showing even if he had to borrow money for his breakfast. And when he had least he was most careless in giving it away. Henry Long has left an account of a typical incident. In January before he first went up to Harrow he had ac-

[2] Unpublished letter, dated January 28, 1808. Berg Collection, New York Public Library. This is the first record of Byron's sending a challenge to a duel. Medwin quoted him, probably inaccurately, as saying: "I have been concerned . . . in many duels as second, but only in two as principal; one was with Hobhouse [Moore?] before I became intimate with him." (Medwin, I, 15.) There is no evidence that Byron actually fought a duel, but he came near it several times, and he thought about it often and sent several challenges. On at least six separate occasions, of which there is record, he was eager to call out an antagonist who had, as he thought, insulted him, but each time he was prevented by his friends, or by apologies or explanations of the other party. The idea that Byron would one day have to fight a duel perhaps contributed to his interest in pistol practice. Captain Gronow records that "When in London, Byron used to go to Manton's shooting-gallery, in Davies Street, to try his hand, as he said, at a wafer. Wedderburn Webster was present when the poet, intensely delighted with his own skill, boasted to Joe Manton that he considered himself the best shot in London. 'No, my lord,' replied Manton, 'not the best; but your shooting to-day was respectable.' Whereupon Byron waxed wroth, and left the shop in a violent passion." (Gronow: *Reminiscences*, I, 152.)

companied his brother to see Byron at Dorant's Hotel, where the impecunious lord was sitting for a miniature.[3] When they departed, "Lord Byron in shaking my hand very cordially, left in it a piece of crumpled paper, which I being totally unversed in those matters was very nearly letting drop, but I looked at it as we were going down stairs, and holding it up to my brother, 'see what he has put into my hand, what is it?' 'What is it? why a tip you fool, put it into your pocket.' It was a £5 banknote."[n] Delawarr was embarrassed by a similar tip.

Hanson came to the rescue with an advance of the whole of Byron's allowance (£125) due at Easter, but a few days later Byron applied to him for a loan of £100.[n] Despite the fact that he had not been in good health, possibly because of his excessive dieting, he did not curtail his amusements.[4]

Following Byron's second visit to Harrow, Henry Drury arranged a reconciliation with Dr. Butler, and all obstacles were removed to his frequent return to the school, where he was now something of a hero, for many of the boys had read his poems. At first Byron had been rather wary when Drury told him that Butler was ready to forget and forgive. But once the reconciliation was effected it seems to have been wholehearted on both sides. Byron wrote immediately to Ridge: "You must *go back* and *cut out* the whole *poem* of *Childish Recollections*. . . . as I am now reconciled to Dr. Butler I cannot allow my satire to appear against him, nor can I alter that part relating to him without spoiling the whole."[n]

Byron's associations at Harrow seem to have been the most innocent of his pastimes, for he soon became involved in excesses in London that undermined his health and all but ended his career. With due allowance for his habit of exaggeration in his correspondence, the records of the winter and spring of 1808 show clearly to what extremes he had abandoned himself in the

[3] The Longs probably saw Byron posing for George Sanders, the Scottish portrait-painter, who had come to London in 1805 and was soon overwhelmed with business among the nobility. By 1806 he was obliged to refuse sitters. His charge then was thirty guineas for a miniature about three inches high by two and one-half inches wide. He painted several portraits of Byron.

[4] Byron boasted to Henry Drury on January 13 that he was only ten stone and a half—147 pounds. (*LJ*, I, 161.)

pursuit of physical pleasure. He wrote to Becher on February 26: "Just rising from my Bed, having been up till six at a Masquerade. . . . to give you some idea of my late life, I have this moment received a prescription from Pearson, not for any *complaint,* but from *debility,* and literally *too much Love.*" Then he treated his reverend friend to a little malicious boasting, perhaps with a recollection of Becher's part in the suppression of his early volume. "You know my devotion to woman, but indeed Southwell was much mistaken in conceiving my adorations were paid to any Shrine there, no, my Paphian Goddesses are elsewhere, and I have sacrificed at their altar rather too liberally.—In fact, my blue eyed Caroline, who is only sixteen, has been lately so *charming,* that though we are both in perfect health, we are at present commanded to *repose,* being nearly worn out.—So much for Venus." [5]

To Hobhouse, who had returned to Cambridge, he wrote the next day a similar confession: "I am buried in an abyss of Sensuality. I have renounced *hazard,* however, but I am given to Harlots, and live in a state of Concubinage. I am at this moment under a course of restoratives by Pearson's prescription, for a debility occasioned by too frequent Connection." [n] And he gave a few additional details for Hobhouse's delectation: "Scrope Davies is meandering about London, feeding upon leg-of-beef soup, and frequenting the British Forum; he has given up hazard, as also a considerable sum at the same time. Altamont is a good deal with me. Last night, at the Opera Masquerade, we supped with seven whores, a *Bawd* and a *Ballet*-master in Madame Catalani's apartment behind the scenes (of course Catalani was *not* there). I have some thoughts of purchasing D'Egville's pupils; they would fill a glorious harem." [n]

In his letter to Hobhouse, Byron had mentioned a circumstance

[5] From the original letter in the Morgan Library. This part of the letter was omitted by Moore and has not since been published. Three days before Byron wrote this seemingly callous letter he composed some verses that must have been intended to refer to his "charming" Caroline in much more romantic terms than he would confess to in his letters. He called on the "Breeze of the night" to "soothe her soul to dreams of love." (*Poetry,* I, 262–3.) The date, February 23, 1808, on the manuscript seems to connect it with his "blue eyed Caroline."

which may in part have been the cause of his dissipations. "As an author, I am cut to atoms by the E[dinburgh] Review; it is just out, and has completely demolished my little fabric of fame. This is rather scurvy treatment for a Whig Review, but politics and poetry are different things, and I am no adept in either. I therefore submit in silence."[6] Byron later pretended to have taken the review in his stride, but Hobhouse, who knew something of his state of mind at the time, said emphatically: "this was not the case—he was very near destroying himself."[n]

Byron's mawkish humility in the Preface had invited ridicule, but the review was unnecessarily provocative and meanly personal. The fact that it appeared in a periodical of such wide circulation and critical prestige made it the harder to bear. "The poesy of this young lord belongs to the class which neither gods nor men are said to permit," the reviewer began pontifically. "His effusions are spread over a dead flat, and can no more get above or below the level, than if they were so much stagnant water." The critic made much of the fact that the noble author was "peculiarly forward in pleading minority. . . . Perhaps, however, in reality, all that he tells us about his youth is rather with a view to increase our wonder than to soften our censures. He possibly means to say, 'See how a minor can write! This poem was actually composed by a young man of eighteen, and this by one of only sixteen!'" The critic ended with a final barb: "We are well off to have got so much from a man of this lord's station, who does not live in a garret, but 'has the sway' of Newstead Abbey."[n]

What cut most deeply was that the critic had laid bare the very vanities he thought he had concealed in his Preface. Byron's immediate reaction was extremely violent. He told Medwin: "When I first saw the review of my 'Hours of Idleness,' I was furious; in such a rage as I never have been in since."[n] And apropos of the *Quarterly* review of Keats, he wrote Murray: "I know, by experience, that a savage review is Hemlock to a sucking author; and the one on me . . . knocked me down—

[6] *LBC,* I, 2. Letter of Feb. 27, 1808. Byron seemed not to be aware that the Edinburgh reviewers would not know his Whig leanings and would attack him as he appeared in his Preface, a conceited young lord.

but I got up again." [n] But the feeling that predominated in the end was anger, the desire for revenge. It "was rage, and resistance, and redress—but not despondency nor despair," he told Shelley.[n] In all his later recollections this was what he stressed. "I heard of it six weeks before," he recorded in his journal of 1813, "read it the day of its denunciation,—dined and drank three bottles of claret (with S. B. Davies, I think,) neither ate nor slept the less, but nevertheless, was not easy till I had vented my wrath and my rhyme, in the same pages, against every thing and every body." [7] His wrath against the Whig reviewers of the *Edinburgh* was such that in his cups he declared in the presence of some of its members his intention to withdraw from the Cambridge Whig Club. When the members took it seriously, however, he told Hobhouse: ". . . perhaps in a moment of intoxication and passion such might be my idea, but *soberly* I have no such design, particularly as I could not abandon my principles. . . ." [n]

Byron had warned his mother through Becher not to be too upset by the review, but when he wrote her after its appearance he was more despondent than she was. "I received a letter from Byron yesterday," she wrote, "and he *abuses* himself worse than the *Edin*[*bu*]*r*[gh] Reviewers, he says if I have any regard for him I never will mention his Poetry to him more as he wishes to forget it, as a Schoolboy it was well enough, but as a Man he has done with it forever. . . . he has really *no* opinion of his talents in that way and has *now* no pleasure in the employment. Now the plain English of all this is that he is really discouraged and depressed, and that this *odious* Review has *convinced* him that he really has *no* Talents. . . . God help him if he is so easily discouraged he will neither be a statesman or an Orator, in short he will do no good." [n]

But Byron's discouragement was soon overcome when he found outlet for his wrath in rhyme. Some friend coming in after he had read the review, seeing his perturbation, asked: "Have you received a challenge?" After he had written twenty lines of his satire he felt better, and when he added a few more lines he was

[7] *LJ*, II, 330. Journal entry of Nov. 22, 1813. But Medwin quoted Byron as saying that after he had drunk the three bottles of claret to drown his rage, "it only boiled the more." (Medwin, I, 174.)

better still.[n] "I remembered only the maxim of my boxing-master," he recalled, "which, in my youth, was found useful in all general riots,—'Whoever is not for you is against you—*mill* away right and left,' and so I did. . . ."[n]

How much the mortification caused by the review contributed to the physical indulgence that had debilitated Byron it is impossible to say, but within the next two weeks he seems to have endangered his health seriously and yet not to have given up his allegiance to Venus. On March 14 Byron wrote Hobhouse in a vein of lightness that was the convention of their set: "The *Game* is almost up. For these last five days I have been confined to my room, Laudanum is my sole support, and even Pearson wears a woeful visage as he prescribes. . . . on disclosing the mode of my life for these last two years (of which my residence at Cambridge constituted the most sober part), my Chirurgeon pronounced another quarter would have settled my earthly accounts, and left the worms but a scanty repast. I have given up the Casta, but I hope to live and re-establish Medmenham Abbey, or some similar temple of Venus, of which I shall be Pontifex Maximus. You have heard of one *nymph*. Rumour has been kind in this respect, for, alas! I must confess that *two* are my *property*—one under my own immediate custody, as the other will be also when I am recovered."[n]

One of these "nymphs" Byron had established in lodgings in the suburbs, possibly with the aid of John Jackson, the pugilist. Moore wrote: "An amour (if it may be dignified with such a name) of that sort of casual description which less attachable natures would have forgotten, and more prudent ones at least concealed, was by him converted, at this period, and with circumstances of most unnecessary display, into a connexion of some continuance,—the object of it not only becoming domesticated with him in lodgings at Brompton, but accompanying him afterwards, disguised in boy's clothes, to Brighton."[8] Medwin tells a similar story, quoting Byron as saying: "Another of the

[8] Moore, I, 147. A girl disguised as a page boy appears in Byron's *Lara*. The faithful Kaled (presumably the Corsair's last love, Gulnare) followed her master to exile and death. Whether she had any of the characteristics of the girl he took to Brighton it would be fruitless to speculate.

wild freaks I played during my mother's life-time, was to dress up Mrs. . . . . , and to pass her off as my brother Gordon, in order that my mother might not hear of my having such a female acquaintance." [n] An episode that Moore recorded in his notes may concern the arrangement of the establishment at Brompton: "Wildman's account of [Miss?] Cameron at Madame D——s [a note says the name is illegible in Moore's MS.]; the first night B. saw her; his going away with her; redeemed her from D—— for 100 guineas. Breakfasted with B. afterwards out at —— [Brompton?]. The separate beds B. *always* had with women. 'Tell Miss Cameron to come down.' Wildman's surprise." [n]

A reviewer of Medwin, presumably someone who knew Byron well, corroborated part of the original account and added a rich bit of scandal: "The story of keeping a girl in boy's clothes, and passing her for his cousin, lest his mother should hear of it, Lord Byron has had abundant cause to repent; but the affair itself had a most ludicrous conclusion, for the young gentleman miscarried in a certain family hotel in Bond Street, to the inexpressible horror of the chambermaids, and the consternation of all the house." [n]

It is quite possible that Byron, in a chivalric mood when he found that she was pregnant, told his friends that he would marry the girl, for some such rumor reached Hobhouse in Cambridge and greatly agitated him. It was more or less expected that a young lord should sow his wild oats before he came of age, but it was a much more serious matter for his friend to become so deeply involved with a girl of no rank or breeding, or, what was worse, with a demimonde character such as the sixteen-year-old Caroline. Hobhouse wrote anxiously: "The story of your engagement with Miss (I forget her name) is all over Cambridge. I did not much wonder at it considering your very long and painful continence, which might induce a more severe saint than yourself to be too frequent in the caresses of the first pretty girl which you chanced to light upon." [n]

Byron probably allayed his friend's fears about the rumored engagement, but he had not given up his favorite "nymph" when he wrote to Hobhouse on March 26: "I am still living with my

Dalilah, who has only two faults, unpardonable in a woman—she can read and write." Then he turned lightly to another matter. "Greet in my name the bilious Birdmore [Davies, who was a fellow of King's College]. . . . The university still chew the Cud of my degree. Please God they shall swallow it, though Inflammation be the consequence. I am leading a quiet though debauched life."[9] Byron was aware that he had small claim to the degree, but he coveted it nevertheless. The rules called for residence at Cambridge for nine terms for the B.A., and he had actually spent only three full terms and a very small part of two others at Trinity, but he was counting on the usual laxness in applying the rules to the nobility.

Toward the end of March he had received copies of his new volume, *Poems Original and Translated.* The contents were even soberer than those of the previous edition. The Preface and all the lighter pieces had been removed, and the five that were added strengthened the impression of nostalgic regret for a boyhood that was gone. The verses beginning "I would I were a careless child" expressed the feelings that swept over him frequently in these months, the reaction to his overstrained pleasures, the secret dissatisfactions and longings that were covered up in the buffoonery of his letters. The greater his disenchantments, the more pathetically he clung to the dreams of his youth.

Since the appearance of the caustic criticism in the *Edinburgh Review* Byron had lost his eagerness to distribute his poems, except to a few sympathetic friends. He sent a copy to Becher, who had seen them through the press, at the same time pretending to be unaffected by the review of the earlier volume: "For my own part, these 'paper bullets of the brain' have only taught me to stand fire . . . my repose and appetite are not discomposed. . . . I think *I* could write a more sarcastic critique on *myself* than any yet published."[n]

Keeping up his jaunty air, he continued: "I am residing with

[9] *B-SP,* I, 40–1. He began this letter: "I have sent Fletcher to Cambridge for various purposes, and he has this *dispatch* for you." This seems to be Byron's first mention of the valet who was to serve him until his death in 1824. William Fletcher had been one of the tenants at Newstead. It may be that Byron took him into his service in 1806 or 1807 when he dismissed Francis Boyce (Frank).

a nymph who is now on the sofa *vis-à-vis* while I am scribbling. I have three females (attendants included) in my custody. They accompany me of course." *n* His health was improved, but his financial situation was hopeless. "*Entre nous,* I am cursedly dipped; my debts, *every* thing inclusive, will be nine or ten thousand before I am twenty-one. . . . Newstead I may *sell;* —perhaps I will not. . . ." *n* Already he was thinking of going down to Newstead in May or June as soon as Lord Grey should leave.

Hobhouse was relieved that Byron was dividing his attentions and would probably not allow himself to be drawn into an unequal marriage, but was again disturbed by the low company he kept. In April, Byron, who had become a familiar of pugilists through "Gentleman" Jackson, arranged a match near the Rubbing House on Epsom Downs between the popular little boxer Tom Belcher and the Irish champion Dan Dogherty, whom he backed. Dogherty was beaten.*n* And on May 10 Byron accompanied another pugilist, Tom Cribb, to a fight between John Gully, champion of England from 1805 to 1808, and Bob Gregson in Sir John Sebright's park in Hertfordshire.[1]

Continuing his inquiries about Byron's London life, Hobhouse asked: "How go you on with your misses two? . . . I believe we are both pretty well agreed as to the matter of matrimony. You will never after all you have said be a Benedict, and as for myself I find my hatred and disgust of that sex . . . every day increasing. You must for certain either have a whore or a termagant. . . ." *n*

Byron was in perfect agreement. He would not make the sacrifice even for an heir. If Augusta had a son, he wrote her, "I will make him my *heir,* for I shall never marry, unless I am ruined, and then his *inheritance* would not be great." *n* During this year Byron made a wager of a hundred guineas with John Hay that he would never marry.[2]

[1] Second letter on the Bowles controversy, *LJ*, V, 579–80. Byron had a taste for low company which continued throughout his life. It was one trait remarked by his schoolfellow Robert Peel. (Moore: *Memoirs,* II, 684.)

[2] A Mr. M. Hawley wrote Byron on January 17, 1815, just after his marriage to Annabella Milbanke, to congratulate him and remind him of his bet

When summer came on, Byron broke the routine of his London life. He had not undergone any moral reformation, but had simply tired of his harem and his other amusements. His renunciation of gambling was probably prompted by the realization that he could not afford it, for he found it exhilarating. In his "Detached Thoughts" he wrote:

"I have a notion that Gamblers are as happy as most people, being always *excited*. Women, wine, fame, the table, even Ambition, *sate* now and then; but every turn of the card, and cast of the dice, keeps the Gamester alive: besides one can Game ten times longer than one can do any thing else.

"I was very fond of it when young, that is to say, of 'Hazard'; for I hate all *Card* Games, even Faro. . . . Upon the whole, I left off in time without being much a winner or loser. Since one and twenty years of age, I played but little, and then never above a hundred or two, or three." [3]

On June 16, Byron left for Brighton, where he was later joined by Hobhouse and Scrope Davies. Except for excursions to Harrow and Cambridge, he spent most of the summer there. The chief

with John Hay in 1808. (Murray MSS.) The bet, which was made while Byron was at Brighton in the summer, was in the nature of a forfeit, the agreement being that he would take a guinea and repay fifty guineas. (There was some dispute as to whether the sum mentioned was fifty or a hundred guineas.)

[3] *LJ*, V, 425. Byron's friend Scrope Davies, though he was several times cleaned out at the gaming-table, did not quit playing until he was completely ruined. It may be significant that Byron and Davies called on Mrs. Massingberd on May 12 (unpublished letter of Byron to Mrs. M., Byron Exhibition Catalogue, Feb. 1915, Nottingham Mechanics Institution), possibly to put Davies in touch with moneylenders. But Davies had uncommon luck at times. "One night," Byron recorded in his "Detached Thoughts" (*LJ*, V, 447), "Scrope Davies at a gaming house (before I was of age), being tipsy as he usually was at the Midnight hour, and having lost monies, was in vain intreated by his friends, one degree less intoxicated than himself, to come or go home. In despair, he was left to himself, and to the demons of the dice-box. Next day, being visited, about two of the Clock, by some friends just risen with a severe headache and empty pockets (who had left him losing at four or five in the morning), he was found in a sound sleep, without a night-cap, and not particularly encumbered with bed-cloathes: a Chamber-pot stood by his bed-side, *brim-full* of—*Bank Notes!* all won, God knows how, and crammed, Scrope knew not where; but *there* they were, all good legitimate notes, and to the amount of some thousand pounds."

attraction was the sea bathing, of which Byron was extravagantly fond, and in which, as in everything else, he indulged to excess.

At the beginning of July, Byron went down to Cambridge to take his degree, which was granted on the 4th. Writing to William Harness later, he said: "*Alma Mater* was to me *injusta noverca;* and the old beldam only gave me my M.A. degree because she could not avoid it.—You know what a farce a noble Cantab. must perform." [n]

While at Cambridge he was roused again by the attacks of Hewson Clarke in *The Satirist.* In May, Clarke had printed quotations from numerous reviews of *Hours of Idleness,* including some of the most caustic things said by the *Eclectic,* the *Monthly Mirror,* and the *Edinburgh Review.*[n] He followed this up in the June number with the ridiculing verses, "Lord B——n to his Bear," which apparently Byron first saw at Cambridge. Flaring up, he wrote a challenging note to Clarke: "Report universally attributes to your pen, passages in the 'Satirist' of this and last month, alluding to me in so marked and unjustifiable a manner, that I can no longer delay requiring an explanation. I shall expect (if you are not the author,) an immediate and unequivocal disavowal. In case this proposal should not meet your approbation, my friend Mr. Hobhouse is instructed how to act." [n] It is probable that Byron again either calmed down or was persuaded by Hobhouse not to send the note, for there is no record of the two satirists coming within pistol shot of each other.[n] But Clarke had not ended his taunts. In the August number of *The Satirist* he reviewed *Poems Original and Translated:* "This pretty little collection of namby-pamby verses. . . . but stay, ladies, 'tis a truly harmless Lord, now—he is without his Bear, and is himself muzzled." [n]

This episode, together with his uncertain health and the aftermath of his affairs with women in London, caused Byron to sink into a fit of depression. He wrote in the back of a volume of Pliny which he had picked up at Cambridge: "I have been perpetually troubled with sickness of late—which has made me so melancholy that the immortality of the soul has been my constant speculation—as the mortality of the body my constant plague.—In good earnest—Seneca is nothing to a fit of illness." [n]

But Hobhouse knew that the cause was deeper. He had already tried to warn him in prose and verse to avoid entanglements with women, and now he saw that Byron had been rescued from the sirens only to be cast on the rocks of his own despair. It may have been with a view to getting him out of London and curing him of his despondency that Hobhouse and Davies accompanied Byron to Brighton after he had taken his degree and had attended another Speech Day at Harrow. There, with fierce plunges in the sea, the writing of disconsolate verses to his lost love,[4] and occasional orgies of drinking, he spent July and August.[n]

The girl he had kept at Brompton Byron took with him to Brighton. "He introduced this young person, who used to ride about with him in male attire, as his younger brother," Moore said; "and the late Lady P** [Perceval],[n] who was at Brighton at the time, and had some suspicion of the real nature of the relationship, said one day to the poet's companion, 'What a pretty horse that is you are riding!'—'Yes,' answered the pretended cavalier, 'it was *gave* me by my brother!'"[5]

John Jackson, the "Professor of Pugilism," as Byron called him in a note to *Don Juan* (XI, 19), "my old friend and corporeal pastor and master," visited him frequently at Brighton during the summer, "the expense of the professor's chaise thither and back being always defrayed by his noble patron."[n] Hobhouse annoyed Byron greatly by writing a lampoon on his association with the boxer.[n] Byron when genuinely attached to someone was less given to snobbishness than were some of his friends. He also,

[4] That he was emotionally involved with one London inamorata, possibly the blue-eyed Caroline, is indicated by the poem "There was a time, I need not name," dated "June 10, 1808," the burden of which is that she has been unfaithful to him but that it is "doubly sweet to find/ Remembrance of that love remain." The whole tone is romantic and melancholy rather than flippant or bitter.

[5] Moore, I, 147. Captain Gronow (*Reminiscences,* I, 152–3) says: "He [Byron] was fond of boating, and was generally accompanied by a lad, who was said to be a girl in boy's clothes. This report was confirmed to me by [Wedderburn] Webster, who was then living at Brighton. . . . I myself witnessed the dexterous manner in which Byron used to get into his boat; for, while standing on the beach, I once saw him vault into it with the agility of a harlequin, in spite of his lame foot."

probably with somewhat different motives, interested himself in a boy by the name of John Cowell, a tradesman's son at Brighton, and later used his influence to have him admitted to Eton.

Byron was planning to return to Newstead now that Lord Grey had left (his lease expired on June 24). His reply to Grey, who had written concerning some matters of property and servants, indicates that his feeling toward him had not changed: "Your Lordship must be perfectly aware of the very peculiar reasons that induced me to adopt a line of conduct which however painful, and painful to me it certainly was, became unavoidable." [n] But, he added, in grateful recognition of favors conferred on him as a boy he would be glad to meet him as a friend.

Two melancholy poems written in August reveal a depth of attachment for one of his "nymphs" not seen in Byron's letters about her. One asked "And wilt thou weep when I am low," and the other expressed with even greater poignancy the sense of loss:

*Remind me not, remind me not,*
*Of those beloved, those vanish'd hours,*
*When all my soul was given to thee. . . .*

*Can I forget—canst thou forget,*
*When playing with thy golden hair,*
*How quick thy fluttering heart did move?* [n]

Early in September, Byron was back at Newstead, making repairs and preparing to welcome some of his friends. Although Lord Grey had taken little care of the park or the lakes, Byron fell in love with the Abbey all over again. He still lacked some months of achieving his majority, but the expansive halls and grounds gave him again the sense of being lord of a manor, and his tentative thoughts of selling Newstead he soon strenuously rejected.[n] He was already dreaming of entertaining as lavishly as his ancestors had done. Hobhouse had come, and they were planning amusements.

Byron had invited Henry Drury and, through him, Hodgson, who could not come because of his duties at Cambridge, but who sent a rhyming reply. He also extended an invitation for a later time to "Gentleman" Jackson, but for the time being the house was "filled with workmen, and undergoing a thorough repair." [n] He could also use that as an excuse to keep his mother from coming over from Southwell, which she was eager to do, for she too liked to contemplate being mistress of an estate and still had visions of being Byron's housekeeper when he came of age. He had quite other notions. "When my rooms are ready I shall be glad to see you," he wrote grandly; "at present it would be improper, and uncomfortable to both parties. You can hardly object to my rendering my mansion habitable, notwithstanding my departure for Persia in March (or May at farthest), since *you* will be *tenant* till my return; and in case of any accident . . . I have taken care you shall have the house and manor for *life*, besides a sufficient income. So you see my improvements are not entirely selfish." [n]

That Eastern voyage, which he had conceived back in January, was very much in his mind throughout the autumn. He felt that somehow the obstacles to it would be removed once he reached his majority. In the meantime he would round out his satire to pay off his critics before he left England. Hobhouse remained with him at Newstead, where they found sufficient amusements while the repairs were going on, and occasionally they patronized balls and masquerades in Nottingham. On October 12 they went to the Infirmary Ball, and later Byron sent to D'Egville in London for a pattern for a Turkish masquerade costume, which he had Nottingham tailors make of lavish materials. The "Rich Masquerade Jacket and Trimmings," the "Full Trimmed Turban," and other fittings increased his already large tailor's bill by £11. 9*s*. 6*d*.[n]

Though he could afford to fit up only a few rooms at Newstead, he spared no expense on them. To his mother, who was fretting about the cost of the refurbishing, he wrote that he would establish her in it before he sailed for India, "which I expect to do in March, if nothing particularly obstructive occurs. I am now fitting up the *green* drawing-room; the red for a bedroom, and the rooms over as sleeping-rooms. They will be soon completed;—at least I hope so. I have paid Barnet 182 pounds, his whole Bill, I think a *large* one." [n] Of his Eastern tour he wrote: "After all, you must own my project is not a bad one. If I do not travel now, I never shall, and all men should one day or other. . . . If we see no nation but our own, we do not give mankind a fair chance. . . ." [n]

Old Joe Murray, who had been the chief servant of the "Wicked Lord" and whom he had granted a small pension, Byron installed as head of his domestic retainers. The others included William Fletcher, his valet, and Robert Rushton, a handsome boy, son of a neighboring farmer, to whom Byron had taken a great fancy. Byron's favorite dog, Boatswain, and the tame bear he had kept at Cambridge were now at the Abbey. Byron and Hobhouse enjoyed the lordly independence of their life in the decayed baronial mansion. They bathed in the lake and rode through the spacious park. "Hobhouse hunts, etc.," Byron wrote Hodgson, "and I do nothing." [n] But he was not idle, for he was constantly adding to his satire. He asked Hodgson to try to find him a copy of Gifford's *Epistle to Peter Pindar*. Gifford's *Baviad* and *Mæviad* were the models he most admired after Pope.

Riding about the estate brought sentimental thoughts of his innocent and romantic youth, so short a time gone and so irrevocably lost, when he had ridden daily to Annesley. When Mary Chaworth, now Mrs. Musters, heard he was at Newstead, she invited him and his guest to dinner at the Hall which had such poignant memories for him. He steeled himself for the ordeal, and might have maintained the nonchalance he assumed for the occasion had not Mary brought her two-year-old daughter into the room. He could not confess such sentimental weaknesses to Hobhouse, who had forsworn the romantic passions and might laugh at him, but a couple of days later he unburdened himself to Hodgson. The other day, he said, "I was seated near a woman, to whom, when a boy, I was as much attached as boys generally are, and more than a man should be. I knew this before I went, and was determined to be valiant, and converse with *sang froid;* but instead I forgot my valour and my nonchalance, and never opened my lips even to laugh, far less to speak, and the lady was almost as absurd as myself, which made both the object of more observation than if we had conducted ourselves with easy indifference. . . . What fools we are! We cry for a plaything, which, like children, we are never satisfied with till we break open, though like them we cannot get rid of it by putting it in the fire." [n] But Hobhouse saw nothing of this, and Byron, to forestall his scoffing, passed the whole matter off lightly and spoke of the Musters marriage with a kind of bitter ribaldry. "Byron told me many particulars of this marriage," Hobhouse wrote later, "something of them very ridiculous which at that time he narrated without the slightest appearance of regret or feeling of any kind." [n]

But in the silence of the Abbey, Byron confided to paper his emotional disturbance and the chagrin of the experience. "Well! thou art happy, and I feel/ That I should thus be happy too," he began. But he confessed:

*I deem'd that Time, I deem'd that Pride,*
*Had quench'd at length my boyish flame;*
*Nor knew, till seated by thy side,*
*My heart in all,—save hope,—the same.*

And so he must cast out the dream in the "sullen calmness of despair." [n] But that revived image was to haunt him for many a year.

Byron's depression was increased by another disturbing experience. Boatswain, the great Newfoundland dog with whom he had romped so often, and who had won his affection more completely than any of his other quadrupeds, went mad and died before his eyes. At the beginning of his fit, Moore says, "so little aware was Lord Byron of the nature of the malady, that he, more than once, with his bare hand, wiped away the slaver from the dog's lips during the paroxysms." [n]

"Boatswain is dead!" Byron wrote to Hodgson on November 18, "he expired in a state of madness on the 10th after suffering much, yet retaining all the gentleness of his nature to the last, never attempting to do the least injury to any one near him." And in a burst of self-pity he added: "I have now lost every thing except Old Murray." [n]

Nursing his grief until it was confounded with all his other disappointments and turned to misanthropy, Byron wrote an epitaph in verse intended to be placed on Boatswain's tomb:

*But the poor dog, in life the firmest friend,*
*The first to welcome, foremost to defend. . . .*
*Unhonour'd falls, unnoticed all his worth. . . .*

He ended with a couplet that Hobhouse, who thought the whole thing silly, knew to be particularly untrue:

*To mark a Friend's remains these stones arise;*
*I knew but one unchang'd—and here he lies.*[6]

When he showed the verses to Hobhouse, that staunch friend altered the ending to "here *I* lies."[n] As a joke he contributed a prose introduction (commonly thought to be Byron's own) in the same spirit: "Near this spot/ Are deposited the Remains of one/ Who possessed Beauty without Vanity,/ Strength without Insolence,/ Courage without Ferocity,/ And all the Virtues of Man without his Vices./ This Praise, which would be unmeaning Flattery/ If inscribed over human ashes,/ Is but a just tribute to the Memory of BOATSWAIN, a Dog. . . ."[n]

Now Byron was more eager than ever to leave England. He had written to no less a person than the Duke of Portland, "as head of his Majesty's Government," to procure him permission to pass through the territories of the East India Company. The Duke's reply Byron thought a little curt,[n] but it did not stop him from making further applications to members of the government. And then he must persuade Hanson of the wisdom of his voyage. "In the first place," he wrote, "I wish to study India and Asiatic policy and manners. I am young, tolerably vigorous, abstemious in my way of living; I have no pleasure in fashionable dissipation, and I am determined to take a wider field than is customary

[6] *Poetry,* I, 281. Byron later altered the last line to read: "I never knew but one,—and here he lies." He had intended to erect the tomb with the inscription on the spot where the altar had been in the ruined Abbey church, but it was eventually put in the garden. He would reserve a place for himself in the tomb. Byron no doubt felt strongly the loss of the dog, but the eulogy at the expense of human folly and wickedness was a common eighteenth-century convention which he could have borrowed from his idolized Pope.

with travellers. If I return, my judgment will be more mature, and I shall still be young enough for politics. . . . A voyage to India will take me six months, and if I had a dozen attendants cannot cost me five hundred pounds; and you will agree with me that a like term of months in England would lead me into four times that expenditure." [n]

Indeed, Hanson had seen enough of Byron's ways to convince him easily of the truth of the latter statement. But Byron's next proposal probably appalled him. "You honour my debts; they amount to perhaps twelve thousand pounds, and I shall require perhaps three or four thousand at setting out, with credit on a Bengal agent. This you must manage for me. If my resources are not adequate to the supply I must *sell*, but *not Newstead*. . . . My debts must be paid, if possible, in February." [n] Byron still had hopes of realizing some cash from the sale of the Rochdale estate as soon as he was of age and it was freed from the legal tangle.

He had another reason for going abroad, or so he told himself. Mary Chaworth-Musters had asked him why he was quitting England in the spring. He committed his reply to verses, which he sent off to Hodgson, since "Hobhouse hates everything of the kind":

*In flight I shall be surely wise,*
*Escaping from temptation's snare;*
*I cannot view my Paradise*
*Without the wish of dwelling there.*[n]

He was flattered by Hodgson's admiration of his poems. There had been a mutiny of the pupils at Harrow, where the boys threw stones at Butler and blocked the roadway from London so that there could be no interference from parents. Several boys were expelled, including Byron's friend Wingfield. Henry Drury had facetiously suggested, Hodgson said, that the reading of Byron's poems had caused the insurrection.[n] "If my songs have produced the glorious effects you mention," Byron replied, "I shall be a complete Tyrtæus, though I am sorry to say I resemble that interesting Harper, more in his person, than Poesy." [n] This reference to the lame poet of Greek legend whose songs had

⁘ *BYRON IN HIS CAMBRIDGE ROBES. BELOW: BYRON IN 1807*

MRS. SPENCER SMITH

stimulated the courage of the Spartans in the field, though made with apparent lightness, indicated the extent to which the sensitivity to his deformity, developed as a child, lingered in his consciousness.

Toward the end of November Hobhouse left him, and other visitors had not appeared. In the loneliness of the Abbey, which he rather enjoyed, Byron cultivated his bitterness and continued working on the extension and revision of his satire. He was determined not to publish until he could make the poem, in the manner of Pope and Gifford, so polished and fortified in wit and sense as to be invulnerable to the shafts of critics.

Byron's mood was not brightened by news from Hanson that the Rochdale cause had been set back again and was likely to drag on interminably. "I suppose it will end in my marrying a *Golden Dolly* or blowing my brains out; it does not much matter which, the remedies are nearly alike,"[n] he wrote Hanson with exasperated humor.

When the gardener brought him a human skull that had been unearthed, it suited his sardonic whim to have it made into a drinking-cup. As he touched up the account later, it was "a skull that had probably belonged to some jolly friar or monk of the abbey about the time it was dis-monasteried. . . . Observing it to be of giant size, and in a perfect state of preservation, a strange fancy seized me of having it set and mounted as a drinking-cup. I accordingly sent it to town, and it returned with a very high polish, and of a mottle colour like tortoiseshell. . . ."[7] It was set in heavy silver resting on four balls; the jeweller's bill—which did not worry Byron, for he had many larger—was £17. 17*s.*[n]

The event was worthy of a poem, "Lines Inscribed upon a Cup Formed from a Skull":

[7] Medwin, I, 71–2. Nanny Smith, the housekeeper at the Abbey, told Washington Irving that Byron "took a notion that there was a deal of money buried about the Abbey by the monks in old times, and nothing would serve him but he must have the flagging taken up in the cloisters." They found nothing but coffins filled with bones. One of the coffins he had put in one end of the great hall. "Several of the skulls were cleaned and put in frames in his room." (Irving: *Newstead Abbey,* p. 78.)

*Start not—nor deem my spirit fled:*
*In me behold the only skull,*
*From which, unlike a living head,*
*Whatever flows is never dull.*[n]

In his loneliness Byron felt the need for a dog. The death of Boatswain had left a great void. The bear was affectionate in his rough way; he used to stand up on his hind legs and lick old Murray's face,[n] a demonstration that the dignified old servant probably did not appreciate. On December 12 Byron wrote to "Gentleman" Jackson, who was a familiar of the sporting world: "You will get the greyhound from the owner at any price, and as many more of the same breed (male or female) as you can collect." [n] He had invited several friends for the Christmas holidays, including such disparate characters as Jackson and Hodgson, but none of them could come and he was left alone with his misanthropic meditations.

After the holiday he began to think of going up to London. His solitary life had become boring to him, and he had important business to tend to. The Rochdale affair had come to a standstill and there seemed no way to satisfy his creditors, who were pressing upon him now that he was approaching his majority. Mrs. Massingberd, hounded by the moneylenders, was worrying Byron, and he passed the unpleasant task of appeasing her and them on to Hanson.[n] The solicitor was disappointed that Byron would not accept his invitation to dine at Chancery Lane on his birthday, which he intended to make a gala occasion. Byron preferred to spend the day according to his own whims and moods in London, but he asked Hanson to represent him at Newstead, where the tenants were preparing a manorial fête for the occasion. "You will be extremely welcome here and your presence will preserve order in my absence, the tenants are to have a good dinner and plenty of Ale & Punch, and the *Rabble* will have an Ox and two Sheep to tear in pieces, with *Ale,* and *Uproar.*" [n]

Another reason for going up to town was to take his seat in the House of Lords. His political notions were still rather vague, but he was determined to maintain his independence in the political muddle and sit with neither party, though he would generally favor the Whig opposition. "I shall take my seat as soon as circumstances will admit," he told Hanson. "I shall stand aloof, speak what I think, but not often, nor too soon." [n]

Poor Mrs. Byron, who was as easily cajoled by her son as she had been by her husband, the irresistible "Mad Jack," also had great expectations for Byron's career as a statesman and looked for extraordinary exploits from him when he came of age. To Hanson she wrote: "My son I am happy to say behaves very well to me, his Heart is good and his *Talents* are *great* and I have *no* doubt of his being a great Man, God grant that he may be a prudent and happy one also." [n] Byron had just allowed her to draw £50 on his account and was preparing to leave Newstead in her care during his foreign tour—he could always get along with her better from a distance, and would do anything to keep her there. As the time approached for his departure, Byron was in good spirits again. Announcing that he would be at Reddish's Hotel in St. James's Street on January 19, he confided to Hobhouse his intention of publishing his satire, which had now grown to 624 lines.[n]

Before Byron left for London he revealed to Hanson in a casual sentence that he had not been entirely without feminine consolation at Newstead. Giving orders for the disposal of his household, he wrote: "You will discharge my Cook, & Laundry Maid, the other two I shall retain to take care of the house, more especially as the youngest is pregnant (I need not tell you by whom) and I cannot have the girl on the parish." [8] This rather astonishing news was buried in a letter complaining of the exorbitant charges of the Nottingham silversmith and the advisability of raising the Newstead rents.

But Byron was never as callous in his human relationships as his letters sometimes suggested. Although he was obviously not in love with the girl and did not pretend to be, he had made a provision for her beyond what was considered, in the code of the

[8] Unpublished letter of Jan. 17, 1809, Houghton Library, Harvard University. On the 16th Byron had written to Hobhouse that nothing of moment had occurred, "except that Lucinda is pregnant [the servant girl's name was Lucy], and Robert has recovered of the cow-pox, with which it pleased me to afflict him." (Unpublished passage, from original letter, Murray MSS.; Hobhouse proof.)

time, just and adequate when a young lord got a servant girl into trouble. He had stipulated an annuity of £100 for her. But on February 4 he requested Hanson to make an alteration in his will; Lucy's annuity was to be reduced to £50 and the other £50 was to go to the bastard.[9]

Byron's first concerns when he reached London were to get his satire published and to take his seat with appropriate dignity at the coming session of Parliament. He dispatched a letter to Dallas, who knew something of the mysteries of publishing, and another to the Earl of Carlisle, who could save him the trouble of presenting credentials by introducing him in the House as a near relation. Dallas called on him Sunday morning. "It was his birthday, (January 22d, 1809,) and that on which he came of age. He was in high spirits; indeed, so high as to seem to me more flippant on the subject of religion, and on some others, than he had ever

[9] Letter of Byron to Hanson, Murray MSS. What became of the child if it lived is not known. This incident might, if Moore misread Byron's date on the manuscript as 1807 instead of 1809, explain the mystery of the poem "To My Son!" (Moore, I, 104), in which Byron said of the mother:

*Her lowly grave the turf has prest,*
*And thou hast known a stranger's breast. . . .*

As was Byron's custom, he allowed himself more sentiment in verse than in his letters:

*Why, let the world unfeeling frown,*
*Must I fond Nature's claim disown?*
*Ah, no—though moralists reprove,*
*I hail thee, dearest child of love. . . .*

He referred to this youthful *faux pas* more lightly in *Don Juan* (XVI, 61). After speaking of a pregnant country girl in a scarlet cloak, he added parenthetically: "I hate the sight to see, since—/ Since—since—in youth, I had the sad mishap—/ But luckily I have paid few parish fees since." Writing to Moore from Italy in 1818, Byron said: "Besides my little legitimate, I have made unto myself an *il*-legitimate since (to say nothing of one before). . . ." (*LJ, IV*, 196. Letter of Feb. 2, 1818.) According to E. H. Coleridge, "He [Byron] told Lady Byron that he had two natural children, whom he should provide for." (*Poetry*, I, 260n.) The gossiping housekeeper at Newstead, Nanny Smith, later told Washington Irving that Byron "had with him a beautiful boy as a page, which the housemaids said was a girl." The servant girls were very jealous; "one of them, in particular, took the matter in great dudgeon. Her name was Lucy; she was a great favourite with Lord Byron, and had been much noticed by him, and began to have high notions . . . . the poor thing dreamt of nothing less than becoming a lady, and mistress of the Abbey . . . . she is now married, and keeps a public-house at Warwick." (Irving: *Newstead Abbey*, p. 78.)

appeared before." But he was so deferential and good-mannered that Dallas was flattered by his attention and told himself that "by adopting forbearance, I might do him some service in an occasional argument or sentiment." Before the interview ended, Byron put his satire into the hands of Dallas, who was "surprised and charmed with the nerve it evinced." [n]

After he had looked over the manuscript, Dallas wrote Byron in a fawning but officious style: "I have read your Satire with infinite pleasure, and were you sufficiently acquainted with my mind to be certain that it cannot stoop to flattery, I would tell you that it rivals the Baviad and Mæviad. . . ." But then he proposed changing the title, which was still "The British Bards" to "The Parish Poor of Parnassus" and recommended a number of alterations to accord with his preferences and prejudices. At the same time he sent two dozen lines of his own to be inserted. Dallas feared that Byron's lines on Lord Carlisle would betray the author, who wished to remain anonymous.[n]

In anticipation of favors from his guardian, Byron had written

*On one alone Apollo deigns to smile,*
*And crowns a new Roscommon in Carlisle.*

In his reply to Dallas he sent a substitution designed to conceal his authorship:

*Nor e'en a hackney'd Muse will deign to smile*
*On minor Byron, nor mature Carlisle.*

But he politely turned down Dallas's own contribution. "My only reason for not adopting your lines is because they are *your* lines. . . . I am determined it shall be all my own, except such alterations as may be absolutely required. . . ." [1] He said nothing about Hobhouse's cleverer lines on Bowles, which he allowed to

[1] *LJ*, I, 211. Letter of Jan. 25, 1809. Dallas may have been responsible for some excisions of Popean coarseness. Crossed out in the proof sheets of "British Bards" is a line referring to "Cloacina's holy pontiff, Lambe," and also deleted is the accompanying note: "We have heard of persons, 'who when the Bagpipe sings in the nose, cannot contain their urine for affection,' but Mr. L. carries it a step further than Shakespeare's diuretic amateurs, being notorious at school and College for his inability to contain anything." (Eg. 2028, ff. 20, 22.)

stand. The title he now suggested was the one that stood in the final printing: *English Bards and Scotch Reviewers.*

In the meantime, Byron was consumed with chagrin by the cold reply he received from Lord Carlisle, who merely informed him of the technical procedure for entering the House, but did not offer to introduce him. "Extremely nettled, he determined to lash his relation with all the gall he could throw into satire," Dallas recorded.[n] And after Byron had reflected on his injuries he added some sharper lines on Lord Carlisle:

*Lord, rhymester, petit-maître, pamphleteer!*
*So dull in youth, so drivelling in his age,*
*His scenes alone had damned our sinking stage.*[2]

Deeply mortified that he was forced by the Earl's snub to go through the formalities of proving his legitimacy to the Chancellor before he could take his seat, something that rarely happened to a young lord, he had Hanson digging up records of the creation of the Barony and sending clerks to Cornwall for family birth records.[n]

In the meantime, Byron was preparing himself for his career in Parliament by reading political memoirs and histories. His bill at the bookseller's went up rapidly. In January and February he purchased such heavy works as Holinshead's *Chronicles, The Memoirs of Grammont,* Cobbett's *Debates* (11 vols.), Cobbett's *Parliamentary History* (4 vols.), and forty-five volumes of the *British Essayists,* in addition to the lighter reading in *Cælebs in Search of a Wife* and *Poetry of the Antijacobin.*[n]

Byron's extravagance in the face of his increasing debts continued to make his mother uneasy. And Byron in London was constantly plagued with creditors. "I am *dunned* from Morn till

[2] In the second edition, published while he was abroad, he added a couplet even more bitter and personal:

*No Muse will cheer with renovating smile*
*The paralytic puling of* CARLISLE.

This remained in successive editions. When it was later called to his attention that the Earl suffered from a nervous disorder, to which this might seem a reference, Byron's comment was "I thank Heaven I did not know it —and would not, could not, if I had. I must naturally be the last person to be pointed on defects or maladies." (*LJ,* II, 331. Journal of Nov. 22, 1813.)

Twilight," he wrote Hanson on February 8, "money I must have or quit the country, and if I do not obtain my seat immediately, I shall sail with Ld. Falkland in the Dervise Frigate for Sicily. ——I have a considerable sum to pay tomorrow morning and not five pounds. . . ." He would not sell Newstead "let my *embarrassments* be what they may! but I would willingly relinquish my Rochdale claims to be out of debt." [n]

On March 4, Mrs. Byron wrote to Hanson again: "I have had a very dismal letter from my son, informing me that he is *ruined.* He wishes to borrow my money. This I shall be very ready to oblige him in, on such security as you approve. As it is my *all,* this is very necessary, and I am sure he would not wish to have it on any other terms. . . . I wish to God he would exert himself and retrieve his affairs. He must marry a Woman of *fortune* this spring; love matches is all nonsense. Let him make use of the Talents God has given him. He is an English Peer, and has all the privileges of that situation." [n]

Through February, pending the delays before he could take his seat, Byron continued to send Dallas corrections and alterations for *English Bards and Scotch Reviewers.* On the 16th he wrote: "Print soon, or I shall overflow with more rhyme." Dallas had taken the manuscript first to his own publisher, Longman, who, he said, "declined publishing it in consequence of its asperity." [3] He finally settled with James Cawthorn to bring out an edition of a thousand copies, which Byron thought too many. Some advance copies were ready by the first of March, when Byron presented one to Scrope Davies.[n] But even while it was going through the press he made changes and additions. Dallas came to see him daily and frequently carried away new lines to be inserted.

One morning when he called, Byron was much distracted by the death of his friend Lord Falkland, killed in a duel the night before. He was chiefly disturbed that he could not do more for the

[3] *LJ,* I, 214; Dallas: *Recollections,* p. 20. Dallas was not unrewarded for his labors. In addition to various gifts of several hundred pounds, Byron presented him with the copyrights of *Childe Harold* (cantos one and two) and the *Corsair,* worth in all more than a thousand pounds. (*Westminster Review,* Vol. III [Jan. 1825], p. 12.)

widow and four children. "I have been endeavouring to assist them," Byron wrote his mother a few days later, "which, God knows, I cannot do as I could wish, for my own embarrassments and the many claims upon me from other quarters." [n] When a posthumous child was born to Lady Falkland, Byron stood godfather, and before he went abroad, putting himself still further into debt to do so, he inserted £500 in a breakfast cup at Lady Falkland's so that it would not be discovered until he had left.[n]

Passing down St. James's Street on March 13, Dallas saw Byron's carriage at the door and went in. Byron was agitated and paler than usual. He said: "I am going to take my seat, perhaps you will go with me." They talked about the satire, the last sheets of which were in the press. Dallas accompanied him to the House of Lords. While they waited in an antechamber, one of the officers went to announce Byron's arrival to the Lord Chancellor. "There were very few persons in the House. Lord Eldon was going through some ordinary business. When Lord Byron entered, I thought he looked still paler than before; and he certainly wore a countenance in which mortification was mingled with, but subdued by, indignation. He passed the woolsack without looking round, and advanced to the table where the proper officer was attending to administer the oaths. When he had gone through them, the Chancellor quitted his seat, and went towards him with a smile, putting out his hand warmly to welcome him; and, though I did not catch his words, I saw that he paid him some compliment. This was all thrown away upon Lord Byron, who made a stiff bow, and put the tips of his fingers into a hand, the amiable offer of which demanded the whole of his. . . . The Chancellor did not press a welcome so received; but resumed his seat; while Lord Byron carelessly seated himself for a few minutes on one of the empty benches to the left of the throne, usually occupied by the Lords in opposition." When Dallas afterward reproached him for his coldness to the Chancellor, he said: "If I had shaken hands heartily, he would have set me down for one of his party—but I will have nothing to do with any of them, on either side; I have taken my seat, and now I will go abroad." [n] The humiliation of the manner in which he was introduced to the House rankled for many years. In his "Detached Thoughts" he wrote that after he had taken the oath "the Chancellor apologized to me for the delay, observing 'that these forms were a part of his *duty.*' I begged of him to make no apology, and added (as he certainly had shown no violent hurry) 'Your Lordship was exactly like "Tom Thumb" (which was then being acted), You did your *duty,* and you did *no more.*'" [n]

*English Bards and Scotch Reviewers* appeared a few days later. Byron sent a copy on the 18th to his old Harrow friend William Harness, then at Cambridge, with the stipulation that the author's name be kept secret, for he hoped to preserve his anonymity until he saw how the book was received. He was now collecting portraits of his favorite schoolfellows, and he asked Harness to pose for his picture to George Sanders, miniature-painter, at Byron's expense. Such a sentimental gesture might seem foolish now, he wrote, "but in a few years, when some of us are dead, and others are separated by inevitable circumstances, it will be a kind of satisfaction to retain in these images of the living the idea of our former selves, and, to contemplate, in the resemblances of the dead, all that remains of judgment, feeling, and a host of passions." [n] In going abroad Byron felt that he was cutting all his ties, and he clung to the Harrow associates, with whom his bonds were sentimental rather than intellectual.

His decision to collect mementos of his classmates was no doubt given impetus by the sad news of the death of Edward Noel Long, who had been closer to him in the subtleties of temperament and personality than most of his other friends. Long was drowned early in 1809 while proceeding to Lisbon with his regiment in the *St. George,* which collided with another ship in the night. Byron wrote that "Hobhouse laughed at my being distressed at Long's death, and amused himself with making epigrams upon his name. . . ." [4] When Long's father wrote to ask Byron to compose an epitaph for his son, he replied: "God knows! his death has been a heavy blow to me, but the expression of my

[4] *LJ,* V, 168–9. Hobhouse's comment in his copy of Moore was: "true in part but not true as to the inferences drawn." Hobhouse and Davies were inclined to make sport of what they considered Byron's melancholy posing. When Byron would say in a melodramatic manner: "I shall go mad," Scrope Davies used to remark quietly in a dry manner: "Much more like silliness than madness." (Hodgson, I, 104.)

own grief, would be a mockery of yours. . . . if I had been required to write an epitaph on a person totally indifferent to me, I should have succeeded better."[n] Nevertheless he promised, "but I had not the heart to complete it," he wrote later.[n]

A copy of *English Bards and Scotch Reviewers* had gone to Hodgson at Cambridge. "As to my satire, I defy the scribblers," Byron told him. But Hodgson had some misgivings. It is not surprising that the cautious and conventional Hodgson should have been somewhat frightened by this bold satire. With youthful brashness Byron had lashed out against almost all contemporary writers, who, compared with Pope or Dryden or his more immediate model, Gifford, were either "little wits" or "knaves and fools": "The cry is up, and scribblers are my game." Only those who followed the Popean model, like Rogers and Campbell, escaped his shaft. "Ballad-monger Southey" was damned for writing too much; Moore, whom Byron had read with avidity as a boy, was upbraided for the immorality of his lays; and Scott accused of writing "stale romance" for money. But despite the imitativeness of the poem, Byron's originality often transcended the limitations of his model. The rollicking mood of his later satires shone through when he wrote of

*That mild apostate from poetic rule,*
*The simple* Wordsworth . . .
*Who, both by precept and example, shows*
*That prose is verse, and verse is merely prose. . . .*
*Thus, when he tells the tale of Betty Foy,*
*The idiot mother of 'an idiot Boy;'*
*A moon-struck, silly lad, who lost his way,*
*And, like his bard, confounded night with day;*
*So close on each pathetic part he dwells,*
*And each adventure so sublimely tells,*
*That all who view the 'idiot in his glory'*
*Conceive the Bard the hero of the story.*

But he added a somewhat pedestrian section on the "Scotch Reviewer" Jeffrey in which he called on the famous hanging judge Jeffries to yield his rope to his namesake, "To wield in judgment, and at last to wear." And he returned to stereotyped phrases again when he called on Gifford to rise and scourge the fools and dull pretenders.

Feeling that he had evened the score with the reviewers, Byron was ready to go abroad. All he lacked was money, and Hanson would have to provide that. In the meantime he would make a farewell visit to his mother and to Newstead. For a last fling and a kind of final farewell to England, he had invited several friends to share his hospitality at the Abbey. Hodgson could not come, but some of Byron's most amusing intimates rode up from London, including Hobhouse, Matthews, Wedderburn Webster, and probably Scrope Davies. The stories of the unholy orgies carried on there, circulated generally in Byron's lifetime and later, grew out of what was actually little more than some spirited horseplay spurred on occasionally by drafts from Byron's stock of choice wines. Byron recalled: "We went down to Newstead together, where I had got a famous cellar, and *Monks'* dresses from a masquerade warehouse. We were a company of some seven or eight, with an occasional neighbour or so for visitors, and used to sit up late in our friars' dresses, drinking burgundy, claret, champagne, and what not, out of the *skull-cup*, and all sorts of glasses, and buffooning all round the house, in our conventual garments." [n] In this exalted foolery Matthews was one of the leaders.

That the party was amusing, but hardly a continual round of debauchery, is indicated in an account which Matthews wrote for his sister a short while after the visit. He started with a description of the Abbey as it then was: "Though sadly fallen to decay, it is still completely an *abbey*, and most part of it is still standing in the same state as when it was first built. There are two tiers of cloisters, with a variety of cells and rooms about them, which, though not inhabited, nor in an inhabitable state, might easily be made so; and many of the original rooms, amongst which is a fine stone hall, are still in use. Of the abbey church only one end remains; and the old kitchen, with a long range of apartments, is reduced to a heap of rubbish. Leading from the abbey to the modern part of the habitation is a noble room, seventy feet in length, and twenty-three in breadth; but every part of the house displays neglect and decay, save those which the present Lord has lately fitted up. . . . But if the place itself appear rather strange to you, the ways of the inhabitants will not appear much less so. Ascend, then, with me the hall steps, that I may introduce you to my Lord and his visitants. But have a care how you proceed. . . . For, should you make any blunder,—should you go to the right of the hall steps, you are laid hold of by a bear; and should you go to the left, your case is still worse, for you run full against a wolf! . . . Our average hour of rising was one. I, who generally got up between eleven and twelve, was always,—even when an invalid,—the first of the party, and was esteemed a prodigy of early rising. It was frequently past two before the breakfast party broke up. Then, for the amusements of the morning, there was reading, fencing, single-stick, or shuttle-cock, in the great room; practising with pistols in the hall; walking—riding—cricket—sailing on the lake, playing with the bear, or teasing the wolf. Between seven and eight we dined; and our evening lasted from that time till one, two, or three in the morning. The evening diversions may be easily conceived." [n]

As he passed down the Long Gallery one night on his way to his sleeping-quarters, Hobhouse saw a stone coffin from which he heard a groan proceeding. When he came near, a figure in a cowl rose from the coffin and blew out his candle. The ghost was Matthews.[n] As for "Paphian girls" singing and smiling in the Abbey, as Byron proclaimed to the world in *Childe Harold,* they must have been the servant girls whom he reserved for his pleasure when he was alone there, for Hobhouse was no ladies' man, though Matthews and others of the party might easily be imagined pursuing a kitchen maid down a long corridor.[5]

The "Haunted Chamber," the small dismal room adjoining

[5] In *Childe Harold* (I, 7) Byron drew a picture suggesting revelry at the Abbey:

> *Monastic dome! condemned to uses vile!*
> *Where Superstition once had made her den*
> *Now Paphian girls were known to sing and smile;*
> *And monks might deem their time was come agen,*
> *If ancient tales say true, nor wrong these holy men.*

But it is possible that Byron in the poem transferred his London harem of 1808 to Newstead.

Byron's bedroom on the top floor near the ruined church—the room in which various visitors to the Abbey were said to have seen a headless monk—was occupied by Robert Rushton, the handsome boy whom Byron had taken as a page. His feminine features may have led to the rumors that Byron kept a girl in boy's clothing at the Abbey.[n]

Byron would isolate himself to write sometimes, and Hobhouse was already busy with his volume of poems which he called his "Miscellany" (Matthews insisted on dubbing it—with justice, as it turned out—the "Miss-sell-any").[n] Byron was thinking of his voyage, and the dilatory Hanson still had procured him no money for it; he had only pointed out the obstacles to raising more while creditors were hounding him on every side. Byron wrote in desperation on April 16: "If the consequences of my leaving England were ten times as ruinous as you describe, I have no alternative, there are circumstances which render it absolutely indispensable, and quit the country I must immediately.—My passage is taken, and the 6th of May will be the day of my departure from Falmouth. I shall be in town on the 22d. of this month, and must raise money on any terms. . . ."[n] On the 19th he wrote again, asking Hanson to collect the £1,000 long overdue from the Duke of Portland.[n] And on the 22nd, still at Newstead, he had fastened his hope on a cash settlement out of court in the Rochdale lawsuit. On Hanson's sanguine assurance that such an event was imminent, he had given a draft to his stonemason for £264. And he was still threatening to go to the usurers if Hanson did not raise money by other means.[n]

In the meantime, Byron was cheered by the news that his satire was selling well and had been praised by the one man he wished most to please, William Gifford. Dallas wrote on April 17 that the publisher (Cawthorn) thought the edition would soon be sold out. He had made inquiries at Hatchard's, the Queen's Bookseller, and found that, "notwithstanding our precautions, you are pretty generally known to be the author.[n]

For that and other reasons Byron was now eager to get to town. Moreover, dissensions had arisen among his too exuberant guests. A few days after their arrival, Matthews, who was in ill-health and probably irritable, had threatened to throw "bold

Webster" out of a window, "in consequence of I know not what commerce of jokes." Webster went to Byron and said that his respect and regard for him as a host would not permit him to call out any of his guests, and that therefore he would go to town the next morning. "He did," Byron wrote. "It was in vain that I represented to him that the window was not high, and that the turf under it was particularly soft. Away he went." [n]

When the other members of the party started back to London, "Hobhouse and Matthews, who were the greatest friends possible, agreed, for a whim, to *walk together* to town," Byron wrote. "They quarrelled by the way, and actually walked the latter half of the journey, occasionally passing and repassing, without speaking. . . . They were reconciled in London again." [n]

Byron arrived at Batt's Hotel, Jermyn Street, on the 25th, eager to have more news of his satire. He sent a note immediately to Dallas, asking him to call.[n] Still determined to sail on the Malta packet, he wrote urgently to Hanson: "I wish to know before I make my final effort elsewhere, if you can or cannot assist me in raising a sum of money on fair and equitable terms and immediately." [n]

But Hanson was unable to raise the necessary money in time, and Byron postponed his sailing until June. In the meantime he enjoyed the stir his satire had made, and set about preparing a second edition, making many changes and additions, bringing the total up to 1,050 lines, and adding a postscript to cast a few parting darts at Jeffrey, whom he still believed to be the author of the *Edinburgh Review* critique of his early poems, and to take his revenge on Hewson Clarke of *The Satirist*.[6]

Dallas was with him constantly and by May 10 the new edition was ready to go to the press. Byron was eager to read the proofs before he left England. Dallas urged him to tone down some of his more caustic attacks on living literary figures and

[6] As for Hewson Clarke, Byron dismissed him in the postscript as "a very sad dog, and for no reason that I can discover, except a personal quarrel with a bear, kept by me at Cambridge to sit for a fellowship, and whom the jealousy of his Trinity contemporaries prevented from success, has been abusing me, and, what is worse, the defenceless innocent above mentioned, in the *Satirist* for one year and some months."

also occasionally to clip the wings of his licentious fancy. At the last moment he tried to get Byron to suppress the personalities in the postscript. Dallas wrote that he was angry with himself for having been weak enough to let the concluding pages go to the printer. "I beseech you to sacrifice these. . . . I WILL NOT LET YOU print them."[n] Byron conceded to the point of modifying some phrases.

Dallas was even more concerned for Byron's state of mind in the last days before he left London. "Misanthropy, disgust of life leading to scepticism and impiety, prevailed in his heart and embittered his existence. . . . Unaccustomed to female society, he at once dreaded and abhorred it; and spoke of women, such I mean as he neither dreaded nor abhorred, more as playthings than companions. As for domestic happiness he had no idea of it. 'A large family,' he said, 'appeared like opposite ingredients mixed perforce in the same salad, and he never relished the composition.'" Dallas believed that in wider circles "he had found no friend, and but few companions, whom he used to receive with an assumed gaiety, but real indifference at his heart, and spoke of with little regard, sometimes with sarcasm."[n]

But there were aspects of Byron's friendships that Dallas did not see or understand. The cynicism and nonchalant fatalism of Hobhouse, Matthews, and Davies appealed to Byron more than the socially accepted hypocrisies of others. And their wit was a refreshing antidote to his melancholy. "One of the cleverest men I ever knew in Conversation was Scrope Beardmore [*sic*] Davies," Byron wrote in his "Detached Thoughts." "Scrope was always ready, and often witty: Hobhouse as witty, but not always so ready, being more diffident."[n]

Byron had now become genuinely attached to Hobhouse for his dependable qualities as well as for his more facetious talents. While they were at Newstead, Hobhouse had agreed to accompany him on his voyage abroad. John Cam, having quarreled with his father, had no ready cash for traveling. But that was no obstacle to Byron, who had no money either and was some thirteen or fourteen thousand pounds in debt; he would lend his friend whatever was needed. He had also invited Matthews to go along, probably on the same terms.[n]

May was passing, and still Hanson had produced no cash. Byron wrote in exasperation on the 23rd: "Your quitting town has put me to the greatest inconvenience. . . . I have not five pounds in my possession. . . ." *n* Two days later Hanson reported that his partner Birch could get him an advance of £6,000 from an acquaintance.[7] But the negotiations dragged on into June and the sailing had to be postponed again.

New vexations plagued him. He had brought his valet Fletcher and his page boy Robert Rushton up to London. It was probably at this time that Sanders painted the full-length portrait of Byron and Robert standing by the sea with a precipitous mountain in the background.[8] But on May 19 Byron reported in great indignation to his mother, then installed at Newstead: "I have detected Fletcher in a connection with prostitutes, and of taking to a woman of the town the very boy whom I had committed to his charge, which lad he sent home with a lie in his mouth, to screen them both, after the most strict injunctions on my part to watch over his *morals*, and keep him from the *temptations* of this *accursed place.* I have sent the lad to his father; before this occurrence he was good-hearted, honest, and all I could wish him, and would have been so still, but for the machinations of the scoundrels, who have not only been guilty of adultery, but of depraving the mind of an innocent stripling. . . . Did you ever hear of anything so diabolical? He did not even deny it, for I found the address of the strumpet written in *his own hand. . . .*" *n* Had Byron been less interested in Rushton, he would have been less

[7] Eg. 2611, ff. 121–2. This acquaintance of Birch was a Mr. Sawbridge, from whom Byron eventually borrowed £6,000, which, like most of his other debts, was not paid back until after Newstead was sold in 1818.

[8] Finding that miniature-painting hurt his eyes, Sanders had given it up for large portraits in oils. By 1811 he was getting 250 guineas for a full-length portrait. (Geoffrey Wills: "A Forgotten Scottish Painter," *Country Life,* [London], Oct. 8, 1953, p. 1120.) Despite his difficulties in raising money for his voyage, Byron paid for the painting before he left. (*LJ*, I, 292.) Moore used the portrait of Byron and Rushton as the frontispiece of the first volume of the quarto edition of his life of Byron, labeling it "Lord Byron at the age of 19." From this it has been assumed that it was painted in 1807. The sittings could have begun in that year. There is a similar painting of Byron alone by Sanders, used as the frontispiece of Moore's first volume in the 1832 edition. It is possible that Sanders copied it, adding Rushton in 1809.

morally incensed. Indeed, Byron had himself boasted of his escapades with prostitutes.

But Byron could not remain angry long. Fletcher and the boy were both forgiven and recalled to London in time to accompany him abroad.[n] In the last days of leave-taking Byron turned back once more to his school friends. He went to Harrow twice for Speech Day, and on June 3 spent the night with Henry Drury. Henry Long wrote to his father: "[Byron] goes the 10th or 12th to—guess!—Constantinople, what for?—why for fun! he tipped me £5 half of which I enclose to you not knowing what to do with it. . . ."[n]

Long recalled one occasion when he observed "the monitors and upper boys all engaged with the perusal of a new book which I afterwards found to be the 'English Bards and Scotch Reviewers.' This poem though anonymous was known to have been composed by Lord Byron and as such was welcomed at Harrow. During the early part of the term, extending from Easter to August, Lord Byron paid many visits to Harrow, previous to his departure to the Continent. He sent for me as usual and we walked about together." Byron took young Long with him on a sentimental tour of his old haunts. They went into the schoolroom to see where their names were carved on the wall and visited the Peachey stone in the churchyard, which had once been his favorite spot. "Near it is an ancient monument surrounded with an iron rail and greatly decayed. 'The Sexton,' he said, talking in what I should call somewhat an affected style and voice, 'the sexton tells me the family to whom this monument belonged is extinct.'—he was rather fond of the notion of families becoming extinct. . . . His visits during this period (May 1809) were always signalized by a tip to me of a £5 note. . . ."[n]

When Dallas came on June 10 to take leave of him he found Byron embittered by what he considered a callous slight. "'Will you believe it,' said he, 'I have just met *** [Clare],[9] and asked

[9] E. H. Coleridge (*Poetry*, II, 22) conjectured that the ungrateful friend was "possibly Delawarr," and most biographers since have accepted his guess as fact. But Hobhouse, with whom Byron was closely associated at the time, and who must have been regaled no less than Dallas with Byron's indignant account of the incident, wrote the name "Clare" in the margin of his copy of Moore (I, 167) opposite the asterisks.

him to come and sit an hour with me; he excused himself; and what do you think was his excuse? He was engaged with his mother and some ladies to go shopping! And he knows I set out to-morrow, to be absent for years, perhaps never to return! Friendship!—I do not believe I shall leave behind me, yourself and family excepted, and perhaps my mother, a single being who will care what becomes of me.' " [n]

When he had overcome his chagrin, however, Byron must have realized that he was not abandoned by his friends. He did not leave town the next day, but lingered on, no doubt held immobile by lack of money, until the 19th. Determined not to be obliged to postpone his sailing again by the slowness of the negotiations with Sawbridge, he had gone to the usurers. "In consequence of the delay," he told Hanson, "I have been under the necessity of giving Thomas an annuity for his bond, and taking up further monies on annuity at seven years purchase to the *tune* of four hundred per annum altogether including T's bond." Hanson could make the payments from Sawbridge's loan when completed. "I am now setting off," he concluded.[n]

Before he and Hobhouse left London, Matthews gave them "a most splendid entertainment, to which we did ample justice." [n] Byron's new edition of *English Bards* and Hobhouse's volume of poems were not yet off the press. Byron had called down from Newstead not only the repentant Fletcher and Robert Rushton, but also old Joe Murray, who was unhappy under Mrs. Byron's governance.[1] And he had added to his entourage a German servant who had been in Persia.

From Falmouth on the 22nd Byron wrote a farewell letter to his mother. "I am about to sail in a few days. . . . I have letters in plenty:—you shall hear from me at the different ports I touch upon; but you must not be alarmed if my letters miscarry. The Continent is in a fine state—an insurrection has broken out at Paris, and the Austrians are beating Buonaparte—the Tyrolese

[1] Mrs. Byron wrote Hanson on June 17: "Old Murray is I believe gone to Lisbon . . . he really is so *troublesome* that I don't think I will have any thing to do with him. . . ." And with a kind of wistfulness she added in a postscript: "Lord Grey de Ruthyn has married a Farmer's Daughter, and Smith Wright is to marry a Lady with two hundred thousand pounds!!!" (Eg. 2611, f. 125.)

have risen. . . . As to money matters, I am ruined—at least till Rochdale is sold; and if that does not turn out well, I shall enter into the Austrian or Russian service—perhaps the Turkish, if I like their manners. The world is all before me, and I leave England without regret, and without a wish to revisit any thing it contains, except *yourself*, and your present residence." Old Murray, who could not withstand the rigors of Eastern travel, he would send back in about a month. "Robert I take with me; I like him, because, like myself, he seems a friendless animal." [2]

But the self-pity was sloughed off when he added a note to Hobhouse's letter to Matthews the same day. They had missed the Malta packet, which sailed on the 18th, and they had several days to wait for another ship. Exhilarated by the new scene, and animated by the prospective voyage, he wrote gaily of the opportunities for gallantry in Falmouth. He wished Matthews could be with them "in this delectable region, as I do not think Georgia itself can emulate in capabilities or incitements to the 'Plen. and optabil.—Coit.' [3] the port of Falmouth & parts adjacent—We are surrounded by Hyacinths & other flowers of the most fragrant nature, & I have some intention of culling a hand-

[2] *LJ*, I, 224–5. It seems likely that, despite his intention when he went north, Byron did not see his mother during his visit to the Abbey in April while his guests were there, or at any rate that he avoided the scene of an avowed farewell. That is indicated by his statement in *Childe Harold* (I, 10):

*Childe Harold had a mother—not forgot,*
*Though parting from that mother he did shun. . . .*

It was always easier for both of them to be reasonable at a distance, as he had learned from bitter experience. "Even a few days before we parted, for the last time, on my leaving England," he told Lord Sligo in Greece, "she, in one of her fits of passion, uttered an imprecation upon me, praying that I might prove as ill-formed in mind as I am in body!" (Moore, I, 242.) But when he did not put her in a passion, Mrs. Byron loved her son as devotedly as any mother and was zealous in looking after his interests. She wrote to Hanson shortly before he left England: "The *grief* I feel at my sons going abroad and the addition of his leaving his affairs in so unsettled a state . . . I think altogether it will kill me." (Eg. 2611, f. 125.)

[3] The Latin abbreviation Byron quoted (with some confusion of cases and genders) in this letter and several times later is of a phrase in the *Satyrica* of Petronius (para. 86, sec. 4): *"coitum plenum et optabilem"* ("complete intercourse to one's heart's desire"). I am indebted to Professor Gilbert Highet for tracing the quotation to Petronius.

some Bouquet to compare with the exotics we expect to meet in Asia.—One specimen I shall certainly carry off." [n] The facetious Matthews would easily understand the Latin abbreviations and the language of flowers.

On the 24th, Hanson sent the disappointing news that Sawbridge had finally remitted only £2,000 (the expected £6,000 could not be had), and some of this had to go to pay debts. Moreover, Sawbridge's draft was not due until July 12. Fortunately, Scrope Davies had had good luck at the gaming-tables and came to the rescue with a loan of £4,800, for which Byron gave his Bond of Indemnity.[4]

Byron wrote a farewell letter to Henry Drury on the 25th in great good spirits: "We sail tomorrow in the Lisbon packet having been detained till now by the lack of wind and other necessaries, . . . by this time tomorrow evening we shall be embarked on the vide vorld of vaters vor all the vorld like Robinson Crusoe.——The Malta vessel not sailing for some weeks we have determined to go by way of Lisbon, and as my servants term it to see 'that there *Portingale*' thence to Cadiz and Gibraltar and so on our old route to Malta and Constantinople, if so be that Capt. Kidd our gallant or rather gallows commander understands plain sailing and Mercator, and takes us on our voyage all according to the Chart. . . . Hobhouse has made woundy preparations for a book at his return, 100 pens two gallons Japan Ink, and several vols best blank is no bad provision for a discerning Public.—I have laid down my pen, but have promised to contribute a chapter on the state of morals. . . . Hobhouse further hopes to indemnify himself in Turkey for a life of exemplary chastity at home by letting out his 'fair bodye' to the whole Divan.—Pray buy his missellingany as the Printer's Devil calls it. . . . P.S. We have been sadly fleabitten at Falmouth." [n]

Despite the frivolity of his letters, Byron had provided himself with a good deal of serious reading for the voyage. During the

[4] Eg. 2611, f. 130–1. Byron finally repaid Davies on March 27, 1814, after he had received some part of the £25,000 finally paid by Claughton before he defaulted on the purchase of Newstead. (*LJ*, II, 407.) The £4,800 paid to Davies at that time may have included interest on the loan. He had previously paid £1,500 on account. An undated letter from Davies to Byron in the Murray MSS. says: "The bond debt is £4633."

spring he had run up a bill of over one hundred pounds at William Miller's, the bookseller at 50 Albemarle Street, not only for political works and Parliamentary debates but also for travel books (Porter's *Travels,* Barrow's *China,* Dallas's *Constantinople*). And for literary recreation he purchased the works of Burns, *Robinson Crusoe, Gulliver's Travels,* twenty-five volumes of *British Theatre,* Gifford's *Baviad* and *Mæviad,* Miss Edgworth's Tales, *Elegant Extracts,* and *Selections from the Gentleman's Magazine.*[n]

Before he finished his farewell letter to Hodgson on the 25th, Byron's facetiousness had become slightly wry: "Hodgson, remember me to Drury, and remember me to yourself when drunk. I am not worth a sober thought. . . . I leave England without regret—I shall return to it without pleasure. I am like Adam, the first convict sentenced to transportation, but I have no Eve, and have eaten no apple but what was sour as a crab;—and thus ends my first chapter. Adieu."[n] But on June 30, though they had gone on board, they were still in Falmouth Roads, and Byron, in good humor again, enclosed some effervescent verses in the letter, which he had held until the last moment:

*Huzza! Hodgson, we are going,*
*Our embargo's off at last;*
*Favourable breezes blowing*
*Bend the canvass o'er the mast.*

. . .

*Now we've reach'd her, lo! the captain,*
*Gallant Kidd, commands the crew;*
*Passengers their berths are clapt in,*
*Some to grumble, some to spew.*

. . .

*Fletcher! Murray! Bob! where are you?*
*Stretch'd along the deck like logs—*
*Bear a hand, you jolly tar you!*
*Here's a rope's end for the dogs.*
*Hobhouse muttering fearful curses,*
*As the hatchway down he rolls;*
*Now his breakfast, now his verses,*
*Vomits forth—and damns our souls.*

*"Here's a stanza*
*On Braganza—*
*Help!"—"A couplet?"—"No, a cup*
*Of warm water."—*
*"What's the matter?"*
*"Zounds! my liver's coming up;*
*I shall not survive the racket*
*Of this brutal Lisbon Packet."*

It was two days more before favorable winds carried Byron and his strange ménage from the coast of England.

# CHAPTER VII

## *1809–1810*

## The Grand Tour

WHEN the Lisbon packet, *Princess Elizabeth*, finally sailed from Falmouth on July 2, 1809,[n] she carried "in all nineteen souls." In addition to Byron, his valet Fletcher, old Joe Murray, the boy Robert Rushton (the "little page" of *Childe Harold*), and Friese, the German servant taken on the recommendation of Dr. Butler because "he has been all among the Worshippers of Fire in Persia, and has seen Persepolis and all that," the passengers included "Hobhouse, two officers' wives, three children, two waiting-maids, ditto subalterns for the troops, [and] three Portuguese esquires and domestics." Captain Kidd, "a gallant commander as ever smuggled an anker," [n] spread the canvas to the fair light wind and they had a rapid passage, arriving in the Tagus four and a half days after leaving Falmouth. While Byron's mind turned to romantic contemplation of the departure his rebellious stomach, in spite of the comparatively smooth passage, turned over in a most disconcerting manner. He confessed to Hodgson: "I have been sea-sick, and sick of the sea." [n]

Romantic visions surged up again, however, when the vessel sailed up the Tagus and they saw Cintra's mountain and Lisbon's beautiful harbor. The exhilaration and strangeness of being in a foreign land struck the young Englishmen when the Portuguese pilots leaped on board. Not even the lice and mosquitoes, the filth and degradation of the Portuguese people could for long dampen the exuberance of Byron in this environment. "I am very happy here," he wrote to Hodgson, "because I loves oranges, and talks bad Latin to the monks, who understand it, as it is like their own,—and I goes into society (with my pocket pistols), and I swims in the Tagus all across at once, and I rides on an ass or a mule, and swears Portuguese, and have got a diarrhœa and bites from the mosquitoes."[1]

Hobhouse, though equally attracted by the novelty of the surroundings, recorded in the diary he began the day they arrived in Lisbon the particularities of the dirt, poverty, and ignorance of the country.[n] The people were, he reported to Matthews, "at least 100 years behind the English in all the improvements of civilized and comfortable life." They saw a man sitting on the steps of a pedestal "pulling lice and fleas, chiefly lice, from his bosom and breeches, and cracking them by the tens on the step. The women who are the ugliest race of animals, really frightful, are as nasty. . . ." He saw no bookseller's shops, "only stalls with a few dirty books." The hotels "appear dirty in the extreme. We are at an English one, of which there are several, kept by one Barnewell at a quarter of the town called Buenos Ayres, situated on a hill where the English used to reside."[n]

The Peninsular War was in full swing. Sir Arthur Wellesley was on the frontier and swore he would be in Madrid in a month, and, according to Hobhouse, was "the god of the city," for the Portuguese had bitter memories of the French occupation. But in spite of the fact that the English were allies and deliverers and theoretically popular, there was enough of wartime roguery and violence in the city to make it wise to go armed, especially at night.[2]

The travelers passed their first night on board the packet. The

[1] *LJ*, I, 233. Letter of July 16, 1809. Byron had been in Lisbon only a few days before he swam the Tagus, a feat that Hobhouse called "a more perilous, but less celebrated passage" than his later swimming of the Hellespont. He swam "from Old Lisbon to Belem Castle, and having to contend with a tide and counter current, the wind blowing freshly, was but little less than two hours in crossing the river." (*Journey*, II, 808.)

[2] In one of his notes to *Childe Harold* (*Poetry*, II, 86), Byron says that his carriage was stopped by some ruffians while he was on the way to the theater. The occasion was probably that mentioned by Hobhouse under the date of July 18 in his diary: "At ½ past nine went with B. in a Calash to Rua dos Condes attacked near the —— by 4 men." There is a local tradition, first set in writing by the historian Alexandre Herculano in 1844, that Byron was struck as he left the San Carlos Theatre by a jealous Portuguese husband with whose wife he had flirted. (See Borst, p. 9.)

next day they went with Captain Kidd to a merchant named Bulkely, who charged them thirteen per cent to change their money.[n] In the evening they attended a sentimental comedy, where "God Save the King" was played and the program supplemented with variety singing. At another performance the following evening in the Rua dos Condes theater they saw some very lascivious Iberian dances which were much applauded by the audience. They witnessed a review of the British troops under General Crauford on July 10, and the same day paid a visit to the Monastery of Bela and were shocked to learn that none of the fifty monks spoke or understood Latin. They dined as usual at Barnewell's with other Englishmen and went again to the theater.

The following day Byron and Hobhouse set out for the picturesque village of Cintra, which made a lasting impression on the poet's mind. The village, he told his mother, "about fifteen miles from the capital, is, perhaps in every respect, the most delightful in Europe. . . . Palaces and gardens rising in the midst of rocks, cataracts, and precipices; convents on stupendous heights—a distant view of the sea and the Tagus. . . ."[n] But the greatest attraction of all was the Moorish palace on the heights of Cintra where the author of *Vathek* had lived. "The first and sweetest spot in this kingdom is Montserrat, lately the seat of the great Beckford," Byron wrote to Hodgson.[n] They dined and spent the night at Cintra and the next day climbed to "Nossa Señora da Peña," a convent on a rock above the Moorish castle. The whole environment of Cintra they found so attractive that they spent a second night, dining with Mr. Turner, who had also come up from Lisbon.

Back in the capital, they continued their sightseeing. After two weeks they were growing tired of Portugal, and, the ship for Gibraltar not being due for some days, they decided to travel overland to Seville and Cádiz on horseback. The stories they heard of Portuguese character (which Hobhouse sedulously recorded in his diary) made them the more willing to leave. During most of their stay they associated almost exclusively with Englishmen, who gave them an unfavorable report of the country and its people.

The night before they left, the two travelers called on J. W. Ward, whom they had seen frequently during their stay in Lisbon. Ward knew nothing about Byron, but (he wrote later) "I had not been half an hour in his company before I perceived that he was a person of no common mind." Ward boasted, however, that the extraordinary mind of Byron "by no means prevented me from cheating him extremely in the sale of some English saddles with which I equipped him at Lisbon to make the tour of Portugal and Andalusia." [n]

Before taking the boat across the Tagus on July 20, Byron and Hobhouse provided themselves with some mosquito netting.[n] They spent the first night in an inn at the small town of Aldea Gallega on the opposite shore of the estuary. There were just four in the party. Byron took Robert Rushton with him, and they had hired a Portuguese servant and guide by the name of Sanguinetti for the trip across the peninsula. The other three servants were to bring the more bulky baggage and equipage to Gibraltar by the packet.

The ardor of the young travelers was not dampened by the inconveniences or dangers of the journey. They felt that they were just starting on their adventures. The fact that part of the country through which they would travel had recently been a battleground increased the excitement. They arose at four o'clock and, hiring five post horses, started for Los Prigones, traveling through vineyards and a beautiful cork woods. It was dark before they came through a forest to Montemenor. They saw "a vast number of crosses signs of murders on the side of the way," but with English regimental uniforms, greatly respected in Spain at the time, they felt safe.

The next day they arrived just before the gates shut on the fortified frontier town of Elvas. They breakfasted the following morning on good goat's milk and coffee and the best French bread. Their next stage was Badajoz across the frontier, three leagues distant, where they arrived at five, but they went on to the little village of Albuena before stopping.

On Monday the 24th they arose at four again. Everywhere there were relics of the recent fighting. They overtook two French prisoners and a seventy-year-old Spanish spy being taken to Seville to be hanged. At Monasterio there were two thousand patriot troops. They lodged in a courier's house, where they were served boiled chicken as usual, and a "large woman bolted into the room & began to dance when Sanguinetti played his flute to a fandango tune."[3]

On the 25th they rode two leagues of their way through the picturesque and rugged Sierra Morena range, which shuts off the northern plains from Andalusia. They took two carriages for the final stage to Seville. Not finding lodgings, Hobhouse recorded, "at Mrs. Latchford's (. . . near the Cathedral whither we were recommended by Mr. Ward) nor at the Possada (where the English men go in general) went to Mr. Wiseman, British Consul conducted by F. Hoffman who recommended us to the lodgings of two unmarried ladies in the Calle de las Cruzes No. 19—Josepha Beltram & sister—went supperless & dinnerless to Bed all 4 in one little room."

Nevertheless, they kept their crowded quarters for the three nights they spent in Seville. The Grand Junta, the revolutionary Spanish government that was allied with the English to drive Napoleon from Spain, had made its headquarters there, and the population, normally 30,000, had swelled to 100,000. The next day Byron and Hobhouse left their names with the English Ambassador, John Hookham Frere,[4] who was at dinner, and then visited the cathedral, which Byron always remembered as the finest he had ever seen. That night they went to bed "after tunes from Sanguinetti and the two ladies."

Before they departed on the morning of the 28th, they were visited by Sir John Carr, a professional writer of travel books, of whom Byron wrote facetiously to Hodgson from Gibraltar: "I . . . have been down on my knees to beg he would not put

[3] This scene in the little Spanish town made so strong an impression on Byron that years later he recalled a number of its details, perhaps with some embroidery, in a satiric ribbing of Wordsworth's prosaic prefatory remarks to "The Thorn." (*LJ*, VI, 381–2.) The picturesque description given in this fragment makes one wish that Byron rather than the sober Hobhouse, concerned with the condition of the roads and the fare at the inns, had kept a diary of the journey.

[4] It is a curious circumstance that Byron first met John Hookham Frere, from whose *Whistlecraft* he was to get the inspiration for the burlesque style of *Beppo* and *Don Juan,* thus early in Spain.

me into black and white." [n] According to Hobhouse, they set off, "after kissing our hostess and sister (one of whom asked Ld. B. why he had not come to bed to her at 2 o'clock according to invitation)."

Byron gave a more extended and amusing account of the episode in a letter to his mother: "We lodged in the house of two Spanish unmarried ladies, who possess *six* houses in Seville, and gave me a curious specimen of Spanish manners. . . . The eldest honoured your *unworthy* son with very particular attention, embracing him with great tenderness at parting (I was there but three days), after cutting off a lock of his hair, and presenting him with one of her own, about three feet in length, which I send, and beg you will retain till my return. Her last words were, *Adios, tu hermoso! me gusto mucho*—'Adieu, you pretty fellow! you please me much.' She offered me a share of her apartment, which my *virtue* induced me to decline; she laughed, and said I had some English *amante* (lover), and added that she was going to be married to an officer in the Spanish army." [n]

While Hobhouse was entering in his diary complaints of the bad dinners and of waiters picking their teeth with pins, Byron was exhilarated by the whole experience in Spain. He wrote to Hodgson of this part of the journey: "The horses are excellent—we rode seventy miles a day. Eggs and wine, and hard beds, are all the accommodation we found, and, in such torrid weather, quite enough. My health is better than in England. Seville is a fine town, and the Sierra Morena, part of which we crossed, a very sufficient mountain; but damn description, it is always disgusting." [n] Later he referred to Seville, the birthplace of his Don Juan, as "a pleasant city,/ Famous for oranges and women." [n]

The violent aspects of Spanish character appealed scarcely less to him. Hobhouse had recorded that at St. Olalla they had witnessed a bitter quarrel between the postmaster and one of the guides, the former challenging the other to fight with knives and using abusive language. Byron recalled at the same place having "heard a young peasant threaten to stab a woman (an old one, to be sure, which mitigates the offence), and was told, on expressing some small surprise, that this ethic was by no means uncommon." [n]

He was also intrigued by stories of the Maid of Saragoza, who had manned the artillery of her native city when all the gunners of a battery had been killed, and had encouraged a renewed defense against the French. While he was at Seville, "she walked daily on the Prado, decorated with medals and orders, by command of the Junta." [n]

The travelers made the first stage to Cádiz in two carriages with four horses each, passing through Alcalá and stopping for the night at the Golden Lion Inn at Utrera. Rising at four, they took to horseback again and broke the journey by visiting Mr. Gordon, the British proprietor of a large winery at Xeres. At a quarter past five they arrived at the bustling port of Puerta de María (Puerta Santa María). They "embarked and arrived in an hour at Cadiz [at] ½ p[ast] seven—no lodgings for servants at Wood's Hotel the Landlady preferring also merchants (as she said) to Lords we went to Bailly's Hotel [Calle de Pedro Conde] where well serv'd."

At the Consul's the next morning, Sunday, July 30, they met Lord Jocelyn and Mr. Wellesley Pole, a wastrel nephew of the Duke of Wellington. After dinner they crossed the bay again to see the bullfight at Puerta Santa María, the only such event then countenanced by the Supreme Junta in Spain. With other principal visitors and military and naval officers they were invited to sit in the box of the governor.

Byron was sufficiently captivated by the picturesque event to devote eleven stanzas of *Childe Harold* to it, but at the same time he was disgusted with the brutality of the performance, being particularly revolted by the "wild plunging of the tortured horse." Hobhouse's later account indicates that the spectacle sickened them both at the time: "An Englishman who can be much pleased with seeing two men beat themselves to pieces,[n] cannot bear to look at a horse galloping round an arena with his bowels trailing on the ground, and turns from the spectacle and the spectators with horror and disgust." [n] Nevertheless, Byron and Hobhouse had recovered sufficiently by the time they returned to Cádiz at nine in the evening to attend a comedy, and to take a peep into what Hobhouse calls the "seraglio," probably a sort of "Moulin Rouge."

Byron's recollection of Cádiz was glowing. "Cadiz, sweet Cadiz!" he wrote to Hodgson from Gibraltar, "it is the first spot in the creation. The beauty of its streets and mansions is only excelled by the loveliness of its inhabitants. . . . Cadiz is a complete Cythera. Many of the grandees who have left Madrid during the troubles reside there, and I do believe it is the prettiest and cleanest town in Europe. London is filthy in the comparison." [n]

On August 1 they were wakened by the cannon firing for the victory of Cuesta and for the landing of Lord Wellesley, who had been sent as Envoy Extraordinary to try to persuade the Spanish government to exert greater efforts in behalf of his brother and the British army. Byron and Hobhouse walked out and "saw the bustle about the ambassador & saw the cobler get up and make a speech refusing a sum of money offered by Ld. Wellesley to the people who drew his carriage thro the city." In the evening they walked again in the Almedea, where they met Byron's Cambridge acquaintance Gally Knight "in blue regimentals of yeomanry" and W. Pole.

On Wednesday, August 2, Byron and Hobhouse boarded the *Atlas* and dined with Admiral Purvis, who arranged for their passage in the *Hyperion* frigate, which was sailing the next day for Gibraltar.

In Cádiz, as in most cities far from the fighting front in wartime, the gaieties of life were unabated. Byron, who had already met some of the Spanish grandees and notables, regretted leaving. At the play that evening Hobhouse was separated from his friend, and later wrote in his diary: "whilst B. was in a box with Miss Cordova, a little mad & apt to fall in love, . . . I went out." Byron wrote his mother that the night before leaving Cádiz he "sat in the box at the opera with Admiral Cordova's family; he is the commander whom Lord St. Vincent defeated in 1797, and has an aged wife and a fine daughter, Sennorita Cordova. The girl is very pretty, in the Spanish style; in my opinion, by no means inferior to the English in charms, and certainly superior in fascination. Long black hair, dark languishing eyes, *clear* olive complexions, and forms more graceful in motion than can be conceived by an Englishman used to the drowsy, listless air of his countrywomen, added to the most becoming dress, and, at the same time, the most decent in the world, render a Spanish beauty irresistible." He continued: "Miss Cordova and her little brother understood a little French, and, after regretting my ignorance of the Spanish, she proposed to become my preceptress in that language. I could only reply by a low bow, and express my regret that I quitted Cadiz too soon to permit me to make the progress which would doubtless attend my studies under so charming a directress. I was standing at the back of the box . . . for fear of incommoding the ladies in front, when this fair Spaniard dispossessed an old woman (an aunt or a duenna) of her chair, and commanded me to be seated next herself, at a tolerable distance from her mamma. At the close of the performance I withdrew, and was lounging with a party of men in the passage, when, *en passant,* the lady turned round and called me, and I had the honour of attending her to the admiral's mansion. I have an invitation on my return to Cadiz, which I shall accept if I repass through the country on my return from Asia." [n]

This experience the night before sailing seemed to fix in Byron's mind an idealized vision of the Spanish women which remained long with him. The adventurous strangeness of the light flirtation with the dark foreign beauty blossomed soon after in his verses to "The Girl of Cadiz":

*Oh never talk again to me*
*Of northern climes and British ladies;*
*It has not been your lot to see,*
*Like me, the lovely Girl of Cadiz.*

. . .

*Our English maids are long to woo,*
*And frigid even in possession;*
*And if their charms be fair to view,*
*Their lips are slow at love's confession;*
*But, born beneath a brighter sun,*
*For love ordained the Spanish maid is. . . .* [n]

The same theme occupied his mind when he wrote to Hodgson from Gibraltar, but his account of the women was tempered with some realism: "The Spanish women are all alike, their education the same. The wife of a duke is, in information, as the wife of a peasant,—the wife of a peasant, in manner, equal to a duchess. Certainly they are fascinating; but their minds have only one idea, and the business of their lives is intrigue." [n]

The travelers, used to early rising by this time, boarded the *Hyperion* (Captain Brodie) on August 3 at seven in the morning, and at seven that night "saw Africa for the first time off Cape Trafalgar." At noon on the 4th they were in sight of Gibraltar. At three they went on shore with Captain Brodie and put up at the Three Anchors or British Hotel. They found, as Hobhouse wrote, a "horrid dirty table (when I pulled up the green baize that covered it) got two rooms very buggy looking and dirty like the rest of this stinking Hotel." The servants, Joe Murray, Fletcher, and Friese, had not yet arrived on the schooner *Triumph* from Lisbon, and Byron and his companion missed their baggage, which was coming on the same boat. After a bad dinner spoiled by greasy cooking, they climbed up the rock in the evening and came down after sunset. They spent a restless night, perhaps because of the bugs, and slept until three the next afternoon. It is small wonder that Byron's thoughts turned back to Spain. To Hanson he wrote: "Cadiz is the prettiest town in Europe, Seville a large and fine city, Gibraltar the dirtiest most detestable spot." [n]

But the days passed more pleasantly after they had discovered the garrison library, filled, as Hobhouse says, with "good common books." It was there that John Galt first saw Byron. A "young man came in and seated himself opposite to me at the table where I was reading," he recalled. "Something in his appearance attracted my attention. His dress indicated a Londoner of some fashion. . . ." Galt began to observe him closely without attracting his attention. "His physiognomy was prepossessing and intelligent, but ever and anon his brows lowered and gathered; a habit, as I then thought, with a degree of affectation in it, probably first assumed for picturesque effect and energetic expression; but which I afterwards discovered was undoubtedly the occasional scowl of some unpleasant reminiscence: it was certainly disagreeable—forbidding—but still the general cast of his features was impressed with elegance and character." [n]

Byron and Hobhouse walked up the rock every evening to watch the sun set and to cast eager glances across the strait toward Africa, for Byron hoped to see another continent before he reached Asia. He had paid fifty guineas to a tailor at Gibraltar to fit him out in "a most superb uniform as a court dress, indispensable in travelling." [n] He intended to sail over to Africa on Saturday, August 12, but though the distance was only six miles, the wind was contrary, and instead he and Hobhouse set off in the afternoon in the governor's barge for Algeciras across the bay with Sir William Drummond, lately retired as British Ambassador at Naples. Drummond, an outspoken freethinker, was alarmed when the sea rose and the barge began to roll. When Byron told him there was no danger, he replied: "It is well for you who think that if you are drowned you will go to another world, but I, who have no such belief, would rather remain a little longer where I am." [n] They dined at the home of Lady Westmorland in Algeciras, where they met General Francisco de Castaños, hero of the Spanish victory over the French at Baylen the summer before.

The servants and baggage had finally arrived from Lisbon, and Hobhouse, who was accountant and practical manager of affairs, was busy packing and making final arrangements for their departure on the Malta packet. Byron reluctantly gave up his excursion to Barbary. He was depressed at parting with Joe Murray, and especially with Robert Rushton, who had been with them on their overland journey from Lisbon. He was sending them home because Joe was too old for the hardships of Eastern travel, and Robert was too young. "I have sent Robert Rushton home," he wrote Hanson, "because Turkey is in too dangerous a state for boys to enter." [n] To his mother he wrote: "Please show the lad kindness, as he is my great favourite. . . ." [n] And he asked the boy's father to deduct £25 a year from his rent for Robert's education. "In case of my death I have provided enough in my will to render him independent." [n] Sanguinetti, their Portuguese guide (who, Hobhouse found, had made a mathematical mistake of ten thousand Spanish reas in his own favor in turning in his bills), they paid off, and apparently the German servant also, for only Fletcher accompanied them from Gibraltar.

On August 15 they took their favorite walk up the rock for the last time, and the next evening boarded the *Townshend Packet* (Captain Western). Galt, who was already on board, recognized Byron as the visitor he had seen in the library. "In the little bustle and process of embarking their luggage," he recorded, "his lordship affected, as it seemed to me, more aristocracy than befitted his years, or the occasion. . . .

"Hobhouse, with more of the commoner, made himself one of the passengers at once; but Byron held himself aloof, and sat on the rail, leaning on the mizzen shrouds, inhaling, as it were, poetical sympathy, from the gloomy rock, then dark and stern in the twilight. There was in all about him that evening much waywardness; he spoke petulantly to Fletcher, his valet; and was evidently ill at ease with himself and fretful towards others." [n]

They got away the next day with a light wind, but were becalmed a good deal. The third day out, according to Galt, "Byron relented from his rapt mood, as if he felt it was out of place, and became playful. . . ." The passengers, including Galt, a Mr. Thomson, a merchant, and Mr. T. Shee, beguiled the time by shooting at bottles. Byron supplied the pistols and was the best shot. During the calms the jolly-boat was lowered and Byron and the Captain caught a turtle or two.

On the passage to Sardinia, Galt observed Byron's abstemious diet. "He ate little; no animal food, but only bread and vegetables." He was sociable enough in the daytime, but, "when the lights were placed, he made himself a man forbid, took his station on the railing between the pegs on which the sheets are belayed and the shrouds, and there, for hours, sat in silence, enamoured, it may be, of the moon." [n]

The evening before they came to anchor at Sardinia's capital city of Cagliari, however, Byron condescended to join the others in the cabin. The whole party landed on the morning of the 27th and went into the town, where a merchant named

Shepherd provided horses for everyone but Hobhouse, who with Galt walked about the town while the others, including Byron, rode into the country, where they saw three heads nailed to a gallows. They had left their cards with the English Minister, Mr. Hill, who invited them to dinner. Byron and Hobhouse returned from the ship dressed in their gaudy red uniforms, which Galt thought an affectation.[n]

When Mr. Hill accompanied the travelers to their boat, Byron made him a speech, thanking him "with more elocution than was precisely requisite," Galt recalled. After the Minister had left, Hobhouse could not refrain from expressing his amusement, and others joined in the laughter. Byron became petulant and, walking beside Galt, asked if he had not acquitted himself with grace and dignity. "Of course," Galt wrote, "though I thought pretty much as Mr. Hobhouse did, I could not do otherwise than civilly assent. . . ."[n]

The next day Byron did not make his appearance until late in the evening, and when he did, Galt thought it was because Hobhouse had made some kind of amends. As they sailed along the coast of Sicily on August 30, Byron was in a very good humor, "overflowing with glee, and sparkling with quaint sentences. The champagne was uncorked and in the finest condition."[n]

Only Byron and Hobhouse were allowed to land in the boat when the mail was put off at Girgenti. They were at sea again on the 31st, plying toward Malta, which they reached at 2:00 p.m., entering the harbor of Valetta. The Captain, who had a letter to Sir Alexander Ball, the Governor, went ashore and dined with him. According to Galt, Byron and Hobhouse were the only passengers who did not leave the ship. "They remained behind for a reason which an accidental expression of Byron let out—much to my secret amusement. . . . They expected—at least he did—a salute from the batteries, and sent ashore notice to Sir Alexander Ball . . . of his arrival; but the guns were sulky, and evinced no respect of persons; so that late in the afternoon, about the heel of the evening, the two magnates were obliged to come on shore, and slip into the city unnoticed and unknown."[n]

They climbed up many steps to get to the heart of the town, but apparently called on no one and returned on board for the night. Going ashore again the following morning, this time with Mr. Shee, they delivered a letter to Colonel Dickens, saw the church of St. John, and returned to the *Townshend*, where at last they found a formal invitation to partake a family dinner with Sir Alexander Ball. Only then did Byron and Hobhouse take final leave of the packet. Without any place yet to stay, they proceeded to the palace. The Governor had no lodging for them, but he advised them to take passage to Smyrna on the brig *Wizard*, which was leaving with a convoy on Sunday. It was then Friday, September 1. From the palace the Governor took them in his carriage to St. Antonio, his country seat. They dined with him and Lady Ball. Hobhouse noted: "dinner all in one course with lectures on temperance and commendation of our abstinence." Returning to town in the Governor's carriage, still not knowing where they were to sleep, they called on Mr. Chabot, a merchant to whom they had a letter. He was at dinner with a party which included John Galt, who was amused again at the predicament of the travelers. "His Lordship was in better spirits than I had ever seen him. His appearance showed, as he entered the room, that they had met with some adventure, and he chuckled with an inward sense of enjoyment, not altogether without spleen—a kind of malicious satisfaction—as his companion recounted with all becoming gravity their woes and sufferings, as an apology for begging a bed and morsel for the night." [n] Mr. Chabot gave them beds for the night, and the next morning they called on the Governor to tell him their difficulty. He dismissed them shortly, but his secretary told them he had arranged for them to have Dr. Moncrieff's house at No. 3 Strada di Forni.

Byron now began to enjoy his stay at Malta. He bought an Arabic grammar to prepare for the Eastern voyage; [n] he and Hobhouse went to bathe at a well-constructed bath; and in the afternoon they dined with General Oakes at his country house. Byron got into a "grand dispute with his aid de Camp a rude fellow who grinn'd—carried off by the General to town for fear of battle."

At Mr. Chabot's the next day Byron and Hobhouse met Spiridion Forresti, a much-traveled gentleman who was full of stories of the diplomatic and political world. They found Forresti an immensely entertaining companion and saw much of him during the rest of their stay on the island. On the 4th he introduced them to the celebrated woman who had incensed Napoleon and had made a dramatic escape from the French. Hobhouse recorded the meeting laconically: "introduced by Mr. F to la celebre Mrs. Spencer Smith. . . . a tall pretty woman with fat arms well made."

Byron found the life pleasant and the inhabitants hospitable, and he was in no hurry to move. The usual routine was to take an Arabic lesson in the morning and then to go by boat to La Pieta for bathing, and to dine with some of the residents in the afternoon, proceeding thence to the theater. On the 8th he and Hobhouse were again at Mr. Chabot's, where Byron "made a bet of 20 guineas with a Mr. Wherry that he get into the female slave market at Constantinople."

Then, on the 9th, Byron's interest in the island life increased greatly, for they called on "a pretty Mrs. Commissioner Fraser and Mrs. Sp[encer] Smith." Later they dined with General Oakes, but in the evening Byron took Hobhouse back to Mrs. Fraser's, "Mrs. Sp. Smith being there." Hobhouse was uncomfortable in the society of women, but Byron was immediately intrigued by the romantic Constance Spencer Smith. She was three years older than he was, and she had all the attraction of a woman who had lived in foreign courts. Byron had seen no women since he left his native land with whom he could talk on a plane of equality; and even in England all of his amours had been with country girls like Julia Leacroft, or ballet dancers and chambermaids. He was captivated by her society, and for the rest of his stay was constantly with her. It is probable that, not used to making love to a woman of his own social station, he was a little diffident at first, and that reserve, together with his Grecian beauty of countenance and the charm of his demeanor when he wanted to be agreeable, swept the lady off her feet even faster than Byron was carried off his.

By the middle of September Byron and Hobhouse were making

preparations to leave; they were to sail on the *Spider,* commanded by Lieutenant Oliver, with a convoy of British merchant vessels to Patras and then Prevesa. Of course the details of the preparation fell to Hobhouse, for Byron was fully occupied with the fascinating Constance, and he was reluctant now to leave. He had written some melancholy verses in her album on the 14th,[n] and she was the chief subject of his letter to his mother the next day. The melancholy arose probably from the reflection that she was then planning to return to her husband in England.

Hobhouse, judging no doubt from his friend's initial reserve and from his subsequent remarks about the affair after time and distance had cooled the passion, thought that Byron was not in love with the lady.[n] John Galt, who, however, had left Malta before the affair had progressed far, retained the same impression. He said Byron "affected a passion for her; but it was only Platonic. She, however, beguiled him of his valuable yellow diamond ring." [n] But the attachment had become stronger on both sides than was generally known at the time. Byron later confessed to Lady Melbourne (while demonstrating that time and distance could cure any passion in three months—apropos of Caroline Lamb): ". . . in the autumn of 1809 in the Mediterranean I was seized with an *everlasting* passion, considerably more violent on my part than this has ever been—everything was settled—and we . . . were to set off for the Friuli: but, lo! the Peace spoilt everything, by putting this in the possession of the French, and some particular occurrences in the interim, determined me to go to Constantinople. However we were to meet next year at a certain time; though I told my *amica* there was no time like the present, and that I could not answer for the future. She trusted to her power, and I at the moment had certainly much greater doubts of her than myself." [n]

It was on September 16 that Byron made his tryst with Mrs. Spencer Smith.[n] He was due to sail on the *Spider* at any moment, but the wind continued contrary. On the 18th the breeze had changed and the convoy was expected to set out early the following morning. Byron and Hobhouse dined at the home of Mrs. Fraser, the friend of Mrs. Smith. At 11:00 that night Byron informed Hobhouse that he had challenged Captain Cary, aide-de-camp of General Oakes, with whom he had come near fighting at the General's shortly after their arrival on the island. The first offense had been the Captain's arrogant manner in discussing politics, but now Byron wrote that he had "been informed that you have since mentioned my name in a public company with comments not to be tolerated. . . . As the vessel in which I am to embark must sail the first change of wind, the sooner our business is arranged the better. To-morrow morning at 6 will be the best hour, at any place you think proper. . . ." [n] No doubt the Captain's comments on this later occasion had concerned Byron and Mrs. Spencer Smith.[n]

Hobhouse says that Captain Cary had accepted the challenge for six the next morning, but that at midnight Major Waddle, his agent in the affair, called. Hobhouse's diary of the 19th tells the rest of the story: "the Spider and convoy under weigh very early, firing guns. detained by Capt. C. insisting to know Ld. B's informants. after 3 messages by Major Waddle to myself, agreed to be satisfied, as Ld. B. had promised secrecy, after having sent a long letter disclaiming every intent to insult Ld. B. got on board at 12." [n] Hobhouse later told Moore of "the cool and manly courage with which he [Byron] conducted himself through the whole affair." [n]

Months later Byron wrote cavalierly of the affair to Henry Drury: "At Malta I fell in love with a married woman and challenged an aid du camp of Genl. Oakes (a rude fellow who grinned at something, I never rightly knew what,) but he explained and apologised, and the lady embarked for Cadiz, & so I escaped murder and adultery." [n]

As the gentle breezes carried the convoy into the Ionian Sea, Byron felt a certain relief. On the morning of the 23rd they were in the channel between Cephalonia and Zante and in the distance they could see the high mountains of the Peloponnesus back of Patras. In the evening they caught sight of Ithaca's two hills northeast of Cephalonia.

By the 26th the brig had come to anchor in the harbor of Patras. Though the *Spider* was leaving shortly for Prevesa, Byron and Hobhouse went ashore so that they might feel that they had actually set foot on ancient Greece—"at half after ten for the first time landed in the Peloponessus in a currant ground to the left (the North) of the Town to shoot Pistols with Lord B. . . . on board after leaving some things to the care of Mr. Strané English consul at Patras, a good kind man very ugly [5]—sail'd for Prevesa. On the right, the North, saw the town of 'Mesaloge' [Missolonghi]." Thus, on his first day in Greece Byron saw in the distance the town where fifteen years later he was to breathe his last.

Passing the next day between Ithaca and Santa Maura (Leucadia), the brig made a prize of a Turkish ship from a French port. Under the spell of the legend-hallowed islands they were passing, Hobhouse read part of the *Odyssey* given him by Matthews. The next evening they were anchored off Prevesa and saw the moon rise over the hills commanding the Bay of Actium. They landed at 11:00 on the 29th in their regimentals, but their dignity and spirits were somewhat dampened by a violent downpour of rain as they disembarked on the classical shores. Mr. Commiuti, the Greek who acted as English Consul at Prevesa, was absent, but his brother, who knew no English and could not read their letter, entertained them at the Consul's house, after which they were shown through Ali Pasha's "palace" by the Albanian governor, "a most merry man who laughed much with little Signior Bosari and told him . . . 'avec une sourire impudent' that one of the rooms was for the 'boys.'" It was but a poor building, a kind of barracks, with bare walls. The ill-dressed and fierce-looking Turks with pistols and long knives in their belts, the dirty quarters in which they were housed by the Consul, the narrow, muddy streets—added to the soaking they got on landing—gave them a sad impression of the country.[6] But the skies cleared the next day, and they rode with Lieutenant Oliver, Signor Bosari, and the brother of the Consul to the ruins of Nicopolis on the plain between the Ionian Sea and the Gulf of Arta. They found the ancient city buried under

[5] Strané had been a fellow passenger on the *Spider* from Malta.

[6] Hobhouse in his diary described the privy or "necessary" of the Consul as being nothing more than a triangular orifice in the floor with a bench board above it. Byron, not understanding its operation, sat down on the triangle with his knees to his nose.

thistles and used for sheep pens. The land was everywhere neglected, but the scene was striking as they rode through olive groves, caught glimpses of the sea, and heard the bleating of the sheep, the tinkling of bells, and the croaking of frogs.

The next morning, October 1, they started on the first leg of their journey toward the isolated town of Jannina [Greek: Ioannina] in the heart of the Epirus, which Ali Pasha had recently made his capital. They were not traveling light (Byron never did). In addition to "four large leathern trunks, weighing about eighty pounds when full, and three smaller trunks," they had a canteen, three beds, with bedding, and two light wooden bedsteads (as a precaution against vermin and the damp of mud floors). And they had brought four English saddles and bridles.[n]

Perhaps on the recommendation of Strané, they had hired in Patras a Greek by the name of George to act as dragoman or interpreter. He served them well enough except that he was bustling, talkative, missed no chance of robbing them, and spoke no Turkish, but the last was not too great a handicap in a country where a large part of the population was Greek.

From Prevesa the caravan went by boat to Salora, the port of Arta, about twelve miles from Prevesa on the Ambracian Gulf. Arriving just in time to escape a storm, they were housed in a barrack next door to ten Albanian soldiers of the Pasha. They took coffee and grapes and smoked a long pipe with the soldiers and observed their manners, "the only unpleasant circumstance being the belches in fashion." Captain Elmas, in charge of the garrison, was captivated by Byron's fine Manton gun, and only the knowledge that it was intended for Ali Pasha restrained him from insisting on a trade. As it rained the next day, they spent a second night in the barrack, where they were entertained by the monotonous nasal singing of Albanian and Greek songs. The travelers were now on easy and familiar terms with the soldiers.

On the morning of October 3 they set out with ten horses, four carrying the baggage, and two soldiers from the barrack as a guard. At Arta they were lodged by a Greek who kept the custom-house. Compared with those at Prevesa, their accommodations were good, but Hobhouse, the John Bull of the party, only exceeded in his complaints by Fletcher, registered his belief that, "Properly speaking, the word comfort could not be applied to anything I ever saw out of England." [n] Byron was more adaptable.

On the 5th they saw Jannina and its lake, "houses, domes, and Minarets, glittering through gardens of orange and lemon trees, and from groves of cypresses—the lake spreading its smooth expanse at the foot of the city—the mountains rising abruptly from the banks of the lake." [n] But the sense of the picturesque was blotted out as they entered the suburbs and saw hanging to a string under a tree a man's arm with part of the side torn from the body. "Ld B and myself a little sick," Hobhouse wrote in his diary.

The travelers made their way to the home of Captain Leake, the official British Resident in Jannina. Leake was ill, but sent word that a house had been provided for them. Their host, Signor Nicolo, a Greek who spoke Italian, was kind and attentive.[7] They dressed in their red uniforms to receive the secretary of Ali and the Greek Primate of the city. The secretary, who spoke French, overwhelmed them "with the news that his Highness had been aware of our intention to visit Jannina, that he had ordered every thing to be prepared for our reception, that he was sorry to be obliged to leave his city to finish a little war, but begged that we would follow him, and that he had ordered an escort to conduct us to his camp." They were further astonished to find that the Pasha had ordered provisions for their table and that they were not to be allowed to pay. They had been expected four days before, and Captain Leake had deferred leaving Jannina to receive them.

There were reasons of policy behind Ali Pasha's hospitality. At the moment of their arrival he was particularly anxious to conciliate the English, for he wanted their co-operation against the French in the Ionian Islands.[n] Byron, however, was immensely flattered by the attention.

[7] The house of Signor Nicolo Argyri still stands in what is now "Byron Street" in Jannina. It is a solid two-story house with projecting bars on the upper window. A plaque in Greek over the door states that Byron and Hobhouse lived there in October 1809.

The young English visitors spent six pleasant days in Jannina. A tailor called and they tried on Albanian costumes, "as fine as Pheasants," Hobhouse called them. Before they left the country Byron had bought "some very 'magnifiques' Albanian dresses. . . . They cost fifty guineas each, and have so much gold, they would cost in England two hundred." *n*

Captain Leake, though he still had a cold, called the day after their arrival to see what he could do for them. They were the first Englishmen Leake had seen in Jannina, for the country was very little traveled. Hobhouse was making copious notes for his book. Signor Nicolo was very helpful.

The next day Byron and Hobhouse called at the palace of Mouctar Pasha, eldest son of Ali. Mouctar was absent, but his son, a boy of ten, gravely entertained them with coffee and sweetmeats and, ordering his father's women to be withdrawn to the inner apartments of the harem, took them for a tour of the palace, a task which so delighted him that he had to fight with himself to maintain his Turkish reserve and dignity. A shabby-looking guard embraced him tenderly with a "strange mixture of familiarity and respect." He took a boyish pride in showing his watch, but drew back when Hobhouse tried to touch a charm hanging round his neck. Byron later wrote his mother that this little Mahmout Pasha, Ali's grandson, "with large black eyes, which our ladies would purchase at any price . . . asked me how I came to travel so young, without anybody to take care of me. This question was put by the little man with all the gravity of threescore." *n*

They were fortunate enough to see a Greek wedding procession that night, and the next day, October 8, the Ramadan, or Mohammedan Lent, began. Pistols and guns were fired in every part of the city at the rising of the moon, and the minarets of the mosques were illuminated. All day the Turks fasted, but the night was a time for visits, for puppet shows, jugglers, dancers, and storytellers. Heavy drums were beaten at midnight to call the faithful to the mosque, but the feasting and carousing lasted until daybreak. They dined with Captain Leake and went one evening to a Turkish bath, full because of Ramadan, but they were "frightened away by a [crooked?] old fellow one of the rubbers so that we did not go into the inner room where the washing takes place and where the operation is performed, as Signior Nicolo said, by belli giovani."

On the 11th the travelers set out for Tepelene to visit the Pasha with Ali's secretary, his servant, a priest, and an Albanian soldier of the city guard, named Vasilly, assigned to look after the Vizier's guests and act as general factotum and guide. Byron loitered behind the others, who hurried on to the village of Zitza to escape an impending storm. George, the Greek dragoman, and the helpless but faithful Fletcher were with him, as well as the priest. When the thunder and lightning crashed upon them and the rain came, the frightened guides ran away, two of the horses fell, George in the excitement "stamped swore cried and fired off his pistols, which manœuvre being performed without due notice alarmed the 'valet' into fears for his life from robbers, . . . the whole situation becoming so serious that Ld B laughed." For nine hours they had been in ignorance of their position, though only an hour's ride from Zitza, where the anxious Hobhouse had ordered fires and firing of guns to guide them.

They stopped near some Turkish tombstones and a rain-swollen torrent, and there, inspired by the flashes of lightning, Byron composed some verses. While "the elements exhaust their wrath," one thought, that of "Sweet Florence" [Constance Spencer Smith], still had the power to keep his bosom warm."[n]

At three in the morning they arrived in the village, both Byron and the baggage unharmed because of the rough woolen capotes that covered them. But Byron recorded that "Fletcher was sorely bewildered, from apprehensions of famine and banditti. . . . His eyes were a little hurt by the lightning, or crying (I don't know which). . . ."[n] They spent the day at Zitza recuperating and visiting the monastery on a hill crowned with fine oak trees, "in the most beautiful situation," Byron wrote, "(always excepting Cintra, in Portugal) I ever beheld."[n]

On the 13th they started out again. In the rainy season it was a hard trip through mountainous country, and it required another week for them to reach Tepelene. In places the roads were completely washed away. Hobhouse complained of not being able to sleep because of fleas or barking dogs or wet bedding.

Reminiscing of this time later, Byron recalled that his friend, "when we were wayfaring men, used to complain grievously of hard beds and sharp insects, while I slept like a top, and to awaken me with his swearing at them: he used to damn his dinners daily, both quality and cookery and quantity, and reproach me for a sort of 'brutal' indifference . . . I was always *out* of bed before him, though it is true that my ablutions detained me longer in dressing than his noble contempt of that 'oriental scrupulosity' permitted."[n] Hobhouse used to lament, Byron said, "that I had no notion of comfort, because I could sleep where none but a *brute* could, and certainly where *brutes did;* for often have the *cows,* turned out of their apartment, *butted* at the door all night, extremely discomposed with their unaccountable ejectment. Thus we lived—one day in the palace of the Pacha, and the next perhaps in the most miserable hut of the mountains. I confess I preferred the former, but never quarrelled with the latter. . . ."[n]

The wild mountain scenery reminded Byron of the Scottish Highlands. He admired the characters and the costumes of the Arnaouts or Albanese. "The Albanians in general . . . have a fine cast of countenance; and the most beautiful women I ever beheld, in stature and in features, we saw *levelling* the *road* broken down by the torrents between Delvinachi and Libochabo."[n]

On October 19 they came down into the plain and saw the towers and minarets of Tepelene. "I shall never forget the singular scene on entering Tepaleen at five in the afternoon, as the sun was going down," Byron wrote his mother. "The Albanians, in their dresses, (the most magnificent in the world, consisting of a long *white kilt,* gold-worked cloak, crimson velvet gold-laced jacket and waistcoat, silver-mounted pistols and daggers,) the Tartars with their high caps, the Turks in their vast pelisses and turbans, the soldiers and black slaves with the horses, the former in groups in an immense large open gallery in front of the palace, the latter placed in a kind of cloister below it, two hundred steeds ready caparisoned to move in a moment, couriers entering or passing out with the despatches, the kettle-drums beating, boys calling the hour from the minaret of the mosque, altogether, with the singular appearance of the building itself, formed a new and delightful spectacle to a stranger." [n]

This was indeed for Byron the high point in his voyage, and he ever remembered it as something approaching the Arabian Nights in the magic of barbarian splendor and strangeness. Not even the capital city of the Turks on the Bosporus, with its grander mosques and minarets, nor the palace of the Sultan himself could vie in captivating interest with the absolute little court which Ali Pasha had established in this remote and inaccessible region of Albania. That it was little known was part of its charm for Byron, as well as for Hobhouse, who was making notes for a book of travels. Later Byron referred with some pride to what Gibbon had said of Albania, that a country "within sight of Italy is less known than the interior of America," and added that "with the exception of Major Leake, then officially resident at Joannina, no other Englishmen have ever advanced beyond the capital into the interior." [n]

When Byron arrived, Ali Pasha had made himself absolute ruler not only over all of Albania, but also over the whole of the Epirus to the Gulf of Corinth, and his son Veli was Pasha of the Peloponnesus, then commonly referred to as the Morea. By cunning, treachery (though no more than was common among rival bandit chieftains at the time), and diplomacy, Ali had raised himself gradually from a petty leader of robber bands to a ruler more powerful in his own domain than the Sultan himself, to whom, as a ruler of the Ottoman Empire, he nominally paid tribute and homage. Having subdued after long and cruel warfare the toughest of his opponents, the Suliotes, who held out for years in their rock-bound fastnesses on the coast of the Epirus north of Prevesa, Ali now held peaceful but despotic sway over the whole of his domain, permitting no robbery but his own, as Hobhouse observed.

If the travelers expected something formal and formidable in their interview with this sanguinary despot, who had murdered more people by treachery and his own hands than had ever been counted, they were soon disillusioned. They were given a good apartment in the palace—welcome after the hardships of the journey—and were introduced to a secretary (actually a

Greek physician of Ali) who spoke German, Latin, French, Italian, Greek, and Turkish. News had just come that the English had taken Cephalonia and Ithaca, in addition to Zante, from the French, a fact that made Ali the more eager to show every courtesy to his English visitors. But Byron was still convinced that the Pasha was most impressed by his rank. Before they went to bed, Hobhouse recorded: "Ld. B gave me a lecture about not caring enough for the English nobility."

They called on the Vizier the next day with the dragoman George and the secretary. Byron had dressed "in a full suit of staff uniform, with a very magnificent sabre, etc." His account of the interview to his mother shows how much he was impressed by the personality of Ali, a man who could be cruel and yet who was suave and luxury-loving, able to live according to his own laws, indulging all his appetites without social restraint. His ruthlessness added to his romantic stature and made him the kind of noble villain that Byron was to celebrate in his Oriental tales.[8] Like the pirate Lambro in *Don Juan,* Ali appeared to be "the mildest mannered man/ That ever scuttled ship or cut a throat." [n]

Byron wrote his mother: "The vizier received me in a large room paved with marble; a fountain was playing in the centre; the apartment was surrounded by scarlet ottomans. He received me standing, a wonderful compliment from a Mussulman, and made me sit down on his right hand. . . . His first question was, why, at so early an age, I left my country?—(The turks have no idea of travelling for amusement). He then said, the English minister, Captain Leake, had told him I was of a great family, and desired his respects to my mother. . . . He said he was certain I was a man of birth, because I had small ears, curling hair, and little white hands, and expressed himself pleased with my appearance and garb. He told me to consider him as a father whilst I was in Turkey, and said he looked on me as his son. Indeed, he treated me like a child, sending me almonds and sugared sherbet, fruit and sweetmeats, twenty

[8] The Pasha Giaffir in *The Bride of Abydos* bears a close resemblance to Ali Pasha. The name "Giaffir," however, Byron apparently took from one of Ali's victims, whose daughter the Pasha married. (*Poetry,* III, 189n.)

times a day. He begged me to visit him often, and at night, when he was at leisure. I then, after coffee and pipes, retired for the first time." [n]

While he was greatly flattered by the Pasha's attention, Byron half sensed, and recognized more fully when he had reflected upon the interview and had seen more of Turkish manners, that Ali's observation of his handsome features had a particular meaning more personal and sensuous than an interest in his noble birth or rank would have elicited.

The Vizier was "affable, good humored," Hobhouse observed. He even laughed aloud, something unusual in the dignified Turk. He wore a high turban with many folds and had an ataghan studded with diamonds. "His highness is sixty years old, very fat, and not tall," Byron wrote, "but with a fine face, light blue eyes, and a white beard; his manner is very kind, and at the same time he possesses that dignity which I find universal amongst the Turks. He has the appearance of anything but his real character, for he is a remorseless tyrant, guilty of the most horrible cruelties, very brave, and so good a general that they call him the Mahometan Buonaparte." [n]

Fletcher, who had, according to Hobhouse, "been lousing all day with great success especially in my lord's shirt," got his reward by being sent the next day to the Vizier with "a gun of Manton's single barrel & a telescope of Berger's with a promise of another gun also of Ld. B's, a rifle of Manton's." Ali, much pleased, gave an order for eighty piasters to Fletcher. Byron and Hobhouse paid their second visit that evening, when the Vizier received them in a more elegantly furnished apartment. He congratulated them on the English victories in the Ionian Islands and said he preferred them for neighbors.

On the evening of the 22nd they had their last audience with Ali. When they told him they wanted to go to the Morea, he gave them a letter to his son Veli Pasha and much practical advice about roads, warning them against certain routes infested by robbers. They could either have an armed guard through Acarnania or he would give orders to the governor of Prevesa to send them in an armed galiot to Patras. Their request to take with them Vasilly, who had proved a much more valuable guide than George, was readily granted. Ali called Vasilly in, gave him instructions about the roads, and playfully warned him that if any accident happened to his guests, he would cut off his head.[n]

They heard many stories of the Vizier's barbarities. The wife of his son Mouctar, who was a favorite of his, complained one day that her husband was neglecting her for other women. Ali demanded to know who they were, and she wrote down in her grief and jealousy (quite at random without positive evidence, it was said) "the names of fifteen of the most beautiful women, some Greeks some Turkish, in the city of Ioannina. The same night they were all seized in their houses, conveyed to the palace in the fortress, thence carried in boats on the lake, and after being tied up in sacks, were thrown into the water." [n] This story was confirmed by Vasilly, who was one of the thirty soldiers of the city guard employed to seize them and to carry out the Pasha's brutal order.

The rains had subsided when Byron and his entourage left for Jannina on the 23rd, and they made in four days the journey of seventy-five miles that had taken them nine days over washed-out roads. They spent the last night comfortably in the monastery at Zitza, and galloped into Jannina at a quarter past five on the 26th, taking up their abode again with Signor Nicolo.

Riding out on the Vizier's horses on the 28th, accompanied by Bosari, Byron and Hobhouse visited the remains of a great amphitheater of antiquity, the largest in Greece, in the hills east of Jannina. They were not aware that it was the fabled Dodona, near which stood the "talking oaks" that echoed the voice of Zeus.[n]

The next evening they called at Ali's great palace, where they met the eldest son of Veli, Pasha of the Morea. This boy of twelve, "a sprightly pretty boy said to be very clever & certain to be spoilt," had all the poise of his cousin.

"I have been introduced to Hussein Bey, and Mahmout Pacha, both little boys, grandchildren of Ali, at Yanina," Byron wrote his mother. "They are the prettiest little animals I ever saw, and are broken into the court ceremonies already." [n]

During his journeys through this picturesque land, for hours in the saddle alone with his thoughts, or at night while Hobhouse and Fletcher were complaining of the hard beds which made sleep impossible, Byron turned over in his mind his own strange life and its purposeless course. This contemplation often brought on that "rapt mood" noticed by Galt, or caused him to gaze, as Captain Leake observed, "with an air distrait and dreamy upon the distant mountains."[n] Byron felt a strong need to record the experiences and sift out the impressions of his youth. He had already written an intimate journal of his early life which Hobhouse persuaded him to burn.[n] Now he turned to verse, which he had already found a happier medium than prose for distilling the materials of existence.

Among the books Byron had brought with him from England was an anthology of English poetry called *Elegant Selections.* In it was a selection from Spenser's *Faerie Queene.*[n] The meter of the Spenserian stanza seemed to lend itself to the adventure and commentary of a voyage. On the last day of October, while Hobhouse was inspecting the free public schools of Jannina, Byron began the first canto of *Childe Harold's Pilgrimage.* That evening Hobhouse wrote in his diary: "Byron is writing a long poem in the Spenserian stanza. . . ."

The travelers left Jannina on November 3, and arrived at Salora on the Gulf of Arta on the 5th. There they rested, bathing in the sea, while Vasilly went on to Prevesa with a letter to Captain Leake, who had preceded them, to get advice on the best route to follow to avoid robbers. When his reply came, they decided to accept Ali Pasha's offer of an armed vessel to Patras. On the 7th they sailed to Prevesa.

The next day they boarded a galiot with forty men and four guns bound for Patras. Ali had good soldiers, but his navy was something of a farce. The captain, a mild man who knew little about sailing, ran aground as they were taking off, and wanted to wait until night, but Byron and Hobhouse, unaware of the total inefficiency of the whole Turkish crew (the four Greeks among them were the only ones who knew anything about the management of a ship), urged him to go on. So they pulled free and got away with a fair breeze about one in the afternoon. But by 4:00, though the wind seemed favorable, the ship was in distress. Fear of running into a headland of Santa Maura, still held by the French, had put the crew into a panic. Putting about and heading for Corfu to the north, the confused steersman ran into a heavy swell. The wind freshened, the sails split, guns broke loose. The captain wrung his hands and the crew gave up and went below deck. The wind increased at sunset, and the ship, though a solid fifty-ton vessel, shook violently. "George our dragoman," Hobhouse wrote, "at every heel the ship took, called loudly on the name of God, and when the main-yard snapped in two, every thing was given up for lost. . . . The ship lay like a log on the water. . . . The Captain being asked what he could do, said, he could do nothing.—'Could he get back to the mainland?'—'If God chuses,' was his answer.—'Could he make Corfu?'—'If God chuses.'" [n]

Fortunately the captain gave up the crippled vessel to the Greeks, who got it at dawn into a bay near a rocky cliff on the coast of Suli, north of Prevesa. No sooner was the anchor dropped than the Turks, realizing that it was the first morning of Bairam, the feast marking the end of the Ramadan, kissed and embraced each other and the captain without taking more thought of the ship.

The whole thing was so ridiculous in retrospect that Byron wrote a humorous account of it to his mother: "Fletcher yelled after his wife, the Greeks called on all the saints, the Mussulmans on Alla; the captain burst into tears and ran below deck, telling us to call on God; the sails were split, the main-yard shivered, the wind blowing fresh, the night setting in, and all our chance was to make Corfu . . . or (as Fletcher pathetically termed it) 'a watery grave.' I did what I could to console Fletcher, but finding him incorrigible, wrapped myself up in my Albanian capote . . . and lay down on deck to wait the worst. I have learnt to philosophise in my travels; and if I had not, complaint was useless." [n]

Proceeding by land back to Prevesa, the travelers decided that they would rather face the robbers to the south than trust themselves again to the seamanship of the Turks. In spite of the hardships and misadventures, Byron had come to like the country and to admire the inhabitants. It was in quite a different mood from that of their first arrival in Prevesa that he sat down on November 12 to write a long letter to his mother. He was in the best of humor. In contrast to an English winter, he found the Albanian climate delightful. "Yesterday . . . I bathed in the sea; to-day is so hot that I am writing in a shady room of the English consul's, with three doors wide open, no fire, or even *fireplace,* in the house, except for culinary purposes." And he admired the Albanians and praised their hospitality. The Albanian chief who helped Byron's party out of the Turkish galley and lodged them, when pressed to accept some money, replied: "No, I wish you to love me, not to pay me." All he wanted was a paper stating that they had been well received.

As for his future plans, Byron wrote: "I am going to-morrow, with a guard of fifty men, to Patras in the Morea, and thence to Athens, where I shall winter. . . . to study modern Greek, which differs much from the ancient, though radically similar. I have no desire to return to England, nor shall I, unless compelled by absolute want, and Hanson's neglect; but I shall not enter into Asia for a year or two, as I have much to see in Greece, and I may perhaps cross into Africa, at least the Egyptian part." [9] It was easy for Byron on occasion to convince himself that he had definite plans, but generally he realized that chance would govern the remainder of his pilgrimage, as it had his journey into Albania.

Byron and his party started out the morning of the 13th to make their way through the wilds of Acarnania, infested as they knew by robbers, to Missolonghi, from which they would have only to cross the Gulf to Patras. Accompanied by thirty-seven Albanian soldiers, they sailed up the Gulf of Arta (or Ambracian Gulf), reaching the fortress of Vonitza at sunset. Spending the night on board, they landed at Utraikee the next afternoon. As

[9] *LJ,* I, 253–6. Writing to Hanson the same day, Byron reiterated his intention never to "revisit England if I can avoid it. . . . Why I say this, is best known to myself; you recollect my impatience to leave it, you also know by what I then and still write that it was not to defraud my creditors." And again in the same letter, after saying that he had no fear of the consequences of his satire, he added: "I never will live in England if I can avoid it. *Why*—must remain a secret, but the farther I proceed the less I regret quitting it." (*LJ,* VI, 446.)

Byron saw the moon shining on Actium's coast, where "The ancient world was won and lost," he thought again of the "Sweet Florence" he had left at Malta, and jotted down his "Stanzas Written in Passing the Ambracian Gulf."

At Utraikee the atmosphere was tense, for a band of robbers had swooped down there only a few days before and had killed two people. Perhaps that very tensity contributed energy to the dancing of the Albanian soldiers around their open fires in the evening after their roasted goat was consumed. Sitting on the ground while the Albanians danced around the flame to the music of their own songs, most of which had to do with their exploits when they were robbers, Byron and Hobhouse stored up some of their most vivid impressions of the picturesque. Byron remembered their "bounding hand in hand, man linked to man," while they sang a song which, according to Hobhouse, began: "when we set sail, a band of Thieves from Parga, we were in number 62," and which had for a refrain: "Robbers all at Parga, Robbers all at Parga." [n] Almost every man in Ali's army had been a robber at one time or another.

The anxious but uneventful journey through the forests to the Gulf of Lepanto took six days. Arriving at Anatolica, a village on a salt sea marsh, on the 19th, they spent the night and entered Missolonghi the next day. As Byron, dressed in his gay regimentals, came into the town, he was met by the English Consul (a Greek) "on a prancing palfry." He had taken Byron for the English Ambassador and spoke French to him. Missolonghi had then a population of about five thousand, part Greek and part Turk, who supported themselves mainly by fishing. It stood on a flat, marshy promontory sticking out into a shallow lagoon accessible only to small boats. Fishermen's huts, built on stakes in the water, and fishing-nets circled the lagoon. It was not attractive, and Byron nowhere in his letters or poems described the fateful town as it appeared to him on his first visit.

At Missolonghi they dismissed their guard, paying each man a sequin. One of the soldiers who had become attached to him, a Turk by the name of Dervish Tahiri, Byron took into his service as an additional guide.[n] The wind proving too strong for the caïque that was to carry them to Patras, the party returned to their lodging, to the horror of the Consul. The next day, the 22nd, they made the crossing in two and one-half hours, and were hospitably welcomed by the Greek acting as English Consul for the Morea, Mr. Strané. They rested eleven days at Patras, repairing and replenishing their supplies and equipage, and enjoying the convenience of tables and chairs again. They were entertained by most of the official population, including Strané's cousin, the Imperial Consul. They rode through the orange, olive, and currant groves near the town and indulged in the luxury of bathing in the sea in December.

At Patras they dismissed the unsatisfactory George and hired another Greek, Andreas, who had lived in Constantinople and who spoke Turkish, Greek, French, Italian, and bad Latin learned while in a choir at Rome. On December 4 they set out on their final trek toward Athens. Passing through orange and lemon groves along the shore, they reached Vostitza the next day. Across the blue waters of the Corinthian Gulf they caught their first sight of Mount Parnassus, covered with snow. At Vostitza they lodged with the Cogia Basha, Andreas Londos, governor under Veli of the town and district. The wealthy young man, only twenty, was the son of Veli Pasha's trusted prime minister, and he had the best house in the Morea.

It was the intention of the travelers to cross the gulf at this point, but, the wind being contrary, they spent several days with their agreeable host, and on rainy days, when they became better acquainted, the Cogia let down the Turkish reserve he tried to cultivate and became a playful boy.[n]

The wind remaining unfavorable, they were still at Londos's on December 9. They went out to shoot woodcocks on the shore and saw none, but Byron shot an eagle. It was only wounded, and the unpleasant experience remained with him a long time. In his journal of 1814 he wrote: "The last bird I ever fired at was an *eaglet*, on the shore of the Gulf of Lepanto, near Vostitza. It was only wounded, and I tried to save it, the eye was so bright; but it pined, and died in a few days; and I never did since, and never will, attempt the death of another bird."[n]

That evening the Cogia Basha was playing draughts with a

local doctor when the latter mentioned the name of Rhiga, the Greek who, twenty years before, had attempted to organize a revolution against the Turkish masters. The young Londos, to the surprise of his guests, who thought it a little odd that a Greek in so high a position under the Turks should express openly such revolutionary fervor, "jumped suddenly from the sofa, threw over the board, and clasping his hands, repeated the name of the patriot with a thousand passionate exclamations, the tears streaming down his cheeks."[1] Then he recited with ecstasy the patriotic war song of the Greeks, "*Deute Paides*," "Greeks arise," an adaptation of the "*Marseillaise*" written by Rhiga. Byron and Hobhouse were both delighted and later made translations of it.[n] They had begun to see, as they had not in Albania, that there was among the Greeks an underlying hatred of their masters which needed only a flame to set it off.

Finally on the 14th they got away in a Cephalonian boat with fourteen men and ten oars and crossed the gulf to Salona. They arrived at midnight, and, in order to sleep at the *han,* or inn, they had to make beds in two small rooms filled with onions.

Their chief reason for crossing the gulf at this point, rather than proceeding by the shorter and smoother route through Corinth to Athens, was of course their desire, fostered by their classical education, to see Delphi, taste of the Castalian spring, and actually walk on the rocks of Parnassus. As they were riding up to the town of Chrisso at its base the next day, they got an inspiring view of the mountain that was the home of Apollo and the Muses. This one sight of it in the clear Greek air gave Byron a livelier sense of the poetry it inspired than all his classical reading. Breaking off his tribute to "Spain's dark-glancing daughters" in the poem he had been composing during all the pauses of their journey, he hailed the wonder that he saw,

[1] *Journey,* II, 586. Constantine Rhiga founded the Hetairia, a society to encourage and foster Greek nationalism. He gathered money for the cause from wealthy Greeks throughout the Turkish dominions, but while at Vienna was given up to the Grand Signor by Joseph II and executed in 1798. His memory and his patriotic songs did much to arouse the Greeks to rebellion a few years after Byron's first visit to Greece. When the revolution broke out in 1821, Andreas Londos was one of the first to take a lead in the war.

*Not in the fabled landscape of a lay,*
*But soaring snow-clad through thy native sky,*
*In the wild pomp of mountain-majesty!* [n]

Going up the mountain to Castri (the site of Delphi), Byron saw some large birds soaring over the rocks. "Upon Parnassus," he later recalled, ". . . I saw a flight of twelve Eagles (Hobhouse says they are Vultures—at least in conversation), and I seized the Omen. On the day before, I composed the lines to Parnassus (in Childe Harold), and, on beholding the birds, had a hope that Appollo had accepted my homage." [n] Hobhouse was right; they were vultures, which if Byron had known he might have used equally effectively as a symbol of what the gods had in store for him.

Delphi was disappointing. There was little to be seen but a dirty village (the excavators' tools had not yet laid bare the ancient ruins), and the travelers had to use their imaginations to picture the throne of the Pythoness in a cave where cattle were sheltered and the amphitheater in a few jutting fragments of wall.

On the 17th they skirted the slopes of Parnassus on their way to Livadia, where they lodged with the Archon Logotheti in a "magnificent mansion." There they met a freethinking bishop by the name of Gregorius.[n] Byron had not expected to find such a frank "esprit fort" in a Greek bishop. "This worthy hypocrite rallied his own religion with great intrepidity (but not before his flock), and talked of the mass as a 'coglioneria.' [n] It was impossible to think better of him for this. . . ." [2]

After visiting the sites of ancient Chæronea and Orchomenus, and stopping to wonder whether the fork of a road was the spot where Œdipus unwittingly killed his father, they proceeded toward Thebes, into which they galloped in a downpour of rain on December 22. While Hobhouse was sightseeing, Byron, now nearing the end of his account of Childe Harold's journey

[2] *Poetry*, II, 188. Byron elsewhere said that his Albanian servant Vasilly, a Greek Christian, "had the greatest veneration for the church, mixed with the highest contempt of churchmen, whom he cuffed upon occasion in a most heterodox manner. Yet he never passed a church without crossing himself. . . ." When Byron pointed out his inconsistency, he answered: "Our church is holy, our priests are thieves." (*Poetry*, II, 175–6.)

through Spain, took time to write some digressive stanzas on an English Sabbath.[n] They set out on the 24th for Athens, spending Christmas Eve at Scourta, "a miserable deserted village." Here they occupied a hovel, the worst of their journey, slightly removed from the racks and mangers of a stable. On Christmas Day they caught their first view of the city from a pine-covered hill on the border of Bœotia and Attica. From this point, near Fort Phyle, Byron recalled, "Athens, Pentilicus, Hymettus, the Ægean, and the Acropolis, burst upon the eye at once."[n] They rode down through the olive groves, crossed the Cephisus, passed through an arched gateway, and entered Athens at 8:30 in the evening.

Entering the city in the dark, the weary travelers, somewhat awed by being under the walls of the citadel of the Acropolis, went immediately up a narrow street to a private dwelling that had been recommended to them as harboring English travelers. It was a double house owned by Mrs. Tarsia Macri, widow of a former British Vice-Consul.[n] The lodgings they took, Hobhouse wrote, "consisted of a sitting-room and two bed-rooms, opening into a court-yard where there were five or six lemon-trees, from which, during our residence in the place, was plucked the fruit that seasoned the pilaf, and other national dishes served up at our frugal table."[3] The widow Macri had three daughters, whom Byron soon noticed, Mariana, Katinka, and Theresa, "all of them under fifteen."[n] The youngest, Theresa, a dark-eyed brunette with a pale but clear complexion and straight nose inclining to aquiline, had just passed her twelfth year when the English travelers arrived.

The day following their arrival Byron and Hobhouse began to look about them. Athens, the capital of Greece in her glory, was in 1809 a small town of narrow streets and squalid appearance crowded around the north and west sides of the Acropolis and enclosed by a wall ten feet high. The whole town, which

[3] *Journey*, I, 291. This house was partly destroyed in the Greek Revolution and disappeared entirely soon after. Prince Pückler-Muskau found it in ruins with only the walls standing in 1836. (Brouzas, pp. 24–7.) Today a modern two-story dwelling stands on the spot, in Hagia Street, on flat land to the west of the Acropolis; a plaque tells in Greek and English that Byron's Maid of Athens lived in a house on the site.

in its great age extended to the hill of Lycabettus and into the plain in every direction from the citadel, then had a population of only ten thousand pressed within the walls that Hobhouse walked around in forty-seven minutes. Of the twelve or thirteen hundred houses, four hundred were occupied by Turks, the rest by Greeks and Albanians. In addition there were seven or eight Frank families, under the protection of the French Consul.[4] There were no hotels or inns, and occasional European visitors were compelled to find lodgings with a few private families. An increasing number of these visitors were coming to Athens since Continental travel had been restricted or cut off by the Napoleonic wars and since renewed interest in the archæological aspects of classical study had stimulated travelers like E. D. Clarke to explore the sites of ancient civilizations.[n]

Athens when they arrived was ruled by a Waiwode appointed by the Disdar Aga, an officer of the Sultan, under whose protection the Athenians placed themselves in the seventeenth century (by paying a voluntary tribute of thirty thousand crowns). So dependent was the Waiwode on the good will of his subjects that he generally treated them with lenity so long as the tribute to the Porte and his own perquisites were handed over regularly. The practical government of the Greek population of Attica and other provinces of Greece was left in the hands of the Cogia Bashis or Archons, Greeks themselves and often ecclesiastical authorities as well, like the freethinking and wealthy bishop in Livadia. They extracted from the people double the taxes required by the Porte and thus enriched themselves. These officers rather than the Turks were considered by many the real oppressors of the people. But, while there was bitterness, there was no organized resistance. One discontented Greek to whom Hobhouse talked said that if there was a revolt against the Archons, "The Turks will be on our side, if we get the better; but, alas! the influence of money is all-powerful. . . ."[n]

On their first day in the city Byron and Hobhouse went to see the English Vice-Consul, Spiridion Logotheti, who, Hobhouse wrote in his diary, "had the imp[udenc]e to propose his gawky

[4] *Journey*, I, 292–3. The term "Franks" was used generally in the Levant to designate all western Europeans.

son as a travelling companion to us." [n] The same day they received a visit from Giovanni Battista Lusieri, the Neapolitan painter employed by Lord Elgin, first to make drawings and then to superintend the dismantling on the Acropolis and elsewhere of the famous sculptures which Elgin was shipping to England. Byron, echoing the common skeptical view in London when the first marbles Elgin had brought home were shown, had made some contemptuous remarks in *English Bards and Scotch Reviewers* about Elgin's "mutilated blocks of art." [n] He was, therefore, inclined to think lightly of the work directed by Lusieri.[5] So from his first day in Athens Byron became involved in the controversy, which, Hobhouse said, had "enlisted all the Frank settlers and the principal Greeks on one or the other side." [n]

On the 27th, Byron and Hobhouse accompanied Lusieri and Logotheti to call on the governor of the town, the Waiwode, "a personable man who had served in Ægypt." They soon began their sightseeing. Hobhouse generally walked out in the morning and explored the ground, while Byron remained at the widow Macri's, probably writing the last stanzas of the first canto of *Childe Harold,* which he finished shortly after arriving in Athens. Then he joined Hobhouse in riding over the same ground, or perhaps a little farther afield. On the 28th they saw the Temple of Theseus and the Columns of Olympian Zeus. The next day they wanted to go to the Acropolis, but were told that they must first send a present of tea and sugar to the governor or Disdar,

[5] Hobhouse diary. Lusieri, commonly known as Don Tita Lusieri, was an accomplished landscape-painter and topographical draftsman. First employed by Sir William Hamilton in 1799 while Hamilton was British envoy at Naples to make topographical studies for him in the Near East, he was later engaged by Lord Elgin while he was British Ambassador in Constantinople to make drawings of the sculptures in Athens. Elgin then got permission from the Turkish authorities to erect scaffolds and make plaster casts. Discovering that many of the ancient marbles were deteriorating and were likely to be lost, he took the liberty of removing and shipping to England some of the statues and friezes, an action not opposed by the Turkish governor or by the authorities in Constantinople (perhaps well rewarded for their acquiescence). Elgin's first shipment had gone to England in 1802, but it was not opened to the public until 1807, in a museum in Park Lane, where Byron saw the collection before he went abroad. Lusieri, who had been in Athens ten years at this work when Byron arrived, was then superintending another shipment.

a poorly paid subordinate of the Waiwode. So, postponing their visit, they rode out to Piræus and saw chests of Lord Elgin's marbles ready to be loaded on a Hydriote ship that was to convey them to England.

They returned galloping to Athens by a road that passed back of the Acropolis, from which both the Parthenon and the Temple of Theseus could be seen in a flattering view that obliterated the ravages of time. They could imagine themselves travelers approaching Athens in its glory. That day they dined with the widow Macri and her three daughters, a communicating door having been made in the wall that separated them from the next house. Byron had now acquired a very comfortable room vacated by Mr. Galton, an Englishman who had been at the Macris' on their arrival. He still had his two Albanian servants, besides Fletcher and Andreas, the polylingual boy they had added to their entourage at Patras, and it was a problem to house them all. Vasilly, by preference, slept in the yard.

As the year ended, the pattern of their life was established, and it was an increasingly pleasant one. Every day Byron rode out one of the city gates with Hobhouse. One day it would be to the north to Pentelicus, from which the ancient Greeks had extracted the marble for the great columns and the statues on the Acropolis. On another they would ride westward to Eleusis and view Salamis and Ægina in the distance, or to a monastery on Mount Hymettus. Sometimes they were joined by Lusieri or some other Franks or Greeks. They dined on red mullet or woodcock. The climate was mild, with more sunshine than Byron had ever seen in the winter. The people were hospitable and agreeable. Soon they had met the principal Greek families and the few Franks who made up the compact social life of the town. Among the latter were two Frenchmen, Nicholas Roque, a merchant (who had married the sister of their landlady, and was the uncle of Mariana, Katinka, and Theresa Macri), and Louis Fauvel, a cultured gentleman who had gained distinction as an illustrator before he settled in Athens, where he could pursue his archæological and artistic interests while acting as French Consul. Byron paid tribute to Fauvel's "talents as an artist, and manners as a gentleman." [n]

But there was a lighter side to their social life that appealed as much to Byron. "They have balls and parties in the winter and spring of the year," Hobhouse wrote, "in their own small circle, to which the principal Greeks are invited, and particularly during the carnival, when they and many of the inhabitants are in masquerade." [n]

At Byron's comfortable lodgings his spirits were lightened by the presence of "the three graces," the Macri sisters, who waited on the guests. The blooming freshness of their youthful charm and innocence, however, aroused thoughts of death and decay, of beauty that passes and joy that is transient. And on his daily rides and excursions the feeling was strengthened by the mellow beauty of the Attic landscape and the relics of a decayed civilization. It oppressed him as much in the character of the people, who, though pleasant, lived too quiescently under the Turkish yoke, as in the ruins of columns and the broken beauty of statues once perfect. While Hobhouse took notes copiously on every detail of archæological and historical interest, Byron merely soaked in general impressions, cultivated the bittersweet mood of the moment, and stored up memories.

Byron had a certain contempt for his friend's antiquarian zeal. "Travelling in Greece," he later told Trelawny, "Hobhouse and I wrangled every day. His guide was Mitford's fabulous History. He had a greed for legendary lore, topography, inscriptions; gabbled in *lingua franca* to the Ephori of the villages, goatherds, and our dragoman. He would potter with map and compass at the foot of Pindus, Parnes, and Parnassus, to ascertain the site of some ancient temple or city. I rode my mule up them. They had haunted my dreams from boyhood; the pines, eagles, vultures, and owls were descended from those Themistocles and Alexander had seen, and were not degenerated like the humans; the rocks and torrents the same. John Cam's dogged perseverance in pursuit of his hobby is to be envied; I have no hobby and no perseverance. I gazed at the stars and ruminated; took no notes, asked no questions." [n]

Delayed by formalities, Byron, accompanied by Hobhouse and Lusieri, Lord Elgin's agent, finally visited the Acropolis on January 8. The marble columns scattered about, the roofless and crumbling Parthenon where Athena's statue had stood, together with the dismantling operations directed by Lusieri, filled Byron's mind at once with the most exalted ideas of Greece's Golden Age and the most depressed feeling of the vanity of human ambitions and hopes. In the prologue to the second canto of *Childe Harold*, which he was just beginning, some of these ideas found expression. Calling on the Goddess of Wisdom, Athena, whose temple was here, to look on the dominion of those "who never felt the sacred glow" that thoughts of her inspired, he asked:

*Where are thy men of might? thy grand in soul?*
*Gone—glimmering through the dream of things that were. . . .*

And then:

*Look on this spot—a Nation's sepulchre!*
*Abode of Gods, whose shrines no longer burn.*
*Even Gods must yield—Religions take their turn:*
*'Twas Jove's—'tis Mahomet's—and other Creeds*
*Will rise with other years, till Man shall learn*
*Vainly his incense soars, his victim bleeds;*
*Poor child of Doubt and Death, whose hope is built on reeds.*

"Athena's wisest son" (Socrates) had uttered the greatest wisdom, Byron thought, when he said: "All that we know is, nothing can be known." [n]

In subsequent visits to the Acropolis in the following weeks and in their rides to Piræus Byron observed with increasing indignation what he considered the depredations and robbery that Lord Elgin was perpetrating in Greece. He began to take a quite different view of the Elgin-marble question. These relics that were being carried away were not now in his eyes worthless stones and "maimed antiques," but the heritage of the finest culture of the Greek race. The indifference of the modern Greeks was no excuse, he felt, for such spoliation—and not all the Greeks were indifferent; he had heard the story of some workmen throwing down a case of the marbles because, they declared, they heard the statue groaning and crying out for his fellow spirits on the Acropolis.[n]

Although Byron did not care much for works of art as such, except for occasional pieces whose realistic portrayal of the beauty of the human form stirred his imagination, he was not one to balance, as did Hobhouse, the good and the bad effects of Lord Elgin's work. One contention of Hobhouse and others was that the preservation of these art treasures in London would benefit "an infinitely greater number of rising architects and sculptors." Byron met that argument by turning it to ridicule. He later wrote: "I opposed, and will ever oppose, the robbery of ruins from Athens, to instruct the English in sculpture (who are as capable of sculpture as the Egyptians are of skating). . . ." [n]

Byron's feelings became savage as he viewed the fresh plaster scars marking the removal of one of the Caryatides. In the first heat of his *sæva indignatio* he castigated his fellow Scot in some stanzas to be added to the prologue of the second canto of *Childe Harold.*

The legend that Alaric the Goth, terrified by phantoms of Minerva and Achilles, or struck with a reverence for the classic city, had spared its treasures and monuments, offered the dramatic contrast that kindled Byron's imagination. He named among the "plunderers" Sir William Hamilton, who had begun the work of removing the marbles for Elgin (and who was famed for recapturing from the French the Rosetta Stone, which eventually unlocked the secrets of the Egyptian hieroglyphs), and Lord Aberdeen, who had done some collecting in Greece. But his ire was mainly reserved for Lord Elgin, whom he accused of having a barren mind and a hard heart.

However unfair the personal attack, which he himself was soon to regret, the fervor of his appeal to Greek patriotism and the generous enthusiasm of his Philhellenism touched chords that resounded far beyond the practical arguments of the day. Byron felt what Hobhouse and others could not foresee: that the Greeks might someday gain their freedom and preserve their own monuments.[6]

[6] Byron's protest against the spoliation of the Greek treasures has transcended practical considerations of art-preservation and even British national pride among Philhellenes to the present day. Sir Harold Nicolson has told how, when he was a young junior clerk in the Foreign Office in 1924, the centenary of Byron's death, he proposed to his superiors that it would be a

Byron had from his arrival formed a more favorable opinion of the Greeks than had his traveling companion and most of the other Franks with whom he was associated in Athens. When the French Consul, M. Fauvel, and the merchant M. Roque (who, according to Hobhouse, supported himself chiefly "by lending money, at an interest from twenty to thirty per cent to the trading Greeks, and in a trifling exportation of oil") came to visit Byron, M. Roque expressed the view common to foreigners in Greece at the time. The Athenians, he said, "are the same *canaille* that existed *in the days of Themistocles!*" This he uttered with "the most amusing gravity," Byron recalled in a note to *Childe Harold*, adding sarcastically: "The ancients banished Themistocles; the moderns cheat Monsieur Roque; thus great men have ever been treated!" [n]

But though he saw through their weaknesses and their vanities, Byron continued to be on excellent terms with both the Greeks and the Franks in Athens. The social life was more congenial than any he had experienced since he had come abroad, for it was informal and spontaneous. There was none of the stiffness of the official dinners he had attended at Gibraltar and Malta. Lusieri, whom Byron never at the time blamed too much for following the instructions of Lord Elgin, was an agreeable companion. Indeed, it was Lusieri himself who pointed out to Byron the extent of the devastation that had been wrought by Lord Elgin on the Parthenon and the Erectheum. Byron and Hobhouse dined with him on January 5, Christmas Day old style.

Early in the month Byron had made the acquaintance of a Greek by the name of Demetrius Zograffo, who accompanied them on many of their rides, acting as guide on jaunts as far as Salamis. And they were feeling constantly more at home with the Macris. They had conceived a project for a tour of the Greek islands in the Ægean, but the captain of the Hydriot vessel at

fine gesture of friendship to Greece if the British Museum, which purchased Lord Elgin's marbles in 1816 for £37,000, would send back one of these, the Caryatid, to its original home on the Erectheum. But they, not being as enthusiastic Byronians as Nicolson, were deaf to the appeal. (See Harold Nicolson: "The Byron Curse Echoes Again," *New York Times Magazine*, March 27, 1949, pp. 12, 13, 33, 35.)

Piræus was for some reason afraid to take them, perhaps because he did not know the waters or was afraid of pirates or warships that would take his cargo for contraband.

It was the holiday season of the Greeks and there was much spontaneous gaiety. One evening the ordinarily staid Hobhouse put on a velvet Turkish cap turban-fashion. On the 12th he and Byron dined in their quarters and, Hobhouse recorded, ". . . had presents of sweet cakes made of sugar and almonds and rose water brought in this being new year's eve by Theresa the girl of 12 years old but quite 'nubila' from the other house." And the next day, after an excursion with Lusieri and Demetrius to Eleusis, from which they returned by moonlight, they "went to B's house to dancing and buffoonery where there was a Greek fiddler and tambourinier—monotonous Greek music—and slow dancing. . . ."

Byron's increasing interest in the Macri girls (it is evident that he did not, at least at first, single out one of them for particular attention), together with his relaxed life in Athens, made the emotional strain of his love for Constance Spencer Smith seem very remote and unreal. It was a pleasant memory, but now he could disburden himself of it and the deceiving delirium that accompanied it. After returning from a ride to the monastery on Mount Hymettus on the 16th, he closed the account of that struggle with the verses:

*The spell is broke, the charm is flown!*
*Thus is it with Life's fitful fever. . . .*[n]

But for Byron there was always a sadness in the farewell to love, even when the feelings that first prompted the affair were gone. Writing of the departure of Childe Harold from the "fair Florence," he bemoaned the loss in the cooler light of reflection. As he saw it now, the passion he had felt consuming him at the time was only an illusion. The lady herself, he reflected, must have been attracted chiefly by the fact that he had withstood, "unmoved, the lustre of her gaze," for she was unaware that he was "not unskilful at the spoiler's art." But Byron had already learned the sad lesson that

*When all is won that all desire to woo,*
*The paltry prize is hardly worth the cost. . . .*[n]

Now he felt that it was better to admire and to be admired by "the three graces," the fresh and innocent Macri sisters, in this unfretted and pleasant relationship, however much his tyrannical urges pressed him to play the gallant. The fact that he could not even communicate with these young girls, except perhaps in a few words of the Romaic that he had learned, made the relationship the more engaging.

By the end of their third week the travelers had visited most of the relics of ancient Greece in and around Athens. One of Byron's favorite excursions was to the port of Piræus and then around the rocky promontory to the gemlike harbor of Munychia and on to the wider bay of Phaleron, returning to Athens through the olive groves with a fine view of the Parthenon and the Theseum against the hills. On January 18 they chose this for their last ride before making an extensive tour of Attica, and they stopped at Munychia to look for the tomb of Themistocles.[7]

On the 19th the caravan, consisting of Byron, Hobhouse, Vasilly, the Albanian servant, and Demetrius, who acted as guide, together with two men to look after the eight horses, set off for Cape Colonni [8] at the extreme southeast tip of Attica, where it reaches out toward the Cyclades Islands in the Ægean. Following around the south end of Hymettus, they spent the first night at Vary, the second at Keratea. Delayed there by rain, they climbed up the near-by mountain of Parne to explore a great cave. They had lighted fir torches at the entrance and carried a supply of strips for relighting. Wandering from one grotto or chamber to another—and these seemed endless—they came to a fountain of pure water. There they lingered awhile, but, seeing

[7] Byron opened *The Giaour* with a description of this rocky promontory, supposed to be the site of the tomb of Themistocles:

*No breath of air to break the wave*
*That rolls below the Athenian's grave,*
*That tomb which, gleaming o'er the cliff,*
*First greets the homeward-veering skiff*
*High o'er the land he saved in vain. . . .*

[8] Byron spelled the name Colonna. The Latin name of Sunium (French Sounion) which Byron used in "The Isles of Greece" still persists.

the torches wasting, they sought the exit only to find themselves after a short while back at the fountain. Terror seized them when the guide confessed that he had forgotten the intricate route they had come. Relying on their own memories and sense of direction, they finally saw a light just as the last torch was being consumed. They might have perished, for the townspeople said there were a thousand chambers in the cave. The relief from the grave danger was so great that Hobhouse picked up a stick and laid blows upon the conductor's back.

What Byron's conduct was on the occasion Hobhouse does not tell, but it is likely that it was not heroic and that he was a little ashamed of it afterward, for, instead of boasting of it as he did of other adventures in which he had found himself in danger, he described this, Galt said, "with spirit and humour. Magnifying both his own and his friend's terrors. . . ." [n]

The next day, Byron's birthday, it rained without ceasing and they did nothing but listen to the stories and songs of Demetrius. But on the 23rd at noon they reached Cape Colonni, or Sounion. On a high cliff at whose base the sea tumbled on shelves of rock stood what remained of the marble columns that had supported an ancient temple, then supposed to be that of Minerva.[9] The white Doric columns, much more startling than the cream-colored ones on the Acropolis, were starkly silhouetted against the sea. On every side the deep-blue Ægean was dotted with steep-sided green islands. These were "The Isles of Greece" that became an indelible memory to Byron. Years later the vivid recollection of the scene furnished the dramatic description in the last stanza of his famous poem:

*Place me on Sunium's marbled steep,*
*Where nothing, save the waves and I,*
*May hear our mutual murmurs sweep. . . .*[1]

[9] All travelers in Byron's day considered this the Temple of Minerva. It was not until 1898 that an inscription was discovered which revealed that it had been erected to Poseidon, God of the Sea. (Borst, p. 100 n.)

[1] *Poetry,* VI, 172. "The Isles of Greece," following stanza 86 of the third canto of *Don Juan.* The "Isles of Greece" visible from the Temple of Poseidon include Hagios Georgios (Belbina of antiquity), Makronesi (Helene), and on a clear day a double row of the Cyclades: Keos (Zea, where Byron

The next goal of the travelers was Marathon, which they reached late the following afternoon. So unimpressive was the site of the ancient battle that they had passed well over the plain before they were aware that they had gone by the mound marking the grave of the Athenians who died fighting the Persian invaders in 490 B.C. But Byron saw more than the flat, marshy ground lying between the gulf, almost invisible from the low land, and the base of the range of Pentelicus. While Hobhouse was anatomizing the site of the battle the next day, Byron was re-creating for himself a heroic picture, contrasting the past with the present of Greece. That imagined scene eventually found shape in words which fired Greek nationalist pride and spurred Philhellenic zeal, and which became almost the most quoted of all Byron's lines:

*The mountains look on Marathon—*
*And Marathon looks on the sea;*
*And musing there an hour alone,*
*I dreamed that Greece might still be free;*
*For standing on the Persians' grave,*
*I could not deem myself a slave.*[n]

Returning by Cephisia at the foot of Mount Pentelicus, the travelers were back in their quarters at the Macri home on the evening of the 25th. Byron's desire to get on with *Childe Harold* and his reluctance to bestir himself again for the inconveniences of overland travel probably determined him not to accompany the indefatigable Hobhouse on a tour to Negroponte.

When Hobhouse returned to Athens on February 13, Byron had formed a new friendship, with Nicolo Giraud, a boy of about fifteen or sixteen, the brother of Lusieri's wife. On the 14th, while Hobhouse was visiting the Waiwode and Lusieri, Byron rode out to Phyle with Nicolo. At the masquerade at the Macris' that night Hobhouse apparently became bold enough to attempt some gallantries, for he recorded pathetically in his diary: "Marianna Consulina dressed in my Albanian clothes.—'futile and con-

---

landed on his return from Constantinople), Thermia, Seriphos, and even Milos; and in the background Eubœa, Andros, and Tinos. Knowing eyes can perceive Hydra off the jutting peninsula of Argolis against the mountains of the Peloponnesus.

founded attempts!!'" Nicolo and another member of the party by the name of Antony were taken up by the guard, perhaps for some mimicry of the Turkish authorities such as that which Hobhouse described in his *Journey*.[n]

Though neither Hobhouse nor Byron was inclined to serious study, occasionally they both made some attempts to learn Romaic. On February 20, John Galt, their companion from Gibraltar to Malta, arrived from Zante and joined them in their rides and in their evening parties. He had already visited Veli Pasha in Tripolitza and had come on by Argos and Corinth. Galt took lodging in the Capuchin monastery, built around the monument to Lysicrates at the northern base of the hill on which the Acropolis stood.

Agreeable as Byron found the life in Athens, he had not given up his intention of going on to Constantinople and from there to Persia and India. Robert Adair, British Ambassador at the Turkish capital, to whom he had written for a traveling firman, on February 7 sent him one giving permission to travel in all the Turkish dominions.[n] But Byron was still waiting for news from his business agent, from whom, in the eight months since his departure from England, he had received no letters and no remittances. With as much restraint as he could command he told Hanson: "I have no redress but to write again and again,—a merry task to one, who hates writing as I do." [n]

Then on March 4 the English sloop-of-war, the *Pylades*, came into port at Piræus. Captain Ferguson, accompanied by a tall young man, Dr. Francis Darwin, son of the author of *The Botanic Garden*, called and offered passage to Smyrna. It was something of a wrench for them to leave Athens on such sudden notice (the ship was leaving the next day), but they accepted. The carnival was on, and they had to show their visitors around the town, and to call on the Consul, Logotheti. The burden of preparations fell again on Hobhouse, who was occupied with "1,000,000 affairs." They rose early on Monday the 5th, but it was half past one before they had sent off the baggage and were riding toward the sea, looking back at the Temple of Theseus and the Parthenon for the last time. They passed through the olive groves to Port Phoron, where the *Pylades* was anchored off Salamis, "galloping at a quick pace," Hobhouse wrote, "in order to rid ourselves, by the hurry, of the pain of parting." [n]

Some of the pain for Byron, and perhaps for Hobhouse too, was caused by the parting from the Macri sisters. Byron, though he had grown attached to all of them, had latterly paid particular attention to the youngest, Theresa, whose fresh youth gave him a curious pang. It may have been on the eve of his departure that he wrote, or at least began, his now famous lines:

*Maid of Athens, ere we part,*
*Give, oh give me back my heart!*

Perhaps Theresa herself had taught him the refrain, Ζωή μου, σᾶς 'αγαπῶ, which Byron said was a Romaic expression of tenderness meaning "My life, I love you!" and which "sounds very prettily in all languages, and is as much in fashion in Greece at this day as, Juvenal tells us, the two first words were amongst the Roman ladies, whose erotic expressions were all Hellenised." [n] The poet's vow at parting suggests the particular attractions of Theresa:

*By those tresses unconfined,*
*Wooed by each Ægean wind;*
*By those lids whose jetty fringe*
*Kiss thy soft cheeks' blooming tinge;*
*By those wild eyes like the roe. . . .*

The opening line of the next stanza, "By that lip I long to taste," indicates what no one who knows Byron's peculiar sensitivity to romantic idealizations of youthful beauty will doubt: that his relations with Theresa thus far had been, if not Platonic, at least in the realm of longing rather than possession. Byron's libertine proclivities were entirely compatible with such a detached admiration, though the two tendencies were frequently at war in him. But he could say with sincerity as he galloped out of Athens: "By love's alternate joy and woe,/ Zoe mou, sas agapo."

Galt went aboard and rode with them to Piræus, where he said farewell as they set out at sunset. He parted reluctantly with his English friends. "One may travel long enough," he wrote, "and come many times even to Athens without meeting with any company equal to theirs." [n] Byron left Athens with as much regret.

Never had his life fitted into such a tranquil pattern among people who, if not heroic, were at least agreeable, nor had he found before a climate and setting so conducive to contentment. As he proceeded on his travels, his homesickness for Attica increased. His realistic judgment of the people did not diminish his admiration for them. "I like the Greeks," he told Henry Drury, "who are plausible rascals,—with all the Turkish vices, without their courage. However, some are brave, and all are beautiful. . . ." *n*

# CHAPTER VIII

## *1810–1811*

## Constantinople and Athens

THE PYLADES came to anchor in the harbor of Smyrna on March 8. Two British frigates were already there, the *Salsette* and the *Frederickstein.* Byron in his splendid regimental uniform and Hobhouse, "much despised on account of my old great coat," dined with a large party of officers and civilians invited on board the *Salsette* frigate by the commander, Captain Bathurst. Among the guests were the British Consul-General, Mr. Francis Werry and his family, who invited Byron and Hobhouse on shore in the evening to their excellent house, long and narrow, "like the gallery and chambers of an Inn," Hobhouse noted, "but every thing is English and comfortable." Byron and Hobhouse readily accepted the hospitality of Werry, "a fine old fellow, fierce and tall and unimpaired by years." They had two good rooms and made the Consul's house their home for the more than a month they stayed in the town. Captain Bathurst of the *Salsette* frigate was also there.

Byron began to realize that he was in the Turkish dominions proper. His two Albanian servants had been mistaken for slaves, and Andreas, whom he had brought along in addition to Fletcher, was taken for their master and asked if he would sell them. On the 13th Byron and Hobhouse set off, with a Janissary borrowed from Mr. Werry for a guide, for the ancient ruins of Ephesus.

This journey, which occupied three days under the guidance of the imperturbable Janissary, who smoked constantly while he rode, made a deep impression on Byron. Passing out of the cultivated coastal region, they were soon in a marshy and desolate country where after dark the whole atmosphere resounded with the croaking of frogs. At night they put up their beds, which were a wonder to the Turks, in a large building meant for horses near a small mud coffeehouse. The Turks loitering there watched every movement while they made up their beds and divested themselves of their garments one by one, "as if they waited until we should strip off our skins."[n] After viewing the desolation and the marble spoils, Hobhouse said: "The decay of three religions is there presented at one view. . . ."[n]

Byron's only comment on the ruins was that "the temple has almost perished, and St. Paul need not trouble himself to epistolize the present brood of Ephesians. . . ."[n] What struck him more was the dramatic barking of jackals heard in that once great but deserted city. Their "mixed and mournful sound" as they "Bayed from afar complainingly" seemed to echo fittingly the melancholy of its moldering marble.[n] He felt for the first time that he had seen the East.

Guided by the slow-moving Suliman, their Janissary, the travelers returned to Smyrna, arriving at Mr. Werry's late at night on the 15th. The *Salsette* was then due to leave for Malta, but Byron and Hobhouse were waiting for an opportunity to go on to the Dardanelles and Constantinople.

Byron was disconsolate and uncertain of the future. He could not plan ahead, for he would not know until he got to Constantinople whether he would have remittances there which would permit him to go on to Persia, or whether he must return. The lethargy he professed ("the further I go the more my laziness increases," he told his mother) stemmed partly from the climate, partly from his reflection on the state of his affairs, and somewhat from the tempo of life in the East. "I keep no journal," he wrote, "but my friend Hobhouse scribbles incessantly."[n] He was not as idle as his letter suggested, however, for he was still adding stanzas to *Childe Harold's Pilgrimage.* He finished the wanderings of Harold in Albania, which of course followed closely his own journey through that wild and colorful land, with the frenzied dancing of the soldiers around their campfire on the southern shore of the Ambracian Gulf. Then he turned his thoughts to Attica, where he had felt himself in the presence of ancient Greece. Byron was still groping for a view of the modern Greeks. About one thing, however, he had formed rather definite ideas: they must trust to their own efforts and their own courage if they would be free.

*Hereditary Bondsmen! know ye not*
Who *would be free* themselves *must strike the blow?*
*By their right arms the conquest must be wrought?*
*Will Gaul or Muscovite redress ye? No!* [n]

Finally, however, his imagination was stimulated by the simple beauty of the land made more lovely by the reminders of its glorious past.

*Where'er we tread 'tis haunted, holy ground;*
*No earth of thine is lost in vulgar mould,*
*But one vast realm of Wonder spreads around,*
*And all the Muse's tales seem truly told. . . .* [n]

On March 28, Byron finished the second canto and laid the manuscript aside. He had reached a climax of the Childe's wanderings in the purple passages on Greece. His subsequent experiences did not inspire him to continue.

When the *Salsette* frigate received orders to proceed to Constantinople to carry Robert Adair, the English Ambassador, back to England, Byron and his friend were invited to go along. The *Salsette* left Smyrna on April 11. One person at least was sorry to see Byron go. Hobhouse wrote in his diary: "B tells me that Mrs. W [Mrs. Werry, wife of the Consul] proh pudor! actually cut of[f] a lock of his hair. I saw her cry at parting—pretty well at 56 years at least."

Skirting the long island of Mytilene or Lesbos the following day, they anchored off the flat plain of Alexandria Troas. Remaining the rest of that day and the next, Byron, Hobhouse, and Captain Bathurst had an opportunity to go ashore and see the ruins of the ancient city and what was said to be the tomb of Ajax. Mount Ida was not visible because of the mist. The morning of the 14th the *Salsette* anchored off Cape Janissary or Sigium, a few miles from the fort on the Asiatic side of the entrance to the Hellespont. The ship being detained for a fortnight by contrary winds and the delays necessary to procure a firman to pass the Dardanelles from the Pasha in charge of the fort, they had ample time to explore the "ringing plains of windy Troy." The Troad was exciting enough, though doubt still existed as to the location of ancient Ilium, or, for that matter, as to whether it had ever existed. Byron, however, was willing to accept the tradition that it lay on the plain stretching south from the Hellespont and east to the range of Ida. The authenticity of the tale of Troy seemed important to him. He wrote in his diary at a later period: "I have stood upon that plain *daily*, for more than a month in 1810; and if any thing diminished my pleasure, it was that the blackguard Bryant [1] had impugned its veracity. . . . But I still venerated the grand original as the truth of *history* (in the material *facts*) and of *place*. Otherwise, it would have given me no delight. Who will persuade me, when I reclined upon a mighty tomb, that it did not contain a hero? . . . Men do not labour over the ignoble and petty dead—and why should not the *dead* be *Homer's* dead?" [2]

Although there were no remains of the ancient Troy except "the tombs of her destroyers," great earthen mounds, he was alive to a magic evocation of the world of Homer as they walked on the plain, crossed the Scamander, and gazed at Mount Ida in the distance. From his cabin window, he told his mother, he could see the supposed tomb of Antilochus.

After reading the first book of the *Iliad* as a preparation, Hobhouse, Byron, Captain Bathurst, and a party from the *Salsette* made their first excursion upon the Trojan plain on the morning of the 15th, crossing a stream flowing out of a swamp which passed for the Scamander. The next day the party went on shore again and crossed the plain to the Dardanelles. Taking a boat across to the European side a little above the castle, Byron and

[1] Byron referred to Jacob Bryant's *Dissertations concerning the war of Troy, and the expedition of the Grecians, as described by Homer; showing that no such expedition was ever undertaken, and that no such city of Phrygia existed*, a book which was first published in 1796.

[2] *LJ*, V, 165–6. Diary of Jan. 11, 1821. It was not until 1882 that the researches and discoveries on the site of Troy made by Heinrich Schliemann established its location as the modern Hissarlik, a village not far from the Dardanelles.

Mr. Ekenhead, a lieutenant of marines on board the *Salsette*, attempted to swim to the Asiatic side, but were obliged by the excessive coldness of the water and the strength of the current, which carried them about one mile and a half below the castle, to give up when they had been an hour in the water and were only halfway across.

After a few days Byron found more to interest him in the Dardanelles than on the Trojan plain. He had not given up his ambition to try his swimming skill in imitation of Leander. Waiting for favorable winds and currents, he bathed almost daily in the bay below the Asiatic fort, or farther up toward Abydos. One of his amusements was to dive for land tortoises flung in on purpose.[n]

Life on the *Salsette* was made pleasant enough for the passengers. The officers occasionally put on plays among themselves, and Captain Bathurst was full of stories, some of them risqué. Byron apparently got along very well with him except that the rough old sailor made a row because the lazy lord slept so late.[n] It was a welcome change when the ship lifted the anchor on May 1 and tried for the strait, but was driven up the Thracian coast toward Lemnos and finally anchored eight miles from the Dardanelles. The next day they tried again, but were obliged by the current to anchor near the Asiatic fort. On Thursday morning, May 3, Byron and Ekenhead tried once more to swim the Hellespont and this time succeeded. Hobhouse recorded excitedly in his diary: "This instant 3 m[inutes] p[ast] 10 a.m. wrote this in the Dardanelles, at anchor. Byron and Ekenhead . . . now swimming across the Hellespont—Ovid's Hero to Leander open before me." He later added to the entry: "Mr. Ekenhead performed this in one hour & 5 minutes setting off two miles above Europe castle & coming out a mile at least below Dardanelles, Ld B. in 1 hour & 10 minutes." At Constantinople on the 26th Byron himself added a note at this point in Hobhouse's diary: "The total distance E & myself swam was more than 4 miles the current very strong and cold, some large fish near us when half across, we were not fatigued but a little chilled; did it with little difficulty." [n]

This was a feat that gave Byron much satisfaction and one in which he took unremitting pride. The day the deed was performed he wrote an enthusiastic letter to Henry Drury, to whom he had not written before during his journey: "This morning I *swam* from *Sestos* to *Abydos,* the immediate distance is not above a mile but the current renders it hazardous, so much so, that I doubt whether Leander's conjugal powers must not have been exhausted in his passage to Paradise." *n*

Although Byron realized that had he followed Leander precisely he would have swum from the Asiatic to the European shore, and would have returned the same night after seeing Hero, he maintained that his purpose had been to prove the practicability of the exploit, since no other traveler on record had attempted the crossing in either direction.[3] Six days after the event, while the *Salsette* was still at anchor by the fort, Byron composed his lighthearted lines "Written after Swimming from Sestos to Abydos."

Whether he literally had the ague, as he asserted humorously in the last line, the chilling did not dampen his spirits. With an exuberance that induced ribaldry he wrote to Drury: "I see not much difference between ourselves & the Turks, save that we have foreskins and they none, that they have long dresses and we short, and that we talk much and they little.—In England the vices in fashion are whoring and drinking, in Turkey, Sodomy &

[3] In a note to his poem "Written after Swimming from Sestos to Abydos" he wrote: ". . . the only thing that surprised me was that, as doubts had been entertained of the truth of Leander's story, no traveller had ever endeavoured to ascertain its practicability." (*Poetry,* III, 13 n.) But when he entered into a controversy with a traveler named William Turner, who had maintained that Byron and Ekenhead had not proved their point (Turner had tried and failed to swim from the Asiatic shore against the tide), Byron stated flatly that there were four instances on record. (*LJ,* V, 247.) Byron was right in believing that it was a considerable feat, but not an impossible one for a good swimmer such as he was. While it was his most memorable swimming adventure, because most romantic in its associations, it was not the most difficult. Hobhouse noted that Byron's swimming of the Tagus at Lisbon had required more endurance against wind and tide. And later his race from the Lido through the Grand Canal kept him longer in the water. Perhaps a hundred swimmers since, from college students to Richard Halliburton, have accomplished the crossing of the Dardanelles, chiefly because Byron threw new glamour over the fabled deed of Leander. (See *The Best of Byron,* ed. by Richard Ashley Rice, pp. 727–9.)

smoking, we prefer a girl and a bottle, they a pipe and a pathic.—They are sensible people. . . . By the bye, I speak the Romaic or modern Greek tolerably. . . . I can swear in Turkish, but except one horrible oath, and '*pimp*' and 'bread' and 'water' I have got no great vocabulary in that language.—They are extremely polite to strangers of any rank properly protected." *n*

Idle and dissatisfied with the aimless current of his existence despite the surface gaiety that burst forth in his correspondence, Byron confessed to Hodgson: "Hobhouse rhymes and journalises; I stare and do nothing. . . . We have been very nearly one year abroad. I should wish to gaze away another, at least, in these evergreen climates; but I fear business, law business, the worst of employments, will recall me previous to that period, if not very quickly. . . . I hope you will find me an altered personage,—I do not mean in body, but in manner, for I begin to find out that nothing but virtue will do in this damned world. I am tolerably sick of vice, which I have tried in its agreeable varieties, and mean, on my return, to cut all my dissolute acquaintance, leave off wine and carnal company, and betake myself to politics and decorum." *n*

At last on May 11 a fair light wind carried the *Salsette* up the straits. When she passed the castles she saluted with seventeen guns, and the compliment was returned by a like volley from the Asiatic fort, which unfurled the Turkish flag in their honor. At two o'clock on the 13th they caught their first sight of Constantinople from the Sea of Marmora, the minarets of the great mosques and the domes and tall cypresses rising gradually out of the mist. Passing the Seven Towers, they anchored under the gloomy walls near the Seraglio point at sunset. No lights were visible, and not a human being could be seen. *n*

At noon the next day Byron and Hobhouse left the *Salsette* with some of the officers in the Captain's gig. Battling against a strong wind and the current of the Bosporus, they came in close under the walls of the Sultan's palace and there saw two dogs gnawing a dead body. *n* Following this ominous introduction to the barbarities of the country, they were pleasantly surprised by the civilized comforts of the inn at which they arrived after landing at Tophana, a suburb by the artillery ground near the mouth of the Golden Horn, and taking horses a mile up the hill to Pera. Their hotel, kept by a Monsieur Marchand, was at the main crossing of the principal street in the section where all the embassies and the Frankish population were located.

At the time Byron arrived in Constantinople no foreigners were allowed to reside within the walls of the old city, Stamboul, between the Bosporus and the Golden Horn. The suburb of Pera, though occupied by many Turks also, was practically governed by the European embassies, who had their own guards of Janissaries. Although Englishmen were respected and liked by the Turks, the English position with the government of the Porte was not entirely secure. Robert Adair, sent to conclude a treaty after the English alliance with Russia, Turkey's enemy, had been broken, had stayed on as Ambassador when the treaty was signed in 1809. But Sultan Mahmoud contrived to play the English against the French and to make all the foreigners feel their subservience when they came on official missions to the palace.

When Byron and Hobhouse two days after their arrival called at the English palace, Adair was ill. They were welcomed by Stratford Canning, the young secretary of the embassy, who had played against Byron in the Harrow-Eton cricket match in 1805, though they had not met at that time. The palace was the social rendezvous of the English colony in Constantinople. Cut off from official connection with the French and their satellites, the Ambassador extended general hospitality to most English travelers who turned up in the Turkish capital, sharing his table and what apartments were available with them. Adair, though in bed, desired to see Byron and his friend. He was "very pale and weak," but he offered them an apartment in the palace and assigned them a Janissary for a dragoman. They declined the apartment, since Byron preferred a private residence to the formalities of the palace, but they dined frequently with the other English there.

The next day, after a visit to Galata, another foreign quarter filled with merchants and traders, they took up new lodgings in Pera.[4] That night they dined at the palace in their uniforms. A

[4] The house was opposite a small convent of nuns and near the mansion of the French embassy.

day or two after his arrival Byron went with his Janissary into a shop to buy some pipes. There he met a strange Englishman who later wrote a vivid description of his countryman:

"He wore a scarlet coat, richly embroidered with gold, in the style of an English aide-de-camp's dress-uniform, with two heavy epaulettes. . . . His features were remarkably delicate, and would have given him a feminine appearance, but for the manly expression of his fine blue eyes. On entering the inner shop, he took off his feathered cocked-hat, and showed a head of curly auburn hair, which improved in no small degree the uncommon beauty of his face." [5]

Byron saw much to justify a growing dislike of the Turks. Though they were tender in their treatment of the thin, gaunt dogs lying everywhere in the filthy streets, their contempt for human life and their arbitrary tyranny seemed revolting to the Englishman. Then, too, he had no opportunity to meet the Turks on a social level. This was in strong contrast to his experience in Greece.

On May 18, Byron and Hobhouse accompanied Captain Bathurst on a formal visit to the Captain Pasha, or Admiral of the Turkish fleet, in a splendid room at the edge of the Golden Horn. Hobhouse noted his "black eye, black beard—reported to be a very savage fellow." Byron recalled his ferocious whiskers. On the 19th, Byron and Hobhouse went with a party of English to the winehouses of Galata, where they witnessed some lascivious dances performed by boys in a style that Hobhouse called inde-

[5] *The New Monthly Magazine,* Vol. XVII (1826), pp. 310–11. Observing that his countryman was having a difficult time with his professional interpreter, to whom he spoke in indifferent Italian, the stranger offered his services and showed Byron some of the curiosities of the town. Byron shook him cordially by the hand and assured him "that he always felt great pleasure when he met with a countryman abroad." But when he was formally introduced to the stranger at the Ambassador's later in the week, he turned his back immediately after the introduction "in the coldest manner." Byron was cordial again, however, when he met the stranger on the street, extending his hand and saying: "I am an enemy to English etiquette, especially out of England; and I always make my own acquaintances without waiting for the formality of an introduction." His manner was so irresistibly attractive that the stranger accepted his apology and they went walking once more. (Ibid., pp. 311–12.)

scribably "beastly." Afterward, perhaps to clear their heads of the winehouse atmosphere, they climbed the 147 steps of the Galata tower, from the top of which they had a "view of every part of this beautiful city."

Before going to the old city they made an excursion across the Bosporus to Scutari. Then on the 21st, with Captain Bathurst and several others, guided by two Janissaries from the embassy, they explored the bazaars in Constantinople. They admired Sultan Achmet's mosque with its six minarets and passed by the Seraglio walls high and gloomy, pausing to observe the heads of criminals (executed for crimes against the state) exposed in niches on either side of the gate. They dined at a kabab house, took coffee and sherbet, and then crossed the water to the arsenal, where they saw another grim spectacle, the headless body of a man recently executed.

But Byron soon tired of the city and returned to his old pastime of riding out each day to some attractive spot in the surrounding country. Nothing in the environs appealed to his imagination so much as the ride around the land walls which had stood for over a thousand years in a semicircle from the Golden Horn to the Sea of Marmora. "The walls of the Seraglio," Byron told his mother, "are like the walls of Newstead gardens, only higher, and much in the same *order;* but the ride by the walls of the city, on the land side, is beautiful. Imagine four miles of immense triple battlements, covered with ivy, surmounted with 218 towers, and, on the other side of the road, Turkish burying-grounds (the loveliest spots on earth), full of enormous cypresses. I have seen the ruins of Athens, of Ephesus, and Delphi. . . . but I never beheld a work of nature or art which yielded an impression like the prospect on each side from the Seven Towers to the end of the Golden Horn." [n]

Spring was transforming the gardens and country places along the Golden Horn and the Bosporus into a luxuriance unimagined in the dull and muddy months of winter. Byron frequently rode to the Valley of the Sweet Water, one of the Sultan's pleasure gardens beyond the head of the Golden Horn.[6] Or he fol-

[6] One of their excursions was to Scutari and Phanari across the Bosporus, where many Greeks lived. In a note to *Childe Harold* Byron wrote: "In the

lowed the Bosporus on the European side to the village of Belgrade, where once had lived the famous Lady Mary Wortley Montagu, whose romantic history fascinated Byron.[7]

The social life at Constantinople, though confined to the limited circle of the officers of the frigate, the officials at the embassy, and a few English travelers, Byron found equally agreeable. There is every indication that he was on the best terms with all of them. Frequently Canning or Bathurst went with him on his rides and his excursions in the town. On May 26, Byron accompanied Captain Bathurst and a large party to see the Minister of the Marine (who stared at the young Mr. Chamier and said: "I love English seamen").

On the 28th the English were all invited to join the official procession when Adair took leave of the Caimacam, the representative of the Grand Vizier, who was himself absent from the city. Byron and Hobhouse dressed in their gay regimentals and went to the Ambassador's palace, but when Byron found that his rank was not recognized and that he would have to march behind Mr. Canning, the secretary of the embassy, he left in a pique. That night he refused to dine at the palace with Hobhouse, who came home to find his traveling companion packing up with the intention of going to Smyrna by way of Mickalitch. Childishly standing on his rights as a peer and feeling that he had been insulted, he was unable to regain perspective for three days. Fletcher, probably because he objected to the long overland voyage which his master proposed, kicked over the traces and came foul of Byron's ugly mood. Byron wrote to Captain Bathurst the next day: "My only English servant proving refractory, I am under the necessity of giving him a 'mittamus' to his own Country.—As I do not wish to be entirely without an Englishman I venture to beg of you (if my request is not improper) to permit me to take a youngster from your ship as a substitute." [n]

Robert Adair's special invitation to Byron to dine at the palace on the King's birthday [n] (June 4), together with Hobhouse's

Fanal [Phanari], and in Yanina, the best Greek is spoken. . . ." (*Poetry*, II, 202.)

[7] Lady Mary had been at Constantinople in 1717–18. Her association with Pope no doubt increased Byron's interest in her.

friendly persuasion, finally brought the testy lord out of his pique, for on the 31st he breakfasted with Hobhouse at the palace and accompanied a party on the Ambassador's cutter up the Bosporus. They went as far as the Black Sea or Euxine and watched the waves breaking on the Cyanean Symplegades. A few days later Byron got a better view of the breakers beating into the mouth of the Bosporus from a hill above the "Giant's Grave" on the Asiatic side.

On June 6 the *Black John* lugger arrived with letters from England. One to Byron from Hodgson contained disturbing news: nasty stories had been spread about his friend Edleston.[8] Another letter of Hodgson quoted one from Cawthorn saying that the second edition of *English Bards and Scotch Reviewers* had been sold out and that he was preparing another. Cawthorn had enclosed to Hodgson a letter addressed to Byron. The letter was from Ireland. "I have not judged it expedient (from the circumstance of the direction) to send it you," Hodgson wrote. "It probably is a challenge, & will keep till you return to England—unless you *wish* me to send it—I shall preserve the seal (which is a very absurd one) unbroken till we meet." [9]

Byron by this post received a remittance of £500 from Hanson (another £500 had been sent to Malta for him), but he had now given up his projected tour to Persia and India, and had determined to return to Greece for another year if possible. He did not know the state of his affairs in England, since he had no explanation from Hanson, but he suspected the worst.[1] Hob-

[8] Hobhouse wrote in his diary on June 6: "messenger arrived from England —bringing a letter from Hodgson to B—tales spread—the *Edleston* is accused of indecency."

[9] Hodgson letter of March 25, 1810. Murray MSS. The letter was from Thomas Moore, the Irish poet, who had taken offense at some lines in *English Bards.* (See Chapter IX, p. 299.)

[1] Things were going badly, and Byron probably had some indication of it in the letters from his mother, several of which had reached him while he was in Athens and Constantinople. Mrs. Byron was constantly harassed by her son's creditors, the most persistent and troublesome of whom was Brothers, the Nottingham upholsterer, who held a bill for £1,600 for renovating and furnishing rooms at Newstead. Mrs. Byron complained pitifully to Hanson on June 2 that the creditors had an execution and that everything was to be sold in a fortnight. (Eg. 2611, f. 194.) Hanson was just as desperate. He replied that daily calls were made upon him for bills of Byron that ran up-

house, unwilling to draw longer on his friend's funds, and eager to get back to England to publish his travels, had apparently intended to return on the *Black John,* but the arrival of his Westminster School friend Charles Cockerell on that ship perhaps caused him to wait for the *Salsette.*

His visit to the mosques of St. Sophia and of Sultans Achmet, Osman, and Suleyman on June 19 roused Byron to more comment than he had devoted to any other sights of the city. St. Sophia, he wrote his mother, "is inferior in beauty and size to some of the mosques, particularly 'Soleyman,' etc., and not to be mentioned in the same page with St. Paul's (I speak like a *Cockney*)." [n]

A few days later, writing to Dallas, Byron expressed indifference to the fate of his satire. What happened to it would not disturb his "tranquillity beneath the blue skies of Greece," where he proposed to spend the summer and perhaps also the winter. He added "that all climates and nations are equally interesting to me; that mankind are everywhere despicable in different absurdities; that the farther I proceed from your country the less I regret leaving it. . . ." [n]

He saw something more of follies of mankind on June 26 in a visit to the "howling" dervishes in the courtyard of a ruined mosque near the archery ground back of Pera. These performers howled in a kind of ritualistic frenzy and worked themselves into what appeared to be a sensual ecstasy. There followed masochistic jugglers' tricks ending in a general orgiastic screaming and jumping and jostling.[n]

---

ward of £10,000 and annuities around £3,000 a year, and that there were not funds to cover a tenth of these sums. (Eg. 2611, f. 187.) Hanson was not as neglectful as Byron thought. He had written four or five letters giving a full account of financial affairs. Sawbridge had paid the remaining £4,000 of his loan, £1,000 of which Hanson had put with Hammersley, the international bankers, to Byron's account. The remaining £3,000 was swallowed up by the annuities, etc. Hanson had sold the Weymondham estate in Suffolk for £4,400, but had not yet received the money because of a legal technicality concerning the title. Newstead had been surveyed and was thought to be worth £4,700 a year, but to gain that yield they would have to lay out considerable sums. The legal tangle of Rochdale continued. Hanson counseled the sale of Newstead. (Hanson Business Letters, Murray MSS.)

On the 27th, Robert Adair, who had invited Byron to attend the ceremony of his final audience with the Sultan, wrote to say that the day was fixed, but warned him that the Turks did not acknowledge any precedence, so that Byron could be assured of no special place in the procession or at the audience. Only persons connected with the embassy were recognized by the government.[n] Byron was not satisfied, however, until the Austrian Internuncio, the highest authority on diplomatic etiquette, had decided against his pretension.[n] On July 4, Byron confessed rather reluctantly and with not too good grace: ". . . your authorities (particularly the *German*) are too many for me. I shall therefore make what atonement I can, by cheerfully following not only your Excellency, 'but your servant or your maid, your ox, or your ass, or anything that is yours.' "[2] Declining another invitation, he added: "I am never very well adapted for, or very happy in, society, and I happen at this time, from some particular circumstances, to be even less so than usual." [n]

What the particular circumstances were can only be conjectured. Whether disturbed by news from England or by nearer sources of irritation, he evinced a like misanthropy when he wrote Hodgson the same day: "Next week the frigate sails with Adair; I am for Greece, Hobhouse for England. A year together on the 2nd July since we sailed from Falmouth. I have known a hundred instances of men setting out in couples, but not one of a similar return. . . . I am confident that twelve months of any given individual is perfect ipecacuanha." [n] But this feeling must have sprung from his general boredom rather than from any particular animus, for on the same date he wrote a jollying but entirely good-natured account of Hobhouse's return and of "that loquacious traveller's" literary luggage.[n] And a few days later he rode out with Hobhouse once more to the Valley of the Sweet Water.

The Ambassador's audience took place on July 10. Hobhouse devoted four pages of his diary to a description of the event. They rose at four, crossed the Golden Horn as the sun rose

[2] *LBC*, I, 9. But Byron bore no grudge against the Ambassador. He wrote later to his mother: "Adair received me wonderfully well, and indeed I have no complaints against any one." (*LJ*, I, 295. Letter of July 30, 1810.)

over the hills of Asia, and were greeted by the salute of the *Salsette*'s cannon. After waiting for some time in a dirty, dark chamber of the executioner's lodge, they were ushered into the Divan, where the Ambassador dined with the Caimacam, while Byron, Canning, Captain Bathurst, and Hobhouse contrived to be seated at a little table with Chelibi Effendi.

Following another long wait under a wooden shed where a dirty stone seat was supplied for the Ambassador, they were ushered, with much jostling and pushing, into the audience chamber. Mahmoud II was sitting on a throne that looked to Hobhouse like a four-posted bed, "but of a dazzling splendour; the lower part formed of burnished silver and pearls. . . . He was dressed in a robe of yellow satin, with a broad border of the darkest sable: his dagger, and an ornament on his breast, were covered with diamonds. . . . He for the most part kept a hand on each knee, and moved neither his body nor head, but rolled his eyes from side to side, without fixing them for an instant upon the Ambassador or any other person present. Occasionally he stroked and turned up his beard, displaying a milk-white hand glittering with diamond rings." *n*

This was Byron's introduction to the Grand Signor against whom he was to be engaged in war on the side of his Greek friends when he died at Missolonghi. The spectacle in the Sultan's palace, where there was displayed a pageantry and richness far surpassing anything at Ali Pasha's court, failed to touch him in the same way precisely because he did not feel himself personally involved in the scene. Although its contrasts of opulence and meanness would have roused his sense of the ironic in other circumstances, the feeling that he was one of a crowd instead of a principal actor in the event must, even more than his present preoccupations, have made the audience seem of little significance to him.[3] When he later praised the Turks, he usually thought of those he had met in Albania.

[3] The anonymous stranger, quoted before, who apparently was also present at the audience, reported that, while Byron was unimpressed by the Sultan, the latter let his wandering eyes fall on the handsome countenance of the young lord. "His youthful and striking appearance, and the splendour of his dress, visible as it was by the looseness of the pelisse over it, attracted

The *Salsette* left Constantinople with Adair, Hobhouse, Byron, and his entourage on July 14. During the voyage Adair observed that Byron was laboring under great dejection of spirits.[4] On the 17th the frigate pulled into the harbor of "Zea" (Keos) just off Cape Colonni. Byron and his servants went ashore, and Hobhouse noted sentimentally in his diary: "Took leave, *non sine lacrymis,* of this singular young person, on a little stone terrace at the end of the bay, dividing with him a little nosegay of flowers; the last thing perhaps that I shall ever divide with him." [n] Byron was happy to get back to the soil of Greece. To Hobhouse a few days later he wrote: "The same day which saw me ashore at Zea, set me forth once more upon the high seas, where I had the pleasure of seeing the frigate in the *Doldrums* by the light of sun and moon. Before daybreak I got into the Attics at Thaskalio, hence I dispatched men to Keratia for horses, and in ten hours from landing I was at Athens." [n]

Though his intention had been to go on immediately to the Morea, where he had some unexplained business with the Consul Strané (possibly to pick up remittances that had been forwarded from Malta and were payable at Patras),[5] Byron lingered for a few days in Athens. He went back to his old apartment at the Macris', where he was greeted on his arrival by his Cambridge friend Lord Sligo (Altamont), who had come into Piræus in command of a brig. When Byron left Athens spring was in the bud, but when he returned the intense heat of summer had settled over the country and might have caused him to hesitate longer before setting out on an overland journey had not the business at Patras seemed urgent and had the "fine

greatly the Sultan's attention, and seemed to have excited his curiosity." (*The New Monthly Magazine,* Vol. XIX [1827], p. 147.) The same writer stated that the Sultan insisted in 1824 that the handsome youth he had seen in the English party was not Byron but a woman dressed in man's clothes.

[4] Moore, I, 235. Moore says that during this voyage, "Perceiving, as he walked the deck, a small yataghan, or Turkish dagger, on one of the benches, he [Byron] took it up, unsheathed it, and, having stood for a few moments contemplating the blade, was heard to say, in an under voice, 'I should like to know how a person feels, after committing a murder!' "

[5] Two references in letters to Hobhouse seem to indicate that Byron had commissioned Strané to cash some drafts for him (possibly because he could get a favorable exchange). (*B-SP,* I, 76, 79.)

prospects" at the Macris' turned out more to his liking. "Your northern gentry can have no conception of a Greek summer," he wrote his mother.[n] But Greece still pleased him more than Turkey. Constantinople, he said, with all its mosques, "cannot be compared with Athens and its neighbourhood; indeed I know of no Turkish scenery to equal this."

And then he added a sentence whose significance is revealed in a later letter: "An usual custom here, as at Cadiz, is to part with wives, daughters, etc., for a trifling present of gold or English arms (which the Greeks set a high value upon)."[n] The fact was that Theresa Macri's mother was willing enough to part with her daughter to the English lord, but she wanted compensation according to Greek custom, or a legal marriage, and the probability is that she had schooled the girl to resist any easy philandering. Byron wrote Hobhouse later in the summer that ". . . the old woman, Theresa's mother, was mad enough to imagine I was going to marry the girl; but I have better amusement."[6]

Lord Sligo was also planning a jaunt into the Morea and jumped at the chance to accompany Byron, to the chagrin and discomfiture of the latter, who was, as he wrote Hobhouse, "already heartily disgusted with travelling in company."[7] On the 20th there was a great bustle of preparation. In the midst of the noise Byron wrote his mother that he was leaving the next day for the Morea, "where I shall probably remain a month or two, and then return to winter here, if I do not change my plans, which, however, are very variable, as you may suppose; but none of them verge to England."[n]

The unwieldy caravan got under way on the 21st,[n] Lord Sligo's

[6] *B-SP,* I, 81. Letter of Aug. 23, 1810. Later, seeing that Byron did not intend to marry, the mother was willing to let him carry Theresa away for a money consideration.

[7] *B-SP,* I, 75. Letter of July 29, 1810. Hobhouse was not too disconcerted by statements of this kind, for he knew that at bottom Byron had a genuine affection for him. Later Byron wrote his mother: ". . . I am woefully sick of travelling companions, after a year's experience of Mr. Hobhouse. . . ." (*LJ,* I, 290–1. Letter of July 20, 1811.) And he repeated the statement in another letter, but added: ". . . not that he was a bad one, but because my nature leads me to solitude, and that every day adds to this disposition." (*LJ,* I, 295. Letter of July 30, 1811.)

companions and servants making it necessary for them to have twenty-nine horses in all. Byron gave Hobhouse a farcical account of the expedition: "He has 'en suite' a painter, a captain, a gentleman misinterpreter (who boxes with the painter), besides sundry idle English varlets. . . . You may suppose that a man of the Marchese's kidney was not very easy in his seat. . . . At Corinth we separated, the M[arquis] for Tripolitza, I for Patras." *n*

On the 25th Byron and his entourage reached Vostitza, where he and Hobhouse had stayed with the Cogia Basha Andreas Londos. There he added to his suite a Greek boy by the name of Eustathios Georgiou, whom he had met on his earlier voyage, possibly at the home of Londos.[8] The absurd jealous attachment of this youth, who was ready to follow him to England or to Terra Incognita, filled him with amusement. The absurdity was increased when "The next morning I found the dear soul upon horseback clothed very sparsely in Greek Garments, with those ambrosial curls hanging down his amiable back, and to my utter astonishment, and the great abomination of Fletcher, a *parasol* in his hand to save his complexion from the heat. However, in spite of the *Parasol* on we travelled very much enamoured, as it should seem, till we got to Patras, where Strané received us into his new house. . . . Next day he went to visit some accursed cousin and the day after we had a grand quarrel. Strané said I spoilt him. I said nothing; the child was as froward as an unbroken colt. . . . I think I never in my life took so much pains to please any one, or succeeded so ill. . . . At present he goes back to his father, though he is now become more tractable. Our *parting* was vastly pathetic, as many kisses as would have sufficed for a boarding school, and embraces

[8] A number of letters in Greek from Eustathios Georgiou are among Byron's papers at John Murray's. These have been summarized for me by George Savidis. The handwriting, which is very bad, may have been that of a public scribe, Savidis suggests, since Georgiou was probably illiterate. The first one, dated Jan. 1, 1809 (probably a mistake for 1810), indicates that Byron had asked to have the boy sent with Strané to him in Athens after he arrived there. But Eustathios, ill with a fever, could not come. The second letter, dated April 7, 1810, says that he (Eustathios) has information that Byron is going to travel again, and that he is eager to accompany him.

enough to have ruined the character of a county in England, besides tears (not on *my* part) and expressions of 'Tenerezza' to a vast amount. All this and the warmth of the weather has quite overcome me." [n]

The ability to see the ridiculous aspects of his own passions as well as those of others was part of Byron's irresistible charm for those who knew him well. The next day he continued his narrative for Hobhouse: "My new Greek acquaintance has called thrice, and we improve vastly. In good truth, so it ought to be, for I have quite exhausted my poor powers of pleasing. . . . We are to go on to Tripolitza and Athens together. I do not know what has put him into such good humour unless it is some Sal Volatile I administered for his headache, and a green shade instead of that effeminate parasol? But so it is. . . . Now is not all this very ridiculous? Pray tell Matthews. It would do his heart good to see me travelling with my Tartar, Albanians, Buffo, Fletcher and this amiable παίδη [boy] prancing by my side." [n]

To Hobhouse, who had gone to Malta on the *Salsette,* he addressed some good-natured banter. "You cannot conceive what a delightful companion you are now you are gone. . . . I amuse myself alone very much to my satisfaction, riding, bathing, sweating, hearing Mr. Paul's musical clock, looking at his red breeches; we visit him every evening. . . ." [n] When these amusements fail, there is my Greek to quarrel with, and a sopha to tumble upon." [n]

Byron had not forgotten that he had letters to Veli Pasha, son of Ali and ruler of the whole of the Peloponnesus. Some time early in August he set out, accompanied by Strané and Eustathios, for Veli's capital at Tripolitza. There is no record of their route, except that Byron later said that he had seen Argos, Napoli, and Mantinea (in Arcadia) in his route to and from Tripolitza.[n] Veli was even more taken with Byron than his father had been and avowed his admiration with less restraint, presenting him with a "very pretty horse." Since Veli was leaving soon on an expedition against the Russians, he extended "a most particular invitation to meet him at Larissa, which last is singular enough, as he recommended a different route to Lord Sligo, who asked leave to accompany him to the Danube." There could be little doubt about Veli's meaning. "He said he wished all the old men . . . to go to his father, but the young ones to come to him, to use his own expression, 'Vecchio con Vecchio, Giovane con Giovane.' He honoured me with the appellations of his *friend* and *brother*, and hoped that we should be on good terms, not for a few days but for life. All this is very well, but he has an awkward manner of throwing his arm round one's waist, and squeezing one's hand in *public* which is a high compliment, but very much embarrasses *'ingenuous youth.'* . . . He asked if I did not think it very proper that as *young* men (he has a *beard* down to his middle) we should live together, with a variety of other sayings, which made Strané stare, and puzzled me in my replies." Byron had finally sent Eustathios home from Tripolitza, for "he plagued my soul out with his whims, and is besides subject to *epileptic* fits . . . which made him a perplexing companion. . . ." [n] When he returned to Athens about August 19, Byron removed his goods and servants from the Macri house, where his strained relations with the mother of Mariana, Katinka, and Theresa had no doubt dampened the spontaneity of his rompings with the girls,[9] and took up his residence at the Capuchin convent at the foot of the Acropolis.[1]

[9] To sift truth from fiction regarding the relations of Byron and Theresa Macri is next to impossible, for many legends grew up about the "Maid of Athens," fathered and frequently distorted by romantic travelers who saw the Macri girls in later years or repeated gossip heard in Athens. C. G. Brouzas has accumulated a number of these travelers' rumors ("Byron's Maid of Athens: Her Family and Surroundings," *West Virginia University Bulletin*, June 1949, p. 35 ff.). One of these stories was that Byron wished to spirit her away, and that she was taken from home and hidden at her uncle, M. Roque's. Moore (I, 224 n.) recollected that Byron told him it was in making love to one of the Macri girls that "he had recourse to an act of courtship often practised in that country,—namely, giving himself a wound across the breast with his dagger. The young Athenian, by his own account, looked on very coolly during the operation, considering it a fit tribute to her beauty, but in no degree moved to gratitude." Theresa eventually married a Mr. Black, but for the rest of her long life she basked in the fame Byron had given her as "The Maid of Athens."

[1] Byron seemed to have the impression that the "Convent" (a term used generally to designate a religious house of retirement from the world, either male or female, and not restricted to the house of nuns, as in modern American usage) was Franciscan, but then occupied by Capuchins. On one occasion he wrote: "I am living alone in the Franciscan monastery with one

These were the quarters which John Galt had occupied while he was in Athens. The convent, built around the fourth-century monument of Lysicrates (commonly known as the Lantern of Demosthenes), served as a school for some of the sons of the Frank families and, in the absence of hotels, as a hostelry for travelers. The circular chamber formed about the monument in the courtyard had been fitted up as a small library. In this little world, where the buffoonery took him back to his happiest school days, Byron was contented enough.

"I am most auspiciously settled in the Convent," he wrote to Hobhouse on the 23rd. It was more commodious than any apartment he had yet occupied, with plenty of room for his now numerous suite. It was not solitary, for in addition to the abbot there were six "Ragazzi," "all my most particular allies." These and Fauvel, the French Consul, and Lusieri were now almost his only associates. Of the present waggeries in the convent Byron recited a few for Hobhouse.

Byron was immensely entertained by the low comedy of these antics, but also flattered by the attention paid to him. "The first time I mingled with these sylphs," he told Hobhouse, "after about two minutes' reconnoitring, the amiable Signor Barthelemi, without any previous notice, seated himself by me, and after observing by way of compliment that my 'Signoria' was the 'piu bello' of his English acquaintance, saluted me on the left cheek. . . . But my friend, as you may easily imagine, is Nicolo, who, by-the-by, is my Italian master, and we are already very philosophical. I am his 'Padrone' and his 'amico,' and the Lord knows what besides." After informing Byron that he would follow him over the world, Nicolo added that they should not only live but die together. "The latter I hope to avoid," Byron told Hobhouse, "—as much of the former as he pleases. . . . Then we have several Albanian women washing in the 'Giardino,' whose hours of relaxation are spent in running pins into Fletcher's backside."

"Intrigue flourishes," he added. In addition to his own affairs, which offered "better amusement" than Theresa, "Andreas is

'fri*ar*' (a Capuchin of course). . . ." (*LJ*, I, 307.) But in his letters he usually referred to it as the Capuchin Convent.

fooling with Dudu,[2] as usual, and Mariana has made a conquest of Dervise Tahiri; Vircillie [Vasilly], Fletcher and Sullee, my new Tartar, have each a mistress—'Vive l'Amour.'"

As was indicated by the sprinkling of the language in his letter, Byron was getting a good deal of pleasure from his study of Italian, even though he was not too regular in his application. He had been translating an ode of Horace into that language. "I chatter with everybody, good or bad, and tradute prayers out of the mass ritual; but my lessons, though very long, are sadly interrupted by scamperings, and eating fruit, and peltings and playings; and I am in fact at school again, and make as little improvement now as I did then, my time being wasted in the same way."

But there were times when he missed Hobhouse's steadying influence. It was as if the balance wheel had flown out of his life, and there was both a heady exhilaration and a slightly dizzying fear in the experience. He wished Hobhouse there to share the nonsensical gaiety, "but then," he remembered, "you are so very crabbed and disagreeable, that when the laugh is over I rejoice in your absence. After all, I do love thee, Hobby, thou hast so many good qualities, and so many bad ones, it is impossible to live with or without thee."[n] Hobhouse, at Malta on his way home to an estranged family, depressed by the failure of his volume of poems and disconsolate at parting from his friend, had no such reservations. He wrote: "I kept the half of your little nosegay till it withered entirely, and even then I could not bear to throw it away. I can't account for this, nor can you either, I dare say."[n]

But Byron was too active in mind and body not to seek some variation from this routine. He was already planning another tour of Attica with Lusieri, "who is a new ally of mine,

[2] This "Dudu" was probably Mariana, daughter of M. Roque; Mariana Macri also bore that nickname, according to Kampouroglou (see Dawson and Raubitschek, pp. 34–5; Brouzas, p. 21). It has been supposed that "Dudu" Roque furnished the name for the plump beauty in the harem in *Don Juan* (VI, 40 ff.). But since "Loula" was one of the nicknames of Theresa (Brouzas, p. 35), it is possible that Byron was thinking of the three Macri sisters when he gave the names of Lolah, Katinka, and Dudu to the three odalisks who took the greatest sentimental interest in Don Juan.

and Nicolo goes with me at his own most pressing solicitation, 'per mare per terras.'" The next day he added: "I am about to take my daily ride to the Piræus, where I swim for an hour despite of the heat. . . . it is a curious thing that the Turks when they bathe wear their lower garments, as your humble servant always doth, but the Greeks not. . . ." [n]

Moore recorded that in his lone wanderings through Greece Byron found seclusion to look within himself, and "One of his chief delights, as he mentioned in his 'Memoranda,' was, when bathing in some retired spot, to seat himself on a high rock above the sea, and there remain for hours, gazing upon the sky and the waters, and lost in that sort of vague reverie, which, however formless and indistinct at the moment, settled afterwards, on his pages, into those clear, bright pictures, which will endure for ever." Moore added that he had become so enamored of these lonely musings "that even the society of his fellow-traveller [Hobhouse], though with pursuits so congenial to his own, grew at last to be a chain and a burthen on him. . . ." [n]

It was not surprising that Hobhouse, with a much closer knowledge of Byron's mind at the time, and with recollections of the letters he had received from Athens and the Morea (most of them not accessible to Moore), should have written rather contemptuously: "On what authority does Tom say this? he has not the remotest grasp of the real reason which induced Lord Byron to prefer having no Englishman immediately and constantly near him." [n]

But there was probably some truth in both interpretations of Byron's motives. He felt constrained by the presence of such a tangible embodiment of British conscience and mores as Hobhouse, despite his veneer of Cambridge sophistication, seemed to be. And he did feel his poetic imagination expand, if not in complete solitude, at least in the company of simple and uncritical human beings who admired him and who furnished a stimulus to his creative faculties rather than a mirror to his shortcomings. The lack of communication on complicated levels (because of the language barrier) was a kind of relief. Swimming or sitting on a rock above the Ægean beaches with the devoted Nicolo Giraud was a relaxed pleasure that he was to remember more fondly than most of the adventures of his travels.

One day when he was returning from his daily bathing at Piræus he observed a curious procession moving down toward the shore under a guard of soldiers. Sending one of his servants to inquire, he learned that it was a party sent to execute the sentence of the Waiwode or Turkish governor of Athens on a girl caught in an act of illicit love. She had been sewed into a sack and was to be cast into the sea. She was a Turkish girl whom Byron undoubtedly knew (though how well, he was careful never to say), and he determined to save her. He ordered the leader of the guard to accompany him, bringing the prisoner, to the Waiwode. The soldier was reluctant to disobey the Governor, but when Byron drew his pistol and threatened to shoot him he complied. With threats and bribery (the latter probably the more effective) Byron was able to persuade the Waiwode to give up the girl on condition that she should leave Athens. He conveyed her to the convent and sent her off at night to Thebes, where she found a safe asylum.[3]

This episode, from which *The Giaour* was later derived, burned itself into his consciousness so deeply that he could never think of it without something of a shudder. Medwin, though he garbled a great many details, was probably not wrong in quoting Byron as saying that the occurrence was one "in which I myself was nearly and deeply interested." [n] The passionate mood of *The Giaour* itself is some indication of the intensity of the experience as a remembered episode. When Galt called on Byron in 1813, after that poem had been published and much talked about, and the facts behind it speculated upon, Byron recorded in his diary: "I showed him Sligo's letter on the reports of the Turkish girl's *aventure* at Athens soon after it happened. . . . I thought it had been *unknown*, and wish it were; but Sligo arrived only some days after, and the *rumours*

[3] This is the story as told by Lord Sligo, which Byron said was "not very far from the truth." (*LJ*, II, 311.)

are the subject of his letter.[4] That I shall preserve,—*it is as well.* Lewis and Galt were both *horrified;* and L. wondered I did not introduce the situation into *The Giaour*. He *may* wonder;—he might wonder more at that production's being written at all. But to describe the *feelings* of *that situation* were impossible —it is *icy* even to recollect them."[5]

A few days later, on September 12, while Byron's mind was still filled with this event, Lady Hester Stanhope, the strong-minded niece of the younger Pitt, with her friend Michael Bruce and her physician Dr. C. L. Meryon, arrived at Piræus by boat from Corinth accompanied by Lord Sligo. The lady had already heard of Byron from Hobhouse, who had seen her at Malta.

[4] In August 1813, Byron asked Sligo to write out what he had known of the affair at the time.

[5] *LJ*, II, 361. Journal, Dec. 5, 1813. Galt (p. 114) believed that the story of *The Giaour* was "founded on an adventure which happened to himself —he was, in fact, the cause of the girl being condemned, and ordered to be sown [*sic*] up in a sack and thrown into the sea." It is impossible to know whether he got this impression from talking with Byron or from the circumstantial account of Medwin (I, 99–102), who quoted Byron as saying that it was his attempt to arrange an assignation with the girl during Ramadan that caused the discovery of their secret and her condemnation to a horrible death. In reviewing and correcting Medwin in an article in the *Westminster Review* (Jan. 1825, p. 27) Hobhouse wrote that "the girl whose life lord Byron saved at Athens, was not an object of his lordship's attachment—but of that of his lordship's Turkish servant." But it must be remembered that Hobhouse was not in Athens at the time and that Byron did not tell him everything that happened during the months he spent alone there. Byron gave clear hints in his letters to Hobhouse at the time that he was engaged in one or more intrigues in Athens. On August 23 he had written: "I have been employed the greater part of today in conjugating the verb 'ασπαζω' [embrace]. . . . I assure you my progress is rapid, but like Cæsar 'nil actum reputans dum quid superesset agendum,' I must arrive at the pl & opte and then I will write to ——. I hope to escape the fever, at least till I finish this affair, and then it is welcome to try." (*B-SP*, I, 82.) The "pl & opte" (elsewhere given as "plen. and optabil. Coit."), which Quennell could not make out from the MS. but which is here supplied from the Murray MSS., was a facetious code, shared by Matthews and others of his circle, meaning an opportunity for sexual gratification. And on October 4, recovering from a fever at Patras and thinking back to his experiences in Attica, Byron wrote again to Hobhouse: "Tell M. that I have obtained above two hundred pl&optCs and am almost tired of them. . . . You know the monastery of Mendele, it was there I made myself master of the first." (*B-SP*, I, 87—again the "indecipherable" word is supplied from the Murray MSS.)

ALI PASHA

ATHENS, CIRCA 1810

When she and her party came into the harbor, Byron was just diving from the molehead. Sligo invited him to dress and join them. For a few days they were closely associated in Athens. Byron tried to be agreeable, but felt himself brow-beaten by the intellectual woman. "I saw Lady Hesther Stanhope at Athens," he wrote a few weeks later to Hobhouse, "and do not admire 'that dangerous thing a female wit.'"[n]

Lady Hester Stanhope recollected Byron quite as uncharitably, if the record of her impressions is not distorted by her physician, who published her *Memoirs:* "I think he was a strange character: his generosity was for a motive, his avarice for a motive; one time he was mopish, and nobody was to speak to him; another, he was for being jocular with everybody. Then he was a sort of Don Quixote, fighting with the police for a woman of the town [an obvious reference to what she had heard of his rescue of the Turkish girl]; and then he wanted to make himself something great. . . . At Athens I saw nothing in him but a well-bred man, like many others; for, as for poetry, it is easy enough to write verses. . . . He had a great deal of vice in his looks—his eyes set close together, and a contracted brow. . . ."[n] The only thing she liked about him was the curve of his neck under the cheek and the curl on his forehead. She was said at a later time to have amused her friends by imitating his little affectations, especially his habit of giving solemn orders to his servant in Romaic.[6]

Whether to escape this formidable lady, or for some other reason, Byron left Athens a few days after her arrival, probably about the middle of September, for a second excursion to the Morea, taking only Nicolo Giraud with him as interpreter and companion. It was an ill-fated voyage from the beginning, but Byron took it in his stride, at least in his letters to his friends in England. He had gone by boat to the Isthmus of Corinth and was blown ashore on the island of Salamis. Then going to Olym-

[6] A. W. Kinglake: *Eothen,* p. 77. Her traveling companion, Michael Bruce, to Byron's surprise, took a great liking to him. On his way home Byron wrote to Hobhouse: ". . . on the night he [Bruce] left Athens he made me a profession of friendship, on the extremity of the Piræus, the only one I ever received in my life, and certainly very unexpected, for I had done nothing to deserve it." (*LBC,* I, 36–7. Letter of June 19, 1811.)

pia to see the remains of the festal center of ancient Greece, he caught a fever,[n] but it did not seize him violently until he was back in Patras. He was recovered enough on September 25 to report the ridiculous aspects of the situation to Hobhouse. After having been confined to bed by Dr. Romanelli and a fever for three days, "by the blessing of God and two glysters, I am now able to sit up, but much debilitated."[n]

He had a relapse, however, and could not conclude his letter until October 2, after "five days bed-riding with Emetics, glysters, Bark, and all the host of Physic." He was then attending poor Nicolo, his sole dragoman, who had waited on him day and night and had himself succumbed to the fever. Byron told Hodgson that "Nature and Jove" had triumphed over the physicians.[n]

On October 4, Nicolo was still ill with the fever, but Byron was well enough to write another long letter to Hobhouse, which he ended by pouncing upon his unsentimental friend's comment on the bouquet they had divided. "Your last letter closes pathetically with a postscript about a nosegay; I advise you to introduce that into your next sentimental novel. I am sure I did not suspect you of any fine feelings, and I believe you were laughing, but you are welcome."[n]

As soon as he and Nicolo were able to travel, Byron started back toward Athens, arriving on October 13. Lord Sligo, who was still there but preparing to go to Constantinople, found him weakened and emaciated by the fever. Standing before a looking-glass one day, Byron said to Sligo: "I look pale; I should like to die of a consumption." "Why?" Sligo asked. "Because the ladies would all say, 'Look at that poor Byron, how interesting he looks in dying.'"[n] Having lost weight from his illness, Byron kept up his thinning regimen, taking Turkish baths three times a week, drinking vinegar and water, and eating only a little rice.

By the end of the month Lord Sligo had left, but Byron's life at the monastery went on as usual. On the 1st of November one of Hanson's straying letters arrived with depressing news of his client's hopeless financial situation. Hanson insisted again that the only hope was to sell Newstead. Byron replied: "Yours arrived on the first Inst. it tells me I am ruined.—It is in the power of God, the Devil, and Man, to make me poor and miserable, but neither the second or third shall make me sell Newstead."[7] But this desperate mood did not prevent Byron from enjoying the social life of Athens. Besides his friendship with Fauvel, the French Consul, and Lusieri, he reported to Hodgson that he was "on good terms with five Teutones and Cimbri, Danes and Germans, who are travelling for an Academy."[n]

These five interesting foreigners, recently arrived in Athens, furnished the sort of mental stimulation he had begun to feel the lack of in the limited though pleasant society to which he had confined himself since the departure of Hobhouse. These were not merely curious travelers; they were men with artistic and scientific education and background. The enthusiastic leaders of the expedition were two young Danish archæologists, Dr. Peter Oluf Brønsted and George H. C. Koës, who had met in Rome and persuaded to join them Baron Haller (Karl Freiherr Haller von Hallerstein) of Nuremberg, architect to Prince Louis of Bavaria; Jacob Linckh, a Bavarian painter with an enthusiasm for archæological subjects; and Otto Magnus Freiherr von Stackelberg, who had studied for a diplomatic career at the University of Göttingen, but whose deep interest in the classical world turned him to archæological pursuits.[n]

They had arrived during Byron's absence in the Morea, but soon after his return he became very friendly with the whole group. His special favorites among them were Dr. Brønsted, "a pretty philosopher as you'd wish to see," with whom, he told Hodgson, he had "contracted an alliance," and Linckh, whom he employed to paint landscapes for him.[n] He went on some expeditions with these and with Baron Haller and Stackelberg. Although he had no special interest in archæology and his own interests were in the picturesque and human aspects of the country, he found them agreeable intellectual companions with whom

[7] Letter of Nov. 11, 1810. Eg. 2611, f. 214–15. This letter was carried by Fletcher, whom Byron sent home sometime after the middle of November with papers the lawyer had sent for Byron to sign, and a note from his master asking Hanson to pay Fletcher's arrears of wages (amounting in all to £250) and to look for a vacant farm at Newstead for him.

he could converse on general topics, and he respected their activities more than those of the mere collectors (and despoilers, as he considered them).

In addition to the Nordic gentlemen, several other English travelers added to the society Byron shared in Athens during the winter. The day after his return from Constantinople he had been visited by three Englishmen, the Hon. Frederick North, youngest son of George III's prime minister; Henry Gally Knight, whom he had known at Cambridge and who had turned up at Cádiz while Byron and Hobhouse were there; and John Nicholas Fazakerly, who later entered Parliament and became known as a scholar and antiquary. These three Byron considered superficial squinting travelers. North (later Lord Guilford), an ardent lover of things Greek, afterward founded the Society for Promotion of Culture at Athens and wore an ancient classical costume while he was chancellor of the Ionian University. Knight was a constant butt of Byron's humor in his later letters to John Murray, who published Knight's *Eastern Sketches* and his writings on architecture. Byron spoke of the "middling mountebank's mediocrity," [n] and wrote two ballads ridiculing his Grub Street productions.

But these travelers soon passed on, and others more congenial to Byron appeared on the scene. Among them was Charles R. Cockerell, Hobhouse's schoolfellow. Byron asked this future president of the Royal Institute of Architecture to paint some scenes that would be useful to Hobhouse in writing his volume of travels.

Byron had an unusual facility for mingling with great varieties of people, and, despite strong preferences and antipathies, he could adapt himself to the ways of foreigners with greater ease than could most Englishmen. Though he did not apply himself with any regularity to their study, he had picked up enough of the languages of the country to talk with the people, and took considerable delight and pride in his ability to converse in several tongues. He had spoken bad Latin with his servant Andreas Zantachi, but when he left and "that timberhead Fletcher" had been sent home, Byron was thrown back upon the native languages. By that time, however, he had learned enough Italian, a language pretty generally spoken in Greece, to get along, with the aid of a few useful phrases of the native tongues. He was studying modern Greek with a master, he told Hodgson, and he was aided by "tolerably fluent Lingua Franca . . . and some variety of Ottoman oaths of great service with a stumbling horse or a stupid servant." *n*

In addition to Lusieri and Fauvel and their families, who had lived long enough in Athens to be almost natives, though they looked down on the Greeks, Byron was on a footing of easy sociability with official and clerical Turks and Greeks. On November 14 he wrote to Hodgson: "The day before yesterday the Waywode (or governor of Athens) with the Mufti of Thebes (a sort of Mussulman Bishop) supped here and made themselves beastly with raw rum, and the Padré of the convent being as drunk as *we*, my *Attic* feast went off with great *éclat*." *n*

No one could be a more lively companion than Byron when he was in the right mood, but whenever he stopped to reflect, boredom settled over him. On November 26 he wrote to Hobhouse: ". . . my life has, with the exception of a very few moments, never been anything but a *yawn*. . . . I have now seen the World, that is the most ancient of the ancient part. I have spent my little all, I have tasted all sorts of pleasure (so tell the Citoyen [Matthews]); I have nothing more to hope, and may begin to consider the most eligible way of walking out of it; probably I may find in England somebody inclined to save me the trouble. I wish I could find some of Socrates's Hemlock, but Lusieri tells me it don't poison people now-a-days." *n*

His association with the brilliant foreigners in Athens was a welcome diversion from his brooding reflections and debilitating pleasures.[8] On November 28 he dined with Sandford Graham; and with Cockerell, Foster, Graham, Baron Haller, and Lusieri he planned another excursion to Sunium. Byron, who had found

[8] In his cryptic facetiousness, he wrote: "Mention to M. that I have found so many of his antiques on this classical soil, that I am tired of pl & opt Cs, the last thing I could be tired of." (Unpublished passage in letter to Hobhouse of Nov. 26, 1810. Murray MSS.; Hobhouse proofs.)

it one of the most beautiful spots in Greece, was happy to be able to guide the others, though some of them knew more about the antiquities.

The expedition set out in the early days of December. They lingered awhile on the inspiring cliff where the temple to Poseidon looks out on the Cyclades, and then retired to the town of Keratia on the peninsula, where they finished off the day with low comedy. Graham and Byron drank to excess, and "the former in his Bacchanism decapitated a large pig with a Highland broadsword, to the horror of Lusieri."[9]

But they learned later that they had very nearly played parts in a much more serious drama. On December 5, Byron added an excited postscript to his letter to Hobhouse. While they were wandering about the ancient temple, "five-and-twenty Mainotes (pirates) were in the caves at the foot of the cliff, with some Greek boatmen, their prisoners. They demanded of these who were the Franks above? One of the Greeks knew *me*, and they were preparing to attack us, when, seeing my Albanians, and conjecturing there were others in the vicinity, they were seized with a panic, and marched off."[n]

Back in Athens life went smoothly enough. "Here be many English," he wrote to Hobhouse on January 10, "and there have been more, with all of whom I have been and *am* on dining terms, and we have had balls and a variety of fooleries with the females of Athens."[n] His plans for the future were still uncertain, though he had vague notions about returning to England in the spring.

In November he had received a letter from Mrs. Spencer Smith, who, true to the tryst made the year before, had returned to Malta and was disappointed not to find Byron there. But the cautious decorum of her letter was not likely to rouse him from his present and less costly pleasures. Not having had a reply to a verbal message sent by a sea captain, she waited

[9] *LBC*, I, 25. P.S. of Dec. 5, 1810. The party apparently returned by way of Marathon, as Byron and Hobhouse had done earlier the same year. Byron told Hobhouse it was "the same tour we made last year." It may have been on this second tour to Sunium that Byron carved his name on the square column of the temple to Poseidon, where it may be seen today.

two months and with what must have seemed to Byron a typical English circumspection wrote: "In case your thoughts are still the same as they were on the 16th of September, 1809, then set out for Malta on the very first opportunity, as I cannot stay here longer without injuring my own interests. . . . Is the seal still in your possession, or have you thrown it into the sea? If you decide upon coming I need not, I trust, recommend you to give your friends any other reason you chuse to give but the real one, for your sudden departure." [n] But for Byron that affair was past. The lady, however, not knowing how completely the spell was broken, lingered on through the winter and spring, while Byron remained in Athens living for the moment and forming impulsive plans, none of which encompassed the lady who waited at Malta.

In writing to his mother on January 14 he indulged in some self-justification, first of his motives for sending Fletcher home, and then of his traveling and residence abroad. His English servant had long been a handicap, he reiterated, and he was now sufficiently master of the languages of the country to get along without him. "Besides, the perpetual lamentations after beef and beer, the stupid, bigoted contempt for every thing foreign, and insurmountable incapacity for acquiring even a few words of any language, rendered him, like all other English servants, an incumbrance."

As for his residence abroad, Byron assured his mother that he had gained immeasurably in becoming a citizen of the world. "Here I see and have conversed with French, Italians, Germans, Danes, Greeks, Turks, Armenians [n] . . . and without losing sight of my own, I can judge of the countries and manners of others. Where I see the superiority of England (which, by the by, we are a good deal mistaken about in many things), I am pleased, and where I find her inferior, I am at least enlightened. Now, I might have stayed, smoked in your towns, or fogged in your country, a century, without being sure of this, and without acquiring any thing more useful or amusing at home." [n]

On January 20, two days before his twenty-third birthday, he wrote exuberantly to Hodgson: "I am living in the Capuchin Convent, Hymettus before me, the Acropolis behind, the Temple of Jove to my right, the Stadium in front, the town to the left; eh, Sir, there's a situation, there's your picturesque! nothing like that, Sir, in Lunnun, no not even the Mansion House. And I feed upon Woodcocks and Red Mullet every day, and I have three horses (one a present from the Pasha of the Morea), and I ride to Piræus, and Phalerum, and Munychia. . . . I wish to be sure I had a few books, one's own works for instance, any damned nonsense on a long Evening." *n*

Needing literary occupation, Byron on the day after his birthday wrote some paragraphs on the Greeks as a people and a nation. These notes summed up his reactions to the books he had read in the monastery library, and also perhaps his own reflections after conversations with the other Franks in Athens, most of whom took a dim view of the modern Greeks. Byron himself at this time felt that they could not rise by their own power from the state of degradation into which they had fallen from centuries of slavery: ". . . the interposition of foreigners alone can emancipate the Greeks, who, otherwise, appear to have as small a chance of redemption from the Turks, as the Jews have from mankind in general.[1] . . . The Greeks have never lost their hope, though they are now more divided in opinion on the subject of their probable deliverers. . . . But whoever appear with arms in their hands will be welcome; and when that day arrives, Heaven have mercy on the Ottomans; they cannot expect it from the Giaours." *n*

Toward the end of January a firman for Syria and Egypt, for which he had applied, arrived, and this new interest moved Byron to spur Hanson into sending remittances. But, still firm in his resolve not to sell Newstead, he told his mother that if he was forced to part with it he would never return, "as my only tie to England is Newstead, and, that once gone, neither interest nor inclination lead me northward. . . . I feel myself so much a citizen of the world, that the spot where I can enjoy a delicious

[1] Byron seems at this time to have forgotten or reversed the opinion he had expressed in *Childe Harold:* "*Who* would be free *themselves* must strike the blow." His statement also goes counter to what he later said in "The Isles of Greece": "Trust not for freedom to the Franks." He seems to have alternated between the two views as he observed the treachery of the Western nations and the slave-tempered character of the Greeks.

climate, and every luxury, at a less expense than a common college life in England, will always be a country to me; and such are in fact the shores of the Archipelago." [n]

To Hobhouse he wrote: ". . . I am off in spring for Mount Sion, Damascus, Tyre and Sidon, Cairo, and Thebes. Pray whisper in Hanson's ear the word remittances, as I shall soon be run out if you don't urge that worthy but snail-paced man." [n] But remittances were slow in coming, and he gradually lost interest in the project. In the meantime he was stirred to composition again. Toward the end of February he began another long poem in heroic couplets in the manner of *English Bards and Scotch Reviewers,* satirizing his contemporaries with the same recklessness as in the earlier poem. Just after he had come out of a Turkish bath on March 5 (he took one every other day and considered it "an immense luxury") he wrote to Hobhouse: "Since my last letter, 27 ult, I have begun an Imitation of the 'De Arte Poetica' of Horace (in rhyme of course) and have translated or rather varied about 200 lines and shall probably finish it for lack of other argument. The Horace I found in the covent where I have sojourned some months." [n] The poem, which he called *Hints from Horace,* was finished by the 12th.[n]

Soon after, he turned to another theme more nearly connected with his observations in Athens, *The Curse of Minerva,* two hundred lines of which he had written by the 17th. In this humorless satire he poured forth all his rancor against Lord Elgin as the despoiler of Greece. His feelings on the subject had grown in intensity as he came to take the side of the Greeks against the foreigners. At the beginning he put those lines, quite in a different mood and perhaps composed as a separate poem, which describe the sun sinking "in one unclouded blaze of living light" over the hills of the Morea and the beauty of a spring night settling over Athens. Then, after comparing Elgin with Alaric, he made Minerva, speaking for her injured land, place the curse "on him and all his seed." In couplets much more intemperate than the lines in *Childe Harold* condemning Elgin, Byron piled opprobrium upon the Scottish lord. England was not responsible for him—he came from Caledonia, "land of meanness, sophistry, and mist." [n]

Some of Byron's best friends among the foreigners had left Athens, and he himself was preparing, though reluctantly, to depart for England. Having finished *The Curse of Minerva,* he sat down to write some notes on the modern Greek language and literature. His conversations with Dr. Brønsted had made him aware of the work of certain modern Greek scholars such as Adamantios Korais (Byron used the French spelling "Coray"), and he himself had talked with the schoolmaster Psalidis in Jannina, who had a great interest in the modern Greek language. His own tutor in the Romaic, Marmarotouri,[n] a leader among the Greek patriots, had no doubt stimulated his interest further in the subject. And it may have been this tutor who called his attention to the long satirical poem which he cited as an example of the literature of the modern Greeks. "The most singular piece I have lately seen," Byron wrote, "is a satire in dialogue between a Russian, English, and French traveller, and the Waywode of Wallachia . . . an archbishop, a merchant, and Cogia Bachi (or primate), in succession; to all of whom under the Turks the writer attributes their present degeneracy." [2]

Although Byron may not have been fully aware of the extent to which pride in the language was tied up with feelings of patriotic nationalism among the Greeks, he saw in their literature, albeit three quarters of it was devoted to theological works, some promising stirrings of intellectual growth. Still determined to be rigidly realistic in his view of the Greeks, he tried to eschew the extremes of those who saw them all as

[2] *Poetry,* II, 199. This sentence was included in a long note to the second canto of *Childe Harold,* dated "Athens, Franciscan Convent, March 17, 1811." Hobhouse described the satirical piece, which he said Byron received as a present, as "a long paper of verses . . . which, in a dramatic colloquy between a Greek patriot, an Englishman, Frenchman, and Russian, a Metropolitan, a Waiwode of Wallachia, a Merchant and a Primate, and by the introduction of Greece, personified as a desolate female in tears, displays the apathy of the privileged classes. . . ." (*Journey,* II, 597.) Mr. K. Th. Dimaras of Athens showed me an extensive fragment of this satire copied from a manuscript that came from the monastery on Mount Athos. Byron could have acquired from this poem his idea that the Greeks could not trust the Franks to free them; he could have found in it too the equally important theme that the higher classes of the Greeks themselves were the friends of tyranny.

"canaille" and those who sentimentally overpraised them because of what they had been.

One specimen of the national literature Byron was eager to preserve, not only as an example of popular Romaic song, but also for its sentimental associations. The song, he noted, "is a great favourite with the young Girls of Athens of all classes, their manner of singing it is by verses in rotation, the whole number present joining in the Chorus.—I have heard it frequently at our balls in the Winter of 1810–11.—the air is plaintive & pretty." [n] The melancholy love plaint, beginning (in Byron's free translation) "I enter thy Garden of Roses/ Beloved & fair Haidée!" [3] sung in the sad monotony of the Greek rhythms, left an imprint in his memory of some of his pleasantest moments in the country that he was soon reluctantly to leave. Shortly before he embarked at Piræus he had the Greek text of the song copied out for him by Marianna ("Dudu") Roque, cousin of the Macri girls.[n]

On March 19, Byron gave a dinner to all the Franks in Athens.[n] Several of them—the ones with whom he had been most closely associated—were also departing shortly, but they lingered until April. Their winter in Athens, he wrote, had been "most social and fantastical." [n]

He looked back on the experience with feelings in which realism was mingled with romance. "I parted, as I lived, friends with all the English and French in Attica, and we had balls, dinners, and amours without number," he wrote. Then he indicated that he had renewed his attentions to Theresa Macri, though not to the exclusion of others.[4] "I was near bringing away

[3] Byron's translation was first published in the quarto edition of *Childe Harold* (pp. 186–8). The name Haidée (Χαίδι) means "caress" (Dawson and Raubitschek, p. 53). It was a name that Byron chose for his most romantic heroine in *Don Juan,* the daughter of the pirate Lambro, who nursed Juan back to life and health when he was shipwrecked on a Greek island.

[4] That the Macri girls and "Dudu" Roque were closely associated with the social activities in which Byron participated during the winter and spring is indicated in a letter from Cockerell to Byron, March 10, 1811: "We rejoice at your proposal of the ball, & are now as always at your service. Shall we assemble the Consulinas Macri Roque &c, if your house is not to your taste would you like to assemble them here or at Logotheti's?" (Murray MSS.)

Theresa, but the mother asked 30,000 piastres! I had a number of Greek and Turkish women, and I believe the rest of the English were equally lucky, for we were all *clapped*." [n]

Byron's irregular life in Athens had brought on several other ailments. "Ever since my fever in the Morea in Septr. . . . my health has been changing in the most tramontane way," he had written Hobhouse on March 5. "I have been fat, and thin (as I am at present) and had a cough and a catarrh and the piles and be damned to them, and I have had pains in my side and left off animal food, which last has done me some service." [n]

But when the actual day for parting came, Byron felt pangs greater perhaps than he had expected. First of all there was a pathetic leave-taking from his faithful Albanians. Vasilly took his piasters with an awkward show of regret at his master's departure. Then he sent for Dervish, who entered "just as Signor Logotheti, father to the ci-devant Anglo-consul of Athens, and some other of my Greek acquaintances, paid me a visit. Dervish took the money in his hand, but on a sudden dashed it to the ground; and clasping his hands, which he raised to his forehead, rushed out of the room weeping bitterly. From that moment to the hour of my embarcation, he continued his lamentations, and all our efforts to console him only produced this answer, 'M'αφεῖνει,' 'He leaves me.' Signor Logotheti, who never wept before for anything less than the loss of a para (about the fourth of a farthing), melted. . . ." [n]

The transport ship *Hydra,* which he boarded at Piræus, ironically carried at the same time Byron, the manuscript of his *Curse of Minerva,* and the last large shipment of Lord Elgin's marbles on their way to England. Byron had his own curious cargo. In addition to Nicolo Giraud, whom he intended to put in school at Malta,[5] he had "four ancient Athenian skulls, dug out of sarcophagi—a phial of Attic hemlock—four live tortoises—

[5] On April 5, 1811, Giraud wrote to Byron in Greek: "I do not know how to express my gratitude to Your Honour; even if I were given a hundred lives, I would consider it of less importance in comparison to the blessing which Your Lordship has bestowed upon me. Yes, my parents have given me birth, but You have presented me with a virtue which enables me to know who I was before and who I am now, thanks to your magnanimity. Therefore I beg to kiss your hands, with all due respect, and remain your obliged and humble servant." (Murray MSS.—translated for me by George Savidis.)

a greyhound . . . two live Greek servants, one an Athenian, t'other a *Yaniote*, who can speak nothing but Romaic and Italian." [n] Lusieri, Byron's friend and Lord Elgin's agent, was also on board, probably to look out for the marbles and to establish his young brother-in-law at Malta.

The ship was first supposed to sail on April 11, but it did not get under way until the 22nd.[n]

Byron had left Athens in the midst of spring. All his thoughts turned eastward. In a note to *Childe Harold* he wrote: "Setting aside the magic of the name, and all those associations which it would be pedantic and superfluous to recapitulate, the very situation of Athens would render it the favourite of all who have eyes for art or nature. The climate, to me at least, appeared a perpetual spring; during eight months I never passed a day without being as many hours on horseback: rain is extremely rare, snow never lies in the plains, and a cloudy day is an agreeable rarity." [n]

Despite the "compelling" circumstances which urged her toward her native country, Austria, Mrs. Spencer Smith, the "Fair Florence," was still at Malta, waiting patiently for her unhurried lover. The *Hydra* came into the harbor at Valetta on April 30,[n] and Byron disembarked, still suffering intermittently from his maladies. He expected (and hoped) that the lady had accumulated enough other admirers to free him from an embarrassing responsibility. Byron later told Lady Melbourne with amusing detachment of their meeting at the palace. "The Governor (the most accommodating of all possible chief magistrates) [n] was kind enough to leave us to come to the most diabolical of explanations. It was in the dog-days, during a sirocco (I almost perspire now with the thoughts of it), during the intervals of an intermittent fever (my love had also intermitted with my malady), and I certainly feared the ague and my passion would both return in full force.

"I however got the better of both, and she sailed up the Adriatic and I down to the Straits. I had, *certes*, a good deal to contend against, for the lady (who was a *select* friend of the Queen of Naples) had something to gain in a few points and nothing to lose in *reputation*, and was a woman perfectly mistress of herself and every art of intrigue, personal or political—not at all in love, but very able to persuade me that she was so, and sure that I should make a most *convenient* and complaisant fellow-traveler."[6]

But, cavalierly as Byron could speak of the affair later to Lady Melbourne, it was not over so soon, for he was a month at Valetta and it is safe to assume that their "explanations" lasted through most of that time and were not confined to one meeting. No doubt they contributed to his depressed state of mind and his unhappy memories of the town.

To Hobhouse he wrote on May 15: "I am in bad health and worse spirits, being afflicted in body with what Hostess Quickly in Henry V. calls a villainous 'Quotidian Tertian'; it killed Falstaff and may me. . . . it returned in quarantine in this infernal oven, and the fit comes on every other day, reducing me first to the chattering penance of Harry Gill, and then mounting me up to a Vesuvian pitch of fever, lastly quitting me with sweats that render it necessary for me to have a man and horse all night to change my linen."[n]

In addition, letters from Hanson were more than ever disquieting. Creditors could not be held off much longer. Both Davies, who had borrowed money and had to meet annuity payments, and Mrs. Massingberd would have to go to jail if their debts were not paid.[n] Hanson was further bedeviled by Mrs. Byron, who wrote despondently: "I am neither well nor happy, and *never expect* to be so in this world."[n] Brothers, desperate because he too might have to go to jail for debts, was constantly threatening to sell the furniture at Newstead to settle his claim.[n] As for Davies, Byron wrote to Hobhouse: ". . . it is with the greatest regret I see him in such a situation, from which he shall be, at all events and at all expense, relieved, for if money is not ready, I will take the securities on *myself*."[n]

[6] *LBC*, I, 78. Letter of Sept. 15, 1812. Byron added as a sequel to the story: "She is now, I am told, writing her memoirs at Vienna, in which I shall cut a very indifferent figure; and nothing survives of this most ambrosial amour, which made me on one occasion risk my life, and on another almost drove me mad, but a few Duke of York*ish* letters and certain baubles, which I dare swear by this time have decorated the hands of half Hungary and all Bohemia. Cosi finiva la musica."

He tried to cheer Hobhouse, whose "Miscellany" had failed, who was not yet reconciled to his father,[7] and who was talking of joining the Militia or trying to get a Foreign Office clerkship abroad. Byron attributed the failure of Hobhouse's book to his own and other contributions, and recommended that his friend follow Matthews's recommendation and go back to Cambridge. Hobhouse was also concerned about his debt to Byron, which amounted at the time of their parting to £818. 3*s*. 4*d*. (Byron had spent nearly twice as much in the same time).[n] But, knowing that his own property was worth more than a hundred thousand pounds, Byron refused to allow his friend to worry about so inconsequential a debt.

Byron had already arranged to sail for England on the *Volage* frigate, which, together with several other British warships, was setting out at the beginning of June with French prizes. As the days dragged out in the oppressive heat, and the fever and his other ailments made him miserable, he grew morbidly introspective. On May 22 he jotted down some notes under the heading "Four or Five reasons in favour of a Change." Before he left off he had found seven reasons:

1st At twenty three the best of life is over and its bitters double. 2ndly I have seen mankind in various Countries and find them equally despicable, if anything the Balance is rather in favour of the Turks. 3dly I am sick at heart.

> "*Me jam nec* fæmina . . .
> *Nec* Spes animi credula mutui
> *Nec* certare *juvat Mero*."[8]

4thly A man who is lame of one leg is in a state of bodily inferiority which increases with years and must render his old age more peevish

[7] A reconciliation took place on February 4, 1811, but the condition of it was that the son apply for a captaincy in the Militia. (Joyce, pp. 26–7.)
[8] Byron was quoting from memory and somewhat inaccurately Horace's first ode of the fourth book ("To Venus"):

> *Nor maid nor youth delights me now,*
> *Nor credulous dream of heart's exchange, nor hours*
> *Of challenged wine-bout, nor the brow*
> *Girt with a wreath of freshly gathered flowers.*

& intolerable. Besides in another existence I expect to have *two* if not *four* legs by way of compensation.
5thly I grow selfish & misanthropical, something like the "jolly Miller" "I care for nobody no not I and Nobody cares for me."
6thly My affairs at home and abroad are gloomy enough.
7thly I have outlived all my appetites and most of my vanities aye even the vanity of authorship.[n]

Four days later his bitterness found vent in some rollicking and slightly malicious verses, his "Farewell to Malta":

> Adieu, *ye joys of La Valette!*
> *Adieu, Sirocco, sun, and sweat!*
> *Adieu, thou palace rarely entered!*
> *Adieu, ye mansions where—I've ventured!*
> *Adieu, ye cursèd streets of stairs!*
> (*How surely he who mounts them swears!*) [n]

A more serious farewell was that to Nicolo Giraud, the boy who was willing to follow him round the world, and the only being, he now felt, who truly loved him.[9] On June 2 Byron sailed on board the *Volage* frigate, which with the *Amphion* was convoying two French prizes. The trip was necessarily dull, for, though some of his illnesses had subsided, they still chased one another alternately through his system and left him weak.

On the 17th they were in the harbor at Gibraltar. They were driven through the strait by an easterly gale, but then the wind slackened and the passage became more tedious. On the 19th, Byron wrote Hobhouse again: "I am recovered from my Tertian, but neither my health nor my hitherto hoydenish spirits are as rampant as usual." Turning to Hobhouse's affairs, Byron pro-

[9] In John Murray's collection are a number of Giraud's letters to Byron, some in Greek, a greater number in Italian, and some later ones in English, expressing his gratitude to his friend and master "*fine alla morte*" and giving news of his progress in school. According to Moore (I, 244), on parting from the boy at Malta Byron gave him a considerable sum of money. On his return to England Byron put a clause in his will leaving Nicolo £7,000 (it was omitted when a subsequent will was made in 1815). He had requested Giraud to write every month. On the 1st of January 1815, Giraud wrote from Athens: "It is now almost three years that I am at Athens; and I have sent to you many letters, but I have not received any answer. . . . I pray your excellency to not forget your humble servant which so dearly and faithfully loves you."

tested against his joining the army. ". . . Santissimi Coglioni!—the militia at five-and-twenty; boys over your head, and brutes under you. . . ." [n] The thing for Hobhouse, he still felt, was "La Bagatelle" (the title proposed for a literary periodical).

To his mother Byron wrote that he was returning to England "with much the same feelings which prevailed on my departure, viz. indifference. . . . You will be good enough to get my apartments ready at Newstead; but don't disturb yourself, on any account, particularly mine, nor consider me in any other light than a visitor. . . . It is my intention to proceed first to town, to see Mr. Hanson, and thence to Newstead, on my way to Rochdale. . . . My prospects are not very promising, but I suppose we shall wrestle through life like our neighbors. . . . I have brought you a shawl, and a quantity of attar of roses. . . ." [1]

Byron whiled away the tedium of the voyage by writing letters to several friends in England to apprise them of his arrival. To Dallas, who was an eager and a useful literary agent, he wrote: "I have an imitation of Horace's *Art of Poetry* ready for Cawthorn, but don't let that deter you, for I sha'n't inflict it upon you." [n] Although he wrote Hodgson that he was "sick of fops, and poesy, and prate," he admitted that he had written some four thousand lines on his travels.[n]

Befogged on the Bay of Biscay on July 2, 1811, just two years after the day he left England, he sat down again to write the companion of his outward voyage: "I have been thinking again and again of a literary project we have at times started, to wit,—a periodical paper, something in the Spectator or Observer way. . . . You must be Editor, as you have more taste and diligence than either Matthews or myself. . . . We must have for each day, one or two essays, miscellaneous, according to circum-

[1] *LJ*, I, 311–12. Letter of June 25, 1811. Mrs. Byron had governed his little empire with a firm hand. She dismissed servants to reduce expenses, kept an eye on the others, including Mealey, the caretaker, and was a screeching terror to trespassers. To a fox-hunting neighbor she had written in September 1809: "You are surely not so ignorant as not to know that breaking down fences and riding through fields of standing corn with your Hounds are most *unjustifiable, arbitrary,* and *oppressive* acts, and will not be submitted to in a *free country,* even if you was the *first Man* in it. . . . If the breed of Fox hunters could be . . . got rid of, the benefit to society in general would be great." (Prothero: "Childhood and Schooldays of Byron," pp. 64–5.)

stances, but now and then political, and always a piece of poetry of one kind or other." [n]

Byron's spirits had risen sufficiently for him to make light of his ailments when he wrote Henry Drury on the 7th while the frigate was becalmed off Ushant, near Brest harbor: "The enclosed letter is from a friend of yours Surgeon Tucker whom I met with in Greece; & so on to Malta, where he administered to me for three complaints viz. a *Gonorrhea* a *Tertian fever;* & the *Hemorrhoides, all* of which I literally had at once, though he assured me the *morbid* action of only one of these distempers could act at a time, which was a great comfort, though they relieved one another as regularly as Sentinels. . . ." [n]

The *Volage* arrived at Portsmouth on July 11, but the squadron was ordered to the Nore and Byron set foot on his native shores once more at Sheerness on the 14th, two years and twelve days after he had sailed from Falmouth.[n] He was perhaps only half aware of the depth of his foreign impressions and of the maturing and mellowing processes that had been at work in him during his grand tour, nor was the change perceptible immediately to his friends, for on the surface he was as devil-may-care as ever. "I don't know that I have acquired any thing by my travels but a smattering of two languages and a habit of chewing Tobacco," he wrote Augusta.[n] But the effects on his character and career were far more pervasive.

His observations abroad had led him to be more than ever contemptuous of a narrow orthodoxy: "I will bring you ten Mussulmans shall shame you in all goodwill towards men, prayer to God, and duty to their neighbors," [n] he wrote Hodgson, who was disturbed by his heterodox opinions. His political views were broadened also by his ability to compare governmental tyrannies at home and in other countries.

But more than anything in his Eastern experiences he had rubbed elbows with life in picturesque surroundings that he would never forget, and these early contacts with all kinds of men he grew to prize as the foundation of his worldly wisdom. In 1821 he wrote: ". . . in the course of my youth, I have seen a little of all sorts of society, from the Christian prince and the Mussulman sultan and pacha, and the higher ranks of their countries, down to the London boxer, the *'flash and the swell,'* the Spanish muleteer, the wandering Turkish dervise, the Scotch highlander, and the Albanian robber. . . ."[n] Henceforth he was drawn constantly toward the warm lands "where the cypress and myrtle/ Are emblems of deeds that are done in their clime."[n] Many times in the next few years, when the complications of his personal life made him long for escape, he was on the point of leaving again for the shores of the Mediterranean. For the East, and particularly Greece, was to be evermore "the greenest island" of his imagination.[n]

"If I am a poet," he told Trelawny, ". . . the air of Greece has made me one."[n] Aside from the perpetual source of literary material most congenial to his spirit which the East had furnished him, there was instilled in him a deep-lying and genuine cosmopolitanism. It was not an accident that he chose a passage from *Le Cosmopolite* as a motto for *Childe Harold.* He had been predisposed to become a citizen of the world even before he had traveled; he came home a confirmed one and would always view the prejudices and dogmas of the "tight little island" in the light of his knowledge of "the ways and farings of many men."

# CHAPTER IX

## *1811–1812*

## London and Newstead: *Childe Harold*

WHEN Byron arrived in London on July 14, he was immediately involved in a whirl of business and a renewal of friendships which left him little time for the melancholy reflections that had haunted him on the long voyage home. His first visitor was Scrope Davies, who came in drunk that same evening with "a new set of jokes." *n* Hobhouse, who had finally succumbed to his father's wishes and joined the Militia as captain, sent a welcome from his barracks in Dover. "The *Travels* are going on swimmingly," he wrote, "plain prose is to be my fate. You shall be immortalised you rogue you shall. . . . You will be overwhelmed with compliments in Town. Ward told me that Sheridan had mentioned *English Bards* to him in terms of the highest praise." *n*

In his letter to Hobhouse the next day, promising to meet him on the 17th at Sittingbourne near Canterbury, Byron announced that he had already delivered his imitation of Horace to Cawthorn, who had sold almost the whole of a fourth edition of *English Bards and Scotch Reviewers.* The eager Dallas, having been forewarned that Byron had a manuscript, lost no time in calling. Byron told him he "believed Satire to be his *forte*," and showed him a copy of the *Hints from Horace.* Having agreed to superintend its publication, Dallas took the manuscript home, but was "grievously disappointed," for he felt that "a muse much inferior to his might have produced them in the smoky atmosphere of London, whereas he had been roaming under the cloudless skies of Greece. . . ." *n*

Dallas came to breakfast the next morning and, trying to conceal his disappointment in the satire, expressed surprise that Byron had written nothing else during his journey, "upon which he told me that he had occasionally written short poems, besides a great many stanzas in Spencer's [*sic*] measure, relative to the countries he had visited. 'They are not worth troubling you with, but you shall have them all with you if you like.'" With this Byron handed him the manuscript of *Childe Harold's Pilgrimage,* together with some shorter poems, which he took from a small trunk. "He said they had been read but by one person, who had found very little to commend and much to condemn: that he himself was of that opinion, and he was sure I should be so too." *n*

Apparently not too sure of his own literary judgment, Dallas called into consultation his friend Walter Wright, former Consul-General of the Ionian Islands and author of a poem called *Horæ Ionicæ* which Byron had praised in *English Bards and Scotch Reviewers.* It was probably Wright who convinced the timid Dallas that *Childe Harold* had great possibilities of popular success.[1] But the two agreed that some of the stanzas expressing skepticism in religion and politics should be deleted or toned down. Dallas wrote an enthusiastic letter on July 16: "You have written one of the most delightful poems I ever read. . . . I would almost pledge my life on its advancing the reputation of your poetical powers, and of its gaining you great honour and regard. . . ." *n*

There the matter rested while Byron went to Sittingbourne. He was as glad to see Hobhouse as he had been relieved to part with him the year before. They had much to catch up on; they spent two days together visiting Canterbury and the vi-

[1] Dallas took the whole credit to himself for discovering *Childe Harold's* merit, but Wright told Crabb Robinson "that he had been reading for Dallas a manuscript poem entitled *Childe Harold's Pilgrimage,* which Lord Byron offered to make him a present of. . . . 'I have told him,' said Wright, 'that I have no doubt this will succeed. Lord Byron had offered him before some translations from Horace, which I told him would never sell, and he did not take them.'" (*Robinson,* I, 2.)

cinity and parted on the 19th.[n] Back in London, Byron was visited by the admiring Hodgson, full of enthusiasm, rhymes, and good advice.[2] Byron kept him up late, regaling him with anecdotes of his life in the East. Before leaving for Harrow to spend a few days with Henry Drury, Byron called on the bookseller and publisher William Miller to arrange for the payment of his long-overdue account and to put in a good word for Hobhouse's book of travels.

On the 23rd he was in London again, trying to cajole and pacify Mrs. Massingberd and the moneylenders and conferring with Hanson, who was preparing copyhold papers for him to sign in connection with the Weymondham estate in Suffolk.[n] Dallas, confident that he had a valuable thing in the poem Byron had given him, asked for permission to find a publisher for it, and was surprised that his friend, though flattered by such enthusiastic praise, was reluctant to have it go to a printer. Whether from genuine diffidence or because he wanted to be further convinced, Byron protested: "It was any thing but poetry —it had been condemned by a good critic—had I not myself seen the sentences on the margins of the manuscript?"[3]

What troubled Dallas more was Byron's flat refusal at first to omit or alter any of the stanzas, especially those expressing doubt concerning immortality. Dallas was also afraid of the attack on the Tory government's foreign policy and its conduct of the war in the Peninsula, particularly in the section on the Convention of Cintra.[4] Offensive to him too were the stanzas

[2] Hodgson, I, 179–81. Hodgson had grand visions of Byron as a moral satirist and reforming statesman. After this visit he sent some inspiring verses: "First let thy country's foes severely feel/ Thy *caustic ardour* for the general weal./ Spread, like a flame, my Byron, through the land/ That natural warmth no scoundrel can withstand."

[3] Dallas: *Recollections,* pp. 75–6. Although Hobhouse took exception to Dallas's statement (quoted by Moore, I, 260) that the poem had been read by only one person before Dallas saw it, he did not recognize himself as the "good critic" referred to by Byron. Opposite this passage in Moore (I, 261) he wrote: "It is true that [Gifford?] objected to the stanzas on the convention of Cintra and on the Sunday excursions of the citizens." But Gifford did not "condemn" the manuscript as a whole. Moreover, Dallas was quoting Byron's arguments against publication before the manuscript came into the hands of Murray, who showed it to Gifford.

[4] *Poetry,* II, 39–41. Byron took the general Whig view that the war against

ridiculing the amusements of the people on a London Sunday.

Confident that he could eventually persuade Byron to remove or modify the dangerous parts, Dallas was eager to get it published, and continued his praise of the poem until he got consent. Dallas thought he had raised Byron's opinion of the composition, which was no doubt high enough already. What made Byron reluctant was the fear—probably increased by his conversation with Hobhouse, who had read part if not all of the manuscript in the East—of what the critics might say about the self-revealing egoism of some of the stanzas.

Byron was easily persuaded, however, by such enthusiasm as Dallas and Wright displayed, for he was in fact eager enough to see the poem in print, though without his name.[5] At any rate, within a few days Dallas was searching for a publisher. He thought first of Cawthorn, who had, he considered, done well with *English Bards.* Byron objected on the ground that Cawthorn "did not then rank high among the brethren of the trade,"[6] and suggested Miller, who had been so cordial toward Hobhouse's *Journey.* Dallas obediently carried the manuscript to Miller, who, however, declined to publish it, not so much because of the objectionable political and religious opinions as because of the attack on Lord Elgin, whom he served as bookseller and publisher.

---

Napoleon had been bungled. But he was particularly bitter in denouncing the generals who signed the Convention of Cintra. On September 3, 1808, Generals Kellerman and Wellesley had put their names to the "Convention" or agreement whereby the French general Junot, defeated at Vimiera, was allowed to withdraw all his troops, artillery, equipment, and cavalry, with a safe convoy into France. Byron's spleen was loosed against the court of inquiry in England which had whitewashed and exonerated the generals and approved of the Convention. The stanzas, as Byron had written them in 1809, went even beyond the current views of the opposition Whigs in condemning all parties concerned. (See Borst, pp. 17–18.)

[5] Hobhouse wrote in the margin of his copy of Moore (I, 260–1) opposite the statement (derived from Dallas) that "it was some time before Lord Byron's obstinate repugnance to the idea of publishing Childe Harold could be removed": "So Mr. Dallas says—but I do not believe the fact."

[6] Dallas: *Correspondence,* p. 129. "As for C[awthor]n," Byron wrote to Hobhouse, "you may rely on it you will have some sneaking conduct before you get from his hands. . . . why deal with a vendor of lampoons?" (Unpublished letter of July 23, 1811, Murray MS; Hobhouse proofs.)

Byron then gave Dallas carte blanche to find a publisher, Cawthorn and Longman being the only ones ruled out, the latter firm because it had rejected *English Bards.* Having been given the manuscript as an outright present for what it would bring him, Dallas first carried it to John Murray (who then had a shop at 32 Fleet Street, opposite St. Dunstan's Church) because Murray, and his father before him, had published Dallas's own work and had expressed a desire to have something from Byron after the success of *English Bards and Scotch Reviewers.*[n] Murray was the second of the name, his father having purchased a bookselling and publishing business from William Sandby in 1768. Succeeding to the business in 1795, John Murray II had already, in 1811, by his good judgment and initiative established a high reputation as a publisher, having brought into his sphere some of the chief literary men of his day, including Walter Scott, Isaac D'Israeli, Robert Southey, and William Gifford. Instrumental in founding the *Quarterly Review* in 1808, he had become its publisher. It was fortunate both for Murray and for Byron that Gifford, whom Byron already regarded as the greatest critic of the age, and who had been pleased by the hero-worshipping praise in *English Bards and Scotch Reviewers,* was, as first editor of the *Quarterly,* Murray's chief literary adviser.

While these negotiations were going forward, two disturbing matters had demanded Byron's attention. To add to the irony of his sailing from Greece on the ship bearing Lord Elgin's marbles, he had acceded to Lusieri's desire that he carry from Malta to England a letter to that same lord whom he was attacking so bitterly for his spoliation of the Greek treasures. Byron had fulfilled his commission by sending on the letter after his arrival, but, embarrassed by a note from Lord Elgin, who wanted to call personally to thank him,[7] Byron felt obliged to warn him of his intention to publish on the subject, so that

[7] Letter of July 29, 1811. Murray MSS. In another letter (July 31) Lord Elgin asked again to call and said that he attached much value to Byron's opinion of the researches at Athens. Since Byron left the next day for Newstead, it is unlikely that the two ever met.

Elgin "might not have an opportunity of accusing me of double dealing afterwards." *n*

More upsetting still—and this may have made him wary of rushing into print with anything so vulnerably autobiographic as *Childe Harold*—was a scurrilously personal attack in the March 1811 number of *The Scourge,* a new periodical even more vitriolic than *The Satirist.* *n* The writer he knew to be his old enemy Hewson Clarke, whom he had ridiculed in a Postscript to the second edition of *English Bards and Scotch Reviewers.* Clarke complained that Byron had released his lampoon only after he had left the shores of Britain. And, referring to Byron's aspersions on his lowly birth, he struck back with more fury than fact: "It may be reasonably asked whether to be a denizen of Berwick-upon-Tweed, be more disgraceful than to be the illegitimate descendant of a murderer; whether to labour in an honourable profession . . . be less worthy of praise than to waste the property of others in vulgar debauchery; whether to be the offspring of parents whose only crime is their want of title, be not as honourable as to be the son of a profligate father, and a mother whose days and nights are spent in the delirium of drunkenness. . . ." *n*

Byron flared up and immediately started an action for libel.[8] In the meantime, Dallas had been busy with Murray and had learned that the publisher was considering the manuscript but was fearful of the public response to some passages. Dallas proceeded to send Byron a formal protest, under six headings, to the unorthodox stanzas in *Childe Harold.* *n*

Byron told Hobhouse on the 31st that his affairs were in "the most lackadaisical posture," so much so that he could not accept Hobhouse's invitation to Dover, for he hadn't money enough to carry him there and back. *n* Yet he was planning to

[8] *LBC,* I, 42. Letter of July 31, 1811. On October 7, Sir Vickery Gibbs gave Byron an opinion on the advisability of prosecuting Clarke. The time that had elapsed and the fact that Byron's own attack on Clarke might raise a prejudice in the minds of the jury caused Gibbs to recommend that it might "be best upon the whole to leave these offensive Papers in the State of Neglect into which they have no Doubt by this Time sunk." (Eg. 2611, ff. 258–9.) On this advice Byron dropped the prosecution.

purchase a carriage. The whole incident is characteristically fantastic. Soon after his return Byron had ordered a *vis-à-vis* built by the carriage-maker Goodall. This he traded to his old friend James Wedderburn Webster for a carriage. "Bold Webster," the unstable character who had been the butt of practical jokes at Newstead, apparently repented of his bargain, and Byron, a little piqued, arranged for Goodall to keep the *vis-à-vis*, himself undertaking to buy the carriage from Webster for two hundred guineas. Byron kept his temper sufficiently to congratulate Webster, though a little wryly, on his matrimonial bliss (he had married Lady Frances Annesley, daughter of Arthur, first Earl of Mountnorris and eighth Viscount Valentia, the year before), adding facetiously: "I shall follow your example as soon as I can get a sufficient price for my coronet." [n]

When the carriage arrived two days later, however, with a faded and worn interior instead of the new one he had stipulated, Byron lost his good humor. "Two hundred guineas for a carriage with ancient lining!!! Rags and rubbish!" [n]

But the next day all this was driven out of his head, for news came that his mother was seriously ill. In this emergency he was completely without money and had to draw £40 on Hanson before he could set out for Newstead.[n] He was still in London when a servant arrived to tell him that Mrs. Byron was dead.[9] The shock did not strike him immediately. From Newport Pagnell he wrote to John Pigot: "My poor mother died yesterday! . . . I heard *one* day of her illness, the *next* of her

[9] "Byron was informed when in London of her being unwell; but the surgeon did not at first perceive any danger, and his departure for Newstead was not, therefore, so speedy as it might have been. The surgeon afterwards became alarmed, and requested B. might be hastened down. A servant was despatched from the Abbey for this purpose; but shortly after, her ladyship [*sic*] died; and Rushton (who was then at the Abbey) was sent on horseback after him with the information, and overtook him near Nottingham; so that *B. knew of her death before he left London.*" "Byroniana. No. III," *Literary Gazette,* June 14, 1828.) Moore wrote (I, 272): ". . . so sadly characteristic was the close of the poor lady's life, that a fit of rage, brought on, it is said, by reading over the upholsterer's bills, was the ultimate cause of her death." What the specific illness was it not known. She was only forty-six when she died.

death. Thank God her last moments were most tranquil. . . . Peace be with her!" [n] But once he was at Newstead, the sense of loss settled more heavily upon him, even though he knew that her own actions had made it impossible for him to have genuine affection or respect for her. Now the ties of blood and of early recollections opened the floodgates of emotion to remorse and self-pity. The night after his arrival Mrs. Byron's maid passed the door of the room where the body lay and heard a heavy sighing; "on entering the chamber, [she] found, to her surprise, Lord Byron sitting, in the dark, beside the bed. On her representing to him the weakness of thus giving way to grief, he burst into tears and exclaimed, 'Oh, Mrs. By, I had but one friend in the world, and she is gone!'" [n]

Before Mrs. Byron was buried, another blow struck. Charles Skinner Matthews, the most brilliant of Byron's Cambridge friends, died horribly on August 3, enmeshed in a bed of weeds at the bottom of the Cam in a pool where he was bathing alone.[n] "Some curse hangs over me and mine," Byron wrote to Scrope Davies. "My mother lies a corpse in this house; one of my best friends is drowned in a ditch. . . . Come to me Scrope, I am almost desolate—left almost alone in the world. . . ." [n]

On the morning of his mother's funeral, Byron could not bring himself to follow the remains to Hucknall Torkard Church, where they were buried in the family vault. He stood in the door of the Abbey, watching until the procession passed out of sight. Then, according to Moore, "turning to young Rushton, who was the only person left besides himself, he desired him to fetch the sparring-gloves, and proceeded to his usual exercise with the boy. He was silent and abstracted all the time, and, as if from an effort to get the better of his feelings, threw more violence, Rushton thought, into his blows than was his habit; but, at last, —the struggle seeming too much for him,—he flung away the gloves, and retired to his room." [n]

Whatever his mother may have said in anger and exasperation, Byron knew that she had been devoted to him in her fashion. She had great pride in his accomplishments and confidence in his future greatness. He must have been touched by finding among her effects a bound volume of literary reviews and notices of all his published poems, together with her own marginal comments.[n]

News of a third death that moved him acutely, that of his Harrow schoolfellow John Wingfield, had reached Byron when he wrote on August 10 to Hobhouse, who had left with his regiment for Ireland. All he could think of to say was that Matthews, in a letter written the day before his death, "spoke of you with that affectionate familiarity, so much more pleasing from those we love, than the highest encomiums of the world." As for himself, Byron confessed: "I am really so much bewildered with the different shocks I have sustained, that I can hardly reduce myself to reason by the most frivolous occupations. . . . There is to me something so incomprehensible in death, that I can neither speak nor think on the subject. Indeed, when I looked on the mass of corruption which was the being from whence I sprung, I doubted within myself whether I *was*, or whether she *was not*. . . . I have neither hopes nor fears beyond the grave, yet if there is within us 'a spark of that Celestial fire,' M[atthews] has already 'mingled with the gods.'"[n]

With his thoughts so closely upon death, Byron sat down to write the draft of a will to be drawn up by Samuel Bolton, Mrs. Byron's Nottingham attorney, "as soon as possible, in the firmest manner." The estate of Newstead was to be entailed on his cousin George Byron. To Nicolo Giraud of Athens he wished to leave £7,000, to be paid on the boy's reaching the age of twenty-one. To Fletcher, Joe Murray, Demetrius Zograffo, and Robert Rushton he would leave £50 per annum each for life, and Fletcher should be given the right to rent the mill at Newstead. Hanson was to get £2,000, and the claims of Davies were to be satisfied. His library and furniture were to go to Hobhouse and Davies, whom he named as executors. (Alternates were the Reverend John Becher of Southwell, and Dallas.)[1] Finally he wrote: "I desire that my body may be buried in the vault of the garden of Newstead, without any ceremony or

[1] The solicitor had left blanks for the Christian names of the executors in drawing up the will; coming to Dallas, Byron wrote in the margin: "I forget the Christian name of Dallas—cut him out." (*LJ*, I, 329n.)

burial-service whatever, and that no inscription, save my name and age, be written on the tomb or tablet; and it is my will that my faithful dog may not be removed from the said vault."

A few days later he added: ". . . in case any of my successors within the entail (from bigotry, or otherwise) might think proper to remove the carcass, such proceeding shall be attended by forfeiture of the estate, which in such case shall go to my sister, the Hon[ble] Augusta Leigh and her heirs on similar conditions." [n]

Byron had not seen Augusta since some months before his departure for the East; having heard that she was hurt by his attack on Lord Carlisle in *English Bards*, he had not written to her while he was abroad. But her letter of sympathy on the death of his mother elicited a good-natured reply, twitting her on the rapid growth of her family: "Notwithstanding Malthus tells us that, were it not for Battle, Murder, and Sudden death, we should be overstocked, I think we have latterly had a redundance of these national benefits, and therefore I give you all credit for your matronly behaviour." And he concluded cynically: ". . . *I* shall marry, if I can find any thing inclined to barter money for rank within six months. . . ." [n]

Scrope Davies had been at Newstead, but now had gone on to Harrogate. "His gaiety (death cannot mar it) has done me service; but, after all, ours was a hollow laughter," Byron told Hodgson. "I am solitary, and I never felt solitude irksome before." [n] To fill up the emptiness he turned to business. Murray, after some cogitation, had finally determined to publish *Childe Harold*, possibly on Dallas's assurance that he could get Byron to soften some of the dangerous stanzas. Byron had already made one concession. He would not change the lines on death and immortality, but he added a "hypothetical" stanza beginning:

*Yet if, as holiest men have deemed, there be*
*A land of Souls beyond that sable shore. . . .*[2]

[2] *Poetry*, II, 103. Byron did eventually suppress one stanza which began: "Frown not upon me, churlish Priest! that I/ Look not for Life, where life may never be. . . ."

Now he agreed to omit the satirical sections on Sunday in London.[3]

Two matters of greater concern to himself, however, Byron took up with Dallas, who, as owner of the copyright that Byron had freely given him, and for which Murray was inclined to make a handsome offer, was very willing to act as mediator while the author was out of town.[4] Knowing Murray's connection with the reviewers, Byron wrote: "Has Murray shown the work to any one? He may—but I will have no traps for applause."[n] His greatest anxiety was that Murray would show the manuscript to Gifford, whose commendation Byron wanted above all others, but independently of any seeking of author or publisher. He had not a little fear that the editor of the Tory *Quarterly*, who had praised the satiric *English Bards*, would find much to displease him in the sentimental tone and liberal political opinions of *Childe Harold.*

And he was anxious on another point. Dallas said that Murray wanted his name on the title page. ". . . you must be aware," Byron replied, "that my plaguy Satire will bring the north and south Grub Streets down upon the *Pilgrimage*. . . ."[n] But though he was most eager to avoid having his own character identified with that of Childe Harold, he finally agreed to let his name appear.[5] He himself was not afraid of the reactions to his unorthodox opinions, but he knew that Murray would have some worry on that score.

Though he did not show it on the surface, neither business nor pleasure could quite fill the void in his life. In reply to the lugubrious piety of Dallas's continued consolations, he wrote: "Your letter gives me credit for more acute feelings than I possess; for though I feel tolerably miserable, yet I am at the same time subject to a kind of hysterical merriment, or rather laughter

[3] *LJ*, I, 335. Letter of Aug. 21, 1811, to Dallas. These stanzas were, however, retained when the poem was published.

[4] In the final arrangement with Murray, Dallas was paid £600 for the copyright.

[5] When Byron began the poem he apparently had no thought of concealing its autobiographical character, for he called his hero "Childe Burun" (so it stands in Byron's original manuscript). This was changed to "Childe Harold" when Dallas persuaded him to publish it. (See *Poetry*, II, pp. xiv, 17 ff.)

without merriment, which I can neither account for nor conquer, and yet I do not feel relieved by it; but an indifferent person would think me in excellent spirits."[n]

In fact, Byron felt a little more comfortable with his less pious friends who, like Davies, would laugh with him instead of offering homilies. He had accepted Davies's invitation to visit him at Cambridge in October, and now he tried to pull the ridiculous but likable Webster out of the "hysterics" into which the confusion about the carriage had thrown him. ". . . you know I wish you well, and if I have not inflicted my society upon you according to your own Invitation, it is only because I am not a social animal, and should feel sadly at a loss amongst Countesses and Maids of Honour. . . ."[n] But a few days later Byron responded to the repeated invitation of the uxorious Webster: "I shall invade you in the course of the winter, out of envy, as Lucifer looked at Adam and Eve."[n]

Byron was still waiting for Hanson to accompany him to Rochdale. Then he would go to Cambridge to see Davies and Hodgson and on to London, where he would take his seat in Parliament if it met in October. Although the enthusiasm he had once felt for a Parliamentary career, the dreams of oratorical brilliance and statesmanlike performance he had had at Harrow and Cambridge and occasionally while abroad, had largely melted, it was still something to do. In the meantime he wandered about the lonely Abbey, solitary and disconsolate. Again as in his boyhood it oppressed him as the symbol of his decaying race. And once more he set down in verses the feelings of the moment:

*In the dome of my Sires as the clear moonbeam falls*
*Through Silence and Shade o'er its desolate walls. . .*

. . .

*And the step that o'erechoes the gray floor of stone*
*Falls sullenly now, for 'tis only my own. . . .*[n]

Boredom rather than dejection weighed upon him while he remained without occupation for his active mind. There was some employment in looking after the publication of his poems, though he would have preferred to leave the details to others.

And he had promised to help Hobhouse with his travel book. About the *Hints from Horace* he wrote Cawthorn: ". . . I am inclined to think it had better be delayed till the Satire is reprinted, & so come out in the humbler light of an appendage to the aforesaid.—Besides I have another thing in Mr. Murray's hands, and I don't like firing on the Public with a *double Barrell.* . . ." [n]

The fact is that Byron was coming to have a much greater liking for *Childe Harold* than for his satires, and, what with the enterprise of Murray and his growing distrust of Cawthorn, he eventually encouraged Dallas to stall the one publication until the other was out. His personal feeling for *Childe Harold* was increased by the tributes he had added to Wingfield and to Matthews.[n]

Augusta had written again, hinting at embarrassments and a changed situation and saying that there was much she wanted to talk over with him. Byron replied with brotherly banter: "The embarrassments you mention in your last letter I never heard of before, but that disease is epidemic in our family. . . . I don't know what Scrope Davies meant by telling you I liked Children, I abominate the sight of them so much that I have always had the greatest respect for the character of Herod." He wished to settle his business in Lancashire "& then if I can't persuade some wealthy dowdy to ennoble the dirty puddle of her mercantile Blood,—why—I shall leave England and all it's [*sic*] clouds for the East again; I am very sick of it already." [n]

The next day he added some more serious lines. He had heard that Augusta's husband, Colonel Leigh, had quarreled with the Prince of Wales, whom he served as an equerry. The consequences might be disastrous to their future. Byron's response was "However, at all events, and in all Situations, you have a brother in me, and a home here. . . . Pray can't you contrive to pay me a visit between this and Xmas? . . . You will do what you please, without our interfering with each other; the premises are so delightfully extensive, that two people might live together without ever seeing, hearing or meeting,—but I can't feel the comfort of this till I marry. In short it would be

*THERESA MACRI, THE MAID OF ATHENS*

BYRON IN ALBANIAN DRESS

the most amiable matrimonial mansion, and *that* is another great inducement to my plan,—my wife and I shall be so happy,—one in each Wing." [n]

And now Byron was involved against his will in a controversy over religion and immortality. The losses he had sustained served to strengthen rather than weaken his skepticism. Dallas continued to argue with him over the freethinking passages in *Childe Harold,* resorting, when theological arguments failed, to the plea of expediency and of danger to his literary reputation. Hodgson, about to take orders, was also disturbed by the failure of his friend to see what he considered the reasonableness of orthodox views. His devotion to Byron increased the earnestness of his plea. "Did we need any proof from reason of the soul's immortality, surely that obvious inference from the shortness of our visible life would be convincing." [n]

Byron's reply was quite open and frank: "I will have nothing to do with your immortality; we are miserable enough in this life, without the absurdity of speculating upon another. . . . As to revealed religion, Christ came to save men; but a good Pagan will go to heaven, and a bad Nazarine to hell. . . . I hope I am sincere; I was so at least on a bed of sickness in a far-distant country, when I had neither friend, nor comforter, nor hope, to sustain me. I looked to death as a relief from pain, without a wish for an after-life, but a confidence that the God who punishes in this existence had left that last asylum for the weary." Byron refused to be catalogued. "I am no Platonist, I am nothing at all; but I would sooner be a Paulician, Manichean, Spinozist, Gentile, Pyrrhonian, Zoroastrian, than one of the seventy-two villainous sects who are tearing each other to pieces for the love of the Lord and hatred of each other. . . . But I will say no more on this endless theme; let me live, well if possible, and die without pain. The rest is with God. . . ." [n]

But Hodgson could not leave the matter there. With deep earnestness he set out to convert his friend from his heresies. Taking Byron's own motto, he pleaded: "Crede, Byron!" [n] Not trusting too much his own powers of reasoning, he called on Byron to read Butler's *Analogy* and Paley's *Evidences,* the books that were coming more and more to be relied upon by ecclesiastics to refute the unbelief that had grown out of the Enlightenment and the increasing trust in science and reason.

Byron, who felt he was being drawn into a futile argument, answered with a little more asperity. "I will neither read *pro* nor *con*. God would have made His will known without books, considering how very few could read them when Jesus of Nazareth lived, had it been His pleasure to ratify any peculiar mode of worship. As to your immortality, if people are to live, why die? And our carcases, which are to rise again, are they worth raising? I hope, if mine is, that I shall have a better *pair of legs* than I have moved on these two-and-twenty years, or I shall be sadly behind in the squeeze into Paradise." *n*

Hodgson was genuinely distressed. He wrote again with a pathetic zeal as if he already had visions of Byron roasting in hell: "Your last painful letter will recur to my thoughts—Let me make one other effort. . . . for God's sake—hear me, Byron. . . . examine the whole of Paley's Evidences—the two volumes may be read carefully in less than a week—Let me for the last time by our friendship implore you to read them." *n*

There Byron was willing to let the matter drop. Dallas, who was constantly making suggestions for alterations in *Childe Harold,* also interlarded his letters with arguments on religion. Byron conformed to a number of his suggestions, but added: "I have brought you and my friend Juvenal Hodgson [6] upon my back, on the score of revelation. You are fervent, but he is quite *glowing;* and if he take half the pains to save his own soul, which he volunteers to redeem mine, great will be his reward hereafter. I honour and thank you both, but am convinced by neither." *n*

Murray, who wrote copious flattery about *Childe Harold,* was also concerned about Byron's iconoclastic opinions, but for purely practical reasons. He wanted the poet to alter "some expressions concerning Spain and Portugal which . . . do not harmonise with the now prevalent feeling," and also "some

[6] Hodgson had published a translation of Juvenal. Byron wrote on September 9 that he had been reading it. "The Tenth Sat[ir]e has always been my favourite, as I suppose indeed of everybody's." (*LJ,* II, 32.)

religious sentiments which may deprive me of some customers amongst the Orthodox." [n]

Byron was straightforward in his reply: "With regard to the political and metaphysical parts, I am afraid I can alter nothing. . . . but if there are any alterations in the structure of the versification you would wish to be made, I will tag rhymes and turn stanzas as much as you please. As for the *'Orthodox,'* let us hope they will buy, on purpose to abuse—you will forgive the one, if they will do the other." [n]

When he learned that Murray had sought and received Gifford's opinion soon after Dallas delivered the poem to him, Byron was furious. The more he thought about it, the more heated he became. "I am not at all pleased with Murray for showing the MS.," he told Dallas. "It is anticipating, it is begging, kneeling, adulating,—the devil! the devil! the devil! and all without my wish, and contrary to my express desire." [n] Against Dallas's remonstrance that Murray was not to be blamed for letting Gifford see the manuscript, Byron retorted: "I *will* be angry with Murray. It was a bookselling, back-shop, Paternoster-row, paltry proceeding. . . ." [n] But such protests, while they relieved his mind of pent-up indignation, were, as he knew, too late to do any good. Gifford's favorable opinion had no doubt encouraged Murray to publish *Childe Harold.*

Dallas had seen, as had most of the others who read the manuscript, that Byron's wish not to identify himself with the Childe was impossible to realize. This added anxiety may subconsciously have influenced Byron in his revisions, though in the main these were merely verbal; he clung tenaciously to the shocking passages.

Byron now found himself in an embarrassing situation with regard to the publication of *Hints from Horace.* He had assured Cawthorn on September 4: "If I had a friend willing and able to correct the press, it should be out with my good will immediately." [n] But by the 23rd, Dallas had persuaded him to let *Childe Harold* come out first.

To Dallas's suggestion that he continue *Childe Harold,* Byron replied that to do that he must return to Greece and Asia. "I must have a warm sun, a blue sky; I cannot describe scenes so dear to me by a sea-coal fire."[7] He was willing to agree that Dallas and Murray and Gifford were all right as to the probable effects of the metaphysical parts of the poem, but, he wrote, "I also feel that I am sincere. . . . My work must make its way as well as it can; I know I have every thing against me, angry poets and prejudices; but if the poem is a *poem,* it will surmount these obstacles, and if *not,* it deserves its fate."[n]

September wore on, and still Hanson did not come. Byron spent his idle moments in devising notes for *Childe Harold.* The motto—"*L'univers est une espèce de livre, dont on n'a lu que la première page quand on n'a vue que son pays,*" etc.—he took from "a little French volume, a great favourite with me, which I picked up in the Archipelago."[8] For the rest, Dallas could sort out and "*cut up* into notes," "to be *cut up* afterwards,"[n] some of his letters written to his mother from abroad and the prose paragraphs he had composed in Athens. He was too lackadaisical to care greatly.

He was not quite alone, but might as well have been for all the stimulation he got from his visitor, John Claridge, who had been his schoolfellow at Harrow. To Hobhouse he gave a devastating account of Claridge. "Now he is a good man, a handsome man, an honourable man, a most inoffensive man, a well informed man, and a—*dull* man, and this last damned epithet undoes all the rest; there is Scrope B. Davies, with perhaps no better intellects, and certainly not half his sterling qualities, is the life and soul of me, and everybody else, but my old friend, with the soul of honour and the zeal of friendship, and a vast variety of insipid virtues, can't keep me or himself awake.—Alas, '*Motley's the only wear.*'"[n] Had he then come into such

[7] Byron said he had projected an additional canto while he was in the Troad and Constantinople, but could not now go on "under existing circumstances and *sensations.*" (*LJ*, II, 28.)

[8] *LJ*, II, 39–40. Letter of Sept. 16, 1811. The little volume was *Le Cosmopolite, ou, le Citoyen du Monde,* by Fougeret de Monbron (London, 1753). The conclusion of the motto is not quite that which Byron was then telling his friends he had derived from his own wanderings. Monbron says he has turned a sufficiently great number of pages (of the universe) and has found them equally bad. But the examination of them was not unfruitful. He had hated his country. But the impertinences of the diverse peoples among whom he had lived had reconciled him to it.

close association with other of his Harrow favorites (even Clare, whom he always idealized), would the verdict have been the same? Travel and a few years of experience of the world had changed his outlook markedly.

Hanson still had not arrived at the end of September. In the meantime, Byron told Hodgson, "I am plucking up my spirits, and have begun to gather my little sensual comforts together. Lucy is extracted from Warwickshire; [9] some very bad faces have been warned off the premises, and more promising substituted in their stead; the partridges are plentiful, hares fairish, pheasants are not quite so good. . . . I have just issued an edict for the abolition of caps; no hair to be cut on any pretext; stays permitted, but not too low before . . . Lucinda to be commander . . . of all the makers and unmakers of beds in the household." [n]

Mellowed by time and better spirits, and desirous of accommodating Dallas and Murray if possible without sacrificing too much, Byron had at last agreed to modify his harsh pronouncement on the Convention of Cintra and had offered to omit the stanza referring to the "unnatural" love practices of Beckford.[1]

He finally left for his Lancashire estate near the end of September and was back at Newstead on October 9. News had come in his absence of an event that shocked him more than anything he had yet felt: Ann Edleston had written that her brother John had died the previous May.[2] To Dallas he wrote: "I have been again shocked with a *death,* and have lost one very dear to me in happier times . . . an event which, five years ago,

[9] Lucy was the Newstead maid Byron had dismissed before he went abroad.

[1] *LJ,* II, 47–8. Letter of Sept. 26, 1811. Byron eventually cut out three stanzas of personal attack on the generals and altered three others to a broader criticism of the Convention of Cintra. (See Dallas: *Correspondence,* pp. 181–3; and *Poetry,* II, 38–40.) The stanza containing the innuendo on Beckford was suppressed and did not appear during Byron's life. It was first published with the title "To Dives. A Fragment" in the Murray edition of Byron's works in 1833 (XVII, 241).

[2] Ann Edleston's letter to Byron, dated Sept. 26, 1811, is now among the Murray MSS. He apparently did not see it until after his return from Lancashire. His first reference to Edleston's death is in his letter of Oct. 10, 1811, to Hodgson. "I heard of a death the other day that shocked me more than any of the preceding, of one whom I loved more than I ever loved a living thing, and one who, I believe, loved me to the last. . . ." (Quoted in H. B. Smith: *A Sentimental Library,* p. 46.)

would have bowed down my head to the earth. It seems as though I were to experience in my youth the greatest misery of age. My friends fall around me, and I shall be left a lonely tree before I am withered. . . . I am indeed very wretched, and you will excuse my saying so, as you know I am not apt to cant of sensibility." [n]

The only relief for such wretchedness was in poetic composition. He poured out his feelings in a poem to "Thyrza." [n] By using a woman's name, he was able to give full release to his sorrow for the loss of Edleston. He could speak freely of "the glance none saw beside":

*The whispered thought of hearts allied,*
*The pressure of the thrilling hand;*
*The kiss, so guiltless and refined,*
*That Love each warmer wish forbore;*
*Those eyes proclaimed so pure a mind,*
*Ev'n Passion blushed to plead for more.*
*The tone, that taught me to rejoice,*
*When prone, unlike thee, to repine;*
*The song, celestial from thy voice,*
*But sweet to me from none but thine;*
*The pledge we wore—I wear it still. . . .*[3]

[3] E. H. Coleridge included in his edition of Byron's poetry a note from an unnamed correspondent [Lord Lovelace]: "There can be no doubt that Lord Byron referred to Thyrza in conversation with Lady Byron, and probably also with Mrs. Leigh, as a young girl who had existed, and the date of whose death almost coincided with Lord Byron's landing in England in 1811. On one occasion he showed Lady Byron a beautiful tress of hair, which she understood to be Thyrza's. He said he had never mentioned her name, and that now she was gone his breast was the sole depository of that secret." (*Poetry,* III, 30–1). The lock of hair was probably the "pledge" mentioned in the poem. A correspondent to *Blackwood's Magazine* (Nov. 1824, p. 540) who signed himself "Harroviensis," probably a fellow Harrovian who knew Byron well, referred to a locket he wore in 1813 "containing a lock of fair soft hair, with a golden skull and cross-bones placed upon it. . . . The hair was of a fair girl, who died before his passion had departed, and whose name I could never prevail on him to mention." E. H. Coleridge wrote in the margin of his copy of Moore's life of Byron (now in the possession of James M. Osborn of New Haven, Conn.): "Lord Lovelace's rambling and meaningless Thyrza-note (see *Poetry,* III, 30) was designed to combat a theory of mine (and the Athenaeum's long ago)—obviously the true one—that Thyrza and Edleston were one and the same person. I main-

The same day (October 11) he wrote an anguished "Epistle to a Friend [Hodgson], In Answer to Some Lines Exhorting the Author to Be Cheerful, and to 'Banish Care,'"[4] but not even writing brought him ease. Two days later he wrote to Hodgson: "I am growing *nervous* (how you will laugh!)—but it is true,—really, wretchedly, ridiculously, fine-ladically *nervous*. Your climate kills me; I can neither read, write, nor amuse myself, or any one else. My days are listless, and my nights restless; I have very seldom any society, and when I have, I run out of it."[n]

The next day Byron sent off to Dallas a stanza to be added to *Childe Harold*, beginning:

*There, Thou!—whose Love and Life together fled,*
*Have left me here to love and live in vain—*[n]

As he had already told Dallas of the death of Edleston, he felt the necessity to cover his tracks: "I think it proper to state to you, that this stanza alludes to an event which has taken place since my arrival here, and not to the death of any *male* friend."[n]

With Hobhouse he could be more frank: "At present I am rather low, and don't know how to tell you the reason—you remember *E.* at Cambridge—he is *dead*—last May—his Sister sent me the account lately—now though I never should have seen him again (and it is very proper that I should not) I have been more affected than I should care to own elsewhere."[n]

But with Hobhouse he could also discuss other matters—the progress of their books, his own financial affairs, and his projected visit to Cambridge. His account of the potentials of his property was perhaps intended in part to suggest that his friend should not worry too much about the debt that Hobhouse senior had not yet paid. "I have been down to Rochdale with Hanson," he announced; "the property there, if I work the mines myself,

---

tained and maintain that Byron's feelings on this point were entirely to his credit, and that Lord Lovelace wilfully or stupidly misunderstood the whole incident. E.H.C."

[4] *Poetry,* III, 28–30. Hodgson, to whom Byron sent the poem, wrote in the margin opposite its bitter ending: "N. B. the poor dear Lord *meant* nothing of this. J. H." (The manuscript, with the last lines crossed out by Hodgson, is now in the Huntington Library.)

will produce about £4000 pr. ann.; but to do this I must lay out at least £10,000 in etceteras. . . .

"Newstead is to be advanced immediately to £2100 pr. ann., so that my income might be made about £6000 pr. ann. But here comes at least £20,000 of debt, and I must mortgage for that and other expenses, so that altogether my situation is perplexing." *n*

On the 16th, Byron wrote Dallas that he was "on the wing for Cambridge." *n* The long-promised visit to Davies, then a Fellow of King's College, was a pleasure, but also an ordeal, for all his old friends were gone but Davies himself (Hodgson was away when he arrived), and the familiar courts were filled with ghostly memories. He had not been on the banks of the Cam since he took his degree in 1808. His first shock was meeting for the first time Charles Matthews's younger brother Henry, "the image, to the very voice, of his brother Charles, only darker: his *laugh* his in particular. . . . I nearly dropped, thinking that it was his Ghost." *n*

The Cam where he and Long used to swim was now haunted too, and the choir brought back memories that were much too painful. "I am very low spirited on many accounts," he wrote Hobhouse. "The event I mentioned in my last [the death of Edleston] has had an effect on me, I am ashamed to think of. But there is no arguing on these points. I could 'have better spared a better being.'" *n*

Everywhere he turned on this familiar ground Byron was reminded of his daily walks and water excursions with Edleston.[5] A sense of desolation and irreparable loss weighed upon him, and he turned again to composition. With this final tribute to the dead chorister he would end *Childe Harold's Pilgrimage:*

*Thou too art gone, thou loved and lovely one!*
*Whom Youth and Youth's affections bound to me;*

[5] From Cambridge Byron wrote to Mrs. Pigot at Southwell, asking for the return of the "Cornelian" Edleston had given him, which he had assigned to Elizabeth for safekeeping. He told her that "the giver of that cornelian died in May last of a consumption, at the age of twenty-one. . . ." (*LJ*, I, 131n. Letter of Oct. 28, 1811.) Byron later told Hobhouse: "I was well enough treated at Cambridge, but glad to leave it, it made me *'leman-choly'* for many reasons and some d——d bad ones." (*LBC*, I, 54.)

*Who did for me what none beside have done,*
*Nor shrank from one albeit unworthy thee.*
*What is my Being! thou hast ceased to be!*
*Nor staid to welcome here thy wanderer home. . . .*

*Oh! ever loving, lovely, and beloved!*

*All thou couldst have of mine, stern Death! thou hast;*
*The Parent, Friend, and now the more than Friend. . . .*[6]

While he lingered in Cambridge waiting for Hodgson's return, Byron received a letter from Thomas Moore, the Irish poet, restating the contents of a letter Moore had sent on January 1, 1810, the epistle with the ridiculous seal which Hodgson had described but held back, sensing it to be a challenge, while Byron was abroad. Moore's Irish blood had risen at Byron's derisive reference in *English Bards and Scotch Reviewers* to his part in a farcical duel with Francis Jeffrey, editor of the *Edinburgh Review,* which he thought he had lived down.[7] Though aimed at Jeffrey, the gibe also put Moore in a ridiculous light:

[6] These were printed as stanzas 95 and 96 of the second canto. The poem actually ended with two others, probably sent at the same time but possibly composed shortly after the news of the event had stunned him. The next-to-the-last stanza, beginning "Then I must plunge again into the crowd," closely parallels the "Banish Care" lines to Hodgson. And the thought in the last stanza is almost a poetic paraphrase of his lament in his letter of October 11 to Dallas: He is left to suffer in youth the greatest ill of age, to see his friends fall around him.

[7] Moore had already made his reputation as a writer of amorous and musical verse under the pen name Thomas Little when the *Edinburgh Review* in July 1806 made some remarks about his *Odes, Epistles, and Other Poems* which roused him to challenge Jeffrey. At the rendezvous, while the seconds were loading the pistols, Jeffrey and Moore walked up and down, trying to preserve the dignity of the occasion and to conceal the fact that they had each taken a liking to the other. Coming in sight of the awkward operations behind the trees, Moore could not refrain from telling his antagonist a story of an Irish barrister who in a similar situation had called out: ". . . sure, isn't it bad enough to take the dose, without being by at the mixing up?" (Moore: *Memoirs,* I, 90.) Jeffrey scarcely had time to smile before they were handed the pistols, but before they could fire, some police officers, warned by some of Moore's friends, intervened and took them to Bow Street. Although the seconds swore that both pistols had been loaded, the story got out that Jeffrey's had no bullet in it. But Moore soon formed a close friendship with Jeffrey and wrote a public statement denying the implication that anything unfair was intended.

*Can none remember that eventful day,*
*That ever glorious, almost fatal fray,*
*When Little's leadless pistol met his eye,*
*And Bow-street Myrmidons stood laughing by?*[8]

But it was only after Byron's name appeared on the title page of the second edition of *English Bards and Scotch Reviewers* after his departure from England that Moore conceived that he owed it to himself to call for an "explanation" of the insult. What concerned him was the lie given to his public statement on the affair. Now that Byron was back in England, Moore felt that honor demanded his writing a second letter; but its tone was much milder, for he had been married in the meantime, and it was evident that he would rather have an explanation than an encounter. He intimated that if a satisfactory explanation were forthcoming, he would be glad of the honor of being ranked among Byron's acquaintances.[n]

It was hardly a letter to stir the blood, and perhaps Byron was a little disappointed that it was not more martial. He had expected something more ferocious from the irate authors whom he had imagined seeking satisfaction on his return. But he had not himself been precipitous in claiming Moore's first letter, which he had not yet seen when he received the second.

Byron replied with caution and reserve: "Your former letter I never had the honour to receive;—be assured in whatever part of the world it had found me, I should have deemed it my duty to return and answer it in person.

"The advertisement you mention, I know nothing of. . . . With regard to the passage in question, *you* were certainly *not* the person towards whom I felt personally hostile. On the contrary, my whole thoughts were engrossed by one, whom I had reason to consider as my worst literary enemy. . . . I can neither retract nor apologise for a charge of falsehood which I never advanced."[n]

[8] *English Bards and Scotch Reviewers,* 2nd ed., lines 458–61. Either because he heard it that way in the current gossip or because he deliberately changed the story to suit his purpose of making Jeffrey lacking in courage, Byron stated that Moore's pistol was leadless. Though this was less insulting to Moore, it still belied the statement in his newspaper account that both were loaded.

Eager as he was to accept Byron's explanation, Moore felt that he must ask for further particulars concerning the miscarriage of his first letter. And he added regretfully: "As your lordship does not show any wish to proceed beyond the rigid formulary of explanation, it is not for me to make any further advances." [n]

Byron left for London on October 28, and the next day he wrote from 8 St. James's Street, suggesting that the first letter, still in Hodgson's keeping, be opened in Moore's presence, "for the satisfaction of all parties." [9] With regard to the other matter, "Was I to anticipate friendship from one, who conceived me to have charged him with falsehood?" [n]

Piqued by such a sparring rebuff to his overtures of friendship, Moore apologized for wandering from the point under discussion and stated that their correspondence might now cease, for he was satisfied with Byron's explanation. [n]

Byron, feeling that he had gained his point, relented and opened his mind more freely. "I felt, and still feel, very much flattered by those parts of your correspondence, which held out the prospect of our becoming acquainted. . . . You have *now* declared yourself *satisfied*, and on that point we are no longer at issue. If, therefore, you still retain any wish to do me the honour you hinted at, I shall be most happy to meet you, when, where, and how you please. . . ." [n] Moore hastened to Holland House, where his bosom friend Samuel Rogers, the banker-poet, was then visiting, to tell him about the correspondence, and Rogers suggested that the meeting take place at his house.[1]

Immediately on arriving in town, Byron called Dallas into consultation concerning his publications. *Childe Harold* was already on the press, and some proofs had been taken, but Byron was constantly adding and changing. Murray had insisted on

[9] Byron did not mention the fact that he knew of the letter while he was abroad; nor that he was in and about London for nearly three weeks before he was called to Newstead. As late as November 17, 1811, Byron was still urging Hodgson to send the letter so that he could turn it over to Moore unopened. (*LJ*, II, 70.)

[1] Moore, I, 312–13. Byron was careful to act according to strict protocol throughout, all messages being sent through Scrope Davies, who would have acted as second in case of a duel.

having a quarto, which Byron thought "a cursed unsaleable size." [n] On October 31 he sent Dallas some more stanzas (probably the lines "To Thyrza") "on a subject which has lately occupied much of my thoughts. They refer to the death of one to whose name you are a *stranger*, and, consequently, cannot be interested. I mean them to complete the present volume. They relate to the same person whom I have mentioned in Canto 2nd, and at the conclusion of the poem." [2]

In London again, Byron felt the eyes of the critics upon him, and, on the verge of making the acquaintance of Moore, Rogers, and others of a higher literary society than any in which he had previously moved, he again had qualms concerning his self-revelations in *Childe Harold.* He warned Dallas: "I by no means intend to identify myself with *Harold,* but to *deny* all connection with him. . . . I would not be such a fellow as I have made my hero for all the world." [n]

When Byron wrote to Hobhouse on November 2, he was full of eagerness for his coming meeting with "Anacreon Moore" and "Pleasures of Memory" Rogers.[n] The next day Byron had some more news of "Bold Webster." "His wife is very pretty, and I am much mistaken if five years hence she don't give him reason to think so. Knowing the man one is apt to fancy these things, but I really thought she treated him, even already, with a due portion of conjugal contempt, but I daresay this was only the megrim of a misogynist.

"At present he is the happiest of men, and has asked me to go with them to a tragedy to see his *wife cry!*"

The more he thought of his present companions, the more Byron longed for Hobhouse's company. He found his earlier school friends insipid, though a kind of loyalty to the memories of the past held him to them. As for Claridge's "attachment," "will attachment keep one awake? or say pleasant things? . . . When I was a child I thought as a child . . . but now give me a man of calibre, a little sense, a sprinkling of information. . . ." [n]

[2] *LJ,* II, 66. This statement seems definitely to connect the Thyrza poems, three of which were printed at the end of the quarto volume of *Childe Harold,* with stanzas 9, 95, and 96 of the second canto, whose content and circumstances of composition make it plain that they were addressed to Edleston.

Though he had acceded to Dallas's request that the publication of the *Hints from Horace* be held back until *Childe Harold* appeared, he had not given up the intention of publishing, and now was contemplating a fifth edition of *English Bards* to which the *Hints* would be added.[3] Dallas was in and out frequently with proofs of *Childe Harold,* and was delighted with the poem.

Byron had been elected a member of the Alfred Club while he was in Greece, and, though he spoke of it condescendingly, he found it agreeable enough. It was a new club, founded in 1808 at 23 Albemarle Street, not far from his rooms at 8 St. James's Street. In after years he remembered it as pleasant, "a little too sober and literary," but "upon the whole a decent resource on a rainy day, in a dearth of parties, or parliament, or an empty season."[4]

The eagerly awaited dinner at the home of Rogers took place on November 4. Rogers had planned to have only Moore and himself there to meet Byron, but Thomas Campbell, having called in the morning, was invited to join the party. Byron must have felt more excitement than he would let himself show when he entered the door, for Rogers, twenty-five years his senior, he had long viewed with awed respect as the most admirable of the poets who had carried on the tradition of Pope.[5] Campbell and Moore retired from the drawing-room by prearrangement and Rogers met Byron alone. Then after a few moments the others returned and were introduced. They were all impressed with the appearance and flattered by the deference of the young lord, who looked with more genuine admiration upon these idols of his earliest literary dreams than he would have upon men of

[3] Though peace had been made with Moore, Byron apparently did not intend to omit the offending lines, for he left the original note, with the exception of one phrase, and added a manuscript note in a copy of the fourth edition, in which he was making corrections for the new edition. (*Poetry,* I, 334 n.)

[4] *LJ,* V, 424 ("Detached Thoughts"). Byron was nevertheless flattered by his election to the Alfred. He told Hodgson there were 354 candidates for six vacancies. (*LJ,* II, 86–7. Letter of Dec. 8, 1811.)

[5] In a footnote to *English Bards and Scotch Reviewers* Byron called "The Pleasures of Memory" and "The Pleasures of Hope" "the most beautiful didactic poems in our language, if we except Pope's *Essay on Man.*" (*Poetry,* I, 361.) Moore was thirty-two when he met Byron and Campbell was thirty-four, while Byron was in his twenty-fourth year.

much greater worldly power and prestige. Dressed in mourning black, which emphasized the paleness of his features, he did not disappoint their expectations.

When they sat down to dinner, the host was embarrassed by the fact that there seemed to be nothing his guest could eat. Rogers asked Byron if he would take soup. "'No; he never took soup.'—Would he take some fish? 'No; he never took fish.'—Presently I asked if he would eat some mutton? 'No; he never ate mutton.'—I then asked if he would take a glass of wine? 'No; he never tasted wine.'—It was now necessary to enquire what he *did* eat and drink; and the answer was, 'Nothing but hard biscuits and soda-water.' Unfortunately, neither hard biscuits nor soda-water were at hand; and he dined upon potatoes bruised down on his plate and drenched with vinegar."[6]

Nothing was said about the subject of the late correspondence between Byron and Moore. The discussion turned upon literary topics, among the subjects being the merits of Walter Scott and Joanna Baillie. Byron became animated and charmed his new acquaintances. The guests as well as the host paid him marked attention, and they talked until a very late hour. Moore wrote: "From the time of our first meeting there seldom elapsed a day that Lord Byron and I did not see each other, and our acquaintance ripened into intimacy and friendship with a rapidity of which I have seldom seen an example."[n]

Only a few days after the first meeting Byron wrote enthusiastically to Hobhouse, still with his regiment in Ireland: "I have lately been leading a most *poetical* life with Messrs Rogers, Moore, and Campbell. . . ."[n] Byron was entering upon a new life, and he took to it with immense zest. He delighted in his new acquaintances because they were not mere inkhorn or Grub Street writers; for the first time he was associating on an equal footing with those he considered the "first" literary men of the land.

[6] Rogers: *Table-Talk*, p. 231. Rogers recalled (pp. 231–2): "Some days after, meeting Hobhouse, I said to him, 'How long will Lord Byron persevere in his present diet?' He replied, 'Just as long as you continue to notice it.'—I did not then know, what I now know to be a fact,—that Byron, after leaving my house, had gone to a Club in St. James's Street and eaten a hearty meat-supper."

Moore and Rogers did not, however, take the same interest in Byron's boon companions. Moore, who was something of a toady to rank, having himself risen from the humblest origins (his father was a Dublin grocer—a trade the most risible among snobs) to a position of ease in the best drawing-rooms in London, thought that Byron's earlier friends were much beneath him. Moore recorded that ". . . at the time when we first met his position in the world was most solitary. Even those coffee-house companions who, before his departure from England, had served him as a sort of substitute for more worthy society, were either relinquished or had disappeared, and with the exception of three or four associates of his college days (to whom he appeared very strongly attached), Mr. Dallas and his solicitor seemed to be the only persons whom even in their very questionable degree he could boast of as friends." [n] Opposite Moore's statement that Byron had a "total want of friends and connexions" during his early years, Hobhouse wrote sarcastically in his copy of Moore's life of Byron: "In fact he had no friends until he knew Mr. Tom Moore."

But there was indeed some justification for Moore's misgivings about Byron's circle in his first contacts with them. The more dependable Hobhouse was in Ireland, and Byron's most frequent visitors, aside from the clownish Webster, were the sycophantic Dallas, full of piety and literary pretensions, the alcoholic Davies, with his coffeehouse tastes and a wit that did not in Moore's eyes compensate for his reckless flouting of the social graces, and a variety of literary clergymen, of whom Hodgson and his friend Robert Bland were fair, but at the moment not very admirable, examples.

The dinner Byron had arranged for Rogers, Moore, and Hodgson was embarrassing, for Hodgson was "drunk and Sensibilitous" for reasons that Byron explained succinctly to Hobhouse: "Bland (the *Revd.*) has been challenging an officer of Dragoons about a *whore,* & my assistance being required, I interfered in time to prevent him from losing his *life* or his *Living.* The man is mad, Sir, mad, frightful as a mandrake, and lean as a rutting Stag, & all about a bitch not worth a Bank-token. She is a common Strumpet, as his antagonist assured me, yet he means to marry her. Hodgson meant to marry her, the officer meant to marry her, her first Seducer (seventeen years ago) meant to marry her, and all this is owing to the *Comet!*

"During Bland's absence [Bland had been abroad for two years, and had returned about the first of November], H[odgso]n was his Dragon, and left his own Oyster wench to offer her his hand, which she *refused.* Bland comes home in Hysterics, finds her in keeping, (not by H[odgso]n. however), & loses his wits. Hodgson gets drunk and cries, and he and Bland (who have been berhyming each other as you know these six past Olympiads), are now the antipodes of each other.

"I saw this *wonder,* and set her down at seven shillings worth." [n]

Bland had asked Byron, as his second, to carry a challenge to the officer of the Life-guards who had stolen the wench from both him and Hodgson, but Byron used his greatest stock of diplomacy and tact to prevent scandal and bloodshed. On top of this, Byron had to be confessor to the blubbering, conscience-stricken Hodgson, who wrote to explain how he had come to offend against his own sense of honor in making love to the girl whom Bland had put in his care during his absence.[n] In spite of Hodgson's imbecilities, Byron stuck by him.

In the meantime Byron was improving his new acquaintance. "I dine to-day with Ward to meet the Lord knows whom," he wrote to Hobhouse on November 16. "Moore and I are on the best of terms. . . . Rogers is a most excellent and unassuming soul, and Moore an epitomé of all that's delightful." [n] Campbell too he had found agreeable because of his praise of *Childe Harold,* which Byron had let him read in proof.[n] He also showed the printed sheets to Rogers, whose prediction was, though no doubt he kept it to himself, that it would never please the public.[7] And while *Childe Harold* was "coming costively into the world," Byron was encouraging Cawthorn to go ahead with

[7] Rogers: *Table-Talk,* p. 232. It is curious that Byron should have shown *Childe Harold* rather than *Hints from Horace* to Rogers and Campbell, for they both were upholders of the Popean tradition; perhaps he wanted praise for the poem that touched him more closely. Moore had been more tactful, though no less discouraging; he told Byron *Childe Harold* would not succeed because "it was too good for the age." (Moore: *Prose and Verse,* p. 428.)

the *English Bards* and the *Hints from Horace*, to which he had now decided to add the "Curse of Minerva" to make "a monstrous vol. of crown octavo." [n]

The town was empty, but, though he was eager to get back to Newstead, he was staying on to try to get something done about the annuities. Mrs. Massingberd, who had had her income seized, couldn't pay her rent, and Byron felt responsible.[8] "I am living as quietly as you can be," he told Hobhouse, "and have long left off wine entirely, and never enter a coffee-house of any description. My meal is generally at ye Alfred where I munch my vegetables in peace." [n] He added a few cynical remarks on Webster, who had taken his wife to the country: "Wr. will be a noble subject for Cuckoldom in three years, though he has managed to impregnate her Ladyship, which consequently can be no very difficult task.—She is certainly very pretty, & if not a dunce, must despise her 'Bud' heartily. She is not exactly to my taste, but I dare say Dragoons would like her." Byron expressed a wish that Hobhouse would come over from Ireland and go down to Notts. with him, and indicated one of the reasons for his own desire to get back to the country. "My establishment at Newstead improves. I have Lucy, Susan, a very pretty Welch girl, & a third of the Notts breed, whom you never saw, all under age, and very ornamental. But my diet is so low that I can carry on nothing carnal." [n]

Toward the end of November, Byron yielded to the entreaties of Hodgson and visited Cambridge again. There he renewed his acquaintance with another of his old Harrow favorites, William Harness. He invited Hodgson and Harness to spend Christmas with him at Newstead. Back in London through the early part of December, he carried on a friendly, slightly defiant corre-

[8] After receiving several distressing letters from Mrs. Massingberd, Byron wrote to Hanson on December 15: "I must take the annuities on myself, & request you will arrange with the Jews on ye subject. There is nothing else left for it. I cannot allow people to go to Gaol on my account, it is better they should tear my property to pieces, than make me a scoundrel. . . . do something for the poor old Soul immediately." (Eg. 2611, ff. 276–7.) Mrs. Massingberd, who was well acquainted with moneylenders, wrote Hanson on December 5, 1811, that Messrs. Blake and Scavel of Norwich could advance Byron £20,000 if the security was good. (Eg. 2613, f. 157.) Hanson had advertised for a loan of that sum. But nothing came of these negotiations.

spondence with both, a little irked by the lip service to piety of the one and the naïve moral seriousness and sentimental attachment of the other, who was still the schoolboy.[9] To Hodgson, who, still hoping to convert Byron to orthodoxy, had recommended that he read Richard Watson's *An Apology for Christianity, in a Series of Letters to Edward Gibbon,* he wrote: "I have read Watson to Gibbon. He proves nothing, so I am where I was, verging towards Spinoza; and yet it is a gloomy Creed, and I want a better, but there is something Pagan in me that I cannot shake off. In short, I deny nothing, but doubt everything."[n]

A few days later he wrote despondently: "To-day is the Sabbath,—a day I never pass pleasantly, but at Cambridge; and, even there, the organ is a sad remembrancer." He heard a song of former days which reminded him of Edleston, whereupon he wrote another poem to Thyrza, "Away, Away, Ye Notes of Woe." But it was something that now he was striving to forget. "I wish parliament were assembled, that I may hear, and perhaps some day be heard;—but on this point I am not very sanguine. I have many plans;—sometimes I think of the East again, and dearly beloved Greece. I am well, but weakly. Yesterday Kinnaird[1] told me I looked very ill, and sent me home happy."[n]

Byron delighted in letting his friends know that he was getting into the most admired literary circles of the capital. He wrote Hodgson: "Coleridge has attacked the *Pleasures of Hope* [by Thomas Campbell], and all other pleasures whatsoever. Mr. Rogers was present, and heard himself indirectly *rowed* by the

[9] Byron wrote facetiously to Harness on Dec. 8, 1811: "You will want to know what I am doing—chewing Tobacco.—You see nothing of my allies Scrope Davies and Matthews, they don't suit you, & how does it happen that I (who am a pipkin of the same pottery) continue in your good graces?" (Pratt, p. 97.)

[1] Douglas Kinnaird, fifth son of the seventh Baron Kinnaird, was a close friend of Hobhouse at Trinity College. Byron began to see him occasionally after his return from the East and later was closely associated with him as a fellow member of the committee for managing Drury Lane Theatre. When Byron went abroad the second time, Kinnaird, a partner of the banking firm of Ransom and Morland, became his banker and business adviser as well as confidant. Some of Byron's most interesting letters from abroad are written to Kinnaird.

lecturer. We are going to a party to hear the new Art of Poetry by this reformed schismatic. . . ."[2] Byron was referring to Coleridge's series of lectures on Shakespeare. On the 15th he wrote Harness: "Tomorrow I dine with Rogers & am to hear Coleridge, who is a kind of rage at present."[3]

Despite the fact that so many of his friends were out of town, Byron was enjoying a full life in London. He had acquired a taste for the theater as early as his Harrow holidays, and now returned to it with zest. On the 9th he saw a farcical performance of Rowes's *Fair Penitent* at the Haymarket with Robert Coates as Lothario. The play was closed in the third act when hysterical laughter greeted the death of the hero.[n] Byron also saw Mrs. Siddons, and on the 14th heard Kemble in Coriolanus —"he was glorious & exerted himself wonderfully."[n]

But as usual Byron's moods rose and fell. At the moment when a song roused his memories of Edleston he was "greeted with an epistle of Hodgson's full of his petty grievances." Writing to explain to Harness why he had been brusque in a previous letter, Byron said: ". . . I was bearing up against recollections, to which *his* imaginary sufferings are as a Scratch to a Cancer." In that humor he became savage in his judgment of his clerical friends. "Bland is ill of a gonorrhea, a clerical & creditable distemper, particularly to a despairing Corydon.—Hodgson I should conjecture to have a Syphilis at least, if I may judge by his querulous letter.—So much for these Sentimentalites, who console themselves in the stews for the loss, the never to be recovered loss, the despair of the refined attachment of a brace of Drabs!"[n]

On the 19th he left for Newstead, taking Hodgson and Harness with him.[n] He had hoped that Moore would come too, but family obligations prevented Moore's leaving at Christmastime.

[2] *LJ*, II, 83. Letter of Dec. 8, 1811. In his letter to Harness, Byron had referred to Coleridge as "this Manichean of Poesy." (Pratt, p. 96.)

[3] Pratt, p. 98. On the following January 20 (1812) Crabb Robinson wrote: "Evening Coleridge's lecture, conclusion of Milton. Not one of his happiest lectures. Among the audience Lord Byron and Rogers the banker. . . ." (Robinson, I, 60.) According to Robinson, "Rogers related that he brought Lord Byron and Wordsworth together to a *tête-à-tête* dinner. Wordsworth tried to talk his best and talked too much—he did not appear to advantage." (Robinson, I, 436.)

The weavers were rioting in Nottingham, "breaking of frames and heads, and out-manœuvring the military."[n] Hodgson was frightened at the prospect of violence; Byron was unperturbed. Joe Murray, who held the fort at Newstead, had grown superstitious in his old age and had been frightened by dreams and ghosts. Byron would have welcomed a ghost or two.

Harness found the Abbey a fit scene for Gothic tales. When they arrived, "It was winter—dark, dreary weather—the snow upon the ground; and a straggling, gloomy, depressive, partially-inhabited place the Abbey was." Having heard tales of the orgies there before Byron went abroad, Harness was perhaps a little disappointed to have to report that "nothing could be more quiet and regular than the course of our days." Byron was not in the humor for rioting, especially with his present company. He was retouching *Childe Harold;* Hodgson was editing the copy for the *Monthly Review;* and Harness was reading for his degree. When they came together at night, they had warm arguments on poetry and religion. The young Harness listened with admiration while the more learned Hodgson with "judicious zeal and affectionate earnestness (often speaking with tears in his eyes)" tried to convert Byron to orthodoxy.[n]

Byron found consolation for these dull evenings in other parts of the Abbey. In the servants' quarters were the three pretty girls he had brought into his household in September. His favorite now was Susan Vaughan, a native of Wales, of whom, he wrote Hobhouse, "I am tolerably enamoured for the present."[n]

When, called by business and the opening of Parliament, Byron left for London on January 11 of the new year, Susan put up a very good show of being inconsolable, and there is little doubt that she was sincere enough in her first lamentations at losing her "dearest friend." Byron sent her a letter from the Newstead Hut (the caretaker's house), another from Nottingham, together with a locket in which to keep his hair, one from Newport Pagnell on the way, and another as soon as he reached London. She was constantly in his thoughts, and he now confessed to Hobhouse that he was "foolishly fond" of her.[n] Her letters show that she had little education or wit, but considerable vivacity and a willingness to please.

The day after he left she wrote: "Yes, working your bosoms [shirt fronts?] I should think will give me a great deal of pleasure. Anything that's yours I *love* and always shall. Can you doubt it, my dearest friend? I have hitherto given you every proof of my affection." [n] Her next letter, written on the 15th, was even more ardent in its protestations: "My dearest friend, you say you believe I love you, that you have tried everything to win my heart. Shall I tell you my heart was yours entirely long—long before you gave me any proof of your *Love?*" [n]

Lucy and Robert Rushton, both jealous of the partiality Byron had shown to Susan, were not slow in spreading tales about her. When Susan wrote on the 18th, she was disturbed by the fear that Byron was angry with her,[n] and in her next letter she reminded him of his past privileges and pleasures in a way that may not have been altogether to his liking, for it showed how little of a secret their affair was likely to be. Susan had apparently been acting as nursemaid to the valet Fletcher's young sons. She wrote: "You, of course, have not forgot the night you come up to our room, when I was in bed—the time you locked the door. You woked the boys and ask'd George if he knew you; and he told you he did, which he did indeed, so well that he as not let it slip his memory yet. He is up stairs with me now, and I have been asking him how he come to tell such storys . . . He looks very earnestly at me, and says he: Why, Susan, have you forgot Lord Byron coming to *bed to us?* . . . Don't you remember, Susan, me Lord putting his hand so nicely over your *bosom?* . . . The D——l may have George Fletcher, if he did not *kiss* you besides, and Bessy too. I could not help laughing at him, and told him it was storys." But the precocious George was not the only one gossiping. Susan added: "I believe I mentioned, in another letter, how remarkable kind *Lucy* and *Robert* are. They cant talk enough about you and me, but they are under the necessity of going into—*R's Bedroom,* so that they may not bee disturb'd in their conversation." [n]

In the meantime Robert was not slow to retaliate with some hints at Susan's misconduct. These aroused Byron's suspicions, and he determined to get at the truth. "I am sure *you* would not deceive me," he wrote to Rushton, "though *she* would. Whatever it is, *you* shall be forgiven. I have not been without some suspicions on the subject. . . ."[n]

Rushton's story was sufficient (perhaps it was confirmed by others) to convince him that Susan, despite all her protestations of eternal devotion, was unfaithful to him. It was a new experience for Byron to be deceived by a kitchen wench upon whom he had lavished so much affection. He confessed to Moore: "I am in a state of ludicrous tribulation. . . .[4] at *this moment,* praise, even *your* praise, passes by me like 'the idle wind.' . . . now I can think of nothing but damned, deceitful,—delightful woman, as Mr. Liston says in the *Knight of Snowdon.*"[n]

On Susan's first letter, in which she had written: "Pray don't forget me, as I shall never cease thinking of you, my Dearest *and only Friend,*" Byron wrote: "This was written on the 11th of January, 1812; on the 28th I received ample proof that the Girl had forgotten *me* and *herself* too."[n] As in other moments of depression, he blamed his deformity for his misfortune. "I do not blame her," he told Hodgson, "but my own vanity in fancying that such a thing as I am could ever be beloved."[n]

To Hobhouse he confessed: "I have dismissed my Seraglio for squabbles and infidelities."[n] The thought of Newstead was now distasteful. He was preparing to sell all his furniture. "The women are gone to their relatives, after many attempts to explain what was already too clear," he told Hodgson. Referring to a severe kidney ailment from which he had just recovered, he added: "If the stone had got into my heart instead of my kidneys, it would have been all the better."

In the shock of his disillusionment he turned once more to thoughts to Edleston. "I believe the only human being, that ever loved me in truth and entirely, was of, or belonging to, Cambridge, and, in that, no change can now take place. . . . I almost rejoice when one I love dies young, for I could never bear to see them old or altered."[n]

And again he set his thoughts into verse:

*The love where Death has set his seal,*
*Nor age can chill, nor rival steal . . .*

[4] Byron apparently told the whole story to Moore, who, however, deleted it when he published the letter, which has since disappeared.

*And, what were worse, thou canst not see*
*Or wrong, or change, or fault in me.*[5]

On January 15, soon after he got back from Newstead, Byron took his seat in the House of Lords again. Parliament was convening for the first time since his return from abroad. In 1809 he had been content to listen and observe,[6] but now, having been at foreign courts, and having taken lessons in comparative government at first hand, he felt that he had sufficient experience of men and policies to raise his voice. Ever since Dr. Drury had praised his performance on Harrow Speech Days, Byron had nursed the dream of making a name for himself as a political orator and statesman. He had delayed his return to Harrow after one of his holidays to listen to the Parliamentary de-

[5] "And Thou Art Dead, As Young and Fair," *Poetry*, III, 42. The manuscript is dated February 1812; the poem was first published in the second edition of *Childe Harold*. In addition to the three stanzas (9, 95, and 96) of the second canto of *Childe Harold* and the three poems naming Thyrza printed at the end of the first edition of that poem ("To Thyrza," "Away, Away, Ye Notes of Woe," and "One Struggle More, and I Am Free"), Byron wrote at least five others inspired by the shock of Edleston's death or later reflections upon that event ("Epistle to a Friend" [the "Banish Care" lines], "Euthanasia," "And Thou Art Dead, As Young and Fair," "If Sometimes in the Haunts of Men," and "On a Cornelian Heart Which Was Broken"). And to this group should be added the last two stanzas (97 and 98) of the second canto of *Childe Harold*. It is possible too that the poem beginning "There be none of Beauty's daughters/ With a magic like thee," commonly believed to have been addressed to Claire Clairmont because it was first published in 1816 not long after Byron met her, was really written to Edleston, perhaps while he was still alive. The lines exactly coincide with Byron's known sentiments; he admitted that he was first captivated by the young chorister's voice:

*And like music on the waters*
*Is thy sweet voice to me. . . .*
*So the spirit bows before thee,*
*To listen and adore thee;*
*With a full but soft emotion,*
*Like the swell of Summer's ocean.*

[6] Contrary to common supposition, based on Dallas's account of Byron's conversation on the day he first took his seat in the House of Lords ("I have taken my seat, and now I will go abroad"—Dallas: *Recollections*, p. 36), Byron attended the sessions seven times in March, April, and May 1809—namely, March 13, 14, 15, 21; April 28; May 10, 15. (Erdman: "Lord Byron as Rinaldo," p. 192.)

bates on the Catholic question. That ambition followed him to Cambridge and was as strong as the persuasion of friends in drawing him into the Cambridge Whig Club and into friendship with Hobhouse. To prepare himself for such a career had been one of his motives for his journey to the East. And contemplation of this aim gave him the most satisfying self-justification for his long residence abroad. This constantly held goal, though only occasionally acknowledged, accounted in large measure for his considering literature a secondary pursuit.

But, while he was confident enough of his own powers of expression, and was possessed of certain basic Whig principles as well as some notions of the fundamental rights of peoples, he had considerable diffidence and misgiving concerning practical political procedure. He was less impressed by the flattering praise and sycophantic hero-worship of Dallas and Hodgson than by his own awareness of his ignorance of particular issues.[7]

In the six times he went down to the House in January he was a listener only and did not speak. As late as the 1st of February, when he wrote Hodgson, he had not determined upon a subject for his maiden speech: "The Catholic Question comes on this month, and perhaps I may then commence. I must 'screw my courage to the sticking-place,' and we'll *not* fail."[8] Though encouraged by the mediocre performances he had witnessed, Byron still looked upon the speech as an ordeal and as worthy of his best efforts.

If the ambitious young lord, eager to enter upon a statesman's duties, could find nothing to try his oratory and wit upon in the interests of good government and the common weal, he was not altogether to blame, for no really great issues were before the House at this session. The mad king, George III, had finally been relieved of his post; the Prince of Wales had been installed as Prince Regent a few months before. On the first day of Byron's attendance he was forced to listen to monotonous and

[7] Hobhouse wrote in the margin of his copy of Moore (I, 126) that Byron "was totally ignorant of the points in dispute in that [Hobhouse's attack on the Whigs] or any other question of politics."

[8] *LJ*, II, 96. Letter of Feb. 1, 1812. Byron had long considered the Catholic-disabilities question as a most important one, and he had followed the debates on it from his Harrow days.

ridiculously solemn evidence on the state of the King's health. Impatient for a job worthy of his mettle, he was appointed on January 20 to a committee to hear some dozens of cases of appeals on writs of error. Divorce evidence read off at interminable length was sometimes amusing, but more often dull.[n]

Three days after his letter to Hodgson, however, Byron had determined upon a subject and was preparing his speech with some enthusiasm. Having decided to speak in favor of measures to alleviate the distress of the stocking-weavers of Nottingham rather than merely repress their rioting, Byron sought the advice of Lord Holland, who, as Recorder of Nottingham, might be expected to have special knowledge of the subject as well as interest in the area. The discontent was growing worse since troops had been sent in to suppress the breaking of frames by the desperate weavers in protest against the introduction of a wide frame that had put more of them out of work.[9]

Lord Holland was willing enough to encourage a potential Opposition member of the upper house, but he wanted to proceed cautiously. The first step should be a question put to the ministers. If their answer was negative or unsatisfactory, Byron then proposed, if Lord Holland approved, to give notice of a motion for a Committee of Inquiry. When he started gathering facts for his speech, Byron did not know—and it was kept a close secret until it was sprung suddenly on the Commons on February 14—that the Cabinet had already concocted a bill offering as sole remedy for the situation an increase in the severity of punishments for frame-breaking. The Tories under the leadership of Lord Eldon, the Lord Chancellor who had sworn Byron in when he took his seat in 1809, were still solidly in

[9] In November 1811, bands of unemployed weavers began breaking into houses and destroying machinery. On the 14th soldiers were first called out to quell the riots. By the 9th of December, 900 cavalry and 1,000 infantry had been sent to Nottingham. But neither they nor the two additional regiments sent on January 8, 1812, succeeded in stopping the violence. (*LJ*, II, 97 n.) In December Major Cartwright had found "men almost in a state of famine." (Cartwright, *Life*, II, 17–21.) The Luddites continued their frame-breaking. (Their leader was known as General Lud, named supposedly from a half-witted boy, Ned Lud, who in 1779 in a fit of passion broke a stocking-frame.)

power, and conciliatory measures were furthest from their thoughts.

Byron's attendance at the sessions of the House only six times in February [n] did not necessarily indicate any slackening of interest in his "senatorial duties," though it may have shown that he had learned to take its routine dullness more lightly. For the first half of the month he was suffering acutely from a cold and from what he believed to be a stone in the kidney. Haunted by thoughts of the unfaithful Susan Vaughan, "in great bodily pain," and harassed by financial worries that were constantly growing more acute,[1] it is not surprising that he abstained from going to the House except when something important was happening.[2]

In the last weeks of February, Byron was reading the final proofs of *Childe Harold* with increasing trepidation. He had told Hobhouse in December that he was alarmed as the moment of publication approached, but now he was even more so, for in imagination he tried to picture what the appearance of such unconventional sentiments and personal revelations would do to his Parliamentary career. With Hobhouse, who had arrived in London on February 21,[3] he called in Fleet Street to see

[1] Byron wrote Hobhouse on February 10, 1812: "I have been most painfully ill, cupped on the loin, glystered, purged and vomited secundum artem, and am condemned to the strictest regimen, and the most durable of disorders for the residue of my life." Possibly at the urging of Hanson, he embarrassedly asked Hobhouse for a note of hand for the amount due him. "In case of any accident befalling yourself or me, you are aware that I possess no *document, note* or *memorial* of the money transactions between us beyond the mention of the sum in one or two of your letters. . . ." He announced further that he was preparing to sell the furniture at Newstead and that he had "almost arranged the annuity business with Scrope Davies, who has behaved very well indeed, much better than he has been treated, though that was not my fault." (*B-SP*, I, 132.) In a letter to his son while the latter was in Ireland (B.M. Add. 36456, ff. 44–5) Benjamin Hobhouse had agreed to pay the debt to Byron of £1,323 by bills payable in six months. But it was March 17, 1812, before Hobhouse drew a draft on his father for the sum due to Byron. (Hobhouse diary.)

[2] On February 10 he wrote Hobhouse that he had been voting for the Catholics. (*B-SP*, I, 132.)

[3] Hobhouse had secured a leave from his regiment to see his book of travels through the press. He later asked for an extension of his leave and never went back to his post, finally getting his father's consent to resign his commission. On February 28 he went into lodgings at No. 4 Manchester Buildings, Westminster.

Murray the publisher, and from time to time returned and talked while the sheets were passing through the press. Having come fresh from the fencing-rooms of Angelo and Jackson, he used, according to Murray's biographer (perhaps to pretend indifference and to fend off embarrassment), "to amuse himself by renewing his practice of 'Carte et Tierce,' with his walking-cane directed against the book-shelves, while Murray was reading passages from the poem, with occasional ejaculations of admiration; on which Byron would say, 'You think that a good idea, do you, Murray?' Then he would fence and lunge with his walking stick at some special book which he had picked out on the shelves before him." Murray later said: "I was often very glad to get rid of him!" [n]

Shortly after Byron's return to London from Newstead, Professor E. D. Clarke had written him that Lord Aberdeen wished to propose his name for membership in the "Athenian Club." Byron replied to Clarke that before his name was put up it should be known that in the notes to his forthcoming poem he was making some remarks on Lord Elgin that would not perhaps be agreeable "to a zealous Antiquarian." He added: "Truth is I am sadly deficient in gusto, and have little of the antique spirit, except a wish to immolate Ld. Elgin to Minerva & Nemesis. But should these omissions & offences be got over, I should feel truly happy in being one of the Elect." [4]

With a kind of fatalistic anticipation of the failure of his Parliamentary career, arising partly from self-distrust and partly from a realistic conception of the inexorable degradation of political life, Byron went recklessly ahead with his plans for publication. He was preparing to launch not only *Childe Harold,* in which he would speak his mind freely, but also the *Curse of Minerva,* to which he now added lines expressing his conviction of the hopelessness of things in England and the futility of his own efforts to right the wrongs by political action.

Byron was still thinking of escape to the sunnier, less demanding life of the East. While his speech was in preparation he

[4] Eg. 2869, ff. 7–8. Letter of Jan. 19, 1812. According to a subsequent letter of Clarke (Murray MSS.), Lord Aberdeen wanted to present Byron's name even after he demurred, but Byron did not become a member.

wrote to Hodgson: "In the spring of 1813 I shall leave England for ever. Every thing in my affairs tends to this, and my inclinations and health do not discourage it. Neither my habits nor constitution are improved by your customs or your climate. I shall find employment in making myself a good Oriental scholar. I shall retain a mansion in one of the fairest islands, and retrace at intervals, the most interesting portions of the East. In the mean time, I am adjusting my concerns, which will (when arranged) leave me with wealth sufficient even for home, but enough for a principality in Turkey." [n]

But events in Parliament aroused his attention again. The Tory riot bill, introduced in the House of Commons on February 14, though vigorously opposed by Sir Samuel Romilly on the second reading on the 17th, passed at the third reading (February 20) and was sent on to the Lords. The bill, which now specified the death penalty for frame-breaking, and which would force those in whose houses the frames were broken to be informers, was introduced in the upper house by Lord Liverpool.[n]

While the bill was being debated, another event added bitterness to the discussion and rallied Whigs of all complexions to oppose the intransigent Tories. The Prince Regent had at length shown his true colors, undeceiving the Whigs, who had hoped that his accession to power would bring a change of regime. Fearing that a reforming Whig government would cut his revenues, but being indebted to the Whigs for support and many favors, he conceived the plan of seeming to invite them to form a government but making it impossible for them to do so. In a letter to the Duke of York he had asked the leaders of the Conservative Whigs to form a coalition with some of their most hated enemies among the Tories. Lords Grey and Grenville replied with some sharpness to this proposal, and the Prince made occasion for a quarrel with his former friends by bitterly criticizing their answer at a banquet at Carlton House on February 22. Lord Lauderdale spoke up to say that the reply voiced the sentiments of the whole party, whereupon the Prince abused all his Whig friends in violent language. His little daughter, Princess Charlotte, who was present, wept at her father's treachery to those who had befriended him and to the party in which she and her mother had put all their hope. She was ordered out of the room with the Duchess of York.[n] This incident came to Byron's ears shortly after and was treasured for future use.

Several times while he was writing his speech Byron consulted Lord Holland, and Rogers brought them together for a personal meeting at Byron's own lodgings. Byron had early sensed that he and the older lord did not see eye to eye on the Frame Bill. While Lord Holland and his associates among the Moderate Whigs avoided a direct attack upon the bill, pressing instead for a Committee of Inquiry, Byron was willing and eager to take the Radical or "democratical" line of arguing on humanitarian grounds for justice to "the industrious poor," and to bring in as a secondary consideration, and as a kind of cynical and ironic appeal to those who had no sympathy for the lower classes, the inefficacy of the brutal legislation proposed. Even the Liberal Whigs were careful, with a few exceptions, to avoid what would seem or could be interpreted as a "Jacobin" defense of the workers. Sir Francis Burdett, who had somewhat less eagerness for martyrdom since his imprisonment for a breach of privilege in a free-speech case in 1810, when he had been embarrassed by popular acclaim that nearly identified him with the mob, merely voted against the measure in the lower house without speaking.[n]

Byron, who, on taking his seat in 1809, had declared his purpose to stand aloof from both parties, to speak what he thought, and to preserve his independence, realized now that he was playing a lone hand, for he was held back by an aristocratic, half-snobbish pride from allying himself openly with the Radical leaders in Parliament whose point of view he more nearly shared. Though he later welcomed the defense and applause of such men as Burdett and Earl ("Citizen") Stanhope, he was more eager now to conciliate and work in harmony with Lord Holland, from whom, however, he did not try to hide his own views. Two days before he made his speech he wrote:

"My own motive for opposing the bill is founded on its palpable injustice, and its certain inefficacy. I have seen the state of these miserable men, and it is a disgrace to a civilized country. . . . The effect of the present bill would be to drive them into actual rebellion."

Then in deference he added: "I believe your Lordship does not coincide with me entirely on this subject, and most cheerfully and sincerely shall I submit to your superior judgment and experience, and take some other line of argument against the bill, or be silent altogether, should you deem it more advisable. Condemning, as every one must condemn, the conduct of these wretches, I believe in the existence of grievances which call rather for pity than punishment." Then, concerned with the impression his letter might make on Lord Holland, he added a postscript: "I am a little apprehensive that your Lordship will think me too lenient towards these men, and half a *frame-breaker myself.*" [n]

Afraid that he might not be able to control his feelings in an extemporaneous talk on this important occasion, Byron wrote out his speech and memorized it like a Harrow oration. Dallas, who heard him practicing parts of it, said: "He altered the natural tone of his voice, which was sweet and round, into a formal drawl, and he prepared his features for a part—it was a youth declaiming a task. This was the more perceptible, as in common conversation he was remarkably easy and natural. . . ." [n]

Byron had chosen to speak on the second reading of the bill (February 27, 1812). He was in a state of high excitement. When the moment arrived, the desire to make a sensation in his maiden speech out-topped his interest in the subject itself. Whatever Lord Holland's advice as to tactics had been, Byron ignored the motion for a Committee of Inquiry, launching a direct and radical attack on the injustice, iniquity, and cruelty of the bill, making dramatic capital of the misery of the workers. With rhetorical questions and balanced sentences, with rolling periods and reasoned arguments as well as ironic contrasts, he appealed to the feelings and the humanity of his audience. Pitt, Burke, and Sheridan were his models, but he himself recognized that his delivery, "loud and fluent enough," was "perhaps a little theatrical." [n]

Byron followed the general Whig Opposition when he blamed part of the distress on the foreign wars (waged by the Tories), but he went further, protesting that "while the exalted offender can find means to baffle the law, new capital punishments must be devised, new snares of death must be spread for the wretched mechanic, who is famished into guilt."

He piled up dramatic contrasts as he approached the climax of his argument. "I have been in some of the most oppressed provinces of Turkey; but never under the most despotic of infidel governments did I behold such squalid wretchedness as I have seen since my return in the very heart of a Christian country." Then he asked: "How can you carry the Bill into effect? Can you commit a whole country to their own prisons? Will you erect a gibbet in every field, and hang up men like scarecrows?"

The solemn Tory lords must have fumed and felt that they were being forced to listen to a new demagogue quoting passages from Cobbett's *Political Register*. The peroration was calculated to make their complexions rise still higher. Suppose the bill passed, Byron said: ". . . suppose one of these men, as I have seen them,—meagre with famine, sullen with despair, careless of a life which your Lordships are perhaps about to value at something less than the price of a stocking-frame;—suppose this man surrounded by the children for whom he is unable to procure bread . . . dragged into court, to be tried for this new offence, by this new law; still, there are two things wanting to convict and condemn him; and these are, in my opinion,—twelve butchers for a jury, and a Jeffreys for a judge!" [n]

Byron told Hodgson: "I spoke very violent sentences with a sort of modest impudence, abused every thing and every body, and put the Lord Chancellor [Lord Eldon] very much out of humour: and if I may believe what I hear, have not lost any character by the experiment." [n] He knew he had shocked many in the House, but he was exhilarated by the experience. "I was born for opposition," he later wrote.[n] The Whigs hastened to congratulate him. Some like Lord Holland had no strong convictions against the bill, though they favored a penalty less severe, but they were glad to encourage a new Opposition member. Their polite comments turned upon his oratory rather than his arguments. "Lord H.[olland] tells me I shall beat them all if I persevere; and Lord G.[renville] remarked that the construction of some of my periods are very like *Burke's!!*" [n] Lord Holland's private opinion was less flattering. He wrote in his *Memoirs:* "His speech was full of fancy, wit, and invective, but not exempt from affectation nor well reasoned, nor at all suited to our common notions of Parliamentary eloquence. His fastidious and artificial taste and his over-irritable temper would, I think, have prevented him from ever excelling in Parliament." [n] But Burdett, who had stepped up from the Commons to hear him, was more genuinely enthusiastic: "*He* says it is the best speech by a *lord* since the '*Lord* knows when,' probably from a fellow-feeling in the sentiments." [n]

As when Byron first took his seat, Dallas was the only one of his personal friends who was there to congratulate him on his maiden speech. In the introduction of that speech he had said rather pathetically, though probably he had not meant it to be plaintive, that he was "a stranger not only to this House in general, but to almost every individual whose attention I presume to solicit." [n] He was "glowing with success, and much agitated," when Dallas met him after the speech. Putting out his hand, Dallas advanced his left one, having an umbrella in the right. " 'What,' said he, 'give your friend your left hand on such an occasion?' " [n] But he was grateful to Dallas, shaking and pressing his hand very warmly, repeating some of the compliments that had been paid to him, and concluding that the speech would be a good advertisement for *Childe Harold.*

The next day he took Hobhouse to dine with Tom Moore at St. Albans. Neither Hobhouse nor Moore had gone down to the House to hear his speech. On the two days following his Parliamentary debut Byron heard himself complimented in the speeches of Lords Holland and Grenville; he was equally flattered that Lords Eldon and Harrowby took the floor to answer him.[n]

He sat on the committee that successfully modified the bill, substituting "fine or imprisonment" for the death penalty as a punishment for frame-breaking.[5] He did not essay a rejoinder to the Tory peers in the House, but took his revenge on Lord Eldon and his colleagues in "An Ode to the Framers of the Frame Bill,"

[5] Erdman: "Lord Byron as Rinaldo," p. 213. The bill, with this amendment, was passed after the third reading in the House of Lords on March 5 and was sent back to the Commons, where the amendment was thrown out.

which he sent off to the *Morning Chronicle,* where it appeared anonymously on March 2. This provocative piece, which ended with the expression of a hope that "the frames of the fools may be first to be *broken,*/ Who, when asked for a *remedy,* sent down a *rope,*" [6] was saucy and personal beyond anything he had said in his speech. A few days later he wrote and sent to the same paper, also to be published anonymously, a "Sympathetic Address to a Young Lady," commemorating the episode at Carlton House. Byron did not venture to put his name to the *lèse-majesté* of these lines:

*Weep, daughter of a royal line,*
*A Sire's disgrace, a realm's decay;*
*Ah! happy if each tear of thine*
*Could wash a Father's fault away!* [7]

Already uncertain of his position in Parliament, Byron was seeking a freer mode of expression, as well as compensation for what he considered his failure. Despite the praise that had greeted his first speech, he remembered his nervousness, his underlying insecurity while facing the critical lords (who may indeed have been gazing at his lame foot), and he was growing impatient with the "Parliamentary mummeries" that bogged down all the business of government. Had it not been for the feeling, imposed half by his own pride and half by the conventions of the time, that writing could not be the serious or main occupation of a gentleman, he might have turned at once to poetry or journalism. As it was, a series of circumstances was forcing him to suppress the form of expression that was most congenial to him—satire.

At the beginning of his Parliamentary career he was facing a dilemma. Although he was pushed by his natural sympathies and his convictions toward a Radical position, he longed for the society, not of those with whom he would have had most in common in political philosophy, but of aristocratic circles of the Mod-

[6] *Poetry,* VII, 13–14. Byron never acknowledged this poem and it was not known to be his until 1880.

[7] The eight lines of this poem were published in the *Morning Chronicle* on March 7, 1812. When Byron acknowledged it by including it with the second edition of *The Corsair* in 1814, there was a great furor.

erate Whig camp, of which Holland House was the center. It argues nothing of snobbery in Byron's nature—for those early friends such as Hobhouse and Davies, whom Moore, the truer snob, slandered as mere "coffee-house" companions, he never for a moment deserted when he had become the lion of London society—to say that he had a kind of psychological urge, built upon the whole background of his early life, to be accepted as a social equal in the aristocratic world. Both his pride and his intellect prevented him from being a social climber, but he was flattered by Lord Holland's overtures, and from the time of their first meeting continued to pay him the greatest deference.

It is not surprising, then, that when Rogers hinted that Lord and Lady Holland would not be sorry if he refrained from any further publication of *English Bards and Scotch Reviewers,*[8] he immediately dropped his work on a fifth edition, together with the *Hints from Horace* and *The Curse of Minerva,* which he had intended to print in the same volume. For many reasons he was not sorry to suppress his early satire. After having mingled more in the literary world during the several months he had been acquainted with Rogers and Moore, he had come to see that his judgments had been youthful, rash, and unfair. He told Leigh Hunt later: "My motive for writing that poem was, I fear, not so fair as you are willing to believe it; I was angry, and determined to be witty, and, fighting in a crowd, dealt about my blows against all alike, without distinction or discernment." [9] He reimbursed Cawthorn and ordered all copies cast to the flames.[1]

[8] Byron had attacked the Hollands in his satire on the mistaken assumption that Holland, as leader of the Whigs, had been responsible for the harsh review of his early poems in the Whig *Edinburgh Review.*

[9] *LJ,* III, 227. Letter of Oct. 22, 1815. Byron told Hunt that his suppression of the poem was "subsequent to my acquaintance with Lord Holland, and was neither expressed nor understood, as a *condition* of that acquaintance."

[1] Cawthorn kept the fifth edition in type, however, and when he could not get Byron's permission to publish it attempted to get out a pirated edition but was stopped by an injunction. (Wise: *A Bibliography of . . . Byron,* I, 32.) He continued to put out spurious printings of the first four authorized editions (Wise counted fifteen of these, and there were probably more) after Byron's fame made the trade profitable. Byron's later opinion of the poem is recorded in notes which he wrote in a copy of the fourth edition after he had gone abroad in 1816. And at the end he recorded his final judg-

Moore had the impression that it was "a friendly remonstrance from Lord Elgin, or some of his connexions" that caused him to suppress *The Curse of Minerva,*[n] but Byron, feeling no particular obligation to Lord Elgin, and still having strong convictions about the rape of the marbles from Greece, had Murray print some copies on quarto sheets for private circulation.[n] The poem's last hundred lines, embodying the savage attack on British policies, had they been made public, would have given their author the reputation of firebrand and Jacobin, and he might have been less welcome at Holland House.

*Childe Harold* had been advertised for publication on March 1, but Murray held it from public sale until the 10th. Byron was visiting Dr. Drury at Harrow and did not see a copy of the handsome quarto volume until March 3, when Dallas brought it to him.[n] Murray had done a good job of predisposing the public to be eager for it by showing the sheets to various people who spread the word abroad. In three days after the official publication date the edition of five hundred had been sold. But Byron had distributed a good many presentation copies before that date. One of the first went to Lord Holland with a letter that showed how uncertain and apprehensive he still was of its reception. Byron pretended to take the whole matter lightly: ". . . your Lordship, I am sorry to observe to-day, is troubled with the gout; if my book can produce a *laugh* against itself or the author, it will be of some service. If it can set you to *sleep,* the benefit will be yet greater. . . ."[n]

If Byron thought he had sufficiently camouflaged the personal parts to avoid identification of himself as Childe Harold, a letter from Professor E. D. Clarke of Cambridge, to whom he had sent a copy by Scrope Davies, must have been disquieting. Clarke had the highest praise for the poem. Clarke's friend Matthias entirely agreed with him. "'Surely,' said I to him," Clarke wrote, "'Lord Byron, at this time of life, cannot have experienced such keen anguish as those exquisite allusions to what older men

---

ment: "The greater part of this satire I most sincerely wish had never been written—not only on account of the injustice of much of the critical, and some of the personal part of it—but the tone and temper are such as I cannot approve." (*Poetry,* I, 381 n.)

*may* have felt seem to denote!' This was his answer: '*I fear he has—he could not else have written such a poem.*' " [n]

But by the middle of the month it no longer mattered what was said or thought. *Childe Harold* had caught on, and overnight the author was famous.

# CHAPTER X

## *1812*

## Fame and Society

EVEN before the first edition of *Childe Harold* had disappeared from Murray's shelves, Byron had become an object of curiosity and interest in the drawing-rooms of the Whig aristocracy. The center of the most recherché society in London was then Holland House, the Kensington mansion of the third Lord Holland and his wife, Elizabeth, whom he had married in 1797 two days after her first husband, Sir Godfrey Webster, had divorced her (naming Lord Holland as corespondent). In a society in which such irregularities of conduct were common enough, being taken for granted as prerogatives of an uninhibited upper class, there could be little embarrassment in sitting down to dine with the best company in London at Holland House. Not only the *haut ton* of the aristocracy—the Whig first families—but also the cream of the talents gathered at the home of the Hollands.[1] It was, it is true, a dominantly masculine company, for the more fastidious ladies who cared for their reputations could not overlook the fact that Lady Holland had *openly* —that was the crime—defied the conventions. Rogers and Moore were frequent visitors, and Byron soon joined them there. His genial and kindly host welcomed him without reserve or rancor. Byron's past indiscretions in *English Bards and Scotch Review-*

[1] The great Whig families, though for the time being they were not in power, had recollections of the period of their prestige in the eighteenth century and looked down on the Tories as lacking in fashion and gauche in literary and cultural matters.

*ers* were obliterated in the new friendship. Though he was slightly more on his guard with Lady Holland, who had a sharp tongue, Byron completely capitulated to their advances and made every effort to be gracious.

But the Hollands did not monopolize Byron for long. The publication of *Childe Harold* soon made him the literary lion of the season, and he was swept into other, more exciting circles. At Melbourne House in Whitehall an erratic and vivacious young lady who had been enraptured by the romantic pilgrimage was burning to meet the author. Lady Caroline Lamb had been married for seven years and had borne a son to her husband, William Lamb, second son of Lord and Lady Melbourne. A creature of impulse, great nervous energy, and immense and almost uncontrollable sensibility, she yet retained a childlike freshness and naïveté that had scarcely been disturbed by marriage, motherhood, or even an affair with the same Sir Godfrey Webster who had been the first husband of Lady Holland. In her irresponsible girlhood Lady Caroline had been something of a tomboy. She recorded in a commonplace book some of the nicknames that were bestowed upon her: "Ariel," "Sprite," "Young Savage," "Squirrel," "The Fairy Queen." [n] Born Caroline Ponsonby, daughter of the Earl of Bessborough and of Henrietta Ponsonby, sister of the beautiful Duchess of Devonshire, she was allowed to develop all her eccentricities in the fabulous atmosphere of Devonshire House, Chatsworth, and Hardwick. Having had no formal education, she could scarcely read when she reached her teens, but she developed a facility for writing verses and drawing.

She had heard nothing of Byron until one day Rogers, who, with Moore, was a frequent visitor at Melbourne House, said: "You should know the new poet," and gave her his copy of *Childe Harold* to read.[n] "I read it," she told Lady Morgan, "and that was enough. Rogers said, 'he has a club-foot, and bites his nails.' I said, 'If he was as ugly as Æsop I must know him.' I was one night at Lady Westmoreland's; the women were all throwing their heads at him. Lady Westmoreland led me up to him. I looked earnestly at him, and turned on my heel. My opinion, in my journal was, 'mad—bad—and dangerous to know.' " [n] Anyone who knew Caroline could easily have interpreted that entry to mean that she was more determined than ever to meet him, but on her own terms, not when she would have to compete with dozens of other women. Her dramatic gesture was not lost on Byron. His interest was piqued by her turning away, and he had no doubt already heard from Rogers and others of this fascinating eccentric.

A few days later while she was sitting (perhaps by prearrangement) with Lord and Lady Holland, Byron was announced. When Lady Holland offered to present him, Byron said to Caroline: "That offer was made to you before; may I ask why you rejected it?" Caroline's reply is not recorded. Nor did she give any further account of that first meeting except to say: "He begged permission to come and see me." *n* Byron was not at first attracted to her physically, at least according to the cold survey he later gave Medwin: "The lady had scarcely any personal attractions to recommend her. Her figure, though genteel, was too thin to be good, and wanted that roundness which elegance and grace would vainly supply." *n*

He went to see her the next day, however, limping up the gray stone stairs at Melbourne House, where William's parents had fitted up rooms for the Lambs on their marriage (the Melbournes lived on the ground floor).[2] "Rogers and Moore were standing by me," Caroline told Lady Morgan. "I was on the sofa. I had just come in from riding. I was filthy and heated. When Lord Byron was announced, I flew out of the room to wash myself. When I returned, Rogers said, 'Lord Byron, you are a happy man. Lady Caroline has been sitting here in all her dirt with us, but when you were announced, she flew to beautify herself.' Lord Byron wished to come and see me at eight o'clock, when I was alone; that was my dinner-hour. I said he might. From that moment, for more than nine months [*sic*], he almost lived at Melbourne House." *n* The last statement being demonstrably untrue, most of Caroline's later romantic reminiscences of the affair must be read with caution, though it was sensational enough in fact.

Byron soon found that what she lacked in beauty she made up

[2] Melbourne House, now the Scottish Office, had been the residence of the Duke of York.

in vivacity and unpredictability. In all the philandering of his dissipated youth and during his foreign travels he had never conceived a romantic attachment to any woman of his own rank and intellect. Mary Chaworth had been only a country girl whose charms were magnified in his adolescent dreams by her inaccessibility. Mrs. Spencer Smith had had an exotic appeal in the narrow society at Malta, but had not possessed the aristocratic assurance of the world into which Byron had so recently been thrown. For the rest, he had always been most successful with girls below his social and intellectual level, with those who flattered his ego and looked up with awe at his title. And he had come to have a kind of Oriental scorn of women as creatures in no way capable of sharing a man's thoughts or feelings.

Among the women he had thus far met in the fashionable Whig society his shyness had caused him to play his own hero, the aloof and melancholy Childe Harold. They did not realize how much of his assumed self-possession and his studied politeness and cynical pose was a mask to hide his lack of ease in an aristocratic society to which he had been a stranger most of his life.[3] He braced himself to enter a drawing-room full of people, and was relaxed only when in conversation with a small group, chiefly with men. The clever acerbities of his undergraduate days, which would have pleased Scrope Davies, were not always appreciated in this company.

Lady Mildmay later told Moore how much she had felt afraid of Byron when meeting him in society, and that "once, when he spoke to her in a doorway, her heart beat so violently that she could hardly answer him. She said it was not only her awe of his great talents, but the peculiarity of a sort of *under* look he used to give, that produced this effect upon her." [n]

In Caroline Lamb, Byron found not only a sensitive and perceptive spirit ready to do homage to his most romantic conception of his own personality, but also a girl born to the patrician

[3] Lord Holland later observed to Moore that "it was *not* from his birth that Lord Byron had taken the station he held in society, for till his talents became known, he was, in spite of his birth, in any thing but good society, and *but* for his talents would never, perhaps, have been in any better." (Moore: *Memoirs,* II, 660.)

world who had both sophistication and apparent naïveté. He had met his equal in more than one sense. Her ability to play a part exceeded his own, and her lack of restraint and carelessness of the world's opinion often shocked him.

Caroline probably would have been attracted by Byron in any case, but she was doubly gratified that she had captured the literary lion of the London season, the man who fulfilled her fondest romantic dream. Soon after their first acquaintance she wrote dramatically in her diary: "That beautiful pale face is my fate." [n]

When Byron met Caroline, she was twenty-seven, boyish-looking, with blond curly hair and a kind of frank innocence in her dark hazel eyes. She had a passion for pages, and used to dress in their scarlet-and-sepia liveries. The engaging Devonshire House drawl and a lisp heightened the startling character of her conversation.

Byron was fascinated, and he went again and again to Melbourne House. But he did not succumb immediately, for the giddiness of Caroline's parties and the numerous company put him off. There were daily sessions at Melbourne House to practice dances recently imported from Germany.

On his second morning visit (March 25) Byron saw for the first time William Lamb's country cousin Annabella Milbanke.[4] The only daughter of Sir Ralph Milbanke, Lady Melbourne's brother, she had been brought up in seclusion in a house overlooking the bleak cliffs of the North Sea at Seaham in Durham. She was the apple of her parents' eye, a spoiled child but a very precocious one who had also been tutored at home and early had acquired an interest in mathematics, classical literature, and philosophy.[5] She had read widely, but knew little of the world

[4] Medwin (I, 36–7) quotes Byron as saying: "It was a fatal day; and I remember that in going upstairs I stumbled, and remarked to Moore, who accompanied me, that it was a bad omen. I ought to have taken the warning. On entering the room I observed a young lady, more simply dressed than the rest of the assembly, sitting alone upon a sofa. I took her for a humble companion, and asked if I was right in my conjecture? She is a great heiress, said he in a whisper . . . you had better marry her, and repair the old place, Newstead." Since Moore does not mention the episode, it may be taken with a grain of salt.

[5] Two of Miss Milbanke's commonplace books, now in my possession, show

of fashion when she went to London for the first time alone in 1811 to stay with her mother's friend Lady Gosford and to imbibe social polish while placing herself as decently as possible on the marriage market. That season was rather disappointing; she had few suitors, and she turned down the most promising of those, George Eden, Lord Auckland's heir. She had exalted ideas of what she wanted in a husband, and her letters and diary show that she was not a little priggish.

But the season of 1812 was more propitious. She was in her twentieth year, and in spite of her "snub face" she had a dark beauty that was heightened by her pensive habits and reserve. This time she had suitors in plenty, some of them rather troublesome. One was Augustus Foster, son of the second Duchess of Devonshire, who hesitated to take a post as Minister to the United States because he did not want to leave her. Another was William Bankes, Byron's Cambridge friend, with £8,000 a year, who was paying her persistent court at the time of the publication of *Childe Harold*. Byron presented him with a copy of the poem on March 4 and soon after he lent it to Annabella,[n] who, however, did not finish reading it until the day before she saw the author at Melbourne House. Her opinion, confided to her

---

with what seriousness, precision, and self-confidence she pursued her studies. In 1809, when she was only seventeen, she was making a critical study of Bacon's *De Augmentis Scientiarum* (*Advancement of Learning*), quoting long passages of the Latin with her own commentary on the justness of his observations and comparing them with those of other writers—Cowley, Cowper (a favorite), Horace, Massinger, and even some of the more daring spirits of the seventeenth and eighteenth centuries such as Sir William Temple, Swift, Bolingbroke, Hume, and Rochefoucauld. Her own comments, written in a meticulous hand, indicate the complacency of her judgments, carefully weighed and balanced. "I think self knowledge is not so difficult as to know the place we hold in the opinions of others," she wrote in one place, and in another: "I presume no one will assert that a man enjoying internally an approving conscience and externally the good opinion of others, is less happy than one whose only gratification is that of a foolish vanity." Miss Milbanke continued her commonplace book while she was in London with her parents in the winter of 1809. On February 10 she recorded: "Last night I was at the Hay Market Theatre and saw John Kemble & Mrs. Siddons in Macbeth." But this did not interfere with her serious studies. She was reading Cowper's life and letters. She quoted with approval his philosophy in misfortune: "We are forbidden to murmur, but we are not forbidden to regret."

diary, was brief: "It contains many stanzas in the best style of poetry. He is rather too much of a *mannerist,* that is, he wants variety in the turns of his expression. He excels most in the delineation of deep feeling, and in reflections relative to human nature." *n*

While he was being flattered by the attentions of all the women the next day, Annabella observed him closely. "Saw Lord Byron for the first time," she wrote in her diary that night. "His mouth continually betrays the acrimony of his spirit. I should judge him sincere and independent—sincere at least in society as far as he can be, whilst dissimulating the violence of his scorn. He very often hides his mouth with his hand while speaking. . . . It appeared to me that he tried to control his natural sarcasm and vehemence as much as he could, in order not to offend; but at times his lips thickened with disdain, and his eyes rolled impatiently. Indeed the scene was calculated to shew human absurdities." *n*

That night she listened eagerly to the gossip that was circulating about Byron. "Mrs. Knight told me authentic anecdotes of Lord Byron which gave me much concern, as they indicated feelings dreadfully perverted." And her letter to her parents the next day was full of this new sensation. It was already evident that for the first time she had met a man who aroused more than apathetic interest in her. That she could not approve of him did not lessen her excitement.

She wrote her mother: "My curiosity was much gratified by seeing Lord Byron, the object at present of universal attention. Lady C. has of course seized on him, notwithstanding the reluctance he manifests to be shackled by her. . . . It is said that he is an infidel, and I think it probable from the general character of his mind. His poem sufficiently proves that he *can* feel nobly, but he has discouraged his own goodness. . . .

"I did not seek an introduction to him, for all the women were absurdly courting him, and trying to *deserve* the lash of his Satire. I thought that *inoffensiveness* was the most secure conduct, as I am not desirous of a place in his lays. . . . so I made no offering at the shrine of Childe Harold, though I shall not refuse the acquaintance if it comes my way."

And the sensible girl added, concerning the party at Melbourne House: "I really thought that Lady Caroline had bit half the company and communicated the *Nonsense-mania*." [n]

Though Byron did not talk with Annabella Milbanke on this occasion, he did not fail to notice her. In fact, he must have had some curiosity concerning this bluestocking, for he had heard of her already as the patroness of the Seaham cobbler-poet Joseph Blackett.[n] He told Medwin: "There was something piquant, and what we term pretty, in Miss Millbank [Medwin's spelling]. Her features were small and feminine, though not regular. She had the fairest skin imaginable. Her figure was perfect for her height, and there was a simplicity, a retired modesty about her, which was very characteristic, and formed a happy contrast to the cold artificial formality, and studied stiffness, which is called fashion. She interested me exceedingly." [n]

But for the moment Caroline Lamb occupied his thoughts sufficiently. Though fascinated and flattered by her obvious preference for him, he was apprehensive that she was merely leading him on to please her vanity. Three days after his first visit to Melbourne House he took her a rose and a carnation, saying with a half-sarcastic smile that covered his insecurity: "Your Ladyship I am told likes all that is new and rare for a moment." [n] Her reply was a studied love message mingling cleverness and fancy with the sentimental, and was calculated to soothe his fears and satisfy his ego. "The Rose Lord Byron gave Lady Caroline Lamb died in despight of every effort made to save it; probably from regret at its fallen fortunes." [n]

Caroline's impulsiveness was at once a delight and an embarrassment to Byron. From this time on, notes and letters and verses flew back and forth between them. Caroline may have exaggerated when she said he wrote ten times a day, but in the first stages of their love and quarrels he must have written often. He was soon overwhelmed by her generosity and her abandon. Once she had fallen in love, she knew no reserve; her violence was frightening. Rogers said: "She absolutely besieged him. He showed me the first letter he received from her; in which she assured him that, if he was in any want of money, 'all her jewels were at his service.'[6] They frequently had quarrels; and more than once, on coming home, I have found Lady C. walking in the garden [Rogers's house was in St. James's Place not far from Byron's lodgings at 8 St. James's Street], and waiting for me, to beg that I would reconcile them. . . . such was the insanity of her passion for Byron, that, sometimes, when not invited to a party where he was to be, she would wait for him in the street till it was over! One night after a great party at Devonshire House, to which Lady Caroline had not been invited, I saw her,—yes, saw her,—talking to Byron, with half of her body thrust into the carriage which he had just entered." [n]

There is ample evidence that this affair did not absorb Byron wholly. He was much in demand everywhere, and basked in the sunshine of the attention of many women to whom he could be agreeable without making commitments. The Duchess of Devonshire wrote to her son Augustus Foster in Washington: "The subject of conversation, of curiosity, of enthusiasm almost, one might say, of the moment is not Spain or Portugal, Warriors or Patriots, but Lord Byron! . . . [*Childe Harold*] is on every table, and himself courted, visited, flattered, and praised whenever he appears. He has a pale, sickly, but handsome countenance, a bad figure, animated and amusing conversation, and, in short, he is really the only topic almost of conversation—the men jealous of him, the women of each other." [n]

"The genius which the poem exhibited," Rogers said, "the youth, the rank of the author, his romantic wanderings in Greece, —these combined to make the world stark mad about *Childe Harold* and Byron. I knew two old maids in Buckinghamshire who used to cry over the passage about Harold's 'laughing dames' that 'long had fed his youthful appetite.'" [n] Byron and

[6] The letter referred to by Rogers was probably not her first, though it may have been among the earliest. In the Berg Collection of the New York Public Library are some lines in Caroline's hand to which she has prefixed the note: "These are the first lines Ld Byron wrote to me—I had made him the present of a gold Neck chain and these lines were written at the moment." The lines sound authentically Byronic: "Ah Caro! do I need the Chain:/ Nor dare I struggle to be free/ Since gifts returned, but pain the giver,/ And the soft band put on by thee/ The Slightest chain, will last for Ever!"

his poem were the subject of discussion at every dinner table. Before his house in St. James's Street the traffic was held up by a press of carriages bringing notes of invitation.[n]

Even the demure and fastidious Annabella Milbanke easily succumbed to his charms. On April 13 there was a large party at Lady Gosford's, where she was staying, "at which Lord Byron . . . shone with his customary glory," she wrote her father. "He certainly is very shy, and in consequence our acquaintance did not proceed that night, as I had not leisure to concert an attack on him. Indeed I was tormented by that impudent Bankes, who seems really to consider me as his property and will not understand any rebuffs." [n] But the next night she went with Mrs. George Lamb to a party at Lady Cowper's (Lady Melbourne's daughter), where for the first time she had an opportunity to talk with Byron. He was careful not to be as sarcastic on the subject of Blackett as he had been in his letters to Dallas. To her mother she wrote: "I have met with much evidence of his goodness. You know how easily the noblest heart may be perverted by unkindness—perhaps the most easily a *noble* heart, because it is the more susceptible to ungenerous indignities. . . . At Lady Cowper's Lord B. and I had some very pleasing conversation—at least I thought it so. Lord B. is certainly very interesting, but he wants that calm benevolence which could only touch my heart." Of another party at Caroline Lamb's she recorded: "Lord Byron is without exception of young or old more agreeable in conversation than any person I ever knew." [n]

She was unaware how deeply her fate was sealed when she wrote in her diary the same night: "I continued my acquaintance with Lord Byron, and was additionally convinced that he is sincerely repentant for the evil he has done, though he has not resolution (without aid) to adopt a new course of conduct and feelings." [n] Byron had an almost feminine sensitivity to the nuances of sympathetic feeling and an uncanny capacity for displaying that part of his personality which would most engage the person with whom he was talking. This accounted for his friendship with such disparate characters as Hobhouse and Tom Moore, Dallas and Davies, chambermaids and duchesses. Instinctively he came forward to meet this simple girl on her own level. For her he was Childe Harold. She felt that she had seen much deeper into his being than had any of the women who were throwing themselves at him when he asked abruptly at a party: "Do you think there is one person here who dares to look into himself?" Remembering this at a later time, she wrote: "I felt that he was the most attractive person [in the crowd]; but I was not *bound* to him by any strong feeling of sympathy till he uttered these words, not to me, but in my hearing—'I have not a friend in the world!' . . . I vowed in secret to be a devoted friend to this lone being." *n*

The idea that it was her duty to rescue a noble spirit from the depths helped to convince her that her motives were disinterested. The growth of her interest through the month of April is indicated in her diary, even in entries reproving some of his remarks with impartial justice. On the 26th she wrote her mother: "I consider it as an act of humanity and a Christian duty not to deny him any temporary satisfaction he can derive from my acquaintance—though I shall not seek to encrease it. He is not a dangerous person to me. . . . *I* cannot think him destitute of natural religion—it is in his heart." *n*

Byron found an irresistible appeal in the virgin innocence of this attractive, modest, and serious girl, and apparently he paid a good deal of attention to her—enough to make Caroline jealous. In her naïveté Annabella had sent through Caroline some of her poems for Byron's opinion. Caroline knew how to deal with this impertinence. She passed along the poems, which she felt would do the writer no good in Byron's eyes, adding the gossip that Annabella was attached, if not promised, to George Eden, her frequent attendant at dances.*n*

When Annabella received an urgent call from Caroline to come at once, she was shrewd enough to guess what was in the wind and to be prepared. Her comment was: "I shall exert my influence to prove to Lady Melbourne that there is no danger in my meeting Lord Byron." *n* The only record of the meeting is the brief statement in Annabella's diary for May 2: "Went in morning to Lady Caroline Lamb, and undeceived her by a painful acknowledgment. . . . Received Lord Byron's opinion of my verses." [n] Did Caroline also make a confession,[7] or did she make the most of the trump she held in her hand, Byron's letter written the day before, part of which she read to her eagerly listening visitor? [n] Philosophical as she might be, not all the home truths of that letter could have pleased Annabella.

Byron wrote: "She certainly is a very extraordinary girl; who would imagine so much strength and variety of thought under that placid Countenance? It is not necessary for Miss M. to be an authoress, indeed I do not think publishing at all creditable either to men or women, and (though you will not believe me) very often feel ashamed of it myself; but I have no hesitation in saying that she has talents which, were it proper or requisite to indulge, would have led to distinction. . . . You will say as much of this to Miss M. as you think proper. I say all this very sincerely. I have no desire to be better acquainted with Miss Milbank [*sic*]; she is too good for a fallen spirit to know, and I should like her more if she were less perfect." [n]

Annabella was morally smug enough to take that last statement, if Caroline revealed it to her, as a kind of grim compliment, but something in the letter or the interview with Caroline Lamb took the pleasure out of her theretofore absorbingly interesting London season. The appearance of her parents, alarmed at last by her preoccupation with this "fallen spirit," may have dampened her enthusiasm; in any case, the entries in her diary touching Byron are briefer and more disillusioned. At one party she observed his "propensity to coquetry"; even when he was good-natured, she found the parties dull. She was "wearied with want of tranquillity, and found no pleasure." On another occasion she wrote: "Lord Byron there—he spoke satirically of one of my *best* friends whom he did not know except by sight and report. This was evidently an effect of that irritability which renders him so wretched." And on the last day of May she recorded: "Lord By-

[7] It is possible that this is a misreading of Annabella's diary. Had she written "undeceived by her painful acknowledgment," it would be easy to understand Annabella's double shock, for it would probably mean that in order to put off her innocent rival Caroline confessed to having yielded herself to Byron in fact as well as fancy.

ron was there, but we never spoke." Before long she wrote: "Danced not," and soon after she gave up her diary for good.[n]

During all this time Byron's tranquillity was frequently destroyed, too, but for reasons unflatteringly remote from Miss Milbanke. Through April and May his affair with Caroline Lamb progressed rapidly to successive heights of wildness and folly. Her utter abandonment of all discretion frequently shocked Byron and led to quarrels and passionate reconciliations. One of their quarrels, Byron told Medwin, "was made up in a very odd way, and without any verbal explanation. She will remember it." [n] Byron, too, could be a moody and demanding lover. The waltzing parties, which had made Melbourne House the gayest place in London, were soon abandoned because they gave pain to the lame poet, who could not dance. "Byron contrived to sweep them all away," she told Lady Morgan.[n] He made Caroline swear to give up waltzing: he could not bear to see her in the arms of another. She said: ". . . he liked to read with me & stay with me out of the crowd." [n] Every day he brought her a book.[n] He sat for hours with her baby in his arms for fear of waking him, and was for a time touched by her trust.[n] But he soon grew jealous of the husband. In his letters he reproached her perpetually with loving William better than himself.[8] Bitterness would overcome him, and he would boast of the blackness of his own character; thinking of his deformity, he would cry that William Lamb was to him as an Hyperion to a satyr.[n]

In his jealousy he would force her to swear that she loved him better than William. When she hesitated, he shouted: "My God, you shall pay for this," adding resentfully: "I'll wring that little obstinate heart." Caroline's own jealousy more than matched his. When she saw him bending attentively over a beautiful woman at a dinner at her grandmother, Lady Spencer's, Lord John Rus-

[8] *LJ,* II, 451. In later years Caroline told Lady Morgan that she loved her husband most, her mother second, and Byron third. (*Lady Morgan's Memoirs,* II, 207.) And she wrote Medwin: "He [Byron] never could say, either, that I had not loved my husband." (*LJ,* II, 451.) But she confessed to Lady Morgan: "He [William Lamb] cared nothing for my morals. . . . I might flirt and go about with what men I pleased. He was privy to my affair with Lord Byron, and laughed at it. His indolence rendered him insensible to everything." (*Lady Morgan's Memoirs,* II, 199–200.)

sell saw her in uncontrollable emotion bite through the glass she was holding.[n]

To say that they were not in love, but were merely playing parts, is to disregard the most obvious symptoms of amorous passion in its most virulent form. True, it was not a well-founded love, and by its nature it could not last, for never did two self-centered egos clash so violently. But it was torturingly real while it lasted, and for Caroline it never ceased to be the greatest and most moving passion of her life. She told Medwin: "I grew to love him better than virtue, Religion—all prospects here. He broke my heart, & still I love him. . . ."[n] Byron wrote honestly to Lady Melbourne after his love had been turned to disgust by Caroline's absurdities: "I do not mean to deny my attachment—it *was*—and it is not."[n] His few surviving letters to her, especially those written in the earlier stages of the affair, display both attachment and tenderness, and are firm confessions of the hold she had upon him, even when his reason told him that it was all madness. While the passion was still fresh, he wrote acknowledging his feeling for her but urging more prudence:

"I never knew a woman with greater or more pleasing talents, *general* as in a woman they should be, something of everything, and too much of nothing. But these are unfortunately coupled with a total want of common conduct. . . .

"Then your heart, my poor Caro (what a little volcano!), that pours *lava* through your veins; and yet I cannot wish it a bit colder. . . . you know I have always thought you the cleverest, most agreeable, absurd, amiable, perplexing, dangerous, fascinating little being that lives now, or ought to have lived 2000 years ago. I won't talk to you of beauty; I am no judge. But our beauties cease to be so when near you, and therefore you have either some, or something better. And now, Caro, this nonsense is the first and last compliment (if it be such) I ever paid you. You have often reproached me as wanting in that respect; but others will make up the deficiency.

"Come to Lord Grey's; at least do not let me keep you away. All that you so often *say*, I *feel*. Can more be said or felt? This same prudence is tiresome enough; but one *must* maintain it, or what *can* one do to be saved? Keep to it."[n]

Dallas noted how absorbed Byron was in writing letters to Caroline Lamb at this time, and he related: "While I was with him the lady's *page* brought him a new letter. He was a fair-faced delicate boy of thirteen or fourteen years old, whom one might have taken for the lady herself. He was dressed in a scarlet hussar jacket and pantaloons. . . . He had light hair curling about his face, and held a feathered fancy hat in his hand, which completed the scenic appearance of this urchin Pandarus. I could not but suspect at the time that it was a disguise; if so, he never disclosed it to me . . . I do not precisely recollect the mode of his exit." [n] Caroline did go several times to Byron's rooms in a page's costume or other disguise, often when he did not expect or want her.[9]

It was Byron's misfortune that he felt impelled to despoil his mistress of those very qualities which had in his romantic imagination made her attractive—the freshness and naïveté of her personality. One of her specific charms which tortured Byron most, and which he was urged by inexorable necessity to destroy, was her fondness for her husband. In one of her many last farewell letters she wrote: "I took my last leave of you when you little thought it & the remembrance of this made me both kind—& cold. But was I cold when first you made me yours—when first you told me in the Carriage to kiss your mouth & I durst not—& after thinking it such a crime it was more than I could prevent from that moment—you drew me to you like a magnet & I could not indeed I could not have kept away—was I cold then—were you so? . . . never while life beats in this heart shall I forget you or that moment when first you said you lov'd me—when my heart did not meet yours but flew before it—& both intended to remain innocent of greater wrong." [n]

Spoiled child that she was, Caroline had imagined that she

[9] Medwin, who is not too much to be relied on in details of episodes which in themselves had a basis of fact, reported Byron as saying: "Even during our intimacy I was not at all constant to this fair one, and she suspected as much. In order to detect my intrigues she watched me, and earthed a lady into my lodgings,—and came herself, terrier-like, in the disguise of a carman." (Medwin, II, 67.) Caroline also made, or attempted to make, a confidant of Fletcher, urging him to receive "the little Foreign page" she was going to send to Byron. (*LJ*, II, 116 n.)

could play with fire without being burned. She had thought she could have the adoration of Byron on her own terms as she had that of the rest of the world in which she lived. Once in the game, however, Byron could not stop with a light flirtation, but must carry on until he had conquered her wholly, though he knew and frequently repented the consequences of the steps he seemed fated to take.

For a few headlong weeks Byron's political career, his new-found social success, which at first meant a great deal to his self-esteem, even his literary reputation—all seemed jeopardized by this hectic love affair. He soon realized what a wild spirit he had released by rousing the emotions of this irrepressible *enfant terrible*. Byron was mistaken when he said (if Medwin is to be believed) that she had never loved her husband, but he was probably right in his belief that passion had never before been thoroughly awakened in her. She was fond of the mild and easygoing William Lamb as she was of her mother and her child. She told Medwin: "Byron did not affect—but he loved me as never woman was loved." [n] Once awakened, she could never forget him.

Caroline had never observed prudence, but now her indiscretion knew no bounds. Her mother (Lady Bessborough) and the Lambs became vexed and extremely worried. Had the affair been carried on secretly and discreetly, no one would have been greatly concerned. Lady Melbourne herself had long been the particular friend of Lord Egremont, whom William Lamb, her second son and Caroline's husband, was said to resemble, and her intimacy with the Prince of Wales was commonly thought to account for the interest he took in her son George. The Duke of Bedford had been her most recent lover. She did not pretend to believe that either men or women were or ought to be monogamous, but she was annoyed and shocked by Caroline's public display of her conquest. Lady Bessborough had possessed some of her daughter's recklessness in her youth, but she had followed the code of her class in keeping from public view so far as possible her early liaison and lifelong devotion to Lord Granville Leveson Gower, who later married her niece Harriet, Georgiana Duchess of Devonshire's daughter. Lady Bessborough's curious affair with Sheridan came nearer to being a scandal because of his indiscretion rather than hers (his last gruesome message being that he would be looking up through the coffin lid at her).

In spite of all her mother could do, however, Caroline's conduct was the talk of high society. On May 4 the second Duchess of Devonshire, after apprising her son Augustus of the hopelessness of his suit for Miss Milbanke's hand, gave the gossip of the hour: "Lord Byron makes up to her a little, but she don't seem to admire him except as a poet, nor he her, except for a wife. Your little friend, Caro William, as usual, is doing all sorts of imprudent things for him and with him; he admires her very much, but is supposed by some to admire our Caroline [Mrs. George Lamb] more; he says she is like Thyrsa [*sic*], and her singing is enchantment to him." *n* And the next week the Duchess reported that Byron "is going back to Naxos, and then the husbands may sleep in peace. I should not be surprized if Caro William were to go with him, she is so wild and imprudent." *n*

This would suggest that Byron was already proposing an elopement, perhaps in the knowledge (or hope?) that she would not have the courage to make such a violent break with her comfortable world, perhaps to test whether she would actually leave her husband for him. Caroline told Medwin that Byron at last ". . . press'd me to leave all and go with him—and this at the very moment when he was made an Idol of, and when, as he and you justly observe, I had few personal attractions." *n* Byron later told Lady Melbourne: "I must let you into one little secret—*her* [Lady Bessborough's] folly half did this. At the commencement she piqued that 'vanity' (which it would be the vainest thing in the world to deny) by telling me she was certain I was not beloved, 'that I was only led on. . . .' I made no answer, but determined, not to *pursue*, for pursuit it was not, but to sit still, and in a week after I was convinced—not that [Caroline] loved me, for I do not believe in the existence of what is called Love—but that any other man in my situation would have believed that he was loved." *n*

Distracted by this stormy love affair and by the social whirlpool into which he had been carried by the popularity of *Childe Harold*, Byron neglected his "senatorial duties" after his maiden speech at the end of February. He attended the House only twice in March and three times in April.[n] But the deprecating manner in which he spoke of his Parliamentary career in later years requires some qualification. He said that to "grow a parliament man," as he had been advised by Dr. Drury and various friends, "it never was my turn of inclination to try. I spoke once or twice as all young peers do. . . . but just after . . . my poem of *C^e H^d* was published, and nobody ever thought about my *prose* afterwards: nor indeed did I; it became to me a secondary and neglected object, though I sometimes wonder to myself *if* I should have succeeded?"[1]

The personal enthusiasm of some of his new-found friends in and out of Parliament, together with the flattering praise and apparent success that greeted his first speech, kept Byron for a time interested in cutting a figure in politics. But his whole conception of political life was that of the classical orator with independent liberal or radical views whose voice would carry, by its rhetoric and good sense, its persuasive and reasoned eloquence, over the heads of the House to sway the nation as a whole.[2] Yet he had an aristocratic distaste for rabble-rousers. And, although he was "born for opposition,"[n] he had no stomach for active cooperation with any of the Whig leaders in Parliament; nor could he compromise or exercise the caution which even the most radical of those who espoused popular causes had learned.[3] Moreover, only an issue that he considered worthy of his powers could stir him to action.

The first opportunity that presented itself after the debate over

[1] *LJ*, V, 415. Byron actually spoke only three times: Feb. 27, 1812, on the Frame-breaking Bill; April 21, 1812, on the Catholic Claims Bill; and June 1, 1813, presenting Cartwright's plea for freedom of petition.

[2] Byron devoted several pages of his "Detached Thoughts" to a consideration of the speeches and speakers in the two houses. He concluded: "Neither house ever struck me with more awe or respect than the same number of Turks in a Divan, or of Methodists in a barn would have done. Whatever diffidence or nervousness I felt (and I felt both in a great degree) arose from the number rather than the quality of the assemblage, and the thought rather of the *public without* than the persons within. . . ." (*LJ*, V, 416.)

[3] As has been seen, Byron's deference to the opinions of Lord Holland did not carry into his speeches in the House, though he did generally vote with the Opposition. The disunity within the Whig ranks and the wide variety of opinions that prevented any concerted action by the Opposition did offer a justification for Byron's reluctance to ally himself with any one faction.

the Frame Bill was that on the perennial Catholic question. When the Earl of Donoughmore presented a motion for a Committee on the Roman Catholic Claims, Byron spoke during the debate on April 21. Hobhouse, who "staid up all night at the House of Lords," recorded in his diary: "heard Byron—who kept the House in a roar of laughter—Ld. Grenville the best." [n] Whether the lords were laughing with or at Byron, Hobhouse does not say, but it is probable that the mirth was caused by the homeliness of Byron's irony in the story of the drummer assigned to administer a flogging to a friend who requested him to flog high, then low, and then in the middle. The patient continued his complaints "until the drummer, exhausted and angry, flung down his scourge, exclaiming, 'The devil burn you, there's no pleasing you, flog where one will!' Thus it is, you have flogged the Catholic high, low, here, there, and every where, and then you wonder he is not pleased." [n] And again, when he called the Union with Ireland that of "the shark with his prey; the spoiler swallows up his victim, and thus they become one and indivisible," [n] there may have been merriment, at least from one side of the House.

But the Tory benches must have been hot and silent when at the end of his speech Byron added an ironic tribute to the esteem in which His Majesty's ministers were held. And one can almost see Lord Eldon's gorge rise as Byron concluded with the brash suggestion that Napoleon himself would be most grateful for the ministerial defeat of Catholic emancipation: "It is on the basis of your tyranny Napoleon hopes to build his own." [n]

On the whole, the speech was more provocative and defiant, though less rhetorically balanced, than his defense of the framebreakers. If the peers listened more carefully and politely to the author of *Childe Harold* at the height of his popularity than they had to the nervous, unknown young lord making his maiden speech a few weeks before, the speech itself left no marked impression. It was on a subject upon which prejudices were too firmly fixed, and many, even of his Whig confreres, felt that its tone was not suited to the House of Lords. When a vote came on the question (July 1), the strength on the two sides of the House was so equal (the motion was finally defeated by one vote) that

Byron was "sent for in great haste to a Ball, which I quitted, I confess, somewhat reluctantly, to emancipate five Millions of people." [n] By then his interest in Parliament had subsided.

Had he been more successful, or had he received more applause and encouragement, it is probable that not even the dissipations of social life would have kept him from continuing his efforts in Parliament. His flagging interests were rekindled later when he met that dynamic inspirer of the Radicals, Lady Oxford, but in the meantime he plunged into the compensating flatteries being offered him in full measure by Whig society. There was balm enough to his self-esteem in the reception given to *Childe Harold.* When even his old enemy the *Edinburgh Review* praised the poem (the review came out about May 1), Byron repented of his harsh criticism of Jeffrey and wrote to apologize for his unfair attack in *English Bards and Scotch Reviewers.* Jeffrey's reply was altogether gracious and conciliatory, and his concluding sentence hinted broadly that Byron had been mistaken about the authorship of the review of his early poems. "It will give me great pleasure," Jeffrey wrote, "to have the honor of being made known to your Lordship—and perhaps I may at some future time disclose some particulars in our Reviewing history which may convince you that your resentment has hitherto been misdirected." [n]

Even more pleasing, though sometimes embarrassing, were the tributes of admirers, often unknown and most frequently feminine, that came in every post after the fame of *Childe Harold* had begun to spread widely. Some of them wanted to convert him from skepticism. Often the ladies wanted to meet him or asked him to criticize their verses.[n] By far the most shamelessly infatuated of the ladies who wrote to him in the first months of his fame was Christina, Lady Falkland, widow of his friend Lord Falkland, who had been killed in a duel before Byron went abroad. She had never forgotten Byron's kindness in leaving £500 in a teacup for her when he found she was destitute. Early in 1812 she had written to reproach him for not answering her letters.

But when *Childe Harold* finally reached her in Derby, she lost her balance entirely and supposed that all the love passages in it referred to her. On June 12 she wrote: "Surely I cannot be mistaken! Byron, my adored Byron, come to me. I shall feel each hour an age until you are pressed to a heart as ardent and warm as your own. . . . Tell me, my Byron, if those mournful tender effusions of your heart to that Thyrza . . . were not intended for myself?" She joyfully accepted his hand before it was offered, "but remember I must be loved *exclusively*—your *heart* must be *all my own*." A lock of her hair was her "pledge of lasting love and amity." [n]

On July 13, having received no reply, she wrote again to say that she knew his silence reflected his nobleness of soul. "I have again read your Romaunt, and feel more than ever convinced that in Greece, Cadiz, Florence, etc. I may trace myself—in Athens—Falkland your old ally—in the 'Maid of Athens' your own Christina. . . . You believe that my affections are buried with Falkland in the tomb. Banish all apprehension on that account —I had long ceased to respect or esteem him. It is not a loveless heart I offer you, but a heart whose every throb beats responsive to your own." [n] Byron finally in desperation asked his agent Hanson to turn over her letters to a Mr. Corbett, "relative to a foolish woman whom I never saw, who fancies I wish to marry her." But when Corbett told her that Byron would neither read nor answer her letters, she still persisted: "Why, my adored boy, don't you return my affection as you did? . . . Pray do tell me, George," etc.[n] Was ever a poet so plagued?

Though never completely at ease in society, Byron gave himself up to the fashionable world that was wooing him. Induced by the urge to find his place in the aristocratic world, by innate politeness, and by the gratifications of flattering attention, to accept invitations to more dinners than he could eat (for he had to diet constantly to keep his figure), he found it a strain.

Among the new friends Byron made during the first weeks of his fame were two women of beauty, influence, and dominant personality. One was Lady Jersey, whom he had seen at Caroline Lamb's waltzing party on the day he first caught a glimpse of the modest Miss Milbanke. After her marriage to the fifth Earl of Jersey in 1804, she became the reigning beauty and wit of the most select London society. As a leading patroness of the fashionable balls at Almack's, the most exclusive social center of the

West End, she had tremendous power as arbiter of taste and manners. Byron called her, without rancor (for she stuck by him at a trying time), "the veriest tyrant that ever governed fashion's fools, and compelled them to shake their caps and bells as she wills it." [n] Nothing daunted her. She dared to refuse admittance at Almack's to the Duke of Wellington when he came late, and to return as cold a stare as she received from the Prince of Wales when he cut her for taking up the cause of his wife. Byron was soon a favorite at the tremendous parties given by Lady Jersey.

The other woman with whom he formed a curious and lasting friendship at this time was Elizabeth, Lady Melbourne, mother of Caroline Lamb's easygoing husband. Byron must have met her soon after he began to frequent Melbourne House in late March 1812, but their friendship did not ripen into intimacy until sometime during the summer when she emerged from the fracas over her daughter-in-law as his most trusted confidante. Still attractive at sixty-two, she had been a dark beauty when she married Sir Peniston Lamb in 1769. It must have been a relief for Byron, after a stormy session with Caroline Lamb, to sit and talk in the relaxed atmosphere that always surrounded Lady Melbourne. She was a man's woman: even-tempered and reasonable, pleasantly feminine and even voluptuous, but with a positive distaste for the caprices of pretty women. Tactful and sympathetic, she was never shocked and was never likely to make a scene. She was generally more understanding and tolerant of the frailties of both men and women than was common even in Whig society.

The feminine qualities of Lady Melbourne appealed most to Byron, while her masculine understanding made it unnecessary for him to play a romantic role in her presence. The feminine traits in Byron's own nature made him the more responsive to the balanced gentleness and sophistication that made her a delightful companion and confidante, mistress of herself and of every situation. He perhaps appreciated her the more for the contrast she formed with his own mother in understanding and temper.

Yet the pleasure of the association was that she aroused something more than a mere filial fondness in him. Byron told Lady Blessington: "Lady M[elbourne], who might have been my mother, excited an interest in my feelings that few young women have been able to awaken. She was a charming person—a sort of modern Aspasia. . . . I have often thought, that, with a little more youth, Lady M—— might have turned my head. . . ." [n]

Yet this was a strange friendship between Lady Melbourne and the lover of her son's wife. Though she was governed by good sense and genuine liking for the handsome poet, no doubt her motives were mixed. She could not have been insensible to the compliment in the fact that the most sought-after literary man of London preferred her company to that of younger women with less-faded charms. And she knew that her methods were much more likely to be effective than Lady Bessborough's in drawing him away from Caroline.

That affair had reached hectic heights early in May, and Byron realized that he must get away somehow, but he had not the strength to do it. He told Medwin: "I am easily governed by women, and she [Caroline] gained an ascendency over me that I could not easily shake off. I submitted to this thraldom long, for I hate *scenes,* and am of an indolent disposition. . . ." [n]

Byron tried to be rational for Caroline's sake as well as his own, but it seemed to do little good. He wrote her sage advice, knowing that it was futile: "M.[oore] is in great distress about us, and indeed people talk as if there were no other pair of absurdities in London. It is hard to bear all this without cause, but worse to give cause for it. Our folly has had the effect of a fault. I conformed and could conform, if you would lend your aid, but I can't bear to see you look unhappy, and am always on the watch to observe if you are trying to make me so. We must make an effort. This dream, this delirium of two months must pass away. . . ." [n]

While Byron was in the thick of emotional crises, he took time out to attend a public execution. A deranged trader named Bellingham, fancying himself wronged by the Ministry, shot and killed Spencer Perceval, the Prime Minister, in the lobby of the House of Commons on May 11. He was rushed through trial and hanged before Newgate on the 18th. Drawn by the same curiosity that had taken him to the bullfight in Spain (the element of grossness that also attracted him to boxing-matches),

Byron had rented a window from which to view the hanging. He was accompanied by Hobhouse's friend "Long Baillie" and a Mr. John Madocks. They arrived at three o'clock in the morning from some assembly, and while Madocks roused the inmates, Byron and Baillie wandered on. "Seeing an unfortunate woman lying on the steps of a door," Moore records, "Lord Byron, with some expression of compassion, offered her a few shillings; but, instead of accepting them, she violently pushed away his hand, and starting up with a yell of laughter, began to mimic the lameness of his gait. He did not utter a word, but 'I could feel,' said Mr. Bailey [*sic*], 'his arm trembling within mine, as we left her.' "[4]

Two days later Byron wrote to Moore: "On Monday, after sitting up all night, I saw Bellingham launched into eternity, and at three the same day I saw *** [Caroline Lamb?] launched into the country." He was already planning to go down to Newstead on June 1, taking with him Hobhouse, "who is endeavouring, like you and every body else, to keep me out of scrapes."[n] Hobhouse, whom Sir Harold Nicolson has aptly called "the balance wheel in Byron's life," was already concerned about the danger to Byron's reputation in the affair with Caroline, for he knew more than most of Byron's other intimates how far things had gone and what danger there was of an elopement.

In his rapid social flight Byron had not left Hobhouse behind, but saw to it that his friend got invitations to most of the great houses where he himself was welcomed. On April 11 they were at a dinner at Lord Glenbervie's when they met among other guests Benjamin Constant, the former lover of Mme de Staël, who, Hobhouse observed, "cut butter with a spoon—from excess of delicacy."[n] Byron told Medwin later with a mingling of contempt and pride: "I received every where a marked attention, was courted in all societies, made much of by Lady Jersey, had

[4] Moore, I, 357n. Moore adds another anecdote illustrating Byron's recurring sensitiveness to his lameness. As he and Rogers were coming from a ball, one of the link-boys ran before Byron crying: "This way, my Lord." "He seems to know you," Rogers said. " 'Know me!' answered Lord Byron, with some degree of bitterness in his tone—'every one knows me,—I am deformed.' "

the *entré* at Devonshire-house, was in favour with Brummel, (and that was alone enough to make a man of fashion at that time;) in fact, I was a lion—a ball-room bard—a *hot pressed* darling!"[5]

Byron and Hobhouse, accompanied by Captain George Byron, heir to the title, left for Newstead on June 4.[n] But Byron could not so easily escape from Caroline Lamb. On June 10, Hobhouse noted, "a page come from Lady C. L. with letters for Byron —dreadful body."[n] A pathetic entry in Hobhouse's diary on the 12th, the day they left, indicates the amusements at Newstead: "This whole week passed in a delirium of sensuality—house maid at N."[6] Poor Hobhouse, awkward and ill at ease in the presence of women, with the constant example of Byron's triumphant libertinism before him, had had up to this point no memories more satisfactory than his fumbling attempt to make love to Marianna Macri in Athens.

Byron returned to London on June 13. In his absence he had been elected to membership in the London Hampden Club, a Reform club originally composed of liberal aristocrats like the Duke of Norfolk and the Earl of Oxford, but now filled with a conglomeration of strange bedfellows. Byron may have been recommended by Sir Francis Burdett, the wealthy Radical, who had taken an interest in him since his first speech. Byron felt ill at ease almost immediately in the dissentient ranks of the reformers. He wrote Hobhouse later: "I am and have been for *reform* always, but not for the *reformers*. I saw enough of them at the Hampden Club. . . ."[n]

Nevertheless, he found some congenial spirits among the members. One of the most active recruiters for the club was Lady Oxford. Just when Byron first met her is not clear, but

[5] Medwin, II, 63. Byron's tailors' and jewelers' bills in 1812 are an index to his aspirations to dandyism. On June 20 he bought "12 Fine white Quilting Waistcoats"; on July 1 "A spfine [superfine] Olive Court dress Coat lined Completely thro wh White Silk, 20 Elegantly Cut & Highly polished Steele buttons, A very rich Embroidered Court dress Waistcoat, [and] A pair rich black Silk Breeches." In August and September he added dozens of other items, bringing the total bill on September 18 to £243. 10*s*.

[6] This seems to indicate that Byron had not dismissed all the attractive house maids at Newstead when he sent Susan Vaughan away.

by mid-June he and Hobhouse were both attending her balls and parties. The beautiful and learned Jane Elizabeth Scott, Countess of Oxford, was a rector's daughter brought up in the rosy glow of French Revolutionary thought, whose ardor for popular and radical causes was equaled only by her love for handsome men who by inclination or conversion were devoted to the same causes. Married in 1794, when she was twenty-two, to Edward Harley, fifth Earl of Oxford and Mortimer, she soon tired of the novelty of being a great lady and devoted herself to reform movements and movers. Her first enthusiasm when the Earl, who had absorbed radical ideas in his college days, had subsided into a mild politician and a milder husband, was the champion of the people, Sir Francis Burdett. Nurtured on the freethinking materialism of Horne Tooke, she was completely emancipated from conventional ideas, and indulged in the satisfaction of her instincts with the readiness that was common among the English aristocracy, but with greater nonchalance. It was not her actions, but her frank avowal of profligate principles that shocked her contemporaries. The Princess of Wales, of whom in 1812 she was a bosom friend, told Lady Glenbervie that "Lady Oxford had acknowledged to her that she had granted the last favours to Sir Francis Burdett." The Princess excused her by saying that Lord Oxford was to blame "for having gone from home and left his wife so young and beautiful for above a week in a house alone in the country with so handsome and enterprising a man." But when Lady Oxford admitted everything to the Earl, he "immediately said her candour and frank confession were so amiable that he entirely forgave her." [n] It was scarcely necessary for her to get rid of so agreeable and tolerant a husband.

And so Lady Oxford proceeded, acquiring as a by-product of her amours a family of beautiful children of uncertain paternity, who were commonly referred to as the Harleian Miscellany (after the publication in 1808 of some manuscripts in the library of Lord Oxford under that title). When Byron met her, Lady Oxford was already tiring of her latest lover, Lord Archibald Hamilton, a Reform Whig M.P., attractive but deaf. She could not have failed to notice the handsome features of the young lord who was then the idol of society. But quite apart from her personal interest was the fact that he was just beginning his career in Parliament, and that he had liberal sympathies.[n]

Soon Hobhouse was also attending Lady Oxford's parties, no doubt drawn into the circle by Byron. On June 24 he wrote in his diary: "Dined at Lord Oxford's, met Sir F. Burdett, Rogers, Monk Lewis, etc. Lady Jane Harley [Lady Oxford's daughter] a delightful creature, but *un peu libre*. . . . Lady Oxford most uncommon in her talk, and licentious—uncommonly civil; made a push to get me into the Hampden Club."[7] But Hobhouse declined the honor. Byron, though he also wished to keep his independence in politics, was more easily swayed by personal considerations and friendships. It is doubtful, however, that, absorbed as he was in his intrigue with Caroline Lamb (she was back in town and the affair had flamed up more disturbingly than before), he gave much attention at this time to the "autumnal charms" of Lady Oxford, who, though still attractive, was sixteen years his senior.

It is possible that Byron had already met the Princess of Wales through one of his many friends who were in her most intimate good graces: Samuel Rogers; Ward (who was reputed to be on terms of suspicious intimacy with the Princess, for she was quite indiscreet); Sir William Drummond, the "professed atheist"; or Lady Oxford, who was a constant visitor at Kensington Palace. In any event, he shared the general Whig sympathy for Princess Caroline, whose cause furnished a focus for the opposition to the Prince Regent.

But when the opportunity presented itself for him to meet the Prince, Byron seized it as eagerly as any Tory. In the last week of June he went to a party at Miss Johnson's, where the Prince, informed of the presence of the author of *Childe Harold*, expressed a desire to see him. Byron was presented to him, and all his embarrassment disappeared immediately, for the Prince's

[7] Broughton, I, 41. On June 27 Hobhouse wrote in his diary: ". . . I should certainly be in love with one of the miscellany if I had £5,000 a year—life might then be a little tolerable. . . ." (Ibid., I, 41–2.) His growing interest in Lady Oxford's amazing daughter is reflected in his diary. On July 23 he wrote: "Lady J. Harley told me she could say all Shakespeare by heart—she is a most surprising girl, and is a good instance of the flexibility of female abilities." (Ibid., I, 45.)

gracious references to Byron's poem as well as his general knowledge of literature broke down the poet's reserve. They conversed for more than half an hour.[n]

Nevertheless, Byron felt constrained to write defensively and lightly of the interview to Lord Holland, for he could not allow his Whig friends to suppose that he had capitulated to the enemy: "The other night, at a ball, I was presented by order to our gracious Regent, who honoured me with some conversation, and professed a predilection for poetry. . . .[8] I have now great hope, in the event of Mr. Pye's decease, of 'warbling truth at court.'. . . Consider, one hundred marks a year! besides the wine and the disgrace. . . ."[9]

But Byron wrote in quite a different tone to Sir Walter Scott. Seizing the Prince's high praise of Scott as an opportunity to apologize and atone for his fractious remarks in *English Bards*,[1] Byron rushed off to John Murray to have him relay the Prince's conversation to Scott. After receiving a gratifying letter from Scott, Byron gave more details of the interview: ". . . I told him I thought you more particularly the poet of *Princes*, as *they* never appeared more fascinating than in *Marmion* and the *Lady of the Lake*. He was pleased to coincide. . . . He spoke alternately of Homer and yourself, and seemed well acquainted with both. . . ."[n] Byron was so carried away by his flattering conversation that he was all ready to go to the Prince's next levee, when the last-moment postponement of it prevented an action that would have been difficult to explain to many of his friends in the Opposition.[n] Soon distracted by other interests and associations, he never again sought to attend a levee. Before long he was calling frequently on the Prince's wife and bitterest enemy, Princess Caroline.

At the invitation of Henry Drury, Byron had gone to Harrow

[8] Byron probably refers to a phrase in the Prince's letter of Feb. 13, 1812, to the Duke of York which precipitated the scene at Carlton House that inspired Byron's lines to Princess Charlotte: "I have no predilections to indulge, no resentments to gratify."

[9] *LJ*, II, 125–9. Letter of June 25, 1812. Part of the Poet Laureate's stipend was traditionally a butt of wine.

[1] Byron had accused Scott of being among those "Who rack their brains for lucre, not for fame." (Line 178.)

for Speech Day. He had not been there since the publication of *Childe Harold,* and no doubt enjoyed the renown which it brought him at his old school. Henry Long wrote his father on July 3: "Speech day yesterday was well attended. . . . Lord Byron is grown so exceedingly thin that it is not everybody that would recognize him. His hand felt like that of a Skeleton when I shook hands with him." *n*

Caroline Lamb's tantrums had grown worse.[2] Lady Bessborough, ignorant of how far the affair had gone, but genuinely alarmed and upset by the public scandal, finally called Hobhouse into consultation and asked him to request Byron to leave town. Hobhouse's diary in late June and July is full of references to the agonizing affair, which was rapidly approaching a crisis. On the 7th he recorded: "went to opera met Lady B & C.L.—wicked wretch." *n* The next day he called on Hanson and "had a full account of Ld B's affairs—find things bad in that quarter & lament my incapacity—poor Newstead." *n* It seemed inevitable that the Abbey must be sold. Byron had put it off as long as possible, and the burden of the decision added to his perplexities.

Hobhouse was with Byron frequently in the days that followed, trying to dissuade him from any rash act and to distract him as much as possible. The crisis that Lady Bessborough had feared came on July 29. Hobhouse recorded the whole dramatic story in his diary:

"Wednesday July 29. Went to Byron's, No. 8 St. James' Street in expectation of going to Harrow, a scheme he had resolved on to avoid the threatened visit of a Lady—at 12 o'clock just as we were going, several thundering raps were heard at the door & we saw a crowd collected about the door & opposite to it—immediately a person in a most strange disguise walked up

[2] Caroline's emotional instability is indicated in this note, undated but no doubt written after one of her scenes: "My dearest Byron There is no cause for alarm—but I have had a wretched night and am still painfully irritable. . . . I am exceedingly grieved I gave you so much uneasiness. I will endeavour by all possible means to avoid a return of anything so painful between us—In justice to myself however I may say that I should not feel this irritation if it were not for my present circumstances. These seem both cause and effect—" (Unpublished letter, Murray MSS.)

stairs—it turned out to be the Lady in question from Brocket—she seeing me ran up the garret stairs on which I went down into Mr. Dollman's shop and ordered a hat. Coming up again to take my hat & stick and go away I did think that to leave my friend in such a situation, when, as Mr. Dollman told me, every soul in the house servants & all knew of the person in disguise, and not to endeavour to prevent the catastrophe of an elopement which seemed inevitable, would be unjustifiable —accordingly I staid in the sitting room whilst the Lady was in the bed room pulling off her disguise—under which she had a page's dress. . . . at last she was prevailed upon to put on a habit, bonnet, & shoes—belonging to a servant of the house and, after much intreaty did come out into the sitting room—in B's presence, I pressed upon her the necessity of instantly leaving the place—she said she would not—then, said B, 'we must go off together, there is no alternative'—Indeed, said I, but there is, you shall not go off this time—the lady said—she would not go off—I continued to urge upon her the absolute necessity of leaving the house—she said—there will be blood spilt—that returned I there will be indeed—unless you go away —To this B assented. It shall be mine then said the Lady. She then began to look quite wild, & to struggle and seeing a court sword lying on the sofa back, made a snatch to get at it but was held back by B. to appease her I went out of the room for five minutes to speak to Mr. Dollman & obtain of him that no violent measures might be taken—but whilst absent I desired Fletcher B's valet to go into the bed room to prevent the possibility of any thing crim[l]. happening, or any thing which might be construed into a possibility of the thing to be dreaded taking place—Returning into the Room—I found her more tranquil. She said she would go away on the condition of seeing B once more before Friday—She was told she should—she should do any thing she pleased if she would be content to go away now—Here was a difficulty she must change her cloathes before she went to her carriage, & this she could not do at B's for fear of being known when she came out of his lodging—after some reflection—I told her she might go in a hackney coach (one had been standing at the door by my orders some time) to my lodgings, where she might put on her own cloathes. . . . She said she would do this if B went with her—I said I cannot consent to let you & B be in my rooms together, such a conduct would not be consistent with what I owe to both of you, to your mother (Lady B) and to myself—she intreated very hard for some time that I would permit her & B to be together in my rooms, but I flatly denied, and B said—indeed it would be wrong to expect it of you—I do not expect it. at last she consented . . . on condition that B might go in the coach with her as far as my lodgings—on this I left the house and went to the bottom of St. James's Street—in a minute or two I saw them (B. & the lady) step into the coach and drive down the street. at that instant, I ran across the Park to my lodgings, and having got my door opened, stood at the corner of the buildings—the hackney coach soon came. I stopt it at the corner before it turned in to the Buildings & desired B to get out, which he did—the hackney coach then drove with the lady to my lodgings—I handed her out, took her up stairs, & showing her my rooms, went away immediately that she might dress herself—desiring her to lock the doors—I went into the street to B whom I found at the corner of the buildings & walked with him to Bailly's coffee house—where I left him & came back to my lodgings—the lady had dressed herself in her own cloathes when I came into my sitting room and I immediately began to press the necessity of her getting to her carriage or to some friends—In a short time a note came to her from B inclosed to me, it stated he wished to see her before she left London. She wrote an answer, which she gave to me. . . . at last she settled to go to a Mrs Conyer's No 5, Grosvenor Gate—a friend of hers, and begged I would go with her—to this I consented & she left my lodgings in a hackney coach with me. . . . she was very much affected—Before I went she made me promise I would not prevent B from meeting her once before she left London—she mentioned Barnet or Highgate on her way back, and I knowing that all apparent opposition would only make her as extravagant as before, & cause a scene, consented to speak to him on the subject—god knows that from the very beginning I have done my best to keep my friend out of the scrape—My first wish was that he should give this lady, who by the common consent of all London has made a dead set at him, no power over him by consenting to any serious folly, and when I knew that every thing had past between them, my next desire was to prevent a public disclosure and an elopement—This latter event would, as B assured me and assures me, have certainly taken place but for the part I played in the transactions of yesterday, which I have here noted down twenty four hours only after they took place . . . . at the time Lady B first begged me to interfere, I knew interference was too late, except to prevent an elopement, but this I could not tell her—for my friend B had trusted me with the secret, & to him I owed a paramount and prior duty. . . . I did tell her that the fault was more on the side of the woman than the man, and that if she would answer for the forbearance of her daughter I would engage for the prudence of my friend." [n]

That Byron was, despite the depth of his involvement and his willingness to elope with Caroline, already seeking an escape from the too exigent lady is indicated in a letter he wrote (the very day of the great scene described by Hobhouse) to Miss Mercer Elphinstone, whom he had first met at Melbourne House. She was one of the young ladies casting eyes at Byron when Annabella Milbanke first saw him there. That she was reputed to be a great heiress was no objection to her in Byron's eyes, but what appealed to him more now was her calm good nature, a welcome contrast to the tempestuous Caroline. Miss Elphinstone had asked him, through Mrs. George Lamb, to pay them a visit at Tunbridge Wells.[n]

There is no record that he actually did go down to Tunbridge, but there is little doubt that he wished to go. He was still ruled by Caroline's caprices, however. She was seldom quiet, and no one could predict when she would burst out anew. She could never keep her promises not to see Byron again. There was another and more serious eruption of that "little volcano" on August 12. Lady Bessborough, at last heeding Hobhouse's warning, had gone to Whitehall in the morning to try to persuade Caroline to go with her to her country house at Roehampton, there to be joined two days later by William, who would accompany them to Ireland. "She was in a bad humour," Lady Bessborough told her ex-lover Lord Granville Leveson Gower, "and in the midst Lord Melbourne came in and reproach'd her for some of the strange things she does." Caroline answered rudely, and her mother ran to call Lady Melbourne. When she returned, Caroline was gone. ". . . Lord Melbourne told us she threaten'd him with going to Lord Byron, and he bid her go and be ——, but did not think he would take her. On this she ran down. We went, Lady Melbourne and I, immediately there, but found him as much astonish'd and as much frighten'd when he heard it as we were. He promis'd to restore her if she was to be found, and kept his word." By threatening and bribing the hackney coachman who brought him a message from her, Lady Bessborough continued, Byron "found her at a Surgeon's House in Kensington . . . he pass'd her for his sister, and brought her away almost by force to C. Square, where, I am mortified to say, it was more by his persuasions than mine, and almost reproaches at her bearing to see me suffer so much, that she was induc'd to return with me to White Hall. I went in before her, and William most kindly promis'd to receive and forgive her. The Melbournes, too, were very good, and she seem'd much touch'd by their reception. But how long will it last?"

Lady Bessborough was completely shaken. She feared that she could never get Caroline to go to Ireland, and she dreaded the public scandal, "for it was noon day, and she ran all up Pall Mall, conceal'd herself in a chemist's shop till she thought pursuit was over, sold a ring by which she got money to pay the Hackney Coach. . . ." [n] Even after her mother had broken a blood vessel and she had been frightened into promising to go with her on the Irish voyage,[n] Caroline tried several times to postpone the day of leaving. She believed (or persuaded herself) that she was going to have a child, and pleaded that the voyage would cause her to miscarry.[n]

Byron was relieved when she finally set out with her husband and mother for Ireland early in September. But sometime before she left, the lovers had a final meeting at which Byron shed tears at parting from her. His farewell letter, which she treasured to the end of her days,[3] is an artful mixture of gallantry and self-denial admirably suited to satisfy her sense of what the dramatic situation demanded. She was not wrong in believing that this letter was ample evidence that he was in love with her, but what she could not have understood is that at the same time he was glad to be rid of her. The very fact that she was departing made it easier for him to avow sentiments which, if he no longer felt them quite completely, he *had* felt.

"My dearest Caroline,—If tears which you saw and know I am not apt to shed,—if the agitation in which I parted from you,—agitation which you must have perceived through the *whole* of this most *nervous* affair, did not commence until the moment of leaving you approached,—if all I have said and done, and am still but too ready to say and do, have not sufficiently proved what my real feelings are, and must ever be towards you, my love, I have no other proof to offer. . . . I am about to go out with a heavy heart, because my appearing this evening will stop any absurd story which the event of the day might give rise to. Do you think *now* I am *cold* and *stern* and *artful*? . . . 'Promise not to love you!' ah, Caroline, it is past promising." And he added a postscript: "You know I would with pleasure give up all here and all beyond the grave for you, and in refraining from this, must my motives be misunderstood? I care not who knows this, what use is made of it. . . . I was and am yours freely and most entirely, to obey, to honour,

[3] This was the letter that Caroline used to convince Medwin that Byron had truly loved her. She wrote: "I have had one of his letters copied in the stone press for you; one just before we parted." (*LJ*, II, 452.) Ethel Mayne questioned the authenticity of this letter (*Byron*, pp. 159–60), but I have one of the facsimiles, of which she made a considerable number to distribute to friends (there are a dozen at John Murray's), and the handwriting in unquestionably Byron's, as comparison with other genuine letters and her own forgery of Byron's hand (facsimile in *LBC*, I, 130–1) will show. That Byron recognized his responsibility in the affair is indicated in an undated letter to Lady Melbourne. (A reference to "auctioneers" suggests that it was written on August 14, the day Newstead Abbey was brought up for auction.) ". . . she never did nor can deserve a single reproach which must not fall with double justice & truth upon myself—who am much much more to blame in every respect—nor shall I in the least hesitate in declaring this to any of her family who may think proper to come forward." (*LBC*, II, 303.)

love,—and fly with you when, where, and how you yourself *might* and *may* determine." [4]

There is little reason to doubt the sincerity of Byron's statement of his feelings at the moment. Once Caroline was gone, however, the reaction set in, but he continued to write to her for some time, partly because he knew she expected it, and, as he tried to assure Lady Melbourne, partly because he wanted to pacify the rash girl and prevent further hysterics.

Before they left for Ireland, Lady Bessborough learned from the Prince Regent how widely the affair had been talked about and how ridiculous they had all appeared. The Prince told her that "Ld. Mel: had been with him very much out of humour complaining that she [Caroline] drove him mad, & *we* were almost as bad, that Ld. Byr. had bewitch'd the whole family Mothers & daughter & all & that nothing would satisfy us but making a fool of him as well as of ourselves, & insisting on his asking Ld. Byn. to his house. The P. said all this so rapidly & so loudly (?), interrupting himself now & then to exclaim, 'I never heard of such a thing in my life—taking the Mothers for confidantes! What would you have thought of my going to talk to Ly. Spencer [Lady Bessborough's mother—her sister Georgiana had been intimate with the Regent] in former times!'—that in spite of the subject & the circle I was near laughing." [n]

Byron never thought very highly of Caroline's mother; later he called her "Lady Blarney." But the Prince was right in believing that Byron had made a confidante of Lady Melbourne. In the correspondence with her that followed, Byron revealed with an amazing frankness the interplay of his emotions and his ego touching Caroline and other women with whom he became intimate. Although he found her an excellent sounding-board for the conception of himself as the cynical man of the world which he had already built up for her, there was an area of his mind that he never let her see. He could not bear to submit to the

[4] *LJ*, II, 135–9. The letter is undated, but the statement, "my appearing this evening will stop any absurd story which the event of the day might give rise to," suggests that it may have been August 12, the day Caroline ran away and Byron found and returned her to Lady Bessborough.

scrutiny of her sharp intellect the softer sentiments that generally found release only in his poetry.

Before Byron left London for Cheltenham following the departure of Caroline and her mother, Newstead had at last been sold. The whole estate, 3,200 acres, including the Abbey and its park and all the farms, had been advertised for sale by auction by Mr. Farebrother at Garraway's Coffee House, 'Change Alley, Cornhill, on August 14. But Byron, on Hanson's advice, accepted none of the bids,[5] and the next day Thomas Claughton of Haydock Lodge near Warrington in Lancashire offered £140,000 for the whole property including the timber and furniture.[n] Within a few days Claughton's offer was accepted. The original conditions of sale called for an immediate deposit of twenty per cent of the purchase price, and for the forfeiture of the deposit if the purchaser defaulted in further payments according to the contract. The final agreement was to accept £25,000 as a deposit and to allow £60,000 to remain in an interest-paying mortgage on the estate for three years. The rest was to be paid on December 25.[n] It was soon evident, however, that Claughton had repented of his bargain shortly after he had made it. By questioning the deeds and by various other ruses he postponed as long as possible, first the payment of the deposit, and then subsequent payments. Byron's correspondence with Hanson through the autumn is full of remonstrances concerning Claughton's dilatoriness.

After the first agreement was reached, Byron left London, which was then dull and empty. By August 24 he had alighted at the "sordid inn" at Cheltenham, where he went partly to take the waters (he still suffered from the kidney trouble that had racked him earlier in the year)[6] and partly to be near

[5] Byron had sent Hobhouse to run up the bidding. After bidding twelve times, he left off at 113,000 guineas for the large lot, which he said was bought in for 113,500 guineas, Byron having set £120,000 as a minimum price. The second lot (the forest farms) was bought in at 13,100 guineas. Hobhouse wrote: "Never having done the like before, I was, before the thing began, in a complete fever, but was told by Hanson . . . that I came off most admirably. I had just then only one pound one shilling and sixpence in the world." (Broughton, I, 45.)

[6] Byron's alternate severe dieting and drinking and feasting had already undermined his health. A medical report dated Oct. 15, 1812, among the

the Jerseys, Melbournes, Hollands, and others of his London friends. After his strenuous spring and summer, he was glad of a little quiet company and relaxed ease. At the end of September he wrote to William Bankes: "In a few days I set out for Lord Jersey's, but return here, where I am quite alone, go out very little, and enjoy in its fullest extent the *dolce far niente.*" [n]

He was not as unoccupied as he would have had Bankes believe. Before he was fairly settled at Cheltenham, Lord Holland, who was on a special committee for Drury Lane Theatre, shortly to be opened in a new building constructed after the destruction of the old one by fire in 1809, called on him to enter the contest for an Address to be read on the opening night. He declined "contending against all Grub Street," [n] and cast into the fire the few lines he had at first essayed, because, he told Lady Melbourne candidly: "I never risk *rivalry* in anything. . . ." [n]

But when the committee found none of the contributions to the contest suitable or worthy, Lord Holland called on Byron to write the Address, which he then consented to do to please his friend, though he knew that such made-to-order poetry was not at all his forte. But he labored infinitely over it, sending correction after correction until the last minute. And through it all he had the greatest uneasiness over the probable reaction among the rejected authors and the critics. He was still in Cheltenham when on Saturday, October 10, Drury Lane reopened with two plays, *The Devil to Pay* and *Hamlet.* Byron's 73-line Address was read by Elliston, one of the most popular actors of the day. As Byron perused the papers, he was relieved that the criticism was not so harsh as he had expected, though he was a little irked that his friend Perry, fellow member of the Hampden Club and editor of the *Morning Chronicle,* had been so brutally frank, pronouncing it "in parts unmusical, and in general tame." [n] But Byron was willing to write off the experience as an act of friendship to Lord Holland. "My own opinion upon it is what it always was, perhaps pretty near that of the public." [n]

---

Byron papers at John Murray's recommends a more nutritious diet and the regular use of animal food.

His greatest relief at Cheltenham was the feeling that he had escaped from the harrowing emotions and humiliations of his liaison with Caroline Lamb. He realized now that he wanted more than anything else to be through with the whole business. To Lady Melbourne he wrote: ". . . you will not regret to hear, that I wish this to end, and it certainly shall not be renewed on my part. It is not that I love another, but loving at all is quite out of my way; I am tired of being a fool. . . . It is true from early habit, one must make love mechanically, as one swims. I was once very fond of both, but now as I never swim, unless I tumble into the water, I don't make love till almost obliged. . . ."[n]

Lady Melbourne realized that breaking away would not be easy, for she knew her daughter-in-law. Caroline had arrived in Ireland by no means tamed and in no mood to give Byron up. She wrote constantly, and was determined not to let her lover forget her. At one time she tried to arouse his sympathy for her forlorn state, at another his jealousy by telling him what a gay time she was having. And she reminded him that "eight guineas, a mail, and a packet could soon bring her to London."[n] Byron did not like to confess to Lady Melbourne just how strong a hold Caroline still had on him, though he had deliberately decided to break it.

Poor Lady Bessborough, not knowing how the land lay, wrote to ask Lady Melbourne not to lose her hold on Byron. His confidante sent the letter on to him, and Byron replied: "Pray don't, *I* repeat, and assure you it is a very firm one. . . ." Now, indeed, he needed Lady Melbourne's help, not only to dispose of the troublesome Caroline, but to explore the ground in another field. Only three days after he had declared that he did not love another, he confessed to his startled confidante: "I was, am, and shall be, I fear, attached to another, one to whom I never said much, but have never lost sight of, and the whole of this interlude has been the result of circumstances which it may be too late to regret." In saying that he cared for no other, he had, he admitted, deceived her and himself, for "there was, and is one whom I wished to marry, had not this affair intervened, or had not some occurrences rather discouraged me. . . . The woman I mean is Miss Milbanke. . . . I know little of her, and have not the most distant reason to suppose that I am at all a favourite in that quarter. But I never saw a woman whom I *esteemed* so much."[7]

It did not require Byron's additional flattering submission, "Now, my dear Lady M., I am completely in your power," to make her take the bait as Byron supposed she would. Here was an opportunity to settle the Caroline affair with finality and to get Byron settled. As soon as she could be sure that Byron was serious in his proposal, she would sound out her niece, though she had some grave doubts as to whether that model of the virtues could cope with the vagaries of Byron's temperament. His reply to her query must not have been very reassuring: "You ask, 'Am I sure of myself?' and I answer no, but *you* are, which I take to be a much better thing. Miss M[ilbanke] I admire because she is a clever woman, an amiable woman, and of high blood, for I have still a few Norman and Scotch inherited prejudices on the last score, were I to marry. As to *love,* that is done in a week (provided the lady has a reasonable share); besides, marriage goes on better with esteem and confidence than romance, and she is quite pretty enough to be loved by her husband, without being so glaringly beautiful as to attract too many rivals. She always reminds me of 'Emma' in the modern Griselda, and whomever I *may* marry, that is the woman I would wish to *have married.*"[n] A proposal in that form was not what Annabella might have hoped for, but Lady Melbourne would sweeten it before it reached her.

Byron was now in more of a quandary than ever with regard to the lady in Ireland. He could not quite admit to Lady Melbourne the whole of his complicated feeling for Caroline. He wanted to be rid of her, and yet he could not wrench her out of his life and thoughts so easily, and the tone of his

[7] *LBC*, I, 73–5. Letter of Sept. 13, 1812. To make it clear to Lady Melbourne that he was not merely seeking a money match, Byron told his confidante: ". . . I know nothing of her fortune, and I am told that her father is ruined, but my own will, when my Rochdale arrangements are closed, be sufficient for both. My debts are not £25,000, and the deuce is in it, if with R[ochdale] and the surplus of N[ewstead], I could not contrive to be as independent as half the peerage."

letters had been such that he did not know how to make a direct break without precipitating a terrible crisis. He was embarrassed when Lady Melbourne discovered how fondly he was still writing to Caroline, who had sent her extracts from his letters. Though he proclaimed that he had put himself in Lady Melbourne's hands, he was reluctant to accept her advice that he write a moderate and friendly letter to Caroline. "But *what* you wished me to write, would be a little too indifferent; and *that* now would be an insult, and I am much [more] unwilling to hurt her feelings now than ever. . . ." [n]

It seemed to him now that the only salvation, the only irrevocable road out of the scrape he had become involved in, was to marry. Certainly that was a line of approach likely to engage Lady Melbourne's best efforts in aid of his suit of Annabella. But he would hedge his proposal about with sufficient props to his self-esteem to ease the blow of a refusal.

"Before I became [become?] candidate for the distinguished honour of nepotism to your Ladyship," he wrote Lady Melbourne, "it will be as well for me to know that your niece is not already disposed of to a better bidder; if not, I should like it of all things, were it only for the pleasure of calling you *aunt!* and soliciting your benediction." [n]

A few days later he had lost most of his eagerness to mate with the estimable Miss Milbanke, the present mild enjoyments of Cheltenham, which included a flirtation with an Italian songstress, being more to his taste. "As to Annabella, she requires time and all the cardinal virtues, and in the interim I am a little verging towards one who demands neither, and saves me besides the trouble of marrying, by being married already. She besides does not speak English, and to me nothing but Italian—a great point, for from certain coincidences the very sound of that language is music to me, and she has black eyes, and *not* a very white skin, and reminds me of many in the Archipelago I wished to forget, and makes me forget what I ought to remember, all which are against me. I only wish she did not swallow so much supper . . . a woman should never be seen eating or drinking, unless it be *lobster salad* and *champagne,* the only truly feminine and becoming viands." [n]

After the Hollands had left early in September, Byron had quit the "sordid inn" and moved to their house in Cheltenham, where he reported himself "quiet and alone, without any wish to add to my acquaintances." [n] But he did add a few acquaintances who were agreeable enough without taxing his emotions. By the end of September he was seeing "the Rawdons and the Oxfords and a family named Macleod."

But he was most taken with the Italian opera singer. She was "not very beautiful, but very much in the style I like: dark and lively. . . . She is very fond of her husband, which is all the better, as thus, if a woman is attached to her husband, how much more will she naturally like one who is *not* her husband. . . ."

Lady Melbourne knew how to take such cynical persiflage on Byron's part; it did not put her off the serious business of inquiring into the feelings of her niece. For before he had finished the letter, Byron had broken off with an exclamation: "*At this moment* another *express* from Ireland!!! More scenes!—this woman will never rest till she has made us all what she and I at least deserve." He added: ". . . I see nothing but marriage, and a *speedy one*, can save me. If your niece is obtainable, I should prefer her; if not, the very first woman who does not look as if she would spit in my face, amongst the variety of spouses provided by your *correspondents*, etc."

Annabella was much in his thoughts. The Jerseys had invited him to their country house at Middleton for October 4, and he was hoping that Lady Melbourne would also be there. He called her playfully "mia carissima *Zia*," and added: "I wish my nepotism was well over." But then a disturbing thought struck him. "Does Annabella *waltz?* It is an odd question, but a very essential point with me. I wish somebody could say at once that I wish to propose to her; but I have great doubts of *her*—it rests with herself entirely." [n] A less ardent suitor would be far to seek. The one thing that spurred him on was the fear of Caroline's return. He confessed: "I do not at all know how to deal with her, because she is unlike anyone else. . . . I would marry before they return: this would settle it at once, but I am new to that business, never having made a proposal in my life. . . . I admired your niece but she is engaged to Eden; besides, she deserves a better heart than mine. What shall I do—shall I advertise?"[n]

At this point Lady Melbourne took matters into her own hands. Without telling her niece who the suitor was, she broached the subject by asking Annabella what qualities she would wish in a husband. That was something upon which her niece had thought long and introspectively. She began with a brief analysis of her own "defects of temper": "I am never irritated except when others are so, and then I am too apt to imitate them. This makes good temper in my companions very necessary for my peace. . . . I am never sulky, but my spirits are easily depressed, particularly by seeing anybody unhappy . . . . if I had not acquired the habit of reflecting before I act, I should sometimes have sacrificed considerations of prudence to the impulse of my feelings—but I am not conscious of ever having *yielded* to the temptation which assailed me."

On the back of the same sheet she wrote:

*husband.*

He must have consistent principles of Duty governing strong & *generous* feelings, and reducing them under the command of Reason.

Genius is not in my opinion *necessary,* though desirable, *if united* with what I have just mentioned.

I require a freedom from suspicion, & from *habitual* ill-humour—also an equal tenor of affection towards me, not that violent attachment which is susceptible of sudden encrease or diminution from trifles.

I wish to be considered by my husband as a *reasonable adviser,* not as a guide on whom he could *implicitly* depend.

. . . I would have fortune enough to enable me to continue without embarrassment in the kind of society to which I have been accustomed. I have no inclination to extravagance, and should be content to practise economy for the attainment of this object.

Rank is indifferent to me. *Good connections* I think an important advantage.

I do not regard *beauty,* but am influenced by the *manners of a gentleman,* without which I scarcely think that any one could attract me.

I would not enter into a family where there was a strong tendency to Insanity.

When Lady Melbourne took her to task for being on stilts, she tried to explain herself further. "I should at present occasion disappointment to a husband who expected to find me possessed of constant self-command & composure." That was one reason why she had deferred matrimony, she said. But her aunt was "mistaken in thinking that I meant to dispense with the amiable feelings. . . . So far from supposing that I could be attached by a character of *dry* Reason, and *cold* Rectitude, I am always *repelled* by people of that description." In conclusion she pleaded: "After so full an explanation you will perhaps take off my *stilts,* and allow that I am only *on tiptoe.*"[n]

It was then that Lady Melbourne tried out her principles by forwarding Byron's proposal to her. Even though it was by proxy it startled her, for he was the one man who had really intrigued and interested her, even while her analytical mind dissected and disapproved of him. Before she had forced herself to put him out of her mind following the interview with Caroline Lamb, she had flattered herself that she could quite innocently offer him the "temporary satisfaction" of her friendship. She was with her parents at Richmond when Lady Melbourne's exciting letter arrived. Characteristically, she took several days to deliberate before replying. In the meantime, she sat down on October 8 to write her Character of Lord Byron, which in her chagrin she had put aside some months before:

"The passions have been his guide from childhood, and have exercised a tyrannical power over his very superior intellect. Yet amongst his dispositions are many which deserve to be associated with Christian principles—his love of goodness in its chastest form, and his abhorrence of all that degrades human nature, prove the uncorrupted purity of his moral sense. . . . There is a chivalrous generosity in his ideas of love and friendship, and selfishness is totally absent from his character. In secret he is the zealous friend of all the human feelings; but from the strangest perversion that pride ever created, he endeavours to disguise the best points of his character. . . . So that his mind is continually making the most sudden transitions—from good to evil—from evil to good. . . . He is inclined to open his heart unreservedly to those whom he believes *good,* even without the preparation of much acquaintance. He is extremely humble towards persons whose character he respects, and to them he would probably confess his errors—" [n]

She did not finish the Character. Perhaps she felt it was drawing near to a confession of her own that she feared to make. In her reply, which she wrote on the 12th and asked Lady Melbourne to pass on to Byron, she said she owed it to him to "speak the truth without equivocation": "Believing that he never will be the object of that strong affection which would make me happy in domestic life, I should wrong him by any measure that might, even indirectly, confirm his present impressions. From my limited observations of his conduct, I was predisposed to believe your strong testimony in his favour, and I willingly attribute it more to the defect of my own feelings than of his character than I am not inclined to return his attachment. After this statement which I make with real sorrow from the idea of its giving pain, I must leave our future intercourse to his judgment. I can have no reason for withdrawing from an acquaintance that does me honour and is capable of imparting so much rational pleasure, except the fear of involuntarily deceiving him." [n]

When half the women of London society wore their hearts on their sleeves wherever Byron appeared, and dozens of others who had never seen him were willing to profess their love, Miss Milbanke refused his offer of honorable marriage because she could not feel a sufficiently "strong affection" for him. Nothing could be more intriguing to Byron, though he protested to Lady Melbourne that he was not embarrassed by the refusal and that his heart had not been "much interested in the business." He accepted the refusal good-humoredly, observing: "I am sure we shall be better friends than before. . . . She is perfectly right in every point of view, and during the slight suspense, I felt something very like remorse. . . ." [n] What he regretted most was having lost the opportunity of being Lady Melbourne's nephew. And though he maintained that he was not at all ashamed of his admiration of "the amiable *Mathematician*," he concluded: "I thank you again for your efforts with my Princess of Parallelograms, who has puzzled you more than the

Hypothenuse. . . . Her proceedings are quite rectangular, or rather we are two parallel lines prolonged to infinity side by side, but never to meet." [n]

Byron was now back in Cheltenham after a pleasant week at Middleton with the Jerseys while Lady Melbourne was there. He had invitations from Lord Oxford and Lord Harrowby, and was debating which to accept. In the meantime his business affairs were going badly again. By October 19, Claughton had not yet made the first payment on Newstead, and creditors were pressing harder than ever, having heard that the estate had been sold.[n]

Amid all the suspense and confusion Byron had found time to pen two hundred lines of a satire on waltzing, which he now offered to Murray. Conceived in the prudishness of his libertinism and born in the pangs of the lame watcher on the sidelines of London and provincial balls, the poem had more of bitterness than of humor. Horace Hornem, the country squire and supposed author, seeing his wife at the Countess's ball, to his surprise, "with her arms half round the loins of a huge hussar-looking gentleman I never set eyes on before; and his, to say truth, rather more than half round her waist, turning round, and round, to a d——d see-saw up-and-down sort of tune," broke out in mock pæans to the "Imperial Waltz! imported from the Rhine" that "wakes to Wantonness the willing limbs."

*Waltz—Waltz alone—both legs and arms demands,*
*Liberal of feet, and lavish of her hands;*
*Hands which may freely range in public sight*
*Where ne'er before—but—pray 'put out the light.' . . .*
*Till some might marvel, with the modest Turk,*
*If 'nothing follows all this palming work?'* [8]

It was not the lush realism of the descriptions, however, which made Byron anxious to preserve his anonymity, but the slighting references to the royal family: the mock homage to the graciousness of George III in begetting George IV; ironic turns of phrase

[8] The poem was published anonymously during the spring of 1813, and when Byron found that it was not well received he asked Murray to contradict the report that he was the author.

on "princely paunches" and "the Royal hip." In poetic composition, always an outlet for his strongest emotions, Byron could never exercise ordinary restraint or prudence. But he realized that this was no time to permit such indiscretions to go before the world with his name. Murray had just reported selling in one day to the booksellers 878 copies of the fifth edition of *Childe Harold.*[n] And Byron was gratified that his old enemy *The Satirist* had capitulated to his popularity and praised his new poem "handsomely, after five years' warfare."[n]

Lady Oxford had already cast an appraising eye upon Byron, and was trying to entice him to Eywood, the country home of the Oxfords near Presteign. Her calm and ripened charms appealed to him in contrast to the nervous histrionics of Caroline, who was always trying to arouse his sympathy or his jealousy by relating "*how* many lovers were all sacrificed to this brilliant fit of constancy."[n] Byron now meant, he told Lady Melbourne, "to play off Ldy O[xford] against her, who would have no objection *perchance*, but she dreads her scenes, and has asked me not to mention that we have met, to C., or that I am going to Eywood. . . ."

Lady Melbourne could tell Annabella, he wrote just before setting off for Eywood on the 24th, "that I am more proud of her *rejection* than I can ever be of *another's acceptance*. . . . the *hope* of obtaining *her* . . . was more pleasing than the possession of St. Ursula and the 11,000 virgins (being a greater number than have ever *since* existed at the *same time* in that capacity) could possibly have been. . . ."[n] As to continued acquaintance with her, that must take its chance, "for it never will be anything more, depend upon it, even if she *revoked.* I have still the same opinion, but I never was enamoured; and as I very soon shall be in some other quarter, *Cossi* [*sic*] *finiva.*"[n]

He was soon established at Eywood as a regular cavalier to Lady Oxford, and he found the situation altogether to his taste. Her experience with men had taught her how to charm without being too exigent or demanding. He later told Lady Blessington that his heart once "became captive to a *donna* of forty-six,[9] who certainly excited as lively a passion in my breast as ever

[9] Lady Oxford was actually forty in 1812, and Byron was twenty-four.

it has known; and even now the autumnal charms of Lady —— [Oxford] are remembered by me with more than admiration. She resembled a landscape by Claude Lorraine, with a setting sun, her beauties enhanced by the knowledge that they were shedding their last dying beams, which threw a radiance around. A woman (continued Byron) is only grateful for her *first* and *last* conquest. The first of poor dear Lady ——'s [Oxford's] was achieved before I entered on this world of care, but the *last* I do flatter myself was reserved for me, and a *bonne bouche* it was."[1]

Lady Melbourne, though glad to know that Byron had formed a liaison that would effectively bar any renewal of the affair with Caroline, did not approve of his devotions to Lady Oxford, for Byron might rely on her as confidante as well as lover. Byron noted Lady Melbourne's "*prudential* silence" and urged her to write as usual. "Do you doubt me, in the 'bowers of Armida?' I certainly am very much enchanted, but *your spells* will always retain their full force. Try them."

He had been lulled into false security by an epistle from Ireland "short and full of resignation." He concluded: "I am sick of scenes, and have imbibed a taste for something like *quiet*."[n] But he should have known that it was only the calm before the storm. His telling Caroline that he was "deeply and seriously engaged elsewhere" was hardly likely to leave her in a mood for passive acquiescence.[2]

For Byron it was a delightful situation indeed at the Oxfords': in addition to his charming mistress he had the companionship of her lovely daughters. They were just at the ages that excited

[1] Blessington: *Conversations*, p. 141. Medwin (I, 76–7) quoted Byron as saying: "The autumn of a beauty like her's is preferable to the spring in others. She told me she was never in love till she was thirty; and I thought myself so with her, when she was forty. I never felt a stronger passion; which she returned with equal ardour."

[2] *LBC*, I, 99–100. Letter of Nov. 4, 1812, to Lady Melbourne. Byron told his confidante: "In my last letter I stated that I was *attached*, but to whom, even in allusion, I did not think myself justified in mentioning." After one of her angry and jealous letters Byron had ceased to write to her, and then, according to Caroline, he added these words to a long letter to her mother: "correct yr. vanity which is ridiculous & proverbial, exert yr. Caprices on your new conquests & leave me in peace, yrs. Byron." (Airlie, p. 150.)

his romantic sentiments most profoundly. Lady Charlotte Harley, then eleven, was his favorite. None could have more poignant sentiments of the beauty of youthful innocence than the disillusioned young lord who had known too early and too well the disappointments of love fading into satiety. His tribute to the child exceeded in warmth of idealization anything he ever wrote of her mother. Nothing could be more glowing than the five stanzas to this "Young Peri of the West," under the name of Ianthe, which he prefaced to the seventh edition of *Childe Harold* (1814).

But of course this idyllic life could not last. He was right in his premonition that Lady Bessborough would never forgive him for being the first to make the break. Byron had said that she would expect her daughter "to be adored (like an Irish lease) for a term of 99 years."[n] Now she accused him of being unfair. But who "could act fairly with people who are sending couriers, and threatening to follow them?"[n] Then came a letter from Caroline, "foolish, headstrong, and vainly threatening herself." Her courier had stirred up the house and made his mission obvious. "She has hurt and disgusted me by her latter conduct beyond expression," Byron wrote to Lady Melbourne, "and even if I did not love another, I would never speak to her again while I existed. . . ." Then with utter candor he continued: "I cannot exist without some object of love. I have found one with whom I am perfectly satisfied, and who as far as I can judge is no less so with me. . . . I have engaged myself too far to recede, nor do I regret it."[n]

Finally the storm broke. On November 9, Lady Oxford received a letter from Caroline, "a long *German* tirade," Byron called it, "evidently to discover on what *terms* we were." It contained "a number of *unanswerable* questions," to all of which he persuaded his mistress to give no reply whatever. He was discovering to what lengths a woman scorned will go, and he could agree that hell had no fury equal to Caroline Lamb's caprices exercised to make him pay for his apostasy. He wrote to Lady Melbourne: "I was in doubt whether Ld Oxford (who knew the writer by Ld Bessborough's franks) would not take ye alarm, but we have foiled her there, if that was her intention.

. . . I must pronounce C. to be the most contradictory, absurd, selfish, and contemptibly wicked of human productions." [n]

He could ignore her epistles to himself, but when she had the impertinence to write to Lady Oxford he could not remain silent. The same day he sat down and wrote with curt but devastating restraint: "Lady Caroline—our affections are not in our own power—mine are engaged. I love another—were I inclined to reproach you I might for 20 thousand things, but I will not. They really are not cause of my present conduct—my opinion of you is entirely alter'd, & if I had wanted anything to confirm me, your Levities your caprices & the mean subterfuges you have lately made use of while madly gay—of writing to me as if otherwise, would entirely have open'd my eyes. I am no longer yr. lover—I shall but never be less than your friend—it would be too dishonourable for me to name her to whom I am now entirely devoted & attached." Caroline added that "he put Lady Oxford's seal—one I had myself shewn him & laugh'd with him about, & he dated his letter Presteign." [3]

Caroline later told Lady Morgan that she received Byron's letter at Dublin when they were on their way home. "There was a coronet on the seal. The initials under the coronet were Lady Oxford's. It was that cruel letter I have published in *Glenarvon:* it destroyed me: I lost my brain. I was bled, leeched; kept for a week in the filthy Dolphin Inn, at Rock. On my return, I was in great prostration of mind and spirit." [n]

[3] Airlie, pp. 151–2. This letter, combined with some phrases from an earlier one, is probably the basis of the one which Caroline printed in her novel *Glenarvon* (III, 79–80). Byron told Medwin: "But I am made out a very amiable person in that novel! The only thing belonging to me in it, is part of a letter; but it is mixed up with much fictitious and poetical matter." (Medwin, II, 79.) The letter in *Glenarvon* reads: "I am no longer your lover; and since you oblige me to confess it, by this truly unfeminine persecution,—learn, that I am attached to another; whose name it would of course be dishonourable to mention. I shall ever remember with gratitude the many instances I have received of the predilection you have shewn in my favour. I shall continue your friend, if your ladyship will permit me so to style myself; and, as a first proof of my regard, I offer you this advice, correct your vanity, which is ridiculous; exert your absurd caprices upon others; and leave me in peace." The author of *Glenarvon* adds: "This letter was sealed and directed by Lady Mandeville [Lady Oxford]; but the hand that wrote it was Glenarvon's; and therefore it had its full effect." (*Glenarvon,* III, 80.)

No doubt Caroline was deflated by the letter and dramatized her reaction, but she exaggerated the effects in her account to Lady Morgan, for Byron wrote Lady Melbourne on the 16th: "A letter from Holyhead proves them in England. She is rational and calm, though rather plaintive, and still presses on the point of *seeing* for the purpose of vindication, from I know not what. . . . To cut that short at once, a *promise* has been *requested* and *given,* that I will not on any account consent to such an interview; and this, if possible, I must adhere to." [n]

Byron had already delayed his return to London, where business was pressing, to try to avoid such a meeting. And now Lady Oxford persuaded him to stay a few days longer. In this amiable atmosphere, "reading, laughing, and playing at blindman's-buff with ye *children,*" [n] he felt relieved that marriage with the "Princess of Parallelograms" had not materialized. "I congratulate A[nnabella] and myself on our mutual escape. That would have been but a *cold collation,* and I prefer hot suppers." [n]

Finally on the 21st he left Eywood with regret and returned to Cheltenham. Three days later he was installed at Middleton with the Jerseys, whom he had promised to visit on his way to town. But he could not help contrasting his present abode with the apartment at the Oxfords', where, significantly, "a print of Rinaldo and Armida was one of the most prominent ornaments." [4] Alas, there was no sorceress here in whose arms he could forget the obligations of life. He was glad to report to Hobhouse that "the connection with Lady Caroline Lamb is completely broken off. . . . I am still remote from *marriage,* and presume, whenever that takes place, 'even-handed justice' will return me cuckoldom in abundance." [5]

He arrived at Batt's Hotel in London on November 30 and was immediately beset with business and vexations. Caroline was not inclined to take her dismissal quietly. Not being able to force Byron to meet her otherwise, she was now clamoring for him to

[4] *LBC,* I, 111. Letter of Nov. 26, 1812. Armida was the sorceress in Tasso's *Gerusalemme Liberata* in whose palace Rinaldo forgot his vow as a crusader.

[5] *LBC,* I, 112. Letter of Nov. 27, 1812. Hobhouse's comment on the end of the affair with Caroline Lamb was: "I congratulate you most sincerely on your release from one who certainly was not the Lamb of God which taketh away the sins of the world." (Joyce, p. 40.)

deliver up her letters, which he was willing enough to do, or to burn them in Lady Melbourne's presence, or hers, or anyone's.[n] But when it came to the performance, she was not willing to return his letters in exchange. ". . . I *will* deliver up her's nevertheless," he told Lady Melbourne, "and mine she may make the most of; they are very like the Duke of York's, and the Editor of any magazine will treat with her for them on moderate terms."[n]

Byron's affairs were in the worst way imaginable. Claughton had put off making the first payment by every excuse and subterfuge he could devise. On the expectation of it Byron had accepted Scrope Davies's bill for £1,500 (a partial payment of the loan of 1809) on October 31, and he was extremely embarrassed that it could not be honored for the patient Scrope. Finally, on November 5, Claughton paid in £5,000 of the deposit money, which was swallowed up immediately, but not before Davies's claim was met.[6] And now Byron was being besieged by the impecunious Hodgson, who took it for granted that his noble friend could supply him with unlimited cash. At the same time that Hodgson reproached his old friend for neglecting him for other acquaintances he asked for an immediate loan of £500.[n]

During the two weeks Byron was in London he attended Parliament twice, December 3 and 7.[n] He was happy to see Hobhouse, with whom he sat so long on the 8th that he was too late for a party at Lady Melbourne's.[n] He also had business (respecting *The Waltz*) with John Murray, who had recently moved from Fleet Street to 50 Albemarle Street, just off Piccadilly and only a short distance from Batt's Hotel in Dover Street, where Byron was staying.[7]

To make more trouble and draw Byron's attention to her, Caro-

[6] *LJ*, II, 180 n. Letter of Hanson to Byron, Nov. 5, 1812, Murray MSS. Some time in December Claughton paid another £5,000. (Undated letter, Hanson to Byron, Murray MSS.) In the meantime Byron tried to economize by giving up his horses and dismissing his groom.

[7] On the strength of his expanding business, to which *Childe Harold* had contributed, Murray mortgaged his copyrights and bought for £3,822 the five-story gray stucco-fronted house and the business of David Miller, the bookseller, and moved to Albemarle Street in October 1812. (*LJ*, II, 180; Paston: *At John Murray's*, p. 9.) He transacted his business in the elegant drawing-room on the first floor (now the "Byron Room" and Sir John Murray's office.)

line now asked for the return of her presents to him, not so much because she wanted them as because she thought he had given them to Lady Oxford and that it would embarrass him if she asked for their return. Byron's reply to Lady Melbourne, who had been the intermediary in all their late correspondence, was: "The trinkets are travelling (at least most of them) in all parts of England and Wales; they certainly are not in the possession of —— [Lady Oxford?]; indeed so anxious was I to get rid of them that most of them had disappeared before my acquaintance with *her*." [n]

He was happy to be back at Eywood, where he arrived the week before Christmas, but he was still apprehensive that Caroline would do something to cause trouble at the Oxfords'. "If she writes to Ld O[xford] I am almost sure that *he* will write to Mr. L[amb]; if so—there will be a pretty scene. . . . He is tolerably obstinate, and it would be as well not to bring it to the proof. . . ." [n] Caroline had now gone down to Brocket, where she had nothing to do but gallop madly on the turnpike and write absurd letters full of vague menaces. One ended: "You have told me how foreign women revenge; I will show you how an Englishwoman can." [n]

Fortunately, the revenge was a vicarious and symbolic one which satisfied her sense of the dramatic, while it seemed only ridiculous to Byron. She gathered at Brocket some children from the neighboring village of Welwyn, dressed some little girls in white, and, having made elaborate preparations, lighted a great bonfire in the park in which she burned "effigies" of Byron's picture, while the troop of girls, quite innocent of the significance of the proceeding, danced round the flames. A page boy recited some curious lines that she had written. She cast in the fire copies of Byron's letters (she could not bear to part with the originals).[8]

A few days later Caroline sent Byron a long account of the bonfire. His reply, "which was good-natured enough, but rather more facetious than befits her taste," brought a "pettish re-

[8] *LJ*, II, 447; Rogers (*Table-Talk*, p. 235) said "she burned, very solemnly, on a sort of funeral pile, *transcripts* of all the letters which she had received from Byron, and *a copy* of a miniature (his portrait) which he had presented to her. . . ."

joinder." He was worn out with her absurdities. "I begin to look upon her as actually mad, or it would be impossible for me to bear what I have from her already." [n]

At Eywood, Byron reported "all very happy and serene—no scenes—a great deal of music—good cheer—spirits and temper—and every day convinces me of the *contrast*." [n] Had it not been for this contrast, Byron might have been bored, but he had experienced too much of its opposite in recent months not to enjoy the tranquillity. And Lady Melbourne, who might have been slightly irked by his complacence, was kept in line by Byron's assurance that she still had the greatest influence over him. "You know I have obeyed you in everything. . . . You have been my director, and are still, for I do not know anything you could not make me do, or undo; and *m'amie* (but this you *won't believe*) has not yet learned the art of *managing* me, nor superseded your authority." [n]

There was prospect of more pleasure ahead. "We have some talk here of a voyage to Sicily, etc., in the spring; if so, I shall be of the party, but this is merely speculation for the present." If that scheme failed, he had some thought of "Levanting" again with Hobhouse. His longing for travel was roused by the preparations of his friend William Bankes for an extensive journey to Albania, Greece, and Turkey. The fever of the East was like an intermittent malaria in Byron's mind; it could be activated by any nostalgic associations. He suggested that Lady Melbourne might not be sorry to find him once more "on the wings of the wind" (because of Caroline), and added: "if it will be any satisfaction to the respectable C$^{e}$ to know that she had some share in disgusting me with this country, she may enjoy it to the full. If it were not for *others* I would set sail to-morrow." [n]

He was in no hurry while Caroline behaved. Looking back over the year that had brought him fame, he could think of nothing pleasanter than his present situation. He wrote to Lady Melbourne on the last day of the year the highest tribute to his "Armida": "I shall not entertain you with a long list of *attributes*, but merely state that I have not been guilty of once *yawning* in the eternity of two months under the same roof—a phenomenon in my history." [n]

# CHAPTER XI

## *1813*

## Fame and Amours—Whig Society

LIFE was even more idyllic at Eywood as the year 1813 began. Lord Oxford had gone up to London early in January, and Byron remained another fortnight with his lady and her beautiful children. On January 2, Byron sent his friend Hobhouse a draft on Hanson for one hundred guineas to pay for a picture of his mistress, to be sent "carefully *packed* and *out of sight*" to John Murray's in Albemarle Street to await his arrival in town.[n] Two days later he wrote to Lady Melbourne: "We all go on without any interruptions or disagreeables—very few guests and no inmates—books, music, &c., all the amusements without the *rigidity* of Middleton. I shall be very *qualmish* at the thoughts of returning to town. . . ."[1]

From one quarter of town a disturbing spirit penetrated frequently the peaceful Eden at Eywood. Caroline Lamb was more than ever determined to make Byron pay for his defection. He had ceased to have any direct communication with her, but now he felt obliged to ask Lady Melbourne to "beseech her, for her own sake, to remain quiet. . . . She is perfectly at liberty to dispose of her necklaces &c. to 'Grimaldi' [the clowning comic actor] if she pleases, and to put whatever motto she may desire on her '*livery buttons.*'" Byron explained that "one of her amuse-

[1] *LBC*, I, 128. Letter of Jan. 4, 1813. Later in the year Byron wrote in his journal: "I remember, last year, ** [Lady Oxford] said to me, at ** [Eywood], 'Have we not passed our last month like the gods of Lucretius?' And so we had." (*LJ*, II, 325. Journal, Nov. 17, 1813.)

ments, by her own account, has been engraving on the said 'buttons' *Ne* 'Crede Byron,' an interesting addition to the motto of my family, which thus atones for its degradation in my acquaintance with her." [n]

Byron was anxious above all else to prevent a public scandal which would have unpleasant repercussions in the Oxford household, but Caroline seemed just as determined to make a scene that would force his attention or make him uncomfortable. Her indiscretion had penetrated as far as Eywood already. "Ld O. had a long sermon upon it from his Mother and *maiden* sisters yesterday. . . ." [n]

But this was only the beginning. Caroline forged a letter in Byron's name to get from Murray the one picture of her former lover that Lady Oxford wanted. Caroline, Byron told Hobhouse, had "pilfered the best picture of *me,* the Newstead Miniature!!!. . . The Devil, and Medea, and her Dragons to boot, are possessed of that little maniac." [n] Lady Melbourne was given the task of trying to recover it, even if she had to promise a copy to the thief.

When Byron returned to London in the third week of January he took lodgings at 4 Bennet Street, just off St. James's, and continued to follow closely in the orbit of Lady Oxford. He was immediately swept, probably at first a little against his will, into the circle of the Princess of Wales.[2] Lady Oxford had for more than three years been the closest confidante of Princess Caroline. Of the court that gathered at Kensington House the leading spirits were the Burdett and Oxford coteries. "Monk" Lewis was a favorite, though the Princess laughed at his obesity and his drolleries, and J. W. Ward, with whom Byron was becoming constantly more intimate, was quite as indiscreet as the Princess in his tête-à-têtes with her.

Byron and his "*Amie*" had been in town only a few days

[2] Byron had written from Eywood on December 27, in response to Lady Melbourne's comment on the Princess of Wales: "*M'amie* [Lady Oxford] thinks I agree with her in *all* her politics, but she will discover that this is a mistake. She insists always upon the P[rincess]'s innocence; but then, as she sometimes reads me somewhat a tedious homily upon her *own,* I look upon it in much the same point of view as I should on Mary Magdalen's vindication of Mrs. Joseph, or any other *immaculate riddle.*" (*LBC,* I, 122.)

when the Princess descended upon Lady Oxford at Mortimer House. Lady Charlotte Campbell, Princess Caroline's lady-in-waiting, recorded that when they arrived "The Princess immediately retired with Lord Byron and Lady Oxford, and her lady staid with Lady Jane [Harley]. Lady [——] [3] told me that she thought Lord Byron was exceedingly wearied, and endeavored to listen to the music, and escape from her Royal Highness and Lady O . . . upon the whole, the Princess was not pleased with her visit." [n]

The Princess was not slow in discovering that all was not perpetually joyous in this new paradise of Armida and Rinaldo. On one occasion she wrote to Lady Charlotte Campbell: "Lady Oxford, poor soul, is more in love this time than she has ever been before. She was with me the other evening, and Lord Byron was so cross to her (his Lordship not being in a good mood), that she was crying in the ante-room." [n]

Before long, however, Byron was a regular visitor at Kensington Palace. As he became better acquainted with the Princess and less restrained in the company, he quite won her over with his charm and gaiety. There was perhaps in her very unrefined earthiness and *grossièreté* something that appealed to him. She wrote later: "He [Byron] was all *couleur de rose* last evening, and very pleasant; he sat beside me at supper, and we were very merry; he is quite anoder man when he is *wid* people he like, and who like him. . . ." [n]

If Byron was sometimes moody at the Princess's dinners the reason was not always that the course of love did not run smoothly. He may occasionally have been annoyed by the attentions paid to Lady Oxford, however Platonic they might now be, by her former lover Sir Francis Burdett, but he was just as likely to be upset by the worry of business affairs, the impossible tangle of which struck him immediately on his return to town. Claughton was still withholding the payments on Newstead on the pretense that the title was not clear, while the creditors

[3] Probably Lady Charlotte Campbell (later Lady Charlotte Bury), who, when she published her diary anonymously in 1838, tried to throw her readers off the scent of the authorship by making casual references to herself in the third person.

swarmed in on every side in the knowledge that a sale had been made. Byron alternately wanted to let Claughton give up the purchase so that he could sell the estate elsewhere, and to hold him strictly and legally to his bargain. Hanson dissuaded him, continuing to hope that Claughton would complete the purchase, for he feared that it would be impossible to get so good a price in a second sale.

What galled Byron as much as anything was the fact that in his straitened circumstances he could not help the friends who were constantly calling on him for aid. It gave him great satisfaction to be free with money, and now the best he could do was to offer to sign a bond with Hodgson for £500 instead of giving him the cash as he would have wished to do. And he could not assist his sister Augusta, whose gambling husband was getting her further and further into financial difficulties.

As an additional irritant, Caroline Lamb's fooleries were never-ending. Byron saw Lady Bessborough, who lectured him for not "Soothing" Caroline more, complained that he had deceived Lady Melbourne and Mrs. George Lamb into thinking he was a "sober, quiet, Platonic, well-disposed person," and was horrified at his "deficiency in *Romance*." But no sooner had Caroline's conciliatory tone induced him to agree to return her letters and to take back the "baubles" he had given her, than a new eruption caused him to revoke his decision.[4]

He was as devoted as ever to Lady Melbourne, to whom he wrote on his birthday: "To-day I am twenty-five years of age, and yours for as many centuries. . . ." [n] She believed in Byron's honesty, but somewhat mistrusted his weakness. Perhaps fear that the danger of a renewal of the affair with Caroline was not entirely past prompted her to offer a distraction in further acquaintance with Annabella. Or the idea may have come from a suggestion of her niece. Byron replied that he would be glad to see Annabella in such a manner as to convince her he bore no grudge for her refusal. "I do not wish to seem piqued at the past, nor as a future *aspirant*." [n]

[4] *LBC*, I, 137. Letter of Jan. 22, 1813 (misdated Feb. in *LBC*). The jewelry she had given him Byron had passed on to Lady Oxford's daughter Lady Charlotte Harley, and he was reluctant to ask for its return.

Had not Lady Oxford urged him to attend to his "senatorial duties," Byron would gladly have given up any further appearance in Parliament. He attended several sessions of the House in February, but was bored with the speeches. Toward the end of March he wrote Augusta that he had "no intention to 'strut another hour' on that stage."[n] Still, he fell back upon that opinion with a sense of frustration and failure, for he could not but look with regret upon the fading of the boyish dream that had buoyed him up during his wasted youth and his aimless travels —that he would one day redeem himself by carving out a brilliant public career.

To Augusta more freely than to Lady Melbourne, who, like Lady Oxford, would have urged upon him the duty of not abdicating his political responsibilities, he could confess the full measure of his defeat. "I am going abroad again in June, but should wish to see you before my departure. You have perhaps heard that I have been fooling away my time with different '*regnantes*'; but what better can be expected from me? I have but one *relative*, and her I never see. I have no connections to domesticate with, and for marriage I have neither the talent nor the inclination."[n]

The consequences of his own foolishness were bearing down upon him with increasing heaviness. Lady Caroline Lamb was now by every means trying to induce him to consent to an interview, and her request for forgiveness struck him as useless and embarrassing. "I have already sent her the requested absolutions and remissions; why must I repeat them?"[n] But when she insisted further, he countered with the proposal that the meeting should be in the presence of Lady Oxford! Lady Melbourne reproached him: "Why, if a third person was necessary, did you not ask me? I would have left the room if she was calm."[n] Byron's excuse was: "She wrote to Ly O. desiring to see *her*, and I thought it as well to *lump* the interviews into one. . . ."[n] The fact is that he would have been less embarrassed to have Caroline recall the sentimental extravagances of their attachment before his present lover than before the confidante to whom he had made sport of that aspect of the affair. Besides, he reckoned correctly that such a proposal would stop the interview entirely.

Escape from England was still his greatest desire, but just how he would go he had not yet decided. "I am in the agonies of three different schemes," he wrote Lady Melbourne on March 18. "The *first* you know [going with or following after the Oxfords], the 2d is Sligo's Persian plan. . . . Then there is Hobhouse, with a Muscovite and Eastern proposal also; so that I am worse off than ever ass was before, to which bundle of hay I shall address myself." *n*

There was a kind of apology for his desertion of the Parliamentary career and his Whig associates in his farewell letter to Lord Holland, written a few days later: "I have neither the verve nor the 'copia fandi' to rival Ld Ellenborough in Molochlike declamation in the House; and without occupation of some kind I cannot exist. Travel, therefore, is the only pursuit left me. . . ." *n*

Byron was glad to retire to the peace of Eywood, where he accompanied the Oxfords on March 28. Before leaving, he sent a last appeal to Lady Melbourne to try to recover the picture from Caroline Lamb. And he added from Eywood: "If she sends you the picture, keep it; but for the love of quiet let me hear no more of or *from* her." His exasperation reached its height as he continued: "The detestation, the utter abhorrence I feel at part of her conduct I will neither shock you with, nor trust myself to express. That feeling has become a part of my nature; it has poisoned my future existence. I know not whom I may love, but to the latest hour of my life I shall hate that woman." *n*

In a mephistophelian mood Byron squared his account with the sentimental Caroline, who had asked for a lock of his hair, by sending her a strand from Lady Oxford's head. "It was a lucky coincidence of colour and shape for my purpose," he told Lady Melbourne with malicious glee, "and may never happen again, and surely it is a very innocent revenge for some very scurvy behaviour." *n* But at last Lady Melbourne had persuaded Caroline to give up the picture.

In her last letter Lady Melbourne had given him an account of an incident that appealed to his sardonic sense of humor.

Alterations in the tombhouse at Windsor had led to the discovery that King Charles I was buried in the vault with Henry VIII. The Prince Regent superintended the opening of the leaden coffin on April 1. He was in good spirits, having just buried his mother-in-law, the Duchess of Brunswick, the day before. He gave the Princess Charlotte the center sapphire of Charles's crown and acted out the manner of the decapitation on the shoulders of one of the guests.[n] Byron commemorated the event with some lines which he sent off to Lady Melbourne:

*Famed for their civil and domestic quarrels,*
*See heartless Henry lies by a headless Charles!*
*Between them stands another sceptred* thing,
*It lives—it reigns, "ay, every inch a king?"*
*Charles to his people—Henry to his wife,*
*The double tyrant starts at once to life.*[n]

About to leave England, he was careless of the treason in these lines. "Will you give Ld. Holland—or anybody you like, or dislike—a copy of this; but I suppose you will be *tender* or *afraid:* you need not mind any *harm* it will do me." [n] The verses were not long in finding wide circulation. On April 23 the Princess of Wales gave a copy to her maid-in-waiting with permission to pass it along to her friends.[n]

On April 19, Byron hinted to Lady Melbourne that unexpected complications in his relations with Lady Oxford might make it advisable to change his plan to sail early in May. "*We* are at present in a slight perplexity, owing to an event which certainly did not enter into my calculations; what it is, I leave to your own ingenious imagination, which will not let one off for a little, I am sure." [n] The suggestion that an addition to the Harleian Miscellany was on the way seems obvious, but since no further mention is made of it, there is every reason to believe that the alarm was premature.

Before Byron left town at the end of March, a private printing of his satire *The Waltz* had been run off for him by Sherwood, Neely, and Jones, Paternoster Row.[n] And Murray had printed a few copies of *The Giaour*, an Oriental poem in couplets which Byron had begun in the autumn of 1812 and which was based

FRANCISCAN CONVENT, ATHENS, BYRON'S RESIDENCE IN 1811

THOMAS MOORE

SAMUEL ROGERS

on the episode of the Turkish girl whom he had saved from being cast into the sea while he was in Athens. He doubted the advisability of publishing either poem under his own name, but he had given copies to various friends.[n]

Caroline's silence could not last. She was pleading again for an interview, but Byron was pledged to avoid it. He saw no use in answering her letter. "Having lately lived with common-sensible people, these heroics are too *Devonshire* for me.[5] Besides," he added, half seriously, "I am very busy educating my future wife [Lady Charlotte Harley]. . . ."[6] He expected to be in town on Sunday, April 25, and wanted to remain there as privately and quietly as possible until he sailed. The Oxfords were going to Cheltenham until the vessel was ready. He would embark separately.

Finally Lady Oxford withdrew her interdiction on the conference with Caroline for fear, Byron said, "of being dragged herself into some scene."[n] On the 29th he wrote a letter, consenting to the interview, to be forwarded through Lady Melbourne; it should in itself have stopped the meeting if Caroline had had any ordinary pride: "You say you will '*ruin* me.' I thank you, but I have done that for myself already; you say you will 'destroy me,' perhaps you will only save me the trouble. . . . It is in a great measure owing to this persecution; to the accursed things you have said; to the extravagances you have committed, that I again adopt the resolution of quitting this country."[n]

Byron left no record of the meeting.[n] He was probably glad to forget it, for he had at the last probably weakened into showing kindness and pity. With due allowance for dramatic exaggeration Caroline's account to Medwin has the ring of agonized sincerity, though she may easily have mistaken Byron's pity for love. She wrote: "Our meeting was not what he insinuates—he

[5] A reference to the madcap reputation of the Devonshire House circle, including Lady Bessborough and her sister, Georgiana Duchess of Devonshire, who in their youth were almost as "heroic" as Caroline herself.

[6] *LBC*, I, 150. Letter of April 22, 1813. Byron had become very fond of Lady Oxford's daughter Charlotte Harley. He wrote Lady Melbourne on April 5 that she was one "whom I should love for ever if she could always be only eleven years old, and whom I shall probably marry when she is old enough, and bad enough to be made into a modern wife." (*LBC*, I, 145.)

asked me to forgive him; he looked sorry for me; he cried. I adored him still, but I felt as passionless as the dead may feel.—Would I had died there!—I should have died pitied, & still loved by him, & with the sympathy of all. I even should have pardoned myself—so deeply had I suffered. But, unhappily, we continued occasionally to meet. Lord Byron liked others, I only him—" [n]

And now there was trouble on another side. Lady Oxford made her bid for sympathy. "I am in some anxiety in consequence of a letter from C[heltenha]m this morning," Byron wrote Lady Melbourne on the 14th; "*she* has burst a small blood-vessel, and is weak and ill; all which she attributes to 'me and my friends in town!!' " [n]

In the meantime Byron was not without company. He saw Rogers frequently and dedicated *The Giaour* to him. And Moore was still his most congenial companion. Lady Oxford's indisposition had not been serious, and Byron remained in London, gayer perhaps than either she or Caroline could have wished. On the 19th, before dressing for a party at Lady Heathcote's, he wrote a rhyming epistle to Moore, who had promised to take him the next day to see Leigh Hunt, whose imprisonment in the Surrey Gaol for libeling the Prince Regent had made him a martyr of the liberal cause. Byron, an admirer of Hunt's verses while he was at Harrow, was eager to meet the man who had had the courage to speak of the Prince openly as "a violator of his word, a libertine over head and ears in disgrace, a despiser of domestic ties, the companion of gamblers and demireps, a man who has just closed half a century without one single claim on the gratitude of his country or the respect of posterity!" [n]

Hunt had asked Byron and Moore to dinner, and the anticipation of this meeting gave wings to his egocentric imagination. He wrote his wife that Byron was a young man "of good natural feelings & a fine improvable sensibility, but led away, I am told, by a town life. Perhaps a friend (if we prove intimate) of a taste like his own & full of quite as much excitability, but luckily induced to more philosophic habits by the nature of circumstances, may be able to render his heart & his understanding a service,

& help to lead him off gradually into enjoyments more congenial to both." [n]

According to Hunt, they "passed a very pleasant afternoon, talking of books, and school, and the Reverend Mr. Bowles. . . ." [n] Moore, knowing Byron's sensitive shyness, had asked that the visitors be limited to themselves, and he and Byron were a little chagrined when some of Hunt's lesser literary friends dropped in after dinner, eager to meet the celebrated author of *Childe Harold*.[n]

But Byron was a frequent visitor thereafter. Three days later he came bringing books that he thought might be useful to Hunt as background for his *Story of Rimini*.[7] "This will please you," Hunt wrote to his prim wife, Marianne. "It strikes me that he and I shall become *friends*,—literally and cordially speaking. . . ." He looked forward with satisfaction to her meeting his lordship—". . . a good domestic female, capable of loving one person sincerely and making sacrifices for him, is, I guess, not one of his everyday acquaintances." [n]

Byron did not give as much thought to Hunt at the time as the latter imagined. He was too preoccupied with other friends and affairs. On the 23rd, after a long delay, Hobhouse's *A Journey through Albania and Other Provinces of Turkey in Europe and Asia* was published in a huge quarto by Cawthorn,[n] and two days later the author set out on a Continental tour, having tired of waiting for Byron to arrange his plans, and having obtained the means of travel by procuring a courier's passport and carrying dispatches for the Crown Prince of Sweden.[8] After taking

[7] Hunt wrote to his wife that Byron requested his acceptance of the books "with the air of one who did not seem to think himself conferring the least obligation." (Letter of May 25, 1813, Morgan Library.) Hunt recalled later that Byron would not allow the footman to carry the books, but brought them under his arm, giving the impression "that he was prouder of being a friend and a man of letters, than a lord. It was thus that by flattering one's vanity, he persuaded us of his own freedom from it; for he could see very well, that I had more value for lords than I supposed." (Hunt: *Lord Byron*, I, 4.)

[8] Broughton, I, 48. Hobhouse, on this semi-diplomatic mission, was gone from England for eight months, visiting most of the central European capitals out of Napoleon's hands, returning in February 1814.

leave of him the night before he left, Byron wrote to Lady Melbourne: "he is ye oldest, indeed ye only friend I have, and . . . in parting with him, I lose 'a guide, philosopher and friend' I neither *can* nor *wish* to replace." *n*

Byron was indeed without a guide, but he had some determination yet to escape his own weaknesses by running away from all his personal entanglements. In spite of himself, his meeting with Caroline had unsettled him. He could see clearly enough through her ruses, but felt helpless to deal with them with adequate harshness, and he could not answer for what might happen if he did not get away. In his present mood even his attachment to Lady Oxford was weakening, though it would no doubt be cemented again when she arrived in town.

To complicate his feelings still more, he had during the spring met Miss Milbanke again—the only girl who had ever refused him. He thought that he would be calm, but he was not, at least by her account. She later wrote in her "Auto-Description": "I was extremely agitated on seeing him—and offered my hand for the first time. He turned pale as he pressed it. Perhaps—unconscious as I was—the engagement was then formed on my part. We met frequently, but every time I felt more pain—and at last I shunned the occasions." *n*

Lady Oxford arrived in London on May 27. It may well have been her encouragement that induced Byron to stand up in the House of Lords on June 1 and present the petition of Major John Cartwright for the right to petition for the "Reform" of Parliament.[9] Cartwright, former crony of Lady Oxford's onetime tutor Horne Tooke, who was anathema to Tories and Moderate Whigs alike, had gone his single and uncompromising way in collecting petitions for Reform until by May 1813 he had gathered 292 bearing 199,000 signatures.*n* But with the increase of unrest and the rise of new Luddite disturbances, he and his supporters had been obstructed, as Byron said in his speech

[9] "Reform" meant, of course, the abolition of "pocket boroughs" and the reapportioning of representation more nearly in accord with population. But many even of the Liberal Whigs owed their seats to patronage or special favor, which made them look with distrust on the general suffrage even of the more propertied classes. No reconstruction of Parliament took place until the Reform Bill of 1832.

before the House, "by the interposition of an abused civil and unlawful military force between them and their right of petition to their own representatives." [n] Just how radical that position was it is difficult now to realize unless we refer it to hysterical periods in our own more recent history when it has taken a brave man to stand up against popular fears and prejudices and speak out for the constitutional rights of free speech. Some indication of what a lone wolf Byron really was on this occasion will be seen in the fact that Cartwright could not get the Reform Whig leader Whitbread to present the petition in the lower house, and that Byron's only defender among the lords was the pariah Earl Stanhope, disowned by all parties for his "Jacobinism." Byron wrote later: ". . . Stanhope and I stood against the whole House, and mouthed it valiantly—and had some fun and a little abuse for our opposition." [n]

The very fact that, like Stanhope, he felt that he had burned his bridges behind him as far as parliamentary influence or success was concerned made it possible for him to speak his mind with a freedom unthinkable to a tactful politician. Nevertheless, he recognized it as his swan song in Parliament and as a farewell to the career in public life that he had so long contemplated.

Happy again in the presence of Lady Oxford, Byron was determined to see her as often as possible before she departed, and to join her at the earliest moment afterward. On June 3 they left town for Salthill near Maidenhead, where she was staying until she sailed. Just before leaving, Byron wrote another desperate appeal to Hanson to provide means somehow for his own departure, which he had now postponed to July. He authorized his agent to sell everything at Newstead not in Claughton's contract, including plate, linen, a silver vase, and a silver cup (not the skull cup), as well as pictures and every movable object. He concluded: ". . . all I want is a few thousand pounds, and then adieu. You shan't be troubled with me these ten years, if ever." [n]

He had finally, after much wavering, consented to let Murray publish *The Giaour*. The first edition was advertised in the *Morning Chronicle* of June 5.[n] He had added some three hundred lines to the poem as it had been circulated among his friends in the private printing. Murray had undertaken to publish it, he told Hodgson, "at his own risk, and peril, and profit (if there be any)." [n] The sycophantic Dallas had been a frequent visitor to Byron during the spring, but the author made no offer of the copyright of *The Giaour* except to the publisher. Dallas was aware that Byron had cooled toward him, but that scarcely stopped his visits, and Byron was too polite to send him away, though he had begun to find him a great bore and, as he told Hobhouse, "a *damned* nincom. assuredly." [n]

Byron left with Lady Oxford for Portsmouth on June 13. But he was not so absorbed with his lady that he could not think of other things. He told Murray he was "tremulous for '*The Giaour*'; but you would publish it—I presume, by this time, to your repentance." [n] A few days later he was immensely flattered by a letter from his early literary master, William Gifford. Nothing could have pleased him more. He told Murray it was "the kindest letter I ever received in my life." [n] Gifford expressed his high opinion of Byron's "poetical excellence" and entreated him "not to squander your extraordinary powers in common efforts." He advised the revival of *Childe Harold.* "His fixed melancholy might be shaken, and glimpses of delight break in occasionally upon his habitual gloom. . . . where religion is concerned, some retention is necessary and even wise." [n]

By the 20th, Byron was back in London. There had apparently been a little trouble with Lord Oxford. Even that most patient of husbands was beginning to chafe under the embarrassment of such an open and constant attachment. But his wife soon brought him to heel. Byron duly reported the event to Lady Melbourne: ". . . on *her* threatening to fill up my 'carte blanche' in her own way, he [Lord Oxford] quietly ate his own words and intentions, and now they are to 'live happy ever after' and to sail in the pleasing hope of seeing or not seeing me again. . . ." [n] In order to avoid any scenes, Byron was to meet his *amie* on the coast just before they sailed.

On the evening of June 20, Byron was invited to Lady Jersey's to meet Mme de Staël, the great literary lady of the Continent, who had just arrived in London. And the next day he dined with her at Lady Davy's along with Sheridan and others, and was amazed by the talents of this extraordinary woman who talked the men into silence. He did not fail to observe that this heroine of the persecutions of Napoleon, this liberal expounder of the new German sensibility and "Romanticism," had quite changed her face politically when she reached English shores. Writing to Moore, he said: "She is for the Lord of Israel and the Lord of Liverpool—a vile antithesis of a Methodist and a Tory. . . ."[n]

Byron recorded his recollections years later when the lady was dead and he was in exile in Italy: "She interrupted Whitbread; she declaimed to Lord L.; she misunderstood Sheridan's jokes for assent; she harangued, she lectured, she preached English politics to the first of our English Whig politicians, the day after her arrival in England; and (if I am not much misinformed) preached politics no less to our Tory politicians the day after. The Sovereign himself, if I am not in error, was not exempt from this flow of eloquence."[n]

Byron had occasion to observe the great lady frequently in the following weeks, at Lady Davy's and other assemblies. At first he was inclined to spar with her and, like Sheridan, to bait her because of her opinionated views and her love of argument. But he recognized her intelligence, and in the end he came to respect and even to like her, though he kept, as he did concerning most of his friends, a reserve of caustic and cynical judgment which in no way detracted from his liking or loyalty. He told Lady Blessington later that "Madame de Staël was certainly the cleverest, though not the most agreeable woman he had ever known." He admitted that she "was very eloquent when her imagination warmed . . . her language was recondite, but redundant; and though always flowery, and often brilliant, there was an obscurity that left the impression that she did not perfectly understand what she endeavored to render intelligible to others. . . . She *thought* like a man, but, alas! she *felt* like a woman. . . ."[n]

Byron found her unaware of how much she sometimes shocked English decorum. "Poor dear Madame de Staël!" he exclaimed to Lady Blessington. "I shall never forget seeing her one day, at table with a large party, when the busk (I believe you ladies call it) of her corset forced its way through the top of the corset, and would not descend though pushed by all the force of both hands of the wearer, who became crimson from the operation. After fruitless efforts she turned in despair to the valet de chambre behind her chair, and requested him to draw it out, which could only be done by his passing his hand from behind over her shoulder, and across her chest, when, with a desperate effort, he unsheathed the busk. Had you seen the faces of some of the English ladies of the party, you would have been like me, almost convulsed; while Madame remained perfectly unconscious that she had committed any solecism on *la décence Anglaise*." [n]

Byron gave Lady Blessington an amusing account of how he had once baited the eloquent oracle. He told her that he considered her novels *Delphine* and *Corinne* "as very dangerous productions to be put into the hands of young women. . . . that all the moral world thought, that her representing all the virtuous characters in 'Corinne' as being dull, commonplace, and tedious, was a most insidious blow aimed at virtue, and calculated to throw it into the shade. She was so excited and impatient to attempt a refutation, that it was only by my volubility I could keep her silent. She interrupted me every moment by gesticulating, exclaiming—'*Quel idée!*' '*Mon Dieu!*' '*Ecoutez donc!*' '*Vous m'impatientez!*' . . . I was ready to laugh outright at the idea that *I*, who was at that period considered the most *mauvais sujet* of the day, should give Madame de Staël a lecture on morals; and I knew that this added to her rage." [n]

But in the meantime Byron had his own embarrassments. The Oxfords sailed before he had a chance to see his *amie* again. Chagrined, he wrote to Lady Melbourne on June 29: "Ly [Oxford] sailed yesterday, and now, my dear Ly Me, without pretending to *affect* or *effect*, will you not mention her name to me for the remainder of my weeks in England? To tell you the truth, I feel more *Carolinish* about her than I expected." [n] But, despite his pique, he was as loyal to Lady Oxford as before. In fact, he grew bold enough to goad Caroline into further madness: "At last," he told Lady Melbourne, "(at a pretty time, you will say) I declared to C. my real sentiments about Ly [Oxford], and I think they had a good effect. Do you know I am Constancy in the abstract, and am much more faithful to people on the 'high seas' than if they were on shore—I suppose from my natural love of contradiction and paradox." [n]

Byron was slightly annoyed at first that his sister Augusta should have appeared in London and thrown herself on his protection at the very moment when Lady Oxford was leaving, though he was glad enough to see her. He asked her to accompany him on June 27 to Lady Davy's, where she could see Mme de Staël. "I think our being together before 3d people will be a new *sensation* to *both*." [n] They had not met since before Byron went abroad and very little since Augusta's marriage to her cousin Colonel Leigh in 1807. The correspondence, interrupted entirely during his journey to the East because Byron had heard she was incensed by his attack on Lord Carlisle in *English Bards and Scotch Reviewers,* had been resumed on his return. He had invited her to Newstead in the melancholy autumn of 1811 when he had been shocked by many deaths, but various domestic obstacles had prevented their meeting. She was now the mother of three daughters. When he visited Cambridge, she was away from her home at Six Mile Bottom near Newmarket. Then came the publication of *Childe Harold* and the absorbing occupations of love and fame.

Augusta's affairs had gone from bad to worse. Herself extremely inept at handling money, she was soon brought heavily into debt by her irresponsible husband, who followed the races from one track to another and was seldom home except for the Newmarket events. Byron was not deaf to her distress calls, which came soon after his return and continued at intervals, but Claughton's delays left him helpless to aid her.

Augusta, five years older than her brother, was soft and voluptuous in face and figure, and, though she was not exactly beautiful, she had the handsome Byron profile and large eyes, the long lip that could curl and pout like his own, a tendency to frown as he did and to laugh unrestrainedly at his witticisms. The motherly interest in her "Baby Byron," whom she remembered as a handsome and amusing boy, the willingness to indulge his whims and forgive his weaknesses and foibles, the understanding she displayed with regard to his unhappy early life with his mother and his sensitivity to his lameness—all this added to his feeling that he had found a friend and relative in whose presence he could be unrestrained. Instinctively they understood each other because they were Byrons. There was no need for explanations or affectation. And the consanguinity was balanced by the charm of strangeness engendered by their separate upbringing; in their formative years they had escaped the rough familiarity of the brother-sister relationship. They were both shy in company, but Augusta was proud of her brother's fame and impressed with the easy manner he had acquired in the London drawing-rooms. He was fortunately free from any serious liaison, and he took his sister to the theater and balls and assemblies during July.

Augusta, who had been tied down with children's illnesses and money worries, was delighted with this interlude in London. Her newly discovered brother was so droll and comical and so handsome and highly admired. They developed an easy familiarity. He was soon calling her "Guss," a nickname which he distorted into "Goose" on account of her silly incoherent gabbling. They laughed together with perfect understanding. It was pleasant to have a sympathetic near relative when one had never had such a luxury. A fortnight after the Oxfords had sailed, Byron felt that he had compensation for his loss. He wrote Moore: ". . . my sister is in town, which is a great comfort,—for, never having been much together, we are naturally more attached to each other." [n]

In the midst of this calm, Caroline Lamb forced her attentions on Byron once more. Against his better judgment he had continued to see her occasionally after the meeting in May, mostly at balls or large gatherings. He permitted Murray to send her a copy of *The Giaour* when it was published.[n] But his kindness to her in private did not compensate her for the indifference of his behavior to her in public. On Monday, July 5, he went to a small party at Lady Heathcote's.[n] When he saw Caroline there, he requested "to know her will and pleasure, if there was anything I could say, do, or not do to give her the least gratification." [n] She turned on her heel without answering, leaving Byron in an embarrassing situation with twenty people looking on. On his way to supper with Lady Rancliffe, he encountered her in a doorway in the interim of dancing (it was a waltzing party). She took hold of his hand as he passed and pressed a sharp instrument against it, saying: "I mean to use this." Byron replied: "Against me, I presume?" and passed on, "trembling," he recalled, "lest Ld Y. or Ly R. should overhear her; though not believing it possible that this was more than one of her, not uncommon, *bravadoes,* for *real feeling* does not disclose its intentions, and always shuns display." He did not want to arouse curiosity by leaving the table to go to her, ". . . though, of course," he told Lady Melbourne, "had I guessed her to be serious, or had I been conscious of offending I should have done everything to pacify or prevent her."

He met her once more after supper, and, according to his own account, "told her it was better to *waltz;* 'because she danced well, and it would be imputed to *me,* if she did not.'" [n] But there may have been more bitterness in his tone or his manner than he was aware of, or than he admitted to his confidante. So at least it appeared to Caroline. She told Medwin later: ". . . he had made me swear I was never to Waltz. Lady Heathcote said, Come, Lady Caroline, you must begin, & I bitterly answered—oh yes! I am in a merry humour. I did so—but whispered to Lord Byron 'I conclude I may walze *now*' and he answered sarcastically, 'with every body in turn—you always did it better than any one. I shall have a pleasure in seeing you.'—I did so you may judge with what feelings. After this, feeling ill, I went into a small inner room where supper was prepared; Lord Byron & Lady Rancliffe entered after; seeing me, he said, 'I have been admiring your dexterity.' I clasped a knife, not intending anything. 'Do, my dear,' he said. 'But if you mean to act a Roman's part, mind which way you strike with your knife—be it at your own heart, not mine—you have struck there already.' 'Byron,' I said, and ran away with the knife. I never stabbed myself. It is false. Lady Rancliffe & Tankerville screamed and said I would; people pulled to get it from me; I was terrified; my hand got cut, & the blood came over my gown. I know not what happened after—but this is the very truth. . . . I never held my head up after—never could. It was in all the papers, and put not truly."[n]

Byron did not know what had passed until four o'clock in the morning, when, he told Lady Melbourne, "Ly Ossulstone looking angry (and at that moment, ugly), delivered to me a confused kind of message from you of some scene—this is all I know, except that with laudable logic she drew the usual feminine deduction that I 'must have behaved very ill.'" Lady Westmorland said to him: "You must have done something; you know between people in your situation, a word or a look goes a great way," but Byron stubbornly assured Lady Melbourne that he was unaware he had offended by either words or looks, and, he complained, "If I am to be haunted with hysterics wherever I go, and whatever I do, I think she is not the only person to be pitied."[n] But underneath he must have realized that it was his indifference that had offended her—the very "downright, innocent, vacant, undefinable *nothing*" that he pleaded in his own defense.

Fantastic stories of the event soon got out. Caroline thought at first that she could contradict the reports in the papers, but she soon realized that she had gone beyond the pale of the shoddy but inexorable moral code of her own class: she had at last brought the walls down upon herself by making a public scene. Nothing now could save her. When the affair was discussed mockingly in the scandal columns of *The Satirist*,[n] William Lamb carried her off to Brocket.

Through all this Byron was continuing his preparations to go abroad. It now seemed possible. On July 2 a Chancery suit had been started against Claughton, and on the very day of the scene at Lady Heathcote's Hanson wrote: "An Interview has taken Place and our opponent is ready to pay ye 15000£ but he wants time to pay the remaining 60,000£."[n] Even before this encouraging report, however, Byron had run up fantastic bills for equipment and presents to take with him, and during July and August his purchases increased still more. In addition to such small items as £52. 0*s*. 6*d*. for swords, guns, and other military equipment, and £46. 4*s*. for mahogany dressing-boxes and writing-desks, he ordered a vast amount of uniforms and other clothing, nankeen trousers by the dozen, scarlet-and-blue staff officers' coats, nine very rich gold epaulets, etc., bringing his tailor's bill up to £896. 19*s.* 6*d.* His bill from Love & Kelly, Goldsmiths & Jewellers, was even more fabulous: the balance brought forward from 1812 was already £657. 10*s.* On July 12 he ordered seven fine gold boxes for presents to foreign potentates and others, one a "Gold & Enameld Musical Box—with figures sett with pearls," valued at £105. The total for the seven boxes was £315.[n]

On July 13, Byron applied to John Wilson Croker, Secretary to the Admiralty, to get him a passage in the *Boyne* or any other ship-of-war bound for the Mediterranean.[n] So unsettled was his mind, however, that he could at the same time make plans and enter into speculations, though it is hard to say how seriously, much nearer home than his foreign voyage. On the same day that he applied for passage on the *Boyne,* he wrote to Moore: "I am amazingly inclined—remember I say but *inclined*—to be seriously enamoured with Lady A[delaide] F[orbes]—but this * * [scandal raised by Caroline Lamb?] has ruined all my prospects. However, you know her; is she *clever,* or sensible, or good-tempered? either *would* do—I scratch out the *will.* I don't ask as to her beauty—that I see; but my circumstances are mending, and were not my other prospects blackening, I would take a wife, and that should be the woman, had I a chance. I do not yet know her much, but better than I did." [n]

And, strangely enough, Annabella Milbanke, that other lady whom he had contemplated marrying with about the same degree of coolness but who had never ceased to think of him, called herself to his attention once more through Lady Melbourne. On the 18th, just before she left London for Seaham, she wrote that she had heard a report, which she didn't believe, that Lord Byron had cruelly taken advantage of the law to make Claughton, who "from the imprudent eagerness of youth bid much more than it was worth," adhere to unfair terms in the purchase of Newstead. Supposing Byron to be leaving England shortly, she added: ". . . however long his absence may be, I shall always have pleasure in hearing that he is happy. . . ." [n]

When Lady Melbourne passed the message on to him he replied that the price was Claughton's own offer and "if he is ruined by this contract, or has been ill treated by me or mine on that subject, he has hitherto been silent, at least to me." But Byron hadn't the inclination to defend himself to Annabella. He would, however, seek an explanation of "the interesting *youth* (a *lawyer* of forty-five years)." [n]

Through July, Byron was busy with revisions and additions to *The Giaour,* a second edition of which, six pages and 131 lines longer than the first, had appeared early that month. Fragmentary as it was, the lushness of its descriptive passages had begun to take hold with the public. Byron's friend Ward wrote: "It has some new passages, one of them beautiful beyond all description." [n] He no doubt referred to the now famous lines beginning "He that hath bent him o'er the dead."

Byron was moving in society more than ever. Looking back on this period and the months that followed, Byron later wrote in his "Detached Thoughts": "I liked the Dandies; they were always very civil to *me,* though in general they disliked literary people. . . . The truth is, that, though I gave up the business early, I had a tinge of Dandyism in my minority, and probably retained enough of it, to conciliate the great ones; at four and twenty. I had gamed, and drank, and taken my degrees in most dissipations; and having no pedantry, and not being overbearing, we ran quietly together." [n]

It was in the salons of *haut ton* rather than in the Dandy gatherings that Byron was bored. And the salons that patronized literary men were often just as bad or worse. He was not quite aware at the time why he found them so dismal, but he stored up impressions which he analyzed later. "In general, I do not draw well with literary men," he wrote in 1821, "not that I dislike them, but I never know what to say to them after I have praised their last publication. There are several exceptions, to be sure; but then they have either been men of the world, such as Scott, and Moore, etc., or visionaries out of it, such as Shelley, etc.: but your literary every day man and I never went well in company. . . ." [n] Matthew Gregory ("Monk") Lewis was one of the worst. "Lewis was a good man," Byron recalled, "a clever man, but a bore, a damned bore. . . ." [n]

William Sotheby, whom Byron first met in the Alfred Club in 1811, was another poet to be avoided when possible. Byron's considered judgment in later years was: "Sotheby is a good man, rhymes well (if not wisely), but is a bore. He seizes you by the button." [n] But the worst ones were the loud, opinionated, and talkative bores, like old Edgeworth, the father of the authoress Maria Edgeworth. Byron told Murray: ". . . I thought him a very tiresome coarse old Irish half-and-half Gentleman, and her a pleasant reserved old woman—with a pencil under her petticoat however—undisturbed in its operation by the vicinity of that anatomical part of female humanity which would have rendered the taking of notes neutral or partial in any other she animal above a cow. That sort of women seem to think themselves perfect because they can't get covered; and those who are seem no better for it—the spayed bitches." [n]

In all this rout there were a few whom Byron genuinely admired for superior talents and individuality. Richard Brinsley Sheridan was one. Byron had no doubt met him at a London assembly soon after *Childe Harold* was published, but they reached intimacy at a dinner at the home of Rogers in the spring of 1813. Byron wrote of that memorable meeting in his journal: "Poor dear Sherry! I shall never forget the day he and Rogers and Moore and I passed together; when *he* talked, and *we* listened, without one yawn, from six till one in the morning." [n] Byron admired him as an orator, though he heard him only once in Parliament, but more as a wit. In his later reminiscences and "Detached Thoughts" he referred to Sheridan more often than to any other of his London companions of his years of fame. "In society I have met him frequently," he recalled: "he was superb! He had a sort of liking for me, and never attacked me—at least to my face, and he did every body else—high names, and wits, and orators, some of them poets also. . . . Poor fellow! he got drunk very thoroughly and very soon. It occasionally fell to my lot to convoy him home—no sinecure, for he was so tipsy that I was obliged to put on his cock'd hat for him: to be sure it tumbled off again, and I was not myself so sober as to be able to pick it up again."[n]

In Byron's opinion, only one man in Regency London was a better drinking-companion than Sheridan. That was George Colman the younger, whom he met occasionally and thought ". . . extremely pleasant and congenial. Sheridan's humour, or rather wit, was always saturnine, and sometimes savage: he never laughed (at least that *I* saw, and I watched him), but Colman did. I have got very drunk with them both; but, if I had to *choose*, and could not have both at a time, I should say, 'let me begin the evening with Sheridan, and finish it with Colman.'"[n]

On July 28, Byron wrote to Moore: "I am in training to dine with Sheridan and Rogers this evening." He thought that this might be a farewell dinner, for he expected to leave England within a few days. ". . . I am quite equipped," he told Moore, "and only wait a passage." He added: "Perhaps I may wait a few weeks for Sligo, but not if I can help it."[n]

But, always an easy prey to his own weaknesses, especially where women were concerned, Byron was soon swept along by circumstances which complicated his departure. Augusta, after staying for about three weeks in London and seeing her brother constantly, had returned to Six Mile Bottom, where Byron visited her twice for several days, and after the second visit took her back to London with him.[n] On August 5 he made the rather surprising announcement to Lady Melbourne: "My sister, who is going abroad with me, is now in town. . . ."[n] How deeply involved he was in that quarter Lady Melbourne did not know, though he wished and yet feared to tell her.

On the 11th, Byron returned to the matter which was preying on his mind and about which he had already "written, and destroyed, two ineffectual notes" to Lady Melbourne. He reported that Caroline Lamb had been relatively quiet. But he confessed: "The few things I wished to have said to you did not at all concern her nor hers. . . . I should have been glad of your advice how to untie two or three 'gordian knots' tied round me. I shall cut them without consulting anyone, though some are rather closely twisted round my *heart* (if you will allow me to *wear* one)."[n] And then, as if he had given up any attempt to divulge the secret or ask advice from his confidante, and yet was drawn by an irresistible force within him to hint at it, he continued: "Perhaps I shall not see you again; if not, forgive my follies, and like as much of me as you can."[1]

His plans were further complicated by news that the plague had broken out in Eastern ports. Nevertheless, he and Sligo, having both made large preparations, were determined to go somewhere. On the 18th he was on the brink of revealing his guilty secret to Lady Melbourne, but he drew back. She had sent an unsigned inquiry about him from someone whose identity he could not guess. "Tell me," he wrote, "and in return I will tell—no I won't." And after a few more lines, he added: "I have scribbled on without saying a single thing I wished to say."[2] Augusta had gone back to Six Mile Bottom, and Byron's uncertainty of mind and of plans increased. He wrote Lady Melbourne on August 20: "When I don't write to you, or see you for some time you may be very certain I am about no good—and *vice versâ*. . . . Make my best respects, and don't be angry with me—which you will, however; first, for some things I have said, and then for others I have not said."[n]

And on the 22nd he wrote to Moore: ". . . I am at this moment in a far more serious, and entirely new, scrape than any of the last twelve months,—and that is saying a good deal. It is unlucky we can neither live with nor without these women."[3]

Within the next few days he revealed the nature of that scrape so clearly to Lady Melbourne that she was shocked and frightened for him. Byron's correspondence with Lady Melbourne hints very strongly that he had become involved in a liaison with

[1] *LBC*, I, 170. Byron actually had intended to sail on the *Boyne*, for the moment he heard from Croker that he had passage he wrote a note (probably to Hanson): "Dear Sir, We sail on board the Boyne,—& must be at Portsmouth on Saturday next.—I have only just heard this—could I see you now?" (Copy, no date, Library of Trinity College, Cambridge.) But when he learned that he could not take Augusta and his servants along, he declined the offer of Captain Carlton.

[2] *LBC*, I, 171–2. Byron began this letter: "I *am* 'a very weak person,' and can only answer your letter. I have already written and *torn* up *three* to you. . . ."

[3] *LJ*, II, 251. Byron probably felt that he could say this much to Moore because he intended to say no more.

his half-sister, Augusta.[4] For Byron there would be a fatal fascination in such an intimacy because it was a "new sensation" and because it was forbidden. Augusta, goodhearted and amiable, was intent only upon giving pleasure to the brother of whom she was fond and whom she had grown to love still more for his generosity and kindly qualities during the weeks in London and in the days at her house in the country. Amoral as a rabbit and silly as a goose, she was scarcely aware of abstract moral questions, though she was full of pious phrases and gave Bibles to her family and friends. Byron was too reflective not to think of the dangers and the social consequences of his actions, and too self-torturing not to feel remorse. Like many of his contemporaries in the nineteenth century, he had escaped rationally but not emotionally from the fear-inspired religious training of his youth. The Calvinistic sense of sin haunted his subconscious mind, a ghost that could never be completely exorcised. But that fatalistic conception of human depravity blended with his own weakness to drive him on to further violation of the inhibitions of his own mind.

Lady Melbourne, usually philosophic and calm, was thoroughly alarmed by this new escapade of Byron's. She now saw his proposed voyage with Augusta in another light, and warned him against this fatal step. Byron replied: "Your kind letter is *unanswerable;* no one but yourself would have taken the trouble; no one but me would have been in a situation to require it. I am still in town so that it has as yet had all the effect you wish." [n] Eventually he retreated so far as to abandon his project of taking Augusta abroad, but only when he had also abandoned his own project of going.

While Byron was occupied, and shaken, by these events, he was surprised to receive a long letter from Annabella Milbanke, the first she had ever sent directly to him. In the dullness of

[4] It is true that the extant evidence does not amount to *legal* proof, for eyewitnesses are out of the question in such a case, certain papers are unavailable, if they have not been destroyed, and some of the witnesses would be dismissed by any judge as prejudiced or unreliable. All that can be said is that the circumstantial evidence in Byron's letters can not be ignored, and that certain aspects of his life and correspondence can not be explained sensibly in any other terms.

Seaham she had pondered long over the most fascinating man she had ever met, the only one who had deeply stirred her interests. On August 22 she sat down to tell him guardedly, under the guise of disinterested friendship, how she felt. "It is my nature to feel long, deeply, and secretly," she told him, "and the strongest affections of my heart are without hope." This was pure invention to justify her contention that she was writing only as a friend. She continued: "Early in our acquaintance, when I was far from supposing myself preferred by you, I studied your character. I felt for you, and I often felt with you. . . . How often have I wished that the state of Society would have allowed me to offer you my sentiments without restraint!" She added some moral advice: "No longer suffer yourself to be the slave of the moment, nor trust your noble impulses to the chances of Life. Have an object that will permanently occupy your feelings & exercise your reason. Do good." And she asked him to keep her letter and its contents a secret, particularly from Lady Melbourne, who would "look for design" and not "understand the plainness of my intentions." [n]

Three days later Annabella wrote in her commonplace book some thoughts of her own on character:

It has occurred to me to form certain collective classes of characters. Here then I will write down whatever hints present themselves, and they may elsewhere be digested into order:—

I will begin by the character most interesting to me, in which the following qualities are united.

1.

Active but secret piety—
Independence of worldly interests.
Undeviating rectitude.
Dauntless Sincerity.
Pride of Honor.
Reserve as to the softer feelings—yet all the capacity for affection which accompanies strong and delicate Sensibility.
Generosity and every virtue composing perfect disinterestedness.—
Sound Sense and Consistency.—

I have yet met with this character only in three persons—Two women and one man—Such are the spirits on whom we may build our trust and know no disappointment—

And then, still on a plane of high disinterestedness and generalization (or so she thought), she opened a second chapter:

Characters determined by Disappointment—or by the want of that happiness which according to Mad[e] de Stael, consists in the concordance of our situation with our faculties.—Hence arise, in most instances, either Misanthropy or Despondency, or the union of the two —but there is also a benevolent despondency, like that of Mackenzie's Harley.—

2.

Natural benevolence changed to suspicious coldness.

Every kind impulse is repelled by the consideration of man's unworthiness.[n]

The shrewd Miss Milbanke perhaps supposed that no one reading this could have guessed that she had a certain young lord in mind when she analyzed the second type of character. Nor was she aware of how partially true and how tragically inadequate was her conception of Byron's nature.

On the same day that she entered these thoughts in her notebook, Byron sat down to reply to her letter. He had read between the lines and was flattered that he was still in her thoughts. He ignored her sermonizing, and wrote some words that were exciting beyond Annabella's expectation: "L[y] M. was perfectly correct in her statement that I preferred you to all others; it was then the fact; it is so still. . . . yet I do not think that my self love was much wounded by the event. On the contrary, I feel a kind of pride even in *your rejection*—" And then followed a confession that startled Annabella and made her regret heartily that she had raised the specter of another lover: "I must be candid with you on the score of friendship. It is a feeling towards you with which I cannot trust myself. I doubt whether I could help loving you. . . ."[n]

A little frightened by the audacity of her own white lie, which had tripped her up, she wrote a hasty farewell: "Nothing in your letter can displease me—the recollection of my own may. . . . I will not regret the friendship which you deem impossible, for the loss is *mine,* as the comfort would have been *mine.*" [n]

Byron, afraid that he had frightened her away by his too great frankness, wrote again to clarify his position. "Your friendship I did not reject—though in speaking of mine I expressed some doubts on the subject of my own feelings." [n] Annabella was relieved that her own folly had not cut off the correspondence, and replied immediately that she would welcome him as a valued friend "at some future period, without a painful exertion on your part." [n]

Byron had kept the secret of his correspondence with Annabella as much for his own sake as hers. He was not too sure of how Lady Melbourne would react to the knowledge that negotiations had been reopened between them. But he soon saw that his confidante seemed eager enough to throw Annabella in his way again, probably as an antidote to his more dangerous liaison. She had sent on to him Annabella's specifications for a husband (probably those written at Lady Melbourne's request the year before). His reply would have shocked the poor girl. "I return you the plan of A[nnabella]'s spouse elect, of which I shall say nothing because I do not understand it. . . . She seems to have been spoiled—not as children usually are—but systematically Clarissa Harlowed into an awkward kind of correctness, with a dependence upon her own infallibility which will or may lead her into some egregious blunder. I don't mean the usual error of young gentlewomen, but she will find exactly what she wants, and then discover that it is much more dignified than entertaining." [n]

Byron was instinctively aware of what this friendship might mean to Miss Milbanke. Speaking of her renewal of the correspondence twelve months after she had refused his first proposal, he told Medwin: "The tenor of her letter was, that although she could not love me, she desired my friendship. Friendship is a dangerous word for young ladies; it is Love full-fledged, and waiting for a fine day to fly." [n]

The next day he wrote Annabella with less restraint and

more naturalness: "Your sweeping sentence 'on the circles where we have met' amuses me much when I recollect some of those who constituted that society. After all, bad as it is, it has its *agrémens.* The great object of life is sensation—to feel that we exist, even though in pain. It is this 'craving void' which drives us to gaming—to battle—to travel. . . ." [n] Annabella could take him as he was or leave him.

And now the "craving void," the irresistible desire for "sensation," drove him, despite his better judgment, back to Augusta. On September 8 he wrote to Lady Melbourne: "I leave town to-morrow for a few days, come what may; and as I am sure you would get the better of my resolution, I shall not venture to encounter you." [n] After announcing the next day that he had postponed his journey, he added: ". . . I am nevertheless very much perplexed; however, that must end one way or the other. You say, 'Write to me, at all events'; depend upon it I will, till the moment arrives (if it does arrive) when I feel that you ought not to acknowledge me as a correspondent. . . ." [n]

Through July and August, Byron had been busily engaged in writing and sending off to Murray additions and emendations for *The Giaour,* which the "Anak of stationers," [n] as Byron called him, was willing enough to receive, for the poem was selling rapidly, and the purple passages in the added matter, as well as the hints of secret crimes which rumor was now willing to ascribe to the author, increased the public interest. Three new editions, the third, fourth, and fifth, each with large additions to the text (the fifth had nearly double the number of lines of the first edition), appeared before the end of August.[n] On the 26th, Byron wrote: "I have, but with some difficulty, *not* added any more to this snake of a poem, which has been lengthening its rattles every month." [n]

Since the composition of *Childe Harold* had given relief to his deepest feelings of despondency and frustration Byron had learned to seek that assuagement in writing. His turning back to *The Giaour* at this time was an escape from the quandary into which recent events, and particularly his relationship with Augusta, had thrown him. Getting back into its moods offered him the truest catharsis. The lines he had written to free himself from another emotional crisis he found most applicable to his present state of mind.

*I loved her—Love will find its way*
*Through paths where wolves would fear to prey; . . .*
*I did not vainly seek, nor sigh:*
*Yet sometimes, with remorse, in vain*
*I wish she had not loved again. . . .*
*But look—'tis written on my brow!*
*There read of Cain the curse and crime. . . .*[n]

In the early hours past midnight, after he had shed the dross of a ball or dull dinner and felt himself alone with his innermost thoughts, his whole being expanded and words flowed from his pen:

*Yes, Love indeed is light from heaven;*
*A spark of that immortal fire*
*With angels shared, by Alla given,*
*To lift from earth our low desire. . . .*
*I grant* my *love imperfect, all*
*That mortals by the name miscall;*
*Then deem it evil, what thou wilt;*
*But say, oh say,* hers *was not Guilt!* [n]

But however readily Byron might identify himself with his heroes, he was perturbed that others should. In the middle of August, to counter among his friends a story circulated by Caroline Lamb (perhaps because he himself had hinted to her something of his Eastern adventures?), he asked Lord Sligo to write out his recollections of what he had heard in Athens of the incident of the saving of the Turkish girl.[n] Byron showed it to Lady Melbourne and then to Moore, to whom he wrote: "This letter was written to me on account of a *different story* circulated by some gentlewomen of our acquaintance, a little too close to the text." [5]

[5] *LJ*, II, 258. Letter of Sept. 1, 1813. Byron wrote to Lady Melbourne: "I enclose you a letter from Sligo with *his Giaour*, which differs from our friend *C.'s* as much as from mine. . . ." (*LBC*, I, 177.) After inking out ten lines of Sligo's letter so completely that they could not be read (the MS. is at John Murray's), Byron sent it to Moore, Lord Holland, "Monk" Lewis, Rogers, and Lady Melbourne. The deleted part, he said, "contained merely

Still in a feverish state of anxiety and perplexity, Byron set off for Six Mile Bottom, probably on September 11.[n] He cannot have stayed more than a day or two. What happened there can only be guessed. Did Byron reveal to Augusta the dangers of their going abroad together? Or had she begun to feel remorse and to draw back from the intimacy they had established? Something of the sort may be surmised from his leaving her on the 13th to go to Cambridge, where he and Scrope Davies drank six bottles of wine in an evening.

It is evident that he was seeking some kind of escape, for on the day he arrived in London he wrote to John Murray: "Will you pray enquire after any ship with a convoy *taking passengers* and get me one if possible? I mean not in a ship of war, but anything that may be *paid* for. I have a friend and 3 servants—Gibraltar or Minorca—or Zante."[n]

Shortly after, he accepted the invitation of his friend Wedderburn Webster to visit at Aston Hall, near Rotherham. From there, after several days in that absurd household, he wrote a long letter to Lady Melbourne on the 21st: ". . . feeling feverish and restless in town I flew off, and here I am on a visit to my friend Webster. . . . His bride, Lady Frances, is a pretty, pleasing woman, but in delicate health. . . . The place is very well, and quiet, and the children only scream in a low voice, so that I am not much disturbed, and shall stay a few days in tolerable repose. W[ebster] don't want sense, nor good nature, but both are occasionally obscured by his suspicions, and absurdities of all descriptions. . . . he preached me a sermon on his wife's

some Turkish names, and circumstantial evidence of the girl's detection, not very important or decorous." (*LJ*, II, 258; letter to Moore of Sept. 1, 1813.) It may be that in asking Sligo for this letter Byron wanted to know just how much had been known in Athens about his part in the affair, and how much Sligo knew, for he wrote to Dr. E. D. Clarke that Sligo "arrived just after my departure, and I did not know till last summer that he knew anything of the matter." He could acknowledge the story (less the deleted part, which may well hold the key to the mystery of Byron's personal interest in the affair) without committing himself too much. After assuring Clarke that it was not far from the truth, he added mysteriously: "There was nothing that led further than to the water's edge; but one part (as is often the case in life) was more singular than any of the *Giaour's* adventures." (*LJ*, II, 311. Letter of Dec. 15, 1813.)

good qualities, concluding by an assertion that in all moral and mortal qualities, she was very like 'Christ!!!' I think the Virgin Mary would have been a more appropriate typification; but it was the first comparison of the kind I ever heard, and made me laugh till he was angry. . . ." [n]

Lady Melbourne was no doubt delighted that her protégé had found so much innocent amusement in the country, but the fact that he had not mentioned his other more serious affair could not have left her quite easy in mind.

Having no relish for the Doncaster races, to which the whole household repaired a few days later, Byron ran away to London for a week, promising to return the following Saturday. In London he found a letter from Annabella Milbanke awaiting him. She had been disappointed by his last letter. It was far too "Byronic," and he had not shown a willingness to be reformed by her appeals. He was still fascinated by the strange intelligent girl and intrigued by the interest she persisted in showing in him, but he would not falsify his character merely to gain her approval. "You don't like my 'restless' doctrines—I should be very sorry if you did; but I can't stagnate nevertheless."

He then turned to a subject which she accused him of having avoided—"an awful one—'Religion.'" He would avoid it no longer. "I was bred in Scotland among Calvinists in the first part of my life which gave me a dislike to that persuasion. . . . I believe doubtless in God, and should be happy to be convinced of much more. If I do not at present place implicit faith in tradition and revelation of any human creed, I hope it is not from want of reverence for the Creator but the created. . . ." [n]

Annabella would not have been flattered had she known how extensively his thoughts were occupied elsewhere. "I had reasons of my own," he wrote Lady Melbourne, then at Brocket, "some bad, and others good, for not accompanying the party to D[oncaste]r. . . ." He had intended to see Augusta again and did not want to become involved with any of the ladies at Aston. "I have tried," he added, "and hardly, too, to vanquish my demon; but to very little purpose, for a resource that seldom failed me before did in this instance. I mean *transferring* my regards to another. . . . and *here* I am—*what* I am you know already." [n] And the next day he wrote his confidante: "I have been signing my will to-day. . . ." This will, which superseded the one of 1811, left half his property to his cousin and heir George Byron and half to Augusta.[n] So Lady Melbourne was disappointed in the hope that Lady Frances Webster would divert him from Augusta. Nor was there any hope in the renewed correspondence with Annabella (he was now apparently showing her letters to Lady Melbourne), for there appeared to be no romantic feeling in his analysis of her self-delusions.

"The epistles of your mathematician (A. would now be ambiguous)[6] continue; and the last concludes with a repetition of a desire that none but papa and mamma should know it; why *you* should not, seems to me quite ludicrous, and is now past praying for; but observe, here is the strictest of St. Ursula's 11,000 what do you call 'ems? a wit, a moralist, and religionist, enters into a clandestine correspondence with a personage generally presumed a great *roué,* and drags her aged parents into this secret treaty." [n]

In the meantime, Holland House offered some mild amusements. On the 26th Byron met Southey there—"the best-looking bard I have seen for some time," he told Moore. "To have that poet's head and shoulders, I would almost have written his Sapphics. He is certainly a prepossessing person to look on, and a man of talent, and all that, and—*there* is his eulogy." [7]

Writing to tell Lady Melbourne that he was going back to Aston, Byron continued the theme of the absurd Webster, who had written that the countess he was pursuing was "inexorable." "What a lucky fellow—happy in his obstacles." As for himself, he commented casually, "I am not exactly cut out for the lady of the mansion. . . . She evidently expects to be attacked, and

[6] This obviously indicates that "A." in his thoughts and his letters to Lady Melbourne now referred to Augusta.

[7] *LJ*, II, 266. Letter of Sept. 27, 1813. Southey's record of the meeting was no less guarded. He said that Byron had asked Rogers "to make for him all sorts of amends honourable for having tried his wit upon me at the expense of his discretion [in *English Bards*]. . . . so we met with all becoming courtesy on both sides, and I saw a man whom in voice, manner, and countenance, I liked very much more than either his character or his writings had given me reason to expect." (*The Life and Correspondence of Robert Southey*, IV, 44. Letter of Sept. 28, 1813, to Mrs. Southey.)

seems prepared for a brilliant defence; my character as a *roué* has gone before me, and my careless and quiet behaviour astonished her so much that I believe she began to think herself ugly, or me blind—if not worse."

And he added what may have seemed to Lady Melbourne an ominous sentence: "I have also reasons for returning there on Sunday, with which they have nothing to do. . . ." [n] Byron had suggested that he would like to have his sister at Aston Hall. On September 30 he wrote to Webster: "I have not yet had my sister's answer to Lady Frances's very kind invitation, but expect it tomorrow." [n]

Lady Melbourne, however, no doubt saw more clearly than Byron suspected that his interest in Lady Frances was piqued beyond what he would at present admit, being uncertain of her response. At any rate, the household intrigued him, and he was going back. Aston Hall, which Webster was renting at the time, was the very mansion to which Byron's father had come with Lady Carmarthen, "with whom," Byron told Moore, "he adulterated before his majority." "I stayed a week with the family," he added, "and behaved very well—though the lady of the house is young, and religious, and pretty, and the master is my particular friend." [n]

Byron left for Aston on October 3. At first he was disappointed that Augusta had pleaded illness and had not accepted the invitation, and was annoyed as well as bored by the impossible jealousies of Webster, who had lost his countess and his temper. His host's conduct was growing intolerable, he told Lady Melbourne. Webster took umbrage at Byron's lending some Italian books (Dante and Alfieri) to Lady Frances, "because, forsooth, it is a language which doth infinite damage!!" In spite of the fact that two other guests, one "handsome, but silly," the other "frightful, but facetious," paid her ten times more attention, Webster, Byron said, "suspects something extraordinary from my nonchalance." [n]

But within three days Byron's passive attitude was paying dividends and his interest in the game had increased. He gave Lady Melbourne a full account of his diversionary employments. "In these last few days I have had a good deal of conversation with an amiable person, whom (as we deal in *letters* and initials only) we will denominate *Ph.*" Lady Frances had been carried all at once out of indifference. Byron announced: "I have made love, and if I am to believe mere *words* (for there we have hitherto stopped), it is returned." They were in the billiard room when Byron "made a speech." "We were before on very amicable terms, and I remembered being asked an odd question, 'how a woman who liked a man could inform him of it when he did not perceive it.' I also observed that we went on with our game (of billiards) without *counting the hazards;* and supposed that, as mine certainly were not, the thoughts of the other party also were not exactly occupied by what was our ostensible pursuit. Not quite, though pretty well satisfied with my progress, I took a very imprudent step with pen and paper, in tender and tolerably turned *prose* periods. . . . (I am this moment interrupted by the *Marito,* and write this before him, he has brought me a political pamphlet in MS. to decypher and applaud, I shall content myself with the last; oh, he is gone again), my billet produced an *answer,* a very unequivocal one too, but a little too much about virtue, and indulgence of attachment in some sort of etherial process, in which the soul is principally concerned, which I don't very well understand, being a bad metaphysician; but one generally *ends* and *begins* with platonism, and, as my proselyte is only twenty, there is time enough to materialize."

Then in his burst of confidence Byron concluded: "I remember my last case was the reverse, as Major O'Flaherty recommends, 'we fought first and explained afterwards.'" He added a postscript to his letter at six that evening: "This business is growing serious, and I think *Platonism* in some peril." [n]

Byron's prophecy in 1811 that Webster would be "a noble subject for cuckoldom in three years" [n] seemed in a fair way to being fulfilled ahead of time. Two days later at Newstead, where Webster had accompanied him, he continued his narrative, while the fatuous *marito* sat opposite drinking Byron's expensive wines, relics of his extravagant Cambridge carousings. He was astonished at the event of the past week. "It has changed my views, my wishes, my hopes, my everything, and will furnish you with additional proof of my weakness. Mine guest (late host) has just been congratulating himself on possessing a partner without *passion.* I don't know, and cannot yet speak with certainty, but I never yet saw more decisive preliminary symptoms. . . . She . . . managed to give me a note and to receive another, and a ring before [Webster's] very face, and yet she is a thorough devotee, and takes prayers, morning and evening, besides being measured for a new bible once a quarter." [n]

The irony of the farcical setting was sharpened by the fact that Webster asked for a loan of £1,000 from Byron, who sent off to Hanson from Nottingham a request for an advance of that sum against Claughton's expected payments.[n] Back at Aston the next day the curtain was raised on a new act, the many scenes of which Byron described with zest. One part of himself was now deeply involved emotionally in the affair, for Lady Frances had the combination of innocence and experience which most appealed to Byron. Almost adolescent and virgin-like in her responses, for she had never been really in love with her husband, having married at seventeen to escape a disagreeable family, she was extremely romantic and at the same time rather wily in self-deception and in deceiving the green-eyed Webster. Without relinquishing the seriousness of his ardor or admitting any insincerity in the pursuit, another part of Byron's mind perceived with clear detachment the high comedy, and he knew that he had a perfect audience in his confidante. And as scene after scene unfolded, each more ridiculous than the preceding, he came to savor the cynical reporting of it more than the poignancy of the experience itself.

Lady Melbourne could enjoy it because she thought he was now safe from worse entanglements. In fact, he had so little time or heart for writing to Augusta that she thought he was angry with her for not coming to Aston, and he had to reassure her that his silence had arisen "from several circumstances which I cannot now detail." [n] After this note he did not write her again for several weeks.

The afternoon of his return to Aston from Newstead he reported: "I began the week so well that I thought the conclusion would have been more decisive. But the topography of this house is not the most favourable." [n] Two days later he wrote, justifying himself to his confidante: "Anything, you will allow, is better than the *last;* and I cannot exist without some object of attachment. You will laugh at my perpetual *changes,* but recollect, the circumstances which have broken off the last three and don't exactly attribute their conclusion to caprice." [n]

The next day the narrative continued: "But this is 'le premier pas,' my dear $L^y$ M., at least I think so. . . . I believe little but 'l'occasion manque,' and to that many things are tending. . . . We have progressively improved into a less spiritual species of tenderness, but the seal is not yet fixed, though the wax is preparing for the impression." [n]

In the spacious ruins of Newstead, where the whole party had gone in the middle of October, the ironic dénouement came sooner than Byron expected. "You were right," he told Lady Melbourne. "I have been a little too sanguine as to the *conclusion*—but hear. One day, left entirely to ourselves, was nearly fatal—another such *victory,* and with Pyrrhus we were lost—it came to this. 'I am entirely at your *mercy.* I own it. I give myself up to you. I am not *cold*—whatever I seem to others; but I know that I cannot bear the reflection hereafter. Do not imagine that these are mere words. I tell you the truth—now act as you will.' Was I wrong? I spared her. There was a something so very peculiar in her manner—a kind of mild decision—no scene—not even a struggle; but still I know not what, that convinced me that she was serious. It was not the mere '*No,*' which one has heard forty times before, and always with the same accent; but the *tone,* and the aspect—yet I sacrificed much—the hour *two* in the morning—away—the Devil whispering that it was mere *verbiage,* etc. . . .

"You ask if I am prepared to go 'all lengths.' If you mean by 'all lengths' anything including duel, or divorce? I answer, *Yes.* I love her. . . . I have offered to go away with her, and her answer, whether sincere or not, is 'that on *my account* she declines it.' . . . Poor thing—she is either the most *artful* or *artless* of her age (20) I ever encountered. . . . The most perplexing—and yet I can't prevail upon myself to give it up—is the *caressing* system. In her it appears perfectly childish, and I do think innocent; but it really puzzles all the Scipio about me to confine myself to the laudable portion of these endearments." *n*

In quiet desperation Byron drank too much after dinner, and then about midnight, goaded by the boasting Webster, he emptied his skull cup, which held more than a bottle of claret, at one draft, and was put to bed by Fletcher. Two days later nothing had happened, and Byron, in the petulance of frustration, proclaimed: ". . . I have thrown away the best opportunity that ever was wasted upon a spoiled child." He and Webster had not come to an open quarrel, but had "subsided into a mortal coldness." *n*

At length the melancholy party came to an end on the 19th. But when Byron left for London, Webster "was seized with a sudden fit of friendship" and insisted on accompanying him. Actually, though Byron did not dwell upon this in his account to Lady Melbourne, Webster had to sign some papers to get his £1,000 loan.[8]

When Byron had had time to reflect on his failure to be "decisive" with Lady Frances, he could not regret his restraint. "I do detest anything which is not perfectly mutual, and any subsequent reproaches (as I know by one former long ago bitter experience) would heap coals of fire upon my head. . . . Perhaps after all, I was her dupe—if so—I am the dupe also of the few good feelings I could ever boast of, but here perhaps I am my own dupe too, in attributing to a good motive what may be quite otherwise." *n*

As soon as he was away from the lady, he could philosophize about the passion, which by that very token was beginning to wane, though he would not yet admit it, and his loyalty held him to a readiness for any eventuality. ". . . you really *wrong* me too," he wrote Lady Melbourne, "if you do not suppose that I would sacrifice everything for Ph—I hate sentiment, and in consequence my epistolary levity makes you believe me as hollow and heartless as my letters are light."

Lady Frances continued to write, with a mixture of boldness

[8] *LBC*, I, 206–7. Letter of Oct. 19, 1813. When they were about to leave for London, Webster said: "Don't you see how the poor girl *doats* on me; when I quit her but for a week, as you perceive, she is absolutely overwhelmed. . . ." (*LBC*, I, 208.)

and prudence, letters showing some bewilderment and fear of betrayal and using "two words, 'effusions' and 'soul,' rather oftener than befits out of the circulating library." [n] Byron still protested to Lady Melbourne his earnestness in the affair, but he was beginning to be occupied with other persons and other things. He had found time immediately on his arrival in London on October 20 to send an enthusiastic recommendation for his friend Hodgson, who had applied for the job of translating Lucien Bonaparte's long poem *Charlemagne.*[n] And before the end of the month he showed a more tangible evidence of his friendship. Hodgson was attached to a Miss Tayler, whose mother would not consent to marriage because of Hodgson's debts. Byron and Henry Drury, who was married to the girl's sister, traveled all night in a post chaise to interview the mother, then at Oxford. All obstacles were removed when Byron assured her that Hodgson would soon be clear of debt. Soon after they returned to London, Byron took his friend to Hammersley's bank and there ordered £1,000 put to his credit (Hodgson previously had received £400 from Byron). Byron asked for no bond or receipt, and intended it as a gift.[n] This was probably part of the money that had been set aside for Byron's proposed journey abroad, but that trip had now become a very remote possibility.

But he had not escaped from the agitations of his frustrated love. For that there was only one sovereign remedy—poetic expression. On November 4 he wrote to Lady Melbourne: "In the last three days I have been quite shut up; my mind has been from *late* and *later* events in such a state of fermentation, that as usual I have been obliged to empty it in rhyme, and am in the very heart of another Eastern tale—something of the *Giaour* cast—but not so sombre, though rather more villainous. This is my usual resource; if it were not for some such occupation to dispel reflection during *inaction,* I verily believe I should very often go mad." [n] Before the tale was published he told her: ". . . it will for some *reasons interest you* more than anybody. These I leave you to discover. . . ." [n]

The composition was the work of a week, he told Moore. "All convulsions end with me in rhyme; and to solace my midnights, I have scribbled another Turkish story. . . ." [n] He had finished

JOHN MURRAY II, BYRON'S PUBLISHER

LADY CAROLINE LAMB IN PAGE'S COSTUME

major revisions by the 12th and sent copies to Gifford and Hodgson for criticism.[n] The poem was first called *Zuleika,* "the *Persian poetical* name for *Potiphar's* wife," [n] which he had taken for his heroine, but before publication he changed the title to *The Bride of Abydos.*

The theme of incest (Selim and Zuleika were brother and sister in the first draft) had a powerful attraction for him, but he shied off from it at the last. ". . . I had nearly made them rather too much akin to each other," he wrote E. D. Clarke; "and though the wild passions of the East, and some great examples in Alfieri, Ford, and Schiller (to stop short of antiquity), might have pleaded in favour of a copyist, yet the time and the north . . . induced me to alter their consanguinity and confine them to cousinship." [n]

Despite the fact that both Augusta and Lady Frances were very much in his mind when he wrote *The Bride of Abydos,* Byron had not written to the former for some time when on November 8 he sent an apology.[n] During his perturbation over Lady Frances he had found no time for the moralizing Miss Milbanke either. On October 23 he had told Lady Melbourne: "My Seaham correspondence has ceased on both sides, and I shall not renew it." [n] But Annabella had no intention of losing contact. "The description of Love [in *the Giaour*] almost makes *me* in love," she wrote Lady Melbourne. "I shall be glad of his stay in England as I may hope to have some share of his agreeable society next year in London. . . . I consider his acquaintance as so desirable that I would incur the risk of being called a Flirt for the sake of enjoying it. . . ." Then she turned to her present studies —". . . metaphysical reasoning, Locke, Dugald Stuart, &c. My early study of Mathematics has contributed to lead me to these pursuits, since they are in fact the Demonstrat[ions] of Moral Philosophy." [n]

It may have been Lady Melbourne's showing him this letter that precipitated Byron's facetious communication to the "Princess of Parallelograms" on November 10. As for mathematics, he wrote, "The only part I remember which gave me much delight were those theorems (is that the word), in which, after ringing the changes upon A B and C D, etc., I at last came to 'which is absurd'—'which is impossible,' and at this point I have always arrived and I fear always shall through life. . . ."[n]

In his next letter he made a confession of a more serious sort: "I by no means rank poetry or poets high in the scale of intellect. This may look like affectation, but it is my real opinion. It is the lava of the imagination whose eruption prevents an earthquake. . . . I prefer the talents of action—of war, or the senate, or even of science,—to all the speculations of those mere dreamers. . . ."[n]

Annabella must have been glad to hear that he saw no obstacle to their seeing each other in London in the spring, but she was taken aback by the reason he gave for it. He could be depended on not to break the pact of undemanding friendship, though he still valued what he had lost. As for "the being to whom I would commit the whole happiness of my future life,—I have never yet seen but two approaching to the likeness. The first I was too young to have a prospect of obtaining [Mary Chaworth]. . . . *The second*—the only woman to whom I ever seriously pretended as a wife—had disposed of her heart already, and I think it too late to look for a third."[n]

Annabella was almost hysterical because of her own deception. She told herself that she was "purified from *Self* in *this* concern; but I feel very uneasy at the idea of keeping up a deception, & especially with one who has undoubtedly practised no deception with me. . . . I shall be unhappy until I can regain *truth*."[n] But before she could "regain *truth*," she heard that Byron had left England.

Actually, he had tried to go, but had been frustrated again. Soon after his return to town, he had planned to go to Holland with J. W. Ward, the projected tour to the Mediterranean now seeming impossible because of the plague. But the illness of an uncle took Ward to Scotland, and the trip was postponed indefinitely.[n]

On November 14, just after he had sent the new Eastern poem to Murray, Byron began a journal. The first entry was a self-examination and recapitulation of his life, which he now saw as mostly a record of disillusionment and failure. "At five-and-twenty, when the better part of life is over, one should be *something*;—and what am I? nothing but five-and-twenty—and the odd months. What have I seen? the same man all over the world, —ay, and woman too. . . . I wish one was—I don't know what I wish. It is odd I never set myself seriously to wishing without attaining it—and repenting." And then referring to *Zuleika,* as his Turkish tale was still called, he wrote: "I believe the composition of it kept me alive—for it was written to drive my thoughts from the recollection of ——

*'Dear sacred name, rest ever unreveal'd'* [n]

At least, even here, my hand would tremble to write it." [n]

In his discontent, thoughts of marriage occurred to him frequently. It was the one thing he had not tried. Half his mind longed for it as a peaceful state, but the other half, disillusioned by observation, shied away from it. And the failure of his political career still rankled and contributed to his general dissatisfaction. "I have declined presenting the Debtors' Petition, being sick of parliamentary mummeries," he confided to his journal on the 14th. "I have never yet set to it *con amore;*—one must have some excuse to one's self for laziness, or inability, or both, and this is mine. 'Company, villainous company, hath been the spoil of me.' . . ." [n]

Byron was going out again a great deal, though he avoided dinners when he could. "I wish I were in the country," he wrote in his journal, "to take exercise,—instead of being obliged to *cool* by abstinence, in lieu of it. I should not so much mind a little accession of flesh,—my bones can well bear it. But the worst is, the devil always came with it,—till I starved him out,—and I will *not* be the slave of *any* appetite." [n]

Moore unfortunately was out of town at this season, and Byron regetted his absence. "In society, he is gentlemanly, gentle, and, altogether, more pleasing than any individual with whom I am acquainted." [n] He had little desire for closer association with other literary men. "Southey, I have not seen much of. . . . he is the only existing entire man of letters. . . . His manners are mild, but not those of a man of the world, and his talents of the first order. His prose is perfect. Of his poetry there are various opinions. . . . He has *passages* equal to any thing." [n]

Byron had taken Lord Salisbury's box for the season at Covent

Garden, but on the evening of the 22nd he joined Lady Holland and her party at Drury Lane. He generally found the best company with the Hollands. The next night he dined with Ward, in a small party of the kind of people he liked—George Canning and John Hookham Frere, onetime writers for the *Anti-Jacobin*, "Conversation" Sharp, "a man of elegant mind, and who has lived much with the best—Fox, Horne Tooke, Windham, Fitzpatrick, and all the agitators of other times and tongues." [n] Here was intellectual stimulation worth a dozen parties in the literary coteries of Miss Berry and her familiars. Byron's respect for Ward was daily increasing. "Ward—I like Ward," he wrote. "By Mahomet! I begin to think I like every body;—a disposition not to be encouraged;—a sort of social gluttony that swallows every thing set before it." [n]

Neither social life nor writing, however, could suppress Byron's feeling that his powers were being wasted. He concluded that "no one should be a rhymer who could be any thing better. And this is what annoys one, to see Scott and Moore, and Campbell and Rogers, who might have all been agents and leaders, now mere spectators. . . .[9] To be the first man—not the Dictator—not the Sylla, but the Washington or the Aristides—the leader in talent and truth—is next to the Divinity! . . . I shall never be any thing, or rather always be nothing. The most I can hope is, that some will say, 'He might, perhaps, if he would.'" [n]

His love affair with Frances Webster was fast degenerating into a kind of comedy which he could not help enjoying at the same time that he continued to feel the serious pangs of the attachment, made more acute by the obstacles of separation. When Frances finally wrote, it was to justify with a ludicrous logic her own deception of her husband. She was anxious above all else to keep the *marito* deceived, and yet she was rash in her actions—". . . she writes; makes me answer through an address to a 3rd person whom she has *not trusted*," and she directed him to send

[9] In his journal Byron made a "Gradus ad Parnassum," putting Walter Scott at the top of the triangle among living writers, Rogers below him, then Moore and Campbell together in third place, followed by Southey, Wordsworth, and Coleridge, and "the many." But he confessed that this was not his own ranking but what he believed popular opinion would assign. (*LJ*, II, 344. Journal, Nov. 24, 1813.)

his portrait by Holmes through the same channel.[n] This picture, which was one of three or four Caroline Lamb had acquired (she had already relinquished one to Lady Melbourne, which probably went to Lady Oxford, and one which Byron gave to Augusta), was, Byron noted, "not a flatterer, but dark and stern,—even black as the mood in which my mind was scorching last July, when I sat for it. All the others of me, like most portraits whatsoever, are, of course, more agreeable than nature." [n] Byron had again forced Caroline to give up his portrait to another woman.[1] When Lady Frances finally received the picture, her only comment was: "Indeed it is like." [n]

In his present state of mind Byron would have welcomed an *éclaircissement* with Webster, or so he told Lady Melbourne. If it led to a duel and he was killed, it would be "so *dramatic* a conclusion; all the sex would be enamoured of my memory, all the wits would have their jests, and the moralists their sermon. C. would go wild with *grief* that *it did not happen about her.* Ly O[xford] would say I deserved it for not coming to Cagliari—and—poor —— [Augusta?] [n] she would be really uncomfortable." And thinking of the undemanding fondness of Augusta again, he wrote: "Do you know I am much afraid that that perverse passion was my deepest after all." [n]

On December 2, *The Bride of Abydos* was published. Byron could have had little to complain of in the critical reception of his late work. Gifford, whose opinion he most valued, had praised it highly, and Murray himself was more than pleased

[1] Byron compensated her by ordering Murray to send her a copy of *The Bride of Abydos.* (*LJ*, II, 288.) Actually, Caroline had already wheedled a copy from Murray. Shortly after the affair of the forged letter, in February 1813, she had become acquainted with Murray (Byron to Lady Melbourne, Feb. 7, 1813, *LBC*, I, 133–4) and cultivated the acquaintance in order to keep a secret contact with Byron. It was one of the strangest friendships in literary history. Murray apparently came under her spell and was frequently torn between loyalty to Byron and pity for Caroline, so that he no longer could allow his right hand to know what his left hand was doing. She several times coaxed Murray to let her see the manuscripts of Byron's poems before they were published, a thing that would have made the author furious had he known. By the autumn of 1813 she was on the footing of a confidante with Murray, often an embarrassing one. In return for some information about Byron she sent him presents.

with his author. When Byron tentatively raised the issue of pay for the new poem after his publisher had expressed a willingness to pay five hundred guineas for the copyright of *The Giaour*, Murray replied: "I restore 'The Giaour' to your Lordship entirely, and for it, the 'Bride of Abydos,' and the miscellaneous poems intended to fill up the volume . . . I beg leave to offer you the sum of One Thousand Guineas. . . ."[n] Byron recorded this handsome offer in his journal, but added that he would not accept it—". . . it is too much, though I am strongly tempted, merely for the *say* of it. No bad price for a fortnight's (a week each) what?—the gods know—it was intended to be called poetry."[n] He was still debating whether he dared or cared to violate his own pride by accepting money for his literary work. He put off the decision by telling Murray that the arrangements could wait for six months, when it would be time enough to know whether the offer was a losing one.[n] But Murray knew his public. The *Bride* sold even faster than the *Giaour*. Within a short time Sir James Mackintosh wrote: "Lord Byron is the author of the day; six thousand of his *Bride of Abydos* have been sold within a month."[n]

Byron had sent copies of the two Turkish poems to Leigh Hunt (still in the Surrey Gaol), who had been long hoping for another visit from the young lord whose society in the summer had been so congenial. Hunt's enthusiastic reply brought an apology from Byron, who gave the excuse of personal affairs for his neglect.[n] In his journal Byron wrote: "Hunt is an extraordinary character, and not exactly of the present age. He reminds me more of the Pym and Hampden times—much talent, great independence of spirit, and an austere, yet not repulsive, aspect. . . . He is, perhaps, a little opinionated, as all men who are the *centre* of *circles* . . . must be. . . ."[n]

Byron's sense of guilt at his neglect of Hunt was not so great as that which he felt at not being able to overcome his inertia and diffidence sufficiently to present in the House of Lords the petition of W. J. Baldwin, a debtor in the King's Bench prison, who had been sending pathetic letters to him describing the inhuman treatment of the prisoners and asking for prison reform. The cause appealed to him as had that of the Nottingham weavers, but the emotional crises of the past months and his loss of confidence in his Parliamentary abilities left him with no stomach for the business. He excused himself in his own mind by reflecting that he now lacked the stimulation and encouragement which Lady Oxford had always given him, but he was not happy in his rationalization, for he always saw through his own weaknesses. "Ah, I am as bad as that dog Sterne, who preferred whining over 'a dead ass to relieving a living mother.' . . ."[2] He finally got others interested in the petition, and it was presented by Lord Holland.

Byron was again the literary idol of the London season, sharing the honors with the loquacious and dominating Mme de Staël, who was his warm admirer since he had praised her in a note to the *Bride*. He was invited everywhere, but declined more dinners than he accepted. One night at Lord Holland's he was talking with Thomas Campbell when their host brought out a vessel that looked like a Catholic censer and, approaching Campbell, exclaimed: "Here is some *incense* for you." Campbell, a little piqued at the rival poet's popularity, replied: "Carry it to Lord Byron, *he is used to it.*" Byron's comment in his journal was: "Now, this comes of 'bearing no brother near the throne.' "[n]

Byron's distaste for society increased with his growing disquiet. His life was now an alternation of dining out and remaining home in solitude. When he did have supper with "Monk" Lewis, he was sorry, both for the boredom he had endured and for the indignities to his abused stomach.

Indecision, purposelessness, and ennui crept over Byron as the days passed. He had taken to smoking cigars, as he had formerly chewed tobacco, to keep down the gnawing pangs of hunger when he abstained from food, though he would have preferred a hookah or chibouk. On December 7 he wrote in his journal: "Went to bed, and slept dreamlessly, but not refreshingly. Awoke, and up an hour before being called; but dawdled three hours in dressing. When one subtracts from life infancy (which is vegeta-

[2] *LJ*, II, 359. Journal, Dec. 1, 1813. On December 6 he wrote: "Another scribble from Martin [*sic*] Baldwin the petitioner; I have neither head nor nerves to present it. That confounded supper at Lewis's has spoiled my digestion and my philanthropy. I have no more charity than a cruet of vinegar." (*LJ*, II, 366.)

tion),—sleep, eating, and swilling—buttoning and unbuttoning—how much remains of downright existence? The summer of a dormouse." [n]

Dr. John Allen, a friend of Lord Holland, had lent Byron "a quantity of Burns's unpublished and never-to-be-published Letters," which gave him subject for comment in the journal: "They are full of oaths and obscene songs. What an antithetical mind!—tenderness, roughness—delicacy, coarseness—sentiment, sensuality—soaring and grovelling, dirt and deity—all mixed up in that one compound of inspired clay!

"It seems strange; a true voluptuary will never abandon his mind to the grossness of reality. It is by exalting the earthly, the material, the *physique* of our pleasures, by veiling these ideas, by forgetting them altogether, or, at least, never naming them hardly to one's self, that we alone can prevent them from disgusting." [n]

Byron was self-conscious enough to be aware of how closely he had touched here upon the paradox of his own nature. In the need to veil the "physique" of his pleasures in some ideal essence and to escape from the grossness of reality, and in the realistic earthiness that prevented him from ever achieving that goal, he came closer to Burns than he wished to admit.

The demon gnawing at his vitals during the first half of December had been aggravated by his feeling for Augusta and the struggle against it, for no matter how much he fought it, he could not escape the feeling that no woman was so comforting and satisfying to his self-esteem as Augusta, so yielding to his every wish, so sensuous and undemanding, and so motherly and protective at the same time. As his resolution weakened, his letters to Lady Melbourne fell off, for he knew her sentiments and fears on the subject.[n] By December 11 he had determined to pay Augusta a visit at Six Mile Bottom, but he delayed his journey, and by the 15th she had arrived in London.[n]

On the 18th his journal ceased. He had reserved it for his thoughts, and now they were such as he could not write. The entry for December 14, 15, and 16 consisted of two short sentences: "Much done, but nothing to record. It is quite enough to set down my thoughts,—my actions will rarely bear introspection." [n]

On the day he laid his journal aside he began another Eastern tale, this one more excoriating and self-revealing than any he had yet written. It was the only way the perplexity of his present situation could be relieved. Prose could no longer carry the burden. "*I suoi pensieri in lui dormir non ponno*"—"His thoughts cannot sleep within him"—was the motto he chose from Tasso's *Jerusalem Delivered.*[n] And at the head of the first canto he placed the famous lines from Dante's *Inferno:*

> "*nessun maggior dolore,*
> *Che recordarsi del tempo felice*
> *Nella miseria. . . .*" [3]

With Conrad, "The Corsair," he could range vicariously over "the dark blue sea" of the lovingly remembered Greek Archipelago. There too he could find another kind of freedom—the expansion of spirit which the creative process gave and which permitted him to look through the veil of fiction at his own ego with a frankness not possible even in his letters to Lady Melbourne.

Once started, he wrote feverishly far into the night at his Bennet Street lodgings, and he carried the manuscript with him when he accompanied Augusta home, continuing it there in the small hours at Newmarket.[n] He was back in London by the 27th, when he completed the first draft, which had been turned out at the rate of nearly two hundred lines a day.[n] The next day Dallas called while he was still busy on the poem (probably revising and writing out a fair copy). Piqued at Murray, who had expressed a fear that he might "out-write" himself, Byron presented the copyright to Dallas with the stipulation that he should give it to some other publisher. "He asked me to call and hear the portions read as he wrote them," Dallas recalled. "I went

[3] *Inferno,* Canto V. Byron later translated this canto as "Francesca da Rimini," rendering the lines of Francesca:

> "*The greatest of all woes*
> *Is to remind us of our happy days*
> *In misery. . . .*"

every morning, and was astonished at the rapidity of his composition. He gave me the poem complete on new-year's day, 1814. . . ." [n]

Before the year ended, two ghosts of Byron's past bobbed up again to haunt him. On Christmas Eve, Mary Chaworth-Musters, whose husband, Jack Musters, was now riding after other game than foxes, wrote to the lame boy with whom as a girl she had flirted and who had become a famous poet: "My dear Lord,—If you are coming into Notts, call at Edwalton near Nottingham, where you will find a *very old* and *sincere friend* most anxious to *see you.*" [n]

He wrote a cautious letter back, and received a still more cautious and complaining one. Her motive for wanting to see him was a *good* one, but the world would interpret it otherwise. He should not frank his letter; it was dangerous. She had been ill, and she hinted at the infidelity of her husband. She was staying with a "dear relative" (Miss Radford), to whom he could address his letters. "You would hardly recognize in me the happy creature you once knew me. I am grown so thin, pale, and gloomy." [n] This was hardly the letter he wanted from his old sweetheart, and it did not make him eager to see her. He preferred to preserve the dream he had been nursing through the years.

A voice out of the more recent past was that of Annabella Milbanke, who wrote him the day after Christmas. She had just heard that he was still in England. She had been ill, and she did not yet have strength enough to "regain truth" by confessing to her white lie about another attachment, but merely inquired whether he was leaving soon and how long he would be gone. "Every blessing attend you—is the wish of your faithful friend." [n] After receiving her previous letter at the end of November he had written in his journal:

"Yesterday, a very pretty letter from Annabella, which I answered. What an odd situation and friendship is ours!—without one spark of love on either side, and produced by circumstances which in general lead to coldness on one side, and aversion on the other. She is a very superior woman, and very little spoiled, which is strange in an heiress—a girl of twenty—a peeress that is to be, in her own right—an only child, and a *savante,* who has always had her own way. She is a poetess—a mathematician—a metaphysician, and yet, withal, very kind, generous, and gentle, with very little pretension. Any other head would be turned with half her acquisitions, and a tenth of her advantages." [n]

The stage was set for tragicomedy of the most exquisite sort in 1814.

# CHAPTER XII

## *1814*

## *The Corsair*—Augusta

THE CORSAIR, which Byron had written "*con amore*, and much from *existence*,"[n] occupied him largely in the first few days of January 1814. As soon as he had made a fair copy he sent the manuscript to Lord Holland, whose good sense and judgment he had come more and more to respect, and then designated that it should go to Gifford.[n] He had soon recovered from his pique with Murray, and easily arranged for Dallas to submit the new poem to him (Dallas eventually received £525 for the copyright).[n] On the 2nd he wrote a dedication to Moore, in which, with a thought to Murray's objections to his coming before the public too often, he proclaimed rashly: ". . . for some years to come, it is my intention to tempt no further the award of 'Gods, men, nor columns.'" In that same dedication he further flouted the public by challenging his readers to seek autobiography in his writing if they wished; he would no longer defend or deny.

Drawn by stronger ties than ever to Augusta since her visit to London in December, Byron was doubly perplexed by the attachment of Lady Frances (then in Scotland with her husband), who seemed "embarrassed with constancy,"[n] and the overtures of Mary Chaworth-Musters. After receiving a second letter from Mary, Byron confided to Augusta: "M. has written again—*all friendship*—and really very simple and pathetic—*bad usage—paleness—ill health*—old *friendship—once—good motive*—virtue—and so forth."[n] And to Lady Melbourne he wrote:

". . . I am not quite so sure that seeing her again, and being on the terms of intimacy we once were, would not bring on the *old attack* on *me*. . . ." [n]

Absence and distance were at the same time slowly dissolving his more recent and more poignant attachment to Lady Frances Webster. "That business will never be renewed, or rather never completed," he told Lady Melbourne.[n] As the romance of this country idyl cooled, he was inclined to feel chagrined at the frustration of the affair. "If people will stop at the first tense of the verb 'aimer,' they must not be surprised if one finishes the conjugation with somebody else—" [n]

Things had become altogether too complicated, not, Byron felt, because he had been aggressive in wickedness, but because he was too eager to avoid hurting the feelings of the women who had become attached to him. He wrote to Lady Melbourne: "I cannot conceive why the D——l should angle with so many baits for one whom, all the world will tell you, belonged to him probably before he was born. But when they give me a character for 'Art,' it is surely most mistaken; no one was ever more heedless. Moore, in a letter to me on a *different subject, you may suppose,* says, 'the only chance of salvation for you—(I never look for any from yourself)—is the, &c. &c.' Now, what he wishes me to avoid [entanglement with Lady Frances], *you* would call 'my salvation.' " [n]

Once more he was pining for escape to the freedom of the Mediterranean world. The East enticed him with the memories of his irresponsible youth. And now following its call seemed the only remedy for the perplexities that surrounded him. Ambition no longer held him: "I never *won* the world," he told Lady Melbourne, "and what it has awarded me has always been owing from it's caprice. My life here is frittered away. . . ." [n] He appealed to his confidante to advise him what to do about Mary Chaworth. "I will tell you why. It is impossible I should now feel anything beyond friendship for her or anyone else in present circumstances; and the kind of feeling which has lately absorbed me has a mixture of the terrible, which renders all other, even passion (pour les autres) insipid to a degree. . . ." [n]

Lady Melbourne was inclined to suspect Augusta of being

chiefly at fault, but Byron came gallantly to her defense. "You are quite mistaken . . . as to *her,*" he wrote, ". . . it was not her fault, but my own *folly* (give it what name may suit it better) and her weakness, for the intentions of both were very different, and for some time adhered to, and when not, it was entirely my own—in short, I know no name for my own conduct. Pray do not speak so harshly of her to me—the cause of all." *n*

He was planning to take Augusta to Newstead with him. Before he left, however, he considered rather speculatively and hopelessly Lady Melbourne's sovereign remedy for the tangles his weakness had got him into. "I wish I were married," he told her, "and don't care about beauty, nor *subsequent* virtue—nor much about fortune. I have made up my mind to share the decorations of my betters—but should like—let me see—liveliness, gentleness, cleanliness, and something of comeliness—and *my own* first born. Was ever man more moderate?" *n*

The only prospect he could think of at the moment was Lady Frances's younger sister, Catherine Annesley, "who is very pretty, but fearfully young—and I think a *fool.* . . . I have no *heart* to spare and expect none in return; but, as Moore says, 'A pretty wife is something for the fastidious vanity of a roué to *retire* upon.' "

But, he confessed, "What I want is a companion—a friend rather than a sentimentalist. I have seen enough of love matches —and of all matches—to make up my mind to the common lot of happy couples. The only misery would be if I fell in love afterwards—which is not unlikely, for habit has a strange power over my affections. In that case I should be jealous, and then you do not know what a devil any bad passion makes me." *n* He knew, however, that this was only idle talk, for he was too easily swept along by the stream of circumstances. Augusta had arrived in London, and on Monday the 17th they set out for Newstead in his huge coach. An extremely heavy snow had made the Great North Road all but impassable. *n*

Once having arrived, they were snowbound in the rambling, empty Abbey. The great park was blanketed in white, and snow weighted down the giant oaks and obliterated the roads. It was impossible to drive even as far as Nottingham, and the mails, when they got through, were carried on horseback. The weather was an excuse for not visiting Mary Chaworth, and the presence of Augusta made it a cozy existence. He wrote Lady Melbourne: ". . . we never yawn nor disagree; and laugh much more than is suitable to so solid a mansion; and the family shyness makes us more amusing companions to each other than we could be to any one else." [n]

On his twenty-sixth birthday Byron wrote a letter to John Murray which to reach him would have to "advance through more Snows than ever opposed the Emperor's retreat. . . . Our coals are excellent, our fire-places large, my cellar full, and my head empty; and I have not yet recovered my joy at leaving London." [n]

Still snowbound, on the first of February Byron wrote to Hanson: "Mrs. L. is with me, and being in the family way renders it doubly necessary to remain till the roads are quite safe." [n]

Even when the roads had been cleared, Byron was reluctant to leave Newstead. He had done no writing, which meant that he had reached a temporary state of contentment. Before leaving on February 6, he had an enthusiastic letter from Murray announcing the amazing success of *The Corsair,* beyond anything he or the publisher had dreamed of. Murray wrote in high excitement: "I sold, on the day of publication,—a thing perfectly unprecedented—10,000 copies. . . ." [n] Moore, Isaac D'Israeli, Ward, Gifford, and others all expressed "unlimited approbation." Gifford even did something Murray had never known him to do before; he repeated several passages from memory, including the closing lines:

*His death yet dubious, deeds too widely known;*
*He left a Corsair's name to other times,*
*Linked with one virtue, and a thousand crimes.*[n]

Murray printed seven editions and sold twenty-five thousand copies in a little over one month. This phenomenal popularity was caused partly by the fine descriptive passages, particularly the lush lines beginning

*Slow sinks, more lovely ere his race be run,*
*Along Morea's hills the setting sun . . .*

which Byron had taken from the unpublished *Curse of Minerva* and tucked in at the beginning of the third canto. Then the swift narrative, sustained by an authentic background known to be derived from personal observation, heightened the interest. But, most of all, readers were entranced by Conrad, "That man of loneliness and mystery," in many of whose traits it was easy to see a thinly veiled portrait of the author.

Hobhouse, shortly after his return from abroad, picked up some strange gossip. "He told me an odd report," Byron wrote in his journal, "that *I* am the actual Conrad, the veritable Corsair, and that part of my travels are supposed to have passed in privacy. Um!—people sometimes hit near the truth; but never the whole truth." [1]

In one quarter, however, the publication of *The Corsair* aroused the greatest hostility, not on literary, but on political grounds. While at Newstead, Byron had written to Murray: "The 'lines to a Lady Weeping' must go with *The Corsair*. I care nothing for consequences, on this point. My politics are to me like a young mistress to an old man—the worse they grow, the fonder I become of them." [n] When the first edition appeared on February 1, there was an eruption of righteous indignation in the Tory press led by *The Courier* and supported by the *Morning Post*. The former paper proceeded to dig up Byron's attack on Lord Carlisle in *English Bards and Scotch Reviewers*, as well as his derogatory remarks on others, such as Lord Holland and Moore, in that poem. Byron kept his resolution not to reply to such attacks, but when Murray, with his Tory associations and publisher's fears, withdrew the offending poem from the second edition of *The Corsair*, the author insisted on its being replaced in the third edition. On his way to town he wrote to Murray: "I see all the papers in a sad commotion with those 8 lines; and the *Morning Post*, in particular, has found out that I am a kind of R[ichar]d. III.—deformed in mind and *body*. The *last* piece of

[1] *LJ*, II, 399. Journal, March 10, 1814. Byron here had in mind, not his more recent escapades, but some part of his life in Greece, for he added: "H. don't know what I was about the year after he left the Levant; nor does any one—nor—nor—nor—however, it is a lie—but, 'I doubt the equivocation of the fiend that lies like truth!'"

information is not very new to a man who passed five years at a public school. I am very sorry you cut out those lines. . . . Pray re-insert them in their old place in *The Corsair.*" [n]

The hue and cry against Byron's verses was at its height when he reached London on February 9 after three days of battling the snowdrifts and the slush. The attacks on him rankled more than he wished the world to know. "My person . . . ," he wrote Moore, "has been denounced in verses, the more like the subject, inasmuch as they halt exceedingly. Then, in another, I am an *atheist,* a *rebel,* and, at last, the *devil* (*boiteux,* I presume). . . . my friends desire me not to be in a passion; and, like Sir Fretful, I assure them that I am 'quite calm,'—but I am nevertheless in a fury." [n] He assured Lady Melbourne that he would not reply, adding: ". . . I have that within me, that bounds against opposition." [n]

*The Courier* and the *Morning Post* continued their sniping daily for a fortnight and intermittently for several weeks. It was only when the former accused him of having "received and pocketted" large sums for his poems that he hinted to Dallas that a refutation from *him* would be welcome.[n] Dallas then came forward with a letter to the *Morning Post* making public acknowledgment of the gift of the copyrights of *Childe Harold* and *The Corsair* and affirming that Byron had "never received a shilling for any of his work." [n]

There were reasons for Byron's disquietude apart from the uproar over his poems. On the way to town he had written to Lady Melbourne: "You seem to think I am in some scrape at present by my unequal spirits. Perhaps I am, but you shan't be shocked, so you shan't." He had not seen Mary Chaworth, who had written often and upbraided him for not replying. Byron had little heart for starting or renewing a friendship where he had once loved, especially as Mary seemed to write about little but her ailments and her disappointments. He continued: "You will very probably say that I ought to have gone over at all events, and Augusta has also been trying her rhetoric to the same purpose, and urging me repeatedly to call before I left the country." [n]

But it was not Mary Chaworth who caused his perturbation and nervous tension. He hinted at the real trouble in a letter to

Lady Melbourne on the 11th: "But all these externals are nothing to *that within*, on a subject to which I have not alluded." [n] And when he wrote Annabella Milbanke on the 19th he startled her with a half-confession: "I am at present a little feverish—I mean mentally—and as usual on the brink of something or other which will probably crush me at last, & cut our correspondence short with everything else." [n]

Hobhouse had returned from his Continental tour on February 8, and he met Byron at Covent Garden the day after the latter arrived in town from Newstead. Hobhouse recorded in his diary: ". . . there I saw & joined my dearest Byron in a private box. It is a long time since I have been so happy. I came home with him and sat until near four in the morning." [n] And, equally delighted, Byron wrote in his journal a few days later: "He is my best friend, the most lively, and a man of the most sterling talents extant." [n] Byron added after seeing him again: "My friend H. is the most entertaining of companions, and a fine fellow to boot." [n] They met frequently thereafter. On the 19th they were joined by Hodgson and went into Byron's private pit box at Drury Lane to see the sensational new Shakespearean actor, Edmund Kean, in *Richard III*.[n] After the play Hobhouse went to a party at Lady Harrowby's, but Byron went home and wrote in his journal: "By Jove, he [Kean] is a soul! Life—nature—truth without exaggeration or diminution. Kemble's Hamlet is perfect;—but Hamlet is not Nature. Richard is a man; and Kean is Richard." [n]

Hobhouse had returned with "ten thousand anecdotes of Napoleon, all good and true," Byron recorded in his journal.[2]

[2] Several of the anecdotes Hobhouse told Byron about Napoleon concerned his little regard for the women who satisfied his appetites. One was "that Napoleon would send for any lady whom he frequented & receive her writing saying, deshabillez vous—which she did, he still writing, & when he saw her prepared saying couchez donc. He would jump into bed and after one heat jump up & resume his task. The Chevalier told the following horrid tale. A young woman who was affianced to an officer in the army was seen by the Emperor, sent for & of course subdued. She wrote a deprecating letter to her lover then on service. This was intercepted and handed over to Napoleon, who sending for the girl ordered her to strip and then applied to her a horsewhip so violently that she ran screaming into the antechamber amongst the guards." (Hobhouse diary, April 24, 1814. This and subsequent quota-

"Napoleon!—this week will decide his fate. All seems against him; but I believe and hope he will win—at least, beat back the invaders. What right have we to prescribe sovereigns to France? Oh for a Republic! . . . The greater the equality, the more impartially evil is distributed, and becomes lighter by the division among so many—therefore, a Republic!" [n]

But neither Hobhouse's company nor the distractions of society and the theater could wean him from his obsessive thoughts. On the 19th he had been to see Waite the dentist: "Teeth are all right and white; but he says that I grind them in my sleep and chip the edges. That same sleep is no friend of mine, though I court him sometimes for half the twenty-four." [n] The next morning Byron got up and tore two pages out of his journal.[n] In the light of day, discretion seemed more important than confession.

The last week in February he was more dissatisfied with himself than ever. On the 23rd, Hobhouse dined with him at the St. Albans and afterward "sat with him at home hearing his confessions." [n] On the 27th, Byron was at home alone with his journal, having declined an invitation to dinner at Holland House. "Hobhouse says I am growing a *loup garou,*—a solitary hobgoblin. . . . If I could always read, I should never feel the want of society. . . . 'Man delights not me,' and only one woman —at a time."

And this brought him to the heart of his own weakness: "There is something to me very softening in the presence of a woman, —some strange influence, even if one is not in love with them— which I cannot at all account for, having no very high opinion of the sex. But yet,—I always feel in better humour with myself and every thing else, if there is a woman within ken. Even Mrs. Mule, my firelighter,—the most ancient and withered of her kind, —and (except to myself) not the best-tempered—always makes me laugh,—no difficult task when I am 'i' the vein.' " [3]

tions from the Hobhouse diary through April 5, 1816, are [unless otherwise noted] from the MS. in the Berg Collection, New York Public Library.)

[3] *LJ*, II, 389–90. Moore wrote concerning Mrs. Mule (I, 502–3 n.): "This ancient housemaid, of whose gaunt and witch-like appearance it would be impossible to convey any idea but by the pencil, furnished one among the numerous instances of Lord Byron's proneness to attach himself to any thing,

Through March, Byron was half bored, half diverted by a social life that he participated in more from politeness and inertia than from inclination. He admitted to Moore that he was "uncomfortable," but could not bring himself to tell the cause beyond some broad hints. "There is nothing, however, upon the *spot* either to love or hate;—but I certainly have subjects for both at no very great distance. . . ." [n] To add to his self-dissatisfaction, reflection and reading had convinced him that his literary work was of little value. ". . . I have lately begun to think my things have been strangely over-rated; and, at any rate, whether or not, I have done with them for ever. I may say to you what I would not say to every body, that the last two were written, *The Bride* in four, and *The Corsair* in ten days,—which I take to be a most humiliating confession, as it proves my own want of judgment in publishing, and the public's in reading things, which cannot have stamina for permanent attention." [n]

Byron was no doubt influenced in this opinion by some of his midnight discussions with Hobhouse, for whom his respect and liking were constantly increasing.[4] He trusted Hobhouse's judgment as he did that of no one else. Byron wrote to Phillips, who was putting the finishing touches on the three portraits he had started some months before: ". . . my friend H. who saw the pictures today suggests to me that the *nose* of the smaller portrait is too much *turned up*. . . ." [n] Byron posed again for Phillips,

however homely, that had once inlisted his good-nature in its behalf, and become associated with his thoughts. He first found this old woman at his lodgings in Bennet-street, where, for a whole season, she was the perpetual scarecrow of his visitors. When, next year, he took chambers in Albany, one of the great advantages which his friends looked to in the change was, that they should get rid of this phantom. But, no,—there she was again—he had actually brought her with him from Bennet-street. The following year saw him married, and, with a regular establishment of servants, in Piccadilly; and here,—as Mrs. Mule had not appeared to any of the visitors,—it was concluded, rashly, that the witch had vanished." But she was still there, in "a new peruke, and other symptoms of promotion. . . . When asked 'how he came to carry this old woman about with him from place to place,' Lord Byron's only answer was, 'the poor old devil was so kind to me.'"

[4] The friendship was appreciated wholeheartedly by Hobhouse, who wrote in his diary on March 31: "Lord Byron, whom I love more and more every day, not so much from his fame as his fondness—I think not equivocal, for me—introduced me, at her desire, to Lady Melbourne." (Broughton, I, 99.)

but when Hobhouse saw the portraits a little later, he could see no resemblance to his friend in any of them.[n]

Shy as Hobhouse was, he went into company more often than Byron did, taking advantage of the introductions and invitations which came independently as well as by reason of his friendship with the most famous poet of the day. When Byron did go out, he preferred the society of true wit and intellect that gathered at the home of Rogers: Mackintosh, Sheridan, Erskine, even Mme de Staël. On the 8th he was at Rogers's in a small party including Mackintosh, Sheridan, and Sharp. "Much of old times —Horne Tooke—the Trials—evidence of Sheridan, and anecdotes of those times. . . ." [n] With increasing interest in the literature and society of the eighteenth century, Byron delighted more in these vicarious journeys into the past than in the insipid gatherings of the Regency *haut ton.* "*What plays!* what wit!—*hélas!* Congreve and Vanbrugh are your only comedy," [n] he exclaimed after seeing Sheridan's adaptation of Vanbrugh's *Relapse* (*The Trip to Scarborough*).

But despite the boredom he felt among the social elite, Byron was stirred from his apathy by an encounter at Lansdowne House with Lady Stafford's eldest daughter, Lady Charlotte Leveson Gower. To his journal he confided: ". . . there is an air of *soul* about her—and her colour changes—and there is that shyness of the antelope (which I delight in) in her manner so much, that I observed her more than I did any other woman in the rooms. . . . After all, there may be something of association in this. She is a friend of Augusta's, and whatever she loves I can't help liking." [n] He would have sought an introduction to her had it not been for the embarrassment that she was related to the Carlisles.

Augusta had been urging him to make up his quarrel with Lord Carlisle. He reflected: "I have refused *every* body else, but I can't deny her any thing. . . . Let me see—Ward, the Hollands, the Lambs, Rogers, etc., etc.,—every body, more or less, have been trying for the last two years to accommodate this *couplet* quarrel, to no purpose. I shall laugh if Augusta succeeds." [n]

On Sunday, March 6, John Hanson had begged Byron, as a

friend of his family, to be present the next morning at the marriage of his daughter Mary Anne to the Earl of Portsmouth. It was altogether a hurried and, Hobhouse believed, a shady affair. The Earl was over forty and the girl twenty-four. Hanson insisted that Byron, who had known her since she was a child, should give away the bride, which he did in a bemused and offhand manner. Byron recorded that "Portsmouth responded as if he had got the whole by heart." [n] What he did not record was that the Earl was rather simple-minded, and that Hanson, finding he had a penchant for Mary Anne (he had known the family for some time), rushed him into the marriage.

"I went very reluctantly, one misty morning (for I had been up at two balls all night)," Byron later recalled, "to witness the ceremony, which I could not very well refuse without affronting a man who had never offended me." [n] But, according to Mary Anne's brother Newton, Byron was somewhat more deeply involved. His sister, Newton said, "had been courted for 3 or 4 years by Byron [probably while he was at Harrow] and she loved him but on his part it was Boyish Love—and he told her tho I can't make you a Lady of Title you shall be a Countess nevertheless." And after the ceremony Byron exclaimed: "I told you I would make you a Countess and I will carry you through with the World." [n]

When, shortly after, the brother of the Earl took out a commission of lunacy to try to annul the marriage, Byron loyally stuck by Hanson and swore an affidavit to the effect that Lord Portsmouth seemed "perfectly calm and rational on the occasion," and that his preferring "a young woman to an old one, and . . . his own wishes to those of a younger brother, seemed to me neither irrational nor extraordinary." [5] If he had considered him insane, he would have advised Hanson not to permit the marriage. Lord Chancellor Eldon, probably influenced by

[5] *LJ*, II, 394–5 n. When Moore was gathering material for his life of Byron he recorded in his diary (*Memoirs*, II, 697): "Denman mentioned Lord Byron's affidavit about Lord Portsmouth as a proof of the influence of Hanson over him; Lord B. swearing that Lord P. had 'rather a *superior* mind than otherwise.'" But that was not the language of the affidavit. Byron did, however, equivocate and avoid saying that he thought Lord Portsmouth a simpleton even if he was not a lunatic.

Byron's statement, ruled on this occasion that Lord Portsmouth was capable of entering into a marriage contract and managing his own affairs.[n] Byron later wrote facetiously that the groom "did not seem to me more insane than any other person going to be married."[n]

The unfortunate business did not end here, however. Within a month the girl's mother, Mrs. Hanson, who had been something of a foster mother to Byron from his earliest school years in London, died. According to her son, Byron was deeply affected.[n] The following year Byron barely prevented a duel between Hanson and Chief Justice Best on account of this marriage, the Justice having called Hanson a rascal for his part in it.[n] And nine years later the whole matter was aired unsavorily, with some reflections on Byron's part in the marriage arrangements, when Lord Portsmouth's brother finally brought the lunacy charge into court.[6]

[6] At that time Hobhouse wrote to Byron, then in Genoa: "You see what a mess Hanson has made of the Portsmouth business. The jury returned unanimously on Friday last a verdict of *lunacy since* 1809. . . . You recollect what a pretty smock-faced girl Laura Hanson [Lady Portsmouth's sister] was in our time, who looked as if butter would not melt in her mouth. Well, it turns out that she used to beat and whip and spit upon this poor crazy creature, and joined in all the cruelties against him. . . . It seems that the lunatic was completely entrapped into the said marriage, being told that if he did not marry on the Monday, he could not marry at all, as also that the parson who married them did not know that he was to do [so] until he was told there was a couple in a pew waiting to be married. I have asserted loudly and long that you were totally unaware of these things, and never knew but that the subject had undergone proper deliberation." (Letter of March 2, 1823. Murray MSS.; Hobhouse proofs.)

Byron replied defensively: "I saw no appearance of entrapment, or compulsion. . . . It was no affair of mine to interfere in, and I thought that if Lord P. got a good, plain, quiet, housekeeping wife,—*young* too, instead of that tough morsel prepared by his brother, it was no bad bargain for either party. I could not foresee horse-whipping and the like of that there. I could not fortell *venality*, for I was told that Lord P's property was in *trust*, well secured; and that Lady P. could have only a jointure of a thousand a year. I could not foresee *lunacy* in a man who had been allowed to walk about the world five and forty years as compos of voting, franking, marrying, convicting thieves on his own evidence, and similar pastimes, which are the privileges of sanity. I could have no interest of my own, for I never performed with the Miss Hansons, nor whipped Lord P. . . . [The last clause of this sentence is here supplied from the Hobhouse proofs.] It struck me as so little an entrapment for Lord P., that I used to wonder whether the *girl*

Byron could not indeed foresee in 1814 the trouble that a simple act of friendship would get him into, but he was never given to calculating the consequences of his human relationships. If he had been, he might not have continued his correspondence with Miss Milbanke. Something different from the ordinary feminine allure attracted him to this pretty girl who preached him sermons, and he took her more seriously than he pretended to Lady Melbourne. Byron had written Annabella of a rumor which had reached him that she had refused him a second time, and she seized the opportunity to encourage him. "As for the report," she said, "it is absurd enough to excite a smile. In avoiding the possibility of being in a situation to refuse, I cannot consider myself as having refused." [n] That was her practical application of metaphysics to the problem of letting him know that she would not be unwilling to have him propose again. Byron did not miss her meaning. He recorded in his journal on March 15: "A letter from *Bella,* which I answered. I shall be in love with her again if I don't take care." [n]

Soon he made a confession that must have delighted her and perhaps also frightened her a little: "You do not know how much I wish to see you. . . . Not that I should ever intrude upon your confidence anything (at least I hope not) you should not hear; yet there are several opinions of yours I want to request, & though I have two or three able & I believe very sincere *male* friends, there is something preferable to me in ye delicacy of a woman's perceptions." [7] It may have been fear of his confidences

would have him, and not whether *he* would take the girl." (*LBC,* II, 250–1. Letter of March 19, 1823.)

Byron could not refrain from adding a ribald allusion to another matter which came up at the trial—the failure of the Earl to perform his duties as a husband: "I knew nothing of his ignorance of 'fuff-fuff-fuff,' as Cheek[s] Chester called it, but as he was of a robust[i]ous figure, though not a Solomon, naturally imagined he was not less competent than other people." (Murray MSS.; Hobhouse proofs.)

[7] Mayne: *Lady Byron,* pp. 92–3. Annabella had finished reading *The Corsair* on February 12 and wrote to Lady Melbourne: "In knowledge of the human heart & its most secret workings surely he may without exaggeration be compared to Shakespeare. . . . It is difficult to believe that he could have known these beings so thoroughly but from *introspection.* . . . I am afraid the compliment to his poetry will not repay him for the injury to his character." (Airlie, pp. 162–3.)

that caused Annabella to wait a month before replying, or it could be that she was merely holding off until she could invite him to Seaham. In the meantime he had much to occupy his mind.

The bitterest winter on record added to Byron's restlessness and gloom, for he was never quite happy when he could not be out of doors, on horseback and in the sun as he had been in Greece. To keep in exercise, Byron went back to sparring with his old friend and boxing-master Jackson. "My chest, and arms, and wind are in very good plight," he recorded, "and I am not in flesh. I used to be a hard hitter, and my arms are very long for my height (5 feet 8½ inches). At any rate, exercise is good, and this the severest of all; fencing and the broad-sword never fatigued me half so much." [n] The voracious reading which he had pursued as a schoolboy he took up again. He was reading Machiavelli in Italian, parts of Chardin's *Voyages en Perse*, Sismondi's *De la littérature du Midi*, and the tales of Bandello. He had read the latest *Edinburgh* with the review of *The Corsair* and was gratified by its praise, but more pleased that Jeffrey (whom he supposed to be the author) had treated him so handsomely.[n]

On the 27th, Byron dined at the Cocoa Tree with Scrope Davies. They were celebrating the final settling of Byron's debt of £4,800, which had stood since 1809. The next day Byron wrote in his journal: "My mind is much relieved by the removal of that *debit*." [n] The same day (March 28) he moved into his new apartments on the ground floor of Albany House in Piccadilly.[n] This was the house in which the Melbournes had lived until 1789, when, to oblige the Duke of York and Albany, who had taken a fancy to it, they traded it for the residence in Whitehall. Samuel Rogers told Moore that Byron's apartment at the Albany was about "thirty by forty feet." [n] Byron had subleased it for a term of seven years from Lord Althorp. This removal from his cramped lodgings in Bennet Street into the roomy bachelor quarters in the Albany indicates that he had given up for the time being any thought of an extensive foreign journey.

No longer able to resist the appeals of Augusta, who was alone, anxious, and approaching her confinement, Byron set off for Six

Mile Bottom of Saturday, April 2. Although Hobhouse, who had gone to King's College, Cambridge, to visit Scrope Davies, expected him on the 5th, Byron remained with his sister until the 7th and did not go to Cambridge at all.[n] On the 8th he confessed to Lady Melbourne: "I have been out of town since Saturday, and only returned last night from my visit to Augusta. . . . [Colonel] L[eigh] was in Yorkshire; and I regret not having seen him of course very much."[n]

Byron, who had maintained an irrational admiration for Napoleon since he had fought for his statue at Harrow, was stunned by the news which reached London on the 6th. Paris had capitulated to the Allies. In his maturer years, though shocked by his hero's brutal attempts at conquest, which he observed at first hand in Spain and Portugal, Byron continued a not always secret admiration for him as a soldier and statesman. This predilection was abetted by his great detestation for the Tory prosecution of the war and the corrupt and tyrannical governments which England had taken for allies. Only a month before, he had sent out his "fine print" of Napoleon in his robes, engraved by Morghen after Gerard, to be framed in gilt.[n]

On April 9 came the completely disillusioning news of the abdication. "I mark this day!" Byron wrote. "Napoleon Buonaparte has abdicated the throne of the world. . . . I am utterly bewildered and confounded. . . . Alas! this imperial diamond hath a flaw in it . . . the pen of the historian won't rate it worth a ducat. . . . But I won't give him up even now; though all his admirers have, 'like the thanes, fallen from him.'"[n]

And, despite his idle boast not to publish again, this was something that called for composition. The mood of his journal was the one he embodied in his *Ode to Napoleon Buonaparte,* ten stanzas and ninety lines of which he wrote in one day. He sent it off to Murray as a gift, telling him he could print it or not as he chose.[n]

When Moore twitted Byron on his about-face concerning publishing, he replied: "There was a mental reservation in my pact with the public, in behalf of anonymes. . . ."[n] But he was aware that this was a subterfuge, for, though he had warned Murray not to put his name to it, he had told him: ". . . you may *say* as openly as you like that it is mine, and I can inscribe it to Mr. Hobhouse, from the *Author*, which will mark it sufficiently." [n] Murray lost no time in making it known. Byron added a few stanzas, Murray hurried it through the press, and soon after it was published on the 16th, all papers were discussing Lord Byron's ode.

In the meantime Hobhouse at Cambridge was growing even more excited than Byron about the turn of events. He had long been an enthusiastic follower of the career of Napoleon, and no doubt Byron had absorbed some of his enthusiasm, for he respected his friend's greater knowledge and critical acumen. When it was announced that Napoleon was retiring to Elba, Hobhouse set off on horseback for London, determined to make his way to Paris "whilst yet any part of the Napoleon vestiges yet remain." He immediately called on Byron, who on the impulse of the moment consented to accompany him, and Hobhouse busied himself trying to get passports. When they dined together at the Cocoa Tree, Byron seemed still enthusiastic about the scheme.[n] But the next morning he wrote to Hobhouse: "I take the earliest opportunity of telling you that to my regret *my* Parisian scheme is knocked up by some intelligence received in letters this morning, on business and other concerns." [n]

Piqued by his friend's changeableness, the disappointed John Cam wrote in his diary: "Byron goes not to Paris. He is a difficult person to live with. He has written an Ode to Napoleon Buonaparte, and offered to inscribe it to me. This I got off." [n] But Hobhouse found a traveling companion in Henry Grattan, Jr., son of the Irish patriot and orator, and from Lord Sidmouth, head of the Home Office, he secured couriers' passes and dispatches for Lord Castlereagh, the Foreign Secretary, then in Paris with the victorious armies. He dined with Byron on the 15th—he could never be angry with him for long—and took the Dover coach the next evening.[n]

More than mere whim lay behind Byron's refusal to accompany his friend on this trip. On the 6th, Claughton had promised to pay another £5,000 on account, but on the 10th he had announced that he had not received the sums expected and could not fulfill his promise.[n] But a deeper reason was Byron's loyalty to Augusta, whom he could not leave at so critical a time.

At this point Annabella, whom he had all but given up as a matrimonial possibility, wrote again tentatively: "Am I mistaken in imagining that you are disposed to visit us?" [n] But Byron was not willing to make a move toward the north until he had the approval of his *Tante,* as he called her. Apparently she put no obstacle in the way of his renewing, or continuing, his correspondence with Annabella and did not forbid him to visit Seaham, for he wrote that he would be glad to avail himself of Sir Ralph's possible invitation.[n]

But before the invitation came, Byron had experienced other emotions and was in another mood. After anxious days he learned that Augusta had given birth to a daughter on the 15th. She named the child Elizabeth Medora.[8] When Lady Melbourne asked him whether the danger he ran in this affair was really worth while, he replied: "Oh! but it is 'worth while,' I can't tell you why, and it is *not* an 'Ape,' and if it is, that must be my fault; however, I will positively reform. You must however allow that it is utterly impossible I can ever be half so well liked elsewhere, and I have been all my life trying to make someone love me, and never got the sort that I preferred before. But positively she and I will grow good and all that, and so we are *now* and shall be these three weeks and more too." [n]

Byron's most casual correspondence at this period reflects the depression of his spirits and the obsession of his mind. He remained in a state of indecision whether to go back to Augusta or accept the invitation to Seaham. "In the mean time," he told Moore on the 20th, "I have bought a macaw and a parrot, and

[8] The date of birth is given in *Astarte,* p. 360. Medora Leigh herself believed that she was Byron's daughter. (See *Medora Leigh; A History and an Autobiography,* edited by Charles Mackay; and Roger de Vivie de Régie: *Le Secret de Byron.*) It is curious, however, that Byron never made any direct reference to his paternity in any extant letter or journal, nor did he show more interest in her, in his letters to Augusta, than in her other children (her eldest, Georgiana, was his favorite). It was unlike him not to acknowledge the paternity of his illegitimate children, but he may have been sufficiently uncertain that he was Medora's father to feel justified in ignoring what in the circumstances he could not very well proclaim in public, and Augusta may have had the good sense to destroy any of his letters which made pointed reference to Medora.

have got up my books; and I box and fence daily, and go out very little."[n] This was a foretoken of the strange menagerie of birds and animals that he was to build up around him in the years to come, which served as a kind of escape from the exigencies of human relationships and an outlet for his recurrent misanthropy.

The 20th was the day the Prince Regent went to meet Louis XVIII and escorted him with much pageantry behind cream-white horses up Piccadilly and into Albemarle Street. The first-floor balcony at John Murray's was an excellent vantage point from which to view the procession. But to Murray's invitation Byron replied: "You know I am a jacobin, and could not wear white, nor see the installation of Louis the gouty."[n]

At this time he was being treated by a physician for "an old complaint, 'troublesome, but not dangerous,' . . . of which I am promised an eventual removal." The physician, "a staid grave man," could not understand why Byron took the whole matter so lightly. "It is very odd," he told Lady Melbourne, "he . . . puts so many questions to me about *my mind,* and state of it, that I begin to think he half suspects my senses."[n] But the ailment, whatever it was, did not stop Byron from going to dinners and parties.

By the time the formal invitation came from Seaham (Sir Ralph Milbanke had written on the 25th), accompanied by a serious letter from Annabella suggesting that they talk over matters of religion, Byron began to be a little fearful of what this might lead to. After jesting about it to Lady Melbourne, he added: "Seriously, if she imagines that I particularly delight in canvassing the creed of St. Athanasius, or prattling of rhyme, I think she will be mistaken. . . . I am not now in love with her; but I can't at all foresee that I should not be so, if it came 'a warm June' (as Falstaff observes), and, seriously, I do admire her as a very superior woman, a little encumbered with Virtue. . . . I am quite irresolute and undecided. If I were sure of *myself* (not of her) I would go. . . ."[n]

His confidante was aware that one of the reasons for Byron's indecision was that he was receiving almost daily letters from Augusta, for he was now sending Lady Melbourne the letters of both women, and they had come in their correspondence to use the terms "my A." and "your A." to distinguish Augusta from Annabella.

Lady Melbourne not only gave her permission, but also urged Byron to visit Annabella. "If you don't like her you may talk only on the Prayer Book & if you should like her that subject will cease to make way for another without any effort." [n]

As for the "other A," Lady Melbourne still thought Augusta to blame for the beginning and continuance of the affair, but Byron came once more to her defense: "*You*—or rather *I*—have done *my A* much injustice. . . . She was not aware of her own peril till it was too late, and I can only account for her subsequent '*abandon*' by an observation which I think is not unjust, that women are much more *attached* than men if they are treated with anything like fairness or tenderness." But he confessed that his feelings toward Augusta were "a mixture of good and diabolical."

Byron concluded his letter with a bit of self-knowledge won from experience: "Your niece has committed herself perhaps, but it can be of no consequence; if I pursued and succeeded in that quarter, of course I must give up all other pursuits, and the fact is that my wife, if she had common sense, would have more power over me than any other whatsoever, for my heart always alights on the nearest *perch*—if it is withdrawn it goes God knows where—but one must like something." [n]

But it was Augusta who occupied his thoughts chiefly: "It, indeed, puzzles me to account for ——[Augusta]: it is true she married a fool, but she *would* have him; they agreed, and agree very well. . . . As for me . . . [I] remember when quite a child reading the Roman history about a *marriage* I will tell you of when we me[et], asking ma mère why I should not marry x [the symbol he sometimes used for Augusta in his letters to Lady Melbourne]." [n]

Whether merely overcome by a revulsion against his poetic production brought on by some personal criticism or disturbed by rumors that came too near home, Byron suddenly on April 29 sent Murray a draft to recompense him for the copyrights and requested the suppression of the *Giaour* and the *Bride*, the destruction of all but two copies of each, and the withdrawal of advertisements of future editions. He gave no excuse but "my own caprice." [n]

When Murray protested (it would almost ruin him—*Childe Harold* and the subsequent works of the same author had lifted him to fame and fortune), Byron relented and wrote two days later: "If your present note is serious, and it really would be inconvenient, there is an end of the matter; tear my draft, and go on as usual: in that case, we will recur to our former basis. . . . Some day, I will tell you the reason of this apparently strange resolution." [n]

To Byron's delight, Moore returned to town at the beginning of May, and they went about together a great deal, particularly to the theater, which Byron had come to love more and more since he had discovered the acting of Kean. Moore was soon aware, as he had already had an inkling from innuendoes in Byron's letters, that a secret love affair was gnawing his friend's vitals and that he was more reticent about it than was his custom. On the 4th, in response to Moore's request that he write the words for a song, Byron sent his impassioned stanzas:

*I speak not, I trace not, I breathe not thy name,*
*There is grief in the sound, there is guilt in the fame:*
*But the tear which now burns on my cheek may impart*
*The deep thoughts that dwell in that silence of heart.*

*Too brief for our passion, too long for our peace,*
*Were those hours—can their joy or their bitterness cease?* [n]
*We repent, we abjure, we will break from our chain,—*
*We will part, we will fly to—unite it again!* [9]

Moore encouraged him in his determination to drown the heaviness of his spirits in social dissipation. On the 7th they saw

[9] E. H. Coleridge thought these stanzas were written to Lady Frances Webster (see *Poetry*, III, 319), but he had not seen Byron's letters to Lady Melbourne and did not know how far past that affair was by May 4, 1814, and how completely absorbed Byron had become in Augusta. In the margin of his copy of Moore (I, 554), however, Coleridge wrote opposite the first stanza: "*Does* this apply to Lady Frances Wedderburn Webster? *does* it?" Coleridge sensed that the feelings expressed in the poem had their origin in some more searing passion than that roused by Lady Frances.

Kean's first performance of Iago in *Othello.* Byron would not go into a box, but sat in the orchestra to be near the actor and watch his expression. "Was not Iago perfection? particularly the last look," he wrote to Moore the next day. "I am acquainted with no *im*material sensuality so delightful as good acting. . . ." [n] Hobhouse returned to London on the 8th full of the historic scenes he had witnessed at Paris and with another store of anecdotes of Napoleon. Byron took him to the theater and to parties and introduced him everywhere.

Moore had tried at one time to promote a match between Byron and Lady Adelaide Forbes, and he would have liked to revive his friend's interest in that direction, but Byron was making tentative overtures to another. He sent the Albanian dress in which Phillips had painted him to Miss Mercer Elphinstone for a masquerade costume.[n] But his heart was not in these mild courtships. He told Lady Melbourne, who he knew wanted him to cultivate some distracting romance: ". . . I am trying to fall in love, which I suppose will end in falling *out* with somebody, for I am perplexed about two and would rather have both." Then he added in a postscript: "I am just elected into Watier's [the famous gambling-house where Brummell lost most of his money]. Shall I resume *play?* That will be a change, and for the better." [n]

Early in May he had sent Augusta £3,000 to clear the debts of her wastrel husband, Colonel Leigh, who was in some kind of trouble. Byron wrote on the 9th: "I have money at Hoare's, and more coming in soon, so don't mind me. You can't be off of this sum now, and I heartily hope it may be useful and adequate to the occasion. Now, don't 'affront' me by any more scruples." [n]

On May 14, Byron began a sequel to *The Corsair.* Conrad, the pirate, now called Lara, followed by the faithful Gulnare (disguised as the page boy Kaled), returned to the feudal castle he had left as a boy. He was the same brooding lonely man, but he no longer had recourse to wild action to purge his sorrows.

Thus in the midnight hours Byron purged his brain with patent self-revelations that he took no pains to conceal. Looking back over his early life, he found there the explanation for Lara's melancholy.

*'Twas strange—in youth all action and all life,*
*Burning for pleasure, not averse from strife. . . .*
*In turn he tried—he ransacked all below,*
*And found his recompense in joy or woe,*
*No tame, trite medium; for his feelings sought*
*In that intenseness an escape from thought. . . .*
*Alas! he told not—but he did awake*
*To curse the withered heart that would not break.*[n]

Byron's demons were dispersed by the rapid composition of the poem, which, he later told Murray, "I wrote while undressing after coming home from balls and masquerades, in the year of revelry 1814." [n] He flung himself into the social stream with a kind of abandon, and in the absorption of the moment, for he really liked people, with real and not affected pleasure. On the 18th he took Hobhouse to "a small party of 100" at Lady Jersey's.[n] The next evening they accompanied Tom Moore into the orchestra at Drury Lane to see Kean again in *Othello.* After the play, the three of them went to the greenroom, where Byron was first introduced to Kean, and poet and actor exchanged compliments.[1]

The round of parties was unceasing. On the 25th, Byron was invited to a large benefit party for Kean, arranged by Lady Jersey, but he preferred to take Moore into a box by themselves where they could enjoy the performance without the interruption of a suffocating crowd. They did not join the others until supper. The next day Byron sent Kean a present of fifty guineas

[1] Broughton, I, 125–6. Douglas Kinnaird, soon to become one of the subcommittee of management of Drury Lane, was there, and he and Hobhouse walked home together. The latter wrote in his diary that night: "We made mutual confessions of frightful suspicions." (Unpublished sentence, Hobhouse diary, entry of May 19, 1814. Berg Collection, New York Public Library.)

That, coupled with a cryptic entry three days earlier after Hobhouse had paid Byron a visit—"today I discover a frightful sign of what I yet know not" —suggests that Byron had hinted at some dark secret in his private life. (Hobhouse diary, entry of May 16, 1814, Berg Collection.) In the margin of his copy of Moore (I, 595), where the biographer is speaking rather naïvely of Byron's brotherly "devotedness and fervour," Hobhouse wrote: "My dear M you know nothing of the matter."

and shortly after gave him "a handsome snuff-box and a costly Turkish sword."[2]

Byron was trying desperately to behave as Lady Melbourne wished, but his lackadaisical flirtations had only stirred up Caroline Lamb, who was back in London again and curious as ever about Byron's affairs. "As for C.," he wrote Lady Melbourne, "we both know her for a foolish wicked woman. . . . as I heard a girl say the other night at *Othello,* when I asked her how she liked it, 'I shall like it much better when that woman is fairly smothered.' "[n]

Inflamed by jealousy again, Caroline wrote a wrathful letter demanding back her letters, pictures, and various gifts with which he had parted. She had even invaded Byron's Albany apartment when he was not in. He protested to Lady Melbourne: ". . . at the same signal it might be as well for her to restore *my* letters, as everybody has read them by this time, and they can no longer be of use to herself and her five hundred sympathizing friends." What provoked him more, however, was her spreading the story that he was to be married. She was out in her calculations if she thought it was Lady Adelaide Forbes, "for not a syllable of love ever passed between us. . . ."[n] To explain his supposed caprice, he wrote to Moore, who had recommended Lady Adelaide to him: "Had Lady [Rancliffe, her sister] appeared to wish it—or even *not* to oppose it—I would have gone on, and very possibly married (that is, *if* the other had been equally accordant) with the same indifference which has frozen over the 'Black Sea' of almost all my passions. It is that very indifference which makes me so uncertain and apparently capricious. . . . The proof of this is, that obstacles, the slightest even, *stop* me."[n]

In this world-weary mood he succumbed out of curiosity to the entreaties of a persistent stranger who had been writing him for some time, and sent her a reply. He was used to receiving letters and proposals from strange young ladies, sometimes brazen, more often expressing Platonic regard and concern for

[2] Moore, I, 552–3. Moore wrote: "Such effect had the passionate energy of Kean's acting on his [Byron's] mind, that, once, in seeing him play Sir Giles Overreach, he was so affected as to be seized with a sort of convulsive fit. . . ."

his soul and his poetry. *The Corsair* had brought an increasing number of these letters from unknown ladies, country girls asking for a lock of hair, an autograph, or criticism of their verses. But this girl was a foreigner and wrote rather amusing letters. At any rate, it would be a new sensation. The name of his correspondent was Henrietta D'Ussières. Her importunity had some novelty about it. "You are not unjust, you are good-natured," she wrote.[n] And it was his good nature, combined with other less generally applauded motives, which prompted him to write at last.

Henrietta was overcome when she received on June 17 the envelope addressed in an unknown hand just as she was writing him again. But on unfolding it with "breathless palpitation," she was delighted with its contents. She wrote: "How good-natured you are! No 'Lord Byron is surprised'—no third person —'*you*'—everywhere—your own stile of writing—familiar questions—complete forgiveness—and you are not in the least offended." She rushed out into the rain to post her letter. But before he saw her, she deluged him with pages of her history, romantically embroidered. "You guessed right—your correspondent is a Swiss mountaineer. I have long been in exile. . . ."[n]

Her father, she said, had been an active liberal and fervent believer in the doctrines of Jean Jacques Rousseau. He loved Liberty in the abstract, but was a tyrant with his children. When he wished to mate her with an elderly, kindly, but ugly man, she ran away to England at the age of fifteen. She wanted to call on Byron, but was frightened and cautious.[n]

Who was she really? A lady's maid perhaps, or more likely a governess. Byron's curiosity was aroused, and he wrote her a remarkable letter offering her an assignation. He could write humorously because he did not care whether she came or not. "Excepting your compliments (which are only excusable because you don't know me) you write like a clever woman, for which reason I hope you *look* as *un*like one as possible. I never knew but one of your country—$M^e$ de Stael—and she is frightful as a precipice. . . . If you will become acquainted with me, I will promise not to make love to you unless you like it. . . ."[n]

Finally she came, no doubt heavily veiled, and was admitted to the poet's private apartment. For half an hour they talked, and she was charmed. She could not have been too hideous, for he ended by making her proposals which shocked her and melted her romantic illusions. She escaped and tremblingly wrote him: "Why did you spoil my joy? The first half hour I was so happy! . . . but for the remainder of the evening it was no longer Lord Byron—indeed it was not. . . . oh! Lord Byron, is it thus you would repay so much admiration—so much esteem?" [n]

Though no other letter of his to her is extant, it seems probable that he apologized, but in any event he was pardoned and she tried to see him again just at the moment when great crowds in Piccadilly were trying to get a glimpse of the foreign sovereigns then being feted in London. Shyly she made her way to his door without previous announcement and found him with male company. She begged in such a supplicating tone to be allowed to wait that Fletcher ushered her into the pantry, amid the mops and brooms, while the servant went to fetch his master. But for Byron the episode was closed. He saw it now as ridiculous, and she was hurt that he did not take the parting more tragically. "Why did you say that word? And you smiled & you laughed when I was ready to cry!" [n] Like most of the other women who met Byron, she could not forget him, and, like Caroline Lamb, though for much less cause, she continued to shower him with letters and proposals for meetings, but he was now bored, and for him the rest was silence.

In spite of all Lady Melbourne's warnings of the consequences of his love for Augusta, he was not cured and he confessed it freely. His confidante wrote him on June 10: "I am shock'd at some of the things you s[d] to me last night, & think the *easy* manner in which two people have accustom'd themselves to consider their situation quite *terrible*—but I shall not say more at present, as I see it is so useless." [n] And Byron replied: "All you say is exceeding true; but who ever said, or supposed that you were not shocked, and all that? You *have* done everything in your power; and more than any other person breathing would have done for *me*, to make me act rationally. . . ." [n]

Byron had brought the luckless Lara to his proper tragic end on June 14, just one month after beginning the tale, and now he entered more fervently than ever into the social whirl of the season. It was "the summer of the sovereigns," as Byron called it.[n] Years later he recalled that summer with nostalgic pleasure. He wrote to Moore from Italy in 1822: "Do you recollect, in the year of revelry 1814, the pleasantest parties and balls all over London?"[n] The close of the war on the Continent had brought during June a flock of royalty, statesmen, and generals of the victorious allies to London, among them Alexander, Czar of Russia, the King of Prussia, Metternich, the great hero Blücher, and all their train. The end of a long winter and a long war had loosed the spirit of festivity. Never had London society been gayer. Byron, though he kept a cynical reserve regarding the sovereigns, enjoyed it in his self-forgetful moods more than he pretended.

But Moore, who lifted Byron's spirits more than any other at a party, had left London. Byron had given Moore the journal he had written between the previous November and April, and now asked him to keep it. ". . . I care not what becomes of it; and if it has amused you, I am glad that I kept it."[3]

The tedious Webster was in town again, seeking another "loan." While he saw through the silly fellow's vanity and referred to him as "Master Shallow,"[n] Byron accepted him as a friend with easygoing tolerance, just as he had accepted Dallas and a dozen others with whom he had really little in common. On the 11th, Webster dragged him, against his will, to a party at Lady Sitwell's in Seymour Road. Webster later wrote a manuscript note on Byron's letter of that date: "He there for the first time saw his cousin, the beautiful Mrs. Wilmot [who had appeared in mourning with numerous spangles on her dress]. When we returned to . . . the Albany, he . . . desired Fletcher

[3] *LV*, III, 94. Byron perhaps thus early intended Moore to be the custodian of the relics of his life, if not his biographer. He later gave him his Ravenna journal and his Memoirs, which last were unfortunately cast into the fire at Murray's after Byron died. Though Byron professed little interest in the journal, it was written with a literary art that suggests he intended it to be read. Byron had at about the same time given the letters he had written to his mother from abroad to Dallas, who had been a willing listener to *Lara* as it was composed. (Dallas: *Correspondence*, III, 74.)

to give him a *tumbler* of *Brandy,* which he drank at once to Mrs. Wilmot's health. . . . The next day he wrote those charming lines upon her—" [n] The lines were those which he later prefixed to the *Hebrew Melodies,* though they had no other relationship to that group of poems than their lyric cadences:

*She walks in Beauty, like the night*
*Of cloudless climes and starry skies. . . .*[n]

In the dullness that had settled over his town life since Moore's departure Byron had some thoughts of going to Newstead again, partly to pay a visit to Moore, who lived in the neighboring county of Derbyshire, and partly with the notion of calling on Mary Chaworth, who had written him more than fifty letters in less than half a year. Although Byron had not replied often enough to please her, her interest in him waxed as he told her more details of his life in the world.[4] On April 10 she wrote: "My dear Friend, I am delighted to hear you are 'neither going to be *married* nor for the *present* abroad.'" [n] She sent him a purse she had made and asked for some little remembrance in return. After a long wait he sent her a seal, recalling to her their trip to Matlock in 1803, over which she sighed: "Those were indeed the happiest days of my life, and believe me they are often thought of and regretted." [n]

By June, Mary was only in the fringe of his desire. What he really cherished was a memory, and he was half attracted, half repelled at the thought of meeting the object of that vision in the too solid flesh. A sentimental correspondence based on the past was safest—besides, the center of his affection and his interest was elsewhere. At Earl Grey's he had met again Lady Charlotte Leveson Gower, "one of the tribe of the Carlisles," the friend of Augusta. To his sister he wrote at length of the "*glows* and stammers" that followed their introduction.[n] He had told himself that he was interested in her because of Augusta, but she was very young, very pretty, and retiring, the qualities which most appealed to him in a woman. A few days later he wrote to

[4] After her separation at the end of March (she was to have £4,300 a year, the house at Annesley, rent free, with fifty acres of land and half the plate and linen), Mary felt freer to correspond with Byron and was eager to see him.

Rogers: "Is there any chance or possibility of making it up with Lord Carlisle, as I feel disposed to do any thing reasonable or unreasonable to effect it?" *n* So it was not Augusta, after all, but Augusta's friend who was responsible for his willingness to seek a reconciliation he had always stubbornly resisted.

After a quiescent winter Caroline Lamb had grown troublesome again, emboldened by a friendly gesture or two at the gatherings where they met perforce—gestures which she easily interpreted as evidence that Byron still loved her, or at least that she could break down his defenses again. Her interest in him had never ceased. She followed his every publication and was jealous for his fame.

Though Caroline had written: "we must and shall meet no more," her good resolutions all crumbled when she saw him again in London. She was aware that Byron could not be cruel to her when he met her face to face. Lady Melbourne knew it too, and she was alarmed. Byron's assurance that he and Caroline could behave with "mutual decorum" caused his confidante to explode: "'Mutual decorum'? how could those two words come into your head as applicable to you two? 'villainous mutualities' it should be read." *n*

Caroline suspected something extraordinary in Byron's love life, but could get no clue. It was, she knew, hopeless to get anything from Lady Melbourne, but she tried to make friends with those women who seemed closest to him. Early in June she wrote to Byron: "I go to the 'squerade—shall you—tell your sister to try & not dislike me—I am very unworthy of her I know it & feel it but as I may not love you nor see you—let her not judge me harshly. . . . try & make her forgive me—if you can—for I love that Augusta with my heart because she is yours and is dear to you—" *n*

Caroline had no knowledge of Byron's present amours, but, crazed by neglect and jealousies, she bedeviled her former lover. She was fond of tragic adieux. "Farewell Mephistocles," she wrote, ". . . you are a man any Woman might live with forever. . . . there is nothing in Heaven or earth or under the earth like you . . . if I am condemned to sail in sulphur hereafter I shall think it hard & cruel for why did God make a Being like you if he did not give us strength not to admire & love it—are you sure that you are a Man—I doubt it. . . . think of my situation how extraordinary! my mother in law actually in the place I held—her ring instead of mine—her letters instead of mine—her heart—but do you believe either she or any other feel for you what I felt—ugly & thin & mad & despis'd as I am. . . ." *n*

Certainly Byron had few lovers so clever in composition, so lively in imagination. Caroline might be mad at times, but she was no fool. There is evidence that he did see her, despite his good resolutions, several times in private as well as in public in May and June.[5] But during June she grew wild again and began to invade Byron's chambers at all hours, indiscreetly unannounced. His detestation was increased tenfold by the fact that she did still have a curious fascination, despite the fact that she was emaciated and had grown so thin that he once said in anger he was "haunted by a skeleton." *n* By the end of June he had had more than enough. He felt hounded, beset by a demon who would never leave him. He had told Lady Melbourne of her visits to the Albany, and when she urged him to do something to prevent it he replied: "You talked to me about keeping her out. It is impossible; she comes at all times, at any time, and the moment the door is open in she walks. I can't throw her out of the window: as to getting rid of her, that is rational and probable, but *I* will not receive her."

The remedy of desperation he suggested was the very one Lady Melbourne feared: to run away with Augusta. "These are strong words," he continued, "but I know what I am writing; they will avail nothing but to convince you of my own determination. . . . If there is one human being whom I do utterly *detest* and *abhor* it is [Caroline]. . . . she has often belied and sometimes betrayed me; she has crossed me everywhere, she has watched and worried and guessed and been a curse to me and mine." *n*

[5] In a letter, probably written about this period, she said: "You have been very generous and kind *if* you have not betray'd me, and I do *not think you have*. My remaining in Town and seeing you thus is sacrificing the last chance I have left." (*LJ*, II, 448. Prothero conjectures the date of the letter to be the summer of 1812; but the context places it later. In it she mentioned Mme de Staël, who was in London from June 22, 1813, to May 8, 1814.)

Two days later he assured his confidante that "all bolts, bars, and silence can do to keep her away are done daily and hourly." [n] But these precautions were ineffective. One day she entered his apartments at the Albany, and, finding him out, picked up a copy of Beckford's *Vathek* from the table and wrote on the first page: "Remember me!" "Yes!" Byron told Medwin, "I had cause to remember her; and, in the irritability of the moment, wrote under the two words these two stanzas:—

*'Remember thee, remember thee!*
*Till Lethe quench life's burning stream,*
*Remorse and shame shall cling to thee,*
*And haunt thee like a feverish dream!*

*Remember thee! Ay, doubt it not;*
*Thy husband too shall think of thee;*
*By neither shalt thou be forgot,*
*Thou* false *to him, thou* fiend *to me!'* " [6]

On July 1, Byron, though he had little admiration for the Duke of Wellington, accompanied Hobhouse to a grand masked ball in the Duke's honor at Burlington House. It was the greatest social event of the season, climaxing a month of festivities for the sovereigns. All of the *haut ton* was there, and also some of the demimonde, safe behind dominoes. Hobhouse wrote in his diary: "I presume the supper in the temporary room, in which 1,700 persons sat at ease, was the most magnificent thing of the kind ever seen. . . . Byron as a monk looked very well. . . . Lady C. Lamb played off the most extraordinary tricks—made Skeffington pull off his red guard's coat—walked up into the private rooms." [n]

Byron was not amused. He told Lady Melbourne: "I was obliged to talk to her, for she laid hold of Hobhouse, and passed

[6] Medwin, II, 68–9. Caroline first saw this in Medwin's *Conversations* in 1824, and in her long letter to the author she said: "I feel secure the lines 'remember thee—thou false to him thou fiend to me'—were his. . . ." (*LJ*, II, 451.) But she did not cease to love his memory. She wrote to Lady Morgan after Byron's death: "Lord Byron, that dear, that angel, that mis-guided and mis-guiding Byron, whom I adore, although he left that dreadful legacy on me—my memory. Remember thee—and well." (*Lady Morgan's Memoirs*, II, 207.)

before where another person and myself were discussing points of Platonism; so frequently and remarkably, as to make us anticipate a scene; and as she was masked, and dominoed, and it was daylight, there could be little harm, and there was at least a probability of more quiet. Not all I could say could prevent her from displaying her green *pantaloons* every now and then; though I scolded her like her grandfather upon these very uncalled for, and unnecessary gesticulations."[7]

The famous courtesan and demimondaine Harriette Wilson was, by her own account, at Watier's that night. And if we are to believe her *Memoirs,* a vivid and entertaining picture of the sins and foibles of the Regency, she also met Byron there and conversed with him. It is more likely, however, that she only *saw* him on that occasion, for she wrote him after he had gone to Italy: ". . . we never shall meet, and never *have* met. . . ."[n]

Harriette had first written to Byron about the time he moved to the Albany. He had not answered, and after three days, not accustomed to being treated thus by men, she had written him a furious letter, by her own account, which brought a courteous but discouraging reply: "I am not unacquainted with your name or your beauty, and I have heard much of your talents;

[7] *LBC,* I, 263. Letter of July 2, 1814. Caroline's last private interview with Byron (he saw her occasionally at public gatherings, to his discomfiture, as at this ball) may have taken place some time before this, but in her own account the chronology is confusing. She wrote to Medwin after his book was published: ". . . the last time we parted for ever, as he pressed his lips on mine (it was in the Albany) he said 'poor Caro, if every one hates me, you, I see, will never change—No, not with ill usage!' & I said, 'yes, I *am* changed, & shall come near you no more.'—For then he showed me letters, & told me things I cannot repeat, & all my attachment went. This was our last parting scene—well I remember it. It had an effect upon me not to be conceived—3 years I had *worshipped* him." (*LJ,* II, 453.) It is difficult to know how much of this may be believed. In the summer of 1814, while Byron was still at the Albany, she had not known him three years, for their affair began in the spring of 1812; three years after they met Byron was married and living in Piccadilly Terrace, and it is very unlikely that she visited him there. On the other hand, there is no evidence that Byron ever saw her privately after the 1st of July 1814, and she was peculiarly quiet for several months. It may be that in exasperation Byron did show her some of Augusta's letters. There are clear indications that Caroline talked of Byron's relations with his sister at the time of the separation of the Byrons. But she wrote him occasionally after what she describes as their last meeting.

but I am not the person whom you would like, either as a lover or a friend. . . . I am not of a nature to be loved, and so far, luckily for myself, I have no wish to be so." [n]

Harriette's rejoinder was not quite so indifferent as she intimated in her *Memoirs*. But the hauteur and sarcasm of his next letter offended her and she grew angry again. On reconsideration, she said, his letter had struck her as "an *affected, prosing, stupid scrawl. . . .*" [n] There the correspondence lapsed. But it was resumed after Byron left England. Her letters were full of friendly familiarity, shrewd worldly criticism of his poems, and devotion to him as a person. And Byron responded generously by sending her money when she was in need. Perhaps she was tired of love by that time and appreciated the intellectual friendship he was willing to give her.

The second day after the masquerade, July 3, Byron left for Six Mile Bottom and Cambridge. He announced his journey casually to Lady Melbourne.[n] He had sent his confidante, as usual, the letters of "both A's," along with a cynical comment on Annabella's prim and plaintive note.[n] But he replied in a different tone to the lady herself, apologizing for his delay on the ground that he wished to be able to fix a definite time before accepting her father's welcome invitation.[n]

Before she had received his letter, however, Annabella had written to announce that her mother had gone to Kirkby Mallory, the Leicestershire estate of her uncle, Lord Wentworth, whose wife was dying. Byron's visit would have to be postponed. But on getting his letter the following day, she was so relieved that she poured out what was almost a confession:

> After each time that I met you last year in London, I was vexed by the idea of having been repulsively cold towards you. . . . I was as anxious then as since to make my real feelings known to you. The recollection of that needless & in part involuntary constraint, only gives me a greater degree of satisfaction in asking you to believe me
>
> Ever affectionately yours.[n]

A little alarmed at this letter, for Annabella was committing herself more than he found comfortable at the moment, Byron was glad for the delay in his visit and for the excuse to accept the invitation of the "other A." He had not seen Augusta since early April, before the birth of her daughter Medora. He did not care for babies in their "mewling and puking" stage, squalling and making messes.

After three days he left Six Mile Bottom for Cambridge, dining on the day of his arrival (the 6th) with Scrope Davies and Hobhouse, who was then sounding out the ground for his chances of representing Cambridge in Parliament if the incumbent, Palmerston, as was expected, was given an English peerage.[n] Davies had won £6,065 at Macao at Watier's on June 10[n] and was doing the entertaining. With the convivial Douglas Kinnaird there, the party was congenial and many bottles were opened.

At two the next afternoon the whole Cambridge party—Byron, Hobhouse, Davies, and Kinnaird—started for London in a big coach.[n] Byron had much sobering and exasperating business in the next week. He was determined to force some conclusion upon Claughton, who had been promising another payment for so long that it was evident he could not or would not complete his contract. Hanson was out of town, and Byron tried to get some action from his son Charles.[n] And when Hanson returned, he renewed his plea, but was told that Claughton wished to return to the country to make one last effort before sacrificing the earnest money already paid in.[n]

Vexed, but helpless to do anything, Byron gave vent to his irritation in a letter to Moore: "I have brought my pigs to a Mussulman market. If I had but a wife now, and children, of whose paternity I entertained doubts, I should be happy, or rather fortunate, as Candide or Scarmentado."[n]

Part of Byron's exasperation was caused by the fact that he wanted to finish the business and leave for the seashore with Augusta. He wrote to Hodgson, then spending his holiday at Hastings to be near his fiancée, Miss Tayler, asking him to find a house. Hodgson replied promptly on the 10th: "Your promised visit to Hastings is the 'comble de ma bonheur.'" He recommended Hastings House for its "retirement and picturesqueness."[n]

Byron settled for this house, which had eight Greek muses in the garden, taking it for a month at ten guineas per week. Hodgson secured it from the 13th, but it was another week before Byron and Augusta arrived.[n] In the meantime, Mrs. Leigh had come to town and was staying at the London Hotel in Albemarle Street.[n] Byron postponed leaving for Hastings two or three times in the hope of a settlement with Claughton, but in desperation on the 19th he wrote to Hanson: ". . . if Mr. Cn. will give up £25,000, or even £20,000, I will close with him, and take back the estate. . . . He has never *once* kept his word since the sale was concluded. . . . *You* will cling and cling to the fallacious hope of the fulfilment, already shewn to be so, till I am ruined entirely. . . . *Close* with him on any terms, and let us have done with the equivocator." In a postscript he added: "Tell Lord and Lady Portsmouth that Mrs. Chaworth is in town. I believe the Countess [Hanson's daughter] knows her; is it not so?" [n]

This was another reason for Byron's anxiety to leave London. Under present circumstances he had no desire to see his once idealized "Morning Star of Annesley" in a London drawing-room, especially not with her "dear friend" Miss Radford, who had shepherded her to the bewildering metropolis. Byron had warned Mary of his own family shyness, and had said that they might be embarrassed when they met. On July 7 she was on her way to London and wrote: "Impossible!—*you* shy and awkward—one who has travelled so much and seen so much." [n] But when she arrived Byron put it off on the Hansons to call on her and escaped with Augusta to Hastings on the 20th without seeing her.

In the sea and in the "retired" house Byron was nearly happy for three weeks. The ocean itself always revived his spirits. Then, in addition to Augusta (if the children were there, the house was big enough so that they would not disturb him), he had pleasant company, not only in Hodgson and young Cowell, whom he had befriended in 1808, but also in his cousin George Anson Byron. He was reading *Waverley*, published on July 7, which he did not yet know to be Scott's, and which he thought "the best and most interesting novel I have redde since—I don't know when." [n] To Hobhouse, who had urged him to come to town on the 26th to vote against the Government Bill providing for a severer enforcement of the laws in Ireland, he wrote: "Ly J[ersey] has written to me to speak and write, and the Devil knows what—I *can* do neither—which is a good excuse for refusing, though self-love won't allow it to be an *alledgeable* one. I shall say politely I *won't*. . . ." [n]

Conviviality and country pleasures now meant more to him than Parliamentary oratory, and, besides, he had none too happy recollections of his last speech for the Irish. To Moore he wrote ten days later: "I have been swimming and eating turbot, and smuggling neat brandies and silk handkerchiefs,—and listening to my friend Hodgson's raptures about a pretty wife-elect of his,—and walking on cliffs, and tumbling down hills and making the most of the *dolce far-niente* for the last fortnight. I met a son of Lord Erskine's, who says he has been married a year, and is the 'happiest of men' . . . so, it is worth while being here, if only to witness the superlative felicity of these foxes, who have cut off their tails, and would persuade the rest to part with their brushes to keep them in countenance." [n]

But Byron was already secretly lifting the ax that would clip his own. Annabella, having received no reply, began to be perplexed how to explain her feelings and so wrote him a confused letter full of cryptic sentences (it was as difficult for her not to run into abstractions as it was for Byron not to be concrete and direct). She acknowledged an attachment for him, but an "imperfect one." [n]

The letter was forwarded to Byron at Hastings, where it reached him on August 1. He sat down immediately to answer it, but, reading her ambiguities again, he was not sure that he understood her at all. "Pray then write to me openly and *harshly*," he wrote, "if you please . . . . you are the last person I would wish to misunderstand." He added in a postscript: ". . . my memory is still retentive enough not to require the repetition that you are attached to another." [8]

[8] Mayne: *Lady Byron*, p. 101. Byron had shown Annabella's letter to Hodgson, who wrote an eight-page rhapsody on what his friend might become if he married this paragon, who, he was sure, was more attached to him than she let him see. Hodgson was convinced "that *this* is the person to call out all the better parts of your character, & to assist you in subduing the worse." (Unpublished letter, Aug. 1, 1814, Murray MSS.)

Poor Annabella was back where she had started. How could she ever "regain truth" without confessing that she had told a lie about her attachment to George Eden? Her answer, in spite of its verbiage and analytical nuances, committed her even further while she tried to indicate that she was heart-free without admitting that she was in love with Byron. Finally she was able to crawl out of the troublesome lie without admitting it to be such: "Some time ago I had meant to acknowledge clearly, knowing that you would not mistake the motives of my acknowledgement, that I had been deceived (and too willingly, inasmuch as you were concerned) in thinking I had ever formed a decided attachment. The reasons which led me to believe the character of one person suited to my own, have disappeared with opportunities of fuller investigation . . . nothing could now induce me to marry him."[9]

But in the meantime other kettles were boiling. While they were at Hastings, Byron and Augusta both came to the conclusion that the only solution was for Byron to take a wife. He later told Lady Melbourne: "She wished me much to marry, because it was the only chance of redemption for *two* persons. . . ."[n] Augusta thought her young friend Lady Charlotte Leveson Gower, whom Byron had admired, was much better suited to him than the more austere Miss Milbanke, whose letters he showed her. She began negotiations at once, pretending that her brother was ignorant of these overtures. Byron later told Lady Melbourne that Lady Charlotte's "frequent epistles, and excessive attachment to X [now Byron's constant symbol for Augusta in his letters to Lady Melbourne] *both* so much more numerous and friendly than ever before, with sentences which were *not* to be answered, or if answered, replied to in a *particular* manner, etc., with a hundred little things, which I don't understand, but which convinced X of her disposition; all produced this episode in our drama."[n]

But there the matter rested, without a yes or no, through the summer. Byron was growing restive and irritable, but he was

[9] Mayne: *Lady Byron*, p. 102. Letter of Aug. 6, 1814. In a postscript Annabella committed herself still further by asking for a print of Byron's portrait.

not sure he wanted anything to happen. "I am, in some respects," he wrote Moore, "happy, but not in a manner that can or ought to last,—but enough of that. The worst of it is, I feel quite enervated and indifferent." [n] One night his servant brought him a bottle of ink that was too full, into which he dipped his pen. When it came out smeared all over, he flew into a passion and flung the bottle out the window into the garden.[n] Next morning, he told Moore, "I was horrified by seeing that it had struck, and split upon, the petticoat of Euterpe's graven image in the garden, and grimed her as if it were on purpose. Only think of my distress,—and the epigrams that might be engendered on the Muse and her misadventure." [n]

It was time to leave before a temper that could besmear the muse of music caused further discords. Besides, pressing business required his presence in town. Hanson had written that Claughton had finally agreed to sacrifice £25,000 of the £28,000 paid in, and to turn the property back to Byron, and there were details to arrange and papers to sign.[n] Hanson also sent some ominous news that made Byron even more eager to quit Hastings: "I called last Night upon Mrs. Chaworth," he wrote. "She looks ill and talks of taking the Sea Air at Hastings—She tells me she is separated from Mr. C—her Children are with her." [n]

Byron and Augusta were back in London by the 11th, having escaped from Hastings just before the arrival of Mary and her children, who took the very house they had lived in.[1] On the 10th, Byron had written to Annabella. She had asked for an honest avowal of his feelings, and he replied with a frankness that startled her: "I will answer your question as openly as I can. I did—do—and always shall love you; and as this feeling is not exactly an act of will, I know no remedy, and at all events should never find one in the sacrifice of your comfort." He had from the first believed that she was the woman most

[1] It was no doubt at this time that Augusta, who had urged Byron to call on Mary while they were at Newstead in January (*LBC*, I, 241), cautioned him against seeing her in the summer, for Augusta was then deep in her scheme to marry him to her friend Lady Charlotte Leveson Gower: " 'For,' said she," Byron wrote later, " 'if you go, you will fall in love again, and then there will be a scene; one step will lead to another, *et cela fera un éclat.*' " (*LJ*, VI, 234. Letter of July 12 [?], 1823, to M. Coulmann.)

likely to render any man happy, but, learning of her supposed engagement, he had not pressed his attentions (a statement of the case which was rather oversimplified). "What your own feelings and objections were and are I have not the right and scarcely the wish to enquire. It is enough for me that they exist; they excite neither astonishment nor displeasure. It would be a very hard case if a woman were obliged to account for her repugnance. You would probably like me if you could; and as you cannot, I am not quite coxcomb enough to be surprised at a very natural occurrence. You ask me how far my peace is, or may be, affected by those feelings towards you. I do not know—not quite enough to invade yours, or request from your pity what I cannot owe to your affection."[n]

He had fairly tossed the matter into Annabella's lap, and she did not quite know what to do with it. In London, Byron was already thinking of other things. While he was in Hastings, Murray had published *Lara* anonymously in a volume with Rogers's sentimental tale *Jacqueline.* When Rogers sent him a privately printed copy of the latter poem in June, Byron had flattered the author by saying that it was "all grace and softness and poetry," admitting at the same time that he had "just 'supped full of horror' in two cantos of darkness and dismay."[n] Reluctant to come before the public again in a separate publication, he had proposed a joint venture, later trying to include Moore, who declined,[n] and then coming to an arrangement with Rogers, one which the publisher was not eager for. But in spite of the handicap *Lara* was immediately known to be Byron's and sold rapidly. When Hobhouse saw Byron and his sister in London on the 11th, he was able to report that Murray had told him (Hobhouse) that he had sold six thousand copies.[n] But Murray was not satisfied. Byron reported to Moore: "Murray talks of divorcing Larry and Jacky—a bad sign for the authors, who, I suppose, will be divorced too, and throw the blame upon one another. Seriously, I don't care a cigar about it, and don't see why Sam should."[n] Murray did divorce the poems, and he paid Byron £700 for the copyright, the first money Byron had ever accepted for his own use from the publisher.[n]

A measure of Byron's extending fame was the letter he received while at Hastings from James Hogg, the "Ettrick Shepherd," asking him to recommend him to Murray. "The said Hogg is a strange being," Byron wrote to Moore, "but of great, though uncouth, powers. I think very highly of him, as a poet; but he, and half these Scotch and Lake troubadours, are spoilt by living in little circles and petty societies." What these "home-keeping minstrels" needed was an "illicit amour or two . . . in the way of essay upon the Passions, beginning with simple adultery, and compounding it as they went along." [n]

But he was in a less gusty mood in London. The anxiety about his financial affairs, the uncertainty of the future (Augusta was still in full pursuit of the shy "antelope," Lady Charlotte), the apparent hopelessness of his advances to Annabella, who continued to pique his interest more than the pretty but insipid girl of his sister's choice, and the feeling that, after all, no one satisfied him quite so well as Augusta herself—all contributed to put him on edge. He had talked earlier of going to Scotland, and he was still undecided.[n] There had been a meaningful lapse in his correspondence with Lady Melbourne since he had left town for Six Mile Bottom in July, but on August 15 he sent her four brace of grouse and asked whether he might call. "I have been at the sea, and in it; and am going to Newstead, I believe for a week or so, and thence I know not whither." [n]

Then came Annabella's reply to his open confession, and it was disappointing. In her "prim and pretty" style she told him at great length why she ought not to select him as her example on earth and her guide to heaven, but tempered this with the assurance that George Eden had never had a place in her heart and that she had great esteem and affection for her present correspondent. Byron answered with a curtness that would have stopped any girl less self-complaisant than Annabella: "Very well—now we can talk of something else. Though I do not think an intimacy which does not extend beyond a few letters and still fewer interviews in the course of a year could be particularly injurious to either party, yet as (if I recollect rightly) you told me that some remarks had been made upon the subject, it is perhaps as well that even that should end. This is a point upon which yourself can best determine, and in which I have nothing to do but acquiesce." *n*

Annabella came back with an even lengthier letter. Ethel Mayne, her biographer, had not the patience to quote this *in extenso* but summarized it: "She dissected herself from the age of seventeen; she gave him the irrelevant information that her health required many hours of sleep and exercise—an unattractive as well as an irrelevant avowal! This prevented her from studying much; she cared only for philosophy and poetry—but (remembering what was Byron's favourite study) she asked him to recommend her some books of modern history. At present she was reading Sismondi's *Italian Republics*." *n*

Byron did not answer for some days. On Saturday the 20th he signed the papers which terminated Claughton's contract and put Newstead back in his hands, and the following day he departed with Augusta and her children for the Abbey.*n* And on the 20th, Mary Chaworth was writing plaintively from Hastings: "Why this long silence, my dear Friend, which after the many professions of regard I have had the pleasure of receiving from you quite surprises and mortifies me. . . . You will think me very intrusive, if not impertinent—but the recollection of early days must plead for me." *n*

Byron did not reply because he did not know what to say. For Mary it was too much. While she was still at Hastings, her mind gave way. The strain of the faithlessness of her husband, of the separation, and now of the abandonment by the man who had for months been the focus of her hopes caused a nervous reaction that brought illness and then the wandering of her mind. It was late October before Byron heard of it, and by then he had committed himself so completely elsewhere that he could give her only passing pity.[2]

At Newstead, Byron once more relapsed into good-humored ennui. On the 25th (just a year after Annabella had written her first letter to him) he wrote her at length, starting with a discourse on historical writers, Italian, French, and English

[2] *LBC*, I, 286–7. Letter of Oct. 31, 1814. After a few months Mary recovered, and was later reconciled with her husband.

("Gibbon is well worth a hundred perusals"), and ending with a casual postscript: ". . . I regret it will not be in my power to proceed to Seaham during the present year." [n]

She took her time to reply. In the meantime Byron was enjoying his native woods and lakes. He wrote to Murray: "I have read the few books I had with me, and been forced to fish, for lack of other argument. I have caught a great many perch and some carp. . . ." In a postscript he added: "Mrs. Leigh and the children are very well." [n] He gave more details of his occupations to Moore: ". . . I have taken to breaking soda-water bottles with my pistols, and jumping into the water, and rowing over it, and firing at the fowls of the air." [n]

Miss Milbanke had written again. She moralized at great length; she dissected herself once more; she accepted his offer of books; she would attempt to read the whole of Gibbon. But she could not hide her disappointment that he was not coming to Seaham: "We had avoided every engagement which might have interfered with that more welcome one." The probability is that the spoiled child had inconvenienced her parents considerably by insisting that they keep the gate open to Byron while she continued her metaphysical sparring with him. She was surprised to find him at Newstead, which she thought he had sold. She ended with a wistfulness that was intended to keep the correspondence going: "If we could have met, all my apparent inconsistencies would have been dispelled." [n]

All this time Augusta, the dear "Goose," had been corresponding furiously with the antelope in a language of innuendoes and backing and starting which Byron confessed he could not understand. Lady Charlotte was even more incomprehensible in her simple way than the "Princess of Parallelograms," some of whose angles might be narrow, but whose lines were straight.

Byron wrote to Annabella on September 7, telling her of Claughton's forfeiture and of his regaining Newstead. He added a backhanded compliment that would have offended anyone less sure of her rightness. "You accuse yourself of 'apparent inconsistencies.' To me they have not appeared; on the contrary, your consistency has been the most formidable apparition I have encountered."

He disposed of her regrets that they had not met by saying: "After one or two letters which lately passed between us, and to which I must request your pardon for recurring we—at least *I* (to speak for myself)—could hardly have met without some embarrassment, possibly on both sides, certainly on one." *n*

Before he could receive an answer, Augusta's fine scheme blew up and the antelope escaped in a flutter of fear. Byron's suspicion that the mother was not ignorant of what was going on was justified. He told Lady Melbourne that Augusta's friend "after a certain time was seized with a panic, on some family scheme (which I will tell you when we meet) of a *compact elsewhere.* The fact is, the little girl had no will of her own; and might not be aware of what she had been doing. . . ." [3]

As Moore recollected the story from Byron's burned Memoirs, Lady Charlotte's flustered refusal arrived while Byron and his sister were sitting together one morning. " 'You see,' said Lord Byron, 'that, after all, Miss Milbanke is to be the person;—I will write to her.' He accordingly wrote on the moment, and, as soon as he had finished, his friend [Augusta], remonstrating still strongly against his choice, took up the letter,—but, on reading it over, observed, 'Well, really, this is a very pretty letter;—it is a pity it should not go. I never read a prettier one.' 'Then it *shall* go,' said Lord Byron, and in so saying, sealed and sent off, on the instant, this fiat of his fate." *n*

Byron told the tale more simply to Lady Melbourne: "I then said to X, after consoling her on the subject, that *I* would try the next myself, as she did not seem to be in luck." *n* The "pretty letter" was not a very ardent proposal, and was more verbose than Byron's letters generally were: "There is something I wish to say; and as I may not see you for some—perhaps for a long time—I will endeavour to say it at once. A few weeks ago you asked me a question which I answered. I have now one to propose—to which, if improper, I need not add that your declining to reply to it will be sufficient reproof. It is this. Are the 'objections' to which you alluded insuperable? or is there any

[3] *LBC,* I, 274. Letter of Oct. 4, 1814. The family scheme did work, for Lady Charlotte was married before the end of the year to young Howard, Earl of Surrey, only son of the Duke of Norfolk.

line or change of conduct which could possibly remove them? I am well aware that all such changes are more easy in theory than practice; but at the same time there are few things I would not attempt to obtain your good opinion. At all events I would willingly know the worst. Still I neither wish you to promise or pledge yourself to anything; but merely to learn a *possibility* which would not leave you the less a free agent.

"When I believed you attached, I had nothing to urge—indeed I have little now, except that having heard from yourself that your affections are not engaged, my importunities may appear not quite so selfish, however unsuccessful. It is not without a struggle that I address you once more on this subject; yet I am not very consistent—for it was to avoid troubling you upon it that I finally determined to remain an absent friend rather than become a tiresome guest. If I offend it is better at a distance.

"With the rest of my sentiments you are already acquainted. If I do not repeat them it is to avoid—or at least not increase—your displeasure." [n]

It seems evident that Byron had not intended this as a proposal, but merely a feeler to determine whether he might try again, whether the door was actually shut to him as Annabella's ambiguous letters had suggested. He gave her plenty of opportunity to withdraw without damaging their friendly relationship. And, not to make his own position too ridiculous, he would not waste love language on so tentative a proposal. He confessed afterward to Lady Melbourne: "The prospect (for A[nnabella] had been bewildering herself sadly, and did not appear to be much better disposed towards me than formerly) was not very promising. . . ." [n]

The fateful letter was posted on September 9. In the interim between that day and the 18th, when her reply came, Byron became increasingly ill at ease and uncomfortable. Divert himself as he would, he could not quiet his anxiety. By the 13th he was no longer sure whether he wanted a favorable reply or not; in any case, he would steel himself against failure by preparing an escape—the old one, departure for the Mediterranean—that would free him from all present perplexities, though it might well involve him in others, for he was thinking again of Lady Oxford, who was still traveling on the Continent. And at this crucial moment he turned to Hobhouse. He had to prefix a condition which he assumed then to think remote: ". . . if a circumstance (which may happen but is as unlikely to happen as Johanna [Southcote]'s establishing herself as the real Mrs. Trinity) does not occur—I have thoughts of going direct and directly to Italy—if so, will you come with me?" He continued: ". . . in short you know, my dear H——, that with all my bad qualities (and d——d bad they are to be sure) I like you better than anybody—and we have travelled together before, and been old friends, and all that, and we have a thorough fellow-feeling, and contempt for all things of the sublunary sort. . . ." [n]

Two days later, with such a pleasant prospect of escape, he could look upon either outcome of the event with an exhilarating expectancy. He wrote to Moore: "Now for a little egotism. My affairs stand thus. To-morrow I shall know whether a circumstance of importance enough to change many of my plans will occur or not. If it does not, I am off for Italy next month. . . . I want to see Venice, and the Alps, and Parmesan cheeses, and look at the coast of Greece, or rather Epirus, from Italy, as I once did—or fancied I did—that of Italy, when off Corfu. All this, however, depends upon an event, which may, or may not, happen." [n]

Just when Byron's letter arrived at Seaham, Miss Mayne does not say. But that it caused a sensation there can be no doubt. Annabella must have been abundantly surprised. The late correspondence had not led her to expect it. She was eager to receive the letters with the flourishing "B" surmounted by the coronet on the seal, but she was not exactly pining away. She had just been walking blindfold in the park for a stunt and writing amusing verses about the adventure that nearly landed her in the horse-pond.[n] She was a clever girl, but she was quite free from guile, too innocent to know that even a designing woman of great experience could hardly have pursued tactics better calculated to arouse Byron's interest and curiosity than those she had quite naturally followed, keeping him at bay until she was sure of his intentions.

But his letter melted all her reserve. She refused to see it as a tentative proposal, and considered it a real one. What matter if there were no love phrases? "With the rest of my sentiments you are already acquainted," he had said, and she remembered well enough that he had once said he loved her. Imagine the commotion in the Milbanke household. She had to get her parents' consent, but they were indulgent to their only daughter, who had always had whatever she wanted. Now she had no doubt that she wanted Byron. She wrote the same day:

"I have your second letter—and I am almost too agitated to write—but you will understand. It would be absurd to suppress anything—I am and have long been pledged to myself to make your happiness my first object in life. . . . I will *trust* to you for all I should look up to—all I can love. . . . This is a moment of joy which I have too much despaired of ever experiencing. . . . There has in reality been scarcely a change in my sentiments. More of this I will defer. I wrote by last post—with what different feelings! Let me be grateful for those with which I now acknowledge myself

Most affectely yours." [n]

On an added sheet she said that she had sent another letter to the Albany, not knowing whether he would be in town, accompanied by a "few lines" from her father, not wishing him to have "a moment's suspense." She suggested that there was a more effusive confession in the epistle sent to London: "I hope you will find in my other letter *all you wish.*" [n]

The effect of her reply at Newstead was just as electric, though in quite a different way. Annabella afterward learned from Augusta, when she had become her trusted confidante: "He [Byron] received it at dinner—the apothecary was the only person present besides A. . . . His remark to her, as he handed the letter across the table, looking so pale that she thought he was going to faint, was: 'It never rains but it pours.'" [4] This

[4] Mayne: *Lady Byron,* p. 112. Moore has a note which he credits to Byron's "Memoranda" (the destroyed "Memoirs"): "On the day of the arrival of the lady's answer, he was sitting at dinner, when his gardener came in and presented him with his mother's wedding ring, which she had lost many years before, and which the gardener had just found in digging up the mould

facetiousness, often a device of Byron to cover his deeper feelings, presumably was the first thing that came to his mind when he learned that she had sent *two* letters of acceptance as well as a letter from her father.

Byron was no doubt surprised and at the same time flattered by her immediate and complete capitulation. He told Lady Melbourne: ". . . the stars, I presume, did it." [n] While the other (Lady Charlotte) was her favorite, "no one could acquiesce in this with a better grace" than Augusta, he said.[n] She said Annabella's letter "was the best and prettiest she ever read." And Byron added: "It was really perfect, and so much the more welcome, as almost all the former ones were written evidently under embarrassment of feeling and expression." [n]

Before the day ended, he sat down to write her in a warmer style than that of his restrained proposal—but his letter was still far from being the passionate outpouring of an ecstatic lover.

"Your letter has given me a new existence—it was unexpected—I need not say welcome—but *that* is a poor word to express my present feelings. . . . I know your worth—and revere your virtues as I love yourself and if every proof in my power of my full sense of what is due to you will contribute to *your* happiness—I shall have secured my own.—It *is* in your power to render me happy—you have made me so already.—I wish to answer your letter immediately—but am at present scarcely collected enough to do it rationally—I was upon the point of leaving England without hope without fear—almost without feeling—but wished to make one effort to discover—not if I could pretend to your present affections—for to those I had given over all presumption—but whether time—and my most sincere endeavour to adopt any mode of conduct that might lead you to think well of me—might not eventually in securing your approbation awaken your regard.—These hopes are now dearer to me than ever; dear as they have ever been;—from the moment

---

under her window. Almost at the same moment, the letter from Miss Milbanke arrived, and Lord Byron exclaimed, 'If it contains a consent, I will be married with this ring.' It *did* contain a very flattering acceptance of his proposal, and a duplicate of the letter had been sent to London, in case this should have missed him." (Moore, I, 582 n.)

I became acquainted my attachment has been increasing & the very follies—give them a harsher name—with which I was beset and bewildered the conduct to which I had recourse for forgetfulness only made recollection more lively & bitter by the comparisons it forced on me in spite of Pride—and of Passions—which might have destroyed but never deceived me.—

"I am going to London on some business which once over—I hope to be permitted to visit Seaham; your father I will answer immediately & in the mean time beg you will present my best thanks and respects to him and Lady Milbanke. Will you write to me?" [n]

Would she write to him? Long afterward she said of this letter: "I thought that I might now show him all I felt. . . . I wrote just what was in my heart." [n] Certainly while he was writing it Byron meant what he had said, but with what uncanny precision did he unconsciously give his correspondents what they wanted to hear! That letter fed her false hope that she could reform him, that he wanted to be reformed by her. By what a narrow margin he had missed one fate and found another! A pen's point could have turned the balance and taken him abroad.

# NOTES

## Notes to Chapter I

*P.4, l.14* Edward Bernard compiled a rather detailed pedigree of the Byrons which was published by C. Wilson, London, 1870. See also Charles H. Pearson: *On the Early Byrons and Robert de Burun* (pamphlet, n.d.); and Burke's *Peerage and Baronetage.*

*p.4, l.26* Gray: *Newstead Priory,* p. 230. It is commonly said that the first Byron to own the Abbey was "Sir John the Little with the Great Beard," but this is probably an error. See note for page 5, l. 25. There is also at Newstead a second grant of the Abbey and other property to John Byron, junr., Knt., for £1,000, dated 1616, in the reign of James I. This is apparently a copy of the original document. Why it should have been necessary for the Byrons to purchase the Abbey a second time is a mystery. (See *The Roe-Byron Collection,* p. 25.)

*p.4, l.28* Irving: *Abbotsford and Newstead Abbey,* Appendix, p. 133.

*p.5, l.2* This matter is adequately discussed in Newstead Abbey Publications—No. 1: *The Story of the Abbey* (pamphlet).

*p.5, l.10* Ibid.

*p.5, l.25* According to Mr. Duncan Gray, Librarian of Newstead Abbey, the appellation "Little Sir John with the Great Beard" has been mistakenly applied to the first lay owner of Newstead and properly belongs to his son. I give Mr. Gray's evidence, which seems conclusive enough: "That the second Byron did possess a notable beard is proved by his portrait, formerly at Newstead, and now in the possession of the Dowager Lady Byron. It is reproduced in Canon Barber's book, *Byron—and where he is buried* (1939) [facing p. 17], and shows him with an exceptionally fine, long white beard. The painting is inscribed: 'Ætatis suæ 73 An. Dom. 1599,' which means that he would have been only about thirteen years old at the time of the purchase of Newstead, which must therefore have been made by his father. The earliest mention of the sobriquet we have found is in documents concerning a poaching dispute between the (later) 1st Baron and Sir George Chaworth in 1634, calendared in State Papers Domestic, 1634–5, p. 200. Chaworth declared 'that *old Sir John with the Long Beard,* when he was lieutenant of the forest under the Earl of Rutland, was taken up for hunting there [i.e., in Annesley] by a person yet living . . .' It is very unlikely that anyone living in 1634 could have taken up the first Byron of Newstead, who had died 67 years previously (1567)." (Letter to me of Oct. 17, 1950.) There is additional evidence in the fact that the tombs, originally in Colwick church but now at Newstead, show the first Sir John as clean shaven and the second (died Feb. 24, 1603–4) with a mustache and an extremely long beard.

*p.6, l.12* Pepys *Diary*, entry for April 26, 1667.

*p.6, l.19* The epitaph is quoted *in extenso* in Elze, p. 4, note 1.

*p.7, l.7* Nichol, p. 5.

*p.7, l.11* "A Famous Duel," *The World of Adventure* [n.d., 1865?], p. 99.

*p.7, l.19* From a MS. narrative of Byron's early years by Newton Hanson, son of Byron's attorney John Hanson. It was never published and remains in the collection of Byroniana at John Murray's.

*p.7, l.25* Newstead Abbey Publications—No. 2: *The Abbey Grounds* (pamphlet). See also Brecknock: *Byron,* p. 13, and Young, I, 140–8n. There is a picture of "Folly Castle" in Brecknock: *The Pilgrim Poet,* facing p. 84.

*p.7, l.29* Moore, I, 22.

*p.7, l.35* *The Yale Edition of Horace Walpole's Correspondence, Correspondence with George Montague,* IX, 299. Letter of Sept. 1, 1760.

*p.8, l.27* *The Life, Writings, Opinions . . . of Lord Byron* (Anonymous), Matthew Iley, London, 1825, I, 14.

*p.8, l.33* The details of the duel and the trial are given in *The Trial of William Lord Byron, Baron Byron of Rochdale, for the Murder of William Chaworth, Esq.; before the Right Honourable the House of Peers, in Westminster-Hall, in Full Parliament.* Published by order of the House of Peers. London, 1765. Accounts were also given in *The Annual Register,* 1765, Vol. VIII, Appendix to the Chronicle, pp. 208–12; and *The Gentleman's Magazine,* Vol. XXXV (May 1765), pp. 227–9.

*p.8, l.37* Dallas: *Recollections,* p. 124.

*p.9, l.10* Newton Hanson narrative, Murray MSS.

*p.9, l.13* Prothero, "The Childhood and School Days of Byron," p. 70.

*p.9, l.24* Moore, I, 21.

*p.9, l.26* *LJ*, VI, 233. Letter of Byron to J. J. Coulmann, July?, 1823.

*p.9, l.30* Moore, I, 20.

*p.10, l.4* Newton Hanson narrative, Murray MSS.

*p.10, l.10* Irving: *Abbotsford and Newstead Abbey*, Appendix, p. 134.

*p.10, l.13* Brecknock: *Byron,* p. 94. He leased certain coal mines to Simon Dearden and John Lomax for twenty-one years.

*p.10, l.17* Jeaffreson, p. 14.

*p.10, l.23* Medwin, I, 61–2; Moore, I, 21.

*p.10, l.32* "Histories of the Tête-à-Tête annexed; or Memoirs of the Nautical Lover and Miss Betsy G——n (No. 34–5), *The Town and Country Magazine,* Vol. V (Dec. 1773), p. 625.

*p.10, l.37* *The Narrative of the Honourable John Byron (Commodore in a Late Expedition round the World) Containing an Account of the Great Distresses Suffered by Himself and His Companions on the Coast of Patagonia, From the Year 1740, till their Arrival in England, 1746. With a Description of St. Jago de Chili, and the Manners and Customs of the Inhabitants. Also a Relation of the Loss of the Wager Man of War, One of Admiral Anson's Squadron.* Written by Himself. London, 1768.

*p.11, l.9* Ibid., p. 47; *Don Juan,* II, 71.

*p.12, l.3* J. K. Laughton: *D.N.B.* article on Admiral John Byron; whence most of the facts in this paragraph.

*p.12, l.18* *The Town and Country Magazine,* Vol. V (Dec. 1773), pp. 626–7.

*p.12, l.21* *Autobiography, Letters and Literary Remains of Mrs. Piozzi (Thrale)*, p. 466. Letter of Aug. 25, 1820, to Miss Willoughby.

*p.12, l.36* George Clinton, p. 33.

*p.13, l.14* *The Town and Country Magazine,* Vol. XI (Jan. 1779), pp. 9–11.

*p.14, l.12* Ibid., p. 11.

*p.14, l.18* Jeaffreson, p. 20.

*p.14, l.23* *LJ*, I, 4. Prothero in the *Letters and Journals* says that there were a son and daughter who died in infancy before the birth of Augusta, but in his article "The Childhood and School Days of Byron" he mentions only the daughter.

*p.14, l.34* *LJ*, VI, 231–2.

*p.15, l.20* Pryse Gordon, II, 330–1.

*p.15, l.22* Prothero: "The Childhood and School Days of Byron," p. 64.

*p.15, l.28* Bulloch, p. 123 (287). Bulloch prints the marriage register. Most of my information about the Gordons comes from this zealous researcher into the history of the Gordon family.

*p.16, l.10* Bulloch, p. 11 (175).

*p.16, l.28* Bulloch, p. 24 (188).

*p.17, l.2* Bulloch, p. 44 (208).

*p.17, l.18* I am indebted for a good deal of information on this head to the late Mr. H. K. Grant of London, who made a special study of Byron's Scottish ancestry, and in his enthusiasm did considerable research especially to help me find books and fill in details.

*p.17, l.26* Bulloch, p. 109 (273).

*p.17, l.30* Bulloch, p. 112 (276).

*p.18, l.7* Bulloch, pp. 115–16 (279–80).

*p.20, l.4* The extracts of the diary of Alexander Russell here given are from a typed copy in a scrapbook of Byron Miscellanies formerly belonging to Clement Shorter and now in my possession. According to Bulloch (p. 125), the original manuscript was (in 1902) owned by Russell's grandson, the then laird of Aden.

*p.20, l.16* *Ancient Ballads and Songs of the North of Scotland. . . .* With explanatory notes by Peter Buchan, Edinburgh, 1875, I, 251.

*p.20, l.31* Symon, p. 8.

*p.21, l.2* The *D.N.B.* article on Admiral Byron says he died April 10, 1786, but it must have been an earlier date, for, according to a letter of his widow, Sophia Byron (Byroniana from the Kaye Dowland collection, II, f.98, Morgan Library), the will was read on April 4.

*p.21, l.8* Byron made several appeals to his father's banker. Unpublished letters, dated May 4 and May 5, 1786, in Byroniana from the Kaye Dowland collection, II, f.99, 100, Morgan Library.

*p.21, l.14* Bulloch, p. 128 (292).

*p.21, l.33* Prothero: "The Childhood and School Days of Byron," p. 67.

*p.21, l.37* Moore, I, 7n.

*p.22, l.14* Cramond, I, 236.

*p.22, l.21* Symon, p. 19. Letter of Feb. 29, 1788, from Mr. Beckett, Mrs.

Byron's London attorney, to the agent of the commissioners in Edinburgh.

*p.22, l.25* Cramond, I, 236.

*p.23, l.6* Symon, pp. 12, 18.

*p.23, l.13* Dallas: Note preceding his *Recollections,* 1824.

*p.23, l.16* Symon, pp. 12–13.

# Notes to Chapter II

*P.24, l.9* Symon, p. 16.

*p.24, l.11* Symon, p. 12.

*p.24, l.17* Unpublished letter, University of Texas Library.

*p.24, l.19* Unpublished letter, Morgan Library.

*p.25, l.13* Captain Byron wrote to Mr. Perregaux, the Paris banker, from Edinburgh on Feb. 2, 1788, concerning a draft he had given his sister on Mr. Watson. (Unpublished letter, Huntington Library.)

*p.25, l.15* *LJ*, I, 5.

*p.25, l.20* *Childe Harold*, III, 118.

*p.26, l.10* Moore, I, 7.

*p.26, l.26* Symon, p. 19.

*p.27, l.9* Symon, p. 21.

*p.27, l.16* Symon, p. 21.

*p.27, l.25* Unpublished letter, dated March 25, 1788, University of Texas Library.

*p.28, l.4* The death of this grandson of the fifth Lord Byron in 1794 made the poet heir presumptive.

*p.28, l.11* A coast defense of Henry VIII.

*p.28, l.14* According to Mr. Beckett's report, he owed £30 there.

*p.28, l.16* Unpublished letter, Morgan Library.

*p.29, l.6* Moore, I, 8.

*p.29, l.12* Byron told Medwin in 1822 that he had preserved the note. (Medwin, I, 60.)

*p.29, l.15* Moore, I, 11.

*p.29, l.24* Moore, I, 8–9.

*p.29, l.28* Jeaffreson, pp. 24, 28–9.

*p.29, l.35* Medwin, I, 60.

*p.30, l.11* Symon, pp. 33–4.

*p.30, l.30* Maurois, pp. 32–3. Maurois quotes from Captain Byron's letters to his sister in the Lovelace papers.

*p.31, l.13* Symon, pp. 35–6.

*p.31, l.29* *LJ*, I, ix.

*p.31, l.31* *LJ*, I, 5.

*p.31, l.37* Maurois, p. 33.

*p.32, l.5* Prothero: "The Childhood and School Days of Byron," p. 71.

*p.32, l.7* Moore, I, 11.

*p.32, l.18* *LJ*, VI, 232n. Misdated 1799 in *LJ*.

*p.32, l.25* Medwin, I, 58, 60.

*p.33, l.2* Symon, p. 38. The doctor with whom Mr. Hunter corresponded was Dr. William Livingstone, Professor of Medicine at Marischal College in Aberdeen.

*p.33, l.5* *LJ*, I, 11n.

*p.33, l.13* Moore, I, 10.

*p.33, l.21* Symon, p. 31; Rogerson, p. 5.

*p.33, l.30* Moore, I, 9.

*p.34, l.17* *LJ*, V, 99. Letter of Oct. 16, 1820.

*p.34, l.25* Symon, p. 63.

*p.35, l.7* Moore, I, 13n.

*p.35, l.20* *LJ*, V, 406. From a notation in Byron's journal in 1821, in a section he called "My Dictionary."

*p.35, l.29* Ibid.

*p.35, l.31* *LJ*, V, 407. This was Joseph Paterson, later minister of Montrose. (Rogerson, p. 8.)

*p.35, l.35* *LJ*, V, 407.

*p.36, l.17* Symon, p. 67.

*p.36, l.25* *LJ*, I, 5–6.

*p.37, l.7* Newton Hanson narrative, Murray MSS.

*p.37, l.12* Unpublished letter, Mrs. Leigh to Farquhar, dated June 5, 1795, University of Texas Library.

*p.37, l.24* Blaikie, p. 411.

*p.37, l.27* *LJ*, V, 407.

*p.37, l.30* Bulloch, p. 141 (305).

*p.38, l.3* Now in the Library of Trinity College, Cambridge.

*p.37, l.34* Moore, I, 14.

*p.38, l.5* Dallas (*Recollections,* p. 1), who, however, was rather inaccurate about many details of Byron's life which he got secondhand, says: "I heard of him when a boy at De Loyauté's Academy, and afterwards, on the death of the old Lord. . . ." It has been assumed from this that he studied French at De Loyauté's in Aberdeen.

*p.38, l.20* Moore, I, 255n.

*p.38, l.25* Gamba, p. 149. Richard Knolles (1550?–1610): *The Turkish History, from the Origin of that Nation to the Growth of the Ottoman Empire, with the Lives and Conquests of their Princes and Emperors. . . .* With a continuation to this present year. MDCLXXXVII. A sixth edition was published in 1750. Byron's reference to "Ricaut" means that he had seen the revision of Knolles: *The General History of the Turks, with a Continuation by Sir Paul Rycaut* (3 vols., folio—1687–1700) or a later abridgment of it.

*p.38, l.31* Moore, I, 255n.

*p.38, l.38* *LJ*, V, 391. Letter of Oct. 9, 1821.

*p.39, l.7* Rogers, p. 244n.

*p.39, l.13* *Poetry,* V, 208–9.

*p.39, l.25* *Poetry,* II, 8. This is Byron's earliest mention of the novel, but as it was published in 1789 and had a considerable popularity, it is probable that he read it early.

*p.39, l.32* John Moore: *Zeluco,* I, 3–4.

*p.40, l.11* Moore, I, 13.

*p.40, l.18* Moore, I, 10.

*p.40, l.28* Moore, I, 19. Moore dates the event in the winter of 1797.

*p.40, l.35* Some information about Admiral Duff was supplied me by the late H. K. Grant of London. A picture of Fetteresso Castle is given in *The Book of the Duffs*, II, 309.

*p.42, l.13* *LJ*, II, 347–8. From Byron's journal of Nov. 26, 1813.

*p.42, l.26* *LJ*, VI, 6. Letter of Jan. 12–27, 1822.

*p.43, l.20* Note to *Don Juan*, X, 18. (*Poetry*, VI, 405n.)

*p.43, l.26* Unpublished letter, March 6, 1798, University of Texas Library.

*p.43, l.30* Unpublished letter, March 31, 1798, University of Texas Library.

*p.43, l.34* Unpublished letter, University of Texas Library.

*p.44, l.6* Letter of May 21, 1798, addressed to Farquhar, Hanson papers, Murray MSS.

*p.44, l.12* Moore, I, 20.

*p.44, l.18* Moore, I, 20.

*p.44, l.23* Marginal note in Hobhouse's copy of Moore.

*p.44, l.32* Unpublished letter, Farquhar to Crombie, University of Texas Library.

*p.44, l.38* Unpublished letter, Crombie to Farquhar, June 1, 1798, University of Texas Library.

*p.45, l.18* Unpublished letter, University of Texas Library.

*p.45, l.24* Unpublished letter, June 4, 1798, University of Texas Library.

*p.45, l.31* Unpublished letter, Hanson to Farquhar, June 22, 1798, University of Texas Library.

*p.45, l.35* Moore, I, 22.

*p.46, l.7* Rogerson, pp. 4–5. Moore (I, 37) says the watch, which was preserved by May Gray, had been given to her by Byron when she left Nottingham.

*p.46, l.9* *Don Juan*, X, 18.

*p.46, l.22* Moore, I, 68.

*p.46, l.24* Symon, p. 70.

*p.46, l.36* *Don Juan*, X, 17.

## Notes to Chapter III

*P.48, l.10* Moore: *Prose and Verse*, p. 416.

*p.48, l.24* Much information concerning Byron and his movements is given in the unpublished manuscript narrative of Newton Hanson in the Murray collection. The Hanson and Birch accounts in the same collection give exact dates of events. The Hansons were absent from London on this trip to Newstead from Aug. 27 to Sept. 16.

*p.49, l.11* Details of the property belonging to the estate were given in Mr. Farebrother's advertisement when Newstead was put up for sale on Aug. 14, 1812.

*p.49, l.17* Hanson and Birch accounts, Murray MSS.

*p.49, l.32* Pratt, p. 2. (From a MS. in the University of Texas Library.)

*p.50, l.10* Hanson narrative, Murray MSS.

*p.50, l.14* From a manuscript account titled "Lord Byron" written by Hobhouse in the summer of 1824 and kept with his diary.

*p.50, l.32* Hanson narrative, Murray MSS.

*p.50, l.36* Hanson and Birch accounts, Sept. 18, 1788.

*p.52, l.1* *LJ*, I, 7–8. Letter of March 13, 1799.

*p.52, l.10* According to *Notes and Queries*, 4th series, Vol. III, p. 561 (June 12, 1869), J. D. Rogers was an American Loyalist pensioned by the English government. He lived at Hen Cross, Nottingham. (*LJ*, I, 7n.)

*p.52, l.15* Moore: *Prose and Verse*, pp. 416–17.

*p.52, l.23* Moore, I, 27–8.

*p.52, l.30* *The Trial of William Lord Byron*, p. 4.

*p.52, l.31* *LJ*, VI, 233.

*p.52, l.35* Moore, I, 27.

*p.54, l.22* Facts and quotations in this and the preceding paragraph are from the Hanson narrative, Murray MSS.

*p.55, l.18* Hanson narrative, Murray MSS. Prothero, who drew considerably on the Hanson narrative for his notes, has an account of this. (*LJ*, I, 9–10n.)

*p.56, l.6* Hanson narrative, Murray MSS.

*p.56, l.10* Mrs. Byron entered in her account book after she arrived at Newstead: "Expenses of bringing Lord Byron from Scotland, 35 *l;* paid May Gray a year's wages, 9 *l.*" (Prothero: "The Childhood and School Days of Byron," p. 73.)

*p.56, l.18* There are copies of these letters in the Hanson narrative. The King's Warrant is printed by Moore (I, 29). The annuity was made to commence on July 5, 1799.

*p.56, l.28* *LJ*, I, 9n. Prothero ("The Childhood and School Days of Byron," p. 76) says Glennie's charge was £86. 10*s.* a year.

*p.56, l.35* *LJ*, I, 10n.

*p.57, l.20* *LJ*, I, 10n. Letter of Sept. 1, 1799.

*p.57, l.26* *LJ*, V, 450.

*p.57, l.31* Marginal note in Hobhouse's copy of Moore (I, 19).

*p.58, l.17* Hobhouse marginal notes in his copy of Moore.

*p.59, l.6* Moore, I, 30–1.

*p.60, l.19* Hanson narrative, Murray MSS.

*p.60, l.32* Ibid.

*p.61, l.18* Moore, I, 31–2.

*p.61, l.35* *LJ*, V, 449–50. There is no basis for the statement that this episode had its setting in Nottingham except that Mrs. Parker apparently was living there, or near there, in 1798 (Byron addressed his first letter to her on Nov. 8 of that year), and that Mrs. Byron probably returned to the north during the summer of 1800. According to local tradition in Nottingham, Byron lived with his mother in a house in St. James's Street during the summer vacation of 1800. (*The Sketch*, Sept. 22, 1897, p. 353.)

*p.62, l.5* *LJ*, V, 450.

*p.62, l.27* Hanson narrative, Murray MSS.

*p.63, l.3* Moore, I, 32.

*p.63, l.19* Moore, I, 38. The date of the interview is given in the Hanson narrative, Murray MSS.

*p.63, l.28* A facsimile of this letter is given in H. B. Smith: *A Sentimental Library*, p. 24.
*p.64, l.6* Hanson narrative, Murray MSS.
*p.64, l.24* Moore, I, 38–9.

# Notes to Chapter IV

*P.66, l.3* Moore, I, 39.
*p.66, l.16* Unpublished letter, Berg Collection, New York Public Library.
*p.66, l.27* *LJ*, V, 453–4.
*p.67, l.1* Moore, I, 42–3.
*p.67, l.3* Minchin, p. 192.
*p.67, l.5* *LJ*, V, 454.
*p.67, l.5* Moore, I, 45–6.
*p.67, l.7* *The Mirror*, May 29, 1824, p. 358. The schoolfellow did not reveal his name.
*p.67, l.10* Moore, I, 42–3.
*p.67, l.19* *LJ*, V, 453.
*p.67, l.23* *LJ*, V, 454.
*p.67, l.29* Hanson narrative, Murray MSS.
*p.67, l.31* Hanson and Birch accounts, Murray MSS.
*p.68, l.8* *Poetry*, V, 609–10n.
*p.68, l.18* *LJ*, I, 76n.
*p.68, l.27* Hanson narrative, Murray MSS. Mrs. Byron still owed Lavender £80 for his treatment of Byron's foot in Nottingham in 1799. There is among the Murray MSS. a receipt for that sum from the guardians "for attendance, dressings, & instruments for Lord Byron's foot."
*p.68, l.36* Hanson narrative, Murray MSS. (Quoted in *LJ*, I, 12n.)
*p.69, l.12* Moore, I, 43.
*p.69, l.32* Pratt, pp. 4–5.
*p.70, l.14* Pryse Gordon, II, 321, 332–3.
*p.70, l.18* Hanson narrative, Murray MSS.
*p.70, l.26* L'Estrange, p. 8.
*p.71, l.6* *LJ*, VI, 69–70.
*p.71, l.18* "On the Death of a Young Lady, Cousin to the Author, and Very Dear to Him."
*p.71, l.31* *LJ*, I, 12n. Letter of Dr. Joseph Drury to Hanson, Feb. 4, 1803.
*p.72, l.12* Hanson narrative, Murray MSS.
*p.72, l.27* *LJ*, V, 455.
*p.72, l.30* *LJ*, III, 171n.
*p.73, l.1* Moore, I, 51. The incident is referred to in his tribute to Tattersall (Davus) in *Childish Recollections*, lines 265–86.
*p.73, l.7* "To D——."
*p.73, l.14* *LJ*, I, 12–14. Letter of May 1, 1803.
*p.73, l.19* *LJ*, I, 13n.
*p.73, l.23* *LJ*, I, 15. In the Bill Book (which gave the standings of

the students) of 1803, Byron's name occurs as top of the fifth form. (Minchin, p. 310.)

*p.73, l.30* Moore, I, 39.
*p.74, l.5* Eg. 2612, f.22.
*p.74, l.11* Eg. 2612, ff.84, 85.
*p.74, l.22* Hanson narrative, Murray MSS.
*p.74, l.27* Eg. 2612, f.98.
*p.74, l.29* Hanson narrative, Murray MSS.
*p.75, l.13* Eg. 2612, f.82.
*p.75, l.16* Eg. 2612, ff.126, 140.
*p.75, l.19* Eg. 2612, ff.123, 130.
*p.75, l.25* Hanson narrative, Murray MSS. Letter of Mrs. Byron to Hanson, Oct. 30, 1803.
*p.76, l.25* *LJ*, V, 441. "Detached Thoughts."
*p.77, l.4* *LJ*, I, 17–18.
*p.77, l.9* Eg. 2612, f.130.
*p.77, l.17* Moore, I, 54.
*p.77, l.25* *LJ*, I, 16n. Letter of Oct. 30, 1803.
*p.77, l.30* *LJ*, I, 16n.
*p.78, l.26* Medwin, I, 65–6.
*p.79, l.19* "On Leaving Newstead Abbey."
*p.80, l.12* Eg. 2612, f.136–7.
*p.80, l.15* Eg. 2612, f.135.
*p.82, l.6* *LJ*, I, 23. Letter of March 26, 1804.
*p.82, l.14* Eg. 2612, ff.149. Letter of March 26, 1804.
*p.82, l.26* *LJ*, I, 27–30. Letter of April 9, 1804.
*p.83, l.4* Gabriel Lackbrain is a character in a comedy by F. Reynolds called *Life*.
*p.83, l.10* Moore, I, 65–6.
*p.83, l.26* *B-SP*, I, 10.
*p.83, l.35* *LJ*, V, 453.
*p.83, l.38* Moore, I, 39.
*p.84, l.13* *LJ*, V, 445.
*p.84, l.26* *LJ*, V, 452–3.
*p.85, l.11* Byron's copy of Pope's poems was sold at auction from the library of the late Rev. Dr. Roderick Terry, American Art Association, Anderson Galleries, Feb. 14, 1935, Sale No. 4154, pp. 28–9. It is a 16$^{mo}$ volume of *The Poetical Works of Alexander Pope*, Vol. II, London, n.d. On the first flyleaf is written in Byron's hand: "Harrow on the Hill, Middlesex —A.D. 1803—Given me by my Friend Boldero."
*p.85, l.21* Moore, I, 60, 95–8.
*p.85, l.26* Marginal notes in Hobhouse's copy of Moore.
*p.85, l.32* Unpublished letter of July 2, 1804, quoted in Maggs Catalogue, No. 801, 1951.
*p.86, l.3* Hanson narrative, Murray MSS. Byron to Hanson (copy), July 17, 1804; Mrs. Byron to Hanson, July 20 and July 24, 1804.
*p.86, l.18* Moore, I, 61. The *Autobiography* of the first Lord Herbert of Cherbury (1583–1648) was first published in 1764 by Horace Walpole in a small edition, illustrated with an engraving of a portrait of the hero

lying on the ground after a duel. The reissue of Walpole's edition in 1770 may have been in Mr. Falkner's library.

*p.86, l.20* Moore, I, 61.

*p.86, l.28* *LJ*, I, 30–1.

*p.86, l.37* Eg. 2612, f.163.

*p.87, l.7* *LJ*, I, 43. Letter of Nov. 2, 1804.

*p.87, l.27* Pratt, pp. 14–15.

*p.87, l.32* *LJ*, I, 34. Letter of Aug. 29, 1804.

*p.88, l.5* Moore, I, 56–7.

*p.88, l.8* Moore, I, 57.

*p.88, l.21* *LJ*, II, 347. Journal of Nov. 26, 1813. The fact that this news came, according to Byron, when he was sixteen, and that Mrs. Byron told it to the Pigots, fixes the time fairly definitely in the summer holiday of 1804 while he was at Southwell.

*p.88, l.24* Hanson narrative, Murray MSS.

*p.89, l.12* *LJ*, I, 35. Letter of Oct. 25, 1804.

*p.91, l.10* Medwin, I, 69.

*p.91, l.22* *LJ*, I, 43–4. Letter of Nov. 2, 1804.

*p.91, l.33* *LJ*, I, 46.

*p.92, l.3* *LJ*, I, 45n. Letter of Nov. 18, 1804.

*p.92, l.12* Hanson narrative, Murray MSS. Letter of Dec. 8, 1804.

*p.92, l.18* Moore: *Memoirs*, II, 624–5; Hanson narrative, Murray MSS. Letter of Dec. 29, 1804.

*p.92, l.26* *LJ*, I, 52n. The letter, dated Dec. 29, 1804, is given in full in the Hanson narrative, Murray MSS.

*p.92, l.37* *LJ*, I, 63–4. Letter of April 25, 1805.

*p.93, l.11* Hanson narrative, Murray MSS.

*p.93, l.17* Ibid.

*p.93, l.23* *LJ*, I, 54. Letter of Jan. 30, 1805.

*p.93, l.26* Hanson narrative, Murray MSS. Letter of Jan. 31, 1805.

*p.94, l.10* Moore: *Prose and Verse*, p. 415.

*p.94, l.14* *LJ*, I, 57. Letter of April 4, 1805.

*p.94, l.21* *LJ*, I, 56–7.

*p.94, l.27* *LJ*, I, 58. Letter of April 15, 1805.

*p.94, l.37* *LJ*, I, 60–2. Letter of April 23, 1805.

*p.95, l.8* *LJ*, I, 64–5. Letter of April 25, 1805.

*p.95, l.24* Moore: *Memoirs*, II, 623; Laborde, p. 46.

*p.95, l.32* Moore: *Memoirs*, II, 623.

*p.95, l.34* "On a Change of Masters at a Great Public School." The manuscript is dated "Harrow, July, 1805." (*Poetry*, I, 17.)

*p.95, l.38* Moore, I, 58–9; Moore: *Prose and Verse*, pp. 415–16.

*p.96, l.18* Moore, I, 61.

*p.96, l.23* Moore, I, 67.

*p.97, l.4* *LJ*, I, 66. Letter of June 5, 1805.

*p.97, l.10* *LJ*, I, 68. Letter of July 2, 1805.

*p.98, l.5* MS. recollections of Byron by Henry Long, Berg Collection, New York Public Library.

*p.98, l.15* *LJ*, V, 427.

*p.99, l.21* *LJ*, I, 72. Letter of Aug. 4, 1805.

*p.100, l.2* Moore, I, 57–8.

*p.100, l.15* *Poetry,* I, 210–11. This poem was first published by Moore, who says (I, 56) that it was written not long after Byron's farewell to Mary in 1804. In the Murray edition of Byron's poems published in 1832 the verses were published with the title "Fragment Written Shortly after the Marriage of Miss Chaworth," which, of course, would be the summer of 1805. Owen Mealey wrote to Hanson on Aug. 28, 1805: "Mrs. [*sic*] Chaworth is married to Mr. Musters and Mr. and Mrs. Clark has quitted Annesly. . . ." (Eg. 2612, f.219.) E. H. Coleridge, though he uses the title of the edition of 1832 and gives 1805 as the date of composition, adds to the confusion by quoting in a note a statement of Miss Pigot that they "were written by Lord Byron in 1804."

*p.100, l.17* Hanson narrative, Murray MSS. Letter of Mrs. Byron to Hanson, Sept. 26, 1805.

## Notes to Chapter V

*P.101, l.9* *LJ,* I, 151–2. Letter of Nov. 19, 1820.

*p.101, l.16* *LJ,* V, 445.

*p.102, l.1* *LJ,* I, 80.

*p.102, l.17* *LJ,* I, 81.

*p.102, l.23* Hanson narrative, Murray MSS.

*p.102, l.28* *LJ,* I, 81–2.

*p.102, l.32* *LJ,* I, 83.

*p.103, l.19* See Trevelyan, pp. 75–83.

*p.103, l.25* Wordsworth: *The Prelude,* Book IX, lines 231–2.

*p.104, l.8* *LJ,* I, 84–5.

*p.104, l.27* *LJ,* V, 168–9.

*p.104, l.32* *LJ,* V, 122, 123. Letter of Nov. 19, 1820, to John Murray.

*p.104, l.34* *LJ,* IV, 411–12. Letter of Jan. (mistakenly dated Feb.) 26, 1820.

*p.105, l.33* *LJ,* I, 86–8. Letter of Nov. 30, 1805.

*p.106, l.4* *LJ,* I, 89. Letter of Dec. 4, 1805.

*p.106, l.14* *LJ,* V, 445–6. "Detached Thoughts."

*p.106, l.26* *LJ,* I, 92.

*p.107, l.5* *LJ,* I, 93–4.

*p.107, l.18* *LJ,* V, 446.

*p.107, l.30* *LJ,* V, 169.

*p.108, l.18* Letter of Oct. 13, 1811, Murray MSS. This paragraph was omitted from the letter as published in *LBC.*

*p.108, l.27* *B-SP,* I, 124. Letter of Oct. 22, 1811. This paragraph was also omitted from *LBC.*

*p.109, l.5* *LJ,* I, 94. Letter of Jan. 7, 1806.

*p.109, l.11* On Jan. 16, 1812, Byron wrote out for Hanson an account of his first dealings with the moneylenders, as well as he could remember them at that time: "Lord Byron to the best of his knowledge and recollection in Decr. 1805 January 1806 applied to *King* in consequence of an advertisement in ye papers who acquainted Ld. B. *that his minority* prevented all money transactions without the security of competent persons; *through Mr. K.* he became acquainted with a Mr. Dellvalley [?] another of the tribes of Israel, and *subsequently* with a Mr. Havard [Hazard] of Golden Square.—After many delays during which Ld. B. had interviews with Havard, once he thinks in Golden Square, but more frequently in Piccadilly, Mrs. M. agreed to become security jointly with her daughter.—The second annuity was *settled at Worthing.* Ld. B. thinks Mrs. M. has some *letters* of Ld. B's at that time written. Ld. B. was not present." (Murray MSS.)

*p.109, l.17* *LJ*, I, 95n.

*p.110, l.12* Hanson narrative, Murray MSS.

*p.110, l.34* *LJ*, I, 94–6.

*p.111, l.4* *LJ*, I, 97n. Letter of March 7, 1806.

*p.111, l.19* *LJ*, V, 575.

*p.111, l.37* Hanson narrative, Murray MSS. Quoted in part, *LJ*, I, 95n. Letter of March 4, 1806.

*p.112, l.7* *LJ*, I, 97–8. Letter of March 10, 1806.

*p.112, l.13* Hanson narrative, Murray MSS. (copy).

*p.112, l.19* *LJ*, I, 95n. Letter of April 24, 1806.

*p.112, l.24* The bill of W. Wilson of Cambridge for these items, addressed to Lord Byron, is among the letters of E. N. Long in the Berg Collection of the New York Public Library.

*p.113, l.10* Eg. 2611, f.16.

*p.113, l.15* Murray MSS.; Hobhouse proofs.

*p.113, l.21* After one of their quarrels at Southwell, each thought the other contemplated suicide and went secretly to the apothecaries to warn them not to supply poison. (Moore: *Prose and Verse*, p. 431.)

*p.114, l.5* Unpublished letter, Berg Collection, New York Public Library.

*p.114, l.13* *LJ*, I, 101–2. Letter of Aug. 9, 1806.

*p.114, l.15* Unpublished letter of Aug. 9, 1806, Berg Collection, New York Public Library.

*p.115, l.6* *LJ*, I, 105–6. Letter of Aug. 16, 1806, to John Pigot.

*p.115, l.9* *LJ*, I, 106–7. Letter to John Pigot.

*p.116, l.18* Unpublished MS. reminiscences of Byron by Henry Long, Berg Collection, New York Public Library.

*p.117, l.4* Moore, I, 77.

*p.117, l.11* Moore, I, 76.

*p.117, l.37* There is some confusion about the date of publication. The last poem in the volume is dated Nov. 16, 1806, but one extant copy has an inscription which reads "October 21st Tuesday 1806—Hæc pœmata ex dono sunt—Georgii Gordon Byron, Vale," and another (now in the Morgan Library) "Nov. 8, 1806, H.P.E.D.S.G.G.B., Southwell.—Vale." The most reasonable explanation is that the volume was printed bit by bit on separate sheets and copies might have been presented before later poems were added and the whole bound.

*p.118, l.11* See above, p. 114.

*p.118, l.16* Moore, I, 84n.

*p.120, l.20* Moore, I, 89.

*p.120, l.28* Moore, I, 90–1.

*p.121, l.24* *Poetry,* I, 114–16. First published in *Poems on Various Occasions* (1807), Byron's second privately printed volume.

*p.121, l.31* Moore: *Prose and Verse,* p. 420.

*p.122, l.5* One copy (Becher's) is now in the Ashley Collection in the British Museum; John Pigot's copy is in the Roe-Byron Collection at Newstead Abbey; a copy with manuscript corrections (possibly the one which had belonged to Elizabeth Pigot and which Byron used in preparing his next volume) is in the Morgan Library; a fourth complete copy is in the Library of the University of Texas.

*p.122, l.11* *Poetry,* I, 213–16. The manuscript is dated Dec. 1, 1806.

*p.122, l.24* Actually there were four poems "To Caroline" in *Fugitive Pieces,* though only one bore that title, the one beginning "You say you love, and yet your eye." This and the poem to Mary were never reprinted in any edition of Byron's poetry. E. H. Coleridge reprinted "To Caroline" but not "To Mary" in his seven-volume edition (1898). "To Mary" is available in two facsimile editions of *Fugitive Pieces* and in Willis Pratt's *Byron at Southwell* (1948).

*p.123, l.8* *LJ,* I, 113. Letter of Jan. 13, 1807.

*p.123, l.14* *LJ,* I, 110–11. Letter of Dec. 7, 1806.

*p.123, l.20* Byron presented an early copy to his neighbor; he inscribed it: "Elizabeth Bridget Pigot, Ex dono, Georgii Gordon Byron, Vale! 1806." (See Pratt, pp. 61–2.) Elizabeth or her mother drew Byron's coat of arms on the title page.

*p.123, l.24* Eg. 2611, f.23. Unpublished letter of Jan. 6, 1807.

*p.123, l.34* Murray MSS.

*p.125, l.3* Letter of Aug. 2, 1807, Huntington Library. This sentence at the end of the letter was omitted by Moore, and Prothero (*LJ,* I, 140–3) copied the letter from Moore without seeing the original.

*p.125, l.13* A letter in the Murray MSS. dated Feb. 5, 1807, from W. Baldwin (perhaps an M.P.), to whom Byron had applied, says: "I cannot with any propriety interfere at present as the Application must first be made by your Lordship to his Majesty by Petition. . . . The case of a Servant & a confidential one too robbing his Master does not in general meet with much favor."

*p.126, l.15* Quoted in Bernard Halliday's Catalogue No. 213 (1937).

*p.126, l.24* The sum was finally made up by a loan of £200 from Wylde and Co., bankers of Southwell; £500 from Mrs. George Byron; and £300 from the Misses Parkyns. (Eg. 2611. Letter of April 9, 1809, Mrs. Byron to Hanson.)

*p.127, l.6* *Poetry,* I, 248. This *jeu d'esprit* was not published in Byron's lifetime.

*p.127, l.15* Letter of Augusta to Hanson, Feb. 7, 1807. Hanson narrative, Murray MSS.

*p.127, l.32* Unpublished letter to Long, dated Feb. 23, 1807, Berg Collection, New York Public Library.

*p.127, l.26* Blessington, p. 97.

*p.128, l.5* Pratt, pp. 65–6.

*p.128, l.30* *LJ,* I, 126–7.

*p.129, l.11* *LJ,* II, 19n. Letter of April 16, 1807.

*p.129, l.28* Henry Long manuscript narrative, Berg Collection, New York Public Library.

*p.129, l.36* *LJ*, I, 129n. Letter of April 29, 1807.

*p.130, l.2* Hanson narrative, Murray MSS.

*p.130, l.11* Unpublished letter, Yale University Library.

*p.131, l.1* *LJ*, I, 133.

*p.131, l.36* *LJ*, I, 152, 156. Letter of Nov. 19, 1820, to John Murray.

*p.132, l.12* Hobhouse has supplied the name, left blank by Moore, in the margin of his copy.

*p.132, l.14* *LJ*, I, 160.

*p.133, l.19* *LJ*, I, 133–6. Letter of July 5, 1807.

*p.133, l.23* *LJ*, I, 138n. Letter of July 8, 1807.

*p.134, l.18* *Hours of Idleness* (1807), pp. v–x.

*p.134, l.30* *LJ*, I, 137.

*p.135, l.18* From the original letter dated Aug. 2, 1807, in the Huntington Library. It is printed in *LJ*, I, 140–3, with many inaccuracies.

*p.135, l.27* Hanson narrative, Murray MSS. Letter of July 1807.

*p.136, l.8* *LJ*, I, 143–4.

*p.136, l.21* Moore, I, 118n.

*p.137, l.2* *LJ*, I, 147. Letter of Oct. 26, 1807.

*p.137, l.9* *The Satirist or Monthly Meteor*, Vol. II (June 1, 1808), p. 368.

*p.137, l.17* *Alma Mater . . . By a Trinity-Man* [J. M. F. Wright], I, 166–7. Wright came to Trinity in 1814, seven years after the bear.

*p.137, l.25* Lines 229–30.

*p.138, l.5* *LJ*, I, 147. Letter of Oct. 26, 1807.

*p.138, l.7* Byron impaled Clarke in *English Bards and Scotch Reviewers* (lines 973–80), and in the "Postscript to the Second Edition" he devoted some space to demolishing him.

*p.138, l.16* Murray MSS.

*p.138, l.25* Moore, I, 95–8.

*p.138, l.29* Now in the Berg Collection, New York Public Library.

*p.139, l.15* Gronow, I, 151.

*p.140, l.9* Later published as the first piece in his *Imitations and Translations* (1809).

*p.140, l.20* Pratt, pp. 88–9.

*p.140, l.22* "D" in *Notes and Queries*, 2nd s., VI (Oct. 16, 1858), 302–3. Quoted in Pratt, p. 90.

*p.141, l.30* *LJ*, I, 149.

## Notes to Chapter VI

*P.142, l.23* Dallas: *Correspondence*, pp. 3–6. Letter of Jan. 6, 1808.

*p.143, l.7* *LJ*, I, 169–71. Letter of Jan. 20, 1808. Such an accusation was leveled against Byron by a review in *The Eclectic*. (Vol. III, part ii, pp. 989–93.)

*p.143, l.9* Dallas: *Correspondence*, pp. 9–11.

*p.143, l.17* *LJ*, I, 172–3. Letter of Jan. 21, 1808.

*p.143, l.25* Dallas: *Recollections*, pp. 9–10.
*p.144, l.17* *LJ*, I, 176. Letter of Feb. 2, 1808.
*p.144, l.22* See Chapter V, p. 138.
*p.144, l.28* *Monthly Mirror*, n.s. Vol. III (Jan. 1808), p. 30. Quoted by W. S. Ward: "Byron's *Hours of Idleness* and other than Scotch Reviewers," *Modern Language Notes*, Vol. LIX (June 1944), pp. 547–50.
*p.145, l.13* *LJ*, I, 174–5. Letter of Jan. 25, 1808. Byron had paid off with a new loan, not due until after his majority, £3,000 of the £3,300 due the moneylenders. See Chapter V, p. 123.
*p.145, l.17* Across one of Dallas's later letters complaining of neglect Byron scratched a memorandum of the sums he had given him. The first was: "Two hundred pounds before I was twenty years old." (Hobhouse's review of Dallas's *Recollections*, *Westminster Review*, Vol. III [Jan. 1825], p. 12.)
*p.146, l.8* Unpublished narrative of Henry Long, Berg Collection, New York Public Library.
*p.146, l.12* Byron's receipt, dated Jan. 25, 1808, is in the British Museum, Eg. 2611, f.48. In a letter of Feb. 1808 (quoted in the Waller Catalogue 111, 1877) he wrote to Hanson: "I shall be particularly obliged by the loan of one hundred *promised* last night, and for this and other sums lent by you, I shall sign a receipt with great pleasure."
*p.146, l.26* *LJ*, I, 181. Misdated Feb. 21 in *LJ*. The date on the MS., now in the University of Texas Library, is Feb. 11, 1808.
*p.147, l.21* Unpublished passage in a letter of Feb. 27, 1808, Murray MSS.
*p.147, l.30* *B-SP*, I, 40. (Here corrected from Murray MSS.)
*p.148, l.9* Written in Hobhouse's copy of Moore (I, 145).
*p.148, l.27* *Edinburgh Review*, Vol. XI (Jan. 1808), pp. 285–9.
*p.148, l.32* Medwin, I, 173.
*p.149, l.1* *LJ*, V, 269–70. Letter of April 26, 1821.
*p.149, l.4* *LJ*, V, 267. Letter of April 26, 1821.
*p.149, l.16* *LBC*, I, 2. Letter of Feb. 27, 1808.
*p.149, l.30* Letter of Thursday, [March] 13, 1808 [to Becher or Hanson?], *Athenaeum*, Dec. 5, 1885, p. 733.
*p.150, l.1* Moore: *Memoirs*, II, 638. Apparently Moore got his information from Rogers, who had it from Byron.
*p.150, l.4* *LJ*, II, 330. Journal of Nov. 22, 1813.
*p.150, l.23* Unpublished letter, Murray MSS.; Hobhouse proofs.
*p.151, l.4* Medwin, I, 74.
*p.151, l.12* Moore: *Prose and Verse*, pp. 418–19.
*p.151, l.21* *Blackwood's Magazine*, Nov. 1824, p. 532.
*p.151, l.35* Joyce, p. 10. Joyce gives the date of the letter as March, but another portion of the same letter is given in *LJ* (I, 219–20n.) with the date May 12, 1808.
*p.152, l.32* *LJ*, I, 185–6. Letter of March 28, 1808.
*p.153, l.3* Quoted in H. B. Smith Catalogue. These three sentences were omitted by Moore, and *LJ* follows the text of Moore.
*p.153, l.7* *LJ*, I, 187.
*p.153, l.17* *LJ*, I, 158–9.
*p.153, l.27* Joyce, p. 12.

*p.153, l.31* *LJ*, I, 188.

*p.155, l.8* *LJ*, I, 218. Letter of March 18, 1809.

*p.155, l.13* *The Satirist*, May 1, 1808, pp. 333–5. The reviews were not wholly unfavorable, and Clarke in a footnote defended Byron against some of his Methodist critics.

*p.155, l.23* Unpublished letter, July 3, 1808, Murray MSS.; Hobhouse proofs.

*p.155, l.26* Since the note remained in the Hobhouse papers, it is more than likely that it was never sent.

*p.155, l.30* *The Satirist*, Vol. III (Aug. 1, 1808), pp. 78–86.

*p.155, l.38* *The Roe-Byron Collection*, C. 43, p. 62.

*p.156, l.11* Hobhouse records that he was with Byron at No. 1 Marine Parade, Brighton, in 1808. (Broughton, II, 101. Diary entry of Aug. 11, 1818.) Captain Gronow (I, 152) said Byron's house at Brighton was opposite the Pavilion.

*p.156, l.15* Hobhouse identified "Lady P **" as Lady Perceval in the margin of his copy of Moore.

*p.156, l.24* Moore, I, 147–8.

*p.156, l.26* *LJ*, V, 115.

*p.157, l.11* Letter dated Aug. 7, 1808, quoted in Maggs Catalogue 306, March–April 1913, pp. 24–5. A quotation is also given from Lord Grey's reply. He was much surprised and puzzled to know the reason for Byron's attitude. "We parted in 1804 the best of friends, your letters were afterwards most affectionate. . . ."

*p.157, l.24* *Poetry*, I, 268–70.

*p.157, l.32* There had been rumors as early as the summer of 1807 that Newstead was for sale, perhaps because it was known that Byron had piled up debts of some magnitude and needed money, or possibly because Byron's mother in her alarm had hinted as much. Owen Mealey, the persistent gossip, had written to Hanson on Aug. 26, 1807: ". . . the talk of this country is that Lord Byron means to sell Newstead. . . ." (Eg. 2613, f.10.)

*p.158, l.4* *LJ*, I, 191. Letter of Oct. 4, 1808.

*p.158, l.16* *LJ*, I, 193–4. Letter of Oct. 7, 1808.

*p.158, l.30* Finn and Johnson's bill, Murray MSS.

*p.159, l.1* This last sentence was omitted from the letter as printed in Dallas: *Correspondence*. The MS. is now in the Morgan Library. Letter of Nov. 2, 1808.

*p.159, l.5* *LJ*, I, 194–5. Letter of Nov. 2, 1808.

*p.159, l.16* *LJ*, I, 197. Letter of Nov. 3, 1808.

*p.160, l.5* *LJ*, I, 198. Letter of Nov. 3, 1808.

*p.160, l.11* Marginal note of Hobhouse in his copy of Moore (I, 57).

*p.160, l.21* *Poetry*, I, 277–9.

*p.160, l.31* Moore, I, 154.

*p.160, l.37* *LJ*, III, 171. There is some confusion about the date of Boatswain's death, for the inscription on the dog's tomb at Newstead says he died on Nov. 18, 1808. Moore also gave this date instead of the 10th in quoting this sentence from Hodgson's letter. But it seems that if he had died on the 18th, Byron, writing on that day, would have said "today" or "this morning" instead of giving a date. To confound matters worse, Byron inserted a note in his mother's copy of Hobhouse's *Imitations and Translations* saying that his epitaph on Boatswain, which first appeared there, was written on Oct. 30. (*LJ*, III, 170n.) But this note could not have been written until after his mother's death (Aug. 1811), and it is possible that by that time he had forgotten the exact date. He mentioned the epitaph first in a letter of Nov. 27, 1808, to Hodgson. Confusion is twice confounded by the fact that he wrote in another copy of *Imitations and Translations*, at the end of the Epitaph: "Nov 1808" and added: "Inscription on the monument of Boatswain a favourite Dog—who was born in Newfoundland May 1803—and died at Newstead Octr. 1808." (Jerome Kern sale catalogue, Anderson Galleries, sale No. 2307, Jan. 1929, p. 61.) The only reasonable assumption is that this also was written long enough after the event for him to be uncertain of the date.

*p.161, l.13* Hobhouse wrote in the margin of his copy of Moore (I, 155) opposite those lines: "which I thus altered & 'here *I* lies.' "

*p.161, l.20* Hobhouse's marginal note in Moore (I, 154) opposite the reference to this inscription is: "written by J.C.H. in joke."

*p.161, l.25* Murray MSS.; Hobhouse proofs. Letter of Nov. 20, 1808.

*p.162, l.6* *LJ*, I, 199–200. Letter of Nov. 18, 1808.

*p.162, l.14* *LJ*, I, 200.

*p.162, l.25* *LJ*, I, 202; *Poetry*, I, 283.

*p.162, l.32* Letter of Hodgson, Nov. 16, 1808, Murray MSS.

*p.162, l.35* *LJ*, III, 171. Letter of Nov. 18, 1808.

*p.163, l.16* *LJ*, I, 205–6. Letter of Dec. 17, 1808.

*p.163, l.29* Murray MSS.

*p.164, l.4* *Poetry*, I, 276.

*p.164, l.8* "Byroniana. No. II," *Literary Gazette*, June 7, 1828.

*p.164, l.13* *LJ*, I, 191n.

*p.164, l.24* Byron wrote to Hanson on Jan. 3, 1809: "You will see by the enclosed Letter from Mrs. Massingberd the necessity of coming to some arrangement immediately." (Murray MSS.)

*p.164, l.33* Unpublished letter of Jan. 15, 1809, Yale University Library. In the same letter Byron announced his intention of drawing on Hanson on Feb. 1 for £258 and asked him to pay forty guineas to Lady Perceval for his opera subscription.

*p.165, l.3* *LJ*, I, 209–10. Letter of Jan. 15, 1809.

*p.165, l.11* Eg. 2611, f.93. Letter of Jan. 5, 1809; see also letter of Dec. 26, 1808, in which Mrs. Byron discusses business affairs with Hanson.

*p.165, l.19* *LJ*, I, 163–7. Letter misdated Jan. 16, 1808, probably because Byron himself had not yet become used to the new year and had written 1808 instead of 1809. The poem was extended to 696 lines before it was published.

*p.167, l.6* Dallas: *Recollections*, pp. 10–11. According to Dallas, what Byron submitted to him was "a number of loose printed sheets in quarto . . . entitled *The British Bards, A Satire*." This was the poem as written at Cambridge and Newstead, with corrections and annotations in the margins of the proof sheets, which he had had printed by a country press. (Dallas: *Correspondence*, Paris, 1825, III, 130.) These proof sheets are now in the British Museum (Eg. 2028).

*p.167, l.17* Dallas: *Recollections*, pp. 12–16. Letter of Jan. 24, 1809.
*p.168, l.8* Ibid., p. 11.
*p.168, l.18* Moore (I, 163) says a delay was caused by the fact that the wedding of Byron's grandfather and grandmother took place in a private chapel and there was no regular certificate of the ceremony. Hanson presented evidence of Byron's title to the Lord Chancellor on Feb. 1, 1809 (Hanson papers, Murray MSS.), but on the 7th Byron was still urging him to "forward my business with the Chancellor" (Eg. 2611, f.100), and on March 3 he asked Hanson to send off his clerk immediately to Carhaes for more affidavits. (Murray MSS.) Hanson's bill for proving and establishing Byron's pedigree was £158. 15*s*. (Hanson and Birch accounts, Murray MSS.)
*p.168, l.26* Bookseller's bill of Ridgeway, running from 1808 to 1811, Murray MSS.
*p.169, l.7* Eg. 2611, ff.101–2.
*p.169, l.17* *LJ*, I, 206n.
*p.169, l.27* Pratt, p. 107n.
*p.170, l.4* *LJ*, I, 216. Letter of March 6, 1809.
*p.170, l.8* Moore, 1892 ed., p. 77n. Mrs. Byron wrote to Hanson on April 9: "He gave Lady Falkland five hundred pounds!!!" (Eg. 2611, f.112.)
*p.170, l.36* Dallas: *Recollections*, pp. 33–6.
*p.171, l.6* *LJ*, V, 431–2.
*p.171, l.20* *LJ*, I, 217–19.
*p.172, l.3* Unpublished letter of Byron to E. B. Long, dated April 14, 1809, Berg Collection, New York Public Library.
*p.172, l.4* *LJ*, V, 170. Diary, Jan. 12, 1821.
*p.173, l.22* *LJ*, I, 153–5. Letter of Nov. 19, 1820, to John Murray.
*p.174, l.19* *LJ*, I, 153–4n. Letter of May 22, 1809.
*p.174, l.24* Broughton, III, 29.
*p.175, l.6* Brecknock: *Byron*, p. 260.
*p.175, l.10* *LJ*, I, 157.
*p.175, l.20* Eg. 2611, f.113.
*p.175, l.22* Eg. 2611, f.114.
*p.175, l.27* Eg. 2611, f.112.
*p.175, l.34* Dallas: *Recollections*, p. 36.
*p.176, l.7* Moore, I, 127. Letter of Nov. 19, 1820, to John Murray. Moore gives the date as Nov. 12; but Prothero, who published the letter from the MS., dated it Nov. 19. In his first edition Moore gave the name as "*bold* W **" and added what was probably his own parenthesis: "(as he was called, from winning a foot-match, and a horse-match, the first from Ipswich to London, and the second from Brighthelmstone)." Hobhouse wrote in the margin of his copy of Moore: "though Webster is & was a very poor creature it is too bad to tell the story." In the second edition, possibly because he had been criticized for mentioning a man still living in these terms, Moore represented the name only by asterisks and removed the parenthesis. In later editions of Moore, toward the end of the nineteenth century (for example, the Murray one-volume edition of 1892), the name is changed to Hobhouse, and this is the reading adopted by Prothero in his edition of the *Letters and Journals* (1898). But Hobhouse was at Newstead until Byron returned to

London. And in writing to Webster on Oct. 10, 1811, Byron says: "I can hardly invite a gentleman to my house a second time who walked out of it the first in so singular a mood. . . ." (*LJ*, II, 49.)

*p.176, l.13* *LJ*, I, 157–8. Letter of Nov. 19, 1820, to John Murray.

*p.176, l.16* *LJ*, I, 220–1.

*p.176, l.20* *LJ*, I, 221. Letter of April 26, 1809.

*p.177, l.6* Dallas: *Recollections*, pp. 39–40.

*p.177, l.20* Ibid. pp. 40–1.

*p.177, l.29* *LJ*, V, 422.

*p.177, l.38* *LJ*, I, 155n.

*p.178, l.4* Eg. 2611, f.119.

*p.178, l.25* Unpublished letter, Murray MSS.; Hobhouse proofs.

*p.179, l.5* On June 6, Byron wrote a hurried note: "Mr. Murray [Joe Murray], the moment you receive this you will set off for London in some of the coaches with Robert, & take care that he conducts himself properly —Be quick." (Quoted in Catalogue No. 379 of Myers & Co., London, Spring 1954.)

*p.179, l.11* Unpublished letter, dated June 4, 1809, Berg Collection, New York Public Library.

*p.179, l.30* Unpublished recollections of Byron, Long papers, Berg Collection, New York Public Library.

*p.180, l.7* Dallas: *Recollections*, pp. 41–2.

*p.180, l.19* Eg. 2611, ff.127–8.

*p.180, l.21* *LJ*, I, 159. Letter of Nov. 19, 1820, to Murray.

*p.182, l.2* Unpublished letter of June 22, 1809, Hobhouse papers.

*p.182, l.31* From the original MS. in the Yale University Library. The letter is printed in *LJ*, I, 225–6, with omissions.

*p.183, l.9* Miller's bill, Murray MSS. Byron also bought an "Arithmetic & Key" and "Smith's Atlas."

*p.183, l.17* *LJ*, I, 230.

## Notes to Chapter VII

*P.185, l.2* *LJ*, I, 236; Borst, p. xxiii.

*p.185, l.11* *LJ*, I, 226, 227.

*p.185, l.17* *LJ*, I, 233. Letter of July 16, 1809.

*p.186, l.8* This diary, a part of which was published in Lord Broughton's *Recollections of a Long Life* (1909–1911) and edited with great liberty and little regard for chronology by Hobhouse's daughter Lady Dorchester, is a most valuable guide to the pilgrimage. Hobhouse began the diary in Latin, but after a few days gave up the exercise as too strenuous and continued in English. The dates are one day ahead until the 19th, when he caught the error.

*p.186, l.18* Unpublished letter, probably of July 8, 1809 (the first page is missing), Hobhouse papers. In the diary the hotel's name is spelled Barnwell. This picture of the Portuguese is similar to that given by Byron in *Childe Harold* (I, 17).

*p.187, l.3* This and succeeding details, unless otherwise indicated, come from the Hobhouse diary. According to Hobhouse's accounts kept for the trip (Murray MSS.), Byron lost by the exchange at Lisbon £13. 12*s.* 6*d.*

*p.187, l.20* *LJ*, I, 237. Letter of Aug. 11, 1809.

*p.187, l.24* Hodgson, I, 163. This sentence was omitted by Moore.

*p.188, l.9* Dudley, p. 163.

*p.188, l.11* Hobhouse's accounts, Murray MSS.

*p.190, l.1* *LJ*, I, 235. Letter of Aug. 6, 1809.

*p.190, l.18* *LJ*, I, 238–9. Letter of Aug. 11, 1809.

*p.190, l.28* *LJ*, I, 234. Letter of Aug. 6, 1809.

*p.190, l.29* *Don Juan*, I, 8.

*p.190, l.38* *Poetry*, II, 72. Note to *Childe Harold*, I, 80.

*p.191, l.6* *Poetry*, II, 91. Note to *Childe Harold*, I, 56.

*p.191, l.31* Perhaps a reference to Byron's interest in the pugilistic sport.

*p.191, l.34* *Poetry*, II, 522. This is from one of the notes that Hobhouse wrote for Byron's fourth canto of *Childe Harold*. The gladiatorial contests in ancient Rome reminded him of the bullfight in Spain.

*p.192, l.8* *LJ*, I, 234–5. Letter of Aug. 6, 1809.

*p.193, l.19* *LJ*, I, 239–40. Letter of Aug. 11, 1809.

*p.193, l.34* *Poetry*, III, 1–2. The MS., which was offered for sale by Charles J. Sawyer, Ltd., London (List No. 6, 1951), is dated Aug. 15, 1809. It was completed, then, the day Byron left Gibraltar. This poem was first intended to be inserted in *Childe Harold*, but the lines "To Inez" were substituted as more in tone with the melancholy mood of that poem. "The Girl of Cadiz" was not published in Byron's lifetime.

*p.194, l.5* *LJ*, I, 235. Letter of Aug. 6, 1809.

*p.194, l.24* Eg. 2611, f.146.

*p.195, l.2* Galt, p. 50.

*p.195, l.8* *LJ*, I, 241. Letter of Aug. 11, 1809. The Hobhouse accounts (Murray MSS.) show an item of 50 guineas paid by Byron to a tailor at Gibraltar.

*p.195, l.18* Add. 36455, ff.584–5. Quoted by Churchman, XI (Avril-Juin 1909), 167.

*p.195, l.32* Eg. 2611, f.143. Letter of Aug. 13, 1809.

*p.195, l.33* *LJ*, I, 242. Postscript dated Aug. 15 to letter of Aug. 11, 1809.

*p.195, l.36* *LJ*, I, 242–3. Letter of Aug. 15, 1809.

*p.196, l.19* Galt, p. 51.

*p.196, l.34* Galt, pp. 51–2.

*p.197, l.7* This is the account as given in Hobhouse's diary.

*p.197, l.16* Galt, pp. 54–5.

*p.197, l.23* Galt, p. 55.

*p.197, l.38* Galt, p. 55.

*p.198, l.27* Galt, p. 56.

*p.198, l.33* According to Galt (p. 56), Byron took lessons in Arabic from a monk, "I believe one of the librarians of the public library."

*p.200, l.7* "Lines Written in an Album, at Malta," *Poetry*, III, 4–5.

*p.200, l.13* This was Hobhouse's later view. On the margin of his copy of Moore he wrote: "Moore was right B was *not* in love with Mrs. S.S." Moore had written (I, 201) that "the notion of his being in love was but a dream," in the belief that the stanzas in *Childe Harold* (II, 30–5), with their greater coldness, represented the true state of affairs at the time he was with her, and that the warmer verses such as "To Florence," "Stanzas Composed during a Thunderstorm," and "Stanzas Written in Passing the Ambracian Gulf," were only Byron's idealization of the experience afterward. The opposite was probably true. The stanzas in *Childe Harold* were written in 1810 after time and distance had done their work. There seems little doubt that Byron was thoroughly smitten at the time. He wrote parenthetically in his diary on Jan. 12, 1821: "I was once *so desperately* in love with a German woman, Constance." (*LJ*, V, 172.)

*p.200, l.17* Galt, p. 56.

*p.200, l.31* *LBC*, I, 77. Letter of Sept. 15, 1812.

*p.200, l.33* *"To Lord Byron,"* pp. 12–13.

*p.201, l.9* *LBC*, I, 5.

*p.201, l.11* In writing to Lady Melbourne on Sept. 15, 1812, Byron referred to "this most ambrosial amour, which made me on one occasion risk my life." (*LBC*, I, 78.)

*p.201, l.20* Moore (I, 202) gives a slightly different account, with some details not in Hobhouse's diary.

*p.201, l.22* Moore, I, 202.

*p.201, l.28* From the original letter, dated May 3, 1810, Trinity College MS. R. Z. 40a; this sentence was omitted by Moore, and hence by Prothero, but was printed by Halleck.

*p.203, l.14* *Journey*, I, 27.

*p.204, l.4* *Journey*, I, 40.

*p.204, l.10* *Journey*, I, 52.

*p.204, l.34* Borst (pp. 60–1) gives a good brief account of Ali's attempts to play the English against the French during the Napoleonic wars.

*p.205, l.6* *LJ*, I, 256. Letter of Nov. 12, 1809.

*p.205, l.27* *LJ*, I, 280. Letter of June 28, 1810.

*p.206, l.24* "Stanzas Composed during a Thunderstorm," *Poetry*, III, 7–11.

*p.206, l.30* *LJ*, I, 254. Letter of Nov. 12, 1809.

*p.206, l.33* *LJ*, I, 249. Letter of Nov. 12, 1809.

*p.207, l.9* *LJ*, V, 115. Letter of Nov. 9, 1820, to John Murray.

*p.207, l.17* *LBC*, I, 176. Letter of Aug. 23, 1813, to Lady Melbourne.

*p.207, l.24* *Poetry*, II, 174, 177. Note to second canto of *Childe Harold.*

*p.208, l.2* *LJ*, I, 249–50. Letter of Nov. 12, 1809.

*p.208, l.17* *Poetry*, II, 174.

*p.209, l.20* *Don Juan*, III, 41.

*p.210, l.3* *LJ*, I, 250–1. Letter of Nov. 12, 1809.

*p.210, l.20* *LJ*, I, 252. Letter of Nov. 12, 1809.

*p.211, l.4* *Journey*, I, 114.

*p.211, l.14* *Journey*, I, 122.

*p.211, l.29* Byron wrote in *Childe Harold* (II, 53):

> *Oh! where, Dodona! is thine agéd Grove,*
> *Prophetic Fount, and Oracle divine?*

not knowing that he had trod upon their site, which was not determined until 1876 by a native of Arta, M. Constantin Carapanos, who made excavations that helped to identify the ruins. (See *Poetry,* II, 132.)

*p.211, l.37* *LJ,* I, 257. Letter of Nov. 12, 1809.

*p.212, l.7* Marsden, p. 32.

*p.212, l.10* George Finlay wrote to the Hon. Leicester Stanhope after Byron's death (June 1824): "Lord B. said he had kept a very exact journal of every circumstance of his life, and many of his thoughts while young, that he had let Mr. Hobhouse see it in Albania, and that he at last persuaded him to burn it. He said Hobhouse had robbed the world of a treat." (Stanhope, 2nd ed., p. 526.) Stanhope added in a note: "Hobhouse is said to have destroyed this manuscript, because there were in it objectionable passages, and he thought it would be discreditable to let an extract of it be spread abroad."

*p.212, l.15* On Nov. 4 Hobhouse recorded that their host at Arta took "Byron for a philosopher! because he was reading 'Elegant Extracts' at dinner time." And on the 6th he wrote: "B. pointed out to me that Spencer [*sic*] in his description of Doubt, talks of the Albanian dress and capot." (*Faerie Queene,* Book III, canto XII, stanza 10: "That at his backe a brode Capuccio had,/And sleeves dependaunt *Albanese*-wyse."

*p.213, l.14* *Journey,* I, 188.

*p.213, l.33* *LJ,* I, 253–4. Letter of Nov. 12, 1809.

*p.215, l.18* The song which Byron gave to the soldiers in *Childe Harold* is not this one but a more national and patriotic song, composed from several versions which he heard or got from his Albanian servant. (See Borst, p. 83.)

*p.215, l.37* *Journey,* I, 210.

*p.216, l.27* *Journey,* I, 225–6.

*p.216, l.36* *LJ,* II, 404–5.

*p.217, l.12* Byron's poem "Translation of the Famous Greek War Song" is a rather free rendition. Hobhouse printed his own version of it in his *Journey* (II, 586–7).

*p.218, l.3* *Childe Harold,* I, 60.

*p.218, l.10* *LJ,* V, 450. "Detached Thoughts" (1821). In his 1814 journal (*LJ,* II, 404) Byron had said there were six eagles; apparently in the intervening years they had grown like Falstaff's men in buckram.

*p.218, l.23* Byron saw the bishop again in 1823 in Ithaca, where Gregorius was then living in exile. His name is given in a letter he wrote Byron on Aug. 8 [Greek calendar—20th by the Western calendar], 1823, Murray MSS.

*p.218, l.26* Byron translates this word: "Nonsense; humbug"; but it had some of the shocking connotations of its literal meaning.

*p.219, l.2* *Childe Harold,* I, 69–70. In a note to line 5 of stanza 70, referring to Œdipus and the Sphinx, Byron said: "This was written at Thebes . . . ."

*p.219, l.9* *Poetry,* II, 189.

*p.219, l.18* Hobhouse is responsible for the error, into which other English travelers readily fell for the same reason, and which has been perpetuated in Byron biography, of confusing the mother of the "Maid of Athens,"

Tarsia Macri, with her sister-in-law, Theodora. Actually Theodora Macri was the younger sister of the Vice-Consul Procopius Macri, who died in 1799, leaving his widow, whose first name was Tarsia, to provide for three daughters, one of whom was Byron's "Maid of Athens." It is not surprising that Theodora, then unmarried and living with her sister-in-law, should have been taken by travelers as the head of the household, since she was said to speak some English and hence dealt with the lodgers they were forced to take in to make a living. Professor C. G. Brouzas has made an extensive study of the complicated family relations of the Macris in his article "Byron's Maid of Athens: Her Family and Surroundings" (*West Virginia University Bulletin* [June 1949]: *Philological Papers,* Vol. VII).

*p.219, l.25* *LJ,* I, 269. Letter of May 3, 1810, to Henry Drury. There is no reason to question Byron's statement, though confusion has reigned concerning the ages of the daughters. Mariana was the eldest and must have been no more than fifteen, for her parents were married Jan. 15/27, 1794. (Brouzas, p. 22; from Kampouroglous: *Old Athens,* p. 282, who found the date in the diary of Procopius Macri.) Katinka, the second daughter, was fourteen, according to Kampouroglous, and Theresa, the Maid of Athens, was twelve on Nov. 16, a few weeks before Byron came to Athens. Shirley C. Atchley (*Bios kai drasis tou Byronos en Helladi,* Athens, 1918, p. 29n.—cited by Borst, p. 103n.) from investigations in Athens found that she was born Nov. 16, 1797.

*p.220, l.14* William Miller (*The English in Athens Before 1821*) gives an account of the English travelers who were in the city before, during, and after Byron's visit. Lionel Cust (*History of the Society of Dilettanti,* London, 1898, pp. 68–106, 125–36) tells of the interest in Greek archæology at the time. Borst (pp. 92–3) gives a good summary of this interest in Near Eastern travel. Edward Daniel Clarke, Professor of Mineralogy at Cambridge (appointed in 1808 after Byron had left the University), had been in Greece just before Byron, who later met him at Cambridge in 1811.

*p.220, l.33* *Journey,* I, 295–7.

*p.221, l.1* The unpublished parts of Hobhouse's diary fill in many lacunæ in the knowledge of Byron's activities in Athens, as well as later in Smyrna and Constantinople. Logotheti was appointed British Vice-Consul after the death of Procopius Macri in 1799.

*p.221, l.9* *English Bards and Scotch Reviewers,* 2nd ed., lines 1007–12.

*p.221, l.13* *Journey,* I, 292.

*p.222, l.38* *Poetry,* II, 190. Note to second canto of *Childe Harold.*

*p.223, l.6* *Journey,* I, 299.

*p.223, l.35* Trelawny: *Records,* p. 27.

*p.224, l.23* *Childe Harold,* II, 1–3, 7.

*p.224, l.36* *Journey,* I, 348n.

*p.225, l.11* *Journey,* I, 347n.; *LJ,* V, 547.

*p.226, l.14* *Poetry,* II, 190.

*p.227, l.26* *Poetry,* III, 12.

*p.228, l.2* *Childe Harold,* II, 30–5.

*p.229, l.15* Galt, p. 85.

*p.230, l.20* *Poetry,* VI, 169.

*p.231, l.4* *Journey,* I, 300.

*p.231, l.19* Murray MSS.
*p.231, l.24* *LJ,* VI, 448. Letter of March 3, 1810.
*p.232, l.2* *Journey,* II, 608.
*p.232, l.16* *Poetry,* III, 16.
*p.232, l.36* Galt: *Letters from the Levant,* p. 231.
*p.233, l.9* *LJ,* I, 266. Letter of May 3, 1810.

# Notes to Chapter VIII

*P.235, l.8* *Journey,* II, 654.
*p.235, l.10* *Journey,* II, 659.
*p.235, l.13* From the original letter, dated May 3, 1810, to Henry Drury, in the Library of Trinity College, Cambridge. (Published, with some inaccuracies and omissions, in *LJ,* I, 268.)
*p.235, l.17* *The Siege of Corinth,* lines 1070–1. In a note (*Poetry,* III, 495) Byron admitted that he had taken a poetical license in transferring the jackals of Asia Minor to Greece. He also referred to other details of the remembered scene on the road to Ephesus.
*p.235, l.32* *LJ,* I, 258. Letter of March 19, 1810, to Byron's mother.
*p.236, l.9* *Childe Harold,* II, 76.
*p.236, l.16* *Childe Harold,* II, 88.
*p.238, l.13* *LJ,* V, 250.
*p.238, l.19* Hobhouse diary. Entry of April 26, 1810.
*p.238, l.37* This note is given (not quite accurately) in Broughton, I, 29.
*p.239, l.7* From the original letter in the Library of Trinity College, Cambridge.
*p.240, l.6* From the original letter, dated May 3, 1810, in the Library of Trinity College, Cambridge. There are omissions in the letter as printed by Moore (I, 220ff).
*p.240, l.20* *LJ,* I, 271–2. Letter of May 5, 1810.
*p.240, l.30* *Journey,* II, 820.
*p.240, l.35* *Poetry,* III, 467–8. Byron used the episode in *The Siege of Corinth,* saying in a note that he had seen the spectacle beneath the wall of the Seraglio at Constantinople.
*p.243, l.31* *LJ,* I, 282. Letter of June 28, 1810.
*p.244, l.32* From an unpublished letter in the possession of Dr. Gregg M. Sinclair of Honolulu.
*p.244, l.34* Letter of May 30, 1810. Murray MSS.
*p.242, l.12* *LJ,* I, 282. Letter of June 28, 1810.
*p.246, l.20* *LJ,* VI, 451–2. Letter of June 23, 1810.
*p.246, l.27* *Journey,* II, 929–35.
*p.247, l.7* The letter of Adair is among the Murray MSS.
*p.247, l.9* Galt, p. 111.
*p.247, l.17* *LBC,* I, 9.
*p.247, l.26* *LJ,* I, 286.
*p.247, l.30* *B-SP,* I, 73. Letter to Edward Ellice.
*p.248, l.20* *Journey,* II, 998–9.
*p.249, l.10* Broughton, I, 32.

*p.249, l.16* *B-SP*, I, 74. Letter of July 29, 1810.

*p.250, l.3* *LJ*, I, 289. Letter of July 20, 1810. (So dated in the original MS. in the Morgan Library; misdated July 25 in *LJ*.)

*p.250, l.10* *LJ*, I, 292–3. Letter of July [21?], 1810.

*p.250, l.28* *LJ*, I, 289.

*p.250, l.29* The evidence for the date is based on the assumption that the letter printed as No. 145 by Prothero (*LJ*, I, 292–3) from Schultess-Young's *The Unpublished Letters of Lord Byron* was misdated July 27. It would be easy for one not well acquainted with Byron's hand to mistake his "1" with a long tail for a "7," and the internal evidence bears this out when the date of the previous letter is established from the manuscript to be July 20. He had said in that letter that he was leaving the next day, and in this he wrote: "Today I go into the Morea." Writing from Patras on July 29, Byron said he had been at Vostitza four days before that date, so that he could not have been in Athens on the 27th.

*p.251, l.8* *B-SP*, I, 75. Letter to Hobhouse, dated July 29, 1810.

*p.252, l.4* *B-SP*, I, 75–6. Letter to Hobhouse, dated Patras, July 29, 1810.

*p.252, l.17* *B-SP*, I, 76. Addition dated July 30 to letter of July 29, 1810.

*p.252, l.23* Mr. Paul, a cousin of Strané, was the Imperial Consul in Patras.

*p.252, l.25* *B-SP*, I, 76–7. P.S. of July 30 to letter of July 29, 1810.

*p.252 l.32* *B-SP*, I, 84. Letter of Oct. 2, 1810.

*p.253, l.16* *B-SP*, I, 78. Letter of Aug. 16, 1810.

*p.255, l.22* *B-SP*, I, 79–82. Letter of Aug. 23, 1810.

*p.255, l.28* *LJ*, I, 305n. Letter of July 31, 1810.

*p.256, l.6* *B-SP*, I, 81–2. Letter of Aug. 23–4, 1810.

*p.256, l.19* Moore, I, 254.

*p.256, l.27* Marginal note in Hobhouse's copy of Moore.

*p.257, l.27* Medwin, I, 99.

*p.259, l.7* *B-SP*, I, 85. Letter of Oct. 4, 1810.

*p.259, l.20* Meryon, III, 218–19.

*p.260, l.2* *LJ*, I, 307. Letter of Nov. 14, 1810, to Hodgson.

*p.260, l.7* *B-SP*, I, 82.

*p.260, l.14* *B-SP*, I, 83; *LJ*, I, 298. Letter of Oct. 3, 1810.

*p.260, l.22* *B-SP*, I, 87.

*p.260, l.30* Moore: *Memoirs*, II, 653.

*p.261, l.8* *LJ*, I, 306–7. Letter of Nov. 14, 1810.

*p.261, l.23* The fullest account of the activities of this group is given in an article by Peter Goessler, "*Nordische Gäste in Athen um 1810*," *Ephemeris Archiaolog* (1937), pp. 69–72. An excellent brief summary is given by Borst, pp. 136–8.

*p.261, l.29* *LBC*, I, 29. Letter of Jan. 20, 1811.

*p.262, l.20* *LJ*, V, 68. Letter of Aug. 31, 1820.

*p.263, l.7* *LBC*, I, 29. Letter of Jan. 20, 1811.

*p.263, l.16* *LJ*, I, 307.

*p.263, l.28* *LBC*, I, 20–2. Letter of Nov. 26, 1810.

*p.264, l.20* *LBC*, I, 24.

*p.264, l.25* *LBC*, I, 25.

*p.265, l.9* *"To Lord Byron,"* pp. 12–13.

*p.265, l.28* Corrected from the original MS. in the Morgan Library; in *LJ* (from Dallas) the word is printed "Americans."

*p.265, l.35* *LJ*, I, 309.

*p.266, l.8* *LBC*, I, 29–30.

*p.266, l.25* *Poetry*, II, 192–3.

*p.267, l.3* *LJ*, I, 310–11. Letter of Jan. 28, 1811. (So dated in original MS., Morgan Library; given as Feb. 28 in *LJ*.)

*p.267, l.7* Murray MSS.; Hobhouse proofs. Letter of Feb. 1, 1811.

*p.267, l.20* *B-SP*, I, 92. Letter of March 5, 1811.

*p.267, l.21* Moore, I, 244.

*p.267, l.38* Byron decided in the end not to publish the poem, and placed the opening descriptive lines (1–54) at the beginning of the third canto of *The Corsair*.

*p.268, l.10* In the appendix of the first edition of *Childe Harold* (1812), pp. 224–5, Byron included "the prospectus of a translation of Anacharsis into Romaic, by my Romaic master Marmarotouri, who wished to publish it in England."

*p.269, l.10* Dawson and Raubitschek, p. 42.

*p.269, l.17* Byron wrote on the back of the manuscript, now in the Yale Library, "Greek Song, copied out for me in Athens April 19th 1811 by Δουδου Roque the daughter of a French Merchant of that City previous to my leaving Greece." (Dawson and Raubitschek, p. 33).

*p.269, l.19* *LBC*, I, 31. Letter of March 18, 1811.

*p.269, l.22* *B-SP*, I, 94. Letter of June 19, 1811, to Hobhouse.

*p.270, l.3* From an unpublished portion of Byron's letter of May 15, 1811, to Hobhouse. (Murray MSS.; Hobhouse proofs.)

*p.270, l.10* *B-SP*, I, 92.

*p.270, l.24* *Poetry*, II, 176.

*p.271, l.3* *LJ*, I, 318. Letter of July 7, 1811, to Henry Drury (July 17 in *LJ*); corrected from MS. in Berg Collection, New York Public Library. The Greeks were Demetrius Zograffo, who had been his guide on various expeditions around Attica, and Spiro Saraci. The names are given in a request for their passports to return to Greece, March 2, 1812. (Eg. 2611, f. 282.)

*p.271, l.7* See Larrabee, pp. 618–19.

*p.271, l.17* *Poetry*, II, 188.

*p.271, l.22* A. H. Smith: "Lord Elgin and His Collection," pp. 281–2.

*p.271, l.28* General Oakes had succeeded Admiral Sir Richard Goodwin Keates (who had followed Sir Alexander Ball, the Governor on Byron's earlier visit to Malta in 1809) on April 27, 1810. (*Poetry*, III, 25.)

*p.272, l.19* *LBC*, I, 32.

*p.272, l.24* Letter of March 5, 1811, Hanson to Byron, Hanson business letters, Murray MSS. From another letter of Hanson in the same collection dated Jan. 14, 1812, it becomes clear that Davies merely used his name with the moneylenders and that the whole sum borrowed went to Byron.

*p.272, l.26* Eg. 2611, f. 219. Letter of Jan. 3, 1811.

*p.272, l.29* Eg. 2611, f. 227. Letter of Feb. 13, 1811.

*p.272, l.32* *LBC*, I, 32. Letter of May 15, 1811.

*p.273, l.9* According to Hobhouse's reckoning when they left Constantinople, Byron had spent on the whole voyage from the day they had left London, £757. 13*s*. 6*d*. plus 14,534 piasters (at about 15 piasters to the pound, this would be nearly £1,000 additional). Hobhouse's total for the same period came to £25. 12*s*., plus 6,748 piasters. (The account sheets are in the Murray MSS.) Hobhouse gave the figure of Byron's expenses in pounds in a letter: £1,617. 18*s*. 2*d*. (Joyce, p. 23.) Before Hobhouse's father paid his son's debt to Byron in 1812 it amounted to £1,325. 10*s*. (Joyce, p. 26.)

*p.274, l.7* Borst, p. 149.

*p.274, l.15* *Poetry*, III, 24.

*p.275, l.3* *LBC*, I, 35–6.

*p.275, l.20* *LJ*, I, 315. Letter of June 28, 1811.

*p.275, l.22* *LJ*, I, 317. Letter of June 29, 1811.

*p.276, l.2* *LBC*, I, 39–40.

*p.276, l.12* From the original letter in the Berg Collection of the New York Public Library. This part of the letter was not published by Moore or Prothero.

*p.276, l.16* Byron wrote "Portsmouth July eleventh eighteen hundred and eleven" on the outside of his letter to Hanson, which has the Portsmouth postmark of July 12. (Eg. 2611, f. 238.) The *Morning Chronicle* for July 13, 1811, reports: "Portsmouth, July 11—Arrived from Malta and sailed again for Chatham, the Amphion, 36 [guns], Captain Hoste, and Volage, 24, Captain Hornby, with their prizes, La Corona and La Bellone, French frigates, which they so gallantly took, in a most gallant action, in the Adriatic." (Quoted by Borst, p. 150.) But in a P.S. to his mother's letter, dated July 14, Byron wrote: "This letter was written to be sent from Portsmouth, but, on arriving there, the squadron was ordered to the Nore, from whence I shall forward it." (*LJ*, I, 313.) He must have gone immediately to London, for Davies called on him that night. (*LBC*, I, 41. Letter of July 15, 1811, to Hobhouse.)

*p.276, l.23* *LJ*, II, 31. Letter of Sept. 9, 1811.

*p.276, l.28* *LJ*, II, 22. Letter of Sept. 3, 1811.

*p.277, l.3* *LJ*, V, 591. In "Further Addenda for insertion in the letter to J.M., Esq., on Bowles, Pope, etc."

*p.277, l.5* *The Bride of Abydos*, lines 1–2.

*p.277, l.10* *LJ*, IV, 7. Letter of Nov. 17, 1816, to Moore. For a more detailed discussion of the significance of Byron's first pilgrimage, see Borst, pp. 151–5.

*p.277, l.12* Trelawny: *Records*, p. 27.

## Notes to Chapter IX

*P.278, l.6* *LBC*, I, 41. Letter of July 15, 1811.

*p.278, l.13* Joyce, p. 28.

*p.279, l.2* Dallas: *Correspondence*, pp. 117–18.

*p.279, l.15* Ibid., p. 125.

*p.279, l.28* Ibid., p. 126.

*p.280, l.1* Broughton, I, 35.
*p.280, l.12* Eg. 2611, f. 238; *LJ*, I, 319.
*p.282, l.9* Dallas: *Correspondence,* p. 130.
*p.283, l.2* *LBC*, I, 43.
*p.283, l.7* *LJ*, I, 321–2n.
*p.283, l.21* *The Scourge; or Monthly Expositor of Imposture and Folly,* Vol. I (1811), p. 211. (Quoted, *LJ*, I, 322.)
*p.283, l.27* Dallas: *Correspondence,* pp. 133–5.
*p.283, l.31* *LBC*, I, 42.
*p.284, l.14* *LJ*, II, 3–4n. Letter of July 29, 1811.
*p.284, l.18* *LJ*, II, 4n. Letter of July 31, 1811, to Webster.
*p.284, l.22* Eg. 2611, f. 246. Letter to Hanson, Aug. 2, 1811.
*p.285, l.2* *LJ*, I, 320–1. Letter of Aug. 2, 1811.
*p.285, l.13* Moore, I, 273–4.
*p.285, l.17* Hodgson, I, 182–5.
*p.285, l.21* *LJ*, I, 324–5. Letter of Aug. 7, 1811.
*p.285, l.33* Moore, I, 274.
*p.286, l.3* Moore, I, 275.
*p.286, l.20* *LBC*, I, 43–4.
*p.287, l.4* *LJ*, I, 327–9. The draft is dated Aug. 12, 1811. The completed document, running to nine pages signed on each page by Byron, is now in the Library of the University of Texas.
*p.287, l.9* *LJ*, I, 331. Letter of Aug. 20, 1811.
*p.287, l.21* *LJ*, I, 332–3. Letter of Aug. 21, 1811.
*p.287, l.26* *LJ*, I, 339. Letter of Aug. 22, 1811.
*p.288, l.9* *LJ*, I, 335. Letter of Aug. 21, 1811.
*p.288, l.20* *LJ*, I, 335. Letter of Aug. 21, 1811.
*p.289, l.3* *LJ*, I, 333. Letter of Aug. 21, 1811.
*p.289, l.13* *LJ*, II, 5. Letter of Aug. 24, 1811.
*p.289, l.16* *LJ*, II, 16. Letter of Aug. 31, 1811.
*p.289, l.33* *Poetry,* III, 27. These verses, which Byron sent to Hodgson, were dated "Newstead Abbey, August 26, 1811."
*p.290, l.7* From the original letter, dated Aug. 25, 1811, in the Morgan Library.
*p.290, l.14* *Childe Harold,* I, 91. Byron's tribute to Matthews was in a prose note. (*Poetry,* II, 94–5.)
*p.290, l.26* *LJ*, II, 10–12. Letter of Aug. 30, 1811.
*p.291, l.3* *LJ*, II, 13–14.
*p.291, l.15* Letter of Aug. 31, 1811, Murray MSS.
*p.291, l.32* *LJ*, II, 18–22. Letter of Sept. 3, 1811.
*p.291, l.35* Letter of Sept. 10, 1811, Murray MSS.
*p.292, l.13* *LJ*, II, 36. Letter of Sept. 13, 1811.
*p.292, l.20* Letter of Sept. [18], 1811, Murray MSS. (Part given in *LJ*, II, 36n.)
*p.292, l.30* *LJ*, II, 43. Letter of Sept. 21, 1811.
*p.293, l.2* Smiles, I, 208. Letter of Sept. 4, 1811.
*p.293, l.9* *LJ*, II, 25–6. Letter of Sept. 5, 1811.
*p.293, l.16* *LJ*, II, 41. Letter of Sept. 17, 1811.
*p.293, l.20* *LJ*, II, 45. Letter of Sept. 23, 1811.

*p.293, l.34* *LJ*, II, 24 n.
*p.294, l.7* *LJ*, II, 27–8. Letter of Sept. 7, 1811.
*p.294, l.15* *LJ*, II, 42. Letter of Sept. 17, 1811.
*p.294, l.29* *LBC*, I, 47. Letter of Sept. 20, 1811.
*p.295, l.14* *LJ*, II, 46. Letter of Sept. 25, 1811.
*p.296, l.6* *LJ*, II, 52–3. Letter of Oct. 11, 1811.
*p.296, l.8* *Poetry*, III, 30; V, 208–9. Byron told Lady Byron later that he took the name, which had always fascinated him, from Gessner's *Death of Abel.*
*p.297, l.9* *LJ*, II, 54.
*p.297, l.13* *Childe Harold*, II, 9.
*p.297, l.17* *LJ*, II, 58. Letter of Oct. 14, 1811.
*p.297, l.23* Unpublished paragraph from letter of Oct. 13, 1811, Murray MSS.; Hobhouse proofs. (See Chapter V, p. 108.)
*p.298, l.7* *LBC*, I, 49–50. Letter of Oct. 14, 1811.
*p.298, l.9* *LJ*, II, 58.
*p.298, l.18* *LJ*, V, 116. Letter of Nov. 9, 1820, to John Murray.
*p.298, l.25* *B-SP*, I, 124. (See Chapter V, p. 108.)
*p.300, l.16* Moore, I, 308.
*p.300, l.33* *LJ*, II, 60–3. Letter of Oct. 27, 1811.
*p.301, l.6* Moore, I, 310.
*p.301, l.12* *LJ*, II, 64. Letter of Oct. 29, 1811.
*p.301, l.16* Moore, I, 311–12.
*p.301, l.24* *LJ*, II, 65. Letter of Oct. 30, 1811.
*p.302, l.2* *LJ*, II, 56. Letter of Oct. 13, 1811, to Hodgson.
*p.302, l.16* *LJ*, II, 66.
*p.302, l.19* *LBC*, I, 53.
*p.302, l.34* *LBC*, I, 56–7. Letter of Nov. 3, 1811.
*p.304, l.24* Moore: *Prose and Verse*, p. 424.
*p.304, l.28* *LBC*, I, 58. Letter of Nov. 9, 1811.
*p.305, l.15* Moore: *Prose and Verse*, p. 425.
*p.306, l.13* Unpublished part of letter of Nov. 16, 1811, Murray MSS.; Hobhouse proofs.
*p.306, l.21* Letter of Nov. 17, 1811, Hodgson to Byron, Murray MSS.
*p.306, l.27* *LBC*, I, 59–60. Letter of Nov. 16, 1811.
*p.306, l.29* *LBC*, I, 60. Letter of Nov. 17, 1811.
*p.307, l.3* *LBC*, I, 60–1. Letter of Nov. 17, 1811.
*p.307, l.11* *LBC*, I, 61. Letter of Nov. 17, 1811.
*p.307, l.24* Unpublished part of letter of Nov. 17, 1811, Murray MSS.; Hobhouse proofs.
*p.308, l.11* *LJ*, II, 72–3. Letter of Dec. 4, 1811.
*p.308, l.22* *LJ*, II, 85. Letter of Dec. 8, 1811.
*p.309, l.12* *LBC*, I, 64–5. Letter of Dec. 9, 1811.
*p.309, l.14* Pratt, p. 98.
*p.309, l.27* Pratt, p. 98. Letter of Dec. 15, 1811, to Harness.
*p.309, l.29* *LBC*, I, 68. Letter of Dec. 17, 1811. Pratt, p. 97.
*p.310, l.2* *LBC*, I, 67. Letter of Dec. 15, 1811.
*p.310, l.21* L'Estrange, pp. 12–13; Hodgson, I, 219–20.
*p.310, l.26* Unpublished letter, Murray MSS., Dec. 25, 1811.

*p.310, l.36* Unpublished part of letter of Jan. 16, 1812, Murray MSS.; Hobhouse proofs.

*p.311, l.5* *"To Lord Byron,"* p. 26.

*p.311, l.9* Ibid., p. 29.

*p.311, l.13* Ibid., p. 30.

*p.311, l.34* Ibid., pp. 33–4. Letter of Jan. 20, 1812.

*p.312, l.2* *LJ,* II, 94. Letter of Jan. 25, 1812.

*p.312, l.11* *LJ,* II, 95. Letter of Jan. 29, 1812.

*p.312, l.16* *LJ,* II, 92–3n.

*p.312, l.19* Hodgson, I, 221.

*p.312, l.21* *B-SP,* I, 132. Letter of Feb. 10, 1812.

*p.312, l.33* *LJ,* II, 99–101. Letter of Feb. 16, 1812.

*p.315, l.5* Erdman: "Lord Byron as Rinaldo," pp. 192–3.

*p.316, l.4* Ibid., p. 193.

*p.317, l.13* Smiles, I, 207.

*p.318, l.10* *LJ,* II, 100. Letter of Feb. 16, 1812.

*p.318, l.18* *LJ,* II, 97n.

*p.319, l.2* *Poetry,* III, 45n (quoted from the *Courier*). Raymond, pp. 49–50; Holland, p. 122.

*p.319, l.22* Erdman: "Lord Byron as Rinaldo," p. 211.

*p.320, l.11* *LJ,* II, 103–4. Letter of Feb. 25, 1812.

*p.320, l.19* Dallas: *Correspondence,* III, 15.

*p.320, l.33* *LJ,* II, 105. Letter of March 5, 1812, to Hodgson.

*p.321, l.23* *LJ,* II, 424–30.

*p.321, l.28* *LJ,* II, 105. Letter of March 5, 1812.

*p.321, l.30* *Don Juan,* XV, 22.

*p.321, l.37* *LJ,* II, 105. Letter of March 5, 1812, to Hodgson.

*p.322, l.6* Holland, p. 123.

*p.322, l.10* *LJ,* II, 105. Letter of March 5, 1812, to Hodgson.

*p.322, l.17* *LJ,* II, 424.

*p.322, l.21* Dallas: *Correspondence,* III, 16.

*p.322, l.30* *LJ,* II, 104. Letter of March 5, 1812.

*p.325, l.3* Moore, I, 352.

*p.325, l.6* *Poetry,* I, 453. The title page of this, one of the rarest of Byron's poems in the first edition, bore the imprint of T. Davidson, Murray's printer. (Wise, I, 69–70.)

*p.325, l.15* Dallas: *Correspondence,* III, 17. There is some confusion about the actual date of publication. Moore (I, 343) says: "It was within two days after his speech in the House of Lords [Feb. 27], that Childe Harold appeared." Dallas, who was watching the publication closely, implies that it was ready on the 1st, which was Sunday, but that he did not get a copy until Tuesday the 3rd. Byron, writing to Hodgson on March 5, however, says: "my poesy comes out on Saturday [March 7]." (*LJ,* II, 106.) Advertisements in the *Courier* and *Morning Chronicle* of Tuesday, March 10, announced the first appearance. (*Poetry,* II, xii.) Statements such as Moore's and Hobhouse's (in his diary of March 4 he says: "Ld. Byron sat with me at home this evening . . . his work out") mean no more than that they had seen copies on those dates.

*p.325, l.26* *LJ,* II, 107. Letter of March 5, 1812.

*p.326, l.2* *LJ*, II, 130n. Dated "Wednesday morning"; probably March 11, 1812.

# Notes to Chapter X

*P.328, l.21* *LJ*, II, 114n.

*p.328, l.31* Morgan, II, 200. Lady Morgan quoted Caroline as saying that Rogers "offered me the MS. of *Childe Harold* to read." But since Caroline did not meet Byron until he was famous and much sought after (after the middle of March 1812), it is more probable that Rogers offered her a copy of the book, possibly before publication, rather than the manuscript.

*p.328, l.37* Morgan, II, 200.

*p.329, l.13* Morgan, II, 200.

*p.329, l.18* Medwin, II, 64–5.

*p.329, l.32* Morgan, II, 200–1.

*p.330, l.30* Moore: *Memoirs*, I, 375–6.

*p.331, l.9* Mayne, p. 151.

*p.332, l.19* In his inscribed copy of *Childe Harold*, Bankes wrote: "Very soon after I had it I lent this book to Miss Milbanke who was then unacquainted with Ld Byron. She returned it to me with a note expressing her admiration of the Poem." (Facsimile in catalogue of the Jerome Kern sale, Anderson Galleries, Sale No. 2307, 1929, Part I, p. 55.)

*p.333, l.5* Mayne: *Lady Byron*, p. 35. Diary of March 24, 1812. She began reading the poem on Sunday, March 22.

*p.333, l.17* Ibid., p. 36. Diary of March 25, 1812.

*p.334, l.3* Ibid., pp. 36–7.

*p.334, l.8* See *LJ*, II, 6–7. Letter of Aug. 25, 1811, to Dallas.

*p.334, l.15* Medwin, I, 37.

*p.334, l.22* *LJ*, II, 451. Letter to Medwin, Nov. (?), 1824. Caroline Lamb included this episode in her novel *Glenarvon* (2nd ed., II, 112), quoting Byron's own words.

*p.334, l.27* *LJ*, II, 446. This is one of the few letters of Caroline Lamb which is dated. At the end she wrote: "March 27th, 1812, *Good Friday.*"

*p.335, l.11* Rogers, pp. 234–5.

*p.335, l.24* Foster, pp. 375–6. Letter without date, but probably late March or April 1812.

*p.335, l.30* Rogers, p. 232.

*p.336, l.3* Cecil, p. 149.

*p.336, l.12* Mayne: *Lady Byron*, p. 38.

*p.336, l.26* Ibid., pp. 38–9.

*p.336, l.32* Ibid., p. 39.

*p.337, l.11* Ibid., p. 39.

*p.337, l.21* Ibid., p. 41.

*p.337, l.30* *LBC*, I, 86.

*p.337, l.35* Mayne: *Lady Byron*, p. 41.

*p.338, l.2* Ibid., p. 42.

*p.338, l.5* Ibid.

*p.338, l.18* *LJ*, II, 121. Letter of May 1, 1812.

*p.339, l.2* Mayne: *Lady Byron*, pp. 43–4.

*p.339, l.11* Medwin, II, 67.

*p.339, l.15* Morgan, II, 201.

*p.339, l.18* *LJ*, II, 452. Letter to Medwin (1824).

*p.339, l.19* Elizabeth Jenkins says (*Lady Caroline Lamb*, p. 107): "In Lord Desborough's library at Panshanger are three books, given, as the inscriptions on the fly-leaves show, to her on three consecutive days."

*p.339, l.20* Jenkins, p. 96.

*p.339, l.25* Cecil, p. 156.

*p.340, l.2* Cecil, p. 156.

*p.340, l.11* *LJ*, II, 452.

*p.340, l.14* *LBC*, I, 111. Letter of Nov. 26, 1812.

*p.340, l.38* *LJ*, II, 116–17. The letter is undated.

*p.341, l.11* Dallas: *Correspondence*, III, 41–2.

*p.341, l.30* Unpublished portion of letter (undated—but Caroline said she had known Byron three years when she wrote it), Murray MSS. Part of this same letter (not the part here quoted) is in *"To Lord Byron,"* p. 61.

*p.342, l.19* *LJ*, II, 452.

*p.343, l.13* Foster, p. 362. George Lamb had married in 1809 Caroline Rosalie St. Jules, daughter of Lady Elizabeth Foster, shortly to become the second Duchess of Devonshire.

*p.343, l.16* Foster, p. 364.

*p.343, l.24* *LJ*, II, 452.

*p.343, l.34* *LBC*, I, 74. Letter of Sept. 13, 1812.

*p.344, l.1* Erdman: "Lord Byron as Rinaldo," p. 193. There were no debates in May. He attended once in June and six times in July 1812.

*p.344, l.20* *Don Juan*, XV, 22.

*p.345, l.6* Hobhouse diary, April 21, 1812.

*p.345, l.16* *LJ*, II, 438.

*p.345, l.19* *LJ*, II, 441.

*p.345, l.27* *LJ*, II, 442–3.

*p.346, l.3* *LJ*, V, 431.

*p.346, l.22* Unpublished letter, May 12, 1812, William Andrews Clark Memorial Library, University of California (Los Angeles).

*p.346, l.28* There are several hundred of these letters to Byron in the Murray collection. A selection from them, edited by George Paston and Peter Quennell, was published in *"To Lord Byron"* (1939).

*p.347, l.8* *"To Lord Byron,"* pp. 17–18.

*p.347, l.18* Ibid., pp. 18–19.

*p.347, l.24* Ibid., p. 19.

*p.348, l.5* Blessington, p. 33.

*p.349, l.4* Blessington, p. 125.

*p.349, l.19* Medwin, II, 66.

*p.349, l.30* *B-SP*, I, 158–9. Corrected from the Hobhouse proofs. Quennell gives the date as Jan. 1813, but a reference to Moore's wife and his having left town, together with the date of "Tuesday" in the proof, makes it probable that the date was May 19, 1812. (See *LJ*, II, 122–3.)

*p.350, l.19* *LJ*, II, 122–3. Letter of May 20, 1812.

*p.350, l.31* Hobhouse diary—unpublished entry.

*p.351, l.6* Broughton, I, 40.

*p.351, l.9* Hobhouse diary.

*p.351, l.27* *LBC*, II, 115. Letter of June 26, 1819.

*p.352, l.28* Glenbervie, II, 81. From the diary entry of Oct. 28, 1810.

*p.353, l.2* An account of Lady Oxford's political activities and associations is given by Erdman: "Lord Byron and the Genteel Reformers," p. 1076ff.

*p.354, l.3* Smiles, I, 212–13.

*p.354, l.23* *LJ*, II, 134. Letter of July 6, 1812.

*p.354, l.27* Dallas: *Correspondence*, III, 29.

*p.355, l.7* Long Papers, Berg Collection, New York Public Library.

*p.355, l.15* From an unpublished entry in the Hobhouse diary.

*p.355, l.17* This passage is garbled in Broughton, I, 44.

*p.358, l.15* From the MS. of the Hobhouse diary, entry of July 29, 1812. The greater part of this entry is given in Joyce, pp. 37–40.

*p.358, l.27* *"To Lord Byron,"* pp. 191–2. Letter of July 30, 1812.

*p.359, l.28* Gower, II, 447–8.

*p.359, l.30* Airlie, p. 129.

*p.359, l.33* Gower, II, 449.

*p.361, l.24* *LJ*, II, 452.

*p.362, l.12* Claughton's offer is first mentioned in a letter of Hanson to Byron, Aug. 15, 1812, Murray MSS. A copy of the contract for the sale of Newstead, dated Aug. 17, 1812, is in the Murrays' Byron Collection. Claughton agreed to pay £140,000 for the estate including all furniture except plate, linen, glass, books, fire irons, swords, sabers, pictures, wines, and liquors.

*p.362, l.19* Newstead Sale Bill, p. 9; *LJ*, II, 162.

*p.363, l.6* *LJ*, II, 162–3. Letter of Sept. 28, 1812. The Hollands, the Melbournes, and the Cowpers (Lady Cowper was Lady Melbourne's daughter Emily) had been there early in September.

*p.363, l.13* *LJ*, II, 145. Letter of Sept. 14, 1812, to Murray.

*p.363, l.15* *LBC*, I, 72. Letter of Sept. 10, 1812.

*p.363, l.32* *Morning Chronicle*, Oct. 12, 1812. (*LJ*, II, 172n.) When James and Horace Smith published their *Rejected Addresses*, the *Chronicle* (Oct. 14, 1812) remarked of "Cui Bono?" the parody of Byron's *Childe Harold* in it, that the author had "assigned to the pen of Lord B. a superior *poem* to that which has gained the prize."

*p.363, l.35* *LJ*, II, 173. Letter of Oct. 14, 1812, to Lord Holland.

*p.364, l.12* *LBC*, I, 72. Letter of Sept. 10, 1812.

*p.364, l.20* *LBC*, I, 74. Letter of Sept. 13, 1812, to Lady Melbourne. The Bessborough-Lamb party went first to Tixal to visit Caroline's cousin Lady Harriet Granville Leveson Gower.

*p.365, l.25* *LBC*, I, 79. Letter of Sept. 18, 1812.

*p.366, l.10* *LBC*, I, 85. Letter of Sept. 25, 1812.

*p.366, l.22* *LBC*, I, 82. Letter of Sept. 21, 1812.

*p.366, l.38* *LBC*, I, 84. Letter of Sept. 25, 1812.

*p.367, l.4* *LBC*, I, 76. Letter of Sept. 13, 1812.

*p.367, l.33* *LBC*, I, 87–8. Letter of Sept. 28, 1812.

*p.368, l.3* *LBC*, I, 89–90. End of a letter, probably late September or early October.
*p.369, l.11* Airlie, pp. 137–40.
*p.370, l.3* Mayne: *Lady Byron*, pp. 48–9.
*p.370, l.21* Airlie, pp. 141–2.
*p.370, l.33* *LBC*, I, 90–1. Letter of Oct. 17, 1812, to Lady Melbourne.
*p.371, l.3* *LBC*, I, 93–4. Letter of Oct. 18, 1812.
*p.371, l.11* Letter of Oct. 19, 1812, Hanson to Byron, Murray MSS.
*p.372, l.7* Smiles, I, 216. Letter of Oct. 22, 1812, Murray to Byron.
*p.372, l.9* *LJ*, II, 178. Letter of Oct. 19, 1812.
*p.372, l.16* *LBC*, I, 93–4. Letter of Oct. 18, 1812.
*p.372, l.27* *LBC*, I, 94–5. Letter of Oct. 20, 1812.
*p.372, l.31* *LBC*, I, 97. Letter of Oct. 24, 1812.
*p.373, l.21* *LBC*, I, 98–9. Letter of Oct. 30, 1812.
*p.374, l.15* *LBC*, I, 80. Letter of Sept. 18, 1812.
*p.374, l.17* *LBC*, I, 102. Letter of Nov. 6, 1812.
*p.374, l.27* *LBC*, I, 103–4. Letter of Nov. 9, 1812.
*p.375, l.2* *LBC*, I, 104–5. Letter of Nov. 10, 1812.
*p.375, l.25* Morgan, II, 201.
*p.376, l.9* *LBC*, I, 108.
*p.376, l.14* *LBC*, I, 110.
*p.376, l.17* *LBC*, I, 107–8. Letter of Nov. 14, 1812.
*p.377, l.2* *LBC*, I, 113. Letter of Nov. 30, 1812.
*p.377, l.7* *LBC*, I, 115. Letter of Dec. 14, 1812.
*p.377, l.20* Hodgson to Byron, Nov. 16, 1812, Murray MSS.
*p.377, l.22* Erdman: "Lord Byron and the Genteel Reformers," p. 1086.
*p.377, l.24* *LBC*, I, 114. Letter of Dec. 9, 1812.
*p.378, l.10* *LBC*, I, 115. Letter of Dec. 14, 1812.
*p.378, l.17* *LBC*, I, 117. Letter of Dec. 15, 1812.
*p.378, l.21* *LBC*, I, 119. Letter of Dec. 21, 1812.
*p.379, l.3* *LBC*, I, 123–4. Letter of Dec. 31, 1812.
*p.379, l.6* *LBC*, I, 118. Letter of Dec. 21, 1812.
*p.379, l.16* *LBC*, I, 121. Letter of Dec. 23, 1812.
*p.379, l.30* *LBC*, I, 118. Letter of Dec. 21, 1812.
*p.379, l.38* *LBC*, I, 124.

## Notes to Chapter XI

*P.380, l.8* Unpublished letter of Jan. 2, 1813, to Hobhouse. Murray MSS.; Hobhouse proofs.
*p.381, l.4* *LBC*, I, 126–7. Letter of Jan. 4, 1813.
*p.381, l.11* *LBC*, I, 128–9. Letter of Jan. 5, 1813.
*p.381, l.17* *B-SP*, I, 159–60. Letter of Jan. 17, 1813. The forged letter, written supposedly to herself and giving her authority to "take which picture you think most like," is reproduced in facsimile in *LBC*, I, 130–1.
*p.382, l.9* Bury (1908), I, 125. Dated "Saturday 23rd." No doubt Jan. 23, 1813, for that date is on a Saturday.

*p.382, l.16* Bury (1908), II, 287.

*p.382, l.25* Bury (1908), II, 280. No date is given, but the letter was probably written in the spring of 1813.

*p.383, l.27* *LBC*, I, 138.

*p.383, l.35* *LBC*, I, 134. Letter of Feb. 12, 1813.

*p.384, l.6* *LJ*, II, 198. Letter of March 26, 1813.

*p.384, l.21* *LJ*, II, 197. Letter of March 26, 1813.

*p.384, l.27* *LBC*, I, 137. Letter of Jan. 22, 1813, to Lady Melbourne. (Misdated Feb. in *LBC*.)

*p.384, l.31* Airlie, p. 152.

*p.384, l.33* *LBC*, I, 141. Letter of March 14, 1813.

*p.385, l.10* *LBC*, I, 142–3.

*p.385, l.16* Ilchester, p. 273.

*p.385, l.27* *LBC*, I, 144–5. Letter of April 5, 1813.

*p.385, l.34* *LBC*, I, 146. Letter of April 7, 1813.

*p.386, l.8* Cornelia Knight: *Autobiography* (1861), I, 227. (*Poetry*, VII, 35.)

*p.386, l.15* *LBC*, I, 148. These lines in a slightly different version were first published in the Paris edition of Byron's *Poetical Works*, 1819, VI, 125.

*p.386, l.19* *LBC*, I, 148. Letter of April 7, 1813.

*p.386, l.22* Bury (1908), II, 389.

*p.386, l.29* *LBC*, I, 148.

*p.386, l.35* *LJ*, II, 202n.

*p.387, l.4* Byron probably referred to *The Giaour* when he wrote Murray on March 24: "Let the 15 copies be struck off—& will you have the goodness to attend to the *few* alterations without sending me another revise.—I want them as soon as possible." (Unpublished letter, Nottingham Free Public Library.)

*p.387, l.17* *LBC*, I, 151. Letter of [April 28–9?], 1813.

*p.387, l.25* *LBC*, I, 152–3.

*p.387, l.26* *LBC*, I, 154. The meeting must have taken place the 9th, 10th, or 11th, for Byron had announced his intention of leaving town on Wednesday the 12th.

*p.388, l.7* *LJ*, II, 452.

*p.388, l.13* *LBC*, I, 155.

*p.388, l.29* *Examiner*, March 22, 1812, p. 179.

*p.389, l.2* Unpublished letter of May 20, 1813, Morgan Library.

*p.389, l.5* Hunt: *Lord Byron*, I, 3.

*p.389, l.9* Moore, I, 402.

*p.389, l.18* From the original letter, May 25, 1813, Morgan Library. (Quoted in part in Blunden: *Leigh Hunt*, p. 78.)

*p.389, l.23* *LJ*, II, 210.

*p.390, l.4* *LBC*, I, 156. Letter of May 24, 1813.

*p.390, l.22* Mayne: *Lady Byron*, p. 55.

*p.390, l.31* Cartwright, *Life*, II, 60.

*p.391, l.3* *LJ*, II, 445.

*p.391, l.15* *LJ*, II, 359.

*p.391, l.35* *LJ*, II, 213–14. Letter of June 3, 1813.

*p.391, l.38* *Poetry*, III, 80.

*p.392, l.4* *LJ*, II, 214. Letter of June 6, 1813.

*p.392, l.10* *B-SP*, I, 159. Letter of Jan. 17, 1813.

*p.392, l.15* *LJ*, II, 219. Letter of June 13, 1813.

*p.392, l.18* *LJ*, II, 220. Letter of June 18, 1813.

*p.392, l.24* *Murray's Magazine*, Feb. 1887, pp. 147–8.

*p.392, l.34* *LBC*, I, 160. Letter of June 21, 1813.

*p.393, l.9* *LJ*, II, 223–4. Letter of June 22, 1813.

*p.393, l.18* *Murray's Magazine*, Jan. 1887. (From a paper dated "Ravenna, August 4, 1821," and entitled "Some Recollections of My Acquaintance with Madame de Staël." The manuscript is now in the Library of the University of Texas.)

*p.393, l.35* Blessington, pp. 20–1.

*p.394, l.13* Blessington, p. 21.

*p.394, l.28* Blessington, pp. 23–4.

*p.394, l.35* *LBC*, I, 161.

*p.395, l.5* *LBC*, I, 162. Letter of July 1, 1813.

*p.395, l.12* *LJ*, II, 226–7.

*p.396, l.28* *LJ*, II, 229–30. Letter of July 8, 1813. On July 7, Byron inscribed a copy of *The Giaour* "To My dearest Sister Augusta Mary—from her friend and brother." (H. B. Smith: *A Sentimental Library,* p. 32.)

*p.396, l.33* *LJ*, II, 210.

*p.396, l.36* Byron preserved the calling-card (now in the William Andrews Clark Memorial Library of the University of California at Los Angeles) bearing Lady Heathcote's invitation to the famous party: "at home Monday July 5th a small Waltzing Party 10 o'clock. 1813." Beneath this Byron had written: "This Card I keep as a curiosity—since it was at the Ball (to which it is an invitation) that L^y^ Caroline L performed ye dagger Scene of indifferent memory."

*p.397, l.1* *LBC*, I, 164. Letter of July 6, 1813.

*p.397, l.18* *LBC*, I, 163. Letter of July 6, 1813.

*p.398, l.3* *LJ*, II, 453.

*p.398, l.16* *LBC*, I, 164–5. Letter of July 6, 1813.

*p.398, l.26* *The Satirist* (Vol. XIII, pp. 150, 151) printed an article entitled "Scandalum Magnatum" under a motto from the *Rejected Addresses:*

> With horn-handled knife,
> To kill a tender lamb as dead as mutton

which told how Lady C.L. in a fit of jealousy of Lord B——n "took up a dessert-knife, and stabbed herself." (*LJ*, II, 242–3n.)

*p.398, l.33* Hanson papers, Murray MSS.

*p.399, l.10* Murray MSS. By Dec. 9, Love and Kelly's bill amounted to £1,079. 15*s.* Most of these bills remained unpaid or only partially paid until the final sale of Newstead to Colonel Wildman in 1818. That Byron had made serious preparations for departure for the Levant is indicated in a long letter, dated July 11, 1813, from E. D. Clarke, the Eastern traveler, to Dr. William Clark, whom Byron had engaged to accompany him, giving a list of material necessary for the voyage. (Trinity College MS. R. Z. 40.) Byron had even enlisted the aid of the Ministers. Lord Castlereagh, Foreign

Minister, whom Byron later satirized bitterly in *Don Juan*, wrote a note of recommendation for him to Sir G. Vaselay: "Lord Byron proposes to visit the East and is very desirous of receiving your assistance in his progress. His own Personal Merits and distinguished Literary Reputation would be his best Passport. . . ." (Quoted in Maggs Catalogue 531, 1930.)

*p.399, l.13* Bixby, pp. 24–5. On Aug. 2, Byron had word from Croker that Captain Carlton of the *Boyne* had consented to receive him into his cabin for the voyage. The ship was due to sail the following Saturday (the 8th), but Byron did not leave.

*p.399, l.26* *LJ*, II, 230–1.

*p.399, l.38* Airlie, pp. 159–60.

*p.400, l.7* *LBC*, I, 166–7. Letter of July 18, 1813.

*p.400, l.14* Dudley, p. 212.

*p.400, l.25* *LJ*, V, 423.

*p.400, l.37* *LJ*, V, 435.

*p.401, l.2* *LJ*, V, 418.

*p.401, l.7* *LJ*, V, 433.

*p.401, l.17* *LJ*, V, 110. Letter of Nov. 4, 1820. Omission supplied from the original manuscript in the British Museum. (Ashley 5160.)

*p.401, l.27* *LJ*, II, 320. Journal, Nov. 16, 1813.

*p.402, l.2* *LJ*, V, 413.

*p.402, l.11* *LJ*, V, 460–1.

*p.402, l.17* *LJ*, II, 239–41. Byron apparently had a tentative passage for July 30, but canceled it. On the 11th he wrote Dr. William Clark: "Our sailing day is the 30th & . . . we should be quite ready to leave London on the 25th." (Trinity College Library.)

*p.402, l.24* On July 25, Byron wrote Moore: "Since I wrote last, I have been into the country. I journeyed by night. . . ." (*LJ*, II, 238.) Since he mentioned passing through Epping Forest, he must have been on his way to Newmarket, but he could then have spent only two days with Augusta, for he wrote Murray on the 22nd from London, and was back in town again on the 25th. On July 31 he announced to Murray his intention of leaving town "early tomorrow." His next letter from London was that of August 5 to Lady Melbourne announcing that Augusta had returned with him. Of his second visit he wrote more specifically to Dr. William Clark of Cambridge: "I am going out of town for a week (near Cambridge) we shall wait for Sligo. . . . you cannot regret any delay in our Departure more than I do but a few days or weeks for a comfortable passage will not I trust be thrown away." (Trinity College Library, Letter of July 31, 1813.)

*p.402, l.26* *LBC*, I, 168.

*p.402, l.38* *LBC*, I, 169–70.

*p.403, l.20* *LBC*, I, 172–4.

*p.404, l.27* *LBC*, I, 177. Letter of Aug. 31, 1813.

*p.405, l.19* Mayne: *Lady Byron*, pp. 57–9.

*p.406, l.14* From a commonplace book of Annabella Milbanke now in my possession.

*p.406, l.33* *LJ*, III, 398–9.

*p.407, l.4* Mayne: *Lady Byron*, p. 60.

*p.407, l.8* Ibid., p. 61. Letter of Aug. 31, 1813.

*p.407, l.12* Ibid., p. 65.
*p.407, l.30* *LBC*, I, 177–8. Letter of Sept. 5, 1813.
*p.407, l.37* Medwin, I, 38.
*p.408, l.6* *LJ*, III, 400. Letter of Sept. 6, 1813.
*p.408, l.13* *LBC*, I, 179.
*p.408, l.18* *LBC*, I, 179–80.
*p.408, l.21* *LJ*, II, 224. Murray had been presented with the copyright and reaped a large profit from the successive editions of *The Giaour*.
*p.408, l.28* The poem reached its final length of 75 pages and 1,334 lines in the seventh edition, published Nov. 27 or after. Seven more editions appeared by 1815, but without the addition of any new material. (See *Poetry*, III, 78–80.)
*p.408, l.31* *LJ*, II, 252.
*p.409, l.9* Lines 1048–9, 1053–5, 1057–8. The passages here quoted appeared first in the 41-page first edition (they were not in the earlier privately circulated printing).
*p.409, l.21* Lines 1131–4, 1141–4.
*p.409, l.28* See Chapter VIII, p. 257.
*p.410, l.2* He had told Lady Melbourne on Sept. 9 that he would probably not leave town until Saturday (Sept. 11) or perhaps Sunday.
*p.410, l.15* *LJ*, II, 265.
*p.411, l.5* *B-SP*, I, 174–5.
*p.411, l.28* *LJ*, III, 401–3. Letter of Sept. 26, 1813.
*p.412, l.1* *LBC*, I, 182–3.
*p.412, l.4* *LBC*, I, 185; Hobhouse notes titled "Lord Byron" with diary of 1824.
*p.412, l.18* *LBC*, I, 184. Letter of Sept. 28, 1813.
*p.413, l.7* *LBC*, I, 186. Letter of Oct. 1, 1813.
*p.413, l.11* *LJ*, II, 269. Letter of Sept. 30, 1813.
*p.413, l.22* *LJ*, II, 267. Letter of Sept. 27, 1813.
*p.413, l.34* *LBC*, I, 189. Letter of Oct. 5, 1813.
*p.414, l.30* *LBC*, I, 190–3. Letter of Oct. 8, 1813.
*p.414, l.32* Letter of Nov. 17, 1811, to Hobhouse, Murray MSS.; Hobhouse proofs.
*p.415, l.8* *LBC*, I, 194–5. Letter of Oct. 10, 1813.
*p.415, l.12* *LJ*, II, 275. Letter of Oct. 10, 1813. The payments already made by Claughton were completely disbursed, and Hanson wrote on the 13th that he was making another application to the purchaser for a promised payment of £20,000. (Hanson papers, Murray MSS.) There was, however, enough money in Byron's account to supply the loan to Webster, who signed a bond for it.
*p.415, l.34* *LJ*, II, 276. Letter of Oct. 10, 1813.
*p.416, l.1* *LBC*, I, 196–7. Letter of [Oct. 11], 1813.
*p.416, l.6* *LBC*, I, 198. Letter of Oct. 13, 1813.
*p.416, l.12* *LBC*, I, 201–2. Letter of Oct. 14, 1813.
*p.417, l.2* *LBC*, I, 203–5. Letter of Oct. 17, 1813.
*p.417, l.11* *LBC*, I, 206. Letter of Oct. 19, 1813.
*p.417, l.26* *LBC*, I, 209. Letter of Oct. 21, 1813.
*p.418, l.3* *LBC*, I, 212–13. Letter of Monday [Oct. 25, 1813].

*p.418, l.9* Butler, I, 89. Letter of Oct. 20, 1813, Byron to Dr. Butler.

*p.418, l.20* Hodgson, I, 268–71; Moore: *Memoirs,* II, 634, 648. Hodgson, to his later embarrassment, insisted on giving Byron a bond, which was used as evidence of debt by the executors after Byron's death, but there were enough living witnesses of Byron's intention to acquit him of it.

*p.418, l.33* *LBC,* I, 214.

*p.418, l.35* *LBC,* I, 219. Letter of Nov. 25, 1813.

*p.418, l.38* *LJ,* II, 293. Letter of Nov. 30, 1813. He wrote Moore again on Dec. 8: "Mine is the work of a week, written, *why* I have partly told you, and partly I cannot tell you by letter—some day I will." (*LJ,* II, 302.) But to his diary he confided: "It was written in four nights to distract my dreams from ** [Lady Frances, no doubt; Moore left out the name]." (*LJ,* II, 321.)

*p.419, l.2* *LJ,* II, 278, 283.

*p.419, l.3* *LJ,* II, 283. Letter of Nov. 13, 1813, to Murray.

*p.419, l.14* *LJ,* II, 309. Letter of Dec. 15, 1813.

*p.419, l.18* *LJ,* II, 277.

*p.419, l.22* *LBC,* I, 211.

*p.419, l.32* Airlie, pp. 161–2. The only date given for this letter is Oct. 1813.

*p.420, l.2* *LJ,* III, 404. Byron kept the letter in his desk for a week and sent it on with a postscript on the 17th.

*p.420, l.8* *LJ,* III, 405. This extract is misdated Nov. 10, 1813, in *LJ.* It should be Nov. 29—see Mayne: *Lady Byron,* p. 77.

*p.420, l.19* *LJ,* III, 406. Letter of Nov. 29, 1813. The letters of Nov. 10 and Nov. 29 were garbled in *LJ*—see Mayne: *Lady Byron,* pp. 71–7.

*p.420, l.24* Mayne: *Lady Byron,* pp. 78–9.

*p.420, l.32* Even after Ward had left, the plan was not given up, for Byron wrote on the 30th: "Ward and I *talk* of going to Holland. I want to see how a Dutch canal looks after the Bosphorus." (*LJ,* II, 293.)

*p.421, l.8* A misquotation of Pope's line in *Eloisa to Abelard:* "Dear fatal name! rest ever unrevealed."

*p.421, l.9* *LJ,* II, 313–14.

*p.421, l.20* *LJ,* II, 318–19. Journal, Nov. 14, 1813.

*p.421, l.27* *LJ,* II, 328. Journal, Nov. 17, 1813.

*p.421, l.31* *LJ,* II, 333. Journal, Nov. 22, 1813.

*p.421, l.36* *LJ,* II, 331. Journal, Nov. 22, 1813.

*p.422, l.8* *LJ,* II, 341–2. Journal, Nov. 24, 1813.

*p.422, l.14* *LJ,* II, 334. Journal, Nov. 23, 1813.

*p.422, l.24* *LJ,* II, 338–40. Journal, Nov. 23, 1813.

*p.423, l.1* *LBC,* I, 217. Letter of Nov. 25, 1813.

*p.423, l.8* *LJ,* II, 350. Journal, Nov. 27, 1813. This was one of the portraits by Holmes.

*p.423, l.11* *LJ,* II, 350.

*p.423, l.19* I have supplied the bracketed name as most probable in the context, especially in view of the sentence that follows.

*p.423, l.22* *LBC,* I, 218. Letter of Nov. 25, 1813.

*p.424, l.7* Smiles, I, 221. Letter of Nov. 18, 1813.

*p.424, l.11* *LJ,* II, 327. Journal, Nov. 17, 1813.

*p.424, l.16* *LJ*, II, 289. Letter of Nov. 28, 1813.
*p.424, l.19* Mackintosh, II, 271.
*p.424, l.24* *LJ*, II, 296–7. Letter of Dec. 2, 1813.
*p.424, l.30* *LJ*, II, 357–8. Journal, Dec. 1, 1813.
*p.425, l.20* *LJ*, II, 365. Journal, Dec. 6, 1813.
*p.426, l.3* *LJ*, II, 369. Journal, Dec. 7, 1813.
*p.426, l.16* *LJ*, II, 376–7. Journal, Dec. 13, 1813.

*p.426, l.31* There are no letters from Byron to Lady Melbourne in *LBC* between Nov. 25, 1813, and Jan. 8, 1814.

*p.426, l.33* On Dec. 11, Byron wrote John Galt: "I leave town for a day or two on Monday [13th]. . . ." (*LJ*, II, 306.) And on the 14th he told Thomas Ashe: "I leave town for a few days to-morrow." (*LJ*, II, 306.) But when he wrote E. D. Clarke on the 15th, he said nothing about leaving town but referred to plans to go abroad the following month. (*LJ*, II, 310.) On the 22nd he wrote to Leigh Hunt: "The nearest relation and almost the only friend I possess, has been in London for a week, and leaves it tomorrow with me for her own residence." (*LJ*, II, 311.)

*p.427, l.2* *LJ*, II, 377.

*p.427, l.9* Tasso: *Gerusalemme Liberata*, canto decimo. This motto was published on the title page.

*p.427, l.23* Sir John Fox says (*The Byron Mystery*, p. 86): "*The Corsair*, part of which was written in Colonel Leigh's house near Newmarket, as Mrs. Leigh told Shelley [*sic*] at the time."

*p.427, l.25* Moore, I, 536n.

*p.428, l.3* Dallas: *Correspondence*, III, 58–9. In a note to Byron's *Poetical Works* (1832), IX, 257, it is stated that *The Corsair* "was begun on the 18th, and finished on the 31st, of December, 1813." But the first page of the MS. is dated "27th of December, 1813," and the last page "December 31, 1813, January 1, 1814." (*Poetry*, III, 220.) It is probable that when Dallas called on Byron he was polishing and transcribing it. The autograph manuscript of the first draft, now in the Morgan Library, is dated Dec. 18, 1813.

*p.428, l.11* *LBC*, I, 223n.
*p.428, l.20* *LBC*, I, 224–5n.
*p.428, l.30* Mayne: *Lady Byron*, p. 80.
*p.429, l.6* *LJ*, II, 357. Journal, Nov. 30, 1813.

## Notes to Chapter XII

*P.430, l.2* *LJ*, II, 382. Journal, Feb. 18, 1814.

*p.430, l.6* *LJ*, III, 1. Letter of Jan. 2, 1814, to John Murray. Byron had dedicated *The Bride of Abydos* to Lord Holland.

*p.430, l.9* *LJ*, III, 2–3. Letter of Jan. ?, [1814], to John Murray.
*p.430, l.20* *LBC*, I, 224. Letter of Jan. 8, 1814, to Lady Melbourne.
*p.430, l.25* *LJ*, III, 7. Letter undated, but about Jan. 8, 1814.
*p.431, l.3* *LBC*, I, 228. Letter of Jan. 11, 1814.

*p.431, l.7* *LBC*, I, 227. Letter of Jan. 10, 1814. An index to his diminishing ardor for Lady Frances may be seen in the fact that Byron changed the heroine's name from Francesca to Genevra on Jan. 6, and finally to Medora (a name which had no associations with her) on Jan. 15. (See *Poetry*, III, 239.)

*p.431, l.11* *LBC*, I, 232. Letter of Jan. 13, 1814.
*p.431, l.24* *LBC*, I, 226. Letter of Jan. 10, 1814.
*p.431, l.31* *LBC*, I, 226. Letter of Jan 10, 1814.
*p.431, l.37* *LBC*, I, 228. Letter of Jan. 11, 1814.
*p.432, l.7* *LBC*, I, 231–2. Letter of Jan. 13, 1814.
*p.432, l.16* *LBC*, I, 234. Letter of Jan. 13, 1814.
*p.432, l.29* *LBC*, I, 237. Letter of Jan. 16, 1814.
*p.432, l.34* *LBC*, I, 238.
*p.433, l.7* *LBC*, I, 239, 241. Letter of Jan. 29, 1814.
*p.433, l.13* *LJ*, III, 16. Letter of Jan. 22, 1814.
*p.433, l.16* *LJ*, III, 20.
*p.433, l.24* Smiles, I, 223. Letter of Feb. 3, 1814. Hobhouse recorded in his diary on Feb. 18, 1814: "13,000 copies sold in a month." (Broughton, I, 86.)
*p.433, l.31* *The Corsair*, lines 1862–4.
*p.434, l.20* *LJ*, III, 17. Letter of Jan. 22, 1814.
*p.435, l.3* *LJ*, III, 27. Letter of Feb. 7, 1814.
*p.435, l.13* *LJ*, III, 33. Letter of Feb. 10, 1814.
*p.435, l.15* *LBC*, I, 243. Letter of Feb. 11, 1814.
*p.435, l.20* *Courier*, Feb. 17, 1814; Dallas: *Correspondence*, III, 61–4.
*p.435, l.24* Dallas: *Correspondence*, III, 65. (*Morning Post*, Feb. 21, 1814.)
*p.435, l.36* *LBC*, I, 241–2. Letter of Feb. 6, 1814.
*p.436, l.2* *LBC*, I, 244.
*p.436, l.7* Mayne: *Lady Byron*, p. 89.
*p.436, l.13* Broughton, I, 84.
*p.436, l.16* *LJ*, II, 382. Journal, Feb. 18, 1814.
*p.436, l.18* *LJ*, II, 383. Journal, Feb. 18, 1814, "Nine o'clock."
*p.436, l.21* Broughton, I, 86.
*p.436, l.26* *LJ*, II, 385–6.
*p.437, l.6* *LJ*, II, 383–4. Journal of Feb. 18, 1814.
*p.437, l.12* *LJ*, II, 387. Journal of Feb. 19, 1814.
*p.437, l.13* *LJ*, II, 387. Journal of Feb 20, 1814.
*p.437, l.18* Broughton, I, 87.
*p.438, l.7* *LJ*, III, 54–5. Letter of March 3, 1814.
*p.438, l.16* *LJ*, III, 56. Letter of March 3, 1814.
*p.438, l.24* Unpublished letter of March 6, 1814, Morgan Library.
*p.439, l.2* Broughton, I, 98. Diary, March 19, 1814.
*p.439, l.12* *LJ*, II, 396. Journal, March 10, 1814.
*p.439, l.16* *LJ*, II, 398. Journal, March 10, 1814.
*p.439, l.28* *LJ*, II, 406. Journal, March 22, 1814.
*p.439, l.37* *LJ*, II, 408. Journal, March 28, 1814.
*p.440, l.8* *LJ*, II, 395. Journal, March 7, 1814.
*p.440, l.15* *LJ*, VI, 176. Letter of March 28, 1823, to Lady —— [Hardy].
*p.440, l.23* Hanson papers, Murray MSS.

*p.441, l.3* *LJ*, II, 393n.
*p.441, l.5* *LJ*, VI, 177. Letter of March 28, 1823, to Lady ——— [Hardy].
*p.441, l.10* Hanson papers, Murray MSS.
*p.441, l.13* Moore: *Memoirs*, II, 681.
*p.442, l.13* Mayne: *Lady Byron*, p. 91. Date not given, but probably early March.
*p.442, l.18* *LJ*, II, 401.
*p.443, l.14* *LJ*, II, 401. Journal, March 17, 1814.
*p.443, l.21* *LJ*, II, 403. Journal, March 20, 1814.
*p.443, l.26* *LJ*, II, 407–8. Journal of March 28, 1814.
*p.443, l.28* *LJ*, II, 407. Byron's apartment was No. 2.
*p.443, l.32* Moore: *Memoirs*, II, 1017.
*p.444, l.4* Hobhouse diary; unpublished entry, April 5, 1814, Berg Collection, New York Public Library.
*p.444, l.8* *LBC*, I, 249.
*p.444, l.20* *LJ*, II, 393. Journal, March 6, 1814.
*p.444, l.27* *LJ*, II, 409–10. Journal, April 9, 1814.
*p.444, l.33* *LJ*, III, 66. Letter of April 10, 1814.
*p.444, l.36* *LJ*, III, 70. Letter of April 20, 1814.
*p.445, l.2* *LJ*, III, 67. Letter of April 11, 1814.
*p.445, l.19* Broughton, I, 105.
*p.445, l.22* Murray MSS.; Hobhouse proofs. Letter of April 12, 1814.
*p.445, l.26* Broughton, I, 105–6. Diary, April 12, 1814.
*p.445, l.33* Broughton, I, 106. Diary, April 15, 16, 1814.
*p.445, l.38* Murray MSS. Letters of April 6, 10, 1814, Claughton to Hanson (copies).
*p.446, l.4* Mayne: *Lady Byron*, pp. 93–4.
*p.446, l.10* Ibid., p. 94. No date given, but probably about April 20, 1814.
*p.446, l.23* *LBC*, I, 251. Letter of April 25, 1814.
*p.447, l.2* *LJ*, III, 70. On April 26, 1814, he wrote to an unidentified correspondent: "The Parrot (I grieve to speak it) is in excellent noise & very troublesome spirits." (From an unpublished letter in the possession of Mr. John S. Mayfield of Washington, D.C.)
*p.447, l.13* *LJ*, III, 72. Letter of April 21, 1814.
*p.447, l.20* *LBC*, I, 252. Letter of April 25, 1814.
*p.447, l.35* *LBC*, I, 253–4. Letter of April 29, 1814.
*p.448, l.7* Unpublished letter, Lady Melbourne to Byron, April 30, 1814. Murray MSS.
*p.448, l.25* *LBC*, I, 254–5. Letter of April 30, 1814.
*p.448, l.33* *LBC*, I, 256–7. Letter of April–May 1, 1814.
*p.449, l.3* *LJ*, III, 77.
*p.449, l.11* *LJ*, III, 78. Letter of May 1, 1814.
*p.449, l.26* Byron had first written and then erased here:

*We have loved—and oh, still, my adored one we love!*
*Oh the moment is past, when that Passion might cease.*

(*Poetry*, III, 414.)
*p.450, l.6* *LJ*, III, 81. Letter of "Sunday Matin" (May 8, 1814).

*p.450, l.15* *B-SP*, I, 282–3. Letter of May 3, 1814.

*p.450, l.23* *LBC*, I, 257–8. Letter of May 16, 1814.

*p.450, l.29* *LJ*, III, 84.

*p.451, l.8* *Lara*, lines 115–16, 119–22, 129–30. Byron wrote some opening lines to *Lara* which were even more revealing of his then state of mind, but he suppressed them before the poem was published. There seems little doubt that they were intended as a dedication to Augusta. They were first printed by Lord Lovelace in *Astarte* (1905), pp. 219–20.

*p.451, l.12* *LJ*, VI, 77. Letter of June 6, 1822.

*p.451, l.15* Broughton, I, 123.

*p.452, l.10* *LBC*, I, 257. Letter of May 16, 1814.

*p.452, l.21* *LBC*, I, 258–59. Letter of May 28, 1814.

*p.452, l.30* *LJ*, III, 86–7. Letter of May 31, 1814.

*p.453, l.8* *"To Lord Byron,"* p. 124. Her first letter was dated May 10, 1814.

*p.453, l.22* Ibid., pp. 129–30.

*p.453, l.28* Ibid., pp. 130–4.

*p.453, l.38* *B-SP*, I, 286. This letter is dated June 8, but this must be an error for 18, for it is obviously a reply to her letter of June 17.

*p.454, l.10* *"To Lord Byron,"* pp. 135–6.

*p.454, l.23* Ibid., p. 137.

*p.454, l.34* Unpublished letter, Murray MSS.

*p.454, l.38* *LBC*, I, 259. Letter of June 10, 1814.

*p.455, l.4* Writing to Moore in 1822, Byron recalled the circumstances of the composition of *Lara*, "which, *you* know, was written amidst balls and fooleries, and after coming home from masquerades and routs, in the summer of the sovereigns." (*LJ*, VI, 81. Letter of June 8, 1822.)

*p.455, l.8* *LJ*, VI, 80. Letter of June 8, 1822.

*p.455, l.23* *LJ*, II, 328.

*p.456, l.3* *LJ*, III, 92n.

*p.456, l.7* Mrs. Wilmot was Byron's second cousin by marriage, having married Robert John Wilmot, son of Sir Robert Wilmot and Juliana, second daughter of Byron's grandfather, the Admiral.

*p.456, l.17* Murray MSS.

*p.456, l.22* *"To Lord Byron,"* p. 173.

*p.456, l.31* *LJ*, III, 97. Letter of June 18, 1814.

*p.457, l.3* *LJ*, III, 102. Letter of June 27, 1814.

*p.457, l.21* *"To Lord Byron,"* p. 62. Letter of April 25, 1814.

*p.457, l.31* Unpublished letter, Murray MSS. No date, but dated by context and by Byron's comment on it.

*p.458, l.6* Murray MSS. Undated except by the reference to June 3 in the text of the letter, part of which is printed in *"To Lord Byron,"* p. 63.

*p.458, l.16* Glenbervie, II, 302.

*p.458, l.33* *LBC*, I, 261–2. Letter of June 26, 1814.

*p.459, l.3* *LBC*, I, 262. Letter of June 28, 1814.

*p.459, l.28* Broughton, I, 156–7.

*p.460, l.15* *"To Lord Byron,"* p. 157.

*p.461, l.3* Harriette Wilson: *Memoirs*, p. 248.

*p.461, l.8* *"To Lord Byron,"* p. 147.

*p.461, l.17* *LBC,* I, 262. Letter of July 2, 1814.
*p.461, l.19* *LBC,* I, 262. Letter of June 28, 1814.
*p.461, l.22* Mayne: *Lady Byron,* p. 98. No date given, but toward the end of June.
*p.461, l.34* Ibid., p. 99. No date given, but about July 1, 1814.
*p.462, l.10* Broughton, I, 154, 157. Hobhouse gave up the attempt.
*p.462, l.10* Ibid., I, 141.
*p.462, l.16* Broughton, I, 157.
*p.462, l.21* *LJ,* III, 104–5. Letter of July 11, 1814.
*p.462, l.24* *LJ,* III, 105. Letter of July 15, 1814.
*p.462, l.29* *LJ,* III, 103–4.
*p.462, l.37* Unpublished letter, Murray MSS.
*p.463, l.3* Hodgson, I, 286.
*p.463, l.5* *LJ,* III, 107. Letter of July 18, 1814, to John Murray. Nowhere, except in the letter of Hodgson about taking the house (July 10), is there any mention of Mrs. Leigh bringing her children. Byron does not refer to them in any extant letter from Hastings, but they were with her later at Newstead and may be assumed also to have been at Hastings.
*p.463, l.15* *LJ,* III, 107–8.
*p.463, l.24* *"To Lord Byron,"* p. 173.
*p.463, l.37* *LJ,* III, 110. Letter of July 24, 1814.
*p.464, l.5* Unpublished letter, July 23, 1814, Murray MSS.; Hobhouse proofs.
*p.464, l.18* *LJ,* III, 117–18. Letter of Aug. 3, 1814.
*p.464, l.25* Mayne: *Lady Byron,* p. 100.
*p.465, l.21* *LBC,* I, 273–4. Letter of Oct. 4, 1814.
*p.465, l.33* *LBC,* I, 274. Letter of Oct. 4, 1814.
*p.466, l.4* *LJ,* III, 120. Letter of Aug. 3, 1814.
*p.466, l.7* Moore, I, 575n; Moore: *Memoirs,* II, 667.
*p.466, l.12* *LJ,* III, 124. Letter of Aug. 12, 1814.
*p.466, l.18* Letter of Aug. 2, 1814, Hanson to Byron. Murray MSS.
*p.466, l.22* Hanson papers, Murray MSS. Letter of July 30, 1814.
*p.467, l.13* Mayne: *Lady Byron,* p. 103. Letter of Aug. 10, 1814.
*p.467, l.22* *LJ,* III, 101. Letter of June 27, 1814, to Rogers.
*p.467, l.25* Moore, I, 567n.
*p.467, l.30* Broughton, I, 160. Diary of Aug. 11, 1814.
*p.467, l.35* *LJ,* III, 125. Letter of Aug. 12, 1814.
*p.467, l.37* According to Murray's biographer (Smiles, I, 231), the publisher paid 500 guineas for the copyright of each poem, but he must have added to this sum when *Lara* was published separately (four editions appeared during the autumn), for Byron wrote Hobhouse on Sept. 13 that he had "a note of Murray for £700 (the price of *Larry*) at a *year's* date last month." (*LBC,* I, 266.) Byron was still refusing to accept money for his writing, however, in 1815 (see Chapter XIV, p. 548.)
*p.468, l.9* *LJ,* III, 119–20. Letter of Aug. 3, 1814.
*p.468, l.18* Byron had planned his Scotch tour with his Harrow friend Sinclair, to the estate of the latter's father, so that he would have an excuse to stop on the way at Seaham, and to plead the tour to escape if he wished. (Mayne: *Lady Byron,* p. 106. Letter of Aug. 25, 1814.)

*p.468, l.23* *LBC,* I, 265–6.

*p.469, l.2* Mayne: *Lady Byron,* p. 104. Letter of Aug. 16, 1814.

*p.469, l.12* Ibid., pp. 104–5.

*p.469, l.16* The date of his departure is established by Murray's statement in a letter to his wife, Aug. 24, 1814 (Wednesday): "Lord Byron set out for Newstead on Sunday." (Smiles, I, 249.)

*p.469, l.22* *"To Lord Byron,"* pp. 174–5.

*p.470, l.3* Mayne: *Lady Byron,* pp. 105–6.

*p.470, l.9* *LJ,* III, 131–2. Letter of Sept. 7, 1814.

*p.470, l.12* *LJ,* III, 136. Letter of Sept. 15, 1814.

*p.470, l.25* Mayne: *Lady Byron,* p. 107.

*p.471, l.5* Ibid., pp. 108–9.

*p.471, l.24* Moore, I, 581. In the margin of his copy of Moore at this point Hobhouse wrote: *"No"*—the implication probably being that Byron told Hobhouse a different story and that the dramatized scene given by Moore is a distortion of the facts.

*p.471, l.27* *LBC,* I, 274–5. Letter of Oct. 4, 1814.

*p.472, l.18* Mayne: *Lady Byron,* p. 111.

*p.472, l.29* *LBC,* I, 275. Letter of Oct. 4, 1814.

*p.473, l.13* *LBC,* I, 266–7.

*p.473, l.24* *LJ,* III, 134–5. Letter of Sept. 15, 1814. Byron's recent absorption in Italian literature and history no doubt contributed largely to his desire to visit Italy.

*p.473, l.33* Mayne: *Lady Byron,* p. 110.

*p.474, l.20* Ibid., pp. 111–12.

*p.474, l.26* Ibid., p. 112.

*p.475, l.7* *LBC,* I, 275. Letter of Oct. 4, 1814.

*p.475, l.9* *LBC,* I, 274. Letter of Oct. 4, 1814.

*p.475, l.13* *LBC,* I, 269. Letter of Sept. 23, 1814.

*p.476, l.11* Mayne: *Lady Byron,* pp. 112–13.

*p.476, l.14* Ibid., p. 112. Miss Mayne does not give the source of this, but unless Annabella used practically the same words in one of her "narratives" which Miss Mayne saw among the Lovelace papers, it comes from Mrs. Stowe's *Lady Byron Vindicated* (1870), p. 156: "At last, she said, he sent her a very beautiful letter, offering himself again. 'I thought,' she added, 'that it was sincere, and that I might now show him all I felt. I wrote just what was in my heart.' "